# AN OCCUPATIONAL INFORMATION SYSTEM FOR THE 21ST CENTURY: THE DEVELOPMENT OF O*NET

# AN OCCUPATIONAL INFORMATION SYSTEM FOR THE 21ST CENTURY: THE DEVELOPMENT OF O*NET

Edited by

**Norman G. Peterson, Michael D. Mumford, Walter C. Borman, P. Richard Jeanneret, and Edwin A. Fleishman**

American Psychological Association•Washington, D.C.

Published by
American Psychological Association
750 First Street, NE
Washington, DC 20002

Copies may be ordered from
APA Order Department
P.O. Box 92984
Washington, DC 20090-2984

In the U.K., Europe, Africa, and the Middle East, copies may be ordered from
American Psychological Association
3 Henrietta Street
Covent Garden, London
WC2E 8LU England

Typeset in Sabon by EPS Group Inc., Easton, MD
Printer: Data Reproductions Corporation, Auburn Hills, MI
Cover Designer: Paul Perlow, New York
Technical/Production Editor: Catherine R. W. Hudson

Unless otherwise noted, information in tables and figures is reprinted with express permission from the Utah Department of Employment Security. An expanded version of these data was originally copyrighted with all rights reserved and presented in the following project reports, prepared under Contract Number 94-542, which is administered by the Utah Department of Employment Security on behalf of the U.S. Department of Labor:

Peterson, N. G., Mumford, M. D., Borman, W. C., Jeanneret, P. R., & Fleishman, E. A. (Eds.). (1995). *Development of Prototype Occupational Information Network (O*NET) Content Model.* Salt Lake City, UT: Utah Department of Employment Security.

Peterson, N. G., Mumford, M. D., Borman, W. C., Jenneret, P. R., Fleishman, E. A., & Levin, K. Y. (Eds.). (1996). *O*NET final technical report.* Salt Lake City, UT: Utah Department of Employment Security.

Rose, A. M., Hesse, B. W., Silver, P. A., & Dumas, J. S. (1996). *O*NET: An informational system for the workplace. Designing an electronic infrastructure.* Salt Lake City, UT: Utah Department of Employment Security.

**Library of Congress Cataloging-in-Publication Data**
An occupational information system for the 21st century : the development of O*NET / edited by
    Norman G. Peterson ... [et al.].—1st ed.
        p.    cm.
    O*NET database can be found at http://
    Includes bibliographical references and index.
    ISBN 1-55798-556-1 (acid-free paper)
        1. O*NET.   2. Occupations—United States—Classification—Databases.
    3. Job descriptions—United States—Databases.   4. Vocational interests—United States—
    Databases.   I. Peterson, Norman G.
    HB2595.0273   1999
    331.7'02'012—dc21                                                                98-44293
                                                                                          CIP

**British Library Cataloguing-in-Publication Data**
A CIP record is available from the British Library.

*Printed in the United States of America*
*First Edition*

# Contents

# Contributors

Lance E. Anderson, American Institutes for Research, Washington, DC

Sharon Arad, Personnel Decisions Research Institutes, Inc., Minneapolis, MN

Wayne A. Baughman, American Institutes for Research, Washington, DC

Barry R. Blakley, Jeanneret and Associates, Inc., Houston, TX

Walter C. Borman, University of South Florida and Personnel Decisions Research Institutes, Inc., Tampa, FL

Michael A. Campion, Purdue University, West Lafayette, IN

Ruth A. Childs, American Institutes for Research, Washington, DC

Ashley E. Cooke, American Institutes for Research, Washington, DC

David P. Costanza, Management Research Institute and George Washington University, Washington, DC

Erika L. D'Egidio, Jeanneret and Associates, Inc., Houston, TX

Joseph S. Dumas, American Institutes for Research, Concord, MA

Marvin D. Dunette, Personnel Decisions Research Institute, Inc., and the University of Minnesota, Minneapolis

Donna Dye, Office of Policy and Research, U.S. Department of Labor, Washington, DC

Edwin A. Fleishman, Management Research Institute and George Mason University, Washington, DC

James Green, Westat, Inc., Rockville, MD

Mary Ann Hanson, Personnel Decisions Research Institutes, Inc., Tampa, FL

Bradford W. Hesse, American Institutes of Research, Washington, DC

P. Richard Jeanneret, Jeanneret and Associates, Inc., Houston, TX

U. Christean Kubisiak, University of South Florida and Personnel Decisions Research Institutes, Inc., Tampa, FL

Kerry Y. Levin, Westat, Inc., Rockville, MD

Joanne Marshall-Mies, Management Research Institute and Swan Research, Inc., Bethesda, MD

Melinda S. Mayfield, Purdue University, West Lafayette, IN

S. Morton McPhail, Jeanneret and Associates, Inc., Houston, TX

Frederick P. Morgeson, Texas A&M University, College Station, TX

Michael D. Mumford, American Institutes for Research, Washington, DC

Dwayne G. Norris, American Institutes for Research, Washington, DC

Norman G. Peterson, American Institutes for Research, Washington, DC

Andrew M. Rose, American Institutes for Research, Washington, DC

Christopher E. Sager, American Institutes for Research, Washington, DC

Robert J. Schneider, Personnel Decisions Research Institutes, Inc., Minneapolis, MN

Marilyn Silver, Aguirre International, Washington, DC

Paul A. Silver, American Institutes for Research, Palo Alto, CA

Mark H. Strong, Jeanneret and Associates, Inc., Houston, TX

Joseph Waksberg, Westat, Inc., Rockville, MD

# Preface

This book describes a 2-year effort to develop a comprehensive occupational information system, suitable for many purposes, that would primarily reside in electronic media. The product of this effort is a prototype of the national occupational information system intended to replace the *Dictionary of Occupational Titles* (U.S. Department of Labor, 1991a) and its supporting technology (as documented in the *Revised Handbook for Analyzing Jobs*, U.S. Department of Labor, 1991b). The new system has come to be called the *Occupational Information Network* or *O*NET*.

Although the work described in this book took place over approximately 2 years, it built squarely on conceptual and empirical work completed, primarily, over the last 35 or so years. We have truly stood on the shoulders of giants in our attempt to build a system that will prove viable in the future.

It is well that we could depend on the solid thinking and empirical work of our esteemed forebears and colleagues, because it is almost a cliché to say that the world of work is experiencing tremendous change. A few of these sources of change can be easily listed: the advent of personal computers and the closely associated startling rise in the use of the Internet and the World Wide Web; the far-flung effects of global competition and the perceived benefits (and costs) associated with mega-mergers in a variety of industries; the increase in the demographic diversity of the national and international workforce; a rise in the prevalence of the virtual workplace, where people work singly, electronically connected to others, and sometimes in a very mobile fashion; and the increasing importance of teams in accomplishing work, often replacing functions previously performed by layers of hierarchical management. The long-lasting effects of these winds of change are difficult to forecast, but it seems safe to say that the ways in which we think about, analyze, and structure occupations must change as well. But how?

That is the question this book proposes to answer. We believed that by drawing on the best available thinking and research about the purposes, methods, and uses of occupational analysis, we could develop a comprehensive yet flexible occupational information system that would have the capability to meet the needs of a diverse set of users in an efficient, timely manner. We developed a working prototype of that system, including a language to describe occupations; instruments to allow members of the workforce to describe their jobs using that language; methods of sampling occupational incumbents and supervisors; ways of analyzing the information to determine its technical quality and to organize it for various applied uses; and an electronic database containing the initial set of data, with an interface that allows the exploration and extraction of occupational information. As we note at the end of the book, we think we have been successful in developing a working prototype, but as in any such large endeavor, much work remains to completely fulfill the promise of O*NET.

The research described in this book was a highly collaborative effort carried out by a consortium of several organizations: American Institutes for Research, Personnel Decisions Research Institute, Jeanneret and Associates, Management Research Institute, and Westat, Inc. Although each of these organizations had major responsibilities for different segments of the work, the project often involved the use of members from several of the organizations. The multiple authorships on most of the chapters reflect the major contributions of the project staff. In addition, the editors are indebted to Marvin Dunnette of the University of Minnesota for his introductory chapter, to Donna Dye and Marilyn Silver, Department of Labor, for their chapter describing the historical context of this effort, and to Michael Campion, Frederick Morgenson, and Michael Mayfield, Purdue University, for their closing overview chapter on the scientific and theoretical implications of the O*NET for the analysis of work requirements.

There are many others to acknowledge, and this has been done in the acknowledgments by the chapter authors, by the extensive citations of previous and related work, as well as in the comprehensive reference section of the book. We hope the last will be particularly useful to other researchers and practitioners in the field. These references provide clear evidence of the debt this effort owes to researchers that came before us.

We would like to provide a special acknowledgment to the earlier work of Sidney A. Fine, whose ideas and developmental efforts provided much of the basis for the fourth edition of the *Dictionary of Occupational Titles*, which had a long history and wide impact on human resource management.

We should note that this book solely expresses the opinion of its authors. Although the Department of Labor and the State of Utah funded the project to develop the O*NET, nothing said in this book should be construed as representing their opinions or official positions.

# Acknowledgments

Many people contributed to the successful completion of the prototype Occupational Information Network (O*NET) described herein and to the preparation of this book. For their valuable advice throughout the course of this effort, the authors would like to thank Mike Campion, Purdue University, technical review committee; Donna Dye, Department of Labor, project officer; Marilyn Gowing, Office of Personnel Management, technical review committee; Anita Lancaster, Defense Manpower Data Center, technical review committee; Kenneth Pearlman, Lucent Technologies, technical review committee; Marilyn Silver, Aguirre International, Inc., Aguirre project director; and Barbara Smith, State of Utah Occupational Analysis Field Center, contract monitor. The authors would also like to thank Jean King, Susan Wright, Ruth Childs, and George Wheaton at the American Institutes for Research (AIR) for their assistance in editing and producing this book. We are deeply grateful to the editors of the American Psychological Association for their expert assistance and saint-like patience.

In addition, many individuals made substantial contributions to individual chapters in this book. In particular, the author of chapter 1, "Introduction," would like to thank Michael Mumford and Norman Peterson for permission to use portions of their introductory chapters from two reports: Mumford and Peterson (1995) and Peterson (1996).

The authors of chapter 2, "The Origins of O*NET," would like to thank the following people for their work in developing the O*NET: Susan Berryman, for her insights into the importance of cognition in the modern workplace; J. W. Cunningham, Mark Wilson, Donald Drewes, Robert Harvey, and Richard Jeanneret, for their work in identifying the potential applications of generalized work activities/behaviors in the development of a revised *Dictionary of Occupational Titles* (DOT); Donald Drewes, Paul Geyer, Linda Gottfredson, and Eleanor Dietrich Morgenthau, for their work in identifying recommendations for skills and other characteristics for inclusion in the DOT; Edwin Fleishman, Joyce Hogan, Kimberly Brinkmeyer, and Michael Lesser, for evaluating the adequacy of the DOT in describing interpersonal, physical, and psychomotor skills; Karl Botterbusch, for developing suggestions for revising the DOT from the perspective of disability and rehabilitation workers; Paul Geyer, for examining issues of reliability of ratings of occupational characteristics in the DOT; Arnold Packer, for his recommendation to incorporate skills from the Secretary's Commission on Achieving Necessary Skills (SCANS) into the DOT; David Stevens, for his work in analyzing the U.S. occupational classification systems; Dixie Sommers, for her work as chair of the APDOT in encouraging members to share opinions openly and to tackle tough technical and policy issues; Sherril Hurd, Michael Dymmel, and other technical contractors, who prepared papers and briefings in support of the DOT review; Kenneth Pearlman, Marilyn Gowing, Anita Lancaster, and Michael Campion, who refined the initial APDOT report; and Donald Drewes and William Cunningham, for their research into converting DOT-analyst-derived data into O*NET format.

The authors of chapter 3, "The O*NET Content Model," would like to thank Christopher Sager at AIR for his noteworthy contributions to the development of the content model. They would also like to recognize Donna Dye, Barbara Smith, Walter Borman, Richard Jeanneret, and Edwin Fleishman, who played key roles in developing the content model. Finally, the authors would also like to thank Kenneth Pearlman, Michael Campion, Anita Lancaster, and Marilyn Gowing for their many useful comments.

The authors of chapter 4, "Research Method," would like to thank Michael Wilson, for conducting the nonresponse analysis; Ronie Nieva, for her creative data collection suggestions and editorial recommendations; Angie Rasmussen, for her tremendous organization during the multiple phases of data collection; Susan Heltemes, for her management of the telephone center operations; and the Occupational Analysis Field Center staff, for their assistance throughout the data collection.

The authors of chapter 5, "Skills," would like to thank Christopher Sager, Lance Anderson, and Neal Thurman for their contributions to the analyses presented in that chapter.

The authors of chapter 6, "Knowledges," wish to express their thanks to all those who assisted in the development of the Knowledges taxonomy and measurement system. Specifically, we would like to thank Leon Wetrogan, Charles Uhlman, and Janelle Gilbert for their assistance in taxonomy development. Christelle LaPolice deserves special thanks for her hard work and contributions to data analysis and report generation. We would also like to thank the working professionals, graduate students, and research assistants who helped with scale development and the innumerable rating tasks required by such an effort.

The author of Chapter 7, "Education, Training, Experience, and Licensure/Certification," would like to thank Christopher Sager for his advice on the experience and education data collection instruments.

The authors of Chapter 8, "Generalized Work Activities," would like to recognize the contributions of the pioneering researchers in behaviorally oriented job analysis, and especially the work of Ernest J. McCormick. We also wish to extend our thanks to Mark H. Strong, with Jeanneret and Associates, for his efforts in revising the GWA content and conducting some of the data analyses.

The authors of Chapter 9, "Work Context," would like to thank our colleagues, especially Tonya Collings and Laura Galarza, for their contributions to earlier drafts of this chapter, and we would like to acknowledge the numerous job analysis researchers who provided the foundation for this taxonomy.

The authors of chapter 10, "Organizational Context," would like to acknowledge Marvin Dunnette's assistance in developing the O*NET organizational context taxonomy and to thank Victor Jockin and U. Christean Kubisiak for their assistance with data analysis.

The authors of chapter 11, "Abilities," wish to acknowledge the assistance of Leon Wetrogen, Charles Uhlman, and Catherine Fleishman for their contributions to the data analyses and generation of reports on the ability requirement measurement system during this project. We also acknowledge the prior contributions of George Theologus, Tania Romashko, George Wheaton, and Maureen Reilly during earlier developmental efforts on the abilities taxonomy and measurement system. We are particularly grateful to many individuals in numerous organizations who contributed data on the development, evaluation, and utility of the ability requirements approach over several decades of research and application.

The author of chapter 12, "Occupational Interests and Values," would like to thank Rene V. Dawis, Michael Mumford, and Norman Peterson for their intellectual guidance.

The authors of chapter 13, "Work Styles," would like to thank Amy McKee, for her help on the work styles taxonomy; Mary Ann Hanson, for assistance and guidance on the data analysis; and Patti Haas, for her help with the manuscript.

The authors of chapter 14, "Occupation-Specific Descriptors," would like to thank the staff of the Occupational Analysis Field Centers, particularly John Nottingham, Jane Golec, and Bruce Paige, for providing archival task descriptions for use in the occupation-specific descriptor study.

The authors of chapter 15, "Occupational Descriptor Covariates," would like to thank Christopher Sager and Michael Campion for their contributions to that chapter.

The authors of chapter 16, "Cross Domain Analyses," are grateful to Ruth Childs, for preparing the data and providing support for the analyses, and to Patti Haas, for her careful work in preparing the manuscript.

The authors of chapter 18, "Database Design and Development," would like to acknowledge the outstanding contributions of Harvey Ollis of the National Occupational Information Coordinating Committee; Eleanor Dietrich, occupational systems and data consultant for Directions in Work; and Larry Patterson of the North Carolina Occupational Analysis Field Center. The authors would also like to thank the following staff at the American Institutes for Research for their hard work and substantive contributions to the project: Mary Anne Arcilla, for her contributions to the O*NET presentation software and the electronic codebook; Albert Chang, for his programming work on the electronic codebook; Natalie Broomhall and Sarah Beaver, for setting up the structure of the O*NET web site; Shannon Daugherty, for developing O*NET's comprehensive on-line help system; Diana Vandra, for developing the data dictionary; Jaclyn Schrier, for human factors support; and Lori Hodge and Andrew Davis, for their numerous quality-control tests.

Finally, all the authors would like to thank the many organizations and their employees who graciously contributed their time and effort in the data collection. Completion of this work would have been impossible without their participation.

# AN OCCUPATIONAL INFORMATION SYSTEM FOR THE 21ST CENTURY: THE DEVELOPMENT OF O*NET

# Introduction

MARVIN D. DUNNETTE

Robert C. Droege (1988) described the early beginnings and continuing development of the *Dictionary of Occupational Titles* (DOT; U.S. Department of Labor, 1991a) in Gael's (1988) job analysis handbook. The Wagner-Peyser Act of 1933 established a federal–state system for providing public employment services. Local offices were set up and proceeded to use their resources in part to develop occupational information for use in matching applicant qualifications to job opportunities. Soon it became apparent that local offices lacked uniformity in the way they developed job information. This lack of uniformity made interoffice communications about jobs and their requirements extremely difficult in a system that was intended to be national in scope.

Accordingly, a program was inaugurated in 1934 under the direction of two vocational psychologists (William Stead and Carrol Shartle) "to develop authentic information concerning industries and jobs and to discover the qualifications required for success in various occupations." An advisory board was formed that comprised many of the prominent applied psychologists of the time.[1] As a result, occupational research was planned, funded, and implemented in federal research centers throughout the country with administrative and technical supervision from Department of Labor headquarters in Washington and federal funding through the United States Employment Service (USES).

During the ensuing 5 years, 54,000 job analyses were completed. Information gathered from these studies formed the basic information incorporated into the first edition of the DOT, published in 1939. This edition, together with supplements published in the years 1942, 1944, and 1945, provided a framework for classifying 17,500 jobs (structured into 550 occupational groups) according to work performed, job content, and skill levels.

Since the publication of the first DOT, occupational information has continued to be gathered and updated, and improved classification methods have developed. Accordingly, over the ensuing 50 years, updated versions of the DOT have been published: a second edition in 1949, a third in 1965, a fourth in 1977, and a fifth in 1991. The current DOT provides descriptive information for more than 10,000 occupations.

Many methods have been used over the years to develop occupational descriptions for the DOT. Although procedures have changed over time, the most common approach relies on the skills of experienced job analysts who typically have interviewed and observed job incumbents at one or more sites. These observations have then been used by the analysts to identify and describe tasks, duties, work activities, and inferred knowledges, abilities, and other characteristics that may be distinguishing features of the job being studied.

In its earlier editions, the DOT was seen as a compendium of comprehensive descriptions of job features across many occupations. The DOT still provides information that can be important in many areas. One of the intended uses, of course, was person–job matching. For example, trained counselors could use the descriptive information in the DOT in conjunction with what had been gleaned about an individual's work history, stated preferences, and inventories of interests, abilities, and temperament to develop inferences and guidance about the kinds of occupations for which that individual might be well suited. Similarly, employers in both private and public sectors often used DOT information to help in developing position descriptions to aid in various human resources management areas—such as hiring, vocational placement, and training. In fact, over the years, the various editions of the DOT have undoubtedly been used to aid in job analyses, vocational and career counseling, and organizational planning.

In one way, the availability of the DOT may have delayed the development of new thinking about occupations and career guidance. However, over the last 25 years, many new approaches have been developed that use more sophisticated methods of job analysis and that incorporate scoring procedures and interpretive guidelines to aid in the vocational placement or counseling process. Typically, such systems

---

[1] In addition to Stead and Shartle, board members included Paul Achilles, W. V. Bingham, Clark Hull, L. J. O'Rourke, D. G. Paterson, A. T. Poffenburger, M. R. Trabue, and Morris Viteles.

or instruments have yielded not only job descriptions but also standard guidelines specifying the knowledges, skills, and other characteristics important for carrying out the occupation being described. These methods have been thoroughly reviewed and discussed by Harvey (1991b).

Many approaches have been devised and instruments designed for the primary purpose of gaining more information about particular jobs and job requirements, and many specialized job analysis efforts have actually been accomplished over the years. One may quite easily assume that such a flood of activity over these years was due to a desire for more extended and detailed information about jobs and worker requirements than had been supplied by the more recent editions of the DOT. In fact, occupational information contained in the DOT has been supplemented by two additional information systems: the Standard Occupational Classification (SOC) and the Occupational Employment Statistics (OES) program. These different systems collect, describe, classify, and track information about occupations in the U.S. economy. Unfortunately, these systems are, for the most part, conceptually and technically incompatible, and it has become apparent that efforts to match information across them have frequently been difficult, if not impossible.

The SOC was developed in the 1970s with the intention of unifying classification systems by providing a way of cross-referencing and aggregating occupational data according to fields of work. Unfortunately, the existing SOC (1980) has not yet provided a unified classification system for the 664 occupations it lists.

The OES classification system was designed to meet the needs of both data users and data producers. It is an empirically based, economywide occupational classification system introduced in 1983 in which 744 occupations are identified by title as well as by a definition that describes primary job duties. The emphasis is on occupations of special interest to many data users because the system was designed for maximum analytical use of data collected by the Bureau of Labor Statistics to meet a wide variety of needs expressed by many types of organizations.

Recognition of the increasingly active use of privately developed job and person analysis systems as well as incompatibilities among DOT, OES, and SOC led the Secretary of Labor in 1990 to appoint an Advisory Panel for the Dictionary of Occupational Titles (APDOT). APDOT was specifically tasked with identifying limitations of the DOT and specifying requirements for a new, comprehensive occupational information system.

The APDOT report (U.S. Department of Labor [U.S. DOL], 1993b) acknowledges the value of information contained in the current edition of the DOT, but it adds that a number of issues have not been dealt with that need to be addressed in a new and more truly comprehensive occupational information system.

The report notes that the framework underlying the current version of the DOT was more appropriate for describing occupations in mass production industries than in the labor force emerging near the 21st century. More specifically, occupations are described according to tasks being performed by people employed in a given occupation. Typically, these tasks, and the information derived from them, are identified through job analysts' observations of incumbents. No one rejects the need to describe the tasks performed in specific occupations. However, the focus on job tasks, and the procedures used to collect descriptive information, have led to a number of problems.

One problem is that the DOT is based on analysts' descriptions of job tasks. These tasks have been defined in different ways, at different levels of generality. Because description is primarily based on occupation-specific information, it becomes difficult to organize the resulting information and make cross-job comparisons. Moreover, because of differences in the nature and level of available task data, it becomes difficult to demonstrate the comparability of inferences being drawn from the data concerning other attributes, such as the level of job demands or required vocational preparation. As Campbell (1993) pointed out, it is somewhat doubtful that this kind of occupation-specific descriptive information can be used to classify jobs and draw conclusions about similarities and differences in performance requirements.

A second problem is that the DOT fundamentally is based on one kind of descriptive information: the tasks workers perform on their jobs. Obviously, task information is an essential component of any truly comprehensive occupational information system, but other types of information that might be used to describe occupations are not currently included in the DOT. For example, information bearing on the interests, knowledges, skills, and abilities needed to perform job tasks is not directly collected. Such information may be crucial to answer questions inherent in person–job matching, training, skill transfer, and wage and salary administration (Harvey, 1991a; McCormick, 1976, 1979). Not only does the current DOT fail to capture crucial information about person requirements, it also largely fails to generate information about the nature and conditions of task performance. The DOT does provide information about work conditions, including noise, temperature, and work schedule. However, it does not contain more complex types of descriptive information, such as level of job stress, exposure to hazards, organizational influences, or the conditions of task performance.

A third problem is the time and expense involved in updating descriptive information. An adequate analysis of tasks requires a substantial investment of time. Rapid changes in technology and patterns of employment have resulted in serious delays in keeping the DOT updated. Accordingly, large portions of the information are out of date at any given time.

It is surprising to note that the classic book on taxonomies of human performance by Fleishman and Quaintance (1984) was published well over a decade ago. The book contains many taxonomies that could have proved useful in developing job information for the 1991 edition of the DOT. As it is, such steps were not taken, with the result that a large portion of the information contained in the current DOT is seriously out of date.

The foregoing brief overview of shortcomings suggests that the current DOT cannot be used for rapid assessment of the skills, knowledges, and other characteristics required by a job family or for showing how skill levels in one job may relate to those of other jobs.

## FORMATION OF THE APDOT

The preceding observations were, in part, responsible for the formation of the APDOT commissioned by the Secretary of Labor. The APDOT not only considered limitations of the DOT but also developed recommendations related to the development of a new occupational system. According to the APDOT, a viable new occupational information system should

> promote the effective education, training, counseling, and employment of the American Work Force. The DOT should be restructured to accomplish its purpose by providing a database system that identifies, defines, classifies, and describes occupations in the economy in an accessible and flexible manner. Moreover, the DOT should serve as a national benchmark that provides a common language for all users of occupational information. (U.S. DOL, 1993b, p. 6)

The above statement of purpose implies a number of requirements that may be classified under the headings of content, structure, and data collection. These three areas are summarized briefly in the following paragraphs.

### Content of a New Occupational Information System

Traditionally, DOT has had an occupation-specific focus that has made cross-classifications and the formulation of general classifications difficult. The current DOT has not provided a common framework for describing occupations. A new occupational information system needs to possess occupational information that will allow an occupation to be described in terms of more general cross-job descriptors. Such a system will facilitate the integration of descriptive information into broader structures.

Second, the content of a new occupational information system should include cross-occupation descriptive information that includes the kind of work being done and conditions under which work is performed. Similarly, it is necessary to describe the requirements imposed on the people doing the work.

These considerations dictate the development of a complex, multivariate, descriptive system that includes attributes of both the occupation and the worker.

Third, content of the new system must take account of intended applications of the information that is gathered. Such cross-occupation descriptors should consider both attributes arising from experience, such as skills and expertise (Chi & Glaser, 1985; Halpern, 1994), and more basic attributes of the individual, such as abilities, interests, and personality characteristics (Dawis, 1991; Hough, 1992, 1997; Snow & Lohman, 1984).

### Structure of a New Occupational Information System

The panel recognized that the new occupational information system should be able to answer a wide range of queries. The ability to respond to the different needs of many different users imposes a number of constraints.

First, different applications will require analyses at different levels of specificity, depending on such factors as focusing on a single occupation or much broader issues such as job matching, retraining, or comparisons across occupational levels. Such needs suggest that descriptors should be hierarchically arranged.

Second, the system needs to be accessible to people with different backgrounds who wish to address differing kinds of issues. Descriptors need to be phrased so they are easily understood by all users, regardless of background, and sufficiently flexible so that they can be combined with various facets of the overall database.

### Data Collection Methodology

If the new occupational information system is to be maximally useful, it must be capable of providing accurate descriptions of work characteristics and worker attributes. Thus, procedures must be developed that ensure effective measurement regardless of the designated variables or types of attributes.

In addition, the system must also remain current; thus, the measurement system must allow for rapid, cost-effective data collection. This is especially important in a rapidly changing workforce; the new information system cannot only focus on well known, existing occupations. The need for a system capable of identifying new, emerging occupations implies that descriptions of work and worker characteristics cannot be rigidly referenced to existing occupation titles. Indeed, information must be collected at position levels in such a way that aggregation across positions will be capable of identifying emerging occupations and occupational families.

## TAXONOMIC ISSUES

The APDOT report establishes a set of criteria for evaluating any new occupational information system. Ideally, a new occupational information system would provide meaningful information about occupations in such a way that it permits users to address the many questions posed by the APDOT report. How might one go about developing a system that will allow users to address these many issues? The answer, as mentioned earlier, lies in developing a common descriptive language.

A meaningful taxonomy essentially is a classification system. The purpose of classification is to provide a set of categories or constructs that allows us to summarize information about a set of objects by assigning objects to a smaller number of categories (Fleishman & Quaintance, 1984). Because people work in a variety of different positions and these positions might be described in a number of different ways, the development of a taxonomy is an essential step in the development of an occupational information system based on a common descriptive language.

Development of any taxonomy involves three major steps (Fleishman & Mumford, 1991; Owens & Schoenfeldt, 1979). First, the domain of objects to be described must be defined. Second, a set of descriptors must be developed that allows us to assess the similarities and differences among all objects lying in this domain. Third, a set of rules must be developed that allows us to group objects together on the basis of this descriptive information.

But, as previously mentioned, many different classification systems are possible, and several have been developed over recent years. They differ in the objects they examine, in the descriptors used to assess those objects, and in the systems used to group objects. Such competing classification systems pose another problem. Specifically, how does one determine whether one classification is superior to another? Traditionally, the answer has been that the most useful is chosen. Recently, however, Fleishman and Mumford (1991) proposed a broader set of criteria (based on construct validity) for evaluating different classification systems (Cronbach, 1971; Landy, 1986; Messick, 1989, 1994).

Within this construct validation framework, the question is whether the classification will lead to more meaningful inferences about the likely behavior or characteristics of objects than the inferences provided by competing classification methods. Evidence for the meaningfulness of the inferences being derived from a classification might be obtained from many sources. Fleishman and Mumford (1991) made a distinction between two basic types of validity evidence: internal and external validity.

Although internal validity is primary for carrying out further research, external validity is critical for developing broader interpretations and uses of any given set of measures. External validity is generated by a series of inferential tests. In essence, knowledge is advanced as hypotheses are confirmed and the number of valid inferences increases (Cronbach, 1971; Landy, 1986). As already implied, external validity of classification represents the strongest evidence for the meaningfulness of a taxonomic system. Even so, procedures used in developing the content model, or descriptors used to summarize information about occupations, must possess internal validity in order for them to properly lay the groundwork for subsequent assessment of the external validity of the classification system.

A first step in undertaking the research described in this volume was to examine the content model proposed by the APDOT in conjunction with reviewing the types of occupational descriptors that might be incorporated into an electronic database that could eventually be used as the DOT replacement. Peterson (1996) noted that much of the research effort undertaken as part of developing the new occupational information system took the form of devising a general approach for organizing occupational description to accomplish the ends outlined by the APDOT report.

Perhaps most important is the notion that the new system should provide a common language for describing and thinking about occupations. The actual definitions and rating scales that accompany each descriptor provide the basic elements of this language, the words. The theoretical and empirical relationships between the descriptors within each domain and across the domains begin to provide a sort of grammar for the occupational universe—the ways in which the words fit together to provide information about occupations. Accompanying this notion is the very real point that language is not static but constantly evolving, although not at a rate that obviates the usefulness of the language.

## CHAPTER ORGANIZATION

Subsequent chapters in this book describe details and results of an initial large-scale attempt to translate the APDOT's recommendations into a new occupational information system known as the O*NET. Chapter 2 provides an insider's overview of the origins of the O*NET model, which stemmed from the APDOT's work. Chapter 3 presents a more complete elaboration of the several components of the O*NET content model. The remaining chapters describe efforts to operationalize the model.

Chapter 4 describes the research methodology, including sampling and data collection procedures, and the general methods of analysis used. This chapter also presents results concerning response rates and describes findings from nonresponse analysis. The next nine chapters (chapters 5 through 13) describe the instruments developed and the data analyses carried out for each domain of the O*NET content model. These domains encompass (a) 46 skills; (b) 33 knowledges; (c) occupational preparation (education, training, licensure, and experience); (d) 42 generalized work activities (actions taken in carrying out job responsibilities); (e) 46 aspects of work context (environmental components, hazards, role relationships, degree of challenge, etc.); (f) 49 aspects of organization context (control, variety, training methods, compensation methods, degree of freedom, etc.); (g) 52 abilities (oral expression, written expression, number facility, dexterities, etc.); (h) 21 occupational values (keeping busy, good working conditions, opportunity to get ahead, getting recognition, etc.); and (i) 17 work style requirements (achieving, persisting, cooperating, handling stress, being dependable, etc.).

Chapter 14 examines a number of methods for collecting O*NET occupation-specific information, and Chapter 15 examines issues related to the accuracy of the O*NET occupational information system. Chapter 16 further assesses the construct validity of measures by examining relationships between descriptors from various content domains, across domains, and assessing the structure of the cross-domain relationships, whereas Chapter 17 presents results of clustering jobs on the basis of responses to two of the instruments developed for this project: 46 basic and cross-functional skills and 42 generalized work activities. Chapter 18 describes design and development of the electronic database and associated software. Chapter 19 is an overview of the results and their implications for future development of the O*NET. Chapter 20 takes a broader and more theoretical look at the issues raised by the development of O*NET.

Obviously, this book represents a significant departure from methods of the past. It is apparent that the impetuses for the actions and results described in this book are the clarity and wisdom of the recommendations developed by the APDOT. These successful beginning steps must be followed with all due haste and vigor to continue and expand on what has been begun.

# The Origins of O*NET

DONNA DYE AND MARILYN SILVER

In January 1995, the Department of Labor (DOL) first used the title Occupational Information Network (O*NET) for the DOL's new occupational information tool. The title was DOL's final touch on a new tool that would be instrumental in revolutionizing the labor exchange process. For the first time, there was a comprehensive conceptual framework to guide activities such as job placement, training, and school curriculum development. By combining a common language and an automated database, O*NET can help transform the current labor exchange process into an efficient and effective self-directed system.

O*NET is both a product and a system. As a product, O*NET is a database that uses a common language for collecting, describing, and presenting valid, reliable occupational information about work and the worker. As a system, O*NET is a network of organizations improving, enhancing, and disseminating the information database. Whether a product or a system, O*NET is an informational hub for language and data, enabling labor exchange members to communicate with each other.

Although still in the developmental stage, O*NET is being viewed as the nation's newest technology for dealing with major workplace issues. It replaces the *Dictionary of Occupational Titles* (DOT; U.S. DOL, 1991a). Since the 1930s, the DOT has been the primary source for occupational information, but in recent years it has become outmoded. The DOT was designed to meet the needs of the 1930s and 1940s. Reflecting a view of work that was mechanistic and hierarchical, the DOT cannot deal with connections between occupations and transferability of skills. Nor can it foster effective integration of technology, skills, and new workplace structures. With its emphasis on a contemporary conceptual framework; a flexible, automated database; a network of developers and vendors to enhance the database; and support by employers and users alike, the O*NET is becoming the nation's new primary source of occupational information.

## THE CHANGING WORLD OF WORK

The origin of O*NET was in the late 1980s, when DOL began to see that changes in the labor market and the workplace were putting a strain on the labor exchange process. Global competition, new technology, and increased skill demands were identified as major forces shaping the 1990s and beyond.

## The Facts Creating the Challenge

The fall 1989 edition of DOL's *Occupational Outlook Quarterly* spelled out the challenges of preparing the new workforce to meet the conditions and demands of the changing world of work:

- A gap was identified between what basic skills business needed and the qualifications of the entry-level workers available to business.
- An imbalance existed between the educational preparation of those entering the labor force and industry's requirements, raising an important concern about the ability of the labor market to be productive.
- Educators and business needed better information in order to identify accurately what was needed to satisfy business requirements for productive workers.
- Managerial, professional, and technical occupations that required the most education would have faster rates of growth than occupations with the lowest educational requirements, some of which are even projected to decline.
- More than half of all new jobs created between 1984 and 2000 would require some education beyond high school, and almost a third would be filled by college graduates.
- At the same time, occupations with the fastest growth would not necessarily provide the most new jobs.
- Employment growth and labor force growth would be slower, primarily because of the declining number of people in the 16- to 24-year-old group.
- A shortage of entry workers was identified in certain geographic areas that have low unemployment rates.
- The service-producing sector was projected to account for most of the job growth into the year

2000; health and services would account for a high percentage; business services industries would account for slightly less; and retail trade would account for the least growth.

- Women, persons with disabilities, and minorities were all projected to increase their share of the labor force (Kutscher, 1989).

In an effort to ensure that the American workforce would have skills to meet the challenges of the future into 2000, DOL implemented the Workforce Quality Agenda. The thrust of the agenda was twofold: first, it would identify skills needed in the labor market and establish workplace competency guidelines and occupational skill standards. Second, it would work toward ensuring that both new entrants and existing workers had those skills and ways to continue updating them, while on the job. The agenda also called for improving labor market efficiency by improving the tools used to identify workplace skills and place workers in jobs. The DOT was identified as a potentially effective labor market tool in the Workforce Quality Agenda. The Secretary of Labor seated three distinct, but complementary, national advisory groups to assist with the agenda. These included the National Advisory Commission on Work-Based Learning, the Secretary's Commission on Achieving Necessary Skills (SCANS), and the Advisory Panel for the Dictionary of Occupational Titles (APDOT).

## O*NET: STARTING WITH THE APDOT

The APDOT was officially chartered by Secretary of Labor Elizabeth Dole on August 28, 1990, for an initial 2-year term. After publishing its *Interim Report* and soliciting public reaction to its potential recommendations in March 1992, the panel requested a brief extension to complete its work. Its charter was extended for a full year by then Secretary of Labor Lynn Martin in August 1992. APDOT held its last official meeting in December 1992 and completed its final report in February 1993. *The New DOT: A Database of Occupational Titles for the Twenty-First Century* was APDOT's final report. It was published in May 1993, when it was presented to the new Secretary of Labor, Robert Reich.

The seating of an official advisory panel to review the issues surrounding the DOT was deemed necessary because the DOT was viewed as an entrenched system. It had been in continuous use for more than 60 years. As the nation's single most comprehensive source of occupational information, the DOT served the needs of a wide variety of users both inside and outside of DOL. For example, reference to the DOT is written into the regulations of the Social Security Administration, where it serves as a tool for making Social Security determinations. The active participation and input of this larger DOT user community were seen as essential to the integrity and success of the review. In addition, DOL acknowledged that in considering the DOT's future, a wide and diversified

range of technical expertise, not available within DOL alone, was needed. The APDOT panel reflected broad user perspectives and technical expertise.

## APDOT's Charter and Members

Officially, the APDOT was chartered to report to and advise the Assistant Secretary for Employment and Training on the development, publication, and dissemination of the DOT. APDOT operated for most of its tenure with only 12 members. They were selected to reflect the points of views of users, specifically from government, vocational training, education, and the private sector, including employers and academic communities.

As identified in the charter, the panel was enlisted to

- Recommend the type, scope of coverage, and level of detail that should be collected on occupations to produce a DOT;
- Advise on appropriateness of methodologies of occupational analysis used to identify, classify, define, and describe jobs in the DOT;
- Advise on new or alternative approaches to the production, publication, and dissemination of the DOT; and
- Recommend options for implementation of improvements to the DOT.

The APDOT was initially established as part of the Secretary of Labor's Workforce Quality Agenda. Facilitating the nation's workforce development efforts and improving the country's labor exchange function are key elements of DOL's mission regardless of the political party in power. For example, the Employment and Training Administration's (ETA's) stated mission is "to contribute to the more efficient and effective functioning of the U.S. labor market by providing high quality job training, employment, labor market information, and income maintenance services primarily through state and local workforce development systems" (p. 3). In reviewing the DOT, APDOT was studying an institutionalized tool that had served DOL's mission for more than half a century. Therefore, the panel's work continued uninterrupted and largely unaffected by changes in Secretaries or administrations.

## APDOT's Operations

Between October 1990 and December 1992, the APDOT held quarterly public meetings during which technical experts and members of the public were invited to offer testimony on all issues under discussion. By the time APDOT completed its work, nearly 50 experts and representatives of user groups had chosen to address the panel. In addition, more than 50 staff papers and technical reports had been commissioned on a range of issues such as occupational classification options; reliability and validity of current DOT descriptors; alternative job analysis methodologies; automation issues and options; coordination and integration of the Standard Occupational Classification (SOC) system with the DOT; needs of special user groups, such as vocational rehabilitation; linkage with other databases, such as the National Assessment of Educational Progress (NAEP); and the status of vendor products based on the DOT.

To make the most efficient use of APDOT members, each was assigned to specific subcommittee activities. APDOT began with two subcommittees: one focused on skills issues and the other on purpose/uses of the DOT. As the project progressed, the APDOT reconfigured and refocused to tackle additional issues. In addition, as part of ongoing subcommittee activities, APDOT members presided over special workshops to educate and inform themselves, as well as the DOT Review staff. APDOT members were always careful to report the results of these sessions at public meetings of the full panel.

## The Changing World of Work: Recognizing the Need to Move Beyond the DOT Into a New Paradigm

DOL implied the possible need for a radical restructuring of the DOT as early as the initial concept paper, published in the *Federal Register* in August 1990 (Department of Labor, Employment and Training Administration, 1990). APDOT members then began to clearly articulate this position at their very first meeting. Most controversial was the call for a new paradigm to conceptualize the changing world of work and the DOT's role in reflecting it. The "dictionary" concept was explicitly described as passé, with suggestions of an "encyclopedia, or multidimensional, electronic framework" offered as a replacement paradigm.

After extended discussion, APDOT members requested a background paper summarizing current trends in the workplace and identifying their potential impact on the DOT. The intention was not to conduct original research but to learn from and summarize previous studies. Donald Drewes wrote *The Changing World of Work: Implications for the DOT Review Initiative* (Meridian Corp., 1991). The issues he identified were viewed as critical to the scope of APDOT's investigation. Although DOL and APDOT repeatedly described the project as a "review" or "revision" of the DOT, awareness that a "replacement" for the DOT would likely be required was recognized early on. A staff management paper summarizing the impact of "The Changing World of Work" (Silver, 1991) depicted the choices faced by APDOT, and ultimately DOL. The choices ranged from "tinkering around the edges" of the current DOT to radically restructuring it, along with the systems and methods used to develop, analyze, and disseminate its information.

At the first meeting, one APDOT member asked Carolyn Golding, then Deputy Assistant Secretary for ETA and the Secretary's representative at the meeting, whether, after the panel devoted the next few years to examining issues involved in revising the DOT and made recommendations that responded to the nation's needs, DOL was prepared to implement those recommendations. Ms. Golding responded that while there were never any guarantees, DOL was committed to this study and would consider all recommendations very carefully. It is testimony both to the quality of APDOT's work and the seriousness of DOL's intentions that most APDOT recommendations have been implemented.

## The Dictionary of Occupational Titles (DOT)

The DOT was created in the 1930s, when American industry and government faced the economic crises of the Great Depression. Within this context, DOL took aggressive action. The nation's public employment system was created to improve linkages between skill demand and skill supply. The DOT was developed as a specific tool to assist the new public employment system in carrying out its labor exchange responsibilities. During the period, national apprenticeship programs were established to determine standards for accreditation of industry programs and certification of individual workers (Meridian Corp., 1991).

The philosophical underpinnings and methodological basis of the current DOT still reflect the work structure of mid-20th century America. Constructed on the findings of 1930s occupational research and with the methodology of classic functional job analysis, the inherent worldview reflected in the DOT is that of a manufacturing company emphasizing product rather than information. The emphasis remains on what is produced rather than what the worker does. Moreover, data on worker activities as collected and described in the DOT favor manual over mental tasks. DOT descriptions assume a Tayloristic worldview that is becoming increasingly obsolete. Although changes have been made to the DOT over the past half century (four separate editions were published), its conceptual core has remained remarkably consistent. In short, the DOT's approach and method reflect a time when work was routinized, repetitive, and organized along hierarchical lines (Berryman & Bailey, 1992).

In proposing that DOL once again take direct action to influence the nation's labor exchange efforts, some argue that the U.S. faces an economic crisis comparable to what it faced in the 1930s. The contemporary workplace is becoming transformed. Global competition is increasing the pressure for high performance. Businesses are reorganizing to develop more flexible and adaptable workforce structures. Organizations are flattening. Midlevel managers are disappearing. Jobs are increasingly performed by self-managed teams, with groups making decisions that were previously in management's domain (Meridian Corp., 1991). A sectoral shift in emphasis from manufacturing to services is creating demand for new skill profiles. Along with other factors, such as the comparative quality of American products and services and the speed with which new products are brought to market, the overall impact of change in today's workplace is a demand for higher skills, or increased human resource requirements (Kantor, 1989).

## The End of the Job = The End of the DOT

These workplace changes directly affect the nature and description of occupations and work itself. When APDOT began its investigation, shifting occupational structures were not as well documented as they are today, but signs were evident nevertheless (Hunter & Schmidt, 1982; NCEE, 1990). Through their investigation, some APDOT members came to believe that a job or occupation as defined by the industrial revolution was being redefined by the information age. In the world of self-directed work teams, tasks and activities were not so neatly or rigidly bundled into jobs. Bureaucratic levels were not so rigidly maintained. The tasks and activities previously performed by supervisors and managers—decisions about resource allocations, time schedules, and quality determinations—were migrating throughout the workforce.

APDOT believed that these changes had profound repercussions for the DOT. The organizing premise of the DOT was that a job is a group of task activities performed by a single individual. Assignment of tasks to a job was seen as sufficiently stable to warrant groupings of jobs into an occupation and a stable description prepared in terms of the common tasks performed. Thus, to the extent that the organization of work becomes more fluid and workers more flexible, the suitability of the "dictionary" approach to describe work becomes questionable. If job boundaries become soft and subject to rapid change, the notion of a universe of jobs that the DOT purports to represent becomes subject to challenge. If the universe of work is not stable, then the descriptions prepared from samples of this universe are limited to the time frame for which the job structure remains relatively constant (Meridian Corp., 1991).

APDOT's recognition of this flexibility was reinforced by its awareness that occupational categories were collapsing and merging as companies broadened their job classification categories and drastically reduced the number of differentiated occupations. Added to the mix was APDOT's awareness that entire industries of "highly skilled" individuals were becoming dislocated for extended periods of time (e.g., aerospace-, computer-, and defense-related industries), as people struggled to identify their "transferable skills." Transferable skills are those skills common to more than one occupation. They enable people to move successfully from one occupation to another and play a critical role in helping us define

and understand occupational mobility patterns both within (career ladders) and across (career lattices) occupational areas (Offerman & Gowing, 1990).

This backdrop provided a strong impetus for APDOT to consider a new conceptual framework to replace the nation's "dictionary" approach to describing occupations. APDOT conceptualized the idea of a database of information. It was framed within a "content model structure" that identified, defined, and described occupations according to the comprehensive elements of job performance. The database was constructed as a virtual "wish list" of everything a typical industrial/organizational psychologist "might want to know" about the work, the worker, and the workplace. APDOT's content model contained hundreds of information units on job requirements, worker attributes, and the content and context of work.

## THE COMMON LANGUAGE AND THE CONTENT MODEL: A LASTING CONTRIBUTION

APDOT believed that developing the DOT database as a national benchmark could help standardize terminology for consistent use across sectors. Today there are few standard definitions in the study of skills and work. If major consumers and producers of occupational information could agree on a common language for identifying and defining worker attributes, work content, and outcomes, then efforts to bridge the gap between workforce skills and workplace requirements would be greatly enhanced. APDOT developed a content model (see Figure 2-1) that offered comprehensive information about work and workers in a common language useful to students, educators, employers, and workers. By attempting to improve communication among these groups, APDOT was trying to help integrate learning, training, and work in ways not currently possible.

The content model is frequently viewed as the single most important contribution of the APDOT. Its primary author was Kenneth Pearlman, although he enjoyed the support of his panel colleagues and, in particular, significant contributions from Marilyn Gowing and Anita Lancaster. APDOT did not view the content model as a finished product but rather "as an initial point of departure and subject to further research and analysis as well as administrative decisions that will be made during implementation" (APDOT, 1993, p. 31). As the APDOT explained,

This content model has been drawn from a thorough analysis of user survey results, public comments and a wide-ranging review of research in such areas as job and skill analysis, human individual differences, and organization analysis. It embodies a view of occupational analysis that reflects the characteristics both of occupations (through use of "job-oriented" descriptors) and of people (through use of "worker-oriented" descriptors) as well as the broader labor market. (APDOT, 1993, p. 31)

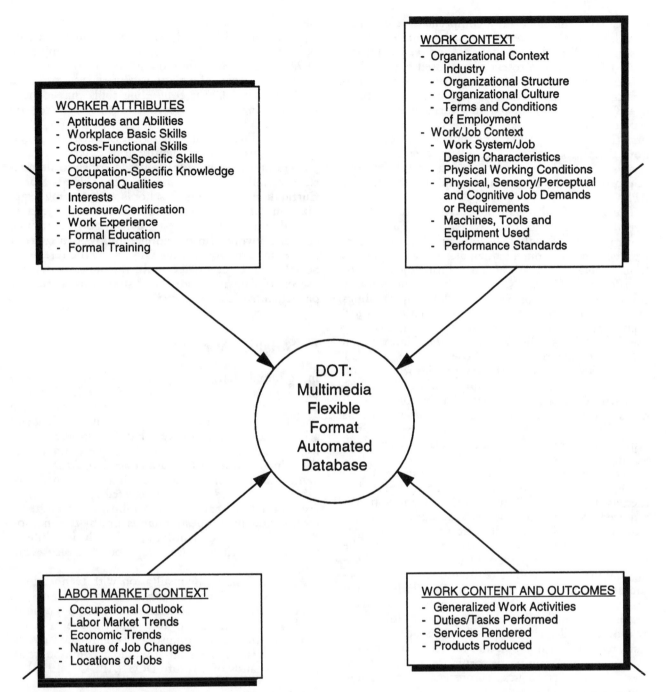

**WORKER ATTRIBUTES**
- Aptitudes and Abilities
- Workplace Basic Skills
- Cross-Functional Skills
- Occupation-Specific Skills
- Occupation-Specific Knowledge
- Personal Qualities
- Interests
- Licensure/Certification
- Work Experience
- Formal Education
- Formal Training

**WORK CONTEXT**
- Organizational Context
  - Industry
  - Organizational Structure
  - Organizational Culture
  - Terms and Conditions of Employment
- Work/Job Context
  - Work System/Job Design Characteristics
  - Physical Working Conditions
  - Physical, Sensory/Perceptual and Cognitive Job Demands or Requirements
  - Machines, Tools and Equipment Used
  - Performance Standards

**DOT:
Multimedia
Flexible
Format
Automated
Database**

**LABOR MARKET CONTEXT**
- Occupational Outlook
- Labor Market Trends
- Economic Trends
- Nature of Job Changes
- Locations of Jobs

**WORK CONTENT AND OUTCOMES**
- Generalized Work Activities
- Duties/Tasks Performed
- Services Rendered
- Products Produced

**FIGURE 2-1.** APDOT content model. *Note.* From *The New DOT: A Database of Occupational Titles for the Twenty-First Century* (p. 32), by the U.S. Department of Labor (1993b), Washington, DC: Author.

## RESEARCH: THE FOUNDATION OF APDOT'S RECOMMENDATIONS

APDOT engaged in extensive research to ensure that it had the best available information. Using the Occupational Analysis Field Center (OAFC) staff to frame each issue, subject matter experts were asked to contribute analyses, opinions, and ideas for some of the most perplexing and complex issues. Highlighted here are those areas that generated the most research: users, job analysis, skills and other occu-

pational characteristics, classification, international review, and dissemination.

## Uses and Users of the DOT: A Customer-Oriented Approach

One significant reason for the DOT project's success was the ongoing effort to discover and reflect what its "customers and stakeholders" wanted. From the beginning, project staff used multiple avenues in this effort. These included (a) a comprehensive user survey, (b) *Federal Register* notices, (c) an interested parties mailing list, (d) presentations, and (e) articles and press releases. More recently, staff used fax mailings and the Internet as major sources of customer information. When the review project began, a team of OAFC analysts conducted structured interviews of representative DOT users. In some cases, this was the first time that the DOT's developers had discussed how their product was used by its customers. The analysts used these data to construct informative, miniprofiles of users, customers, and stakeholders for APDOT.

The APDOT also had information from a DOT User Survey conducted by Westat, Inc. The Westat work provided a global view of the DOT user. Users wanted coverage on all occupations at the current level of detail. And, athough users used the DOT for transferability of skills, it was not their primary source. A summary of Westat's (1993) major findings indicated that certain areas of occupational information are consistently treated as very important by users in all fields, whereas other types of information are very important only for those who use the DOT for specific purposes. For example, information on basic skills, thinking skills, duties, and tasks associated with occupations are viewed as important in all fields, whereas information on the interest patterns associated with occupations appears to be especially important for those who use the DOT for career and vocational rehabilitation counseling.

The following examples were considered by APDOT as they learned what had been expected in the past from the DOT and identified what would be required to serve the country's occupational information needs. Because all military service occupational classification systems are cross-coded to the DOT, it is the most powerful tool available for linking military and civilian occupations, a critical resource during downsizing efforts. Similarly, human resource professionals in both the public and private sectors use the DOT to create or modify job classifications, to determine qualifications for selection tests, to establish skill and training requirements, and to develop job training performance appraisals, career planning strategies, competency certification, and job design.

DOL officials traditionally use the DOT in training, retraining, and placement programs especially within the Employment Service, Job Training Partnership Act programs, Job Corps, and Bureau of Apprenticeship and Training. The Bureau of Labor Statistics (BLS) uses the DOT in its development of occupational and career information. DOT-type information also is critical to support planned workforce investment efforts such as one-stop career centers and school-to-work transition programs.

The Social Security Administration identifies the DOT as a major source of information used to determine disability benefits. Vocational rehabilitation practitioners use the DOT extensively to identify potential new occupations for persons with disabilities.

The DOT is central to counseling and guidance in high school and beyond, where it is used to identify skills and to plan career options. For example, in 1992, more than 4 million people used the state-supported career information delivery systems based on DOT data. Other counseling tools that identify wage earnings and employment outlook also rely on the DOT.

The DOT is used in the nation's foreign labor certification program to identify jobs offered by employers and held by applicants, in order to demonstrate eligibility to work in the United States. Curriculum developers in schools and training organizations use the DOT to match training objectives with descriptions of tasks and to modify curricula. Agencies involved in developing and reporting labor market information use the DOT as a core reference. Social science researchers have also made extensive use of its data in hundreds of studies of workforce participants (APDOT, 1993).

## Job Analysis Methods

In its initial charge to the APDOT, DOL suggested that on-site data collection used in the DOT methodology was becoming cost prohibitive for collecting data on all occupations. Using its own experience as a base, the APDOT believed that data should be collected using structured job analysis questionnaires as the primary strategy for data collection. APDOT began by identifying 60 current job analysis methods. Of the 60 methods, 14 were selected for closer study and evaluation, based on the following criteria: (a) the method used questionnaires or (b) the method could contribute to identifying and analyzing skills in the new knowledge-based, high-performance economy.

After analysis and consultation with technical experts as well as the developers of various job analysis approaches, APDOT concluded that although high-quality results are achievable with the use of structured questionnaires and properly conducted surveys, no single system existed that would accommodate all of the demands of a future DOT (APDOT, 1993).

### Cognitive Psychology and Cognitive Task Analysis

Although traditional job analysis has focused on observable behaviors, cognitive analysis is concerned with forms of thinking that determine the quality of observable behaviors (Gitomer, 1992). Cognitive theories typically explain a specific behavior in terms of its underlying cognitive structures and processes (American Psychological Association, 1992). From her work with high-performance companies, APDOT member Sue Berryman provided considerable insights into the importance of cognition in the modern workplace. Furthermore, she prompted an investigation into the use of cognitive psychology and cognitive task analysis for the new DOT. To assist the APDOT, the American Psychological Association (APA) was asked to make recommendations on how cognitive psychology may be used in revising the DOT. The APA commissioned five papers and conducted a workshop that focused on specific questions and the five papers. The APA submitted two practical recommendations and concluded that, with a number of qualifiers, cognitive psychology and cognitive task analysis could be useful in the DOT (APA, 1992).

### Skills Transferability

APDOT defines transferable skills as those skills that are common to more than one occupation. They enable individuals to move successfully from one occupation to another. Information about transferable skills plays a critical role in helping to define and understand occupational mobility patterns both within and across occupational areas. Consequently, the identification of these skills and their determinants has been a focal point for educators and human resources professionals concerned with individual employability and training. APDOT as well as users believed that providing information relevant to the analysis and determination of transferable skills would be essential in a revised DOT.

### The Role of Generalized Work Activities/ Behaviors in Skills Transferability

The potential for using generalized work activities or behaviors to help in the determination of transferable skills was recognized early on by APDOT members. As it developed the content model, the APDOT studied both generalized work behaviors (worker oriented) and generalized work activities (job oriented). APDOT defined general work behaviors as a category of skill-related information that is more specific than cross-functional skills. The components of this domain represent aggregations of similar occupation-specific skills into broad activity statements. Generalized work activities (GWAs) were defined as aggregations of related duties or tasks into somewhat more general activity statements that do not include highly job-specific content.

Several technical experts and developers of systems were asked to speculate on the potential application of generalized work activities and behaviors in the development of a revised DOT. Although each qualified his response in some way, all concluded that GWAs/generalized work behaviors (GWBs) would be useful in a revised DOT. Harvey (1992) concluded that "GWBs should be included in the DOT, and that doing so would allow it to address many functions for which it is now unsuitable (e.g., grouping jobs for validity generalization; describing jobs for synthetic validity studies; identifying transferable skills; planning career paths; providing linkages to detailed task-level databases)," (p. 3). Jeanneret (1992b) wrote, "The effect GWBs would have on the validity of transferable skills information should be extremely positive" (p. 11). Drewes (1993) stated, "General work activities can be expected to contribute to the development of a future DOT in five major areas: SOC Standard Occupational Classification descriptors, intra-occupational clustering, new/emerging occupations, linkage to ability requirement, and skills transferability determinations" (pp. 29–30). Cunningham and Wilson (1993) commented, "GWBs should prove very useful in defining generalizable knowledge and skill modules. In fact, the GWBs themselves might be viewed as manifestations of knowledges and skills (KSs)" (p. 8).

## Skills and Other Characteristics

Several staff papers and workshops contributed to the development of APDOT recommendations for skills and other characteristics by addressing such topics as skill complexity, skill definition, and skill transferability.

Several experts evaluated the adequacy of the DOT for describing interpersonal, physical, and psychomotor skills. They concluded that the DOT did not contain adequate information on these skills,

> None of the major worker-based job analysis methods reviewed in the Job Analysis Handbook for Business, Industry and Government can provide a comprehensive description of the interpersonal, physical, and psychomotor requirements of jobs. We suggest that the skills within each domain can be used to generate a checklist which, in turn, can be used to describe the requirements of jobs. These checklists are the means by which skill information can be translated into job analysis methods that yield job descriptions and database information. (Hogan, 1992, pp. 3–4)

Other experts contributed to APDOT's deliberations and development of the content model for psychomotor, physical, and interpersonal requirements of work. For example, one expert observed that "It is probably true that no one system will meet all the requirements for the revised DOT, and that several systems may need to be coded for use in classifying jobs, especially with regard to the level of detail and aggregation of information required for specialized purposes" (Fleishman, 1992b, p. 5).

Disability and rehabilitation workers are serious users of the DOT. To ensure that the APDOT understood this community's needs and uses, one expert was asked to develop suggestions for revising the DOT. He made five suggestions: more expanded worker characteristics should be included; newer technologies need to be included in the work fields and materials, products, subject matter, and services; the number of occupational definitions needs to be reduced (the use of generalized work behaviors appears to be the most feasible method to do this); and a skills-based classification could be very useful (Botterbusch, 1992).

Another expert examined issues of reliability in ratings of occupational characteristics in the DOT for the purpose of making recommendations for retaining, revising, or replacing DOT occupational characteristics. He concluded that no current DOT item should be dropped; some items should be added, such as interpersonal requirements and organizational requirements; and other occupational characteristics should be revised. He also made recommendations for research areas (Geyer, 1992).

At the time of the DOT review, the Secretary's Commission on Achieving Necessary Skills (SCANS) was finishing its work of identifying the skills needed to be successful in the modern workplace. The question of including these SCANS skills in the DOT was addressed, and the director of the SCANS commission recommended the inclusion of SCANS in the DOT job descriptions and a significant role for the DOT in effective development and use of the American workforce: "The DOT can play a more important role if the DOT establishes a universal language that employers routinely use. The language should be the focus for job analyses performed by all the organizations involved in the Learning-A-Living system" (Packer, 1992, p. 6). (Learning-A-Living is a system for effective development of the workplace.)

## Classification

One of APDOT's principal charges was to advise the Secretary of Labor on the most appropriate classification system for the DOT. For the previous 60 years, the DOT had had its own separate and distinct classification system. In the last (1991) edition of the DOT, more than 12,000 "different" occupations were identified. In addition, thousands more alternate titles were listed. Not only was this level of "occupational" differentiation unmanageable, it also was incorrect. Although people might not be able to agree completely on the appropriate level of description for an occupation, there was general consensus that 12,000 was too many! In fact, staff provided APDOT with examples like "sewing machine operator," in which the differentiating characteristic among 78 different sewing machine operators was the type of equipment or sewing machine used. APDOT favored a dramatic decrease in the number of occupations to be detailed in the DOT and saw this position as consistent with the future direction of the American economy.

APDOT members believed that the standardization of classification systems across all major sources of occupational information, including the DOT, would lead to one system in which both occupational (job content) information and labor market (wages, supply, demand) information would be technically and conceptually compatible. Using a standardized classification for the new DOT would assist labor market analysts and those interested in the counting functions, without harming those who prefer a skills-based system for classifying data. This was possible because an electronic DOT database would no longer need be tied to one rigid classification method. The database structure would allow for presentation and manipulation of the data in whatever manner was desired by the user, thereby serving a broader range of user needs. This potential for multiple ways to classify the data is extremely important for workforce development efforts in that it would facilitate users' capacities to identify transferable skills (APDOT, 1993).

To provide information to test its hypotheses on classification and to help in developing recommendations, APDOT examined an array of methods for classifying occupational information in a revised DOT. Options included classifying (a) by skills, (b) by type of work performed, or (c) by some other method.

An economist and user of the DOT analyzed the complexities of the U.S. occupational classification systems and built a convincing case for consolidating them:

> Like a catamaran, this case rests on twin hulls. One foundation is counting statistics—figures, such as Census data, that are reported in occupational "cells." Published occupational figures mask within-cell differences that cannot be detected in a practical way using today's collection methods and classification systems.
>
> "The other foundation is transaction uses—such as career counseling, assessment and referral to job openings, and alien worker certification, each of which relies upon the three components . . . personal qualification, job requirement, and projected opportunity.
>
> Today's hulls don't match. The occupational information vessel is not seaworthy. This isn't surprising. Independent design teams, with different specifications, worked on each hull. Therefore, this paper also builds a case for future collaboration between the Federal agencies that have primary responsibility for counting statistics and transaction uses, respectively" (Stevens, 1993, p. 214).

After reviewing systems used in the U.S. and internationally, APDOT recommended that DOL designate a single classification system for use throughout DOL. This single system would be used to develop the DOT database, report labor market data, design and evaluate training programs, and assist in job placement.

After much consideration, APDOT recommended a single standardized occupational classification for a revised DOT. By using modern relational database design, however, the single system can serve all the multiple users of the data. Some APDOT members referred to this as "multiple classifications."

### Classification Issues and the DOT's Temporary Move to the Occupational Employment Statistics Program (OES)

In its final report, APDOT recommended that ETA and BLS work closely together to coordinate the revision of the SOC with the DOT. Working across agencies, this group would develop the classification structure of the DOT as well as the SOC (APDOT, 1992). In particular, it was hoped that a single classification could be developed. This hope was based on the stated mutual interest of BLS and the Office of Management and Budget in coordinating proposed revisions of the SOC with the DOT to produce a system that better served the needs of federal agencies. Today that group exists as the Steering Committee to Revise the Standard Occupational Classification. The revised SOC and a new single classification system is expected to be implemented in the 2000 census.

On the basis of its research and its own experience with occupational classification, APDOT recognized that the DOL needed to adopt interim measures regarding the DOT's classification structure. It recommended using the OES classification system, developed by BLS for collecting employment data, as an interim classification. Using the OES, the only existing national labor market information system, allowed DOL to use empirical data on employment patterns for DOT sample designs and to relate information in the new DOT to other data sources linked with the nation's OES. However, OES remains a rigid classification system. The O*NET prototype still relies on OES. Consequently, APDOT's recommendation for a new, flexible classification structure remains unrealized. Occupational units that subcluster OES categories into 1,120 categories have been developed, but this O*NET classification system does not yet possess the flexibility needed to capture ongoing changes in skill profiles among occupations. Work to develop an alternative system is ongoing, but much work remains to be done.

### International Issues

To ensure that APDOT had the best available information, DOL commissioned studies of labor market tools used by economic trading partners, including Australia, Canada, France, Germany, Japan, Sweden, and the United Kingdom. Experts at the International Labour Office in Geneva identified individuals to prepare the reports. These representatives not only filed individual country reports but in some cases addressed the APDOT to answer questions in public session. Additional expertise was hired to study changes to the Canadian occupational information system. The Canadian system, modeled on the DOT, is also being revised.

These reports were summarized and analyzed in two papers: "Mapping The World of Work" (Hoffmann, 1991) and "International Practices: Occupational Classification and Description," (Morgenthau & Lenz, 1992). Both papers reported issues in the international arena that were similar to those found in the U.S.

### Dissemination

To assist the APDOT in studying the implication of changes to the DOT, a paper was commissioned to identify private sector developers and vendors of career information products that publish and disseminate data from the DOT either in whole or in part. Although the paper identified 115 commercial products that had some degree of relationship to the DOT, it also cautioned that not all commercial products were identified. This paper was instrumental in APDOT's recommendation that DOL encourage the vendor industry to develop specialized, value-added applications (Morgenthau, 1992).

## APDOT REPORTS AND PUBLIC RESPONSES

Throughout the project, concept papers and reports were published in the *Federal Register* and widely distributed to interested parties for public comment. A report summarizing responses to the first concept paper concluded in December 1990 that the public believed that (a) "The DOT is important—the nation has a need for an independent, recognized, reputable source of unbiased data concerning typical occupational requirements," and (b) "the next edition of the DOT should be disseminated electronically while preserving a hard copy edition for those without computer access" (Silver, 1990, p. 1).

In March 1992, the APDOT submitted an interim report to the Secretary of Labor, published it in the *Federal Register*, and distributed copies to some 5,000 interested persons to generate public response. The report discussed activities undertaken to date, tentative findings, and potential recommendations. It laid out a series of principles that informed the public about APDOT's position on key issues and stated that the panel would rely on these principles as it made final recommendations for the DOT.

## FINAL REPORT

The APDOT final report, *The New DOT: A Database of Occupational Titles for the Twenty-First Century*, begins with a quotation from President Clinton: "The only way America can compete and win in the twenty-first century is to have the best-educated, best-trained workforce in the world, linked together by transportation and communication networks second to none" (Clinton & Gore, 1992, p. 6).

The panel saw the DOT database as a key information tool for empowering people within President Clinton's vision. In its final report, APDOT described the new DOT as the technological infrastructure that could support the new administration's planned investment in people. The panel called for replacing the old DOT with a new, computerized database that could be expanded, updated, and retrieved for multiple purposes into the 21st century.

At the end of its tenure, APDOT made a deliberate policy decision to make its final report a general communication tool for DOL management and decision makers rather than just a comprehensive technical compendium. The intention was to encourage as many people as possible to actually read the report, or at least its executive summary. At the same time, the panel sought to maintain credibility in all relevant professional communities by making extensive technical papers and background materials available to those who were truly interested in the details. As its recommendations indicate, APDOT also added new content to the DOT to help capture data on (a) the increasingly cognitive demands of jobs and (b) new ways of thinking and managing that focus on quality, variety, speed, and customer service.

## FROM APDOT FINAL REPORT TO IMPLEMENTATION OF O*NET PROTOTYPE

DOL reviewed the APDOT final report and developed a plan to test the feasibility of the approach. DOL management believed that APDOT had identified the right track for future development of the DOT. However, as anyone who has ever tried to create something new knows, it is very difficult for people to judge the usefulness or value of something that does not yet exist. APDOT staff identified a low-key research strategy, using current OAFC/DOT staff supplemented by numerous technical contractors, including the American Institutes for Research and its consortium and Aguirre International, to build a prototype of the proposed database.

This initial plan was refined with assistance from a "transitional team" of psychologists. The revised plan included a definition of the data descriptors to be included in the new content model, a rationale for inclusion, measurement options, issues or problems raised, and recommendations for testing new approaches to data collection, analysis, and dissemination. On a concurrent track, the OAFC staff, with assistance from Don Drewes and Bill Cunningham, engaged in vigorous research to convert DOT analyst-derived data into the O*NET format. The goal was to help move the O*NET research project along more quickly by demonstrating the practical feasibility of the new system in five pilot state sites (California, Minnesota, New York, South Carolina, and Texas) as early as 1996–1997. The analyst-derived data provided immediate information on all 1,120 occupations and thus a "more complete O*NET content model/database" than could otherwise be constructed for testing and research purposes.

For the first few years, the project was regarded as highly technical and was allowed to evolve quietly. The underlying assumption behind this strategy was that by the time O*NET's feasibility had been proven (estimated to be 2 years), its significance would have been recognized and it would be embraced as the key technical infrastructure needed to address a multitude of workforce development issues. In January 1995, the name of the project was changed to O*NET, the Occupational Information Network, in an effort both to discard the baggage associated with the old DOT name and also to help people envision the forward-thinking, high-tech nature of the project.

## THE FUTURE OF O*NET

Although O*NET is still in its developmental, research stage, many people have begun to recognize its potential. Interest and support for the O*NET concept have come from special interests as diverse as union members, educators, entrepreneurs, corporate human resource professionals, and staff from the U.S. Chamber of Commerce. This broad base of potential support is welcomed because a massive data collection effort will be needed to fill the database. Today, the completion of the prototype database and associated interface software demonstrates the validity of the O*NET concept or "proof of concept." We now know what is possible. The consortium of technical experts who have helped develop the O*NET content model have already made a solid contribution to our knowledge base. Moreover, the relative ease with which the "common language" of O*NET's skill-related terms is being accepted by disparate groups of users across the country has been both surprising and gratifying.

O*NET's usefulness will expand as its database becomes populated and increasingly accessible to the public. Containing information on skills, knowledge, abilities, work content, and the context in which work is performed, O*NET will be able to help all Americans make informed employment decisions. Fulfillment of the O*NET vision means that people will be able to get the facts they need from workstations, whether located at home, in school, at community libraries, in malls at one-stop career centers, or on the job. Worker and job requirements will finally mean the same thing to everyone: small business owners, corporate human resource experts, employees, education and training counselors, program planners, curriculum designers, and students.

No one effort, public or private, can capture all aspects or target all dimensions involved in the changing workplace. DOL's participation helps ensure objectivity and fairness in data collection and equity in data dissemination. However, DOL alone cannot build the extensive occupational information network today's economy demands. Collaboration with the private sector will ensure that O*NET's data will provide the foundation on which other developers can build as they assist career counseling, employment, and job-training activities. The O*NET database is expected to become the publicly funded hub of a vast network of developers, agencies, and organizations working with a common goal: to enhance the employment potential of all Americans.

The ongoing, evolving nature of the O*NET project can be seen by the current impact of the Internet. In 1993, when the APDOT produced its recommendations, the power and influence of Internet had not yet been widely recognized. Today, the general public expects at least part of the O*NET to be available on the Internet. The project has already begun working with America's Job Bank to help make this vision a reality. O*NET reflects what is happening in the workplace. Issues such as global competition, the need for speed, customization of products, and easy access are evident with O*NET as well. One way to describe what is happening to occupational information with O*NET is to see it as "the ultimate in customization" (Davis, 1987). The database concept illustrates that what is important about an occupation in today's world is not a standard definition. Rather, what is important now is easy access to occupational information so that the individual can define what he or she wants to know, when he or she wants to know it.

Although this has not been the case so far, technological advancements and the rapid pace of change could also threaten the capability of O*NET to adapt (Meridian Corp., 1991). Failure to continually accommodate change could lead to inadequate occupational definitions. For example, without a new classification structure more flexible than the OES, O*NET may be left with methods and procedures that are insensitive to or incapable of responding to the changing work environment. In that case, O*NET, like the DOT it is replacing, could eventually become obsolete.

In conclusion, O*NET is made possible today because of technology. APDOT recognized the ability of technology to improve the current DOT, to make its data collection and analysis methods faster and more efficient. APDOT also recognized the ability of technology to make the current DOT more effective (e.g., the use of sampling strategies that result in higher quality information). What is now being envisioned by those involved in O*NET's development is the capacity of technology to be transformational (Gerrity, 1988). Combining the O*NET database with America's Job Bank and applying artificial intelligence to the data recovered may one day enable continuous diagnosis to predict occupational skill changes as well as "emerging occupations." In the world of occupational information, the O*NET future is now.

## CHAPTER 3

# The O*NET Content Model: Structural Considerations in Describing Jobs

MICHAEL D. MUMFORD AND NORMAN G. PETERSON

The world of work is changing. Some scholars—Drucker (1994) and Reich (1992), for example—argue that the kinds of jobs found in tomorrow's economy will be different from those predominating during the age of mass production. Others argue that change in technology and increased global competition will create new types of jobs (Cappelli, 1995; Howard, 1995a). Still others argue that jobs, at least as we know them, represent a dated view of work (Mohrman & Cohen, 1995).

These fundamental changes in the nature and conditions of work present a host of pressing questions. Workers wonder how they can find jobs. Employers wonder what skills they should develop in their workforce. Policymakers and educators wonder what capacities must be developed in our children to promote access to fulfilling, high-skill, high-wage jobs.

To answer these questions, one must be able to describe jobs. In this chapter we present the general structural model used in the Occupational Information Network (O*NET). We begin by examining the concerns influencing our development of this model and then consider the major types of variables included in the model.

## BACKGROUND

### Describing Jobs

People's work shapes the structure of their lives and the nature of the economy. Many systems have attempted to describe jobs as they would any other phenomenon that could so pervasively and dramatically affect our lives.

One approach to describing jobs may be found in the outcome-oriented systems commonly used in labor market studies (Cappelli, 1995). Here jobs are described in terms of the outcomes associated with the work. Thus, jobs might be described in terms of pay, turnover, or health considerations. Another approach used to describe jobs focuses on patterns of movement from one position to others. The idea underlying this labor market approach is that jobs can

be defined by transitions from one position to another, resulting in career paths of the type described by Morrison (1994). Jobs can also be described in terms of the industry where the work is being done. This kind of approach is evident when we describe someone as a steel worker or an auto worker.

Information about outcomes, labor markets, and industries is certainly useful in describing jobs. Nonetheless, these descriptive systems all leave a key question unanswered. They do not tell us what is required of the people doing the work. Of course, any truly useful descriptive system must be able to answer this one crucial question. As a result, most current systems for describing jobs, in one way or another, seek to determine exactly what is required of the people doing the work.

Jobs, however, are complex, and so the requirements they impose can be described in a number of different ways using rather different frames of reference (Harvey, 1990b; McCormick, 1979). For example, Fleishman and Quaintance (1984) identified four major approaches commonly used to describe the requirements associated with different jobs: (a) the information theoretic approach, (b) the task strategies approach, (c) the ability requirements approach, and (d) the task characteristics approach. Each of these approaches has its strengths and weaknesses.

### Job Task Descriptors

Although a number of different types of descriptors might be used to assess the requirements imposed by a job, most attempts to describe jobs are based on the job task paradigm. The job task paradigm developed out of conditions confronting American industry at the turn of the last century. With the development of mass production, work was atomized and divided into component parts. The intent of job task analyses was to identify essential component production activities required on the job and to establish more effective ways for carrying out these activities (Holland, 1973).

Within this paradigm, description is in terms of tasks or component production activities occurring on a particular job. Thus, a task statement for clerical workers might say "check weekly purchase order to ensure accuracy." A job was viewed as being defined by the total set of discrete production activities, or tasks, that workers needed to perform. These tasks were identified by analysts after they had observed the work or through discussion with workers employed on the job and their supervisors.

The success of the job task approach in addressing the needs of industry during the first half of the 20th century has led to widespread acceptance of the approach. Indeed, this approach was the basis for what was perhaps the most widely used collection of occupational titles, the *Dictionary of Occupational Titles* (DOT; U.S. Department of Labor, 1991a).

The DOT provides narrative descriptors of the key tasks involved in some 12,000 jobs in the United States economy. A variety of procedures has been used over the last 50 years to obtain these descriptors. Although these procedures have changed over time, they still reflect an emphasis on job tasks. More specifically, one or two analysts interview and observe workers at one or more sites. This information, primarily qualitative in nature, is then used by analysts to identify the tasks performed on the job. These tasks, and other available qualitative data, are used to formulate job descriptors and draw inferences about characteristics of the occupation. The basic descriptive information is then used to answer a host of questions about people and their jobs, ranging from placement and compensation decisions to decisions about disabilities and naturalization.

Although the DOT has proven useful in addressing some issues, over the years a number of problems inherent in this task-based descriptive system have become apparent. The report of the Advisory Panel for the Dictionary of Occupational Titles (APDOT) describes many of these problems (U.S. Department of Labor, 1993b). Broadly speaking, these problems appear to derive from three characteristics of this kind of descriptive system: (a) its specificity, (b) the lack of a cross-job organizing structure, and (c) the limitations of task data.

Turning first to the specificity issue, it should be apparent that the DOT, like most other job-task approaches, formulates descriptors for a specific job. This job-specific inductive approach requires that a new set of tasks be identified for each and every job. The need to develop new descriptors for each job makes job description a costly and time consuming venture, limiting the availability of timely, up-to-date information. Furthermore, because each job must be studied and understood on its own terms, it becomes impossible to formulate a truly general, common language for describing jobs.

The second issue addresses the inability of the current approach to provide a set of variables for organizing descriptive information and comparing jobs. As noted above, tasks are necessarily job-specific and may or may not occur across jobs. As Campbell (1993) pointed out, without variables that provide a common metric for contrasting the similarities and differences among jobs, it becomes difficult to use the resulting descriptive information to address issues involving cross-job comparison. This limits the system's use in placement, job classification, career planning, and policy development. Furthermore, the lack of a general framework for organizing job-specific information often means that the essence of the job is lost in a sea of detail.

The third and final set of problems is attributable to the nature of the descriptive data provided by task-based systems. Tasks describe discrete production activities. Tasks, however, do not tell us what characteristics workers must possess to perform these activities nor about the conditions under which these activities are performed. Therefore, task-based systems may omit certain kinds of necessary descriptive information, such as knowledge and skill requirements. Moreover, it is questionable whether this kind of molecular, behaviorally based descriptive strategy adequately captures the more complex, difficult-to-observe influences on work behavior. These influences (e.g., team relationships and problem solving skills) may represent key determinants of performance on the jobs of the future (Cappelli, 1995; Mohrman & Cohen, 1995).

## Structural Characteristics

The O*NET described in this and following chapters was intended to provide a new, truly comprehensive occupational information system that would replace the DOT. In designing the O*NET, it was necessary to take into account the limitations of the DOT as well as the intended applications of this new occupational information system. The intended applications of the O*NET are well summarized in the APDOT report (U.S. Department of Labor, 1993b), which states that a new occupational information system should

> promote the effective education, training, counseling, and employment of the American work force. The DOT should be restructured to accomplish its purpose by providing a database system that identifies, defines, classifies, and describes occupations in the economy in an accessible and flexible manner. Moreover, the DOT should serve as a national benchmark that provides a common language for all users of occupational information. (U.S. Department of Labor, 1993, p. 6)

This vision presents a challenge. It calls for a flexible, comprehensive descriptive system that can be used to address a variety of concerns. The O*NET content model was intended to provide a framework for the development of this descriptive system. In the following sections of this chapter, we consider the key assumptions underlying development of the content model. We begin by considering the relevant structural assumptions and then examine the assumptions made about the model content.

## Structural Considerations

One cannot develop a descriptive system without making certain assumptions about the nature and structure of the underlying phenomenon. In developing the O*NET content model, three key assumptions shaped the structure of the resulting descriptive system. These structural assumptions called for (a) the use of a multiple-windows approach, (b) a focus on cross-job descriptors, and (c) a hierarchical organization of variables.

### Multiple Windows

In developing descriptive systems, including job analysis systems, one must attend to the intended applications of the resulting information (Fleishman & Quaintance, 1984). In other words, we must construct descriptive systems that allow us to draw the inferences of interest (Cronbach, 1971; Messick, 1989, 1995). The O*NET was intended to promote a variety of inferences about jobs (e.g., decisions about job similarity and wage and salary administration) and about people seeking employment in jobs, including suitability to disability assessments. As a result, it was clear that no one type of descriptor—for example, abilities—would provide a fully adequate descriptive system. Instead, what was required was a multiple-windows approach in which different types of descriptors could be used to address different issues.

The multiple-windows approach holds that jobs can be described and understood from a number of different perspectives. For example, one might describe a job in terms of the environment in which it occurs (i.e., work context variables), such as working outdoors. Alternatively, one might describe jobs in terms of the skills people need to do the work. The multiple-windows approach holds that each of these different types of descriptors (e.g., work context vs. skills) can be used to describe a job. These different types of descriptors are held to reflect distinct, albeit interrelated, domains that might be used to answer different types of questions about jobs or about how people "fit" to jobs.

One advantage of this multiple-windows approach is that it permits people to work with the kinds of descriptors most appropriate for the questions they are asking. A second advantage is that it permits one to examine the relationships among variables lying in different domains. Thus, one might be able to make statements about the skills required for different work activities. A third advantage is that by focusing taxonomy development on a specific domain—skills, for example—it becomes possible to develop stronger, substantively based descriptive systems that explicitly consider prior research in a given area (Fleishman & Mumford, 1991).

### Cross-Job Descriptors

In any job analysis system, the phenomenon of interest is clearly the work being done on a job or set of jobs. Although we clearly want to focus on jobs, jobs can be described at a number of different levels. As noted earlier, most task-based systems seek to describe each job as a unique entity in its own right. These kinds of job-specific descriptive systems clearly have real value. However, jobs might also be described in terms of broader variables that cut across jobs. The O*NET descriptive system is based on a cross-job approach.

A number of considerations led to the use of a cross-job approach in the development of the content model. In a cross-job system, there is no need to create a new descriptive system for each and every job. Instead, jobs are described in terms of a common set of variables. The resulting gains in efficiency make it possible to collect descriptive data more rapidly and maintain up-to-date information. Furthermore, although specific content can, and often does, change quite rapidly, broader variables capturing key characteristics of multiple jobs tend to be more stable.

More important, the intended applications of the O*NET system and the kinds of questions it would be used to answer dictate a cross-job approach. As Campbell (1993) pointed out, jobs can only be compared if cross-job descriptors are available that provide a common metric for identifying relevant similarities and differences. Thus, use of a job-specific descriptive system would effectively prohibit many key applications, including job classification and person–job matching, while making it impossible to formulate a common language for talking about jobs in general. Accordingly, the O*NET system was based on cross-job rather than job-specific descriptors.

One limitation of a cross-job descriptive system, however, is that generality is often obtained at the price of specificity. As McCage (1993, 1995) pointed out, many applications of job analysis data—training system design, for example—require highly detailed, job-specific information. One way to resolve this tension between the need for generality and the need for specificity is to view job-specific descriptors as instances of a broader cross-job variable within the context of a particular job. For example, jobs may differ in requisite reading skills. In the context of telecommunications jobs, for example, general reading skills may be manifested in reading technical manuals. Thus, within the O*NET system, cross-job descriptors provide a framework for identifying, organizing, and understanding job-specific descriptors such as tasks, tools, and occupation-specific skills.

### Hierarchical Structure

In developing descriptive systems, including job analysis systems, there also is a tension between the need for parsimony and the need for comprehensive description. One might propose a system with a few key cross-job variables, or alternatively, one might develop a system that includes a relatively large number of more narrowly defined variables. For example, one might use a parsimonious, one-variable general intelligence model (Spearman, 1931). Alternatively, one might formulate descriptors to capture a larger number of more discrete variables, such as convergent and divergent thinking (Guilford & Hoepfner, 1967; Thurstone, 1938).

A potential solution to the problem is suggested by Vernon (1950). In his studies of abilities, he argued that these different levels of description do not necessarily reflect incompatible descriptive systems. Instead, broad, general descriptors can be seen as subsuming more narrowly defined descriptors within a hierarchical structure of the sort illustrated in Figure 3-1.

In developing the O*NET content model, we used this kind of hierarchical organization for the variables specified in each of several domains. Besides the merits of this approach in resolving the tension between the need for parsimony and the need for comprehensiveness, this kind of hierarchical within-domain structure is useful in addressing other issues. First, this kind of structure permits integration of multiple systems, thereby facilitating common language development. Second, by explicitly considering multiple levels, users can employ descriptors at the level of parsimony most appropriate for the kind of inferences they are trying to draw. Third, this kind of hierarchical structure allows the initial descriptive system to be extended to incorporate more detailed information in areas of special interest, while allowing the cross-job descriptors to be used in organizing more narrowly defined occupation-specific descriptors.

## Content Considerations

In the preceding section, we considered the general structural characteristics of the O*NET content model. Essentially we argued that what is needed is a system that includes multiple descriptors, drawn from a number of domains and organized hierarchically, that could be applied in describing a number of jobs. Although these observations tell us a great deal about the structure of the content model, they tell us little about the specific kinds of variables to be used in describing people's jobs. In this section we examine some of the major considerations leading to the content domains included in the O*NET content model.

### People and Jobs

Earlier, we noted that a variety of different types of variables might be used in describing jobs. Jobs might be described in terms of abilities, skills, interests, work environment, or work activities, among other types of variables. This wealth of potential descriptors poses a question: How should we structure the types of variables to be used in describing jobs?

One attempt to address the issue may be found in the APDOT report (U.S. Department of Labor, 1993b). The APDOT report considers the different types of variables that might be used in describing jobs and develops the model presented in Figure 2-1 (see chap. 2). Essentially, this model holds that the various types of job descriptors might be organized into four general categories: (a) worker attributes, (b) work context, (c) labor market context, and (d) work context and outcomes.

The APDOT model is consistent with most descriptors of the various kinds of variables that might be used to describe people's jobs. This model, furthermore, underscores the point that in describing people's jobs, we need to consider both the characteristics of the people doing the work (a worker-oriented job description) and the characteristics of the work itself (an occupation-oriented job description; Landy, 1989). Worker-oriented analyses consider attributes such as skills and abilities, whereas occupation-

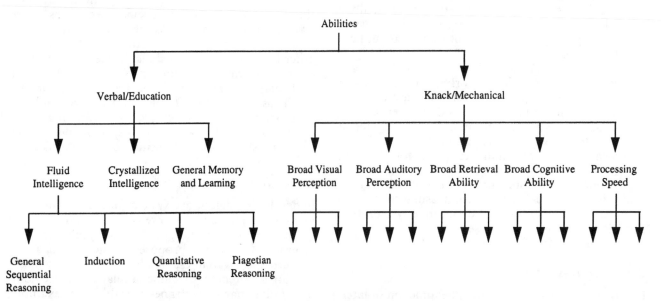

**FIGURE 3-1.** Hierarchical arrangement of abilities.

oriented analyses consider attributes such as production activities and the nature of the job environment.

Of course, any job analysis system intended to provide a comprehensive description of people's jobs must consider both the worker and the work. Moreover, any application of a truly comprehensive occupational analysis system requires both types of information. We cannot match people to jobs without considering both the characteristics of the people and the characteristics of the jobs. Accordingly, the O*NET content model was structured specifically to consider descriptors drawn from each of these two broad domains.

### Requirements and Characteristics

When one considers the nature of people and the nature of jobs, a second distinction of some importance to development of the content model emerges. Both people and jobs are complex entities that develop over long periods of time. As a result, there are many attributes of people and their work that are best viewed as preexisting characteristics outside the control of the individual or the organization for which they are working. Examples of these kinds of preexisting attributes may be found in abilities, temperament, economic conditions, and industry.

Other attributes of workers and their work are more pliable. For example, as a function of experience on their jobs, people acquire knowledge and skills (Ericsson & Charness, 1994). Organizations can change not only the nature of the work to be done but also the climate and conditions of the work (West & Farr, 1989).

Typically, we look at more controllable characteristics of people and their work for different reasons than we look at the givens. For example, we may focus on abilities when our concern is personnel selection. Knowledge and skills, however, are often of greater interest in attempts to train and develop workers. Thus, in formulating the content model it seemed necessary to consider both malleable characteristics (worker requirements and occupational requirements) and preexisting attributes (worker characteristics and occupation characteristics).

### O*NET Content Model

Figure 3-2 summarizes the specific types of variables that would be needed to adequately describe characteristics and requirements of both the worker and the work. This figure also indicates that, in addition to worker requirements, a comprehensive occupational analysis system would consider experience re-

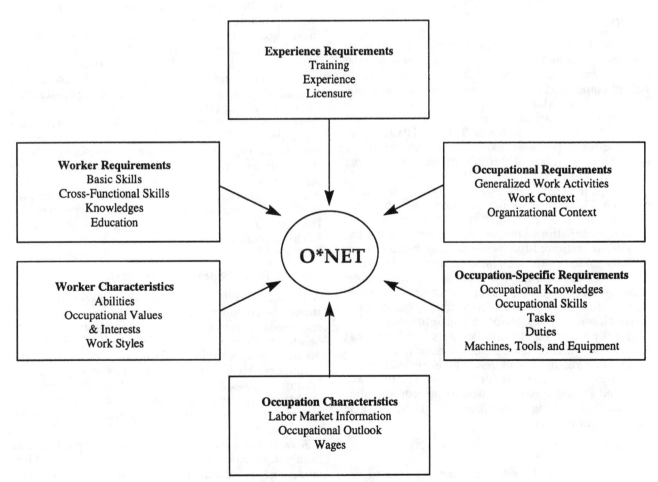

**FIGURE 3-2.** O*NET content model.

quirements that serve to develop performance capacities (e.g., training). This system would also extend to capture occupation-specific characteristics (e.g., tasks, tools, and occupation-specific skills) using the kind of hierarchical structure described earlier. In the following section, we consider in greater detail the specific kinds of variables included in each of these areas.

## CONTENT MODEL DOMAINS

### Worker Characteristics

People's enduring characteristics influence the capacities that they can develop as a function of experience, as well as their willingness to engage in certain types of activities (Fleishman, 1982; Snow, 1986). This point has long been recognized by counselors who commonly use information about a person's characteristics as a basis for placing people in jobs (Dawis, 1990; Holland, 1973). Along similar lines, information about worker characteristics is commonly used to select people for jobs (Guion, 1966; Schmidt, Hunter, & Pearlman, 1981). As might be expected from these observations, information about requisite worker characteristics often provides a basis for describing and comparing occupations.

#### Abilities

Since the 1920s, one of the most common techniques for describing and comparing jobs in terms of relatively enduring characteristics of the person has involved comparing jobs in terms of requisite abilities. Initially, these ability comparisons involved little more than comparisons of incumbents' mean scores on ability tests (Thorndike & Hagen, 1959). More recent efforts, however, have focused on describing occupations in terms of their ability requirements per se (Fleishman & Quaintance, 1984; Lopez, 1988).

Perhaps the best developed system along these lines may be Fleishman's ability-requirements approach (Fleishman & Mumford, 1988). Within this approach, occupations are described in terms of the basic abilities required for successful task performance. Initially, factor analytic techniques were used to identify the abilities that could account for task performance within certain broad, cross-occupation performance domains, such as cognitive, psychomotor, physical, and sensory performance. Subsequently, behaviorally anchored rating scales were developed that would allow incumbents, supervisors, or job analysts to identify requisite abilities. These evaluations of performance requirements in terms of abilities have provided a valid system for identifying requisite abilities and classifying occupations in terms of their ability requirements.

#### Work Style

Although few people would dispute the need to describe occupations in terms of their ability require-

ments, abilities represent only one type of enduring attribute of the individual that would influence the capacity or motivation to perform various work activities. Recent studies by Sackett, Zedeck, and Folgi (1988) drew a distinction between typical and maximal performance, noting that the attributes conditioning maximal performance may not be identical to the attributes conditioning typical day-to-day performance. Usually, abilities are viewed as the enduring characteristics of individuals that determine maximal performance, whereas personality or work style variables (including motivation, integrity, and other characteristics such as openness or mastery motives) are held to influence typical task performance. The evidence compiled by Dweck (1986) and Schmeck (1988) indicates that these kinds of characteristics can have a marked influence on how people adapt to new tasks, while also influencing the development and maintenance of skilled performance in various domains.

Although there is reason to suspect that these stylistic variables may represent an important influence on people's day-to-day work performance, these variables have not traditionally been used for describing jobs in terms of requisite person characteristics. In part, this viewpoint derives from the position that nonnormative, clinical syndromes do not provide an appropriate basis for describing occupations. This point is difficult to dispute. However, it may well prove possible to describe occupations in terms of more general, nonclinical attributes—such as achievement motives, self-discipline, and integrity—that influence how people typically approach work-related tasks. In fact, Guion and his colleagues (Guion, Sept. 15, 1994, personal communication) have shown that job activities can be described using these kinds of nonclinical personality attributes when attributes have been expressly selected to capture key aspects of typical, day-to-day performance. Given this evidence and the need for a comprehensive descriptive system that considers influences on both maximal and typical performance, it seems necessary to consider information about personality—particularly personality constructs bearing on work style—in the content model.

#### Occupational Values and Interests

A third issue relevant to worker characteristics that should be considered in the development of the content model is interests. It is not enough for people to be able to do the work; they must also be willing to do the work. Worker characteristics bearing on the willingness to invest in a certain type of work are commonly subsumed under the rubric of interests. As might be expected, based on these observations, interests are commonly used as a basis for person–job matching.

A variety of taxonomies for describing interests has been proposed over the years (Campbell, 1971; Holland, 1973; Strong, 1943). Furthermore, interests have shown some value as a basis for describing the similarities and differences among occupations (Borgen, 1988). However, the unique value of interests as a basis for describing occupations is often limited because they focus primarily on personality patterns. This kind of system for describing interests is well illustrated in the work of Holland (1973). An alternative approach for describing the interests involved in various jobs may be found in the work of Dawis (1990). Dawis' (1990) approach attempts to describe interests in terms of preferences for certain types of occupational reinforcers. This kind of occupation-based approach to the definition of interests is particularly attractive, in part because it clearly distinguishes interests from personality and in part because it references the definition of interests against occupation-relevant attributes. However, a truly comprehensive system might consider both approaches.

## Worker Requirements

Worker characteristics such as abilities, work styles, and interests are important not only because they influence how people approach work tasks but also because of the influence that these variables have on the development of work-relevant skills (Ackerman, 1987; Fleishman & Hempel, 1955; Snow, 1986).

### Knowledges

Worker requirements, broadly speaking, refer to developed attributes of the individual that might influence performance across a range of work activities. People acquire a variety of attributes that influence performance as a function of education and experience (Anderson, 1993). One effect of education and experience is that people acquire knowledge or an organized set of facts and principles pertaining to the characteristics of objects lying in some domain. Prior studies of expert–novice differences (Chi et al., 1989; Chi & Glaser, 1985; Feltovich, Spiro, & Coulson, 1993) indicate that expert performers in domains ranging from medicine to foreign affairs typically differ from novices. These experts have a more extensive set of concepts available, organized on the basis of underlying principles, which facilitate recall, recognition, and problem solving. Although knowledge appears to develop as a function of domain-specific, episodic experiences (Medin, 1984), the organization of experience in terms of the principles applying in a domain suggests that a general, cross-occupation framework for describing requisite knowledge might be developed by identifying interrelated bodies of principles.

### Skills

Experience in working within a domain also provides people with a set of procedures for working with knowledge (Anderson, 1993; Campbell, McCloy, Oppler, & Sager, 1992). These procedures are what people commonly refer to when they apply the term *skills*. Skills, however, might be conceived of in two different ways. First, when people use the term *basic skills*, they are commonly referring to procedures, such as reading, that would facilitate the acquisition of new knowledge. Second, cross-functional skills refer to procedures that extend across general domains of work activities. Examples are problem solving and social skills. These cross-functional skills develop as a function of experience, although their development may also be influenced by more basic skills and by relevant worker characteristics, such as abilities (Snow & Lohman, 1984).

Although requisite knowledge and skills have been used to describe occupations (Mitchell, Ruck, & Driskell, 1988), the description of requisite knowledge and skills is commonly phrased in terms of a specific occupation or set of positions. As a result, the kind of descriptive information provided by these procedures is of limited value in formulating a general cross-occupation descriptive system. Recent work by Mumford, Fleishman, and their colleagues (Baughman & Mumford, 1995; Mumford, Mobley, Uhlman, Reiter-Palmon, & Doares, 1991) suggests that it might be possible to identify cross-occupation knowledges and skills. These skills would be identified by discovering the general bodies of principles and the procedures that influence performance across domains of activities that extend across occupations.

### Education

Worker requirements, such as knowledge, basic skills, and cross-functional skills, develop in part as a function of experience in performing a certain set of tasks. However, educational background also seems to represent a significant influence on the development of these general knowledges and skills (Snow & Swanson, 1992; Ward, Byrnes, & Oventon, 1990). Recognition of the relationship between education and the acquisition of general knowledge and relevant basic skills (Halpern, 1994) has led many investigators to use educational experience as a proxy for information bearing on general knowledges and skills. Because educational experiences represent a developed capacity of the individual influencing the acquisition of knowledge and basic skills, requisite educational background may also represent another characteristic of the person that must be used to describe cross-occupation differences in terms of relevant worker requirements.

## Experience Requirements

Like education, training and licensure represent structured experiences that are a property of an individual. In contrast to education, which is expressly intended to provide general knowledge and basic or cross-functional skills, training and licensure are variables that are explicitly linked to the nature of certain kinds of work activities. Training and licensure, of course, may be specific to the tasks being performed in a particular position (Goldstein, 1990).

However, training and licensure may also apply to tasks occurring in a number of positions. For example, a training program may seek to develop general leadership or problem solving skills. When training and licensure are intended to extend across a specific set of position activities, these kinds of experiences may provide still another potentially useful type of cross-occupation descriptor. Indeed, prior training and licensure are often used as a basis for personnel selection, counseling, and job matching.

Training and licensure requirements have been used to describe occupation requirements, using a number of different approaches. For example, people have been asked which specific types of training they have completed or what licenses they possess. However, Ash (1988) noted that many of these variables lack sufficient generality to be useful as cross-occupation descriptors. One common approach used to address this issue is to ask when and where training or a license was acquired. Another approach suggested by Peterson (1992b) is to examine the amount of training required or when this capacity was acquired. This latter approach might prove particularly useful in assessing training and licensure requirements if it is linked to a broader taxonomy of requisite knowledges and skills that might potentially be developed in training.

## Occupational Requirements

As noted above, person requirements, such as knowledges and skills, as well as training and licensure, are in part a function of a person's experiences. In the description of people's work activities, these experiences are commonly framed in terms of the requirements of the occupation or the set of positions under consideration. Although these work requirements might be assessed in terms of a number of different descriptors—for example, tools used, products and services provided, or functional duties—the most common procedure is to describe work requirements through definition of the tasks performed in the occupation (McCormick, 1976, 1979). A task is commonly defined as a specific activity performed on some object to meet some functional occupation requirement.

With regard to development of a comprehensive occupation description, the identification of requisite tasks represents an essential step. However, well-developed task statements are usually specific to a particular occupation or set of occupations (Harvey, 1990b). As a result, task statements may be of limited value in describing the kinds of cross-occupation similarities and differences that must be captured by the envisioned occupational information system. Thus, a viable system may require a somewhat broader approach to describing occupation activities.

### Generalized Work Activities

One approach that might be used to address this specificity problem is suggested by the work of McCormick (McCormick, 1976, 1979), Cunningham (Cunningham, Boese, Neeb, & Pass, 1983), and Harvey (1990b). Essentially, this approach attempts to identify generalized work activities (GWAs) or dimensions that summarize the specific kinds of tasks occurring in multiple occupations. For example, the descriptor *controlling machines or processes* might subsume a number of tasks occurring in specific occupations, such as driving heavy machinery or working on a manufacturing production line.

Prior factor analyses of task inventories suggest that it is indeed possible to identify general dimensions of work activities that summarize more specific tasks occurring in a variety of occupations (Campbell, McHenry, & Wise, 1990; McCormick, Jeanneret, & Mecham, 1972). Thus, it might be possible to formulate a taxonomy of GWAs by examining the results obtained in these factor analytic efforts in relation to a general theory of work performance. This taxonomy of GWAs might provide both a viable cross-occupation framework (for the description of differences in requisite work tasks) and a basis for generating more specific descriptive information. This specific information would concern the tasks, tools, and duties that apply in a particular occupation or set of occupations.

### Work Context

A second set of variables used to measure cross-occupational characteristics are work-context variables. These variables describe the conditions under which job activities must be carried out. They include physical conditions (e.g., temperature and noise) as well as social–psychological conditions (e.g., time pressure and dependence on others) that might influence how people go about performing certain activities. Although some occupations are carried out across a wide range of settings, many others can be said to have a typical work context, such as indoor/outdoor work, degree of danger and exposure to elements and hazardous materials, and degree of involvement or conflict with other persons.

### Organizational Context

A third set of cross-occupational variables measure organizational context. These are variables that might interact with the occupational environment and how people go about doing their work. For example, a flatter, more open organizational structure may require workers who possess a broader range of skills, placing a premium on problem-solving skills and an independent work style. O*NET organizational context variables were identified after a review of studies assessing the impact of organizational structure on how work gets done, with a special focus on high performance organizations. Though conceptually relevant, it is important to note that organizational context variables are virtually ignored in the DOT and are the most experimental aspect of O*NET. Thus, the ultimate usefulness of this type of information for selection and training is still unclear.

## Occupation-Specific Requirements

The preceding sections have focused on the cross-job variables that provide the foundation for the O*NET descriptive system. Many questions of interest in describing jobs can, of course, be answered solely on the basis of these cross-job descriptors (Pearlman, 1993). However, as McCage (1995) pointed out, cross-job descriptors may not prove sufficient to answer certain types of questions. For example, training program design and job redesign efforts often require more specific types of descriptive information.

### Tasks

The occupation-specific descriptors traditionally used to answer these kinds of questions are task statements (McCormick, 1976). A task is an activity that occurs in order to produce some product or outcome required on the job (Gael, 1979). These tasks are identified by job analysis based on observations or interviews with people performing the job. Because tasks, by virtue of their focus on the production activities occurring on a specific job, are necessarily job-specific, they are difficult to use in a cross-job descriptive system. However, it is possible that tasks might be incorporated in this type of descriptive system by viewing them as examples of GWAs occurring within the context of a particular job. In fact, Mumford and his colleagues (Mumford & Supinski, 1995a, 1995b; Mumford, Threlfall, Costanza, Baughman, & Smart, 1992) have provided evidence indicating that the tasks performed in telecommunications and financial occupations can indeed be identified and organized on the basis of GWAs.

### Duties, Machines, Tools, and Equipment

Tasks, however, are not the only kind of occupation-specific descriptors that should be considered in a comprehensive descriptive system. Tasks might be grouped into duties on the basis of the products or services being provided by a set of tasks. This duty-based description of job activities often provides a basis for the development of performance appraisal instruments.

In jobs where machines, tools, or other equipment structure the fundamental nature of the work being done—molding, for example—it may be useful to have a description of the machines, tools, and equipment, including computer software that are involved in the job.

### Knowledge Structure and Skills

Two other kinds of occupation-specific information, knowledge, and skills are commonly used in describing people's jobs. Sometimes jobs are described in terms of the knowledge structures people must acquire to display expert performance (Halff, Hollan, & Hutchins, 1986). This expertise-structure approach to job description has been applied in fields such as programming, medicine, and foreign rela-

tions, where it has proven useful in training program design (Feltovich et al., 1993; Rist, 1989; Voss, Wolfe, Lawrence, & Engle, 1991). Along similar lines, one might seek to identify occupation-specific skills for accreditation and career development efforts. In both these cases, however, there is reason to suspect that the relevant knowledge and skills might, like tasks, be identified and organized on the basis of relevant cross-job descriptors (Mumford & Supinski, 1995b).

Although there is a need for these kinds of occupation-specific information, occupation-specific descriptors represent a somewhat unique problem. By virtue of their specificity, these descriptors cannot provide the kind of general framework for describing jobs that was the primary goal of the O*NET descriptive system. Instead, what is required are techniques for incorporating job-specific descriptors into a broader, more encompassing cross-job structure. To the extent that the cross-job descriptors included in the O*NET content model provide a basis for gathering and organizing these more specific descriptors, this model may have helped us take an important step toward the goal of developing a truly common language for describing jobs (Campion, 1995a).

## Occupation Characteristics

O*NET does not directly include variables in the domains of labor market information, occupational outlook, or wages, but it is designed so that connections can be made readily to databases that do contain those variables. Some of the most salient variables in these domains include current occupational employment, overall and by industry; completions in professional, technical, and other occupational education programs; and occupational compensation and earnings. These variables are important to a variety of people, including students, counselors, jobseekers, and policy analysts, all of whom are interested in the current and future availability of openings in occupations and the level of wages or other financial rewards associated with them.

## CONCLUSIONS

Our foregoing observations about the occupation-specific descriptors included in the O*NET occupational information system point to a broad set of conclusions. Traditionally, most occupational information systems have treated each job as a unique, distinct entity. This strategy has resulted in a wealth of information. Unfortunately, this information has proved of limited value because it cannot be understood in terms of a broader organizing framework. Furthermore, it has proven difficult to obtain up-to-date information about jobs because new descriptive systems must be individually created for each and every job.

The O*NET content model circumvents these problems by using a set of common, cross-job variables to describe jobs. Instead of viewing each job as a unique entity, jobs are defined and described in terms of the similarities and differences they display on cross-job descriptors, such as skills and GWAs. Because jobs are seen as differing with respect to cross-job descriptors, new descriptive systems need not be formulated for each and every job. In fact, it becomes possible to describe jobs within a common framework.

The ability of this model to provide a common framework allows us to answer a host of questions about jobs that otherwise would prove difficult to answer. Many of the questions we ask about jobs either implicitly or explicitly require a comparative statement that involves an assessment of the similarities and differences between jobs. Person–job matching requires a statement that a person is more suited for one job rather than another. We cannot classify jobs and develop job families unless we can identify their similarities and differences. By framing measures in terms of cross-job descriptors, the O*NET content model, a direct descendent of the APDOT model, makes it possible, perhaps for the first time, to answer these and a host of other questions that require us to establish how jobs are similar to or different from each other.

In considering the cross-job descriptors included in the content model, another noteworthy characteristic of this descriptive system becomes apparent. The content model expressly considers multiple types of cross-job descriptors, allowing users to look at jobs through different windows. Use of multiple windows helps ensure a comprehensive description of both the work and the worker. Furthermore, by including multiple types of cross-job descriptors and organizing descriptors hierarchically, it becomes possible to answer a wider range of questions about workers and their work by using the descriptors and level of description most appropriate for the situation at hand. For example, when counseling recent graduates, one might focus on information about broad basic abilities. When counseling displaced workers, however, information about skills and prior work activities might prove more useful.

The multiple-windows strategy used in developing the content model has another important implication. Traditionally, occupational information systems have been primarily used as a simple descriptive tool. Description is indeed important, and the O*NET model is intended to provide a truly comprehensive descriptive system. Use of the multiple-windows approach, however, adds another capability. It allows us to draw inferences based on the relationships observed among the variables included in different domains of the content model. As a result, this model might be used to establish the relationship between skills and GWAs. If these relationships can be established, it might be possible to identify the workers qualified for a new job simply by determining the GWAs likely to represent important components of job performance.

Although it appears that the O*NET content model might provide the kind of general flexible information system we need as we move into the 21st century, a host of issues have not yet been addressed. To apply this model, we need to develop descriptors within each domain specified by the content model. Furthermore, evidence needs to be provided indicating that these descriptors can indeed provide an accurate, meaningful assessment of the similarities and differences among jobs. In chapters 5 through 13, we provide a more detailed description of the variables used in each domain of the content model and some initial evidence for the reliability and validity of these measures. Before reviewing the evidence bearing on the reliability and validity of those descriptors, however, we next describe the general procedures used to develop and field test the content model.

# Research Method: Development and Field Testing of the Content Model

NORMAN G. PETERSON, MICHAEL D. MUMFORD, KERRY Y. LEVIN,
JAMES GREEN, AND JOSEPH WAKSBERG

Our objective in developing the taxonomies of cross-occupation descriptors was to provide a basis for measuring the similarities and differences observed among occupations. A variety of procedures might be used to describe occupations with respect to their status on these variables. One might, for example, develop an objective, formal test intended to assess workers' expressions of each characteristic. Alternatively, one might ask occupational analysts to observe worker performance and then rate the extent to which each variable was required for effective performance.

In fact, ratings represent the technique most commonly used to obtain descriptions of occupation characteristics. To obtain these ratings, definitions of the variables of interest are presented to persons familiar with the occupation. They are then asked to describe how the variables manifest themselves in job performance, using rating scales that examine different ways the variables might be expressed. For example, one might ask knowledgeable persons to describe how frequently an activity is performed and how important it is to job performance.

As Messick (1995) pointed out, selection of a particular rating scale should be based on the nature of the variable at hand and the type of inferences to be drawn. Thus, work context variables (e.g., noise) might be assessed in terms of frequency or intensity. Frequency and intensity scales, however, would not be appropriate for assessing skills and abilities. Thus, in developing the O*NET, different types of rating scales were used to assess the variables included in different taxonomies (Mumford, Weeks, Harding, & Fleishman, 1987). Selection of rating scales was based on (a) the key manifestations of the variable on people's jobs, (b) the feasibility of applying the scale across occupations, (c) the usefulness of the descriptive information provided, (d) the appropriateness of the scale for observational ratings, and (e) the available evidence bearing on the reliability and validity of the resulting descriptive information (Friedman & Harvey, 1986; Harvey & Lozada-Larsen, 1988).

Although rating scales were necessarily specific to the particular types of variables under consideration, certain general characteristics of these scales should be noted. In most cases, multiple types of ratings were obtained for a given set of variables. Multiple ratings forced people to carefully consider the questions being asked and to distinguish among constructs—a feature of multiple rating tasks that contributes to the reliability and validity of the resulting descriptive information (McCormick, 1964b). Second, in all cases where level ratings were applicable—abilities and skills, for example—level ratings were obtained on the basis of their demonstrated reliability (Fleishman & Mumford, 1988; Fleishman & Quaintance, 1984) and the merits of level ratings in addressing questions about job demands. In accordance with the procedures recommended by Fleishman and Mumford (1988), these level ratings were obtained using 7-point behaviorally anchored rating scales. Scale anchors were developed using standard judgmental scaling procedures (Childs & Whetzel, 1995; Peterson, Mumford, Borman, Jeanneret, & Fleishman, 1995). Most other ratings, however, were obtained on standard 4- or 7-point Likert scales.

In developing the rating scales, a number of other steps were taken to help ensure the reliability and validity of the resulting descriptive information. First, all rating scales were constructed using operational, rather than technical, definitions written to clearly convey the nature of the variables. Second, operational definitions, along with the associated rating scales, were administered to some 250 people working on jobs ranging from construction worker to college professor (Peterson et al., 1995). Finally, several experienced occupational analysts were asked to review the rating instructions, variable labels, operational definitions, and rating scale anchors for clarity, readability, and appropriateness for use in describing people's jobs. This task resulted in rating procedures that could be expected to yield adequate reliability and validity, while casting scales in a common-language framework intended to facilitate communication and minimize the burden placed on raters.

Figure 4-1 presents the rating scales developed for one skill and one generalized work activity (GWA).

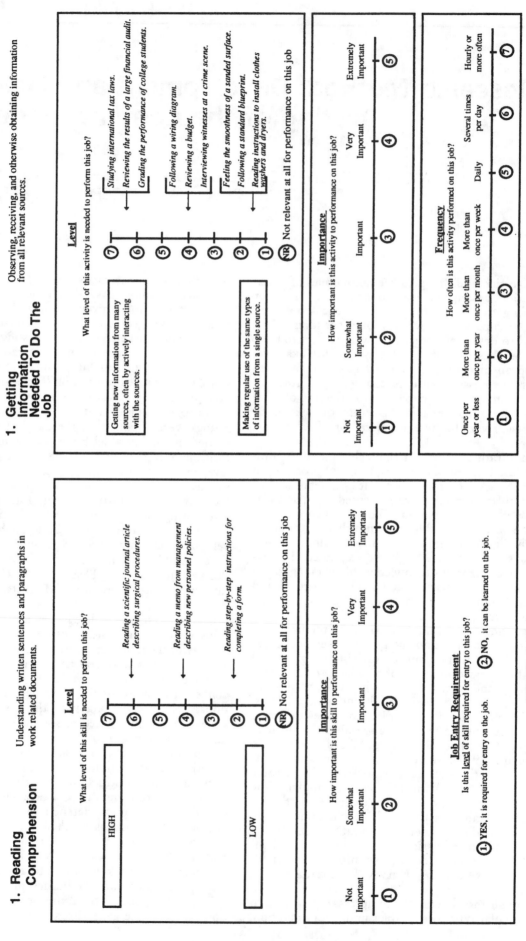

**FIGURE 4-1.** Example pages from the Skills and Generalized Work Activities Questionnaires.

### Instructions for Making Skill Ratings

In this questionnaire you will be presented with a list of 46 skills. Some of the skills are developed over time and are used not only to do work but to learn other skills; examples include Reading Comprehension, Writing, and Speaking. Other skills are important for performance on many jobs; examples include Idea Generation, Troubleshooting, and Time Management.

For each skill, please make the following three ratings: **LEVEL**, **IMPORTANCE**, and **JOB ENTRY REQUIREMENT.**

(1) **LEVEL.** Ask yourself, "What level of this skill is needed to perform this job?" To help you make this judgment, the LEVEL scale includes descriptions of activities requiring high, medium, and low levels of the skill. These are only examples, so they may or may not apply to the specific job you are describing.

Use the example descriptions to select the number on the scale that indicates the skill level required by the job, and mark through the appropriate number, from 1 (indicating that a very low level of the skill is required) to 7 (indicating that a very high level of the skill is required) on the LEVEL scale. For example, the level of "Reading Comprehension" needed for one job might be much higher than that needed for another job.

**THE NOT-RELEVANT (NR) RESPONSE.** If the skill is NOT RELEVANT at all to performance on the job, mark through the NR circle that appears at the bottom of the LEVEL scale. Carefully read all of the level descriptions before selecting the NR option. If you select NR, however, there is no need to complete the IMPORTANCE and JOB ENTRY REQUIREMENT ratings described below.

(2) **IMPORTANCE.** (Complete only if a 1 to 7 LEVEL rating was selected.) Ask yourself, "How important is this skill to performance on this job?" For example, "Information Gathering" might be very important for one job, but less important for another job. For the second job, however, "Listening/Questioning" might be very important.

Rate the IMPORTANCE of the skill for performance on the job by marking through the appropriate number, from 1 (indicating that the skill is of little or no importance) to 5 (indicating that the skill is very important) on the IMPORTANCE scale.

(3) **JOB ENTRY REQUIREMENT.** (Complete only if a 1 to 7 LEVEL rating was selected.) Bearing in mind the LEVEL of the skill that is needed to perform the job, ask yourself, "Is this level of the skill required for entry to this job?" For example, "Reading Comprehension" might be needed by an employee before starting one job. However, "Troubleshooting" might not be necessary before starting a different job. "Troubleshooting" might be learned during on-the-job training.

Rate the JOB ENTRY REQUIREMENT for the job by marking through the appropriate number, either 1 (indicating that the level of the skill is required for entry on the job) or 2 (indicating that the level of the skill can be learned on the job).

Notice that the LEVEL of a skill and the IMPORTANCE of the skill are different. For example, "Reading Comprehension" can be high in IMPORTANCE for two different jobs, but the LEVEL of "Reading Comprehension" that an employee in one job needs is not as high as the LEVEL of "Reading Comprehension" for an employee in another job.

[two completed examples were included here]

Turn the page to begin the Skills Questionnaire.

**FIGURE 4-2.** Example instructions for the Skills Questionnaire.

The instructions accompanying these rating scales are illustrated in Figure 4-2, which presents the instructions developed for the Skills Questionnaire. These rating scales typify the basic instruments used to assess similarities and differences among occupations with respect to the cross-occupation descriptors.

In developing these measures, it was necessary to address two other procedural issues: (a) What source would be used to obtain ratings? and (b) What data collection formats would be used to gather these ratings? When occupation characteristics are to be de-scribed using judgmental techniques such as ratings, it is necessary to obtain descriptive information from people who have the expertise needed to provide accurate, meaningful assessments of occupational requirements (Cornelius, Denisi, & Blencoe, 1984). Broadly speaking, three types of raters are available who have the background needed to provide adequate assessments of occupation characteristics: (a) workers, or incumbents, (b) supervisors, and (c) occupational analysts. Occupational analysts' ratings are often seen as the best source of descriptive ratings, in part because analysts are viewed as more objective, and also because analysts are seen as having a better understanding of how the occupation at hand compares with other occupations (Henderson, 1988).

On the other hand, a variety of available evidence indicates that analysts may not necessarily yield superior descriptions, at least under conditions where there is no overt motive for faking. In one study along these lines, Fleishman and Mumford (1988) examined the degree of agreement observed on ability requirement ratings obtained from incumbents, supervisors, and occupational analysts. They found that in the kind of high-ability populations examined in this study, all three types of raters provided virtually identical descriptions of ability requirements. The results obtained in the Fleishman and Mumford (1988) study are by no means unique. Peterson, Owens-Kurtz, Hoffman, Arabian, and Whetzel (1990) had soldiers, their supervisors, and occupational analysts assess the knowledge, skill, ability, and work style requirements of a sample of Army jobs. Again, it was found that these three types of judges displayed substantial agreement.

Taken as a whole, these studies suggest that occupation descriptions might be obtained from any of these three types of judges. Incumbents, however, seemed best able to provide information across all descriptor domains, especially complex, difficult-to-observe occupation characteristics, such as work styles and organizational context variables. Large samples of knowledgeable incumbents are available, which should contribute to the reliability of the resulting descriptive system. This same consideration, of course, recommends the use of incumbent, as opposed to supervisor, ratings because it generally is easier to obtain sizable samples of incumbents.

Although these considerations recommend the use of incumbent ratings, one further point should be raised. Incumbent ratings base description on the smallest possible unit of analysis: the positions of individual workers. By basing description on these discrete units, without the imposition of an up-front structure, it becomes possible to formulate a more flexible occupational information system than would be the case if analyst or supervisor ratings were used. Regarding type of rater, we were able to take advantage of a related Department of Labor project to convert the *Dictionary of Occupational Titles* (DOT; U.S. Department of Labor, 1991a) information to O*NET information. Occupational analysts used DOT task information about occupations to rate occupations on O*NET descriptor scales. This permitted comparisons of the two kinds of ratings.

Not only can ratings be obtained from a number of different types of judges, but ratings might also be obtained using a number of different data collection techniques. The most common procedure used to collect ratings is the traditional paper-and-pencil measure. Paper-and-pencil questionnaires represent a flexible data collection technique that minimizes

costs while ensuring that the measures can be applied across a wide range of job settings. Nonetheless, a number of other techniques are available. For example, computer-assisted telephone interview (CATI) or survey "fax back" techniques might at some time represent viable alternatives to traditional paper-and-pencil surveys. Rating questionnaires might also be administered using computer-assisted data collection techniques, such as *DOS*- or *Windows*-based administration of the paper-and-pencil surveys or use of the World Wide Web as a basis for survey administration. Computer-assisted survey administration, of course, reduces data coding costs while opening up the possibility of applying new types of unobtrusive measures during data collection. On the other hand, these techniques cannot readily be applied on many lower level jobs lacking easy access to the requisite technology.

On the basis of the flexibility of paper-and-pencil techniques and the need to cover a wide range of occupations, the paper-and-pencil approach was chosen as the primary method to use in administering the rating scales in the present effort.[1]

This background discussion of the rating procedures used to quantify occupational information sets the stage for detailed consideration of how the O*NET occupational analysis instruments were used to collect data on a sample of occupations. The remainder of this chapter describes the sampling methods, data collection procedures, obtained response rates and associated issues, and the general analyses that were conducted to evaluate the O*NET system.

## SAMPLING

Substantial effort was devoted to obtaining a representative sample of occupations for use in assessing the O*NET descriptive system, using a multistage sampling design. The following section details each of the three sampling stages: selecting occupations, identifying establishments, and selecting incumbents.

### Selecting Occupations

The framework used for sampling occupations was based on the 1984 Occupational Employment Statistics (OES) classification, which describes occupations in terms of a six-digit code. The first two digits of this six-digit system describe the job family, whereas the third digit identifies occupations within this job family. The occupational sampling frame for the

---

[1]The feasibility of using computer-administered versions of the paper-and-pencil surveys was assessed in a sample of 10 occupations in which incumbents were likely to have access to the requisite technology. Rating scales were also developed for possible administration over the World Wide Web. However, Web-based administration, because it prohibits systematic sampling, was considered a purely exploratory technique.

baseline study was created by merging the 1991, 1992, and 1993 OES data files with the job family codes from the National Crosswalk Service Center's (NCSC) data file. The merged OES data files provided a file of occupational data with multiple records by year for a given occupation. One record was created for each unique occupation code by collapsing multiple occurrences of a given occupation code and cumulating total employment.

The OES and NCSC file merge was largely successful, with only 14 NCSC occupations not receiving OES codes. The NCSC file then provided additional codes for 10 of the nonmatching OES occupations. The four remaining unmatched occupations were removed from the sampling frame. Their occupation codes, titles, and total employment are as follows: 22514—Drafters, total employment = 286,920; 79014—Gardeners and Groundskeepers, total employment = 127,660; 87705—Pile Driving Operators, total employment = 1,400; 93951—Engraving & Printing Workers, Hand, total employment = 3,850.

One further restriction applies to the occupation sampling frame. Occupations unique to federal government entities are not represented in the occupation sampling frame. Therefore, employment counts for those occupations underestimate the total U.S. employment counts by the number of federal employees in those occupations.

The resulting sampling frame is presented in Table 4-1. This table provides counts of occupations, total employment, and sample size by two- and three-digit job family code. Each cell in the table provides information for a particular three-digit job family. These cells represent areas of analytic interest and were therefore used as strata for the sample of occupations. Cells with fewer than 200,000 employees were excluded from the sample design (i.e., they were assigned sample sizes of zero). There was no information in the OES files for some job families (e.g., job family "104"), and a small amount of employment was reported for three-digit job family codes that did not appear in the original job family matrix provided to us. Both types of cells were excluded from the sample design.

There are several reasons for the selection of a probability sample of occupations, using probability proportionate to size. A major reason for using probability sampling was to have an objective method of picking the occupations to study, thereby avoiding conscious or unconscious biases in selection choices. This type of sampling tends to result in the selection of larger occupations (in terms of number of employees), thereby permitting wide coverage of the workforce with relatively few jobs. Additionally, when probability proportionate to size is used for the first stage of selection and a constant number of employees is chosen per occupation, the sample produces close to equal probabilities of choosing employees. This was a desirable property of the sample, even though no national estimates were planned. Therefore, we allocated 70 occupations across the 14

columns of the job-family matrix with the probability proportional to the column total employment. This simply means that occupations with larger employment totals received a larger number of job families to sample. Adjustments were made to the column sample sizes so that at least one occupation could be selected within each cell. For example, we allocated two occupations to job family column "10" to ensure selection of one occupation each in rows "101" and "102" instead of the 0.65 total occupations warranted under strictly proportional allocation. We allocated the resulting column sample sizes across cells in a similar manner. The final sample size for each cell is given by the last entry in each table cell. A sampling macro was then used to select the specified number of occupations within each cell with probability proportional to total employment. The 70 occupations selected in this manner represent approximately 45% of the workforce, consistent with our goal in using probability sampling.

Because employer demands are placing greater emphasis on computer and technical skills, there was a need to ensure that the prototype included occupations considered to be highly technological in nature. A limitation of the OES sampling frame is that it taps occupations proportional to the amount of current employment and does not necessarily include emerging or highly technological occupations. Thus, it was necessary to adopt an additional sampling technique in order to include the emerging, technological occupations.

A literature review suggested that highly technological occupations are prevalent in many high-performance organizations (Arad, Schneider, & Hanson, 1995). These organizations emphasize the importance of innovation and technology in the workplace. Employment within high-performance organizations tends to set industry standards, and the organizations are often used as benchmarks for job and market trends. Thus, high-performance workplaces seemed a logical place to find the types of occupations absent from the sample selected using traditional statistical techniques.

The literature review indicated that many high-performance organizations were concentrated within a few industries. Thus, we chose the most commonly represented industries in the literature and used the concatenated OES data files from those industries to select additional occupations. Occupations considered for selection were those that were commonly found within high-performance industries and were technological in nature. Ten occupations that met those criteria were chosen to supplement the original sample of 70 occupations.

Taken together, the sample of occupations used for initial development of the O*NET system consisted of 80 unique occupations—70 of which were selected proportional to current employment size using the OES sampling technique, and 10 of which were selected from industries frequently represented in the high-performance literature. Table 4-2 provides job family code, occupation code, occupation title, and

**TABLE 4-1**

## Counts of Occupations, Total Employment, and Sample Size, by Job Family

| Preparation level | Distinguishing activity | "02" Adminstrative and finance occupations | "05" Natural and applied science occupations | "06" Health service occupations | "07" Law, social science, community service |
|---|---|---|---|---|---|
| Management education, training, or experience | Job family | "020" | "050" | "060" | "070" |
| | # occupations | 7 | 1 | 1 | 1 |
| | Total employment | 4,509,870 | 348,760 | 158,680 | 69,280 |
| | Column % | 0.19 | 0.09 | 0.02 | 0.03 |
| | $E(n)$ | 3.38 | 0.26 | 0.12 | 0.05 |
| | $n$ | 3 | 1 | 0 | 0 |
| University degree | Job family | "021" | "051" | "061" | "071" |
| | # occupations | 11 | 34 | 16 | 13 |
| | Total employment | 1,635,760 | 2,518,990 | 2,823,910 | 1,239,950 |
| | Column % | 0.07 | 0.65 | 0.44 | 0.60 |
| | $E(n)$ | 1.23 | 1.89 | 2.12 | 0.93 |
| | $n$ | 1 | 1 | 2 | 1 |
| 2–3 years postsecondary education or equivalent | Job family | "022" | "052" | "062" | "072" |
| | # occupations | 12 | 17 | 15 | 8 |
| | Total employment | 2,110,950 | 1,023,140 | 1,374,570 | 761,760 |
| | Column % | 0.09 | 0.26 | 0.21 | 0.37 |
| | $E(n)$ | 1.58 | 0.77 | 1.03 | 0.57 |
| | $n$ | 1 | 1 | 1 | 1 |
| High school degree preferred | Job family | "023" | | "063" | |
| | # occupations | 65 | | 9 | |
| | Total employment | 16,061,900 | | 2,088,850 | |
| | Column % | 0.66 | | 0.32 | |
| | $E(n)$ | 12.03 | | 1.57 | |
| | $n$ | 11 | | 2 | |
| High school degree not required | Job family | | | | |
| | # occupations | | | | |
| | Total employment | | | | |
| | Column % | | | | |
| | $E(n)$ | | | | |
| | $n$ | | | | |
| | Column total | 24,318,480 | 3,890,890 | 6,446,010 | 2,070,990 |
| | $E(n)$ | 18.22034423 | 2.915205027 | 4.829599592 | 1.551665675 |
| | $n$ | | 3 | 5 | 2 |

| Preparation level | Distinguishing activity | "09" Education, training, and instructional occupations | "10" Art, culture, and recreation occupations | "12" Retail and wholesale sales occupations | "14" Protective service occupations |
|---|---|---|---|---|---|
| Management education, training or experience | Job family | "090" | "100" | "120" | "140" |
| | # occupations | 1 | Not available | 1 | Not available |
| | Total employment | 298,680 | Not available | 432,250 | Not available |
| | Column % | 0.05 | | 0.03 | |
| | $E(n)$ | 0.22 | | 0.32 | |
| | $n$ | 1 | | 1 | |
| University degree | Job family | "091" | "101" | "121" | "141" |
| | # occupations | 21 | 11 | 4 | Not available |
| | Total employment | 4,403,740 | 491,270 | 703,120 | Not available |
| | Column % | 0.76 | 0.56 | 0.05 | |
| | $E(n)$ | 3.30 | 0.37 | 0.53 | |
| | $n$ | 2 | 1 | 1 | |
| 2–3 years postsecondary education or equivalent | Job family | "092" | "102" | "122" | "142" |
| | # occupations | 2 | 9 | 10 | 9 |
| | Total employment | 706,950 | 356,120 | 3,335,220 | 538,500 |
| | Column % | 0.12 | 0.41 | 0.26 | 0.26 |
| | $E(n)$ | 0.53 | 0.27 | 2.50 | 0.40 |
| | $n$ | 1 | 1 | 2 | 1 |
| High school degree preferred | Job family | "093" | "103" | "123" | "143" |
| | # occupations | 2 | 2 | 4 | 3 |
| | Total employment | 365,080 | 23,410 | 4,139,480 | 661,960 |
| | Column % | 0.06 | 0.03 | 0.32 | 0.32 |
| | $E(n)$ | 0.27 | 0.02 | 3.10 | 0.50 |
| | $n$ | 1 | 0 | 2 | 1 |

*Table 4-1 continues*

**TABLE 4-1 (Continued)**

| Preparation level | Distinguishing activity | "09" Education, training and instructional occupations | "10" Art, culture, and recreation occupations | "12" Retail and wholesale sales occupations | "14" Protective service occupations |
|---|---|---|---|---|---|
| High school degree not required | Job family | | "104" | "124" | "144" |
| | # occupations | | Not available | 5 | 4 |
| | Total employment | | Not available | 4,369,530 | 895,070 |
| | Column % | | | 0.34 | 0.43 |
| | $E(n)$ | | | 3.27 | 0.67 |
| | $n$ | | | 3 | 1 |
| | Column total | 5,774,450 | 870,800 | 12,979,600 | 2,095,530 |
| | $E(n)$ | 4.326440909 | 0.652436984 | 9.724817502 | 1.570051991 |
| | $n$ | 5 | 2 | 9 | 3 |

| Preparation level | Distinguishing activity | "15" Personal and commercial service occupations | "17" Craft occupations | "18" Transportation and equipment occupations | "19" Occupations unique to agriculture, forest, and fishing |
|---|---|---|---|---|---|
| Management education, training, or experience | Job family | "150" | "170" | "180" | "190" |
| | # occupations | 2 | 2 | Not available | 2 |
| | Total employment | 359,420 | 193,050 | Not available | 17,940 |
| | Column % | 0.03 | 0.05 | | 0.02 |
| | $E(n)$ | 0.27 | 0.14 | | 0.01 |
| | $n$ | 1 | 0 | | 0 |
| University degree | Job family | "151" | | | |
| | # occupations | Not available | | | |
| | Total employment | Not available | | | |
| | Column % | | | | |
| | $E(n)$ | | | | |
| | $n$ | | | | |
| 2–3 years postsecondary education or equivalent | Job family | "152" | "172" | "182" | "192" |
| | # occupations | 7 | 25 | 2 | 4 |
| | Total employment | 1,337,660 | 2,403,950 | 121,130 | 59,450 |
| | Column % | 0.10 | 0.67 | 0.03 | 0.06 |
| | $E(n)$ | 1.00 | 1.80 | 0.09 | 0.04 |
| | $n$ | 1 | 1 | 0 | 0 |
| High school degree preferred | Job family | "153" | "173" | "183" | "193" |
| | # occupations | 15 | 11 | 32 | 12 |
| | Total employment | 4,230,730 | 282,450 | 3,596,780 | 710,770 |
| | Column % | 0.33 | 0.08 | 0.93 | 0.75 |
| | $E(n)$ | 3.17 | 0.21 | 2.69 | 0.53 |
| | $n$ | 3 | 1 | 3 | 1 |
| High school degree not required | Job family | "154" | "174" | "184" | "194" |
| | # occupations | 24 | 14 | 2 | 3 |
| | Total employment | 6,965,810 | 698,080 | 138,370 | 162,820 |
| | Column % | 0.54 | 0.20 | 0.04 | 0.17 |
| | $E(n)$ | 5.22 | 0.52 | 0.10 | 0.12 |
| | $n$ | 4 | 1 | 0 | 0 |
| | Column Total | 12,893,620 | 3,577,530 | 3,856,280 | 950,980 |
| | $E(n)$ | 9.660397966 | 2.680423615 | 2.889273879 | 0.712510936 |
| | $n$ | 9 | 3 | 3 | 1 |

| Preparation level | Distinguishing activity | "20" Occupations unique to extractive operations | "21" Occupations unique to manufacturing, process, etc. | Totals |
|---|---|---|---|---|
| Management education, training, or experience | Job family | "200" | "210" | |
| | # occupations | Not available | 1 | 19 |
| | Total employment | Not available | 211,670 | 6,599,600 |
| | Column % | | 0.03 | |
| | $E(n)$ | | 0.16 | |
| | $n$ | | 1 | 8 |

*Table 4-1 continues*

**TABLE 4-1** (*Continued*)

| Preparation level | Distinguishing activity | "20" Occupations unique to extractive operations | "21" Occupations unique to manufacturing, process, etc. | Totals |
|---|---|---|---|---|
| University degree | Job family | | | |
| | # occupations | | | 110 |
| | Total employment | | | 13,816,740 |
| | Column % | | | |
| | $E(n)$ | | | |
| | $n$ | | | 9 |
| 2–3 years postsecondary education or equivalent | Job family | "202" | "212" | |
| | # occupations | 97 | 52 | 269 |
| | Total employment | 6,055,050 | 2,551,710 | 22,736,160 |
| | Column % | 0.95 | 0.35 | |
| | $E(n)$ | 4.54 | 1.91 | |
| | $n$ | 4 | 1 | 16 |
| High school degree preferred | Job family | "203" | "213" | |
| | # occupations | 8 | 60 | 223 |
| | Total employment | 160,080 | 3,359,710 | 3,581,200 |
| | Column % | 0.03 | 0.46 | |
| | $E(n)$ | 0.12 | 2.52 | |
| | $n$ | 0 | 2 | 27 |
| High school degree not required | Job family | "204" | "214" | |
| | # occupations | 1 | 7 | 60 |
| | Total employment | 164,550 | 1,200,250 | 14,594,480 |
| | Column % | 0.03 | 0.16 | |
| | $E(n)$ | 0.12 | 0.90 | |
| | $n$ | 0 | 1 | 10 |
| | Column total | 6,379,680 | 7,323,340 | 93,428,180 |
| | $E(n)$ | 4.779902595 | 5.486929104 | |
| | $n$ | 4 | 5 | 70 |

total employment of the 80 occupations selected for inclusion in the baseline study.

## Identifying Establishments

Once the 80 occupations were approved, a list of establishments that were likely to employ people in those occupations was obtained. Dun and Bradstreet (D&B) maintains complete and up-to-date files of all establishments in the United States and provides names, addresses, and phone numbers to customers. These data files were used to identify establishments —business units—likely to employ people on the targeted jobs.

In communicating project requirements to D&B, the assumption was that four standard industrial classifications (SICs) were sufficient to represent each occupation. Thus, a total of 320 SICs were initially requested (4 SICs × 80 occupations); however, because some occupations mapped to fewer than four SICs in D&B's files, only 143 SICs were actually selected. These SICs were chosen on the basis of having a high probability of employing people in the 80 occupations of interest.

D&B was instructed to randomly select a sample of 2,160 establishments from their file. They were asked to stratify the sample across the 143 three-digit SICs and across the following four employment size classes: (a) 5–24 employees, (b) 25–99 employees, (c) 100–499 employees, and (d) 500 or more employees. Establishments that employed fewer than five people were excluded because they were not expected to yield enough employees in each sampled occupation.

Once the sample was received from D&B, it was partitioned into a baseline sample (*n* = 1,240 establishments) and a reserve sample (*n* = 720 establishments). The reserve sample was used only when employer cooperation was less than anticipated.

For roughly 20 occupations, these procedures failed to provide the requisite number of establishments needed to obtain the targeted sample size. In some cases, the problem was due to the need for greater specificity in sampling occupations (e.g., photographers). In other cases, it was attributed to the number of people employed on the job at a given establishment (e.g., butchers). Accordingly, a two-phase plan was developed to address these problems. The first phase involved extending the number of establishments sampled by an additional 400, but using more specific SIC codes. The second phase involved identifying the remaining occupations for which a sufficient number of potential participants had not been identified and then identifying people employed in these jobs, using alternative sources for identifying workers, such as trade associations, unions, and public announcements of the project.

**TABLE 4-2**
**Eighty Occupations Sampled in Initial O*NET Data Collection**

| Job family | Occupation code | Occupation title | Total employment |
|---|---|---|---|
| 020 | 19005 | General Managers & Top Executives | 2,868,700 |
| 020 | 13002 | Financial Managers | 716,050 |
| 020 | 13014 | Administrative Managers | 248,210 |
| 021 | 21108 | Loan Officers & Counselors | 200,060 |
| 021[a] | 25315 | Financial Analysts, Statistical | 29,960 |
| 022 | 51002 | First Line Supervisors, Clerical & Administrative | 1,229,930 |
| 023 | 55347 | General Office Clerks | 2,660,890 |
| 023 | 55108 | Secretaries, except Legal & Medical | 2,440,560 |
| 023 | 55338 | Bookkeeping, Accounting, & Auditing Clerks | 1,812,510 |
| 023 | 55305 | Receptionists & Information Clerks | 927,730 |
| 023 | 55307 | Typists, including Word Processing | 612,490 |
| 023 | 53102 | Tellers | 554,640 |
| 023 | 55344 | Billing, Cost & Rate Clerks | 319,940 |
| 023 | 56011 | Computer Operators, Except Peripheral Equipment | 226,240 |
| 023 | 53121 | Loan & Credit Clerks | 178,860 |
| 023 | 53311 | Insurance Claims Clerks | 104,190 |
| 023 | 57105 | Directory Assistance Operators | 27,270 |
| 050 | 13017 | Engineering, Mathematical, & Natural Sciences Manager | 348,760 |
| 051 | 22302 | Architects, Except Landscape & Marine | 60,070 |
| 051[a] | 22114 | Chemical Engineers | 53,930 |
| 051[a] | 22127 | Computer Engineers | 207,490 |
| 051[a] | 22135 | Mechanical Engineers | 228,850 |
| 051[a] | 25102 | Systems Analysts | 39,354 |
| 051[a] | 25105 | Computer Programmers | 448,190 |
| 052 | 32905 | Medical & Clinical Laboratory Technicians | 100,600 |
| 052[a] | 32902 | Medical & Clinical Laboratory Technologists | 148,800 |
| 061 | 32502 | Registered Nurses | 1,764,950 |
| 061 | 31114 | Nursing Instructors | 46,430 |
| 062 | 32926 | Electrocardiograph Technicians | 15,870 |
| 063 | 66008 | Nursing Aides, Orderlies, & Attendants | 1,117,980 |
| 063 | 66005 | Medical Assistants | 198,090 |
| 071 | 31502 | Librarians, Professional | 130,180 |
| 072 | 27311 | Recreation Workers | 191,050 |
| 090 | 15005 | Education Administrators | 298,680 |
| 091 | 31305 | Teachers, Elementary School | 1,313,510 |
| 091 | 31303 | Teachers, Preschool | 356,740 |
| 092 | 31321 | Instructors & Coaches, Sports & Physical Training | 257,680 |
| 093 | 53905 | Teachers' Aides & Assistants, Clerical | 355,580 |
| 101 | 34051 | Musicians, Instrumental | 47,140 |
| 102 | 34023 | Photographers | 53,910 |
| 120 | 13011 | Marketing/Advertising/Public Relations Managers | 432,250 |
| 121 | 49002 | Sales Engineers | 66,000 |
| 122 | 49008 | Salespersons, Except Scientific & Retail | 1,167,870 |
| 122 | 21302 | Buyers, Except Farm Products | 157,380 |
| 123 | 49011 | Salespersons, Retail | 3,438,510 |
| 123 | 49014 | Salespersons, Parts | 287,910 |
| 124 | 49023 | Cashiers | 2,660,370 |
| 124 | 49021 | Stock Clerks, Sales Floor | 1,088,520 |
| 124 | 49017 | Counter & Rental Clerks | 323,340 |
| 142 | 61005 | Police & Detective Supervisors | 84,860 |
| 143 | 63014 | Police Patrol Officers | 380,230 |
| 144 | 63047 | Guards & Watch Guards | 829,530 |
| 150 | 15026 | Food Service/Lodging Managers | 337,120 |
| 152 | 65026 | Cooks, Restaurant | 573,510 |
| 153 | 65008 | Waiters & Waitresses | 1,748,910 |
| 153 | 65005 | Bartenders | 369,830 |
| 153 | 53805 | Reservation & Transportation Ticket Agents | 116,180 |
| 154 | 67005 | Janitors & Cleaners | 1,806,380 |
| 154 | 65038 | Food Preparation Workers | 1,194,610 |
| 154 | 65041 | Combined Food Preparation & Service Workers | 1,116,790 |
| 154 | 68014 | Amusement & Recreation Attendants | 230,650 |
| 172 | 87814 | Structural Metal Workers | 41,780 |
| 173 | 87902 | Earth Drillers, Except Oil & Gas | 12,170 |
| 174 | 98312 | Helpers, Carpenters | 155,540 |
| 183 | 97102 | Truck Drivers, Heavy or Tractor-Trailer | 1,259,450 |
| 183 | 97105 | Truck Drivers—Light, Include Delivery/Route Workers | 884,040 |
| 183 | 97111 | Bus Drivers, Schools | 381,540 |
| 193 | 79855 | General Farmworkers | 175,290 |

*Table 4-2 continues*

**TABLE 4-2 (Continued)**

| Job family | Occupation code | Occupation title | Total employment |
|---|---|---|---|
| 202 | 85132 | Maintenance Repairers, General Utility | 1,118,560 |
| 202 | 85302 | Automotive Mechanics | 563,960 |
| 202 | 85119 | Other Machinery Maintenance Mechanics | 50,230 |
| 202 | 85123 | Millwrights | 68,720 |
| 202[a] | 85705 | Data Processing Equipment Repairers | 79,520 |
| 202[a] | 89108 | Machinists | 343,780 |
| 210 | 15014 | Industrial Production Managers | 211,670 |
| 212 | 83002 | Precision Inspectors, Testers, & Graders | 180,220 |
| 213 | 92974 | Packaging & Filling Machine Operators | 324,910 |
| 213 | 89802 | Slaughterers & Butchers | 60,020 |
| 213[a] | 93905 | Electrical & Electronic Assemblers | 213,410 |
| 214 | 93938 | Meat, Poultry & Fish Cutters & Trimmers, Hand | 127,820 |

*Note.* The occupation code for Teachers, Preschool was corrected from 31302 to 31303.
[a]Occupations in the high-performance sample

## Selecting Incumbents

### Screening

Once establishments employing people in the targeted occupations had been identified, attempts were made to contact each of those establishments, solicit their cooperation, and obtain a sample of incumbents—people currently working on the targeted job. Because of the dynamic nature of businesses, the D&B sample contained a certain amount of out-of-date or missing information. For this reason, telephone interviewers contacted sample establishments prior to negotiating study participation. Interviewers called each company in the sample to confirm the name, address, and size of the organization and to obtain the name and title of the appropriate person to send an advance letter explaining the study. (These points of contact were generally human resource personnel.) The screening interview was designed to be answered by a receptionist and took about 5 minutes to administer. The 3-day screening resulted in a sample of 1,054 establishments. Of the original sample, 110 were ineligible to participate because they employed fewer than five people. One hundred and seventy-five establishments were out of business, duplicates, or not locatable, or refused to participate.

Establishments qualified to participate in the study were mailed an advance letter. The advance letter described the purpose of the study, discussed how they could help, and provided a fact sheet about the O*NET project that was used to support the solicitation for study participation.

### Negotiation and Incumbent Selection

Perhaps the most important aspect of the data collection effort involved negotiating study participation with the employer sample. Due to the complexity of these negotiations and the high level of expertise needed, Occupational Analysis Field Center (OAFC) staff took primary responsibility for this activity. The OAFC analysts were provided with training in negotiation procedures. The negotiation involved contacting point-of-contact personnel (POCs) at each sampled establishment by telephone and providing information about the study, gaining agreement to participate, and making appointments for later interviews. Before negotiation, a list of occupations likely to be present within each sampled establishment was generated from matching the establishment with its major SIC. No more than 10 occupations were assigned to an establishment. During the negotiation, POCs were asked to confirm that these occupations were present in the organization and to provide the number of incumbents (employees) in each of those occupations. Following negotiations, all of the information about the number of incumbents within an occupation was entered into an employee sampling database.

Finally, the number of employees to sample per occupation within an establishment was generated on the basis of targeted sample sizes. Sampling rates were based on overall employment within the occupation studied. For example, occupations such as secretary yielded large numbers of employees in the sampling database. These large numbers led to low sampling rates, meaning that the sample of secretaries was spread across many establishments, with any one establishment being asked for only a small number of employees in that occupation.

On the other hand, a different outcome occurred for occupations such as librarians, which yielded smaller counts of employees in the sampling database. Occupations like this resulted in higher sampling rates, thereby requiring more employees to be sampled within each establishment.

### Organizational Representative Interview

Following the negotiation phase, the POCs of organizations that agreed to participate were contacted again to complete a 40- to 45-minute computer-assisted telephone interview (CATI). At the conclusion of this interview, the POC was told which occupation or occupations at his or her establishment were recommended for sampling and the number of incumbents needed in each occupation. During this discussion, the POC's responsibilities in collecting job analysis questionnaires from his or her organization's employees were reiterated.

Following completion of the CATI interview, the POC was sent a package containing (a) a letter thanking the POC for participating; (b) instructions for implementing the project; (c) a list containing the number of incumbents needed to complete job analysis questionnaires in each of the selected occupations; (d) job analysis questionnaire packets, one for each incumbent; and (e) materials that could be distributed to explain the study to managers and incumbents. The POC was asked to select incumbents in the designated occupations randomly from among those who had been employed on the job for 6 months or more and to coordinate the distribution and collection of job analysis questionnaires from participating incumbents.

The selected incumbents received from the POCs a packet containing (a) a letter introducing the study, (b) instructions for completing questionnaires, (c) supporting materials and information, (d) a background information questionnaire, (e) an occupation-specific task questionnaire, and (f) two to four general across-occupation questionnaires. Incumbents were asked to complete the questionnaires at work and return them in a sealed envelope to the POC. The POC then forwarded these packets for processing. Follow-up telephone calls were conducted to prompt nonresponding employers. The purpose of the follow-up was to answer POC questions and to encourage study participation. An interview form was used in carrying out the telephone follow-up calls. One follow-up phone call was made approximately every 2 weeks for the following 6 weeks after the POC had received his or her package of questionnaires.

## DATA COLLECTION PROCEDURES

The sampling procedures used in initial development of the O*NET occupational information system were designed to provide 30 incumbents on each measure for a given job. This targeted cell size was based on two considerations. First, samples of 20 to 30 individuals typically yield stable means and standard deviations (Winer, 1971)—a point of some importance if these measures are to be used in describing people's jobs. Second, prior research by Fleishman and his colleagues (e.g., Fleishman & Mumford, 1988; Fleishman & Quaintance, 1984) and others (e.g., Hunter, 1980) indicates that 15 to 30 incumbents are typically sufficient to obtain adequate interrater agreement coefficients, given the type of measures being used to describe people's jobs.

To minimize testing time and ensure that the relationships among measures could be examined, we used a rotation design in administering the rating scales. In this rotation design, the measures developed for a given description domain—skills, for example—were treated as a distinct questionnaire.

The questionnaires were grouped into packets, where each packet contained two or three distinct questionnaires, accompanied by background material and a short task inventory. Each packet took 60 to 90 minutes to complete. In all, 15 different packets were assembled. These packets were rotated across five administration sets such that each questionnaire was paired at least once with every other questionnaire. Figure 4-3 presents this rotation design, noting both the time needed to complete each questionnaire and the time needed to complete all questionnaires included in the packet.

This design required 100 incumbents on each job in order to obtain 33 incumbents who responded to each questionnaire and a smaller number (minimum = 6) of incumbents who responded to any given pair of questionnaires. Accordingly, this design required 8,000 incumbents overall across the 80 occupations considered.

With regard to this design, four other points should be mentioned. First, questionnaires were rotated across packets to minimize potential order and priming effects (Morgeson & Campion, 1996). However, within a questionnaire, order was fixed to maintain the structure of the taxonomies and reduce burdens placed on the incumbents. Second, all packets began with an introduction describing the study, stressing that the data were being gathered as part of a national research study. Third, following this introductory material, all incumbents were asked to complete a short background information form, where they were asked to indicate age, sex, educational level, and years of experience. Fourth, once they had completed the various questionnaires included in their packet, all incumbents were asked to rate the frequency with which they performed and the importance of certain tasks on their jobs. These tasks had been identified by occupational analysts using available DOT data for the targeted occupations.

## RATER COMPARISON STUDY

The intent of this study was to determine whether the descriptions obtained from incumbents—people working on the job—were similar to descriptions obtained from occupational analysts. Occupational analysts providing these ratings were analysts employed by the OAFCs and industrial/organizational psychology graduate students. The analysts rated 1,122 occupational units, where occupational units represented a taxonomy of jobs with a level of specificity in between the more general OES taxonomy and the more specific DOT taxonomy.

The occupational analysts rated the following O*NET content model categories: basic and cross-functional skills, GWAs, abilities, work context, and knowledges. It is important to note that although most of the rating scales used by the occupational analysts were identical to those used by job incumbents, some were not. In particular, the scale used by

| Set 1 | Set 2 | Set 3 | Set 4 | Set 5 |
|---|---|---|---|---|
| Letter/Background/Instructions 1<br>Background Questionnaire<br>Skills 27.5<br>Abilities 24.0<br>Occupation Specific Tasks<br>68.5 | Letter/Background/Instructions 4<br>Background Questionnaire<br>Work Context 23.0<br>Skills 27.5<br>Occupation Specific Tasks<br>67.5 | Letter/Background/Instructions 7<br>Background Questionnaire<br>GWAs 30.0<br>Occ. Values 5.4<br>Skills 27.5<br>Occupation Specific Tasks<br>81.9 | Letter/Background/Instructions 10<br>Background Questionnaire<br>T/E/L/E 11.1<br>Skills 27.5<br>Work Styles 8.8<br>Occupation Specific Tasks<br>66.4 | Letter/Background/Instructions 13<br>Background Questionnaire<br>Knowledges 14.0<br>Org Context 10.6<br>Skills 27.5<br>Occupation Specific Tasks<br>71.1 |
| Letter/Background/Instructions 2<br>Background Questionnaire<br>Knowledges 14.0<br>Org Context 10.6<br>Work Context 23.0<br>Occupation Specific Tasks<br>66.6 | Letter/Background/Instructions 5<br>Background Questionnaire<br>GWAs 30.0<br>Occ. Values 5.4<br>Abilities 24.0<br>Occupation Specific Tasks<br>78.4 | Letter/Background/Instructions 8<br>Background Questionnaire<br>Org Context 10.6<br>Abilities 24.0<br>Knowledges 14.0<br>Occupation Specific Tasks<br>67.6 | Letter/Background/Instructions 11<br>Background Questionnaire<br>Abilities 24.0<br>Work Context 23.0<br>Occupation Specific Tasks<br>64.0 | Letter/Background/Instructions 14<br>Background Questionnaire<br>Abilities 24.0<br>Work Styles 8.8<br>T/E/L/E 11.1<br>Occupation Specific Tasks<br>62.9 |
| Letter/Background/Instructions 3<br>Background Questionnaire<br>Occ. Values 5.4<br>Work Styles 8.8<br>GWAs 30.0<br>T/E/L/E 11.1<br>Occupation Specific Tasks<br>76.3 | Letter/Background/Instructions 6<br>Background Questionnaire<br>Work Styles 8.8<br>T/E/L/E 11.1<br>Knowledges 14.0<br>Org Context 10.6<br>Occupation Specific Tasks<br>65.5 | Letter/Background/Instructions 9<br>Background Questionnaire<br>Work Styles 8.8<br>Work Context 23.0<br>T/E/L/E 11.1<br>Occupation Specific Tasks<br>61.9 | Letter/Background/Instructions 12<br>Background Questionnaire<br>Occ. Values 5.4<br>Knowledges 14.0<br>Org Context 10.6<br>GWAs 30.0<br>Occupation Specific Tasks<br>81.0 | Letter/Background/Instructions 15<br>Background Questionnaire<br>Work Context 23.0<br>GWAs 30.0<br>Occ. Values 5.4<br>Occupation Specific Tasks<br>77.4 |

KEY:

minutes for administration of questionnaire → 

questionnaire name →

| | |
|---|---|
| Letter/Background/Instructions | 1 ← packet number |
| Background Questionnaire | |
| Skills | 27.5 |
| Abilities | 24.0 |
| Occupation Specific Task | 68.5 ← minutes for administration of entire packet including instructions |

NOTES:

1. Skills=Skills questionnaire; Abilities=Abilities questionnaire; Knowledges=Knowledges questionnaire; Work Context=Work Context questionnaire; Occ. Values=Occupational Values questionnaire; Work Styles=Work Styles questionnaire; GWAs=Generalized Work Activities questionnaire; T/E/L/E=Training, Education, Licensure, and Experience questionnaire.

2. Generalized Work Activities and Knowledges times were estimates based on modifications made since the tryout, actual times from the tryouts were 21.7 and 18.5, respectively.

3. Packet administration times include 2 minutes between questionnaires, 10 minutes for the cover letter, overall instructions, and background information questionnaire, and 5 minutes for the occupation-specific Tasks questionnaire.

FIGURE 4-3. Rotation design.

occupational analysts to rate the frequency with which a generalized work activity is performed in an occupation differed from that used by job incumbents. The scales differed in two ways: (a) the scale used by the analysts had 4 scale points, whereas the scale used by the job incumbents had 7; and (b) the scale anchors on the analysts' version did not reference particular time intervals (e.g., one anchor on the analysts' scale was *sometimes*, whereas a comparable anchor on the incumbents' scale was *more than once a month*). In addition, analysts completed only a subset of the work context ratings and did not rate job entry requirements for skills or job specialty requirements for knowledges.

For all 1,122 occupational units, each unit was independently rated by at least five analyst raters. During a rating cycle, each rater rated a set of 125 occupational units on one O*NET content model category for level, importance, and frequency, when applicable. The 80 occupations targeted for data collection from incumbents are a subset of the 1,122 occupational units.

## RESPONSE RATES

Because of the many stages of the study design, response rates are described according to each of the steps in the study design. Initially, 1,240 establishments were screened for a POC. Of the 1,240 establishments, 1,054 (85%) were eligible to participate in the study (see Table 4-3). As noted previously, those ineligible to participate included establishments that were out of business, duplicates in the data file, and those having fewer than five employees. The percentage of ineligible organizations obtained from the D&B file is typical of that found during the initial screening of organizations for an establishment survey.

On the basis of this initial screening, 1,054 establishments were identified for negotiations. During this phase of the project, an additional 80 establishments (7%) indicated that they did not have employees in the jobs we were studying. During negotiations, 218 establishments (21%) refused to participate in the study for a variety of reasons including time constraints, no interest in the study, and company policy regarding participation in outside studies. Overall, 756 establishments (72%) agreed during the negotiations to participate in all aspects of the study design.

The next stage of the study involved administration of the organizational interview. During this stage an additional 92 establishments (12%) refused to participate even though they had initially agreed during project negotiations. Organizational interviews were conducted with 661 organizational representatives, for a response rate of 88% at this stage.

The next stage of the project involved mailing a number of incumbent questionnaires to each POC for distribution within the establishment. Of the 661 POCs who completed the organizational interview,

**TABLE 4-3**

**Phase I, Baseline (Paper and Pencil) Response Counts**

| | Counts |
|---|---|
| **Screening (receptionist)** | |
| Total to screening | 1,240 |
| Ineligible[a] | 143 |
| Possible ineligible[b] | 42 |
| Refusal | 1 |
| Complete | 1,054 |
| Response rate | 100% |
| Survival rate | 85% |
| **Negotiations (human resources representative)** | |
| Total to negotiation | 1,054 |
| Ineligible[a] | 80 |
| Refusal | 218 |
| Complete | 756 |
| Response rate | 72% |
| **Organizational representative interview (human resources representative)** | |
| Total to interview | 756 |
| Ineligible[a] | 3 |
| Refusal | 92 |
| Complete | 661 |
| Response rate | 88% |
| **Mailout: Employer level (mailed October 18 to December 15)** | |
| Total to mailout | 661 |
| Ineligible[a] | 2 |
| Refusal | 174 |
| Nonresponse | 304 |
| Complete | 181 |
| Response rate | 27% |
| **Mailout: Total employees** | |
| Total to mailout | 15,529 |
| Ineligible[a] | 25 |
| Refusal/nonresponse | 13,015 |
| Complete | 2,489 |
| Response rate | 16% |
| **Mailout: Employees (employers who have returned data)** | |
| Total employers who have returned data | 181 |
| Total employee packets sent | 4,125 |
| Total employee packets returned | 2,489 |
| Response rate | 60% |
| **Mailout: Employees (employers who have returned data)** | |
| Total employers who have returned data with at least 1 general manager or secretary | 96 |
| General Managers | |
| Total employee packets sent | 198 |
| Total employee packets returned | 145 |
| Response rate | 73% |
| Secretaries | |
| Total employee packets sent | 335 |
| Total employee packets returned | 245 |
| Response rate | 73% |

[a]Ineligible cases include duplicates, fewer than 5 employees, English not spoken, out of business, no one in chosen occupations.    [b]Possibly ineligible cases include no answer at location; not locatable; phone number not in service.

181 returned at least one incumbent survey. This resulted in a response rate at the employer level of 27%. During the fielding of the incumbent survey, it became apparent early on that POCs were not returning questionnaires at the rate anticipated. In fact, once employers received the incumbent packages, an additional 174 establishments (26%) refused to participate.

## Identifying Response Rate Problems

A number of actions were taken to identify reasons for the low incumbent response rates and to increase POC participation in the distribution and collection of incumbent questionnaires. These attempts to increase participation did not, however, significantly affect POCs' willingness to distribute questionnaires to incumbents. The high rate of refusal at this stage in the study was not anticipated because POCs had been carefully informed at earlier stages about the time needed for incumbents to complete the questionnaires and the majority of POCs had agreed to participate. Consequently, it appeared that the primary factor contributing to slow response rates was the POC's unwillingness to distribute incumbent questionnaires—a gatekeeper effect.

Careful examination of the baseline response rates supports this contention. Results presented in Table 4-3—in "Mailout: employees (employers who have returned data)"—show that participating establishments had an incumbent response rate of 60%, which was 44% higher than the incumbent response rate obtained overall. This finding indicates that when employers actually distributed questionnaires to incumbents in their establishment, participation rates were quite satisfactory.

To gain a better understanding of this gatekeeper problem, phone calls were made to nonresponding establishments. The comments provided by POCs fell into several categories:

- Excessive POC burden associated with distributing and collecting survey packets,
- Too much time required of incumbents to complete the surveys,
- Too short a fielding period during which to collect data,
- No incentives for participation, including stipends or access to the O*NET database, and
- Questionnaire too difficult for some incumbents to comprehend.

## Attempts to Improve Response Rate

Because of the feedback received from POCs, a small pilot test was conducted. A sample of 175 establishments was selected from the reserve sample. Two occupations likely present in these establishments were studied: general managers and secretaries. The study design specifically incorporated steps intended to reduce the burden required from sampled establishments:

- *Reduction in time.* The questionnaire modules were changed so that each incumbent received fewer questionnaires. This revision resulted in the time for completion changing from 60–90 minutes to 30 minutes.
- *Fewer incumbents sampled within an establishment.* POCs were asked to administer questionnaires to no more than five incumbents.
- *No formal sampling of incumbents within establishments.* Although procedures for selecting a representative sample of incumbents were described (e.g., range of experience, range of ability), POCs were not asked to follow formalized sampling procedures.
- *Change in the order of the organizational interview.* The organizational interview was conducted with some of the sample used in this pilot test. However, when the survey was administered, it was given at the end (rather than the beginning) of the data collection process. That is, POCs were first asked to distribute and collect incumbent questionnaires. Then, a small sample of the POCs were asked to participate in the organizational interview.

The results were informative. Following screening, a total of 169 out of 175 establishments (97%) reached the negotiation phase. A total of 11 establishments (17%) refused participation, and 23 establishments (14%) were ineligible (e.g., did not have incumbents in the chosen occupations or they had fewer than 5 incumbents). At the employer stage, 65 employers (51%) responded by sending back incumbent surveys (compared with 27% in the original sample; see Table 4-3). Ten (7%) refused to participate, and 52 (39%) neither directly refused nor sent back surveys. Of the questionnaires mailed, the incumbent response rate was 41% (compared with 16% in the original sample; see Table 4-3). Finally, in establishments that returned any data at all, 85% of the selected incumbents returned packets (compared with 73% for the same two jobs in the original sample; see the last part of Table 4-3). In summary, the procedures used in this pilot test resulted in much higher incumbent response rates than those achieved in the main study. Reducing burden for employers appeared to affect their willingness to distribute and collect questionnaires from incumbents. Clearly, the revised procedures implemented in this test should be incorporated into any future data collection.

## Nonresponse Analysis

Because the response rates in this study were low, it is possible that the survey results obtained are seriously biased. That is, the responding employees might include or exclude particular kinds of people or people employed in particular industries. If that was the case, appropriate caveats would need to be stated prior to any discussion of findings. To partially address the issue of bias, a nonresponse analysis was conducted.

### Nonresponse Analysis Procedures

A total of 1,240 cases was provided for the nonresponse analysis. Table 4-4 summarizes the distribution of cases and completed questionnaires by their final survey disposition. The preponderance of nonrespondents and refusals underscores the need for examining establishment characteristics by disposition to determine whether systematic differences exist by category. For this analysis, cases found to be ineligible during any phase of the data collection effort were dropped, leaving a total of 1,054 cases to be analyzed.

The analysis proceeded in two stages. First, establishment characteristics known for all cases were examined. These included the SIC code of the establishments, the number of employees at the selected location, a status indicator (branch or HQ), and the state in which the establishment was located. Each of these items was supplied by D&B. The distribution of these characteristics across disposition categories was examined to determine whether systematic concentrations of particular firm types were occurring in particular disposition categories.

The second stage of the analysis examined survey results arrayed by disposition status. The majority of establishments did not respond at the mailout phase of the project, as shown in Table 4-4.

### Nonresponse Analysis Summary

Although analyses such as those summarized here cannot definitively establish the presence or absence of nonresponse bias in survey findings, they can provide general indications of survey response coverage. Generally, it was established that, when categorized by final disposition, both establishment characteristics and questionnaire responses were more similar within categories than across them. This observation

is tempered by findings indicating that establishment size and occupational grouping do, in certain cases, affect survey administration outcome. Larger establishments are more likely than others to terminate the survey process through "mail refusal," and certain occupational groupings display greater or lesser propensities to cooperate and provide completed surveys. Regarding high-performance practices as measured via a telephone interview, goal-setting practices showed differences across disposition categories.

Viewed as an ensemble of findings, the nonresponse analyses provide some lessons. Administration of an establishment survey is difficult, and some of the difficulty is a function of the establishments themselves. Obviously, establishment size, area of occupational focus (e.g., construction, service, or justice), and bureaucratic structure (as reflected in human resource practices) affect survey response differentially. When reviewing survey responses, few indications of bias were observed. Of the 14 scales evaluated and the 42 comparisons made, only 2 scales revealed significant differences in responses by disposition. It is less the case that bias has been discovered than that some administrative difficulties with the procedures have been underscored.

## DATA PREPARATION AND PROCESSING

All returned questionnaires were cleaned and coded prior to data entry. On receipt of incumbent packets, identification numbers were entered into a receipt control system that kept track of which questionnaires were completed by each incumbent. As the mail arrived, it was opened, and each form was checked to make sure it had at least some responses. A form number was written at the top of the questionnaire to aid in data entry. Refusals were also entered into the receipt control system. If a company returned all of the incumbent packets blank or indicated a refusal by telephone, this information was entered into the database by company name. After this step, questionnaires were then sorted by form type and coded.

Once the coding was completed, the questionnaires were key punched and verified by experienced data entry operators. Once the data were keyed, various edit checks were run. After these edits, data-quality checks were made and rules for inclusion of data were invoked. These checks occurred within each domain or questionnaire (e.g., within the skills, within generalized work activities). If a data-quality check detected unusable data within one domain, it had no effect on the checks in another domain.

If a respondent had more than 10% missing data within any domain, the entire case (i.e., all of the respondent's responses for that questionnaire) was deleted. If a respondent had fewer than 10% missing responses, but had some missing responses, then the mean descriptor value for that occupation was substituted for the missing response.

**TABLE 4-4**

**Distribution of Cases and Completed Questionnaires by Disposition Category**

| Disposition category | Count | % |
| --- | --- | --- |
| Cases | | |
| Negotiation refusal | 218 | 20.7 |
| CATI refusal | 92 | 8.7 |
| Mail nonrespondents | 323 | 30.6 |
| Mail refusals | 174 | 16.5 |
| Mail completes | 162 | 15.4 |
| Ineligible any phase | 85 | 8.1 |
| Completed questionnaires | | |
| Mail nonrespondents | 304 | 46 |
| Mail refusals | 174 | 26 |
| Mail completes | 181 | 27 |

*Note.* CATI = computer-assisted telephone interview.

An occupation was retained for analysis if four or more respondents had provided data surviving these data-processing and quality checks. Although our goal was to obtain 30 respondents for each domain for each questionnaire, 4 respondents were sufficient to carry out investigative analyses for evaluative purposes.

When these rules were invoked, there were 29 occupations that had at least four respondents across all the O*NET content domains. These occupations are listed in Table 16-1 in chapter 16, which describes the cross-domain analyses. There were somewhat larger numbers of occupations available within each domain, where the requirement only was for four respondents to the relevant questionnaire, not across all questionnaires; those occupations are displayed in chapters 5 through 13, which describe their respective domain analyses.

## GENERAL DATA ANALYSES

The initial O*NET data collection effort was not intended to provide a comprehensive description of all jobs in the United States economy. Instead, it was part of a prototyping effort intended to provide evidence bearing on the meaningfulness of the descriptive information provided by these measures.

The nature of the measures used in any particular domain sometimes dictated unique kinds of analyses. In all cases, however, the basic questions of concern dictated a relatively straightforward set of core analyses carried out within each domain.

The basic within-domain analyses are generally described here; details specific to a given domain are covered in its respective chapter. The results of the below-described analyses are presented in the domain chapters, chapters 5 through 13, of this volume. Each of these chapters presents the results of analyses for one of the O*NET questionnaires. The tables within these chapters are generally named and numbered uniformly for ease of location and comparison, but not all analyses, and therefore not all tables, apply to all chapters.

### Descriptive Statistics

Means and standard deviations of occupational means for the various scales within each domain are provided to give a general impression of the overall centrality and variance of the descriptors within our sample of occupations.

### Reliability

By *reliability* we primarily mean interrater agreement. No rate-rerate data were collected. We computed interrater agreement coefficients for each descriptor measure, using standard intraclass coeffi-cients (Shrout & Fleiss, 1979). Such coefficients were computed for the Level, Importance, Frequency, or other scales available within each domain. We used Spearman-Brown corrections for estimating the reliability coefficients for the 1-rater and 30-rater cases, to allow ready comparisons across domains and to other studies. We used the harmonic mean of the number of raters available for each occupation as our estimate of $k$ for making these calculations. This is a conservative estimate of $k$.

### Scoring

In some cases—most notably, level and importance—different methods of using the responses to arrive at scale scores were available. These methods primarily differed in the way in which the *not relevant* (NR) response was used. The intended and default method was to use *not relevant* as the zero point on the Level scale and to indicate "not important" on the Importance scale. We labeled this the "full scale" method. Alternatively, we examined the case when *not relevant* responses were treated as missing (i.e., only those selecting *not relevant* were excluded from the reliability analyses). Finally, we also examined a dichotomous case for the Level scale, where *not relevant* = 0 and any other response was coded as 1.

### Analyses of Variance

We also computed an analysis of variance with occupations as a between-raters variable and descriptors as a within-raters variable. Aside from describing the sources of variance in the descriptor measures, these analyses allowed a second, stringent method of computing the interrater agreement. We computed the intraclass correlation coefficient using the descriptor by occupation source of variance as the "true" variance and the descriptor by raters within occupation source of variance as the "error" source of variance. Note that the descriptor source of variance, which certainly is a nonerror source of variance, is excluded from the calculation. Only the source of variance that serves to accurately describe each occupation as it differs from other occupations is included as true variance. This is, of course, the most appropriate coefficient for our purposes, but it is most likely an underestimate of within-occupation, interrater agreement. This kind of analysis was also applied to higher level descriptor scores derived by computing the mean values for descriptors combined according to the a priori hierarchical structures for the content model domains. Because these higher level scores would no doubt be used in some applications of the O*NET database, it was useful to determine the interrater agreement coefficients for such scores.

All of these reliability analyses serve to evaluate the degree to which incumbents appear to agree on the description of their occupations using the O*NET job analysis measures. Such analyses are the bedrock on which all other analyses depend.

## Descriptor and Scale Relationships

### Correlations Between Scale Type

In most domains, more than one scale was used to collect information about descriptors. Most notably, level and importance were used in most domains. To estimate the redundancy of information for the different scales, intercorrelations were computed in two different ways: across descriptors within each occupation and across occupations within each descriptor.

### Relationships of Descriptor Scale Scores

To assess the internal structure of the descriptor variables, correlations were computed between the Level scale scores and between the Importance scale scores or other appropriate scores. These correlations were computed at the occupational level (i.e., occupational means were the scores that were correlated) and at the individual level (i.e., individual incumbent scores were correlated, but only four randomly selected incumbents from each occupation were entered into these calculations in order to equally weight the occupations). Because the primary focus of the O*NET is at the occupational level, only the occupational-level data were examined and discussed.

## Factor Structure

Principal-components analyses were also conducted using the occupational-level correlational data. The correlational and principal-component analyses, of course, provide evidence for evaluating the meaningfulness of the relationships observed among the measures (Harvey, Friedman, Hakel, & Cornelius, 1982).

## Occupation Differences

Six representative and relatively distinct occupations were selected, and their profiles of descriptor scores were compared within each domain. The pattern of differences across these occupations was used to illustrate the ways in which each domain's descriptors served to separate occupations, and they served as a check on the "sensibility" of the resulting occupational descriptions.

## Convergence With Analysts' Ratings

Because we had incumbent and occupational analyst ratings for a subset of occupations, we could compare these ratings. We were able to complete these analyses for five of the nine content domains, because analysts had completed their ratings for those five domains. We calculated and displayed the means, standard deviations, and interrater agreement coefficients for all descriptors for both the Level and Importance scales in these five domains, except for the work context domain, which used a different set of scales. In addition we calculated $t$ tests for mean differences, $F$ tests for variance differences, correlations between incumbent and analyst mean descriptor scores (within descriptor, across occupations), and mean $d^2$ values (i.e., the mean across all occupations of the summed, squared differences between incumbent and occupational mean values for all descriptors within an occupation). This set of statistics allowed us to thoroughly evaluate the degree to which the two types of raters converged or diverged in the information they provided. The correlations indicate the degree of agreement in the pattern of the mean ratings, whereas the $d^2$ values indicate the averaged, absolute level of disagreement between mean ratings of the two types of raters. Thus, large correlation coefficients and small $d^2$ values indicate convergence between the raters.

We also conducted principal-component analyses of the correlations between descriptor level scores for the analyst data (i.e., a parallel analysis of that completed for the incumbent data). These two solutions were compared and contrasted to shed further light on the similarities and differences of the information provided by the two types of raters.

## SUMMARY

This chapter has briefly described the rationale for using certain kinds of job descriptive methods in the O*NET prototype development effort (i.e., Level, Importance, and Frequency scales administered to job incumbents via paper-and-pencil questionnaires). The methods for identifying establishments to sample and procedures for collecting data from incumbents in those establishments have been described, as well as the obtained rates of return for those procedures. An analysis of possible improvement in data collection procedures was presented along with an analysis of possible bias in the obtained sample. Finally, the types of analyses conducted on the data were presented in overview. The next nine chapters present the results of those analyses for each of the distinct domains in the O*NET.

## CHAPTER 5

# Basic and Cross-Functional Skills

MICHAEL D. MUMFORD, NORMAN G. PETERSON, AND RUTH A. CHILDS

Throughout industry, government, and education, people are worried about worker skills. This concern with "skills," however they may be defined, is evident in a number of initiatives, including the 1990 Secretary's Commission on Achieving Necessary Skills (SCANS) and the 1994 Congressionally mandated National Skill Standards Board. These new initiatives can be traced to the problems confronting workers as we enter the 21st century (Cascio, 1995; Howard, 1995a). No longer can one go to school for 12 years, take a job, and then do much the same thing for the next 30 years. Instead, changes in technology, global competition, and the emergence of new organizational structures have created a dynamic workplace where people are confronted with a host of complex new duties and are asked to take responsibility for their own work and their own careers.

These changes, indeed, stress the need for complex performance skills and ongoing skill development. This apparently straightforward statement, however, raises many more questions than it answers. How are we to define skills in the first place? Assuming we can define the skills of interest, how are we to identify the kinds of skills likely to be required on different jobs? What do these job skill requirements, in turn, tell us about how we should go about preparing people for the jobs of the future?

In this chapter we hope to provide some initial answers to these and a number of other questions about occupational skill requirements. We begin by briefly reviewing what is known about occupational skills and proposing a working definition for them. Next, we propose a taxonomy of occupational skill requirements and a strategy for obtaining measures of the skill requirements of different occupations. Finally, we present some initial evidence bearing on the reliability and validity of these measures and examine its implications for answering certain questions about workforce skills.

## DEFINITIONAL ISSUES

Skills have not been a major focus of prior research examining the nature and structure of occupational requirements. This point is well illustrated by noting that Gael's (1988) *Handbook of Job Analysis* and Harvey's (1990b) chapter on job analysis in the *Handbook of Industrial and Organizational Psychology* both devote little, if any, attention to the topic of occupational skills. The tendency of job analysts to ignore skills may be attributed to the tradition of examining the work to be done (e.g., tasks) rather than the capacities people must possess to do the work (e.g., skills; Cascio, 1995). Even when occupational analysts consider the capacities needed to do the work, they have tended to focus on abilities and interests—relatively stable, enduring characteristics likely to be useful when one is making initial decisions (Fleishman & Reilly, 1992b; Tyler, 1965).

For many reasons, however, one might argue that skills represent an important missing element in the way we go about describing people's jobs. When we describe the person doing the work, we cannot consider just abilities and interests. Quite often we need to know what capacities people must develop if they are to be able to perform. Clearly, information about those developed characteristics that influence performance, such as skills, is needed to answer a number of questions. Information bearing on occupational skill requirements might be used to identify requisite developmental experiences, establish training requirements, and determine how easily people can move from one job to another.

Although information bearing on occupational skill requirements might prove useful in answering a host of questions, it has proven difficult to arrive at a conceptual definition of the key skills of concern when we describe people's jobs. Some scholars define skills in terms of task performance. Others define skills in terms of educational requirements—the old three "Rs" of reading, writing, and 'rithmetic. Still others see skills as a set of broad new capacities, as illustrated in the literature on critical and creative thinking (Halpern, 1994).

These many different conceptions of skills point to a noteworthy conclusion. We are unlikely to make much progress in identifying and assessing occupational skills unless we can find a scientifically sound definition of the term *skills*. Initial research into the nature of skilled performance defined skills operationally in terms of gains in performance with practice on a certain task. The primary objective of these early studies was to identify the variables contributing to more rapid acquisition of skilled performance. For example, initial studies by Fleishman and his colleagues (e.g., Fleishman, 1972a, 1982; Fleishman & Hempel, 1955; Fleishman & Quaintance, 1984) showed that abilities, such as verbal reasoning, represent an important influence on the development of skilled performance. More recent work by Ackerman (1994) and Kanfer and Ackerman (1989) has shown that motivational and dispositional variables also influence the acquisition of skilled performance.

Although this research proved useful in elucidating the sources of individual differences in skill acquisition, it did not directly examine the nature of skilled performance. This issue, however, has been the question of concern in a number of studies following the cognitive paradigm. Here, techniques such as protocol analysis and comparison of expert–novice differences are used to identify the key characteristics of skilled performance (Anderson, 1993; Chi & Glaser, 1985; S. Ward, Byrnes, & Overton, 1990). Broadly speaking, these studies indicate that skilled performance requires expertise or a principle-based organization of relevant information (Ericsson & Charness, 1994). Associated with expertise, however, skilled performance also appears to involve acquisition of a set of strategies, procedures, and processes for acquiring and working with relevant information (Anderson, 1993; Campbell, McCloy, Oppler, & Sager, 1993; Greeno & Simon, 1988; Sternberg, 1986). These procedures for acquiring and working with knowledge appear to represent the key components we refer to when we use the term *skills*.

This conception of skills is implicit in Hayes and Flower's (1986) work on writing skills. In their research, they analyzed the work of writers and found three general procedures involved in virtually all writing tasks: (a) planning, (b) generation, and (c) revision. In subsequent studies, they found that interventions intended to encourage more effective application of these processes led to gains in performance on new writing tasks. Other research (Baer, 1988; Bull, Montgomery, & Baloche, 1995; S. Ward et al., 1990) also indicates that training in requisite procedures—skill training—can lead to improved performance on transfer tasks.

By defining skills in terms of procedures for acquiring and working with information, three points come to the fore. First, skills are not necessarily stable, enduring characteristics of workers. Instead, they depend on experience and practice. Second, skills can be defined at different levels of generality. In some cases skills refer to a rather narrow set of procedures (e.g., revision skills) and in other cases to broader, more complex sets of procedures (e.g., writing skills). Third, skills cannot be defined apart from some performance domain involving the acquisition and application of certain types of knowledge.

## THE STRUCTURE OF OCCUPATIONAL SKILLS

If skills are referenced against certain performance domains, it becomes clear that there are a variety of different types of skills. One might, for example, speak of citizenship and child-rearing skills; alternatively, one might speak of the skills involved in ice fishing. However important the skills required in those performance domains may be, the skills are not especially useful as a basis for describing the requirements imposed by different occupations.

This observation brings us to a fundamental problem that must be addressed if we are to formulate a systematic framework for identifying and assessing occupational skills. We must be able to specify broad performance domains that represent common, essential aspects of performance on most jobs. In other words, we must be able to identify general domains of job performance.

One way this might be accomplished is by examining general theories of work behavior. Over the years, a number of different models have been proposed that might be used to understand people's behavior in the workplace (Pfeffer & Salanick, 1978). Of those theories, sociotechnical systems theory continues to provide the most widely accepted model of workplace behavior. Broadly speaking, systems theory sees work as a process of transforming raw materials into useful products through the use of technology and division of labor (Katz & Kahn, 1978). This complex sociotechnical system, however, is seen as a dynamic entity in which autonomous social organs strive to achieve a variety of goals. This general framework, in turn, suggests that all jobs will involve five general performance domains that might provide a basis for defining skills. More specifically, those general domains of workplace skills, referred to as *cross-functional skills*, would include the following:

- solving problems (problem-solving skills),
- working with technology (technical skills),
- working with people (social skills),
- working within an organizational system (systems skills), and
- working with resources (resource management skills).

This theoretical definition of the major domains of cross-functional skills—skill domains applying across jobs—in fact finds some support in earlier analyses of workplace skills. For example, Kane and Meltzer (1990), as part of the SCANS project, interviewed a number of executives to identify the kinds of skills they thought would be required in the workforce of the future. They found that executives proposed skills falling in these general domains of cross-functional skills. Along similar lines, in his book on the *Dictionary of Occupational Titles* (DOT; U.S. Department of Labor, 1991a), Fine (1988) proposed the now-classic taxonomy of data, people, and things as a way of structuring the major domains of people's work performance. Fine's taxonomy, of course, maps quite well onto the general structure of cross-functional skills proposed above.

Within this framework, cross-functional skills refer to production-relevant activities likely to occur on any job. This framework might provide an adequate basis for defining occupational skill requirements if our only concern were immediate performance. In a rapidly changing workplace, however, people must constantly master new materials (Osborne, 1994). This straightforward observation implies that a comprehensive definition of skills must consider performance over the long haul—more specifically, those basic skills that provide a foundation for acquiring new knowledge. These basic skills include skills such as reading and speaking that provide a basis for acquiring and conveying information, as well as skills such as critical thinking and monitoring that promote learning in a variety of different domains. Thus, basic skills should be seen as subsuming content skills involving the acquisition and use of information, as well as process skills or learning-to-learn skills.

## SKILLS TAXONOMIES

These broad domains of skills relevant to understanding performance in the workplace provide a framework for developing taxonomies of the basic and cross-functional skills that might be used to describe people's jobs. To specify the skills involved in each of those domains, Mumford and Peterson (1995) reviewed the literature bearing on performance. Table 5-1 presents the technical and operational definitions for each of the basic and cross-functional skills identified by Mumford and Peterson. These skills provided the basis for development of the measures used to describe occupational skills in the O*NET effort.

## Basic Skills

### Content Skills

Basic skills have been defined in a number of ways. The most common approach, however, defines basic skills with respect to the fundamentals that should be provided by any sound educational system (Cureton, 1951; Schmidt, Porter, Schwille, Floden, & Freeman, 1983). In developing their taxonomy of basic skills, Mumford and Peterson (1995) used a related but somewhat different approach. They argued that learning is intimately tied to the acquisition and application of knowledge. Thus, basic content skills can be defined in terms of those capabilities that allow people to acquire information and convey this information to others.

The two most common ways people acquire new knowledge are through reading and talking to others. This new knowledge is then conveyed to others

through writing and speaking. Accordingly, Mumford and Peterson propose that Reading Comprehension, Active Listening, Writing, and Speaking should be viewed as basic skills, or skills likely to promote further learning. These four basic content skills are consistent with most prior discussions of basic skills (e.g., Schmidt et al., 1983) and are the first four shown in Table 5-1.

Mumford and Peterson (1995), however, go on to argue that two other skills, mathematics and science, should also be included in an initial taxonomy of basic skills. Of course, mathematics and science can be viewed as particular forms of knowledge. By the same token, mathematics and science courses also provide a special language and a unique set of procedures for acquiring, working with, and communicating knowledge in a number of different domains. This observation suggests that there is a distinct skill component to learning in those areas that warrants viewing mathematics and science as distinct basic skills.

### Process Skills

Learning in its most basic form can be viewed as acquiring and applying knowledge. At a more complex level, however, there is reason to suspect that the ways in which people work with information during learning will also play a role in knowledge acquisition and performance. In fact, a study by Chi, Bassock, Lewis, Reimann, and Glaser (1989) that contrasts the characteristics of good and poor learners indicates that good learners actively work with new information, searching for organizing principles and their implications. Other studies by Schneck (1988) and Schneck and Grove (1979) also indicate that students who actively work with information, personally elaborating principles and applications, are more likely to show gains in knowledge. Thus, this Active Learning appears to represent an important process in learning-to-learn skills.

Research into general strategies, processes, and procedures that facilitate learning is still in its infancy (Mumford, Baughman, Supinski, Costanza, & Threlfall, 1996). Nonetheless, the evidence available at this juncture indicates that at least three other process skills may play an important role in learning, both in school and on the job. First, it appears that students who flexibly apply strategies for acquiring and working with information, and use multiple strategies, master new material more quickly and perform better on novel problem-solving tasks (Kazier & Shore, 1995; Van Meter, Yoki, & Pressley, 1994a). Thus, Learning Strategies may be viewed as another requisite basic skill. Second, the evidence compiled by Van Meter, Yoki, and Pressley (1994b), as well as by Sternberg (1986), indicates that Monitoring, or ongoing appraisal, of the success of one's efforts and subsequent shifts in strategy or approach when pursued goals are not met will also contribute to learning in a variety of settings. Third, in learning it is not enough simply to monitor how well one is doing. One must also take into account the quality of the

**TABLE 5-1**
**Descriptions and Definitions of Basic and Cross-Functional Skills**

| Construct label | Operational definition | Level scale Level | Level scale Example |
|---|---|---|---|
| | | Content skills | |
| Reading Comprehension | Understanding written sentences and paragraphs in work-related documents | High<br>Medium<br><br>Low | Reading a scientific journal article describing surgical procedures.<br>Reading a memo from management describing new personnel policies<br>Reading step-by-step instructions for completing a form. |
| Active Listening | Listening to what other people are saying and asking questions as appropriate | High<br>Medium<br>Low | Presiding as judge in a complex legal disagreement.<br>Answering inquiries regarding credit references.<br>Taking a customer's order. |
| Writing | Communicating effectively with others in writing as indicated by the needs of the audience | High<br>Medium<br>Low | Writing a novel for publication.<br>Writing a memo to staff outlining new directives.<br>Taking a telephone message. |
| Speaking | Talking to others to effectively convey information | High<br>Medium<br>Low | Arguing a legal case before the Supreme Court.<br>Interviewing applicants to obtain personal and work history.<br>Greeting tourists and explaining tourist attractions. |
| Mathematics | Using mathematics to solve problems | High<br><br>Medium<br><br>Low | Developing a mathematical model to simulate and resolve an engineering problem.<br>Calculating the square footage of a new home under construction.<br>Counting the amount of change to be given to a customer. |
| Science | Using scientific methods to solve problems | High<br><br>Medium<br><br>Low | Conducting analyses of aerodynamic systems to determine the practicality of an aircraft design.<br>Conducting product tests to ensure safety standards are met, following written instructions.<br>Conducting standard tests to determine soil quality. |
| | | Process skills | |
| Active Learning | Working with new material or information to grasp its implications | High<br><br>Medium<br><br>Low | Identifying the implications of a new scientific theory for product design.<br>Determining the impact of new menu changes on a restaurant's purchasing requirements.<br>Thinking about the implications of a newspaper article for job opportunities. |
| Learning Strategies | Using multiple approaches when learning or teaching new things | High<br><br>Medium<br><br>Low | Applying principles of educational psychology to developing new teaching methods.<br>Identifying an alternative approach that might help trainees who are having difficulties.<br>Learning a different method of completing a task from a coworker. |
| Monitoring | Assessing how well one is doing when learning or doing something | High<br><br>Medium<br><br>Low | Reviewing corporate productivity and developing a plan to increase productivity.<br>Monitoring a meeting's progress and revising the agenda to ensure that important topics are discussed.<br>Proofreading and correcting a letter. |
| Critical Thinking | Using logic and analysis to identify the strengths and weaknesses of different approaches | High<br>Medium<br><br>Low | Writing a legal brief challenging a federal law.<br>Evaluating customer complaints and determining appropriate responses.<br>Determining whether a subordinate has a good excuse for being late. |
| | | Complex problem-solving skills | |
| Problem Identification | Identifying the nature of problems | High<br>Medium<br>Low | Analyzing corporate finances to develop a restructuring plan.<br>Identifying and solving customer complaints.<br>Comparing invoices of incoming articles to ensure they meet required specifications. |
| Information Gathering | Knowing how to find information and identifying essential information | High<br><br>Medium<br>Low | Analyzing industry indices and competitors' annual reports to determine feasibility of expansion.<br>Conducting an employee opinion survey.<br>Looking up procedures in a manual. |
| Information Organization | Finding ways to structure or classify multiple pieces of information | High<br>Medium<br>Low | Developing a prototype for a new database system.<br>Classifying library materials according to subject matter.<br>Laying out tools to complete a job. |

*Table 5-1 continues*

**TABLE 5-1** (*Continued*)

| Construct label | Operational definition | Level scale Level | Level scale Example |
|---|---|---|---|
| | | **Complex problem-solving skills** | |
| Synthesis/Reorganization | Reorganizing information to get a better approach to problems or tasks | High | Determining the best order in which to present evidence in a criminal trial. |
| | | Medium | Redesigning a floor layout to take advantage of new manufacturing techniques. |
| | | Low | Rearranging a filing system to make it easier to get needed material. |
| Idea Generation | Generating a number of different approaches to problems | High | Developing alternative transportation plans for a growing urban area. |
| | | Medium | Developing recruitment strategies. |
| | | Low | Finding alternative routes while making deliveries. |
| Idea Evaluation | Evaluating the likely success of idea in relation to the demands of the situation | High | Analyzing probable outcomes of public health policies to combat a disease epidemic. |
| | | Medium | Evaluating and selecting employee suggestions for possible implementation. |
| | | Low | Determining which procedure to apply to get a report typed more quickly. |
| Implementation Planning | Developing approaches for implementing an idea | High | Developing and implementing a plan to provide emergency relief for a major metropolitan area. |
| | | Medium | Scheduling deliveries on the basis of distance between sites, staffing time, availability of vehicles, and cost. |
| | | Low | Scheduling and coordinating a 1-day meeting. |
| Solution Appraisal | Observing and evaluating the outcomes of problem solution to identify lessons learned or redirect efforts | High | Reviewing, assessing, and modifying the implementation of a new business plan. |
| | | Medium | Measuring customer satisfaction after introduction of new billing procedures. |
| | | Low | Identifying and correcting an error made in preparing a report. |
| | | **Social skills** | |
| Social Perceptiveness | Being aware of others' reactions and understanding why they react the way they do | High | Counseling depressive patients during a crisis period. |
| | | Medium | Being aware of how a coworker's promotion would affect a work group. |
| | | Low | Noticing that customers are angry because they have been waiting too long. |
| Coordination | Adjusting actions in relation to others' actions | High | Working as director of a consulting project calling for interaction with multiple subcontractors. |
| | | Medium | Working with others to put a new roof on a house. |
| | | Low | Scheduling appointments for a medical clinic. |
| Persuasion | Persuading others to approach things differently | High | Changing the opinion of the jury in a complex legal case. |
| | | Medium | Convincing a supervisor to purchase a new copy machine. |
| | | Low | Soliciting donations for a charity. |
| Negotiation | Bringing others together and trying to reconcile differences | High | Working as an ambassador in negotiating a new treaty. |
| | | Medium | Contracting with a wholesaler to sell items at a given cost. |
| | | Low | Presenting justification to a manager for altering a work schedule. |
| Instructing | Teaching others how to do something | High | Demonstrating surgical procedures to interns in a teaching hospital. |
| | | Medium | Instructing a coworker in how to operate a software program. |
| | | Low | Instructing a new employee in the use of a time clock. |
| Service Orientation | Actively looking for ways to help people | High | Directing relief agency operations in a disaster area. |
| | | Medium | Making flight reservations for customers when using airline reservation system. |
| | | Low | Asking customers if they would like cups of coffee. |
| | | **Technical skills** | |
| Operations Analysis | Analyzing needs and product requirements to create a design | High | Identifying the control system needed for a new process production plant. |
| | | Medium | Suggesting changes in software to make a system more user friendly. |
| | | Low | Selecting a photocopy machine for an office. |
| Technology Design | Generating or adapting equipment and technology to serve user needs | High | Creating new technology for producing industrial diamonds. |
| | | Medium | Redesigning the handle on a hand tool for easier gripping. |
| | | Low | Adjusting exercise equipment for use by customer. |

*Table 5-1 continues*

**TABLE 5-1 (*Continued*)**

| Construct label | Operational definition | Level | Example |
|---|---|---|---|
| | | Level scale | |
| | | Level | Example |
| | | *Technical skills* | |
| Equipment Selection | Determining the kind of tools and equipment needed to do a job. | High | Identifying the equipment needed to produce a new product line. |
| | | Medium | Choosing a software application to use to complete a work assignment. |
| | | Low | Selecting a screwdriver to use in adjusting vehicle carburetor. |
| Installation | Installing equipment, machines, wiring, or programs to meet specifications. | High | Installing "one of a kind" process production molding machine. |
| | | Medium | Installing new switches for a telephone exchange. |
| | | Low | Installing a new air filter in an air conditioner. |
| Programming | Writing computer programs for various purposes | High | Writing expert system programs to analyze ground radar geological data for probable existence of mineral deposits. |
| | | Medium | Writing a statistical analysis program to analyze demographic data. |
| | | Low | Writing a program in BASIC to sort objects in a database. |
| Testing | Conducting tests to determine whether equipment, software, or procedures are operating as expected | High | Developing procedures to test a prototype of a new computer system. |
| | | Medium | Starting a machine to obtain a first-run workpiece and verify dimensional tolerances. |
| | | Low | Using a test station to assess whether a car meets emission requirements. |
| Operation Monitoring | Watching gauges, dials, or other indicators to make sure a machine is working properly | High | Monitoring and integrating control feedback in a petrochemical processing facility to maintain production flow. |
| | | Medium | Monitoring machine functions on an automated production line. |
| | | Low | Monitoring completion times in running a computer program. |
| Operation and Control | Controlling operations of equipment or systems | High | Controlling aircraft approach and landing at a large airport during a busy period. |
| | | Medium | Adjusting the speed of assembly line equipment on the basis of the type of product being assembled. |
| | | Low | Adjusting the settings on a copy machine to make reduced-size photocopies. |
| Product Inspection | Inspecting and evaluating the quality of products | High | Establishing and monitoring quality-control procedures for a large manufacturing operation. |
| | | Medium | Measuring new part requirements for tolerance to specifications. |
| | | Low | Inspecting a draft of a memorandum for clerical errors. |
| Equipment Maintenance | Performing routine maintenance and determining when and what kind of maintenance is needed | High | Conducting maintenance checks on an experimental aircraft. |
| | | Medium | Clearing moving parts in production machinery. |
| | | Low | Adding oil to an engine as indicated by a gauge or warning light. |
| Troubleshooting | Determining what is causing an operating error and deciding what to do about it | High | Directing the debugging of control code for a new operating system. |
| | | Medium | Identifying the circuit causing an electrical system to fail. |
| | | Low | Identifying the source of a leak by looking under a machine. |
| Repairing | Repairing machines or systems using the needed tools | High | Repairing structural damage to a building following an earthquake. |
| | | Medium | Replacing a faulty hydraulic valve. |
| | | Low | Tightening screw to get a door to close properly. |
| | | *Systems skills* | |
| Visioning | Developing an image of how a system should work under ideal conditions. | High | Creating a new vision for a large manufacturing organization that lets the company respond to changes in market and technology. |
| | | Medium | Preparing a presentation detailing the role of a work unit in relation to the organizational structure. |
| | | Low | Understanding of coworkers' roles in finishing a job. |
| Systems Perception | Determining when important changes have occurred in a system or are likely to occur | High | Identifying how changes in tax laws are likely to affect preferred sites for manufacturing operations in different industries. |
| | | Medium | Observing conditions that may impede the flow of work on an assembly line and notifying personnel that corrective action is necessary. |
| | | Low | Identifying how an argument among team members might affect the day's work. |
| Identification of Downstream Consequences | Determining the long-term outcomes of a change in operations | High | Determining changes that might occur in an industry if a new piece of legislation is passed. |
| | | Medium | Determining how the introduction of a new piece of equipment will affect production rates. |
| | | Low | Determining how loss of a team member will affect completion of a job. |

*Table 5-1 continues*

**TABLE 5-1** (*Continued*)

| Construct label | Operational definition | Level scale | |
|---|---|---|---|
| | | Level | Example |
| Systems skills | | | |
| Identification of Key Causes | Identifying the things that must be changed to achieve a goal | High | Identifying the changes in organizational policy needed to encourage research and development efforts. |
| | | Medium | Identifying the major reasons why a client might be unhappy with a product. |
| | | Low | Determining which route to take to deliver a passenger to a destination quickly. |
| Judgment and Decision Making | Weighing the relative costs and benefits of potential action | High | Deciding whether a manufacturing company should invest in new robotics technology. |
| | | Medium | Evaluating a loan application for degree of risk. |
| | | Low | Deciding how scheduling a break will affect work flow. |
| Systems Evaluation | Looking at many indicators of system performance, taking into account their accuracy | High | Evaluating the long-term performance problem of a company. |
| | | Medium | Determining why a manager has underestimated production costs. |
| | | Low | Determining why a coworker was overly optimistic about how long it would take to complete a task. |
| Resource management skills | | | |
| Time Management | Managing one's own time and the time of others | High | Allocating the time of scientists to multiple research projects. |
| | | Medium | Allocating time of subordinates to projects for the coming week. |
| | | Low | Keeping a monthly calendar of appointments. |
| Management of Financial Resources | Determining how money will be spent to get the work done and accounting for these expenditures | High | Developing and approving yearly budgets for a large corporation and obtaining financing as necessary. |
| | | Medium | Preparing and managing a budget for a short-term project. |
| | | Low | Taking money from petty cash to buy office supplies and recording the amount of the expenditure. |
| Management of Material Resources | Obtaining and seeing to the appropriate use of equipment, facilities, and materials needed to do certain work | High | Determining the computer system needs of a large corporation and monitoring use of the equipment. |
| | | Medium | Evaluating an annual uniform service contract for delivery drivers. |
| | | Low | Renting a meeting room for a management meeting. |
| Management of Personnel Resources | Motivating, developing, and directing people as they work, identifying the best people for the job | High | Planning, implementing, and managing recruitment, training, and incentive programs for a high performance company. |
| | | Medium | Directing the activities of a road repair crew with minimal disruption of traffic flow. |
| | | Low | Encouraging a coworker who is having difficulty finishing a piece of work. |

information one is working with. In other words, one must be able to separate the "wheat from the chaff"—an observation that underscores the importance of Critical Thinking in the learning process (Chaffee, 1994; Paul, 1990; Perkins, Jay, & Tishman, 1994). Collectively, these 10 content and process skills constitute the basic skills in our descriptive system.

## Cross-Functional Skills

### Problem-Solving Skills

Knowledge, of course, is acquired for a purpose. Thus, the processes and procedures involved in applying knowledge to work-related tasks represent another manifestation of skilled performance and provide a framework for identifying cross-functional skills. One common domain of work performance is problem solving. Few of us would dispute that knowledge is a prerequisite for problem solving (Anderson, 1993). A number of recent studies, however,

indicate that problem solving is not simply a matter of expertise. It also depends on the kinds of processes and procedures people apply when working with information. Accordingly, Mumford and Peterson's (1995) taxonomy of problem-solving skills seeks to articulate those processes commonly applied in attempts to solve complex, novel problems.

Drawing from prior taxonomic work (Davidson, 1995; Finke, Wand, & Smith, 1992; Merrifield, Guilford, Christensen, & Frick, 1962; Mumford, Mobley, Uhlman, Reiter-Palmon, & Doares, 1991; Mumford & Gustafson, in press; Runco, 1991, and Sternberg, 1986), Mumford and Peterson (1995) argued that eight distinct processes are, to some extent, involved in virtually all problem solving efforts (see Table 5-1). Typically, problem solving begins with problem identification, when the problem is specified and its general structure defined (Getzels & Csikszentmihalyi, 1976; Redmond, Mumford, & Teach, 1993; Runco, 1994). Following problem identification, people must gather information about the problem and organize this information, using relevant concepts

(Perkins, 1992). In the case of novel problems, it may be necessary to combine concepts and reorganize available information to arrive at an understanding of the problem (Baughman & Mumford, 1995; Finke, Wand, & Smith, 1992). As a result, Mumford and Peterson argue that Information Gathering, Information Organization, and Synthesis/Reorganization will be involved in virtually all problem-solving efforts.

It is not enough, however, to understand the problem. In the "real world," people must be capable of generating workable solutions. Solution generation typically begins by using one's understanding of the problem to generate ideas or approaches for solving the problem (Finke et al., 1992; Mumford & Gustafson, in press). After generating potential approaches for use in problem solving, these solutions must be evaluated, and a plan for implementing the best or most workable solution must be constructed within the constraints imposed by the situation (Arlin, 1990; Covington, 1987; Hayes-Roth & Hayes-Roth, 1979). Of course, solution implementation is not axiomatic. Instead, standards for evaluating implementation must be devised and used as a guide to revise one's approach, ideas, understanding, and potentially one's definition of the problem. Those observations imply that Idea Generation, Idea Evaluation, Implementation Planning, and Solution Appraisal also represent necessary problem-solving skills.

### Social Skills

At work, problems are defined and solved in relation to other people (Hackman & Morris, 1975; Steiner, 1972). Accordingly, social skills are likely to represent an essential component of performance in the workplace, especially in organizations in which a premium is placed on teamwork and customer service (Mohrman & Cohen, 1995; Nelson, 1996). Broadly speaking, two distinct approaches have been used to identify requisite social skills. The first approach, flowing from studies of social intelligence, seeks to identify the capacities people need to acquire and apply social information in problem solving (e.g., Cantor & Kihlstrom, 1987; Ford & Tisak, 1983; Moss, Hunt, Omwake, & Woodward, 1955; Zaccaro, Gilbert, Thor, & Mumford, 1991). The second approach is based on a more pragmatic empirical methodology and involves analysis of the performance requirements involved in tasks requiring social interaction (e.g., Gilbert & Fleishman, 1992; Peterson, 1992a).

In their review of these taxonomies of social skills, Mumford and Peterson (1995) found that both approaches yield remarkably similar sets of social skills. For example, regardless of the approach applied, virtually all prior efforts propose a dimension labeled "Social Sensitivity" or "Social Perceptiveness." More empirically oriented approaches, however, typically place more emphasis on social performance skills, such as negotiation and persuasion. This observation led Mumford and Peterson to propose a six-variable taxonomy of social skills (see Table 5-1), which begins with information acquisition—Social Perceptiveness—and then calls for adjusting one's behavior in relation to others—Response Coordination. These adjustments of one's behavior are then used for Persuasion, Negotiation, Instructing, or Service Orientation.

### Technical Skills

Problem-solving and social skills have long been of interest to psychologists. Technical skills, in contrast, have received relatively little attention. From time to time, one does find studies examining discrete technical skills, such as programming (Ward et al., 1990), design (Smith, 1992), and troubleshooting (Barsalow, 1989). Unfortunately, a few scattered studies cannot provide the framework needed to develop a comprehensive taxonomy of technical skills.

This observation led Mumford and Peterson (1995) to apply an alternative strategy in developing their taxonomy of technical skills. They began by reviewing prior analyses of the tasks performed on technical jobs. In all, 48 job analyses were considered in this review, covering a wide range of technical occupations. This revealed a common process structure evident in virtually all of these jobs. More specifically, these jobs, in one way or another, all involved activities calling for design of equipment, set-up of equipment, operation of equipment, and operations maintenance.

By organizing the key procedures involved in each of these general activity areas, it proved possible to develop a reasonably comprehensive taxonomy of technical skills. To illustrate, "design" (the development of tools and equipment) appears to involve three basic procedures: Operations Analysis, Technology Design, and Equipment Selection. In setting up equipment once it has been produced, Installation, Programming, and Testing appear to represent key skills occurring in a variety of settings. When equipment is being used to produce something, operating equipment typically involves Operation Monitoring, Operation and Control of the equipment, Product Inspection, and routine Equipment Maintenance. Even given the best maintenance, equipment breaks down. To get equipment up and running again, technical jobs typically call for Troubleshooting to identify the source of the problem, and then Repairing. Thus, in all, 12 distinct technical skills were identified. It is of note that these skills appear to provide a reasonably comprehensive description of technical skills, accounting for more than 90% of the technical tasks found on the 48 jobs used in developing this taxonomy.

### Systems Skills

On their jobs, people work in and with a sociotechnical system. Thus, it seems plausible to argue that a distinct set of systems skills should also be used in describing people's jobs. In recent years, the leadership literature has attempted to identify the kinds of skills that allow people to effectively work within a complex social system. For example, House and Howell (1992) argued that organizational leaders often use a vision or a mental model describing optimal system operations to guide action and influence efforts in a dynamic environment. Thus, visioning is a potential important systems skill.

Bass (1994) noted that in complex organizational systems it may not be clear how actions in one part of the system will influence actions in other parts of the system. These observations led Mumford and Peterson (1995) to conclude that Systems Perception, Identification of Downstream Consequences, and Identification of Key Causes may also represent important systems skills.

Organizational systems differ from simpler systems in two other important ways. In any complex social system where change is an ongoing event and many consequences flow from an action, feedback will be ambiguous, and no one course of action will optimize all potential outcomes (Arlin, 1990; Mumford & Connelly, 1993). As a result, it appears that effective performance in complex organizational systems requires judgment and decision making, as well as complex Systems Evaluation skills where multiple sources of feedback are sought and objectively evaluated.

### Resource Management Skills

One tenet of organizational systems theory is that all jobs require us to work with resources in creating products. This proposition, of course, implies that resource management skills may represent important influences on performance across a variety of job settings. In a comprehensive review of 64 taxonomies of managerial behavior, Fleishman, Mumford, Zaccaro, et al. (1991) identified two general kinds of resource management skills involved in people's day-to-day work: managing material resources and managing personnel resources.

Although it appears that material and personnel represent the basic physical resources that must be managed to accomplish any job, this taxonomy does not address the resources needed to obtain people and requisite materials. As Peterson (1992a) pointed out, people and materials must be managed within the constraints of time and money. This observation led Mumford and Peterson (1995) to propose four resource management skills: (a) Time Management, (b) Management of Financial Resources, (c) Management of Material Resources, and (d) Management of Personnel Resources.

## MEASURES AND SAMPLES

### Measures

To this point, we have presented a series of taxonomies. Although these taxonomies specify the kinds of variables that might be used to describe occupational skill requirements, they beg a question crucial to the present effort: Can these taxonomies be used to develop valid and reliable measures of occupational skill requirements?

We began by providing operational definitions of each of the skills included in the taxonomies of basic and cross-functional skills. These operational definitions are presented in Table 5-1 and flow from definitions used in the initial taxonomy development. They differ from the technical definitions, however, in that each skill is defined in simple English. This step was taken to ensure that the resulting rating scales could be applied across a range of jobs.

These operational definitions of the basic and cross-functional skills provide the foundation needed to obtain ratings of occupational skill requirements. These definitions, however, do not say exactly what manifestations of a skill should be used to describe people's jobs. Skill expression, for example, might be assessed in terms of the level of the skill required to perform job tasks (Fleishman, 1992a; Fleishman & Mumford, 1991). Alternatively, skill expression might be assessed in terms of the time needed to learn to apply the skill (Mumford & Supinsky, 1995b).

For the purpose of the present effort, each skill was to be assessed with respect to three variables using rating scales, exemplified in Figure 5-1. First, ratings of level, or the amount of the skill needed to perform job tasks, were to be made on an absolute, 7-point, behaviorally anchored rating scale. Second, ratings on a 5-point scale were to be made indicating the importance of each skill to job performance. Third, a dichotomous rating was required indicating whether the level of the skill indicated earlier must be possessed at the time of job entry. These three rating scales were selected for use in describing skill requirements because they provided substantively meaningful ways of assessing skill expression that could be used in answering a variety of questions about occupational skill requirements.

Because level ratings were made on an absolute scale, referenced against common job tasks, some attention was devoted to development of these anchors. Initially, the anchors were developed by an industrial psychologist familiar with the skills literature. In developing these anchors, prior job analyses, such as those conducted in the SCANS project, along with extant theory, were used to generate tasks that called for high, medium, and low levels of the relevant skill and were likely to be familiar to most people.

To provide some evidence for the meaningfulness of these anchors, three studies were conducted (Childs & Whetzel, 1995). In the first study, 20 judges, all experienced job analysts, were asked to assign the already-written task anchors to the skills and then indicate whether each was a high, medium, or low anchor. It was found that most judges matched anchors to the targeted skills at the appropriate level. The judges, however, did have some difficulty in discriminating medium and high task anchors. In the second study, five judges were asked to

**1. Reading Comprehension**    Understanding written sentences and paragraphs in work related documents.

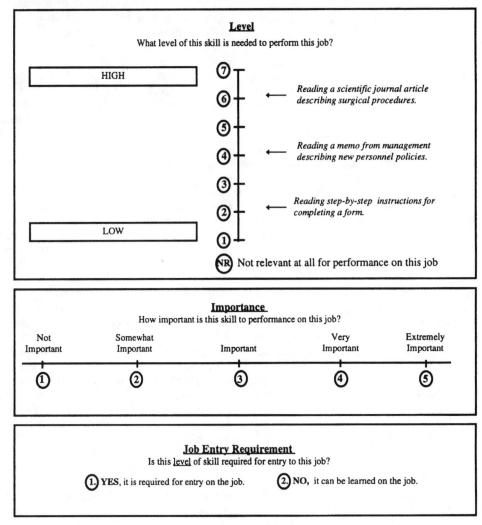

**FIGURE 5-1.** Example page from the Skills Questionnaire.

rate, on a 7-point scale, the level of the targeted skill needed to perform the anchor tasks. In this study, the high anchors received a median rating of 6.25. The medium anchor was 4.82, and the low anchor was 2.36. Although these data provided some further support for the anchors in use, they indicated the need to replace 15 mid- and low-level anchors.

To generate new mid- and low-level anchors, a panel of 10 experienced job analysts was assembled and asked to develop replacement anchors for the problematic anchors. The resulting replacement anchors, along with the original anchors, were presented to a second panel of 10 job analysts, who were asked to rate the anchor skill level requirements on a 7-point scale. For these revised scales, the high anchors had a median rating of 6.45, the midscale anchors had a median rating of 4.24, and the low anchors had a median rating of 2.32. In the third study, 15 experienced job analysts were asked to review all proposed anchors for clarity, readability, and sensitivity.

In applying these rating scales to assess job skill requirements, judges (either job analysts or job incumbents) were asked to read the operational definition of the skill and review the associated Level scale anchors. They were then asked to indicate whether the skill was relevant to the job being analyzed and, if relevant, to rate the level at which it was required, the importance of the skill to job performance, and whether it must be present at the indicated level prior to job entry. Thus, all level, importance, and entry requirement ratings were made only if the skill was deemed relevant.

## Samples

The general procedures used to obtain an incumbent sample were described in chapter 4. As noted earlier, 80 jobs with 30 incumbents per job were targeted to assess the occupational characteristics for each domain specified in the content model. Overall, 29 jobs had at least four incumbents who provided data across all nine domain questionnaires. Considering only the Skills Questionnaire, however, 35 jobs had at least four incumbents who provided usable data. Table 5-2 lists each of these jobs and the number of incumbents within each job who completed the skills measures.

Across jobs, the Skills Questionnaire, which included measures of both basic and cross-functional skills, was completed by 648 job incumbents and supervisors (referred to hereinafter simply as *incumbents*) drawn from 138 different establishments. On average, about 18 incumbents were available for each job. The number of incumbent respondents per job, however, ranged from 4 to 90. More than half of the respondents had 6 or more years of experience on their current jobs. Most respondents had at least some postsecondary school training, and 26% had a college degree.

The incumbent sample provided the primary data to be used in establishing the reliability and validity of the measures for describing occupational skill requirements. To provide evidence bearing on the convergent validity of these ratings, analysts' ratings were also obtained through the North Carolina OAFC. Six experienced job analysts were asked to rate the level at which each skill was required and the importance of the skill for the 35 jobs for which incumbent data were available. Analysts reviewed a list of 10 to 20 tasks (drawn from the DOT, U.S. Department of Labor, 1991a) commonly performed on the job, before making their ratings. The interrater agreement coefficient for analyst ratings was in the low .90s.

## RESULTS

### Interrater Agreement

Table 5-3 presents the means and standard deviations of scores on each skill scale across all jobs. This table also presents the interrater agreement coefficient obtained for each scale, across jobs, and the associated standard error of measurement. When ratings are used to describe people's jobs, one must address a crucial inferential question: Do incumbents, or other judges, agree in their description of a job? The interrater agreement coefficients presented in Table 5-3 provide an initial answer to this question.

Within the sample at hand, where an average of 18 incumbents provided ratings of each job skill requirement, it is clear that these scales yielded reliable descriptions of people's job requirements. The Level scale produced a median interrater agreement coefficient of .84 when *not relevant* responses were included as a part of the scale. When *not relevant* responses were included, the Importance scale also yielded sizable interrater agreement coefficients, with the median coefficient across scales being .83. The ratings bearing on the job entry requirements produced somewhat lower interrater agreement coefficients, with the median across scales being .72. These agreement coefficients are adequate for research purposes. Nonetheless, they suggest that a larger number of judges may be required to achieve good agreement for this type of dichotomous scale.

Above, we allude to the fact that the degree of interrater agreement depends on the number of judges. Although the data presented above indicate that 10 to 15 judges are sufficient to produce adequate agreement among job incumbents in describing occupational skill requirements on the Level and Importance scales, it is well to consider the results that would have been obtained if 1 judge or 30 judges were available. Analyses revealed that single-judge estimates for the Level and Importance scales were quite good—a finding justifying the inclusion of jobs with as few as four raters. Thirty judges, however, would ensure fully adequate interrater agreement for the job

**TABLE 5-2**

**Thirty-Five Occupations With Four or More Incumbents Completing the Skills Questionnaire**

| Occupation code | Occupation title | Number of respondents |
|---|---|---|
| 15005 | Education Administrators | 9 |
| 19005 | General Managers & Top Executives | 45 |
| 22135 | Mechanical Engineers | 6 |
| 25105 | Computer Programmers | 5 |
| 27311 | Recreation Workers | 5 |
| 31303 | Teachers, Preschool | 4 |
| 31305 | Teachers, Elementary School | 13 |
| 31502 | Librarians, Professional | 4 |
| 32502 | Registered Nurses | 32 |
| 32902 | Medical & Clinical Laboratory Technologists | 4 |
| 49008 | Salespersons, Except Scientific & Retail | 11 |
| 49011 | Salespersons, Retail | 13 |
| 49017 | Counter & Rental Clerks | 4 |
| 49021 | Stock Clerks, Sales Floor | 8 |
| 49023 | Cashiers | 28 |
| 51002 | First Line Supervisors, Clerical/ Administrative | 51 |
| 53121 | Loan & Credit Clerks | 4 |
| 53311 | Insurance Claims Clerks | 7 |
| 53905 | Teachers' Aides & Assistants, Clerical | 8 |
| 55108 | Secretaries, Except Legal & Medical | 90 |
| 55305 | Receptionists & Information Clerks | 12 |
| 55338 | Bookkeeping, Accounting, & Auditing Clerks | 32 |
| 55347 | General Office Clerks | 73 |
| 61005 | Police & Detective Supervisors | 13 |
| 63014 | Police Patrol Officers | 21 |
| 65008 | Waiters & Waitresses | 16 |
| 65038 | Food Preparation Workers | 17 |
| 66008 | Nursing Aides, Orderlies, & Attendants | 18 |
| 67005 | Janitors & Cleaners | 23 |
| 85132 | Maintenance Repairers, General Utility | 27 |
| 87902 | Earth Drillers, Except Oil & Gas | 7 |
| 89108 | Machinists | 4 |
| 92974 | Packaging & Filling Machine Operators | 8 |
| 97102 | Truck Drivers, Heavy or Tractor Trailer | 17 |
| 97111 | Bus Drivers, Schools | 9 |

**TABLE 5-3**
**Descriptive Statistics Across All Occupations and Reliability Estimates for Rated Differences Between Occupations: Basic and Cross-Functional Skills**

| | Variable | | | | | | | | | | | |
|---|---|---|---|---|---|---|---|---|---|---|---|---|
| | Level | | | | Importance | | | | Job entry requirement | | | |
| Descriptor | M | SD | SEM[a] | $r_k$[b] | M | SD | SEM | $r_k$ | M | SD | SEM | $r_k$ |
| 1. Reading Comprehension | 4.42 | 0.89 | .36 | .84 | 3.65 | 0.61 | .25 | .83 | 1.18 | 0.20 | .11 | .71 |
| 2. Active Listening | 4.28 | 0.95 | .39 | .83 | 3.63 | 0.56 | .26 | .78 | 1.34 | 0.21 | .12 | .66 |
| 3. Writing | 3.82 | 1.07 | .34 | .90 | 3.22 | 0.64 | .23 | .87 | 1.36 | 0.27 | .11 | .82 |
| 4. Speaking | 4.20 | 0.80 | .38 | .77 | 3.54 | 0.49 | .24 | .75 | 1.33 | 0.22 | .13 | .65 |
| 5. Mathematics | 3.26 | 1.16 | .50 | .82 | 2.96 | 0.65 | .33 | .74 | 1.37 | 0.25 | .14 | .67 |
| 6. Science | 1.53 | 1.35 | .42 | .90 | 1.88 | 0.82 | .26 | .90 | 1.78 | 0.27 | .09 | .88 |
| 7. Critical Thinking | 3.68 | 1.02 | .46 | .80 | 3.12 | 0.70 | .30 | .81 | 1.50 | 0.21 | .11 | .72 |
| 8. Active Learning | 3.62 | 1.14 | .49 | .81 | 3.01 | 0.67 | .31 | .79 | 1.59 | 0.22 | .12 | .72 |
| 9. Learning Strategies | 3.83 | 0.91 | .42 | .78 | 3.12 | 0.50 | .27 | .71 | 1.62 | 0.22 | .12 | .70 |
| 10. Monitoring | 3.26 | 1.19 | .42 | .88 | 2.81 | 0.65 | .27 | .83 | 1.66 | 0.22 | .12 | .71 |
| 11. Social Perceptiveness | 3.62 | 1.08 | .44 | .83 | 3.06 | 0.61 | .30 | .76 | 1.62 | 0.19 | .13 | .52 |
| 12. Coordination | 3.57 | 1.07 | .48 | .80 | 2.99 | 0.63 | .31 | .75 | 1.66 | 0.19 | .12 | .59 |
| 13. Persuasion | 3.19 | 1.15 | .42 | .86 | 2.65 | 0.68 | .26 | .85 | 1.75 | 0.21 | .11 | .72 |
| 14. Negotiation | 2.90 | 1.26 | .44 | .88 | 2.62 | 0.69 | .28 | .84 | 1.75 | 0.20 | .10 | .75 |
| 15. Instructing | 3.78 | 1.08 | .49 | .79 | 3.18 | 0.57 | .30 | .71 | 1.65 | 0.21 | .11 | .73 |
| 16. Service Orientation | 3.28 | 1.02 | .51 | .75 | 2.86 | 0.67 | .35 | .73 | 1.69 | 0.18 | .11 | .61 |
| 17. Problem Identification | 4.16 | 1.08 | .43 | .84 | 3.45 | 0.62 | .29 | .79 | 1.59 | 0.19 | .11 | .66 |
| 18. Information Gathering | 3.92 | 1.07 | .43 | .84 | 3.25 | 0.72 | .30 | .83 | 1.64 | 0.21 | .13 | .62 |
| 19. Information Organization | 3.21 | 1.11 | .51 | .78 | 2.79 | 0.65 | .32 | .76 | 1.69 | 0.21 | .14 | .54 |
| 20. Synthesis/Reorganization | 3.24 | 1.15 | .45 | .84 | 2.79 | 0.60 | .28 | .78 | 1.70 | 0.20 | .11 | .66 |
| 21. Idea Generation | 3.33 | 1.26 | .45 | .87 | 2.79 | 0.69 | .26 | .86 | 1.72 | 0.23 | .10 | .80 |
| 22. Idea Evaluation | 3.07 | 1.25 | .46 | .86 | 2.67 | 0.72 | .30 | .83 | 1.73 | 0.25 | .11 | .80 |
| 23. Implementation Planning | 2.83 | 1.39 | .47 | .88 | 2.54 | 0.84 | .29 | .88 | 1.77 | 0.22 | .10 | .80 |
| 24. Solution Appraisal | 3.02 | 1.40 | .44 | .90 | 2.68 | 0.76 | .29 | .86 | 1.75 | 0.22 | .11 | .77 |
| 25. Operations Analysis | 2.02 | 1.37 | .56 | .83 | 2.06 | 0.79 | .33 | .82 | 1.84 | 0.16 | .09 | .65 |
| 26. Technology Design | 1.76 | 1.40 | .51 | .87 | 1.92 | 0.75 | .30 | .84 | 1.84 | 0.17 | .10 | .63 |
| 27. Equipment Selection | 2.57 | 1.32 | .57 | .82 | 2.36 | 0.77 | .33 | .81 | 1.82 | 0.14 | .10 | .50 |
| 28. Installation | 1.28 | 1.54 | .46 | .91 | 1.69 | 0.88 | .24 | .92 | 1.90 | 0.15 | .06 | .83 |
| 29. Programming | 0.83 | 1.20 | .57 | .78 | 1.49 | 0.78 | .33 | .82 | 1.90 | 0.17 | .10 | .65 |
| 30. Testing | 1.53 | 1.60 | .60 | .86 | 1.85 | 0.95 | .34 | .87 | 1.86 | 0.17 | .09 | .70 |
| 31. Operation Monitoring | 1.69 | 1.75 | .50 | .92 | 1.97 | 0.94 | .29 | .90 | 1.86 | 0.16 | .09 | .73 |
| 32. Operation and Control | 2.05 | 1.39 | .56 | .84 | 2.13 | 0.80 | .35 | .80 | 1.84 | 0.16 | .09 | .71 |
| 33. Product Inspection | 2.31 | 1.34 | .62 | .78 | 2.34 | 0.75 | .36 | .77 | 1.80 | 0.16 | .09 | .68 |
| 34. Equipment Maintenance | 1.67 | 1.63 | .47 | .92 | 1.95 | 0.96 | .26 | .93 | 1.88 | 0.17 | .07 | .84 |
| 35. Troubleshooting | 2.25 | 1.74 | .61 | .88 | 2.27 | 1.01 | .36 | .88 | 1.83 | 0.16 | .08 | .74 |
| 36. Repairing | 1.33 | 1.49 | .42 | .92 | 1.75 | 0.85 | .25 | .91 | 1.89 | 0.15 | .06 | .82 |
| 37. Visioning | 2.34 | 1.15 | .48 | .82 | 2.31 | 0.63 | .30 | .78 | 1.80 | 0.19 | .10 | .76 |
| 38. Systems Perception | 2.22 | 1.23 | .48 | .84 | 2.27 | 0.68 | .31 | .79 | 1.80 | 0.20 | .10 | .77 |
| 39. Identification of Down-stream Consequences | 2.19 | 1.13 | .44 | .85 | 2.22 | 0.65 | .26 | .84 | 1.81 | 0.18 | .09 | .75 |
| 40. Identification of Key Causes | 3.17 | 1.17 | .43 | .86 | 2.74 | 0.66 | .27 | .84 | 1.77 | 0.19 | .10 | .75 |
| 41. Judgment and Decision Making | 2.93 | 1.33 | .44 | .89 | 2.70 | 0.79 | .29 | .86 | 1.70 | 0.24 | .10 | .84 |
| 42. Systems Evaluation | 2.02 | 1.36 | .46 | .89 | 2.09 | 0.75 | .28 | .87 | 1.84 | 0.15 | .08 | .73 |
| 43. Time Management | 3.61 | 1.18 | .48 | .83 | 3.20 | 0.67 | .29 | .81 | 1.64 | 0.24 | .12 | .76 |
| 44. Management of Financial Resources | 1.84 | 1.50 | .50 | .89 | 2.10 | 0.90 | .32 | .87 | 1.81 | 0.22 | .10 | .80 |
| 45. Management of Material Resources | 1.94 | 1.29 | .47 | .87 | 2.09 | 0.73 | .28 | .85 | 1.85 | 0.18 | .08 | .77 |
| 46. Management of Personnel Resources | 2.67 | 1.38 | .45 | .89 | 2.57 | 0.80 | .30 | .86 | 1.75 | 0.23 | .09 | .86 |

*Note.*   Statistics are based on 35 occupations with Skills Questionnaire responses from at least 4 incumbents (mean number of incumbents = 18.51, *Mdn* = 12, harmonic mean = 9.01).
[a]This estimate of the standard error of measurement was calculated as $SEM = SD^* \sqrt{(1 - r_k)}$.
[b]This estimate of reliability was obtained by calculating the intraclass correlation for *k* ratings across occupations: $ICC(1, k) = [BMS - WMS]/BMS$ (Shrout & Fleiss, 1979), where *k* is the harmonic mean of the number of ratings provided on each occupation.

entry requirements scale and exceptional reliabilities, in the .90s, for the Level and Importance scales.

Of course, all of these findings were obtained under conditions in which *not relevant* responses were treated as the lowest score on all scales. In the job analysis literature, use of this scoring procedure has been criticized because of the belief that it results in inflated interrater agreement coefficients. Thus, we also computed the interrater agreement coefficients obtained when (a) only *relevant* responses are scored, and (b) *relevant/not relevant* responses on the Level scale are coded dichotomously. Inclusion of *not relevant* responses had little influence on the reliability of the Level, Importance, and When-Acquired scales.

Furthermore, dichotomously coding relevance on the Level scale yielded sizable interrater agreement coefficients, although these coefficients were smaller than those obtained for the continuous scores. This finding is noteworthy because it suggests that some useful information is contained in *not relevant* responses, thereby justifying the full-scale scoring, including *not relevant* responses, in analysis of the skills data.

Before turning to the substantive implications of our findings, we need to address two other questions. First, do the different rating scales provide any unique information about occupational skill requirements? Second, are there any marked differences in the consistency with which judges rate different types of skills? In other words, do judges agree more about basic skill requirements than about the requirements associated with cross-functional skills?

Turning first to the relationships among the rating scales, Table 5-4 presents the mean correlation, across skills, in the mean ratings of jobs on each scale. As may be seen, across jobs and across descriptors, level and importance ratings displayed sizable positive correlations ($r = .95$). Thus, if a skill was judged to be required at a high level, it was generally regarded as important to performance. As a result, it appears that analysis of occupational skill requirements can generally focus on level, ignoring importance as redundant. In fact, we will follow this convention throughout the rest of this chapter.

However, job entry requirement ratings displayed a somewhat smaller relationship. The median scale correlation of entry requirement with level and importance was $-.70$. The direction of the correlation merely indicates that if level and importance were high, then the indicated skill level was likely to be required at job entry (i.e., 1 = *required*; 2 = *can be learned on the job*). The $-.70$ relationship indicates that this scale might provide some unique information. Nonetheless, given the interrater agreement coefficients obtained for this scale, some caution should be exercised in drawing strong conclusions in this regard.

Turning now to our second question, the relationship between the type of skills being assessed and the resulting interrater agreement coefficients, there is

one straightforward conclusion. As indicated by the interrater agreement coefficients presented in Table 5-3, marked differences were not observed among the median interrater agreement coefficients obtained in the different skill domains. On the Level scale, the basic skills (Descriptors 1–10) and resource management skills (Descriptors 43–46) yielded median interrater agreement coefficients of .82 and .88, whereas the social (Descriptors 11–16), problem-solving (Descriptors 17–24), technical (Descriptors 25–36), and systems (Descriptors 37–42) skills yielded median interrater agreement coefficients of .81, .85, .86, and .85. Apparently, incumbents can accurately appraise jobs on more "abstract" skills, provided that skills are defined in a straightforward fashion and concrete examples are provided.

## Skill Structure

The evidence presented to this point provides a compelling argument for the reliability of our measures of occupational skill requirements. The fact that incumbents display substantial agreement in their assessment of job skill requirements, however, tells us relatively little about the meaningfulness or validity of the resulting descriptive information (Fleishman & Mumford, 1991). Thus, there is a need to examine the available evidence bearing on the meaningfulness of inferences derived from these measures. One way this might be accomplished is by examining the internal structure of the skill measures (Fleishman & Mumford, 1991; Messick, 1989, 1995).

### Domain Differences

One way to assess the meaningfulness of the descriptive information provided by our skill measures is to examine the overall, cross-job means of ratings on the Level scale. As may be seen in Table 5-3, the traditional basic skills of Reading Comprehension (Descriptor (D1), Active Listening (D2), Writing (D3), and Speaking (D4) had the highest average scores on the Level scale ($M_M = 4.18$, $M_{SD} = .93$, where $M_M$ is the mean of the skill means and $M_{SD}$ is the mean of the skill standard deviations) when com-

**TABLE 5-4**

**Means and Standard Deviations of Correlations Between Level, Importance, and Job Entry Requirement Scales Across Occupations and Descriptors: Basic and Cross-Functional Skills**

| Scale | Level | | | Importance | | | Job Entry Requirement | | |
|---|---|---|---|---|---|---|---|---|---|
| | $n^a$ | M | SD | n | M | SD | n | M | SD |
| Level | — | — | — | 35 | .96 | .04 | 35 | −.71 | .18 |
| Importance | 46 | .95 | .04 | — | — | — | 35 | −.74 | .17 |
| Job Entry Requirement | 46 | −.66 | .11 | 46 | −.69 | .12 | — | — | — |

*Note.* All correlations were calculated on the basis of the mean of ratings assigned by raters for a given occupation, descriptor, and scale. Level–Importance means above the diagonal were calculated by taking the Level scale means on a given occupation for all descriptors, correlating them with Importance scale means for that occupation, and then averaging them with the correlations for other occupations. Level–Importance means below the diagonal were calculated by taking the Level scale means on a given descriptor for all occupations, correlating them with Importance scale means for that descriptor, and averaging them with correlations for other descriptors. Other means in the table were calculated in a similar manner.
[a]Number of correlations averaged, not number of observations on which correlations were calculated.

pared with all other skills ($M_M$ = 2.81, $M_{SD}$ = 1.25). Moreover, incumbents typically felt that these skills had to be present at the requisite level prior to job entry, resulting in mean scores on the job entry requirement scale ($M_M$ = 1.30, $M_{SD}$ = .23) that were lower (where 1 = *required for job entry* and 2 = *not required*) than the overall average job entry requirement ratings ($M_M$ = 1.71, $M_{SD}$ = 0.20).

Incumbents across the job sample viewed three other types of skills as being required at moderate levels upon job entry. Incumbent ratings indicated that learning to learn, or learning-process skills, such as Critical Thinking (D7), Active Learning (D8), Learning Strategies (D9), and Monitoring (D10), were required at moderate levels ($M_M$ = 3.60, $M_{SD}$ = 1.07) and should be at least partially present upon job entry. Similar results were also obtained for the complex problem-solving skills (D17–24; $M_M$ = 3.34, $M_{SD}$ = 1.19), such as Problem Identification (D17) and Information Gathering (D18), and the social skills (D11–16; $M_M$ = 3.39, $M_{SD}$ = 1.11). Apparently, most jobs place some premium on problem solving and social skills, as well as learning process skills and basic skills.

A somewhat different pattern of findings emerged for the remaining skills. In general, the technical (D25–36; $M_M$ = 1.77, $M_{SD}$ = 1.48), systems (D37–42; $M_M$ = 2.48, $M_{SD}$ = 1.23), and resource management skills (D43–46; $M_M$ = 2.52, $M_{SD}$ = 1.34) received relatively low ratings on all three rating scales. A similar pattern of findings emerged for the Science (D6) skill, which produced the lowest level ratings of all of the basic skill scales ($M$ = 1.53, $SD$ = 1.35 vs. $M_M$ = 3.59, $M_{SD}$ = 1.05). Those statements should not be taken to imply that science and technology—or, for that matter, the systems and resource management skills—are of little use in understanding people's jobs and the world of work. One must remember that we have, in the present study, examined only a limited number of the more populous jobs. Thus, those skills may be important on certain jobs that are not examined in the present effort. Furthermore, it is quite possible that even in those jobs, technical, systems, and resource management skills will become progressively more essential as science and technology become an integral part of the world of work and workers are given greater latitude in structuring their own activities (Howard, 1995a).

### Factor Structure

Our foregoing observations bearing on the meaningfulness of inferences derived from our measures of the basic and cross-functional skills were primarily based on the comparison of level requirements in different skill domains. Another way to accrue some evidence for the meaningfulness of the descriptive information provided by these scales would be to examine the nature of the relationships among our skill scales. To address this issue, correlations among level ratings were obtained at both the occupation and individual levels.

Individual-level correlations were obtained by drawing only four individuals from more populous jobs to control for differences in the number of respondents drawn from different occupations. Given our use of this procedure, it is hardly surprising that the relational structures observed at the individual and occupation levels were quite similar. Bearing in mind, however, that our primary unit of analysis is jobs, we will reference our review of those correlations against the job-level data.

Level scores on the basic, problem-solving, and social skills scales were closely related. Typically, some of these scales yielded correlations above .60. The basic, problem solving, and social skills, however, were not as strongly related to the various technical skills, which were closely related to each other. The exception to this general rule, however, occurred for the design skills, Operations Analysis (D25), Technology Design (D26), and Equipment Selection (D27), which did evidence sizable positive correlations with the basic, problem-solving, and social skills. This finding, however, is not surprising when one recognizes that design, as opposed to machine operation, requires problem solving, working with others, and a substantial amount of reading and writing.

The systems skills and resource management skills produced a somewhat different pattern of relationships. As might be expected, the level ratings of all of the systems and resource management skills displayed sizable positive correlations, typically exceeding .70. This overlap may well reflect the fact that the skills lying in both of these domains involve interacting with and managing complex sociotechnical systems. The systems and resource management skills correlated positively with both technical skills and measures of the basic, problem-solving, and social skills. This pattern of relationships is consistent with the nature of sociotechnical systems, which require people to work with technology and people in solving significant organizational problems (Hackman & Walton, 1986; Mumford, Zaccaro, Harding, & Fleishman, in press).

To summarize these relationships and further explore the structure of occupational skill requirements, the job-level ratings were factor analyzed using a principal-components solution with varimax rotation. Inspection of the resulting eigenvalues and the variance accounted for by each factor indicated that a three-factor solution provided the best available description of the relationships among the skill scales. Table 5-5 presents the loadings of the skills on each of the three factors, along with the resulting eigenvalues and communality estimates.

The first factor extracted in this analysis accounted for 38.26% of the total variance in level ratings. All of the basic, social, and problem-solving skills yielded loadings above .30. Among the basic skills, Writing (D3, $r$ = .89), Active Listening (D2, $r$ = .87), Speaking (D4, $r$ = .85), and Critical Thinking (D7, $r$ = .85) yielded the highest loadings. Among the cross-functional skills, Synthesis/Reorganization (D20, $r$ =

**TABLE 5-5**
**Principal-Components Analysis Pattern Matrix for the Level Scale: Basic and Cross-Functional Skills**

| Descriptor | Factor | | | Communality |
|---|---|---|---|---|
| | F1 | F2 | F3 | |
| 1. Reading Comprehension | .82 | .12 | .15 | .71 |
| 2. Active Listening | .87 | −.17 | .16 | .82 |
| 3. Writing | .89 | −.04 | .24 | .84 |
| 4. Speaking | .85 | .01 | .16 | .75 |
| 5. Mathematics | .56 | .54 | .04 | .60 |
| 6. Science | .58 | .70 | .05 | .82 |
| 7. Critical Thinking | .85 | .25 | .23 | .84 |
| 8. Active Learning | .82 | .42 | .19 | .88 |
| 9. Learning Strategies | .75 | .07 | .28 | .64 |
| 10. Monitoring | .80 | .11 | .40 | .81 |
| 11. Social Perceptiveness | .67 | −.32 | .39 | .70 |
| 12. Coordination | .80 | .29 | .31 | .82 |
| 13. Persuasion | .80 | .02 | .46 | .86 |
| 14. Negotiation | .58 | −.08 | .68 | .80 |
| 15. Instructing | .74 | .12 | .13 | .59 |
| 16. Service Orientation | .61 | −.30 | .47 | .68 |
| 17. Problem Identification | .83 | .22 | .19 | .77 |
| 18. Information Gathering | .87 | .22 | .22 | .85 |
| 19. Information Organization | .77 | .28 | .33 | .78 |
| 20. Synthesis/Reorganization | .89 | .16 | .25 | .88 |
| 21. Idea Generation | .82 | .29 | .28 | .83 |
| 22. Idea Evaluation | .73 | .36 | .44 | .86 |
| 23. Implementation Planning | .76 | .18 | .43 | .79 |
| 24. Solution Appraisal | .75 | .16 | .50 | .83 |
| 25. Operations Analysis | .60 | .58 | .34 | .82 |
| 26. Technology Design | .41 | .82 | .23 | .90 |
| 27. Equipment Selection | .39 | .74 | .33 | .81 |
| 28. Installation | .05 | .90 | .22 | .85 |
| 29. Programming | .23 | .67 | −.07 | .51 |
| 30. Testing | .19 | .94 | .03 | .93 |
| 31. Operation Monitoring | −.09 | .88 | .15 | .81 |
| 32. Operation and Control | −.09 | .87 | .16 | .79 |
| 33. Product Inspection | .13 | .81 | .30 | .76 |
| 34. Equipment Maintenance | −.12 | .87 | .17 | .80 |
| 35. Troubleshooting | .15 | .96 | .06 | .95 |
| 36. Repairing | −.02 | .92 | .13 | .86 |
| 37. Visioning | .30 | .50 | .71 | .85 |
| 38. Systems Perception | .35 | .58 | .66 | .90 |
| 39. Identification of Downstream Consequences | .39 | .34 | .78 | .88 |
| 40. Identification of Key Causes | .66 | .27 | .54 | .80 |
| 41. Judgment and Decision Making | .64 | .29 | .56 | .81 |
| 42. Systems Evaluation | .45 | .47 | .68 | .89 |
| 43. Time Management | .74 | .04 | .52 | .82 |
| 44. Management on Financial Resources | .41 | .19 | .81 | .85 |
| 45. Management of Material Resources | .35 | .36 | .80 | .90 |
| 46. Management of Personnel Resources | .42 | .17 | .83 | .90 |
| % of variance | 38.00 | 25.00 | 17.00 | — |
| Eigenvalue | 17.60 | 11.56 | 7.98 | — |

*Note.* $N = 35$. The correlation matrix was based on means calculated at the occupation level. F1 = Cognitive Skills, F2 = Technical Skills, F3 = Organizational Skills. These loadings are based on an orthogonal varimax rotation.

.89), Information Gathering (D18, $r = .87$), Problem Identification (D17, $r = .83$), and Idea Generation (D21, $r = .82$) produced the highest loadings. This pattern of loadings suggests that this factor reflects skills involving the active application of general intelligence and education. We have labeled it a *Cognitive Skills* factor.

This interpretation, although an apparently straightforward one, is complicated by the tendency of the social skills to yield sizable loadings on this factor. For example, both Persuasion (D13, $r = .80$) and Coordination (D12, $r = .80$) produced sizable loadings, whereas all of the remaining social skills

produced loadings above .60. Persuasion and Coordination, however, require applying cognitive capacity in a social setting (Simonton, 1995). A variety of evidence indicates, furthermore, that basic social skills may have a noteworthy cognitive component (Ford & Tisak, 1983). Thus, it appears that this factor can plausibly be labeled "Cognitive Skills" if it is recognized that it includes the application of cognitive capacity in social performance settings.

The second factor that emerged in this analysis was easily interpreted and was labeled *Technical Skills*. This factor accounted for 25.13% of the total variance. As might be expected, all of the technical skills yielded loadings above .50. Troubleshooting (D35, $r = .96$), Testing (D30, $r = .94$), Repairing (D36, $r = .92$), and Installation (D28, $r = .90$) had the highest loadings.

The third factor accounted for 17.35% of the total variance. This factor, like the first factor, has a distinctly social component, with both Negotiation (D14, $r = .68$) and Persuasion (D13, $r = .46$) yielding sizable loadings. This factor, however, was primarily defined by the various systems and resource management skills—in particular, Identification of Downstream Consequences (D39, $r = .78$), Visioning (D37, $r = .71$), Management of Personnel Resources (D46, $r = .83$), and Management of Material Resources (D45, $r = .80$). Apparently, skills involving interaction with social systems emerge as a distinct factor in describing jobs. Recognizing that these skills appear to represent key determinants for organizational raters, we labeled this factor *Organizational Skills*.

Perhaps the most important conclusion flowing from this analysis is that the skills scales evidence a coherent structure reflecting something more than a simple overall level of complexity rating. This finding is noteworthy because it provides an essential justification for treating skills as a unique domain of descriptors. In reviewing the results obtained in this factor analysis, it also is tempting to conclude that this domain has a relatively simple structure including cognitive, technical, and organizational skills. This kind of general summary statement does capture a grain of truth. Some caution is required, however, in making this kind of general statement, because the findings pertain only to variable structure, telling us little about how skills act to discriminate jobs from each other.

## Job Differences

When we develop job analysis systems, our ultimate concern is distinguishing one job from another. In other words, a truly useful set of descriptors must be able to tell us something about the similarities and differences among jobs. Accordingly, evidence bearing on the ability of job analysis measures to meaningfully document jobs is commonly considered to be the key piece of evidence bearing on the external validity of a descriptive system (Fleishman & Mumford, 1991). To begin to address this issue, we conducted a set of analyses to examine job profiles.

## Job Profiles

Table 5-6 presents the means and standard deviations of ratings on the Level scale for (a) General Managers and Top Executives, (b) Computer Programmers, (c) Registered Nurses, (d) Police Patrol Officers, (e) Janitors and Cleaners, and (f) Maintenance Repairers, General Utility.

The mean scores of incumbents on these skill scales, of course, reflect the general trends noted in our earlier discussion of these overall descriptive data. For example, across jobs, problem-solving and social skills typically received high ratings with respect to level requirements. Even bearing these general trends in mind, however, a review of mean ratings for these jobs does indicate that they show an interpretable pattern of differences on the Level scale. For example, Computer Programmers indicated the highest level of Programming skills (D29, $M = 6.40$, $SD = .89$) of all the jobs under consideration. However, incumbents in this occupation tended to indicate that their jobs did not require a high level of Social Perceptiveness (D11). As might be expected, General Managers and Top Executives had the highest level ratings on the four resource management skills vis-à-vis the five other jobs under consideration: Time Management (D43, $M = 5.42$, $SD = 1.16$), Management of Financial Resources (D44, $M = 4.93$, $SD = 1.76$), Management of Material Resources (D45, $M = 4.50$, $SD = 1.80$), and Management of Personnel Resources (D46, $M = 5.44$, $SD = 1.44$).

Viable measures, of course, should not just tell us what we already know. They should also extend our knowledge about and understanding of occupational skill requirements. The measures of basic and cross-functional skills also appear to lead to some noteworthy, but perhaps unexpected, inferences about people's jobs. For example, we typically see janitorial and cleaning jobs as involving few, if any, noteworthy skills. In fact, Janitors and Cleaners did receive the lowest scores on most skills. They did, however, obtain higher scores on Equipment Maintenance (D34, $M = 3.17$, $SD = 2.41$) than did General Managers, Computer Programmers, Registered Nurses, and Police Patrol Officers. Along similar lines, despite the fact that police must consistently work with the public, news reports sometimes lead us to lose sight of the importance of social skills in police work. Police Patrol Officers, however, report a level of social skill requirements comparable to those imposed on general managers and top executives. In particular, Police Patrol Officers reported needing high levels of Active Listening skills (D2, $M = 5.86$, $SD = .79$) and Negotiation skills (D14, $M = 5.14$, $SD = 1.28$). Findings of this kind indicate these skill scales may allow us to paint a very accurate picture of occupational skill requirements.

## Analyst Comparisons

Differentiation of occupations is not the only way one might go about accruing evidence for the external validity or meaningfulness of a set of job analysis measures. Another way would be to examine convergence with descriptive information obtained from other types of raters (Fleishman & Mumford, 1989, 1991; McCormick, 1976). Accordingly, Table 5-7 presents the correlations across jobs of incumbents' and analysts' ratings of level requirements for the basic and cross-functional skills.

**TABLE 5-6**
**Descriptor Means and Standard Deviations on the Level Scale on Six Example Occupations: Basic and Cross-Functional Skills**

| | Occupations | | | | | | | | | | | |
|---|---|---|---|---|---|---|---|---|---|---|---|---|
| Descriptor | General Managers & Top Executives (n = 45) | | Computer Programmers (n = 5) | | Registered Nurses (n = 32) | | Police Patrol Officers (n = 21) | | Janitors & Cleaners[a] (n = 23) | | Maintenance Repairers, General Utility (n = 27) | |
| | M | SD | M | SD | M | SD | M | SD | M | SD | M | SD |
| 1. Reading Comprehension | 5.27 | 1.37 | 5.20 | 0.45 | 5.59 | 1.16 | 4.90 | 1.00 | 3.26 | 1.54 | 3.77 | 1.69 |
| 2. Active Listening | 5.33 | 1.07 | 4.80 | 1.30 | 5.38 | 1.36 | 5.86 | 0.79 | 2.43 | 2.21 | 3.52 | 1.74 |
| 3. Writing | 5.16 | 1.07 | 4.80 | 1.10 | 5.16 | 1.02 | 5.33 | 0.91 | 2.00 | 1.88 | 3.26 | 1.51 |
| 4. Speaking | 5.11 | 1.09 | 4.40 | 0.89 | 4.84 | 1.83 | 5.52 | 0.93 | 2.43 | 2.25 | 3.70 | 1.51 |
| 5. Mathematics | 4.18 | 1.35 | 4.60 | 0.55 | 3.97 | 1.47 | 2.62 | 1.16 | 1.87 | 2.05 | 3.56 | 1.93 |
| 6. Science | 2.62 | 2.07 | 4.80 | 1.79 | 3.69 | 1.93 | 1.76 | 1.84 | 1.48 | 1.93 | 1.93 | 2.13 |
| 7. Critical Thinking | 5.32 | 0.99 | 5.40 | 1.14 | 4.19 | 1.79 | 4.76 | 1.18 | 2.70 | 2.32 | 3.11 | 1.89 |
| 8. Active Learning | 5.27 | 0.89 | 5.60 | 1.14 | 4.66 | 1.86 | 4.38 | 1.28 | 2.52 | 2.31 | 3.41 | 1.93 |
| 9. Learning Strategies | 4.58 | 1.44 | 3.80 | 1.48 | 4.97 | 1.28 | 4.19 | 1.33 | 3.52 | 1.86 | 3.85 | 1.59 |
| 10. Monitoring | 5.28 | 1.21 | 3.20 | 1.79 | 4.59 | 1.81 | 3.52 | 1.40 | 1.35 | 1.85 | 2.67 | 1.98 |
| 11. Social Perceptiveness | 4.93 | 1.56 | 2.60 | 0.89 | 5.38 | 1.56 | 5.14 | 1.74 | 2.43 | 2.11 | 3.56 | 1.58 |
| 12. Coordination | 5.20 | 1.60 | 4.60 | 1.14 | 4.16 | 1.82 | 4.81 | 1.08 | 2.17 | 2.23 | 4.33 | 1.54 |
| 13. Persuasion | 5.02 | 1.14 | 3.60 | 0.55 | 4.34 | 1.38 | 4.76 | 1.04 | 2.09 | 1.78 | 3.07 | 1.82 |
| 14. Negotiation | 4.98 | 1.47 | 2.80 | 1.30 | 3.91 | 1.84 | 5.14 | 1.28 | 1.87 | 2.07 | 2.93 | 2.15 |
| 15. Instructing | 4.60 | 1.51 | 4.20 | 1.30 | 5.19 | 1.38 | 4.33 | 0.73 | 2.91 | 1.95 | 4.00 | 1.49 |
| 16. Service Orientation | 4.69 | 1.66 | 2.00 | 1.41 | 4.91 | 1.94 | 4.52 | 1.75 | 2.22 | 1.88 | 3.33 | 1.80 |
| 17. Problem Identification | 5.56 | 0.97 | 5.40 | 0.89 | 5.16 | 1.25 | 5.38 | 0.67 | 2.39 | 2.25 | 4.67 | 1.04 |
| 18. Information Gathering | 5.39 | 1.03 | 4.60 | 1.82 | 4.78 | 1.52 | 4.95 | 1.40 | 2.87 | 1.94 | 3.74 | 1.91 |
| 19. Information Organization | 4.69 | 1.77 | 5.60 | 1.67 | 4.00 | 1.83 | 3.81 | 1.54 | 2.39 | 1.95 | 3.19 | 1.66 |
| 20. Synthesis/Reorganization | 4.75 | 1.58 | 5.20 | 1.48 | 3.84 | 1.83 | 3.33 | 2.03 | 1.74 | 2.05 | 3.11 | 1.74 |
| 21. Idea Generation | 5.00 | 1.31 | 6.00 | 1.41 | 3.77 | 1.81 | 3.81 | 1.36 | 1.70 | 1.84 | 3.56 | 1.65 |
| 22. Idea Evaluation | 5.02 | 1.34 | 5.60 | 1.67 | 3.97 | 1.47 | 3.38 | 1.99 | 2.26 | 1.98 | 3.04 | 1.60 |
| 23. Implementation Planning | 5.09 | 1.29 | 6.20 | 0.84 | 3.75 | 1.88 | 3.10 | 1.89 | 1.48 | 1.97 | 2.89 | 1.87 |
| 24. Solution Appraisal | 5.27 | 1.39 | 4.40 | 1.34 | 4.28 | 1.87 | 3.10 | 1.92 | 1.09 | 1.62 | 2.74 | 1.97 |
| 25. Operations Analysis | 3.96 | 2.16 | 6.00 | 0.71 | 2.88 | 2.15 | 1.29 | 1.71 | 0.96 | 1.74 | 2.63 | 2.32 |
| 26. Technology Design | 2.08 | 2.91 | 2.15 | 5.20 | 1.30 | 2.63 | 1.93 | 1.29 | 1.62 | 1.87 | 2.24 | 3.52 |
| 27. Equipment Selection | 3.91 | 1.99 | 3.80 | 1.64 | 3.88 | 1.64 | 1.76 | 1.87 | 2.96 | 2.29 | 4.26 | 1.53 |
| 28. Installation | 1.07 | 1.79 | 2.60 | 1.14 | 1.03 | 1.77 | 0.10 | 0.44 | 2.22 | 2.09 | 4.70 | 1.54 |
| 29. Programming | 0.78 | 1.64 | 6.40 | 0.89 | 0.41 | 1.19 | 0.33 | 0.86 | 0.83 | 1.87 | 1.44 | 2.19 |
| 30. Testing | 1.56 | 2.11 | 6.00 | 1.22 | 1.47 | 1.76 | 0.24 | 0.62 | 1.83 | 2.53 | 2.85 | 2.07 |
| 31. Operation Monitoring | 0.78 | 1.48 | 2.00 | 1.22 | 2.97 | 2.46 | 0.38 | 0.74 | 2.22 | 2.45 | 4.07 | 2.00 |
| 32. Operation and Control | 1.49 | 2.04 | 2.00 | 2.55 | 2.34 | 1.99 | 0.86 | 1.31 | 1.70 | 2.08 | 3.89 | 2.12 |
| 33. Product Inspection | 2.73 | 2.27 | 2.80 | 0.45 | 2.47 | 1.83 | 0.81 | 1.25 | 2.04 | 2.44 | 3.19 | 2.18 |
| 34. Equipment Maintenance | 1.09 | 1.83 | 1.60 | 1.52 | 1.72 | 1.87 | 2.38 | 1.91 | 3.17 | 2.41 | 5.07 | 1.38 |
| 35. Troubleshooting | 1.98 | 2.44 | 6.20 | 0.84 | 3.13 | 2.11 | 1.24 | 1.48 | 2.96 | 2.55 | 4.96 | 1.29 |
| 36. Repairing | 0.69 | 1.52 | 3.00 | 2.55 | 0.78 | 1.18 | 0.71 | 1.19 | 2.65 | 2.39 | 5.04 | 1.34 |
| 37. Visioning | 4.18 | 2.00 | 3.40 | 2.07 | 2.19 | 1.93 | 1.67 | 1.80 | 2.78 | 2.00 | 3.44 | 2.01 |
| 38. Systems Perception | 3.89 | 2.16 | 2.80 | 1.92 | 2.91 | 2.22 | 1.19 | 1.60 | 1.96 | 1.66 | 3.19 | 1.92 |
| 39. Identification of Downstream Consequences | 4.67 | 1.80 | 2.60 | 2.61 | 3.19 | 2.18 | 1.10 | 1.48 | 2.26 | 2.32 | 2.67 | 2.29 |
| 40. Identification of Key Causes | 5.18 | 1.37 | 4.00 | 1.22 | 4.03 | 2.16 | 2.33 | 1.68 | 2.04 | 2.18 | 3.33 | 1.92 |
| 41. Judgment and Decision Making | 5.20 | 1.47 | 3.80 | 1.10 | 3.97 | 2.15 | 4.05 | 2.48 | 1.91 | 2.33 | 3.41 | 1.58 |
| 42. Systems Evaluation | 4.76 | 1.57 | 3.40 | 1.52 | 2.69 | 1.97 | 0.90 | 1.37 | 1.74 | 2.03 | 2.74 | 2.19 |
| 43. Time Management | 5.42 | 1.16 | 3.20 | 1.10 | 4.50 | 1.97 | 3.90 | 1.37 | 2.70 | 2.27 | 3.85 | 1.94 |
| 44. Management of Financial Resources | 4.93 | 1.76 | 1.20 | 1.79 | 1.50 | 2.00 | 0.52 | 1.40 | 1.17 | 2.12 | 1.96 | 2.41 |
| 45. Management of Material Resources | 4.50 | 1.80 | 1.40 | 1.67 | 3.28 | 2.11 | 0.90 | 1.64 | 1.87 | 2.44 | 3.37 | 2.39 |
| 46. Management of Personnel Resources | 5.44 | 1.44 | 1.60 | 2.19 | 3.22 | 2.17 | 2.05 | 1.83 | 2.26 | 2.16 | 3.00 | 2.42 |

[a]The full title for this occupation is "Janitors and Cleaners, except Maids and Housekeeping."

**TABLE 5-7**

**Comparison Between Incumbent and Analyst Descriptive Statistics Across All Occupations and Reliability Estimates for Rated Differences Between Occupations for the Level Scale: Basic and Cross-Functional Skills**

| | Incumbent | | | Analyst | | | | | | |
|---|---|---|---|---|---|---|---|---|---|---|
| Descriptor | M | SD | $r_k$ | M | SD | $r_k$ | t | F | $r_{ia}$ | $d^2$ |
| 1. Reading Comprehension | 4.42 | 0.89 | .84 | 3.53 | 1.15 | .94 | 7.77* | 1.66 | .81 | 1.22 |
| 2. Active Listening | 4.28 | 0.95 | .83 | 3.23 | 1.04 | .93 | 8.04* | 1.18 | .71 | 1.66 |
| 3. Writing | 3.82 | 1.07 | .90 | 3.11 | 1.08 | .94 | 5.77* | 1.01 | .77 | 1.02 |
| 4. Speaking | 4.20 | 0.80 | .77 | 3.13 | 1.14 | .95 | 7.75* | 2.02 | .70 | 1.79 |
| 5. Mathematics | 3.26 | 1.16 | .82 | 2.72 | 1.14 | .95 | 3.89* | 1.04 | .74 | 0.95 |
| 6. Science | 1.53 | 1.35 | .90 | 1.24 | 1.41 | .96 | 2.15* | 1.10 | .84 | 0.67 |
| 7. Critical Thinking | 3.68 | 1.02 | .80 | 2.63 | 1.38 | .95 | 7.19* | 1.83 | .78 | 1.84 |
| 8. Active Learning | 3.62 | 1.14 | .81 | 2.49 | 1.44 | .96 | 7.85* | 1.59 | .81 | 1.96 |
| 9. Learning Strategies | 3.83 | 0.91 | .78 | 2.38 | 1.29 | .94 | 9.73* | 2.03 | .73 | 2.85 |
| 10. Monitoring | 3.26 | 1.19 | .88 | 2.78 | 1.08 | .93 | 4.18* | 1.22 | .83 | 0.67 |
| 11. Social Perceptiveness | 3.62 | 1.08 | .83 | 2.50 | 1.30 | .96 | 6.82* | 1.46 | .68 | 2.16 |
| 12. Coordination | 3.57 | 1.07 | .80 | 2.56 | 1.43 | .95 | 5.56* | 1.80 | .67 | 2.13 |
| 13. Persuasion | 3.19 | 1.15 | .86 | 1.64 | 1.16 | .93 | 10.22* | 1.00 | .70 | 3.19 |
| 14. Negotiation | 2.90 | 1.26 | .88 | 1.46 | 1.11 | .93 | 9.26* | 1.29 | .71 | 2.87 |
| 15. Instructing | 3.78 | 1.08 | .79 | 1.97 | 1.32 | .92 | 9.07* | 1.48 | .53 | 4.61 |
| 16. Service Orientation | 3.28 | 1.02 | .75 | 2.49 | 1.09 | .91 | 4.63* | 1.14 | .54 | 1.63 |
| 17. Problem Identification | 4.16 | 1.08 | .84 | 3.15 | 1.16 | .94 | 7.04* | 1.16 | .72 | 1.70 |
| 18. Informaton Gathering | 3.92 | 1.07 | .84 | 2.96 | 1.23 | .96 | 7.46* | 1.32 | .79 | 1.49 |
| 19. Information Organization | 3.21 | 1.11 | .78 | 2.95 | 1.09 | .93 | 1.94 | 1.02 | .73 | 0.70 |
| 20. Synthesis/Reorganization | 3.24 | 1.15 | .84 | 2.13 | 1.11 | .93 | 8.61* | 1.06 | .77 | 1.80 |
| 21. Idea Generation | 3.33 | 1.26 | .87 | 2.24 | 1.23 | .95 | 7.60* | 1.04 | .77 | 1.87 |
| 22. Idea Evaluation | 3.07 | 1.25 | .86 | 2.31 | 1.25 | .96 | 5.70* | 1.00 | .80 | 1.19 |
| 23. Implementation Planning | 2.83 | 1.39 | .88 | 2.04 | 1.35 | .94 | 4.86* | 1.06 | .75 | 1.55 |
| 24. Solution Appraisal | 3.02 | 1.40 | .90 | 2.64 | 1.17 | .95 | 2.86* | 1.43 | .82 | 0.76 |
| 25. Operations Analysis | 2.02 | 1.37 | .83 | 1.63 | 1.27 | .92 | 2.62* | 1.16 | .78 | 0.90 |
| 26. Technology Design | 1.76 | 1.40 | .87 | 1.25 | 1.15 | .95 | 3.20* | 1.47 | .75 | 1.11 |
| 27. Equipment Selection | 2.57 | 1.32 | .82 | 2.18 | 0.93 | .89 | 3.02* | 2.04 | .82 | 0.73 |
| 28. Installation | 1.28 | 1.54 | .91 | 1.17 | 1.07 | .86 | 0.63 | 2.06 | .69 | 1.21 |
| 29. Programming | 0.83 | 1.20 | .78 | 0.37 | 1.06 | .93 | 4.82* | 1.28 | .88 | 0.52 |
| 30. Testing | 1.53 | 1.60 | .86 | 1.19 | 1.25 | .93 | 2.22* | 1.63 | .82 | 0.94 |
| 31. Operation Monitoring | 1.69 | 1.75 | .92 | 1.55 | 1.04 | .91 | 0.72 | 2.81* | .81 | 1.16 |
| 32. Operation and Control | 2.05 | 1.39 | .84 | 2.14 | 0.79 | .74 | −0.46 | 3.07* | .63 | 1.13 |
| 33. Product Inspection | 2.31 | 1.34 | .78 | 2.40 | 0.81 | .88 | −0.56 | 2.71* | .72 | 0.86 |
| 34. Equipment Maintenance | 1.67 | 1.63 | .92 | 1.36 | 1.07 | .91 | 1.75 | 2.32* | .78 | 1.14 |
| 35. Troubleshooting | 2.25 | 1.74 | .88 | 1.48 | 1.18 | .93 | 4.41* | 2.17* | .82 | 1.61 |
| 36. Repairing | 1.33 | 1.49 | .92 | 1.25 | 1.08 | .90 | 0.44 | 1.89 | .73 | 1.03 |
| 37. Visioning | 2.34 | 1.15 | .82 | 1.88 | 1.32 | .94 | 2.38* | 1.32 | .59 | 1.43 |
| 38. Systems Perception | 2.22 | 1.23 | .84 | 2.00 | 1.25 | .92 | 1.31 | 1.04 | .65 | 1.09 |
| 39. Identification of Downstream Consequences | 2.19 | 1.13 | .85 | 1.82 | 1.30 | .93 | 2.30* | 1.32 | .71 | 1.00 |
| 40. Identification of Key Causes | 3.17 | 1.17 | .86 | 2.45 | 1.22 | .93 | 5.34* | 1.09 | .78 | 1.14 |
| 41. Judgment and Decision Making | 2.93 | 1.33 | .89 | 2.51 | 1.25 | .93 | 2.95* | 1.13 | .79 | 0.86 |
| 42. Systems Evaluation | 2.02 | 1.36 | .89 | 1.60 | 1.35 | .94 | 2.79* | 1.02 | .78 | 0.95 |
| 43. Time Management | 3.61 | 1.18 | .83 | 2.19 | 1.19 | .93 | 8.35* | 1.00 | .64 | 2.99 |
| 44. Management of Financial Resources | 1.84 | 1.50 | .89 | 1.37 | 1.42 | .94 | 2.16* | 1.12 | .62 | 1.78 |
| 45. Management of Material Resources | 1.94 | 1.29 | .87 | 1.99 | 1.10 | .92 | −0.31 | 1.37 | .69 | 0.89 |
| 46. Management of Personnel Resources | 2.67 | 1.38 | .89 | 1.56 | 1.54 | .95 | 5.51* | 1.24 | .68 | 2.59 |

*Note.* Incumbent statistics are based on 35 occupations with Skills Questionnaire responses from at least 4 incumbents (mean number of incumbents = 18.51, *Mdn* = 12, harmonic mean = 9.01). Analyst statistics are based on the same 35 occupations with Skills Questionnaire responses from at least 6 analysts (mean number of analysts = 10.29, *Mdn* = 12.0, harmonic mean = 8.66). The estimate of reliability was obtained by calculating the intraclass correlation for *k* ratings across occupations: $ICC(1, k) = [BMS − WMS]/BMS$ (Shrout & Fleiss, 1979), where *k* is the harmonic mean of the number of ratings provided on each occupation. The *t* statistic tests for differences in the incumbent and analyst group means. The *F* statistic tests for differences in the incumbent and analyst group standard deviations. The $r_{ia}$ correlation indicates the degree of relationship between incumbent and analyst mean occupational ratings. The $d^2$ statistic indicates the squared differences between incumbent and analyst mean occupations ratings.
*$p < .05$.

This analysis revealed a surprisingly high degree of convergence between incumbents' and analysts' level ratings across the 35 jobs for which adequate incumbent skills data were available. The median correlation between analysts' and incumbents' ratings of skill requirements was .75. This agreement indicates that judges having different perspectives and somewhat different knowledge describe the patterns of occupational skill requirements on these scales in much the same way. This high level of agreement becomes even more impressive when one recognizes that both incumbents' and analysts' ratings were less than perfectly reliable. When one corrects this initial coefficient for attenuation due to unreliability in incumbents' and analysts' ratings, the median correlation between analysts' and incumbents' ratings of requisite skills increases to .87. Even taking into account Schmidt and Hunter's (1996) advice to interpret corrected reliabilities with caution, it appears that analysts and incumbents agree in their descriptions of occupational skill requirements.

Of course, agreement here refers to the patterns of skill ratings; it does not speak to other differences in variances of ratings or differences in the level of skill ratings. To address these issues, a series of t tests and F tests was conducted, contrasting incumbents and analysts in terms of the means and standard deviations of the level ratings for each skill. The results of these analyses are also presented in Table 5-7, along with an overall $d^2$ index describing the pattern of the differences observed between analysts' and incumbents' ratings.

Conventional wisdom holds that analysts typically produce lower skill requirement ratings than incumbents, in part because analysts, as objective outside observers, are less prone to inflate ratings. The results obtained in the t and F tests indicate that with regard to basic, social, and problem solving skills, such differences do exist. Generally, analysts' ratings were roughly a full scale point lower than incumbents' ratings, with the largest differences occurring on social skills. It is of note, however, that analysts' ratings also showed somewhat greater variability, perhaps because analysts lack intimate familiarity with the job. However, much smaller, essentially insignificant differences in both means and standard deviations were obtained on the technical, systems, and resource management skills, with the notable exceptions of Time Management (D43) and Management of Personnel Resources (D46).

These differences in analyst and incumbent mean ratings might reflect differences in the kinds of information used in making ratings. Analysts may indirectly make ratings on a comparative basis, whereas incumbents are likely to focus on what they know—their own jobs. As a result, skills that tap into broad evaluative standards, particularly skills that have strong overall intellectual demand implications (e.g., basic, problem solving, and social skills) may receive higher ratings from incumbents. Analysts may see the job in the context of other, more demanding jobs, resulting in lower ratings. Incumbents, however, may

focus on the more salient and demanding parts of their jobs, resulting in somewhat higher ratings. This "contrasting frameworks" explanation for the mean differences is attractive in part because (a) the salience of social interactions to incumbents helps explain the peculiarly large differences observed on the social skill dimensions and (b) the skills resulting in small differences (e.g., technical, systems, and resource management) are less likely to activate analysts' stereotypes with regard to overall job demands.

Regardless of the interpretation applied, however, it should be recognized that incumbents' and analysts' ratings of skill requirements were not widely divergent. In fact, these differences in mean ratings were typically within 1 point on a 7-point scale. Furthermore, as noted earlier, the pattern of the ratings was essentially identical. Thus, our comparison of the incumbents' and analysts' ratings appears to provide evidence for the convergent validity of the descriptive information provided by our measures of job skill requirements.

## STUDY LIMITATIONS

Before turning to the broader conclusions flowing from our findings, certain limitations of the present study must be noted. First, the reader must recognize that we have examined only two types of skills: basic and cross-functional. Thus, the findings obtained in this effort cannot and should not be viewed as an exhaustive investigation of the skills domain. Clearly, our findings have little to say about citizenship skills in a direct sense, nor do they have much to say about child-rearing skills. Instead, the findings obtained in the present effort bear most directly on those skills likely to influence job performance.

The limitation on the domains of skills under consideration is linked to another caveat. In the present effort, we have expressly focused on those basic and cross-functional skills likely to be involved in all jobs to some extent. In fact, the finding that level scores are high across a variety of jobs tends to reiterate this point. By the same token, however, in this chapter we have made no attempt to identify those skills particular to a single occupation or a limited set of occupations. For example, no attempt was made here to assess multiplexer installation—an occupation-specific skill commonly found on telecommunications jobs.

In a later chapter on occupation-specific skills, we address the procedures needed to identify occupation-specific skills. In this regard, however, it is worth noting that the procedures used to identify occupation-specific skills take as their starting point this general taxonomy of basic and cross-functional skills. For the moment, however, the reader should bear in mind this point—that our measures and findings pertain primarily to the general basic and cross-functional skills likely to influence performance in a variety of different settings. Accordingly, these skills may be more useful in describing the similarities and differences across jobs than in assessing requirements or designing training programs for a particular job.

## CONCLUSION

### Reliability

The findings indicate that our measures of the basic and cross-functional skills clearly provide a reliable description of general occupational skill requirements. Not only were incumbents likely to see some amount of all of the basic and cross-functional skills as being required across a wide range of jobs, but they also displayed a high degree of agreement in assessing the level at which the skill was required, its importance, and whether the indicated level was required at job entry. This high degree of agreement about basic and cross-functional skill requirements might be attributed, in part, to the use of clear, unambiguous definitions of the skills to be assessed and the use of well-designed rating scales that provide concrete exemplars for anchoring ratings. Scaling issues aside, however, it appears that incumbents can make consistent, agreed-upon assessments of skill requirements using their scales. Furthermore, their judgments were consistent, at least in terms of pattern, with the assessments of occupational skill requirements obtained from external observers, the occupational analysts.

### Validity

This apparent convergence of the pattern of skill requirement ratings across incumbents and analysts also speaks to the validity of the descriptive information provided by these rating scales. Although we have primarily focused on the Level scale, it should be noted that substantial convergence was also observed when incumbents' and analysts' ratings of skill importance were correlated with each other. Thus, this finding does not appear to be specific to a particular type of scale. In addition to this convergent validation evidence, it also was clear that ratings of basic and cross-functional level requirements were consistent with known occupational characteristics, while reminding us that occupations are not always what they seem. These points were well illustrated in our comparison of jobs on the Level scale, where it was found that general managers had the highest scores on the resource management skills but were comparable to police officers in terms of requisite social skills.

Our evidence for the validity of the descriptive information about jobs provided by our measures of the basic and cross-functional skills is not limited to convergence across raters and the consistency of skill ratings with known job characteristics. In the present effort, we conducted a number of analyses intended to provide some evidence for the internal and exter-nal validity of the resulting descriptive system. For example, some evidence for the internal validity was provided by our factoring of the skills, which revealed an interpretable structure of relationships among the rating scales, indicating that these scales captured cognitive, technical, and organizational skills.

Evidence for the external validity of the skills scales was accrued in a variety of different analyses. For example, our findings indicate that basic content skills (e.g., Reading Comprehension, Writing, Active Listening) are required at a high level on most jobs and must be present at this level prior to job entry—a finding that is consistent with current educational theory and prior research (Peterson, 1992a). Nevertheless, as an aside, our findings, particularly with regard to cross-job requirements for problem-solving and social skills, indicate that it may be useful to try to develop high levels of these skills prior to job entry as well, to facilitate school-to-work transition (Pearlman, 1996).

### Taxonomy Representativeness

Although the findings obtained in this effort provide some compelling initial evidence for the reliability and validity of our measures as they stand, we might ask another question: Do these taxonomies provide adequate representation of the domain of occupational skill requirements? Of course, this question can only be answered with regard to the intent of the proposed descriptive system (Fleishman & Quaintance, 1984). As noted earlier, it is open to question whether the kind of broad basic and cross-functional skills of concern here will prove fully adequate when one must develop training courses for a particular occupation. Our intent in creating this taxonomy of basic and cross-functional skills, however, was to provide a system capable of capturing the similarities and differences among jobs in terms of their skill requirements. The ability to distinguish among occupations might prove useful in answering a variety of questions about people and their work. For example, this information might be used to guide transfers or find new jobs for disabled veterans. Alternatively, these skills might be used to determine how skill levels are related to pay. Those questions, of course, all implicitly call for cross-job comparisons. Thus, the ultimate question to be asked in appraising our taxonomy of basic and cross-functional skills is whether it provides an adequate basis for distinguishing among jobs. Comparison of the skill profiles across jobs seems to indicate that good differentiation among jobs can be made with the O*NET skills.

Although it appears that the proposed taxonomy of skills is not unduly complex and that these skills can describe the similarities and differences among jobs, our findings cannot rule out the possibility that something is missing. It is possible, furthermore, that new skills may well arise with the development of new technologies or the emergence of new types of organizations. Bearing this caveat in mind, however, the evidence supports the comprehensiveness of the taxonomies of basic and cross-functional skills. First, the domains governed by those taxonomies were developed in relation to a general model of work performance—specifically, sociotechnical systems theory (Katz & Kahn, 1978). Second, in developing the taxonomies within a given area (e.g., problem solving), variables were specified in relation to a general model of performance (Mumford & Peterson, 1995). Third, Mumford and Peterson (1995), in their review of the skills literature, identified 11 prior studies proposing general taxonomies of occupational skills. In a subsequent content analysis, they found that more than 90% of the skills appearing in these taxonomies had direct analogs in the current taxonomy of basic and cross-functional skills. Thus, there is reason to believe that the O*NET basic and cross-functional skills provide a reasonably comprehensive description of general occupational skill requirements.

## Implications for Future Research

Although the present study has provided some important initial evidence for the meaningfulness of our taxonomy of basic and cross-functional skills, we have not answered every question that might be raised about the meaningfulness of the descriptive system. For example, our interest in skills, particularly basic and cross-functional skills, is often based on the hope that developing these skills in the workforce will improve performance across a variety of settings. The evidence provided by Baer (1988) and Ward et al. (1990) suggests that these skills can be developed with appropriate training interventions and that training will result in enhanced performance on transfer tasks. Nonetheless, no attempt has been made in the present study to address either the training or transfer issues.

Further studies need to be conducted, both to elucidate the implications of our taxonomy of basic and cross-functional skills and to demonstrate how this kind of descriptive information may be used in guiding policy decisions about human resources. Nonetheless, we believe the present effort represents an important first step along these lines. We hope that by presenting a valid, reliable system for describing occupational skill requirements, this effort has provided the basic structure needed to guide the kind of systematic research needed to address these and a number of other questions about occupational skill requirements.

# Knowledges

DAVID P. COSTANZA, EDWIN A. FLEISHMAN,
AND JOANNE MARSHALL-MIES

Given the ever increasing amount of information required in today's fast-changing work environment, employers are becoming concerned that their employees, both current and future, will not have the knowledge base necessary to perform their jobs. Requests from managers for increased employee training and formal schooling and for new employees who have the requisite knowledges are indicative of this desire to ensure that workers possess or acquire and are able to apply this knowledge base. These calls for increased training and education have occurred despite a paucity of data about what knowledge areas are relevant to the workforce in general and which areas are most important for performance in a specific job or occupation.

Without defining the nature of different job-relevant knowledges and without specification of the particular knowledge areas that are most germane to specific jobs or occupations, efforts to increase the knowledge of workers are unlikely to result in the desired increase in performance and flexibility required by the changing workplace. The study of occupational knowledge affects any effort concerning person–job matching, job training and retraining, career counseling, vocational interests, and creation of job families or clusters.

Several steps need to be taken before employers will be able to ensure that their employees have the requisite knowledge to perform their jobs. First, knowledge must be defined in job-relevant terms. Second, a taxonomy of knowledge areas that are relevant to the wide variety of jobs in the economy must be identified, and a measurement system for identifying and quantifying the knowledges must be developed. Third, data must be gathered to provide evidence for the comprehensiveness of the new knowledge taxonomy and the reliability and validity of the measurement system.

This chapter describes the development and evaluation of a taxonomy of job-required knowledges and its associated measurement system. We also dis-

cuss the implications of our findings for a variety of human resource functions in the world of work.

## KNOWLEDGE DEFINITION

*Knowledge* is defined as a collection of discrete but related facts and information about a particular domain. It is acquired through formal education or training or accumulated through specific experiences. Job-relevant knowledges are those facts and structures that are necessary for successful job performance. The fact that these pieces of information are organized into some coherent structure is critical to the definition (Chase & Simon, 1973; Chi, Glaser, & Rees, 1983; Halff, Hollan, & Hutchins, 1986; Lesgold, 1984). Discrete facts and figures are not knowledges unless they are also organized in some meaningful way. Although the actual number of pieces of information may vary greatly from domain to domain, the underlying structure is what defines them as knowledges.

The challenge to defining job-relevant knowledges lies in identifying and clarifying which ones are most job-relevant and the level of specificity that is appropriate. Some knowledge domains are more general than others because they include a wider variety of discrete facts. In terms of the work world, this suggests that some knowledges may be more important to successful performance in a greater variety of jobs, as they are broader and more generalized, whereas others are more narrow and specific to a particular job or limited set of jobs.

Thus, the definitional issue is part and parcel of the taxonomic development process. It follows that in developing a taxonomy of knowledges for describing job requirements, it is very important to deal with this issue of specificity so that a comprehensive but parsimonious taxonomic system can be identified. The ideal taxonomy would strive to make uniform the level of specificity of the knowledge constructs so that they will be broad enough to cover multiple domains but not so encompassing that they will be useless as components in differentiating the knowledge requirements of different jobs.

## EARLIER DEVELOPMENT OF KNOWLEDGE REQUIREMENTS TAXONOMY AND MEASUREMENT SYSTEM

An objective of the current effort was to identify relatively broad knowledge areas that are relevant to a wide variety of jobs. This objective was intended to both direct our efforts and to ensure that the resulting taxonomy could serve a number of job-related purposes such as training, career counseling, selection, and person–job matching. The effort evolved from earlier work by Costanza and Fleishman (1992a, 1992b) that attempted to describe and measure a wide variety of job-relevant knowledge areas as part of the Fleishman Job Analysis Survey (F-JAS; Fleishman, 1992a).

The first step in this previous effort to develop the taxonomy, hereinafter referred to as the *Knowledge Requirements Taxonomy*, was to conduct a literature search to identify previously identified job knowledges. Historically, cognitive scientists have emphasized the structure of knowledge and have defined experts as those with complex knowledge structures. Thus, the focus has often been on the structures and processes involved in developing and analyzing knowledge rather than on the knowledges themselves. A few existing limited knowledge lists or taxonomies were identified, including those that contained several articles (e.g., Peterson, 1992a; Prediger, 1989), the original F-JAS knowledge component (Fleishman, 1991a, 1992a), and several government reports and studies (e.g., Secretary's Commission on Achieving Necessary Skills [SCANS], 1992) regarding the demands placed on workers and the knowledges required to perform job duties.

Given this initial literature review and the limited list of existing taxonomies, it was determined that an empirical rather than a rational approach to developing the taxonomy would be more appropriate and pragmatic. Although a purely rational strategy often is a more appealing one, the existing literature and research did not support this approach. Accordingly, we decided that the better approach would be to empirically identify as many job knowledge areas as possible and then to rationally and empirically refine and revise the list until a comprehensive taxonomy was obtained. The resulting taxonomy could then be compared with existing groupings to identify points of convergence and divergence and to ensure the comprehensiveness of the taxonomy.

One technique of finding the knowledges was to use job descriptions. In job analysis, it is common to use job descriptions as a starting point for determining what the critical knowledges, skills, abilities, and personality characteristics (KSAPs) are for a particular job or set of jobs. Therefore, it was decided to use job descriptions to identify the knowledges themselves as well as any job-relevant behaviors and characteristics that were indicative of underlying knowledges. Of course, the only way to include all possible job-relevant knowledges was to review descriptions of all possible jobs. Although no such collection can be totally comprehensive, a particularly useful source of job descriptions does exist in which almost all jobs are explicitly identified and described. This source is the Department of Labor's (DOL) *Dictionary of Occupational Titles* (DOT; U.S. DOL, 1991a).

Each job description in the DOT was read and examined. Because the DOT's descriptions are task based, the tasks in each job description were examined, and the relevant knowledges specified as necessary to perform those tasks were listed. The objective was to be neither too specific (e.g., knowledge of how to insert a drill bit into a drill) nor too general (e.g., knowledge of science). However, whenever there was any question about an identified item, we favored inclusion and included the knowledge. As each job description in the DOT was reviewed and analyzed, potential job-relevant knowledges were compared with ones identified for other jobs. If a new knowledge appeared, it was added to the list. As each knowledge was identified, a prototype definition was generated using the job tasks and content as a starting point.

This analysis of the DOT job descriptions initially yielded 68 qualitatively different knowledges such as *computers, meteorology,* and *safety/security*. Reviews of several prior research efforts noted above (e.g., Campbell et al., 1990; Fleishman, 1992a; McKinney & Greer, 1985; Prediger, 1989) provided additional knowledges to extend the list to a total of 86. The final phase of this step was to generate prototype task examples indicating high, medium, and low amounts of the knowledge, using the job descriptions from which the knowledges were derived.

## IDENTIFICATION OF KNOWLEDGE CATEGORIES

At this stage, it was apparent that the level of specificity still varied across the knowledges. Given the definitional issues discussed above and the importance of comparable levels of specificity, our efforts moved toward trying to equalize the level of specificity. First, we looked for broader, superordinate knowledge areas that might help to clarify and reduce redundancy. Hence, we searched for preexisting taxonomies of job families or job groups into which the knowledges could be categorized. By grouping the knowledges into larger categories on the basis of similarity, the specificity issue could be addressed to improve the usefulness of the taxonomy. Not only could this process simplify the list of knowledges and improve its organization, it could also provide initial evidence for the knowledges' validity. If each knowledge could be grouped with others into larger categories, this would support their meaningfulness in terms of their relationship to each other.

A starting point for this grouping effort was Holland's (1976) six vocational interest areas. Other work by Guilford, Christensen, Bond, and Sutton (1954); Lorr and Suziedelis (1973); Rounds and Dawis (1979); Kuder (1977); Zytowski (1976); and Pearlman (1980) provided potential schemes for categorizing interest areas, work-oriented knowledges, and job families as well as information about the categorization process. The previously mentioned SCANS report and the knowledges identified from the DOT also provided potential categories. From the above references, seven general knowledge categories were identified as capturing many of the proposed knowledges; these categories included artistic/creative, business/administrative, mechanical/skilled trades, outdoor work, professional, scientific, and service sector. The initial 86 knowledges were sorted by the research team into these seven categories and reviewed for completeness, clarity, and reasonableness. The team's comments and suggestions, using the superordinate categories as guides, were incorporated. The result was a consolidation of the list of 86 into a reduced group of 52 knowledges.

## Scaling of Knowledges

Next, using the preliminary task statements culled from the DOT as well as some additional tasks generated by the reviewers, a survey of task examples for the 52 knowledge areas was created. The survey was completed by 19 raters, including psychologists, nonacademic professionals and managers, and doctoral students in psychology. Following the procedures used in the development of the F-JAS (Fleishman, 1975a, 1975b, 1975c, 1992a; Fleishman & Quaintance, 1984), raters were asked to make two determinations about each task for a given knowledge area: (a) Does the task require any amount of that knowledge? If so, (b) on a scale of 1 to 7, what level of that knowledge is required for the task? Raters also were instructed to suggest changes to the definitions of each of the knowledge areas.

This task example survey yielded several important findings. First, the raters were able to agree on whether the tasks were representative of the knowledges and their level ratings of each task. Overall, interrater reliabilities ranged from .89 to .98, indicating substantial agreement among raters. Second, the tasks were rated as representing varying amounts of the knowledges in that certain tasks were clearly rated as high, medium, or low in requiring a particular knowledge. This suggested that the tasks could prove useful as anchors in a behaviorally anchored rating scale (BARS)-like measurement system. Third, there was a general consensus that two of the knowledge areas could be combined and one could be de-

leted. This was done, and the resulting list of 49 was considered to be reasonably complete and representative of job-relevant knowledge areas. These knowledges were used in preliminary forms of the FJAS (Costanza & Fleishman, 1992a, 1992b); Table 6-1 provides a list of these 49 knowledges.

Following the FJAS methodology (see chap. 11), a next step in this prior research was the selection of three task anchors for each knowledge area. Anchors were selected on the basis of the dispersion of their means along the entire range of the scale; their low standard deviations, indicating high rater agreement; and their familiarity and accessibility to the general population.

**TABLE 6-1**
**The Knowledge Requirements Taxonomy**

| Descriptor no. | Title |
| --- | --- |
| 1 | Administration & Management |
| 2 | Art |
| 3 | Biology and Physiology |
| 4 | Building and Construction |
| 5 | Chemistry |
| 6 | Clerical |
| 7 | Computers |
| 8 | Designing |
| 9 | Ecology |
| 10 | Economics and Accounting |
| 11 | Education and Training |
| 12 | Electricity |
| 13 | Electronics |
| 14 | Engineering and Technology |
| 15 | Food Preparation |
| 16 | Food Production |
| 17 | Geography and Map Reading |
| 18 | Geology and Mineralogy |
| 19 | History and Archaeology |
| 20 | Legal, Government Relations, and Jurisprudence |
| 21 | Maintenance and Repair |
| 22 | Materials |
| 23 | Mathematics |
| 24 | Measurement |
| 25 | Mechanical |
| 26 | Medicine and Dentistry |
| 27 | Meteorology |
| 28 | Money |
| 29 | Music |
| 30 | Personal Care and Hygiene |
| 31 | Personnel and Human Resources |
| 32 | Philosophy and Theology |
| 33 | Physics |
| 34 | Politics and Lobbying |
| 35 | Production and Processing |
| 36 | Psychology |
| 37 | Public and Customer Service |
| 38 | Safety and Security |
| 39 | Sales and Marketing |
| 40 | Sanitation and Cleaning |
| 41 | Sociology and Anthropology |
| 42 | Supply, Packing, and Shipping |
| 43 | Technical Drawing |
| 44 | Telephone and Telegraph |
| 45 | Television and Radio |
| 46 | Therapy and Counseling |
| 47 | Transportation |
| 48 | Weapon and Military |
| 49 | Writing, Language, and Grammar |

*Note.* From Costanza and Fleishman (1992a, 1992b).

## Evaluation of the Initial Taxonomy and Measurement System

Data from job incumbents and supervisors were obtained in several earlier efforts to provide some evidence for the validity of both the taxonomy and the empirical technique used to develop it. One large-scale study involved 18 of the knowledge scales (Costanza et al., 1995). Here, a governmental agency was interested in validating a key selection measure used by the agency for entry-level positions. The objective was to cluster the jobs into job families and to select those jobs in these families that best met the requirements for a test validation study. Additionally, because the organization was facing staff reductions, there also was interest in information about job families that could be used in cross-training or job placement.

Job incumbents were asked to rate these knowledges (e.g., *engineering and technical, computers, personnel,* and *physics*) on the level necessary for successful job performance. Across 75 different jobs, the knowledge scales evidenced substantial reliability, using an average of approximately 20 raters per job, with interrater reliabilities averaging over .90.

The ratings for level of abilities and knowledges required in each job were also used to create job families on the basis of similarities and differences in profiles among jobs. A Ward and Hook (1963) clustering technique was employed to group jobs using the abilities and knowledges separately and then combined. The parsimony of the solutions was evaluated empirically, using scree plots; and rationally, on the basis of the understanding by the organization's experts of what the jobs entailed. It was found that the best solution, with 15 job families, was obtained using a combination of the ability and knowledge ratings. The inclusion of the knowledge scales substantially improved the quality and parsimony of the solution.

In another study, for a large financial firm, the critical tasks performed by sales representatives and the knowledges, skills, abilities, and personality characteristics (KSAPs) that contributed to performance on these tasks were identified. A task-based job analysis was conducted and subject matter experts (SMEs) were asked to identify and then rate the importance of a number of KSAPs to task performance. Specifically, the job incumbents identified four of the knowledges from the taxonomy as important to job performance: *economic, government regulations and legal, sales and marketing,* and *language and grammar.* The results here gave some initial indication that the knowledge scales, albeit a limited number in this study, were useful in helping to understand job performance.

In a third effort, the knowledge scales were used in a study of several state police jobs (Trooper, Corporal, Sergeant, Lieutenant). Again, interrater reliabilities for knowledge profiles were from .90 to .95 when 23 raters were used (Wetrogan, Uhlman, & Fleishman, 1995), and the knowledge profiles obtained again helped differentiate the occupations.

From the foregoing efforts, it was apparent that the initial development effort of the FJAS Knowledge Scales had produced a useful taxonomy for describing and analyzing occupational knowledge requirements. Although these earlier projects were limited in terms of number of knowledges covered or the scope of the jobs analyzed, as a group they did provide initial evidence for the reliability and validity of the taxonomy and of the measurement system.

## ADAPTATION AND EVALUATION OF THE KNOWLEDGE REQUIREMENTS SCALES FOR O*NET

For the present effort, the 49 Knowledge Requirements Scales, initially developed for the FJAS, were pilot tested by O*NET project staff on a sample of job incumbents from approximately 30 occupations. The results of this pilot administration and subsequent feedback from the DOL Occupational Analysis Field Center (OAFC) staff provided guidance for making revisions to the knowledge taxonomy and rating scales. On the basis of this feedback, staff undertook a systematic process to review and edit the knowledges, the measurement scales, and the instructions for completing these scales.

This process involved the following four steps: (a) update and extend the literature review; (b) revise the knowledges and knowledge clusters; (c) revise the knowledge rating scales; and (d) identify and incorporate specialty areas into the knowledge rating scales.

## Updating and Extending the Literature Review

The first step in refining the Knowledge Requirements Taxonomy and measurement system for use in O*NET was to update and extend the literature review. This review was extended to cover research related to the acquisition and application of knowledge and to update the previous review of literature on the content and structure of knowledge in both the job and educational domains.

### Knowledge and Expertise

Generally speaking, there have been three fundamental approaches for studying knowledge and expertise (Ericsson & Charness, 1994). The first, the human-information-processing approach, developed by Newell and Simon (1972), explains expert performance in terms of knowledges and skills obtained through practice and experience. The emphasis in the information-processing approach is on the cognitive processes underlying human knowledge acquisition and not on the knowledge content per se.

A second paradigm, the individual-differences approach, focuses on the individual differences of expert performers that would account for their extraordinary success in a particular domain. This approach is illustrated by the works of Gardner (1983, 1993a, 1993b), who advanced a theory of multiple intelligences to describe human knowledge acquisition.

A more recent approach to the study of expertise is illustrated by the work of Ericsson and colleagues (Ericsson & Charness, 1994; Ericsson & Faivre, 1988; Ericsson, Krampe, & Tesch-Romer, 1993; Ericsson & Simon, 1993; Ericsson & Smith, 1991a, 1991b). A series of experimental studies conducted under laboratory conditions have examined empirical, reproducible examples of superior performance. The major finding of this approach has been to identify the central role of very large amounts of focused training. Extended, deliberate practice is believed to alter the cognitive and physiological process of experts to a greater degree than previously believed possible, thereby enabling them to display unusual performance.

All three approaches to studying knowledge and expertise concentrate on the mechanisms of human cognition. Accordingly, the findings from all three areas of inquiry have implications for the processes underlying knowledge acquisition. For purposes of job description, however, they do not explicitly define the knowledge content areas that are occupationally relevant to our nation's workforce.

### Knowledge Content and Structure

Earlier in this chapter we reviewed an initial search of the literature in the identification and classification of knowledges related to the world of work (i.e., knowledges required to perform the population of jobs). As indicated earlier, the DOT and several other sources (e.g., Campbell, McHenry, & Wise, 1990; Fleishman, 1992a; McKinney & Geer, 1985; Prediger, 1989) were the primary sources for the Knowledge Requirements Taxonomy (Costanza & Fleishman, 1992a, 1992b). Unfortunately, these sources did not provide a mechanism for classifying or grouping the large numbers of knowledges required across jobs.

To ensure the comprehensiveness of the initial knowledge taxonomy, project staff again reviewed the literature on the structure and content of knowledge, with an emphasis this time on hierarchical structures for classifying knowledges related to the world of work. In addition, the review was extended to the classification of knowledges in the educational domain.

Several of the sources identified, although not providing a direct list of knowledges, served as a means of verifying the comprehensiveness of the taxonomy. Among these sources were the SCANS list of skills needed for employment (Peterson, 1992a) and the list of competencies in the Multipurpose Occupational Systems Analysis Inventory—Close-Ended (MOSAIC; Corts & Gowing, 1992). Although these systems are broader in definition than is desired, a mapping of these skills and competencies against the knowledge taxonomy confirmed that no major knowledges had been omitted in the taxonomy.

In addition to the DOT, SCANS, and MOSAIC, other systems exist for classifying jobs. One such system, the Occupational Employment Statistics (OES) survey, conducted by the Bureau of Labor Statistics, provides data related to national employment. As with most existing systems for classifying jobs, the OES informs but does not directly reflect the knowledges required by the U.S. labor force.

In addition to literature related to the job domain, literature dealing with specific knowledge content in the educational literature was covered. An example of this literature is the *Classification of Instructional Programs* (CIP; Morgan, Hunt & Carpenter, 1990), a document that lists academic courses of instruction being offered through U.S. colleges and universities. Although this literature is relevant, it is not comprehensive enough for our purposes. Because it focuses on the curriculum taught by our educational institutions, it does not reflect all knowledge requirements of U.S. jobs. For example, many jobs require knowledges that are acquired on the job or are learned in nonacademic settings (e.g., apprenticeships).

The expanded search did not reveal a comprehensive taxonomy of job-related knowledges. However, it did reveal an emerging system for combining and classifying OES occupational information and CIP educational information. This system, currently under development by the National Occupational Information Coordinating Committee (NOICC), is an evolving hierarchical system for grouping 244 national units of analysis (NUAs) into 42 broad groups and 15 superclusters (NOICC, 1995). The NOICC clustering hierarchy links these NUAs to more than 800 OES occupations and more than 1,400 CIP programs. This clustering hierarchy provides a mechanism for matching job market demand and institutional supply data gathered at the state level by state occupational information coordinating committees (SOICCs).

Although the NOICC clustering hierarchy is still under development, the system was deemed most appropriate for evaluating the comprehensiveness and classification of the knowledges in the knowledge taxonomy. The NOICC information served as a basis for revising the knowledges and knowledge clusters and for identifying and designing a mechanism for adding specialty area information to the knowledge rating scales.

### Revising the Knowledges and Knowledge Clusters

In this step we revised the knowledges and knowledge clusters by examining the comprehensiveness and organization of the knowledge list and the level of specificity across the knowledges. The goal was to develop a more parsimonious set of knowledges classified into broader clusters. One means of establishing the content validity of the knowledge classification scheme was to compare it with the NOICC scheme.

Although not identical, the NOICC and our knowledge classification schemas were very similar in terms of the numbers and content of knowledge clusters and knowledges. For example, the Knowledge Requirements Taxonomy had 14 knowledge clusters and 49 knowledges compared with 15 NOICC superclusters and 42 broad groups. This comparability in the numbers and content of the clusters and knowledges suggests a similar overall level of specificity in the two systems.

A more direct comparison of the Knowledge Requirements Taxonomy and NOICC structures provided additional information related to the comprehensiveness and level of specificity of the knowledges. Each of the 49 knowledges was mapped onto the 42 NOICC broad groups by five research psychologists familiar with the original knowledge definitions and measurement system. This mapping revealed that the knowledges covered all areas contained in the NOICC system. In some instances, the two classification systems were virtually identical. For example, the Legal, Government, & Jurisprudence knowledge mapped directly onto the NOICC Legal Services, and the Education & Training knowledge mapped onto the NOICC Education broad group, and so on. In other instances, a single knowledge covered several NOICC broad groups and vice versa. For example, the single Sales & Marketing knowledge covered two NOICC broad groups of Marketing/Advertising and Sales, and the single NOICC broad group of Management covered two knowledges of Administration & Management and Personnel & Human Resources.

These differences between the Knowledge Requirements Taxonomy and the NOICC knowledge classification system were carefully reviewed to determine the most appropriate level of specificity for the knowledges to be used in O*NET. In instances where NOICC provided several broad groups to cover a single knowledge area or where several of the knowledges covered a single NOICC broad group, research staff determined whether the knowledge should be combined with others or further broken down. On the basis of this evaluation and a requirement to reduce the demands on raters, several of the 49 knowledges were combined. The result was a more parsimonious set of 33 knowledges. Once these revisions were made, the 33 revised knowledges were grouped into 10 knowledge clusters, again examining the 15 NOICC supercluster structure for comparability.

Attention was given to the order of presentation of the revised knowledge clusters and the specific knowledges within each cluster. Initial data from the limited range of jobs in the pilot study suggested that some of the original 49 knowledge constructs differed according to their general applicability across occupations. That is, some of the knowledges appeared to be applicable to a broader range of jobs, whereas other knowledges seemed to apply to a narrower range of jobs. Therefore, a decision was made to organize the clusters and knowledges in a more meaningful way.

A panel of four psychologists rationally grouped the knowledges into clusters on the basis of their perceived similarity and relatedness. Cluster headings were then reviewed to ensure their meaningfulness to the raters. Next, the knowledges were independently rated by another panel of four psychologists to determine the likelihood that they would be relevant across the general population of jobs in the economy. Knowledges that were found to apply to a broader variety of occupations were labeled *cross-functional*, and knowledges considered likely relevant to a smaller range of jobs were called *occupation-specific*. Within each cluster, the knowledges were arranged so that the more general cross-functional knowledges appeared first, followed by the more occupation-specific knowledges. These clusters along with their associated knowledges were made part of the survey. Table 6-2 presents the revised Knowledge Requirements Taxonomy, including the cluster headings. Clusters with a higher proportion of cross-functional knowledges were placed toward the beginning of the survey. This reordering was done to ensure that more raters would encounter knowledges relevant to their jobs earlier in the survey.

## Revising the Knowledge Rating Scales

The original Knowledge Requirements Taxonomy and rating scales were created from an extensive review of the cognitive, vocational, training, and job analysis literatures. The knowledge categories were then broadened, narrowed, altered, or discarded on the basis of the review, ratings, and comments of multiple professional psychologists. Task-anchored type measurement scales also were developed so that the task anchors represented different levels of a particular knowledge and had high reliability with regard to their positions on the scales. Project staff reexamined this work and revised it to improve the rating scales while maintaining the integrity of the original measurement system.

A panel of six research psychologists reviewed the 33 knowledge rating scales. The goal of this review was to combine the definitions, level descriptors, and task anchors from any scales that had been combined. The panel, first independently and then as a group, edited each knowledge rating scale, including the knowledge definition, the high- and low-level descriptors, and the task anchors. In those instances where several knowledges had been combined, the definitions and high–low descriptors were revised to reflect the broader knowledge; task anchors were revised, deleted, or added as needed. All scale values for task anchors were reviewed to ensure their proper

**TABLE 6-2**
**Descriptions and Definitions of Knowledges**

| Construct label | Operational definition | Level scale |
|---|---|---|
| | Business and Management | |
| 1. Administration and Management | Knowledge of principles and processes involved in business and organizational planning, coordination, and execution. This includes strategic planning, resource allocation, manpower modeling, leadership techniques, and production methods. | High—Managing a $10 million company. Low—Signing a pay voucher. |
| 2. Clerical | Knowledge of administrative and clerical procedures and systems, such as word processing systems, filing and records management systems, stenography and transcription, forms design principles, and other office procedures and terminology. | High—Organizing a storage system for company forms. Low—Filing letters alphabetically. |
| 3. Economics and Accounting | Knowledge of economic and accounting principles and practices, the financial markets, banking, and the analysis and reporting of financial data. | High—Keeping a major corporation's financial records. Approving a multimillion dollar loan to a real estate developer. Low—Answering billing questions from credit card customers. |
| 4. Sales and Marketing | Knowledge of principles and methods involved in showing, promoting, and selling products or services. This includes marketing strategies and tactics, product demonstration and sales techniques, and sales control systems. | High—Developing a marketing plan for a nationwide phone system. Low—Selling cakes at a bake sale. |
| 5. Customer and Personal Service | Knowledge of principles and processes for providing customer and personal services, including needs assessment techniques, quality service standards, alternative delivery systems, and customer satisfaction evaluation techniques. | High—Responding to a citizen's request for assistance after a major natural disaster. Low—Processing customer dry-cleaning drop-off. |
| 6. Personnel and Human Resources | Knowledge of policies and practices involved in personnel/human resources functions. This includes recruitment, selection, training, and promotion regulations and procedures; compensation and benefits packages; labor relations and negotiation strategies; and personnel information systems. | High—Designing a new personnel selection and promotion system for the Army. Low—Filling out a medical claim form. |
| | Manufacturing and Production | |
| 7. Production and Processing | Knowledge of inputs, outputs, raw materials, waste, quality control, costs, and techniques for maximizing the manufacture and distribution of goods. | High—Managing a food processing plant. Low—Putting a computer back into its packing materials. |
| 8. Food Production | Knowledge of techniques and equipment for planting, growing, and harvesting of food for consumption, including crop rotation methods, animal husbandry, and food storage/handling techniques. | High—Running a 100,000 acre farm. Low—Keeping an herb box in the kitchen. |
| | Engineering and Technology | |
| 9. Computers and Electronics | Knowledge of electric circuit boards, processors, chips, and computer hardware and software, including applications and programming. | High—Creating a program to scan computer disks for viruses. Low—Operating a VCR to watch a prerecorded training tape. |
| 10. Engineering and Technology | Knowledge of equipment, tools, mechanical devices, and their uses to produce motion, light, power, technology, and other applications. | High—Designing an efficient and clean power plant. Low—Installing a door lock. |
| 11. Design | Knowledge of design techniques, principles, tools and instruments involved in the production and use of precision technical plans, blueprints, drawings, and models. | High—Developing detailed design plans for a new high-rise office complex. Low—Drawing a straight line 4 3/16 inches long. |
| 12. Building and Construction | Knowledge of materials, methods, and the appropriate tools to construct objects, structures, and buildings. | High—Building a high-rise office tower. Low—Sawing a board in half. |

*Table 6-2 continues*

**TABLE 6-2 (Continued)**

| Construct label | Operational definition | Level scale |
|---|---|---|
| 13. Mechanical | Knowledge of machines and tools, including their designs, uses, benefits, repair, and maintenance. | High—Overhauling an airplane jet engine.<br>Low—Replacing the filters in a furnace. |

Mathematics and Science

| Construct label | Operational definition | Level scale |
|---|---|---|
| 14. Mathematics | Knowledge of numbers, their operations, and interrelationships, including arithmetic, algebra, geometry, calculus, statistics, and their applications. | High—Deriving a complex mathematical equation.<br>Low—Adding two numbers. |
| 15. Physics | Knowledge and prediction of physical principles, laws, and applications, including air, water, material dynamics, light, atomic principles, heat, electric theory, earth formations, and meteorological and related natural phenomena. | High—Designing a cleaner burning gasoline engine.<br>Low—Using a crowbar to pry open a box. |
| 16. Chemistry | Knowledge of the composition, structure, and properties of substances and of the chemical processes and transformations that they undergo. This includes uses of chemicals and their interactions, danger signs, production techniques, and disposal methods. | High—Developing a safe commercial cleaner.<br>Low—Using a common household bug spray. |
| 17. Biology | Knowledge of plant and animal living tissue, cells, organisms, and entities, including their functions, interdependencies, and interactions with each other and the environment. | High—Isolating and identifying a microscopic virus.<br>Low—Feeding domestic animals. |
| 18. Psychology | Knowledge of human behavior and performance, mental processes, psychological research methods, and the assessment and treatment of behavioral and affective disorders. | High—Treating a person with a severe mental illness.<br>Low—Monitoring several children on a playground. |
| 19. Sociology and Anthropology | Knowledge of group behavior and dynamics, societal trends and influences, cultures, their history, migrations, ethnicity, and origins. | High—Developing a new theory about the development of early civilizations.<br>Low—Identifying two cultures in a story as being different. |
| 20. Geography | Knowledge of various methods for describing the location and distribution of land, sea, and air masses, including their physical locations, relationships, and characteristics. | High—Developing a map of the world showing mountains, deserts, and rivers.<br>Low—Knowing the capital of the United States. |

Health Services

| Construct label | Operational definition | Level scale |
|---|---|---|
| 21. Medicine and Dentistry | Knowledge of the information and techniques needed to diagnose and treat injuries, diseases, and deformities. This includes symptoms, treatment alternatives, drug properties and interactions, and preventive health-care measures. | High—Performing open-heart surgery.<br>Low—Using a small bandage. |
| 22. Therapy and Counseling | Knowledge of information and techniques needed to rehabilitate physical and mental ailments and to provide career guidance, including alternative treatments, rehabilitation equipment and its proper use, and methods to evaluate treatment effects. | High—Counseling an abused child.<br>Low—Putting ice on a sprained ankle. |

Education and Training

| Construct label | Operational definition | Level scale |
|---|---|---|
| 23. Education and Training | Knowledge of instructional methods and training techniques, including curriculum design principles, learning theory, group and individual teaching techniques, design of individual development plans, and test design principles. | High—Designing a training program for new employees.<br>Low—Showing someone how to bowl. |

Arts and Humanities

| Construct label | Operational definition | Level scale |
|---|---|---|
| 24. English Language | Knowledge of the structure and content of the English language, including the meaning and spelling of words, rules of composition, and grammar. | High—Teaching a college English class.<br>Low—Writing a thank-you note. |

*Table 6-2 continues*

**TABLE 6-2 (Continued)**

| Construct label | Operational definition | Level scale |
|---|---|---|
| *Arts and Humanities* | | |
| 25. Foreign Language | Knowledge of the structure and content of a foreign (non-English) language, including the meaning and spelling of words, rules of composition and grammar, and pronunciation. | High—Providing spoken translation of a political speech while listening to it at an international meeting.<br>Low—Saying "please" and "thank-you" in a foreign language. |
| 26. Fine Arts | Knowledge of theory and techniques required to produce, compose, and perform works of music, dance, visual arts, drama, and sculpture. | High—Composing a symphony.<br>Low—Attending a popular music concert. |
| 27. History and Archaeology | Knowledge of historical events and their causes, indicators, and impact on particular civilizations and cultures. | High—Determining the age of bones for placing them in the fossil history.<br>Low—Taking a class in U.S. history. |
| 28. Philosophy and Theology | Knowledge of different philosophical systems and religions, including their basic principles, values, ethics, ways of thinking, customs, and practices, and their impact on human culture. | High—Comparing the teachings of major philosophers.<br>Low—Watching a TV program on family values. |
| *Law and Public Safety* | | |
| 29. Public Safety and Security | Knowledge of weaponry, public safety, and security operations, rules, regulations, precautions, prevention, and the protection of people, data, and property. | High—Commanding a military operation.<br>Low—Using a seatbelt. |
| 30. Law, Government, and Jurisprudence | Knowledge of law, legal codes, court procedures, precedents, government regulations, executive orders, agency rules, and the democratic political process. | High—Being a judge in a federal court.<br>Low—Registering to vote in a national election. |
| *Communications* | | |
| 31. Telecommunications | Knowledge of transmission, broadcasting, switching, control, and operation of telecommunication systems. | High—Developing a new, worldwide telecommunication network.<br>Low—Dialing a phone. |
| 32. Communications and Media | Knowledge of media production, communication, and dissemination techniques and methods, including alternative ways to inform and entertain via written, oral, and visual media. | High—Producing a combined TV, radio, and newspaper campaign to inform the public about world hunger.<br>Low—Writing a thank-you note. |
| *Transportation* | | |
| 33. Transportation | Knowledge of principles and methods for moving people or goods by air, sea, or road, including their relative costs, advantages, and limitations. | High—Controlling air traffic at a major airport.<br>Low—Taking a train to work. |

placement. In cases in which new task anchors were added to the scales, the precise scale values of all existing and new task anchors were determined, first by individual ratings and then by group consensus.

## Identifying and Incorporating Specialty Areas into the Knowledge Rating Scales

The final step in refinement of the knowledge rating scales was designed to allow raters to identify their specialties within each of the 33 knowledges, without placing an undue burden on the raters. This step relied heavily on NOICC's current work in grouping job demand and institutional supply information as represented by OES occupations and CIP programs.

To identify specialty areas within each of the 33 knowledges, staff generated a crosswalk between NOICC information and O*NET knowledges. For each knowledge area, five research psychologists rated the extent to which the knowledges and the NOICC broad groups were related. For each knowledge, the staff examined all related NOICC broad groups, units of analysis, and their associated demand and supply information. It was from the 244 NOICC units of analysis and related demand and supply information that representative specialty areas were derived. The goal was to generate between 2 and 10 specialty areas within each knowledge.

The result of this exercise was a set of 214 specialty areas arrayed across the 33 knowledges. Specialty area information is obtained only for those knowledges that apply to incumbents' jobs. When a given knowledge is deemed not applicable to a job, no specialty area ratings are required.

Figure 6-1 shows an example of the final knowledge rating scales. These rating scales ask the respondent to answer three questions for each knowledge. First, using a 7 point scale, "What level of this knowledge do I need to perform this job?" If the knowledge is not relevant (NR) at all for performance on the job, then the rater moves to the next knowledge. Second, if the knowledge is relevant for performance on the job, the rater is asked, using a 5 point scale, "How important is this knowledge to performance on this job?" Third, the rater selects the relevant specialty areas.

In revising the scales, improvements were pursued while trying to maintain the integrity of the original development process. In addition to revising the knowledge scale content, the editing process increased the scales' clarity and made the reading level more appropriate for incumbents whose jobs require less demanding reading levels and cognitive skills. All scale anchors were checked and, if necessary, replaced to make them less esoteric and more readily identifiable by different incumbent populations. Other anchors were reviewed to ensure that they reflected sufficient amounts of the knowledge required and did not appear trivial to job incumbents. This completed the revision and modification process of the Knowledge Requirements Scales for use in the O*NET data collection. Each knowledge requirement scale (consisting of the knowledge, its definition, three to four task anchors, and high and low clarification statements) was included in the packet administered to incumbents in a sampling of 80 occupations.

## THE SAMPLE

Two sets of judges provided ratings on the knowledges for a variety of occupations. (See chap. 4 for a detailed description of the sampling procedures.) The first sample of raters included job incumbents from 80 occupations. Because of the desire for reliability and stability of the ratings, only occupations for which at least four incumbents provided ratings were used in the analyses. This criterion resulted in a final sample of 645 incumbents from 32 occupations (listed in Table 6-3). It is important to note that these incumbent ratings served as the primary data for subsequent analyses.

The second set of judges consisted of occupational analysts provided by the OAFCs. In this sample, at least six analysts rated the knowledge requirements for each of the 80 occupations. Because of the smaller number of occupations represented in the incumbent sample, however, analyses for the analysts were carried out only on the 32 occupations included in both samples. The data from job analysts were used in later analyses to compare incumbent ratings with analyst ratings.

## RESULTS

### Descriptive Statistics

Table 6-4 presents the means, standard deviations, standard errors of measurement, and intraclass correlations for incumbents' ratings on both the Level and Importance scales for the 33 knowledges. This information helps to address two key issues: (a) the scales' ability to assess a broad range of knowledges required by the diverse sample of occupations and (b) the reliability of the knowledge scale ratings.

Concerning the first issue, the means and standard deviations suggest that, in fact, the knowledge ratings did cover the range of occupational requirements. For example, the knowledges with the highest level ratings, including Clerical (D2; $M = 3.30$), English Language (D24; $M = 3.18$), and Mathematics (D14; $M = 2.93$), are all more general knowledge areas that apply to a wide variety of government or public service jobs. On the other hand, the knowledges receiving the lowest ratings—for example, Fine Arts (D26; $M = .58$) and Food Production (D8; $M = .68$)—are more esoteric knowledge areas that apply to only a few specific occupations. Furthermore, we see from the fairly high standard deviations that there was a wide range of responses, as we would expect given the diversity of the 32 occupations represented. In fact, the average standard deviation was almost 2.0 for level and over 1.0 for importance. These results provide evidence that the knowledge scales were acting as intended; that is, they tap relatively domain-specific knowledge areas that might help better differentiate among occupations.

### Reliabilities

Table 6-4 provides evidence for the reliability of the ratings. In general, high agreement was found among the job incumbents across occupations. The majority of the reliabilities for level and for importance were above .80, and those that exhibited unusually low reliabilities had the lowest mean ratings. Given these relatively high overall reliabilities, it is not surprising that the standard error of measurement results were reasonable, with almost all being below 1.0 for level ratings and .75 for importance ratings.

#### Effect of Number of Raters

The coefficients in Table 6-4 were based on an average of approximately 20 raters; that number of raters seemed to provide acceptable reliability. However, it is reasonable to assume that in some cases there may be fewer or many more raters available. Accordingly, reliability estimates were calculated for 1 rater and 30 raters. These results are consistent with the reliabilities previously observed in Table 6-4. Single-rater reliabilities are mostly in the .20s and .30s, whereas the 30-rater reliabilities are consistently in the .80s and .90s. These reliabilities indicate that, for

## 1. Administration and Management

Knowledge of planning, coordination, and execution of business functions, resource allocation, and production.

### Level

What level of this knowledge is needed to perform this job?

| | Requires knowledge of high-level business administration such as being the CEO of a major industrial company. |

7

6 ← *Manage a $10 million company.*

5 ← *Administer a large retirement and nursing care facility.*

← *Monitor progress of a project to ensure timely completion.*

4

3

← *Plan an effective staff meeting.*

2 ← *Sign a pay voucher.*

| Requires knowledge of basic management such as monitoring a group filling out job applications. |

1

**NR** Not relevant at all for performance on this job.

### Importance

How important is this knowledge to performance on this job?

| Not Important | Somewhat Important | Important | Very Important | Extremely Important |
|---|---|---|---|---|
| 1 | 2 | 3 | 4 | 5 |

### Job Specialty Requirements

Which of the following specialties are relevant to this job?  (Mark "R" for Relevant and "NR" for Not Relevant.)

R  NR  Business Administration

R  NR  Construction Management

R  NR  Engineering, Mathematical, and Sciences Management

R  NR  Food Service and Lodging Management

R  NR  Medical Service Management

R  NR  Personnel and Human Resource Management

R  NR  Public Administration

Other(s) _____

(Please specify)

**FIGURE 6-1.** Example page from the Knowledges Questionnaire.

**TABLE 6-3**
**Thirty-Two Occupations With Four or More Incumbents Completing the Knowledges Questionnaire**

| Occupation code | Occupation title | Number of respondents |
|---|---|---|
| 15005 | Education Administrators | 8 |
| 19005 | General Managers & Top Executives | 50 |
| 22114 | Chemical Engineers | 4 |
| 25105 | Computer Programmers | 9 |
| 27311 | Recreation Workers | 6 |
| 31303 | Teachers, Preschool | 5 |
| 31305 | Teachers, Elementary School | 7 |
| 32502 | Registered Nurses | 22 |
| 32902 | Medical & Clinical Laboratory Technologists | 4 |
| 49008 | Salespersons, Except Scientific & Retail | 11 |
| 49011 | Salespersons, Retail | 20 |
| 49021 | Stock Clerks, Sales Floor | 9 |
| 49023 | Cashiers | 23 |
| 51002 | First Line Supervisors, Clerical/Administrative | 58 |
| 53905 | Teachers' Aides & Assistants, Clerical | 4 |
| 55108 | Secretaries | 83 |
| 55305 | Receptionists & Information Clerks | 13 |
| 55338 | Bookkeeping, Accounting, & Auditing Clerks | 28 |
| 55347 | General Office Clerks | 83 |
| 61005 | Police & Detective Supervisors | 12 |
| 63014 | Police Patrol Officers | 19 |
| 65008 | Waiters & Waitresses | 14 |
| 65026 | Cooks, Restaurant | 6 |
| 65038 | Food Preparation Workers | 32 |
| 66008 | Nursing Aides, Orderlies, & Attendants | 18 |
| 67005 | Janitors & Cleaners | 26 |
| 85119 | Other Machinery Maintenance Mechs | 4 |
| 85132 | Maintenance Repairers, General Utility | 36 |
| 87902 | Earth Drillers, Except Oil & Gas | 5 |
| 92974 | Packaging & Filling Machine Operators | 10 |
| 97102 | Truck Drivers | 7 |
| 97111 | Bus Drivers, Schools | 9 |

the knowledge scales, one rater is not enough, 10–15 are sufficient, and 30 are plenty.

### Comparison of Level and Importance Scales

The final reliability issue was whether the Level and Importance scales had substantially different or nearly the same reliabilities. Analyses of variance and subsequent correlational analyses suggested that, across all occupations and knowledges, reliability was similar for both level and importance ratings ($r_k$ = .85 and .86, respectively). Furthermore, mean correlations between the two scales were substantial: .95 for descriptors across occupations and .90 for occupations across descriptors. This suggests that, as has been found elsewhere in the job analysis literature, the level and importance ratings are highly redundant. Accordingly, we only focus on the level data in the remainder of the analyses, although some of the findings for the importance ratings are also referenced when appropriate.

### Factor Structure

Discussion of the general descriptive nature of the ratings and their reliabilities provided validation evidence for the knowledges' comprehensiveness, reli-

ability, and ability to differentiate between jobs. The discussion in this section focuses on whether the relationships among the knowledges can provide useful information and increase understanding about the occupations rated. A series of analyses was undertaken to explore these relationships and to better understand the knowledges and their ability to describe jobs.

Correlations were calculated among the knowledges on the Level scale at the occupational level. The results show that certain knowledges were, as expected, highly correlated with other knowledges in their a priori cluster (i.e., the superordinate groupings shown in Table 6-2). For example, Administration and Management (D1) was highly correlated with the other knowledges in its a priori "Business and Management cluster," which also includes Economics and Accounting (D3; $r$ = .66 ) and Personnel and Human Resources (D6; $r$ = .85). In addition, Administration and Management (D1) was positively correlated with other conceptually related areas, such as English Language (D24; $r$ = .74), that are necessary for managerial communication, and Legal, Government, and Jurisprudence (D30; $r$ = .52). In the Engineering and Technology cluster, the Engineering and Technology (D10) knowledge was highly correlated with Design (D11; $r$ = .80), Building and Construction (D12; $r$ =

**TABLE 6-4**

**Descriptive Statistics Across All Occupations and Reliability Estimates for Rated Differences Between Occupations: Knowledges**

| | Variable | | | | | | | |
| | Level | | | | Importance | | | |
| Descriptor | $M$ | $SD$ | $SEM^a$ | $r_k^b$ | $M$ | $SD$ | $SEM$ | $r_k$ |
|---|---|---|---|---|---|---|---|---|
| 1. Administration and Management | 2.35 | 2.16 | .76 | .88 | 2.51 | 1.45 | .50 | .87 |
| 2. Clerical | 3.30 | 2.55 | .57 | .95 | 2.83 | 1.45 | .37 | .93 |
| 3. Economics and Accounting | 1.82 | 2.21 | .87 | .84 | 2.09 | 1.33 | .54 | .83 |
| 4. Sales and Marketing | 1.41 | 2.10 | .75 | .87 | 1.81 | 1.22 | .42 | .87 |
| 5. Customer and Personal Services | 2.75 | 2.48 | 1.11 | .80 | 2.63 | 1.47 | .71 | .76 |
| 6. Personnel and HR | 2.17 | 2.25 | .95 | .82 | 2.27 | 1.36 | .61 | .79 |
| 7. Production and Processing | 1.21 | 2.08 | 1.13 | .70 | 1.64 | 1.13 | .60 | .71 |
| 8. Food Production | .68 | 1.70 | 1.15 | .54 | 1.35 | .88 | .49 | .68 |
| 9. Computers and Electronics | 2.43 | 2.06 | .85 | .83 | 2.50 | 1.36 | .53 | .84 |
| 10. Engineering and Technology | 1.10 | 2.00 | .98 | .76 | 1.57 | 1.07 | .49 | .78 |
| 11. Design | 1.14 | 2.03 | 1.22 | .63 | 1.56 | 1.06 | .66 | .60 |
| 12. Building and Construction | 1.06 | 2.09 | .90 | .81 | 1.53 | 1.08 | .43 | .84 |
| 13. Mechanical | 1.21 | 2.04 | .79 | .85 | 1.60 | 1.06 | .73 | .87 |
| 14. Mathematics | 2.93 | 1.82 | .76 | .82 | 2.82 | 1.14 | .51 | .79 |
| 15. Physics | .91 | 1.82 | .91 | .75 | 1.46 | .95 | .44 | .78 |
| 16. Chemistry | 1.21 | 2.00 | .82 | .83 | 1.66 | 1.13 | .46 | .83 |
| 17. Biology | .87 | 1.92 | .84 | .81 | 1.44 | 1.02 | .41 | .83 |
| 18. Psychology | 2.49 | 2.38 | .84 | .88 | 2.35 | 1.36 | .51 | .85 |
| 19. Sociology and Anthropology | 1.22 | 1.89 | .79 | .82 | 1.60 | 1.01 | .42 | .82 |
| 20. Geography | 1.31 | 1.98 | 1.22 | .62 | 1.65 | 1.04 | .62 | .64 |
| 21. Medicine and Dentistry | 1.17 | 2.02 | .86 | .82 | 1.73 | 1.27 | .46 | .86 |
| 22. Therapy and Counseling | 1.39 | 2.13 | .82 | .85 | 1.77 | 1.20 | .46 | .84 |
| 23. Education and Training | 2.30 | 2.31 | 1.00 | .81 | 2.23 | 1.28 | .55 | .81 |
| 24. English Language | 3.18 | 2.01 | .78 | .85 | 2.98 | 1.23 | .53 | .81 |
| 25. Foreign Language | .86 | 1.71 | 1.36 | .37 | 1.41 | .84 | .63 | .43 |
| 26. Fine Arts | .58 | 1.52 | 1.04 | .53 | 1.28 | .75 | .45 | .63 |
| 27. History and Archaeology | .71 | 1.61 | .92 | .67 | 1.35 | .86 | .45 | .72 |
| 28. Philosophy and Theology | .99 | 1.75 | .87 | .75 | 1.49 | .93 | .45 | .76 |
| 29. Public Safety and Security | 1.71 | 2.11 | .76 | .87 | 2.10 | 1.35 | .54 | .83 |
| 30. Law, Government, and Jurisprudence | 1.54 | 2.05 | .82 | .84 | 1.90 | 1.24 | .49 | .84 |
| 31. Telecommunications | 1.42 | 1.73 | 1.25 | .47 | 2.08 | 1.15 | .77 | .55 |
| 32. Communications and Media | 1.72 | 1.88 | 1.06 | .68 | 2.00 | 1.13 | .70 | .61 |
| 33. Transportation | 1.02 | 1.67 | 1.00 | .64 | 1.57 | .97 | .57 | .65 |

*Note.* Statistics are based on 32 occupations with Knowledges Questionnaire responses from at least 4 incumbents (mean number of incumbents = 19.66, $Mdn$ = 11.00, harmonic mean = 9.18). ᵃThis estimate of the standard error of measurement was calculated as $SEM = SD*\sqrt{(1 - r_k)}$. ᵇThis estimate of reliability was obtained by calculating the intraclass correlation for $k$ ratings across occupations: $ICC(1, k) = [BMS - WMS]/BMS$ (Shrout & Fleiss, 1979), where $k$ is the harmonic mean of the number of ratings provided on each occupation.

.75), Mechanical (D13; $r = .65$), and Mathematics (D14; $r = .59$). Several other groupings emerged, including one representing the Arts and Humanities cluster. In this cluster, Foreign Language (D25) and Fine Arts (D26) were highly related ($r = .76$), as were English Language (D24) and Philosophy and Theology (D28; $r = .69$). Overall, the Level scale correlations seemed to support the a priori clusters that group related knowledges together. It is worth noting that the Importance scale correlations were less systematic, although there were similar patterns of correlations, especially in the Engineering and Technology cluster and the Math and Science cluster.

The next step was to conduct a principal-components analysis of the knowledge-level scales. The knowledges were factored using a varimax rotation. The resulting scree plot and eigenvalues suggested that seven components/factors should be retained. These are shown in Table 6-5. Although there were fewer factors than a priori clusters, the final components were very clean and interpretable. Factor 1

accounted for 35% of the total variance and was marked by Geography (D20; $r = .89$), Fine Arts (D26; $r = .86$), History and Archeology (D27; $r = .84$), Foreign Language (D25; $r = .75$), and English Language (D24; $r = .55$), among others. Accordingly, it was called *Arts and Humanities*. Factor 2 (accounting for 16% of the variance) was equally identifiable and was termed *Science and Technology* by virtue of high loadings on Mechanical (D13; $r = .94$), Engineering and Technology (D10; $r = .92$), Building and Construction (D12; $r = .92$), Design (D11; $r = .89$), Physics (D15; $r = .74$), Chemistry (D16; $r = .64$), and several other related knowledge areas. The principal knowledges for Factor 3 were Public Safety and Security (D29; $r = .86$) and Law, Government, and Jurisprudence (D30; $r = .86$). This factor was termed the *Law Enforcement* factor and accounted for approximately 11% of the variance. Additionally, several other knowledges that might reasonably be expected to contribute to law enforcement also showed high loadings. These included elements of law enforcement work

**TABLE 6-5**
**Principal-Components Analysis Pattern Matrix for the Level Scale: Knowledges**

| Descriptor | F1 | F2 | F3 | F4 | F5 | F6 | F7 | Communality |
|---|---|---|---|---|---|---|---|---|
| 1. Administration and Management | .21 | .34 | .40 | .56 | .05 | .50 | .02 | .88 |
| 2. Clerical | .06 | −.16 | .02 | .82 | −.04 | .04 | .19 | .73 |
| 3. Economics and Accounting | .09 | .30 | .14 | .50 | −.25 | .58 | −.01 | .76 |
| 4. Sales and Marketing | .02 | .02 | −.05 | −.00 | .02 | .95 | .07 | .91 |
| 5. Customer and Personal Services | .22 | −.39 | .12 | .18 | .23 | .71 | −.00 | .80 |
| 6. Personnel and HR | .14 | .12 | .46 | .51 | .14 | .55 | −.20 | .87 |
| 7. Production and Processing | .02 | .75 | .04 | .14 | .02 | .12 | −.28 | .67 |
| 8. Food Production | .36 | .27 | −.09 | −.14 | −.09 | −.00 | −.78 | .84 |
| 9. Computers and Electronics | .02 | .26 | .06 | .56 | .04 | .03 | .66 | .82 |
| 10. Engineering and Technology | −.11 | .92 | .10 | .11 | .13 | −.16 | .13 | .94 |
| 11. Design | .14 | .89 | .10 | .10 | −.17 | .03 | .08 | .87 |
| 12. Building and Construction | .19 | .92 | .03 | −.13 | −.06 | .12 | −.04 | .91 |
| 13. Mechanical | .03 | .94 | .04 | −.09 | .18 | −.01 | −.06 | .92 |
| 14. Mathematics | .09 | .53 | .02 | .46 | .28 | .29 | .46 | .87 |
| 15. Physics | .33 | .74 | .05 | .08 | .43 | −.20 | .04 | .89 |
| 16. Chemistry | .01 | .64 | .12 | −.01 | .72 | −.05 | .14 | .96 |
| 17. Biology | .19 | −.04 | .02 | .09 | .95 | .00 | .02 | .94 |
| 18. Psychology | .41 | −.02 | .68 | .21 | .29 | .17 | .21 | .83 |
| 19. Sociology and Anthropology | .68 | −.01 | .63 | .20 | .11 | .14 | .06 | .93 |
| 20. Geography | .89 | .03 | .16 | .05 | −.00 | .01 | .22 | .86 |
| 21. Medicine and Dentistry | .13 | .10 | .29 | −.11 | .81 | .15 | −.00 | .80 |
| 22. Therapy and Counseling | .76 | −.02 | .44 | .10 | .13 | .11 | −.27 | .88 |
| 23. Education and Training | .51 | .10 | .36 | .42 | .46 | .21 | −.04 | .82 |
| 24. English Language | .55 | .03 | .37 | .68 | .05 | .12 | .01 | .91 |
| 25. Foreign Language | .75 | .14 | .26 | −.03 | −.03 | .19 | −.39 | .83 |
| 26. Fine Arts | .86 | .11 | −.11 | .14 | .10 | .04 | −.34 | .92 |
| 27. History and Archaeology | .84 | .16 | .15 | .13 | .27 | −.12 | .18 | .89 |
| 28. Philosophy and Theology | .66 | .01 | .60 | .10 | .20 | .25 | −.02 | .91 |
| 29. Public Safety and Security | .22 | .22 | .86 | −.00 | .01 | −.13 | −.14 | .88 |
| 30. Law, Government, & Jurisprudence | .16 | .10 | .86 | .18 | .16 | .08 | .25 | .90 |
| 31. Telecommunications | .35 | .50 | .34 | −.09 | −.25 | .07 | .46 | .77 |
| 32. Communications and Media | .59 | .11 | .36 | .46 | .17 | .23 | .35 | .90 |
| 33. Transportation | .46 | .32 | .15 | −.05 | .01 | .13 | −.25 | .42 |
| % of variance | 35 | 16 | 11 | 8 | 6 | 5 | 3 | |
| Eigenvalue | 11.71 | 5.32 | 3.57 | 2.70 | 2.12 | 1.65 | 1.09 | |

*Note.* N = 32. The correlation matrix was based on means calculated at the occupational level. F1 = Arts & Humanities, F2 = Science & Technology, F3 = Law Enforcement, F4 = Clerical, F5 = Medicine, F6 = Business Administration, F7 = High Technology. These loadings are based on an orthogonal varimax rotation.

such as Sociology and Anthropology (D19; $r$ = .63), Psychology (D18; $r$ = .68), and Therapy and Counseling (D22; $r$ = .44). These principal-components analysis findings preview the findings reported later regarding the mean level ratings for certain knowledges among police patrol officers (see Table 6-6).

Factor 4 (accounting for 8% of the variance) was a *Clerical* factor and was marked by high loadings for Clerical (D2; $r$ = .82), English Language (D24; $r$ = .68), Computers and Electronics (D9; $r$ = .56), and Administration and Management (D1; $r$ = .56)—all of which are relevant to various aspects of clerical (D2) work. Factor 5, accounting for 6% of the variance, was also clearly identifiable as a *Medical* factor by its markers, which included Biology (D17; $r$ = .95), Medicine and Dentistry (D21; $r$ = .81), and Chemistry (D16; $r$ = .72). Of interest is that Education and Training (D23) also loaded relatively highly on Factor 5 ($r$ = .46), suggesting that the medical personnel surveyed may have had some educational responsibilities as part of their jobs. Factor 6 (accounting for 5% of the variance) was similar to Factor 4, except that it seemed to represent broader ar-

eas of administrative and managerial activities and therefore was named *Business Administration*. Factor 6 knowledge areas included Sales and Marketing (D4; $r$ = .95), Customer and Personal Service (D5; $r$ = .71), Economics and Accounting (D3; $r$ = .58), Personnel and Human Resources (D6; $r$ = .55), and Administration and Management (D1; $r$ = .50). The final factor, Factor 7, was a little unusual. It had one very high positive loading—Computers and Electronics (D9; $r$ = .66)—and one very high negative loading—Food Production (D8; $r$ = −.78). Despite changes in technology, Food Production (D8)—the growing, producing, and preparation of food—remains a relatively "low-tech" domain, populated by many traditional, manual, or mechanical processes. Thus, as a knowledge area, Food Production (D8) can be seen as rather opposite to the high-tech areas of Computers and Electronics (D9). For this reason, Factor 7, which accounted for 3% of the variance, was named *High Technology*. In sum, the seven factors were able to account for 84% of the variance and produced clear and identifiable factors to describe the occupations of interest.

## Job Differences

As noted above, the knowledges were designed to be relatively domain specific. Therefore, by examining the descriptive statistics for specific occupations (as opposed to the averaged results in Table 6-4), we should begin to see differentiation. In this regard, the results presented in Table 6-6 are most interesting. Means and standard deviations were calculated on the Level scale for six sample occupations; these included (a) General Managers and Top Executives, (b) Computer Programmers, (c) Registered Nurses, (d) Police Patrol Officers, (e) Janitors and Cleaners, and (f) Maintenance Repairers, General Utility. The results shown in Table 6-6 support the specificity of the knowledge scales. For example, the knowledge area Administration and Management (D1) showed the expected high mean for General Managers and Top Executives ($M = 4.84$) and a low mean for Janitors and Cleaners ($M = .88$). General Managers' and Top Executives' jobs were also rated higher on knowledge requirements such as Personnel and Human Re-

sources (D6; $M = 4.52$), Customer and Personal Service (D5; $M = 4.66$), Psychology (D18; $M = 4.28$), Mathematics (D14; $M = 4.08$), Economics and Accounting (D3; $M = 3.94$), and English Language (D24; $M = 4.20$). However, General Managers' and Top Executives' jobs were rated low on the level of knowledge required for History and Archeology (D27; $M = 1.00$), Fine Arts (D26; $M = .50$), and Food Production (D8; $M = .54$)—knowledge areas that most managers would be unlikely to need.

Computer Programmers rated high in the knowledge requirements one might expect, with Computers and Electronics (D9) receiving the highest rating ($M = 6.56$) and no other job receiving a rating on this descriptor greater than 3.18. The Mathematics (D14) requirement rating was also highest ($M = 4.67$) for this job. Computers and Electronics (D9) knowledge requirements were rated low for Maintenance Repairers, General Utility ($M = 1.61$) and for Janitors and Cleaners ($M = 1.08$). Registered nurses showed an expected pattern, with incumbents in these positions rating the knowledge level require-

**TABLE 6-6**
**Descriptor Means and Standard Deviations on the Level Scale on Six Example Occupations: Knowledges**

| | Occupations | | | | | | | | | | | |
|---|---|---|---|---|---|---|---|---|---|---|---|---|
| | General Managers & Top Executives ($n = 50$) | | Computer Programmers ($n = 9$) | | Registered Nurses ($n = 22$) | | Police Patrol Officers ($n = 19$) | | Janitors & Cleaners[a] ($n = 26$) | | Maintenance Repairers, General Utility ($n = 36$) | |
| Descriptor | M | SD | M | SD | M | SD | M | SD | M | SD | M | SD |
| 1. Administration and Management | 4.84 | 1.27 | 3.33 | 1.32 | 2.68 | 1.52 | 2.05 | 1.99 | .88 | 1.95 | 1.89 | 2.11 |
| 2. Clerical | 3.16 | 2.24 | 2.89 | 2.26 | 2.68 | 1.99 | 2.68 | 1.63 | 1.19 | 2.04 | 1.42 | 1.84 |
| 3. Economics and Accounting | 3.94 | 2.10 | .33 | 1.00 | 1.00 | 1.66 | .84 | 1.57 | .96 | 2.07 | 1.06 | 1.82 |
| 4. Sales and Marketing | 3.31 | 2.25 | 1.56 | 1.33 | 1.86 | 2.05 | .47 | 1.22 | 1.00 | 2.12 | .81 | 1.69 |
| 5. Customer and Personal Services | 4.66 | 2.05 | 1.89 | 1.27 | 3.18 | 2.91 | 3.74 | 2.84 | 1.35 | 1.96 | 1.44 | 1.95 |
| 6. Personnel and HR | 4.52 | 1.53 | 1.44 | 1.59 | 2.36 | 2.13 | 2.21 | 2.35 | 1.32 | 2.11 | 1.92 | 2.32 |
| 7. Production and Processing | 2.12 | 2.34 | .33 | .71 | 1.00 | 1.93 | .58 | 1.43 | .50 | 1.53 | 1.53 | 2.22 |
| 8. Food Production | .54 | 1.39 | .00 | .00 | .73 | 1.80 | .37 | 1.12 | 1.08 | 2.35 | 1.42 | 2.41 |
| 9. Computers and Electronics | 3.18 | 1.69 | 6.56 | .73 | 2.82 | 1.84 | 2.94 | 1.99 | 1.08 | 2.08 | 1.61 | 1.84 |
| 10. Engineering and Technology | 1.88 | 2.24 | 2.33 | 2.40 | 1.18 | 2.06 | .89 | 1.33 | 1.15 | 1.89 | 2.80 | 2.35 |
| 11. Design | 2.12 | 2.34 | 2.00 | 2.87 | 1.09 | 2.16 | 1.05 | 1.39 | 1.77 | 2.69 | 2.72 | 2.41 |
| 12. Building and Construction | 1.56 | 2.23 | .00 | .00 | 1.14 | 2.21 | .32 | 1.00 | 1.76 | 2.61 | 3.86 | 2.15 |
| 13. Mechanical | 1.94 | 2.31 | .44 | 1.01 | 1.05 | 1.84 | .89 | 1.41 | 1.96 | 2.39 | 4.31 | 2.11 |
| 14. Mathematics | 4.08 | 1.12 | 4.67 | 1.22 | 3.55 | 1.14 | 2.32 | 1.34 | 1.69 | 2.29 | 2.58 | 1.98 |
| 15. Physics | 1.34 | 2.02 | .44 | .88 | 1.50 | 2.11 | .94 | 1.08 | .65 | 1.57 | 2.42 | 2.17 |
| 16. Chemistry | 1.82 | 2.17 | .11 | .33 | 3.18 | 2.17 | .95 | 1.31 | 1.60 | 2.08 | 2.56 | 2.21 |
| 17. Biology | 1.34 | 2.18 | .00 | .00 | 3.68 | 2.75 | .58 | 1.07 | .92 | 2.15 | .91 | 1.92 |
| 18. Psychology | 4.28 | 2.24 | 1.44 | 1.88 | 5.77 | .87 | 4.68 | 1.49 | 1.23 | 2.29 | 1.67 | 2.14 |
| 19. Sociology and Anthropology | 2.52 | 2.21 | .67 | 1.12 | 3.09 | 2.16 | 2.68 | 1.57 | .73 | 1.66 | .75 | 1.65 |
| 20. Geography | 2.16 | 2.26 | .56 | 1.13 | 1.59 | 2.40 | 2.11 | 1.45 | 1.15 | 2.44 | .89 | 2.07 |
| 21. Medicine and Dentistry | 1.40 | 2.20 | .11 | .33 | 4.91 | 1.06 | 1.47 | 1.22 | 1.19 | 2.42 | 1.31 | 2.04 |
| 22. Therapy and Counseling | 2.62 | 2.30 | .33 | .71 | 4.50 | 1.41 | 1.89 | 1.66 | 1.08 | 2.28 | 1.28 | 1.99 |
| 23. Education and Training | 3.72 | 2.04 | 2.33 | 2.12 | 4.05 | 2.26 | 2.84 | 2.06 | 1.88 | 2.45 | 2.33 | 2.41 |
| 24. English Language | 4.20 | 1.18 | 4.22 | .83 | 4.36 | 1.59 | 4.05 | 1.22 | 2.12 | 2.36 | 2.08 | 1.87 |
| 25. Foreign Language | 1.57 | 1.95 | .44 | 1.01 | 1.41 | 2.17 | 1.42 | 1.43 | .96 | 2.09 | .83 | 1.96 |
| 26. Fine Arts | .50 | 1.39 | .22 | .67 | 1.32 | 2.15 | .00 | .00 | 1.00 | 2.08 | .81 | 1.94 |
| 27. History and Archaeology | 1.00 | 1.80 | .22 | .67 | 1.45 | 2.06 | .63 | 1.16 | .62 | 1.77 | 1.06 | 2.00 |
| 28. Philosophy and Theology | 1.72 | 1.93 | .00 | .00 | 3.23 | 2.02 | 1.89 | 1.91 | .65 | 1.62 | .94 | 1.72 |
| 29. Public Safety and Security | 2.04 | 2.13 | .22 | .44 | 2.23 | 2.33 | 5.79 | .79 | 1.85 | 2.13 | 2.67 | 2.04 |
| 30. Law, Government, and Jurisprudence | 2.78 | 1.89 | .00 | .00 | 2.59 | 2.22 | 5.00 | 1.11 | 1.27 | 2.44 | 1.11 | 1.95 |
| 31. Telecommunications | 1.96 | 1.96 | 2.22 | 2.33 | 1.82 | 1.89 | 2.21 | 1.13 | 1.42 | 2.52 | 1.67 | 1.93 |
| 32. Communications and Media | 2.86 | 1.81 | 1.89 | 1.54 | 2.91 | 2.14 | 1.74 | 1.63 | .64 | 1.38 | 1.42 | 2.03 |
| 33. Transportation | 1.72 | 1.74 | .56 | 1.13 | 1.77 | 2.25 | 1.11 | 1.49 | .92 | 2.06 | 1.21 | 1.86 |

[a]The full title for this occupation is "Janitors and Cleaners, except Maids and Housekeeping."

ments of Medicine and Dentistry (D21; $M = 4.91$), Psychology (D18; $M = 5.77$), and Therapy and Counseling (D22; $M = 4.50$), English Language (D24; $M = 4.36$), and Education and Training (D23; $M = 4.05$) the highest. Of interest is that Police Patrol Officers also rated the requirements for Psychology (D18; $M = 4.68$) and English Language (D24; $M = 4.05$) very high. As expected, the Officers also gave very high ratings for the levels of Public Safety and Security (D29; $M = 5.79$) and Law, Government, and Jurisprudence (D30; $M = 5.00$) needed. These ratings reflect the primary activities of Police Patrol Officers in enforcing the law and in mediating disputes and handling difficult, tense, and dangerous situations.

The Janitors' and Cleaners' ratings were characterized by low ratings on almost all of the knowledges, including Design (D11; $M = 1.77$), Mechanical (D13; $M = 1.96$), and English Language (D24; $M = 2.12$), although the standard deviations were generally a bit higher than for the other example occupations. Maintenance Repairers, General Utility rated what was apparently the most relevant knowledge, Mechanical (D13; $M = 4.31$), highest and gave moderate ratings for Building and Construction (D12; $M = 3.86$), Design (D11; $M = 2.72$), and Engineering and Technology (D10; $M = 2.80$). As with the overall ratings shown in Table 6-4, certain knowledges were rated very low by all six example jobs, reflecting the relative rarity of these knowledge requirements among the sample occupations studied. These knowledges included areas such as Food Production (D8), Fine Arts (D26), and History and Archeology (D27). The results for the importance ratings, although not presented here, are generally consistent with those obtained from the Level scale. This is to be expected given the high correlation between the two scale types.

## Incumbent–Analyst Comparisons

Having both analysts and job incumbents complete the survey allowed us to make comparisons between two types of raters. Points of convergence between data sources had the potential of providing additional evidence for the validity of the ratings. Accordingly, we ran a series of analyses that compared the incumbents' and analysts' ratings of the 32 overlapping jobs.

Overall, the results of the analyst and incumbent analyses led to similar conclusions about the occupations represented and their knowledge requirements. Most important, the analysts and the incumbents generally agreed in their knowledge ratings. This finding is encouraging in that descriptive information about the jobs was obtainable through two independent sources of ratings. The average correlation across knowledges between the analysts' and incumbents' ratings was .65 when either the Level scale or Importance scale was used. This indicates that the two types of raters were in general agreement on the level and importance of the various knowledges

across occupations. Nevertheless, there are several differences and unique findings worth reporting.

Table 6-7 shows a summary of the means, standard deviations, reliabilities, and several comparisons between the two sets of ratings. Several interesting findings emerge. First, the analysts tended to provide somewhat more reliable ratings than the incumbents on the Level scale ($M_{analysts} = .86$ vs. $M_{incum.} = .76$), despite the smaller number of analysts rating the target occupations ($M_{analysts} = 9.81$ vs. $M_{incum.} = 19.66$). Nonetheless, both analysts' and incumbents' reliabilities were sufficiently high given the job analysis context and the number of targets and raters.

The second finding is that there were a number of significant differences in both the mean ratings and the variance of those ratings between the incumbents and analysts. Overall, 20 of the $t$ tests showed significant differences, as did 21 of the $F$ variance tests. Although for the most part the incumbents tended to rate the knowledges higher than did the analysts, there were several scales for which the analysts provided higher ratings. These scales included the levels of Mechanical (D13; $t[971] = -6.51$) and Law, Government, and Jurisprudence (D30; $t[971] = -5.11$) knowledge required. In general, however, the incumbents' ratings tended to be less than one-half a standard deviation higher than the analysts' ratings. Furthermore, the $d^2$ statistics showed that the averaged, absolute mean score difference was generally about 1 point on the 7-point Level scale (using the square root of the mean $d^2$ as the indicator) and about .50 to .75 points on the 5-point Importance scale. This suggests that the incumbents' ratings were inflated as compared with the analysts' ratings (which is not unexpected) but that the actual difference in the ratings was generally rather small.

Next, we did a principal-components analysis on the analysts' data, using the same assumptions and rotation that had been used with the incumbents' data. It was hoped that the comparison between the two solutions would shed further light on the relationship of the ratings provided by these two groups. The results of this analysis are presented in Table 6-8. In general, the two groups' factors were relatively similar except for differences in the order in which the factors appeared. The first analyst factor was termed *General Management*, as it included the Administration and Management (D1) knowledge along with several others. The second analyst factor was a narrower version of the incumbents' science and technology factor, here called *Engineering*. Analyst Factor 3 continued the "not quite the same" trend with a broader version of the incumbents' medical factor. This grouping was called *Allied Health Services*. Analyst Factor 4 was very similar to the arts and humanities incumbent factor, and was also called *Arts and Humanities*.

Factor 5 was very similar to the law enforcement incumbent factor (also termed *Law Enforcement* here), with similar markers. This factor was slightly broader than the incumbents' factor and also had no fewer than five other knowledges with loadings

**TABLE 6-7**

**Comparison Between Incumbent and Analyst Descriptive Statistics Across All Occupations and Reliability Estimates for Rated Differences Between Occupations for the Level Scale: Knowledges**

| Descriptor | Incumbent | | | Analyst | | | $t$ | $F$ | $r_{ia}$ | $d^2$ |
|---|---|---|---|---|---|---|---|---|---|---|
| | $M$ | $SD$ | $r_k$ | $M$ | $SD$ | $r_k$ | | | | |
| 1. Administration and Management | 2.35 | 2.16 | .88 | 1.90 | 1.85 | .96 | 3.41* | 1.37 | .69 | 1.43 |
| 2. Clerical | 3.30 | 2.55 | .95 | 2.80 | 1.64 | .94 | 3.71* | 2.43* | .77 | .83 |
| 3. Economics and Accounting | 1.82 | 2.21 | .84 | 1.75 | 1.65 | .96 | .56 | 1.79 | .62 | 1.20 |
| 4. Sales and Marketing | 1.41 | 2.10 | .87 | 1.38 | 1.62 | .94 | .31 | 1.67 | .77 | .82 |
| 5. Customer and Personal Services | 2.75 | 2.48 | .80 | 2.86 | 1.79 | .85 | −.84 | 1.93 | .54 | 1.44 |
| 6. Personnel and HR | 2.17 | 2.25 | .82 | 1.61 | 1.70 | .95 | 4.27* | 1.74 | .61 | 1.34 |
| 7. Production and Processing | 1.21 | 2.08 | .70 | .96 | 1.48 | .85 | 2.18* | 1.97 | .70 | .86 |
| 8. Food Production | .68 | 1.70 | .54 | .37 | .90 | .84 | 3.71* | 3.60* | .33 | .74 |
| 9. Computers and Electronics | 2.43 | 2.06 | .83 | 2.01 | 1.51 | .85 | 3.58* | 1.87 | .81 | .63 |
| 10. Engineering and Technology | 1.10 | 2.00 | .76 | 1.25 | 1.39 | .92 | −1.37 | 2.06* | .84 | .43 |
| 11. Design | 1.14 | 2.03 | .63 | .79 | 1.39 | .84 | 3.15* | 2.12* | .62 | .87 |
| 12. Building and Construction | 1.06 | 2.09 | .81 | .61 | 1.23 | .89 | 4.17* | 2.86* | .63 | 1.28 |
| 13. Mechanical | 1.21 | 2.04 | .85 | 2.03 | 1.73 | .95 | −6.51* | 1.38 | .84 | .96 |
| 14. Mathematics | 2.93 | 1.82 | .82 | 2.52 | 1.26 | .94 | 4.07* | 2.11* | .56 | 1.23 |
| 15. Physics | .91 | 1.82 | .75 | 1.12 | 1.27 | .92 | −2.09* | 2.04* | .79 | .48 |
| 16. Chemistry | 1.21 | 2.00 | .83 | 1.43 | 1.62 | .96 | −1.87 | 1.53 | .75 | 1.00 |
| 17. Biology | .87 | 1.92 | .81 | 1.07 | 1.54 | .96 | −1.72 | 1.55 | .86 | .47 |
| 18. Psychology | 2.49 | 2.38 | .88 | 2.14 | 1.61 | .90 | 2.70* | 2.18* | .71 | 1.08 |
| 19. Sociology and Anthropology | 1.22 | 1.89 | .82 | 1.30 | 1.18 | .86 | −.84 | 2.58* | .78 | .41 |
| 20. Geography | 1.31 | 1.98 | .62 | 1.35 | 1.28 | .88 | −.47 | 2.37* | .61 | .70 |
| 21. Medicine and Dentistry | 1.17 | 2.02 | .82 | 1.11 | 1.35 | .95 | .56 | 2.24* | .79 | .66 |
| 22. Therapy and Counseling | 1.39 | 2.13 | .85 | 1.24 | 1.57 | .88 | 1.27 | 1.83 | .66 | 1.12 |
| 23. Education and Training | 2.30 | 2.31 | .81 | 2.17 | 1.99 | .96 | .94 | 1.35 | .72 | 1.41 |
| 24. English Language | 3.18 | 2.01 | .85 | 2.73 | 1.19 | .95 | 4.37* | 2.86* | .59 | 1.02 |
| 25. Foreign Language | .86 | 1.71 | .37 | .64 | .83 | .77 | 2.72* | 4.23* | .20 | .64 |
| 26. Fine Arts | .58 | 1.52 | .53 | .40 | .87 | .89 | 2.35* | 3.07* | .52 | .58 |
| 27. History and Archaeology | .71 | 1.61 | .67 | .72 | 1.10 | .74 | −.08 | 2.16* | .76 | .36 |
| 28. Philosphy and Theology | .99 | 1.75 | .75 | .70 | .99 | .68 | 3.28* | 3.15* | .63 | .58 |
| 29. Public Safety and Security | 1.71 | 2.11 | .87 | 2.09 | 1.37 | .92 | −3.41* | 2.39* | .79 | .70 |
| 30. Law, Government, and Jurisprudence | 1.54 | 2.05 | .84 | 2.11 | 1.39 | .87 | −5.11* | 2.17* | .70 | .96 |
| 31. Telecommunications | 1.42 | 1.73 | .47 | 1.23 | .96 | .73 | 2.21* | 3.24* | .13 | .79 |
| 32. Communications and Media | 1.72 | 1.88 | .68 | 1.88 | 1.28 | .88 | −1.57 | 2.14* | .58 | .63 |
| 33. Transportation | 1.02 | 1.67 | .64 | 1.30 | 1.35 | .90 | −2.84* | 1.54 | .60 | .72 |

*Note.* Incumbent statistics are based on 32 occupations with Knowledge Questionnaire responses from at least 4 incumbents (mean number of incumbents = 19.66, $Mdn$ = 11, harmonic mean = 9.18). Analyst statistics are based on the same 32 occupations with Knowledge Questionnaire responses from at least 6 analysts (mean number of analysts = 9.81, $Mdn$ = 12, harmonic mean = 8.30). The estimate of reliability was obtained by calculating the intraclass correlation for $k$ ratings across occupations: $ICC(1, k) = [BMS − WMS]/BMS$ (Shrout & Fleiss, 1979), where $k$ is the harmonic mean of the number of ratings provided on each occupation. The $t$ statistic tests for differences in the incumbent and analyst group means. The $F$ statistic tests for differences in the incumbent and analyst group standard deviations. The $r_{ia}$ correlation indicates the degree of relationship between incumbent and analyst mean occupations ratings. The $d^2$ statistic indicates the squared differences between incumbent and analyst mean occupations ratings.
*$p < .05$.

above .30 (the cutoff for inclusion). Factor 6, *High Technology*, was similar to the incumbent factor. The final analyst Factor 7 was termed *Clerical* and was notable for high positive loadings on Clerical (D2; $r$ = .44) and high negative loadings on Building and Construction (D12; $r = −.56$) and Mechanical (D13; $r = −.43$).

These results suggest that the ratings received from the analysts were somewhat less cogent in terms of the relationships among the knowledges for the given set of occupations. For example, many of the analysts' factors were less "clean" than were the incumbents', with sometimes extraneous or only tangentially related knowledges appearing on a factor. Furthermore, the analysts' factor solution showed more loadings below .50 (34 for analysts vs. 26 for incumbents) and more negative loadings (10 for analysts vs. 4 for incumbents). This result suggests that the analysts had a less clear picture of how the

knowledges were related to each other within the given set of occupations. Although the above is only a qualitative assessment, it does provide evidence for the general similarity of the incumbents' and analysts' ratings (i.e., the similar means and factor structures). At the same time, there is some evidence that these two groups differed somewhat in their perceptions of the specific knowledge requirements for the rated occupations. These differences are worthy of further study.

Overall, the conclusion is that the incumbents and analysts produced generally similar ratings and factor structures. Both the descriptive and inferential statistics showed convergence on the highest rated knowledges, reliabilities, and underlying patterns of relationships among the descriptors. These results supporting the validity of the taxonomy are encouraging for the O*NET project as it tries to better and more completely describe occupations.

**TABLE 6-8**
**Principal-Components Analysis Pattern Matrix for the Analyst Level Scale: Knowledges**

| Descriptor | Factor | | | | | | | Communality |
|---|---|---|---|---|---|---|---|---|
| | F1 | F2 | F3 | F4 | F5 | F6 | F7 | |
| 1. Administration and Management | .88 | .10 | .15 | .27 | .14 | .00 | .05 | .89 |
| 2. Clerical | .37 | −.38 | −.08 | −.14 | −.08 | .57 | .44 | .84 |
| 3. Economics and Accounting | .84 | −.04 | −.19 | −.19 | .06 | .12 | .19 | .83 |
| 4. Sales and Marketing | .67 | −.08 | −.36 | .25 | .01 | −.27 | .02 | .71 |
| 5. Customer and Personal Services | .43 | −.58 | .27 | .42 | .23 | −.06 | −.15 | .85 |
| 6. Personnel and HR | .88 | −.09 | .13 | −.04 | .06 | −.07 | −.20 | .85 |
| 7. Production and Processing | .30 | .66 | −.24 | −.19 | .02 | −.46 | .13 | .83 |
| 8. Food Production | .13 | −.13 | −.03 | .14 | −.17 | −.81 | .14 | .75 |
| 9. Computers and Electronics | .40 | .13 | −.06 | .07 | −.32 | .72 | .20 | .85 |
| 10. Engineering and Technology | .00 | .91 | .13 | −.21 | .08 | .05 | −.18 | .94 |
| 11. Design | .17 | .84 | −.16 | .12 | −.10 | .16 | −.02 | .81 |
| 12. Building and Construction | .01 | .56 | −.24 | .03 | −.07 | −.04 | −.57 | .70 |
| 13. Mechanical | −.42 | .65 | .01 | −.33 | .03 | −.03 | −.43 | .88 |
| 14. Mathematics | .71 | .45 | −.07 | .18 | −.18 | .31 | .29 | .94 |
| 15. Physics | −.22 | .92 | .20 | .01 | .13 | −.06 | .00 | .95 |
| 16. Chemistry | −.05 | .66 | .66 | .00 | −.08 | −.09 | .09 | .89 |
| 17. Biology | .04 | .22 | .86 | .18 | −.15 | −.08 | .20 | .89 |
| 18. Psychology | .60 | −.21 | .53 | .39 | .28 | .04 | −.08 | .92 |
| 19. Sociology and Anthropology | .44 | −.15 | .34 | .64 | .44 | .10 | −.09 | .94 |
| 20. Geography | .06 | .07 | .00 | .43 | .82 | .10 | .25 | .94 |
| 21. Medicine and Dentistry | −.03 | −.14 | .95 | .04 | .04 | .08 | −.06 | .93 |
| 22. Therapy and Counseling | .27 | −.14 | .80 | .39 | .14 | .11 | −.07 | .91 |
| 23. Education and Training | .70 | .00 | .28 | .55 | −.02 | .05 | −.11 | .88 |
| 24. English Language | .72 | .00 | .30 | .35 | −.07 | .38 | .22 | .92 |
| 25. Foreign Language | .39 | −.21 | .40 | .49 | .46 | −.17 | .11 | .84 |
| 26. Fine Arts | .04 | −.18 | −.07 | .80 | −.12 | −.26 | −.15 | .79 |
| 27. History and Archaeology | .08 | .07 | .16 | .85 | .15 | .14 | .19 | .83 |
| 28. Philosophy and Theology | .35 | −.06 | .30 | .75 | .33 | .02 | .02 | .88 |
| 29. Public Safety and Security | .27 | .22 | .45 | −.02 | .60 | .03 | −.36 | .81 |
| 30. Law, Government, & Jurisprudence | .66 | .00 | .38 | .06 | .57 | .03 | .08 | .90 |
| 31. Telecommunications | .24 | −.22 | .07 | .12 | .45 | .65 | .06 | .75 |
| 32. Communications and Media | .80 | −.16 | .07 | .29 | .04 | .32 | .10 | .87 |
| 33. Transportation | −.08 | −.02 | −.20 | .01 | .82 | .04 | −.10 | .74 |
| % of variance | 33 | 15 | 13 | 9 | 8 | 6 | 3 | |
| Eigenvalue | 10.83 | 5.10 | 4.20 | 2.79 | 2.53 | 1.89 | 1.07 | |

*Note.* N = 32. The correlation matrix was based on means calculated at the occupational level. F1 = General Management, F2 = Engineering, F3 = Allied Health Services, F4 = Art and Humanities, F5 = Law Enforcement/Public Safety, F6 = High Technology, F7 = Clerical. These loadings are based on an orthogonal varimax rotation.

## DISCUSSION

The results reviewed here suggest that the proposed taxonomy of job-related knowledges is a useful descriptive and interpretative tool for trying to understand and measure the types and levels of knowledges required in a wide variety of occupations. The Knowledge Requirements Taxonomy and measurement system described herein is based on an extension of the ability requirements approach developed by Fleishman and his colleagues (see Fleishman, 1975a, 1975c, 1991a; Fleishman & Mumford, 1991; Fleishman & Quaintance, 1984). This methodology has been used to develop constructs and associated measurement scales exhibiting high reliability, internal validity, and external validity. Creating the knowledge scales began with a review of the cognitive, vocational, training, and job analysis literatures. Knowledge categories were broadened, narrowed, altered, or discarded on the basis of the review, ratings, and comments of many professional psychologists. Task-anchored measurement scales were also developed empirically so that the task anchors represented

different levels of a particular knowledge and had high reliability with regard to their positions on the scales. Special attention was given to making the scales readable, understandable, and "user friendly."

The present study demonstrates that the knowledge scales have high reliabilities when used with job incumbents or with occupational analysts and establishes their utility in describing and understanding worker performance for multiple jobs. As part of the DOL's O*NET, the knowledge taxonomy and measurement system should make an important contribution in the understanding of worker characteristics required to successfully perform a very wide variety of jobs.

## Limitations

Before continuing discussion of the implications of these results, a limitation needs to be mentioned. The approach selected for developing the taxonomy and the measurement system was but one of several possible techniques that could have been selected. As noted above, it has been suggested by colleagues that we might have looked at school curricula as an alternative source for knowledges. We also considered a review and assessment of the job analysis literature, vocational guidance materials, and selection and placement tests. However, in our view, none of these alternatives provided the comprehensiveness and richness of data necessary to adequately capture the broad range of knowledges operative in the world of work.

There also was the possibility of pursuing a more rational approach through the cognitive and expertise literature. Once again, as our purpose was to identify job-relevant knowledges, we felt our approach was more appropriate and efficient toward those ends. It is prudent to recognize that alternate techniques might have produced a slightly different list of knowledges or even levels of specificity. Furthermore, we did not intend to identify any knowledges other than those that are job related. Hence, the knowledges should not be viewed as a comprehensive taxonomy covering all structured information and data that people need to acquire and apply, both within and beyond the world of work. Instead, we encourage follow-up efforts to expand and extend the taxonomy within and beyond the job domain into areas such as family, personal, and social knowledges.

## Evidence of Taxonomy Usefulness

### Interrater Agreement

The findings supply evidence for the reliability of the measures of job-related knowledges covering a wide variety of occupations. Several pieces of information support this conclusion. First, interrater agreement coefficients for the knowledge scales were substantial and more than sufficient, given the number of raters and the diversity of the occupations represented. This interrater agreement was apparent at the discrete knowledge level, across knowledges, across occupations, for both incumbents and analysts, and for both the Level and Importance scales. Such consistency across analyses speaks well for the reliability of the measures.

Second, we revealed substantial agreement between the job incumbents and the job analysts. That both current workers and those with expertise across a variety of jobs would be in such close agreement, both on the level and importance ratings and in the pattern of relationships among the knowledges as represented by the correlations and principal-components analysis, also supports the reliability of the system. To a certain extent, this overall consistency is attributable to the knowledges themselves and to the systematic and empirically driven generation procedures followed for developing the definitions, anchors, and clarification statements used on the measures. Such procedures have, in the past, successfully led to reliable and valid measurement systems in a variety of rating efforts (Fleishman et al., 1995).

### Internal Validity

Turning to the issue of the validity of the taxonomy, we also have a number of findings that support the knowledges' validity. As noted earlier, the convergence between the structure and the discrete knowledge elements of the factors between two independent sets of data provide evidence of the internal validity of the taxonomy. Furthermore, the fact that the principal-components analyses of the data from the incumbent and analyst groups resulted in very similar factors and loadings suggests underlying agreement and consistency in terms of the knowledges and their relationships to each other. The correlational findings that showed reasonable groupings of knowledges around broader domains, such as the "management" and "engineering" groups, also support the internal cohesiveness of the taxonomy.

### Content Validity

The next issue deals with whether we have covered the entire domain of job-related knowledge (i.e., content validity). Here, we feel that the review of the DOT and the crossing of the findings of that review with other existing taxonomies and lists of knowledges has ensured a reasonably complete coverage of the domain of job-relevant knowledges. There is little doubt that the DOT is a comprehensive listing of the jobs present in the current workforce. The fact that every one of the job descriptions therein was reviewed and knowledges extracted suggests that the domain was relatively well covered. Furthermore, the comparison of the taxonomy elements to those represented by the NOICC clustering structure provided additional validity evidence. This effort showed that the taxonomy was able to capture the knowledge areas covered in the NOICC clusters, although some changes were made in the measurement system on the basis of the NOICC findings. In addition, the taxonomy/NOICC linkage provides a mechanism for matching job market demand and institutional supply data gathered by SOICCs with knowledge requirements. The inclusion of occupational specialty data with each rating scale in this study should allow linkage of the knowledges to other national occupational and educational databases as well.

### External Validity

There are several pieces of information that speak to the external validity of the taxonomy. First, the results from previous efforts that used the knowledges (Costanza et al., 1995; Wetrogan et al., 1995) suggest that job-relevant knowledges are predictive of job performance in a wide variety of jobs and are correlated with variables such as education and experience. Second, in terms of the present effort, we found patterns of responses on the knowledges among certain occupations, such as police patrol officers and janitors and cleaners, that support the high level of job-relevant knowledges required to perform the job.

## Summary Statement

The present effort provided a wealth of information in support of the Taxonomy of Knowledges as a reliable, valid, and useful tool in helping to understand and describe a variety of occupations. We see this effort as a further step in developing a knowledge taxonomy and a measurement system that are truly complete and usable. Future efforts should focus on refining and defining the domain and the knowledges themselves, providing additional evidence as to the external validity of the Taxonomy of Knowledges, and expanding its use to a wider pool of jobs, incumbents, and managers. Finally, efforts to tie this taxonomy to both individual and organizational performance would provide valuable information about the taxonomy and its elements.

Overall, the current system was successful in describing, understanding, and classifying occupations in terms of the underlying knowledges needed to perform them. Accordingly, the knowledges, their structure, and the measurement system should prove useful in areas such as job analysis, person–job matching, job training and retraining, career/occupational counseling, vocational interest assessment, and the development of job families. Used in concert with descriptors from other domains of O*NET, the knowledge scales will help us to more completely and accurately describe and understand the world at work. Specifically, they should help researchers and managers to first identify and then train or select for those knowledges that are most important to the work and the job at hand. As part of the DOL's O*NET, the knowledge taxonomy and measurement system made an important contribution to the understanding of worker characteristics required to successfully perform a very wide variety of job tasks.

# Occupational Preparation: Education, Training, Experience, and Licensure/Certification

## LANCE E. ANDERSON

Education, training, experience, and licensure/ certification are all types of information that describe the preparation needed before entering an occupation. Education, training, and experience are commonly recognized as mechanisms for acquiring general knowledge and basic skills (Halpern, 1994), and licensure and certification are ways of demonstrating the acquisition of those knowledges and skills. There are many potential users of the O*NET who will be interested in having information on occupational preparation for every job in the economy, and it is only logical that such information should be collected and available.

However, various issues must be addressed when measuring, collecting, and reporting data on occupational preparation. What kind of information should be collected? How should it be collected? How useful will this information be in informing us about how people should prepare for occupations?

In this chapter we hope to provide some initial answers to these and a number of other questions about education, training, experience, and licensure/ certification. We begin by briefly reviewing the rationale for collecting information on occupational preparation. Then we discuss how we developed the measures for collecting this information. Finally, we present some initial evidence on the reliability and validity of these measures and examine their implications for answering certain questions about workforce occupational preparation.

## BACKGROUND

Education, training, and experience requirements have traditionally been important in characterizing occupations. The reason for this is simple: there is a clear intuitive link between these forms of occupational preparation and the development of basic skills and knowledge (Snow & Swanson, 1992; Ward et al., 1990). These forms of occupational preparation have and will continue to have a significant role in the selection of employees (Ash, Johnson, Levine, & McDaniel, 1989; Dye & Reck, 1988; Hunter &

Hunter, 1984). In fact, research has indicated that over the past 30 years there has been a growing reliance on education for selecting employees (Monahan & Muchinsky, 1983). This is so because evaluations of education are relatively cheap and easily accessible.

Changes in the U.S. workplace will likely lead to even greater emphasis on education, training, and experience. Individuals who will enter the workforce in the next 15 years have already been born, so future trends in labor force participation can be predicted with reasonable accuracy (Fullerton, 1985). The many projected changes in the workforce will affect how organizations manage their human resources (Cascio & Zammuto, 1987). Perhaps the most important change is the decrease in the growth of the workforce. Fewer and fewer young people will be available for entry-level jobs (Fullerton, 1985). Increasing numbers of the young people who will be available will lack the necessary skills for doing the work. This is due to two factors: (a) jobs will likely increase in complexity with changes in technology, shifts from manufacturing to service jobs, and increases in the impact of the global marketplace; and (b) the poor and uneducated segments of our population are growing the fastest (Goldstein & Gilliam, 1990). Various commissions (Commission on Workforce Quality and Labor Market Efficiency, 1989) have agreed that our present workforce too often is poorly prepared for high-performance work because of outmoded current work skills and schools and training institutions that are not changing fast enough to provide appropriate skills. To remain competitive under these circumstances, American industries will have to have highly competent workforces.

National action has been taken to improve the occupational preparation of the workforce. The Department of Labor (U.S. DOL) created the Secretary's Commission on Achieving Necessary Skills (SCANS) to examine the demands of the workplace and to define a set of competencies and foundation skills needed by today's and tomorrow's workforce (*What Work Requires of Schools*, SCANS, 1991; *Learning a Living: A Blueprint for High Performance*, SCANS,

1992). The Department of Education (DOE) set forth Education 2000, which is a broad policy initiative meant to achieve two goals: (a) to provide information on what citizens of all ages should know and be able to do to live and work productively and (b) to indicate what educational and training institutions must do to help meet those needs. DOL and DOE have jointly launched National Skill Standards to promote the development of voluntary skill standards in different industries by involving all stakeholders, industry associations, unions, and educators.

As education, training, and experience become recognized as more important, licensure/certification programs will become more prevalent. Scholars and blue-ribbon commissions appointed by the government and Congress (e.g., Dertouzos, Lester, & Solow, 1989; U.S. Congress, Office of Technology Assessment, 1990) agree that licensure/certification of employees is important to the high-performance workplace.

## DEVELOPMENT OF MEASURES OF OCCUPATIONAL PREPARATION

Our approach to developing measures for occupational preparation descriptors in O*NET was to

- define user needs;
- examine literature for existing taxonomies relevant to those needs;
- develop new taxonomies or augment these taxonomies when necessary;
- examine how educational data are gathered in organizations; and
- develop brief, clear, and easy-to-read items.

Table 7-1 contains a summary of the descriptors that we have developed for the occupational preparation domain. We will refer to this table throughout our discussion of the development of these descriptors.

### Education

Information on education provided through O*NET will be of great interest to many different kinds of users. According to a recent survey of *Dictionary of Occupational Titles* (DOT; U.S. DOL, 1993) users (Westat, 1993), a majority of users in virtually every user group viewed information on education to be "very important." Some of the current uses of this information include (a) career selection, (b) career planning, (c) curriculum development, (d) human resources management, and (e) vocational rehabilitation counseling. This means that education data collected on jobs are currently used (at a minimum) by career counselors, employers, students, training developers, and job seekers.

Recent DOT user surveys (Campion, Gowing, Lancaster, & Pearlman, 1994; Westat, 1993) indicated

that the following information is important to users regarding education and training:

- the amount of education needed to enter the occupation, including the degrees and certificates required; and
- the type of education needed to enter the occupation, including (a) course major or instructional program and (b) coursework.

We explored the literature for taxonomies relevant to these user needs. Although there are various education-oriented taxonomies described in the literature (e.g., Bloom, 1956; Gagne, 1985), we found only one set of taxonomies relevant to user needs. This set of taxonomies is called the *Classification of Instructional Programs* (CIP; U.S. DOE, 1990). The CIP provides classifications of education by type and amount. The "amount" taxonomy found in the CIP classifies education into categories such as high school, undergraduate, and graduate. The "type" taxonomy found in the CIP classifies education according to academic and occupation-specific instructional programs.

The second CIP taxonomy has three levels of specificity. The shortest, most general level lists 40 program categories. At a more specific level, these 40 categories are subdivided into at least 300 programs, and a yet more specific level subdivides these 300-plus programs into upwards of 1,800 programs. Table 7-2 provides examples from each level of the CIP taxonomy of Academic and Occupationally Specific Programs. We chose to use the most general level of the taxonomy (Level 1) to describe occupations using O*NET because users would not likely need more specific information. In addition, a more specific instructional program taxonomy would be more likely to change over time, which would lead to higher maintenance costs. The CIP taxonomy that we used to develop a descriptor relevant to the type of education is shown in Table 7-1, where each member of the taxonomy is an option for Instructional Program Required (D2).

Thus, by using the CIP taxonomies as the basis for descriptor measure development, we would be able to address both kinds of information of interest to users. Another advantage of the CIP taxonomies is that items in the CIP are matched to relevant items in the current DOT and the Occupational Employment Statistics (OES) job families. The revised CIP taxonomy that we used to develop a descriptor relevant to the amount of education is shown in Table 7-3.

Although descriptors based on these two taxonomies should largely address the needs of potential O*NET users, information on the different types of coursework required might be of additional use. This conclusion is based on the notion that instructional programs with the same name vary in their coursework emphasis. Because we were unable to locate any taxonomies that tapped coursework at this level of specificity, we decided to develop a taxonomy of

**TABLE 7-1**
**Descriptions and Definitions of Education, Training, Licensure/Certification, and Experience Descriptors, Listed by Item Type and Scale Type**

| Category | Descriptors | Item type | Scale type |
|---|---|---|---|
| 1. General Education Level | | Check one | 12-point degree level (1 = *less than a high school diploma*, 12 = *postdoctoral certificate*) |
| 2. Instructional Program Required | | Check one | Agriculture Business/Production<br>Agricultural Sciences<br>Architecture<br>Area/Ethnic/Cultural Studies<br>Biological/Life Sciences<br>Business Management/Administrative Services<br>Communications<br>Communications Technologies<br>Computer Information Sciences<br>Conservation<br>Construction Trades<br>Education<br>Engineering<br>Engineering Technologies<br>English Languages/Literatures<br>Foreign Languages/Literature<br>Health Professions<br>Home Economics<br>Law/Legal Studies<br>Liberal Arts/Sciences<br>Library Science<br>Marketing/Distribution<br>Mathematics<br>Mechanics/Repairers<br>Military Technologies<br>Interdisciplinary Studies<br>Parks/Recreation/Leisure/Fitness<br>Personal/Miscellaneous Services<br>Philosophy/Religion<br>Physical Sciences<br>Precition Production Trades<br>Protective Services<br>Psychology<br>Public Administration/Services<br>ROTC<br>Science Technologies<br>Social Sciences/History<br>Theological Studies<br>Transportation/Moving<br>Visual/Performing Arts<br>Vocational Home Economics<br>No Specific Major |
| 3. Subject Area Education Level (15 descriptors): | a. Technical Vocational<br>b. Business Vocational<br>c. English/Language Arts<br>d. Oral Communication<br>e. Languages<br>f. Basic Math<br>g. Advanced Math<br>h. Physical Sciences<br>i. Computer Sciences<br>j. Biological Sciences<br>k. Applied Sciences<br>l. Social Sciences<br>m. Arts<br>n. Humanities<br>o. Physical Education | Check one | 5-point level scale (0 = *not required*, 4 = *graduate school or other post undergraduate*) |
| 4. Licenses Required (2 descriptors) | Commercial Vehicle License<br>Nonvehicle license | yes/no | (0 = *no*, 1 = *yes*) |
| Licenses Named | Licenses Named | Open ended | Analyzed two ways: qualitative and quantitative (0 = *no license listed*; 1 = *one or more licenses listed*) |

*Table 7-1 continues*

**TABLE 7-1 (Continued)**

| Category | Descriptors | Item type | Scale type |
|---|---|---|---|
| 5. Requirement to Obtain a License (6 descriptors) | Postsecondary Degree<br>Graduate Degree<br>On-the-Job Training<br>Examination<br>Character References<br>Coursework | yes/no | (0 = *no*, 1 = *yes*) |
| 6. Who Requires License (3 descriptors) | Law<br>Employer<br>Union/Association | yes/no | (0 = *no*, 1 = *yes*) |
| 7. Related Work Experience (4 descriptors) | Related Work Experience<br>On-Site Training<br>On-the-Job Training<br>Apprenticeships | Check one | 11-point scale (0 = *not applicable or none,*<br>10 = *over 10 years*) |

coursework. This taxonomy was developed on the basis of reviews of (a) previous applied research dealing with coursework subject area as a variable (National Center for Education Statistics, 1993), (b) high school curriculum guides, and (c) coursework descriptions included in various college and university course catalogs. In consideration of the small amount of space available in the O*NET instruments and the rather general needs of users for this type of information, we decided to use a short list of 15 subject matter areas. The taxonomy that we used to develop the subject area descriptors is shown in Table 7-1, where each member of the taxonomy is a separate descriptor (D3a through 3o; these descriptors are listed with the letters D3a through 3o for subsequent tables in this chapter).

## Training/Experience

For many reasons, experience is an important construct to consider when describing occupations. A recent survey of DOT users (Westat, 1993) showed experience data were viewed as "very important" by users to assist in (a) career counseling, (b) vocational rehabilitation and counseling, (c) employment placement, and (d) human resource management. These users are generally most interested in the amount of experience needed to obtain and keep a job.

Amount of experience usually refers to the tenure, or the amount of time an incumbent has been working in an occupation. This certainly is a useful operationalization of experience, as direct, self-report questions about tenure have been positively related to measures of job performance (Hunter & Hunter, 1984; McDaniel, Schmidt, & Hunter, 1988). However, there are various ways of acquiring this experience. For example, apprenticeships are widely recognized as useful ways of gaining experience, but as a method of gaining experience, they differ greatly from in-plant training experience. This difference needs to be reflected when examining the experience required to perform in an occupation. Clearly a taxonomy of different ways of acquiring training/experience was needed.

We developed a taxonomy that includes the various types of occupation-related training and experiences. Then we developed a descriptor to tap each member in the taxonomy. The resulting descriptors are shown in Table 7-1. The types of experience we

**TABLE 7-2**
**Classification of Instructional Programs (CIP): Academic and Occupationally Specific Programs. Examples From the Three Levels of Specificity**

| Level 1<br>(40 categories) | Level 2<br>(300+ categories) | Level 3<br>(1,800+ categories) |
|---|---|---|
| Agricultural Business and Production | Agriculture/Agricultural Sciences, General | Plant Sciences, General |
| **Agricultural Sciences** | Animal Sciences | Agronomy and Crop Science |
| Conservation and Renewable Natural Resources | Food Sciences and Technology | Horticulture Science |
| Agriculture and Related Programs | **Plant Sciences** | Plant Breeding and Genetics |
| Area, Ethnic, and Cultural Studies | Soil Sciences | Agricultural Plant Pathology |
| Marketing Operations/Marketing Distribution | Agriculture/Agricultural Sciences, Other | Plant Protection (Pest Management) |
| Communications | | Range Science and Management |
| Communications Technologies | | Plant Sciences, Other |

*Note.* Items in boldface type are expanded at lower levels in the example.

**TABLE 7-3**
**Revised Amount of Education Taxonomy**

| Level of Education | Explanation (if needed) |
|---|---|
| a) Less than a high school diploma | |
| b) High school diploma (or high school equivalence certificate) | |
| c) Postsecondary certificate | Awarded for training completed after high school (e.g., in Personal Services, Engineering-Related Technologies, Vocational Home Economics, Construction Trades, Mechanics and Repairers, Precision Production Trades). |
| d) Some colleges courses | |
| e) Associate's degree (or other 2-year degree) | |
| f) Bachelor's degree | |
| g) Postbaccalaureate certificate | Awarded for completion of an organized program of study requiring 30 credit hours beyond the bachelor's degree; designed for persons who have completed a baccalaureate degree but do not meet the requirements of academic degrees carrying the title of master. |
| h) Master's degree | |
| i) Postmaster's certificate | Awarded for completion of an organized program of study of 60 credit hours beyond the master's degree but does not meet the requirements of academic degrees at the doctoral level. |
| j) First professional degree | Awarded for completion of a program that requires at least 2 hours of college work before entrance into the program, includes a total of at least 6 academic years of college work to complete, and provides all remaining academic requirements to begin practice in a profession. |
| k) Doctoral degree | |
| l) Postdoctoral certificate | |

identified included Related Work Experience (D7a), On-Site or In-Plant Training (D7b), On-the-Job Training (D7c), and Apprenticeships (D7d). Related work experience (D7a) refers to experience in related jobs. Entry to jobs or acceptable performance in some jobs requires a certain amount of experience in related jobs. For example, many managerial occupations require a particular number of years of experience in a related technical or supervisory job. On-Site or In-Plant Training (D7b), On-the Job Training (D7c), and Apprenticeships (D7d) refer to training experiences that occur in the work context. On-Site or In-Plant Training (D7b) is organized classroom study required and provided by an employer. On-the Job Training (D7c) is when an individual serves as a learner or trainee on the job under the instruction of a more experienced worker (U.S. DOL, 1991). Finally, Apprenticeships (D7d) are training experiences that require 1 or more years of On-the-Job Training (D7c) through work experience supplemented by related instruction. Such experience is often required before one can be considered a qualified and skilled worker (U.S. DOL, 1991). We developed the scale used to measure each of these types of experience so that it would coincide with the scale currently used by the DOT to reflect Specific Vocational Preparation (U.S. DOL, 1991).

Another alternative for determining experience requirements is to examine training/experience requirements for specific skills. Indeed, previous research suggests that experience linked to certain skills is a valid predictor of job performance (Hough, 1984).

Thus, we developed and applied a procedure to gather data about requirements for specific types of experience by asking the question, "Is [the level of skill that you have identified above] required for entry into this job?" We are only collecting this information with regard to basic and cross-functional skills. A simple yes/no scale is provided for the response. This item format is similar to that used in previous work (Peterson, 1992b) where the item stem asked respondents to indicate the percentage of a skill acquired before entry. In that study, respondents were asked to respond on a 5-point percentage scale. Researchers in the current study opted for a 2-point scale because it was thought that (a) this would reduce the complexity of the question for respondents and (b) this format would make it clear that this was not another level scale (like other ratings being made on the same page). On the O*NET instrument, this scale follows a level and importance rating. Note that this scale is also discussed in chapter 5 of this book.

One might, of course, also look at specific experience requirements in terms of knowledge and generalized work activities as well as skills. Skills, however, provide a more appropriate basis for the assessment of experience requirements because they (a) incorporate experience acquired outside the work context and (b) focus on what one can do rather than what one knows.

## Licensure/Certification

As licensure/certification becomes more common in various occupations, the interest in information about these programs will naturally increase. According to a recent survey of DOT users (Westat, 1993), information about licensure/certification was viewed as "very important" by at least 30% of individuals in various user groups. Data from this study indicate that information about licensure/certification is particularly relevant for career vocational counseling and occupational information development/dissemination.

Although much has been written about licensure/certification requirements (e.g., Barnhart, 1994; Shimberg, Esser, & Kruger, 1973) and some well known job analysis instruments include an item on licensure (e.g., Harvey, 1993; McPhail, Jeanneret, McCormick, & Mecham, 1991), little research has been done to determine the best methods to collect licensure/certification information in the context of a job analysis questionnaire. This is likely due to the apparently straightforward nature of the information. Indeed, a review of the methods used to collect licensure/certification data in organizations (e.g., AT&T) revealed little other than the use of an extensive list of possible licenses/certificates. Therefore, the best approach, given the lack of research on the topic, is to carefully define the information that is needed by various users, examine how licensure/certification data were collected in similar contexts (e.g., Canadian Job Classification System), and write items in simple English that could be understood by a variety of respondents.

In line with the uses identified in a recent Westat report (1993), it became clear that information about licensure/certification would be of greatest value if it described the requirements for entry and advancement in an occupation. We determined that users would be most interested in (a) the name of the license/certificate relevant to the occupation, (b) the criteria that must be satisfied to obtain/retain the license/certificate, and (c) the entities that require the license.

The first two types of information focus on identifying the name of the license/certificate relevant to the occupation and then determining the basic requirements needed to achieve and retain licensure/certification. This data would be of obvious interest to career/vocational counselors. The last type of information acknowledges that a license/certificate may be required by law, the employer, or a union or professional organization.

We developed the descriptors so that incumbents would describe the licenses/certifications that were relevant to their jobs. This tactic allows us to capitalize on the first-hand knowledge of the incumbent and allows for description of only those licenses/certificates that are relevant. Descriptors pertaining to licensure/certification are shown in Table 7-1.

The descriptors do not address one important issue with respect to licensure/certification: the issue of reciprocity across states. A state grants reciprocity for a license if individuals who are allowed to practice in the state also hold a valid license from another state (Shimberg et al., 1973). Naturally, this is an important variable to consider, as it may be of interest to users. However, this information varies across time and location. The best way to obtain this information would be to ask the states/localities directly.

## Sample

A detailed description of the sampling procedures is provided in chapter 4. A total of 722 incumbents returned questionnaires that were at least partially completed. From these data, we eliminated occupations with fewer than four respondents, resulting in 598 remaining cases. Table 7-4 lists the 34 occupations and the number of incumbents who completed the ratings. Note that incumbents whose responses were retained are employed at more than 100 establishments. We used these data for most of our analyses.

## RESULTS

We conducted various analyses on the data to assist in evaluating the effectiveness of these descriptors. Our analyses included calculation of descriptive statistics for each descriptor, reliability analyses for each descriptor, application of analysis of variance (ANOVA) procedures meant to examine sources of variation in the ratings, reliability analyses for each major area of occupational preparation, intercorrelations of the descriptors, and factor analyses.

Before presenting the results, a note on the Instructional Program descriptor (D2) is necessary. The Instructional Program (D2) was intended to be a single descriptor (Anderson, 1995) indicating the instructional program required for an occupation. It was not intended to gather information on the relevance of 42 separate instructional programs. However, to facilitate presentation of the descriptive statistics on the descriptor and to allow for an evaluation of the descriptor as 42 separate descriptors, we present statistics for 42 separate descriptors in many of the tables that follow. For purposes of presenting these results, each of the 42 programs is defined as a dichotomous variable, with 0 indicating *not checked* and 1 indicating *checked*.

## Descriptive Statistics

Table 7-5 presents the basic descriptive statistics obtained for each scale. This table presents the overall, cross-occupation mean and standard deviation of the ratings where occupations were treated as the unit of analysis. The associated interrater agreement coefficients and standard errors of measurement are also presented.

**TABLE 7-4**
**Thirty-Four Occupations With Four or More Incumbents Completing the Education, Training, Experience, and Licensure/Certification Questionnaire**

| Occupation code | Occupation title | Number of respondents |
|---|---|---|
| 15005 | Education Administrators | 11 |
| 19005 | General Managers & Top Executives | 38 |
| 22135 | Mechanical Engineers | 6 |
| 25105 | Computer Programmers | 6 |
| 31305 | Teachers, Elementary School | 7 |
| 31502 | Librarians, Professional | 4 |
| 32502 | Registered Nurses | 29 |
| 32902 | Medical & Clinical Laboratory Technologists | 8 |
| 49008 | Salespersons, Except Scientific & Retail | 7 |
| 49011 | Salespersons, Retail | 22 |
| 49017 | Counter & Rental Clerks | 5 |
| 49021 | Stock Clerks, Sales Floor | 8 |
| 49023 | Cashiers | 27 |
|  | Tellers | 4 |
| 51002 | First Line Supervisors, Clerical/Administrative | 57 |
| 53121 | Loan & Credit Clerks | 4 |
| 53311 | Insurance Claims Clerks | 11 |
| 55108 | Secretaries, Except Legal & Medical | 66 |
| 55305 | Receptionists & Information Clerks | 6 |
| 55338 | Bookkeeping, Accounting, & Auditing Clerks | 23 |
| 55347 | General Office Clerks | 68 |
| 61005 | Police & Detective Supervisors | 11 |
| 63014 | Police Patrol Officers | 17 |
| 65008 | Waiters & Waitresses | 15 |
|  | Cooks, Restaurant | 4 |
| 65038 | Food Preparation Workers | 14 |
| 66008 | Nursing Aides, Orderlies, & Attendants | 14 |
| 67005 | Janitors & Cleaners | 29 |
|  | Other Machinery | 4 |
| 85132 | Maintenance Repairers, General Utility | 36 |
| 87902 | Earth Drillers, Except Oil & Gas | 8 |
| 92974 | Packaging & Filling Machine Operators | 10 |
| 97102 | Truck Drivers, Heavy or Tractor Trailer | 9 |
| 97111 | Bus Drivers, Schools | 10 |

The descriptive statistics are consistent with the results we expected given the occupations included in our sample. The results on general level of education are typical: the mean indicates that the average amount of education is somewhere between "high school diploma" and "some college courses." In fact, more than 50% of our respondents indicated that the general level of education required for their occupation is high school or less. This is in line with the general level of education found in the U.S. (National Center for Education Statistics, 1993).

The descriptive statistics on Instructional Program Requirement (D2) indicate that 43% of the sample endorsed No Specific Major (D2pp). Also, 26% of the sample endorsed more than one instructional program. The responses also appear to be consistent with the occupations in the sample. Note that at least 10% of the sample indicated that their occupations required a major in computer sciences, education, or health professions. This is not surprising when one considers that the sample included Computer Programmers, Education Administrators, Elementary School Teachers, Registered Nurses, and Medical and Clinical Laboratory Technologists.

Descriptors pertaining to training/experience and licensure/certification also provided results in line

with our expectations. In terms of the different types of experience, Related Work Experience (D7a) was viewed as required more often than the other types of experience, with Apprenticeship Experience (D7d) being reported as the least frequently required type of experience. Licensure/Certification (D4b) was reported as required nearly 30% of the time. The most frequently reported requirement for a license was examination. A license was most frequently required by the employer, the law, and a union/association, respectively.

## Reliability

We examined the reliability of each descriptor score by calculating an intraclass correlation for each of the ratings across occupations (Shrout & Fleiss, 1979). With this type of intraclass statistic, reliability increases as the between-occupations variance becomes greater and the within-occupations variance becomes smaller. These interrater agreement coefficients are based on a harmonic mean of 9.04 raters per occupation and are presented in Table 7-5, along with the associated standard errors of measurement.

**TABLE 7-5**

**Descriptive Statistics Across Occupations and Reliability Estimates for Rated Differences Between Occupations: Education, Training, Licensure, and Experience**

| Descriptor | | Variable | | | |
|---|---|---|---|---|---|
| | | M | SD | SEM[a] | $k_k$[b] |
| 1. | General Education Level | 3.43 | 2.01 | .37 | .97 |
| 2. | Instructional Program | | | | |
| 2a. | Agriculture Business/Production | .01 | .05 | .03 | .59 |
| 2b. | Agricultural Sciences | .01 | .05 | .04 | .43 |
| 2c. | Agriculture | .00 | .02 | .01 | .52 |
| 2d. | Area/Ethnic/Cultural Studies | .02 | .05 | .03 | .57 |
| 2e. | Biological/Life Sciences | .03 | .07 | .04 | .75 |
| 2f. | Business Management/Administrative Services | .12 | .15 | .08 | .74 |
| 2g. | Communications | .10 | .11 | .09 | .30 |
| 2h. | Communications Technologies | .01 | .03 | .03 | .00 |
| 2i. | Computer Information Sciences | .12 | .18 | .11 | .66 |
| 2j. | Conservation | .00 | .02 | .02 | .22 |
| 2k. | Construction Trades | .03 | .10 | .04 | .81 |
| 2l. | Education | .10 | .15 | .09 | .64 |
| 2m. | Engineering | .03 | .08 | .05 | .63 |
| 2n. | Engineering Technologies | .03 | .10 | .05 | .76 |
| 2o. | English Languages/Literature | .07 | .09 | .08 | .25 |
| 2p. | Foreign Languages/Literature | .03 | .09 | .06 | .59 |
| 2q. | Health Professions | .11 | .23 | .05 | .96 |
| 2r. | Home Economics | .01 | .02 | .02 | .43 |
| 2s. | Law/Legal Studies | .05 | .17 | .03 | .96 |
| 2t. | Liberal Arts/Sciences | .01 | .02 | .02 | .08 |
| 2u. | Library Science | .03 | .17 | .03 | .97 |
| 2v. | Marketing/Distribution | .04 | .08 | .06 | .47 |
| 2w. | Mathematics | .11 | .13 | .09 | .51 |
| 2x. | Mechanics/Repairers | .08 | .17 | .05 | .91 |
| 2y. | Military Technologies | .01 | .02 | .02 | .46 |
| 2z. | Interdisciplinary Studies | .02 | .04 | .03 | .41 |
| 2aa. | Parks/Recreation/Leisure/Fitness | .00 | .02 | .02 | .22 |
| 2bb. | Personal/Miscellaneous Services | .02 | .05 | .03 | .51 |
| 2cc. | Philosophy/Religion | .01 | .03 | .03 | .08 |
| 2dd. | Physical Sciences | .01 | .03 | .03 | .30 |
| 2ee. | Precision Production Trades | .01 | .05 | .02 | .73 |
| 2ff. | Protective Services | .02 | .04 | .03 | .51 |
| 2gg. | Psychology | .04 | .06 | .05 | .38 |
| 2hh. | Public Administration/Services | .03 | .06 | .05 | .32 |
| 2ii. | ROTC | .00 | .02 | .02 | .34 |
| 2jj. | Science Technologies | .01 | .02 | .02 | .00 |
| 2kk. | Social Sciences/History | .01 | .02 | .03 | .00 |
| 2ll. | Theological Studies | .01 | .05 | .02 | .73 |
| 2mm. | Transportation/Moving | .04 | .11 | .05 | .77 |
| 2a. | Visual/Performing Arts | .01 | .03 | .02 | .44 |
| 2b. | Vocational Home Economics | .03 | .07 | .04 | .75 |
| 2c. | No Specific Major | .43 | .26 | .12 | .81 |
| 3. | Subject Area Education Level | | | | |
| 3a. | Technical Vocational | .69 | .44 | .24 | .71 |
| 3b. | Business Vocational | 1.08 | .41 | .23 | .67 |
| 3c. | English/Language Arts | 1.55 | .68 | .31 | .79 |
| 3d. | Oral Communications | 1.61 | .67 | .30 | .80 |
| 3e. | Languages | .99 | .46 | .41 | .20 |
| 3f. | Basic Math | 1.40 | .56 | .24 | .81 |
| 3g. | Advanced Math | 1.28 | .78 | .36 | .78 |
| 3h. | Physical Sciences | 1.19 | .77 | .38 | .76 |
| 3i. | Computer Sciences | 1.36 | 67 | .35 | .73 |
| 3j. | Biological Sciences | 1.15 | .75 | .35 | .78 |
| 3k. | Applied Sciences | 1.31 | .71 | .37 | .73 |
| 3l. | Social Sciences | 1.29 | .77 | .34 | .80 |
| 3m. | Arts | .81 | .52 | .37 | .49 |
| 3n. | Humanities | 1.06 | .70 | .39 | .68 |
| 3o. | Physical Education | .71 | .47 | .32 | .53 |
| 4. | Licenses | | | | |
| 4a. | Commercial Vehicle License | .15 | .28 | .07 | .93 |
| 4b. | Nonvehicle License | .29 | .33 | .08 | .94 |
| 4c. | Licenses Named | .27 | .33 | .07 | .95 |

*Table 7-5 continues*

**TABLE 7-5 (Continued)**

| Descriptor | Variable | | | |
|---|---|---|---|---|
| | *M* | *SD* | *SEM*[a] | $k_k$[b] |
| 5. Requirements to Obtain a License | | | | |
| 5a. Postsecondary Degree | .13 | .26 | .05 | .96 |
| 5b. Graduate Degree | .04 | .06 | .05 | .50 |
| 5c. On-the-Job Training | .24 | .30 | .08 | .93 |
| 5d. Examination | .25 | .31 | .07 | .95 |
| 5e. Character References | .17 | .24 | .08 | .89 |
| 5f. Coursework | .20 | .28 | .07 | .93 |
| 6. Who Requires License | | | | |
| 6a. Law | .28 | .33 | .08 | .94 |
| 6b. Employer | .34 | .36 | .09 | .94 |
| 6c. Union/Association | .17 | .22 | .07 | .90 |
| 7. Experience | | | | |
| 7a. Related Work Experience | 3.80 | 1.69 | .64 | .86 |
| 7b. On-Site Training Experience | 1.76 | .85 | .54 | .59 |
| 7c. On-the-Job Training Experience | 2.49 | .97 | .58 | .65 |
| 7d. Apprenticeship Experience | .81 | .79 | .39 | .75 |

*Note.* Statistics are based on 34 occupations with Education, Training, Licensure, and Experience questionnaire responses from at least 4 incumbents (mean number of incumbents = 17.50, *Mdn* = 11, harmonic mean = 9.04).
[a]This estimate of the standard error of measurement was calculated as $SEM = SD*\sqrt{(1 - r_k)}$. [b]This estimate of reliability was obtained by calculating the intraclass correlation for *k* ratings across occupations: $ICC(1, k) = [BMS - WMS]/BMS$ (Shrout & Fleiss, 1979), where *k* is the harmonic mean of the number of ratings provided on each occupation.

The reliabilities for most of the descriptors were good. The descriptor General Education Level (D1) had a reliability of .97. Most of the descriptors pertaining to training/experience and licensure/certification had acceptable reliabilities (i.e., greater than .75). The exceptions include Requirements to Obtain a License: Graduate Degree (D5b), which has a low mean and low variance in this sample, and Experience: On-Site Training Experience (D7b), a descriptor that likely varies with different organizational training expectations and thus varies within occupation.

When analyzed as separate descriptors, Instructional Program (D2) provided reliabilities that varied greatly. Some of these descriptors (e.g., Health Professions [D2q], Mechanics/Repairers [D2x], and Law/Legal Studies [D2s]) had reliabilities above .90, whereas others had reliabilities below .10 (e.g., Social Sciences/History [D2kk], Science Technologies [D2jj], and Philosophy/Religion [D2cc]). However, more than half of these descriptors had reliabilities of less than .60. It is of note that descriptors with particularly low reliabilities also had low mean scores and low standard deviations. It is likely that for some of these descriptors that have such an obvious tie to specific occupations (e.g., Architecture [D2c]), reliabilities would increase if these occupations were part of the sample.

Overall, these initial analyses indicate that virtually all independent descriptors of occupational preparation yielded adequate, consistent descriptions of occupational requirements, whereas Instructional Program (D2), when analyzed as separate descriptors, showed great variance in the size of the reliability coefficients. We obtained these results with relatively small samples of incumbents within each occupation. Because the size of interrater agreement coefficients depends on the number of raters, it is instructive to examine how these reliabilities vary as a function of the number of raters. Accordingly, we conducted separate analyses where we adjusted the reliability coefficients to both 1 and 30 raters.

The pattern of the results for different numbers of raters is naturally the same, whereas the general level of the reliability coefficients changes. Adjusting the reliability coefficient estimates for 30 raters increases the reliability coefficients among the various domains so that approximately half of the coefficients exceed .90; however, some coefficients still lie below .60. All but one of these low-reliability estimates come from the Instructional Program (D2) descriptors. The single rater reliability coefficients show that General Education Level (D1) and descriptors pertaining to licensure/certification continue to have acceptable reliability (most of them are above .60), while the reliabilities for Instructional Program (D2) are generally inadequate.

Another way one might examine interrater agreement is under conditions where descriptors within a domain or typology are treated as a repeated measures variable. In such an analysis, ANOVA is used to compute an "occupations" main effect, a "descriptor" main effect, and a "descriptor by occupation" interaction. We conducted such analyses for descriptors D2, D3, D4, and D7.

The findings were in line with our expectations, showing significant results for all three effects. They indicate that the mean ratings vary across occupations and across descriptors and that the pattern of ratings across descriptors differs from occupation to occupation. The interrater agreement coefficients derived from these analyses indicate that the ratings evidenced good interrater agreement, yielding coefficients of .78, .74, .85, and .79 for the Instructional Program (D2), Level of Education Required in Specific Subject Areas (D3), Licensure/Certification (D4), and Training/Experience (D7) descriptors, respectively. The reliabilities of these descriptors are generally lower when examined in the one-way analyses (Table 7-5) than in the repeated measures analyses. The reason for the difference is that the one-way analyses examine differences across occupations within descriptor only, whereas the repeated measures analyses examine differences across occupations across all descriptors within an area. Thus, these findings are not in conflict.

The applicability of these different reliability estimates depends on the way the data are being used. If the difference of individual descriptor scores across occupations is the only difference that is relevant, then the reliability estimates associated with the one-way analyses apply. If the mean differences between the patterns of descriptor ratings across occupations also are relevant, then the repeated-measures estimate is more appropriate. Thus the one-way estimates apply when the data are examined on a descriptor by descriptor basis, and the repeated measures estimates apply when examining the results on a set of descriptors. For example, if the query were "Is the instructional program of Architecture (D2c) required for this job?," then the one-way estimate (.52) would be relevant, and one might conclude that the data lack sufficient reliability to respond to the query. However, if the query were "What instructional program is relevant?," then the repeated measures estimate (.78) would be relevant, and one might conclude that the reliability is more than adequate to respond to the query.

## Descriptor Relationships

We examined the correlations among the descriptors at the occupation level, obtained by correlating the occupation means on each descriptor. In examining the occupational correlations among descriptors, it is clear that descriptors pertaining to a given type of occupational preparation correlated highly with one another. For example, virtually all 15 descriptors pertaining to education level, with the exception of Subject Area Education Level: Technical Vocational (D3a) and Subject Area Education Level: Business Vocational (D3b), had intercorrelations above .50. Most descriptors pertaining to licensure/certification also had high positive intercorrelations. Finally, all descriptors pertaining to training/experience had positive intercorrelations. Training/experience descriptors that include a training *element* (e.g., On-Site Training Experience [D7b], On-the-Job Training Experience [D7c], and Apprenticeship Experience [D7d]) had intercorrelations above .50.

Instructional Program (D2), when examined as separate descriptors, had largely uninterpretable intercorrelations. The low correlations are likely due to the low reliability associated with these descriptors when viewed individually, which in turn is due to the understandably very low endorsement rates of the descriptors, owing to the fact that we had just 34 occupations. Also of note is the fact that more than 50% of the sample indicated that only one instructional program was required. As any correlation among these descriptors would be driven by the fraction of the sample for which more than one instructional program is required, these correlations may not reveal the true relationships among the various instructional programs. The correlations between these descriptors and other descriptors pertaining to education, training/experience, and licensure/ certification were also uninterpretable.

## Factor Structure

To further examine the pattern of relationships among the various descriptors, we conducted a principal-components factor analysis. We applied this factor analysis to the occupation-level correlations among all of the descriptors of occupational preparation, except for those pertaining to Instructional Program (D2). We chose not to include Instructional Program (D2) as separate descriptors because of the generally low reliability and low base rate associated with these descriptors. Table 7-6 summarizes the results obtained in this analysis following a varimax rotation.

Inspection of the eigenvalues and a scree test indicated that a three-factor solution provided a clear structure for summarizing the relationships among the descriptors. These factors accounted for 75% of the total variance in the ratings.

The first factor extracted in this analysis, accounting for 39% of this variance, was labeled *Education*. General Level of Education (D1) had a high loading on this factor ($r = .87$). Also, most of the descriptors pertaining to Subject Area Education Level (D3) yielded sizable loadings on this factor. For example, Oral Communications (D3d; $r = .93$), Advanced Math (D3g; $r = .93$), English/Language Arts (D3c; $r = .92$), and Social Sciences (D3l; $r = .92$) all produced sizable loadings. Two descriptors pertaining to Subject Area Education Level (D3) failed to load highest on this factor: Technical Vocational (D3a; $r = .34$) and Business Vocational (D3b; $r = .32$). These loadings make sense, however, given that these subject areas typically result in somewhat lower levels of education (in terms of years completed) and tend to occur for different types of occupations.

The second factor extracted in this analysis, accounting for 26% of the total variance, was labeled *Licensure*. Virtually all variables pertaining to licensure/certification had high loadings ($r > .90$) on this factor. Two descriptors pertaining to licensure/ certification did not have a particularly high loading on this factor: Licenses: Commercial Vehicle License (D4a; $r = .40$) and Requirements to Obtain a License: Graduate Degree (D5b; $r = .41$). The first of these two descriptors likely had a low loading because of the different nature of commercial vehicle licenses relative to other licenses. The loading for Requirements to Obtain a License: Graduate Degree (D5b)

**TABLE 7-6**
**Principal-Components Analysis Pattern Matrix for the Level Scale: Education Training, Licensure/Certification, and Experience**

| Descriptor | Factor | | | Communality |
|---|---|---|---|---|
| | F1 | F2 | F3 | |
| 1. General Level of Education | .87 | .08 | −.19 | .79 |
| 3. Subject Area Education Level | | | | |
|   3a. Technical Vocational | .34 | .13 | .68 | .59 |
|   3b. Business Vocational | .32 | −.55 | .27 | .48 |
|   3c. English/Language Arts | .92 | .07 | −.03 | .86 |
|   3d. Oral Communications | .93 | −.01 | .02 | .87 |
|   3e. Languages | .71 | −.18 | .15 | .56 |
|   3f. Basic Math | .90 | .02 | −.02 | .81 |
|   3g. Advanced Math | .93 | .01 | .03 | .87 |
|   3h. Physical Sciences | .91 | .25 | .05 | .88 |
|   3i. Computer Sciences | .84 | −.33 | .04 | .81 |
|   3j. Biological Sciences | .86 | .32 | −.10 | .86 |
|   3k. Applied Sciences | .86 | .25 | .10 | .81 |
|   3l. Social Sciences | .92 | .26 | −.04 | .91 |
|   3m. Arts | .79 | .00 | .00 | .63 |
|   3n. Humanities | .84 | .14 | −.01 | .72 |
|   3o. Physical Education | .72 | .19 | .19 | .60 |
| 4. Licenses | | | | |
|   4a. Commercial Vehicle License | −.28 | .40 | .16 | .26 |
|   4b. Nonvehicle License | .17 | .97 | .04 | .97 |
|   4c. Licenses Named | .17 | .96 | .02 | .96 |
| 5. Requirements to Obtain a License | | | | |
|   5a. Postsecondary Degree | .48 | .67 | −.17 | .71 |
|   5b. Graduate Degree | .35 | .41 | .00 | .29 |
|   5c. On-the-Job Training | .11 | .97 | .04 | .95 |
|   5d. Examination | .11 | .96 | .04 | .93 |
|   5e. Character References | .08 | .92 | −.02 | .84 |
|   5f. Coursework | .16 | .95 | −.01 | .92 |
| 6. Who Requires License | | | | |
|   6a. Law | −.06 | .95 | .11 | .92 |
|   6b. Employer | .11 | .94 | .05 | .90 |
|   6c. Union/Association | .15 | .86 | .02 | .75 |
| 7. Experience | | | | |
|   7a. Related Work Experience | .34 | −.42 | .29 | .38 |
|   7b. On-Site Training Experience | −.01 | −.06 | .79 | .63 |
|   7c. On-the-Job Training Experience | −.13 | .05 | .82 | .69 |
|   7d. Apprenticeship Experience | −.07 | .02 | .85 | .72 |
|   % variance | | 40.00 | 26.00 | 9.00 |
|   Eigenvalues | | 11.28 | 9.76 | 2.82 |

*Note.* $N = 34$. The correlation matrix was based on means calculated at the occupational level. F1 = Education, F2 = Licensure, F3 = Training. These loadings are based on an orthogonal varimax rotation.

was likely attenuated by the low base rate and variance associated with this type of degree. Subject Area Education Level: Business Vocational (D3b) had a moderately high but negative loading on this factor. This loading likely occurred because that subject area is not typically associated with occupations that require licensure.

The third and final factor extracted in this analysis accounted for 9% of the variance in descriptor ratings. This factor, labeled *Training*, was defined in terms of occupation-specific training, including Apprenticeship Experience (D7d; $r = .85$), On-the-Job Training Experience (D7c; $r = .82$), On-Site Training Experience (D7b; $r = .79$), and Subject Area Education Level: Technical Vocational (D3a; $r = .68$).

Taken as a whole, the results of this analysis provide some initial evidence for the meaningfulness of different types of occupational preparation. Each factor describes different types of occupational prepa-

ration that receive different emphasis depending on the occupation at hand.

Although the factor analysis provides information as to the relationships among the descriptors, it does not directly address the issue of how the various descriptors differentiate occupations. Thus, it should not be assumed that these factors necessarily provide an adequate summary system when our concern is describing the similarities and differences among occupations.

## Occupation Differences

Some initial evidence bearing on the ability of these descriptors to capture the similarities and differences among occupations was obtained by contrasting the mean profile of six occupations on the various scales. We computed the means and standard deviations of the descriptors for six occupations selected to reflect distinct types of employment: (a) General Managers and Top Executives, (b) Computer Programmers, (c) Registered Nurses, (d) Police Patrol Officers, (e) Janitors and Cleaners, and (f) Maintenance Repairers, General Utility.

The mean scores of incumbents on these descriptors meet with our expectations of the education, training, experience, and licensure/certification requirements for these occupations. According to the mean General Level of Education (D1), these six occupations rank in terms of our expectations, with General Managers and Top Executives indicating the highest and Janitors and Cleaners indicating the lowest requirements. Subject Area Education Level (D3) ratings were generally higher for Computer Programmers and Registered Nurses than they were for the other occupations included in the six. Ratings on individual subject areas also met with our expectations. Computer programmers provided the highest ratings of the six on Computer Science (D3i), Advanced Math (D3g), and English/Language Arts (D3c). Registered Nurses received the highest ratings of the six occupations on Biological Sciences (D3j), Applied Sciences (D3k), and Physical Sciences (D3h).

Instructional Program Requirements (D2) were generally in line with our expectations. The most frequently endorsed Instructional Program Requirements (D2) were as follows:

- Management and Administration (D2f) for General Managers and Top Executives (53%);
- Computer Information Sciences (D2i) for Computer Programmers (83%);
- Health Professions (D2q) for Registered Nurses (97%);
- Law and Legal Studies (D2s) for Police Patrol Officers (82%);
- No Specific Major (D2pp) for Janitors and Cleaners (68%); and
- Mechanics/Repairers (D2x) for Maintenance Repairers, General Utility (62%).

Licensure/certification descriptors were generally rated highly by Registered Nurses and Police Patrol Officers, with 100% of the incumbents in both occupations indicating that licensure/certification/ registration is required by their employer. Licensure/ certification ratings were moderately high for Maintenance Repairers, General Utility, with 51% of incumbents indicating that licensure/certification/ registration is required by their employer. These ratings were lowest for Computer Programmers, among whom 100% of incumbents marked "no" in response to all descriptors pertaining to licensure requirements.

Finally, in terms of training and experience, General Managers and Top Executives indicated the most years of experience required in related occupations. Maintenance Repairers, General Utility provided the highest ratings on three descriptors pertinent to training (On-Site Training Experience [D7b], On-the-Job

Training Experience [D7c], and Apprenticeship Experience [D7d]).

The evidence presented above does lead to a noteworthy conclusion. Specifically, it appears that the various descriptors provide a meaningful description of the similarities and differences among occupations in terms of education, training, experience, and licensure/certification. This point is of some importance because ultimately a viable descriptive system must be capable of capturing and accurately reflecting meaningful differences in all types of occupational preparation.

## CONCLUSIONS

In this section, we consider the findings for each type of descriptor, draw conclusions as to the usefulness of these descriptors, and recommend improvements. Before we turn to the conclusions, we should note that these analyses are necessarily limited in scope, and our conclusions may change as additional analyses are done, or as the data on education, training, experience, and licensure/certification are compared with the data from other domains.

### Implications of Results

Even bearing this caveat in mind, we believe that the findings obtained in the present study have some important implications for the assessment of education, training, experience, and licensure/certification requirements. To begin, it appears that it is possible to formulate questions and rating scales that can be used to obtain reliable, meaningful data on these descriptors. The apparent feasibility of assessing these descriptors through an incumbent survey strategy is noteworthy because it represents a relatively low-cost procedure for describing education, training, experience, and licensure/certification requirements.

### *General Education Level*

This descriptor was meant to determine the education level required for the occupation at hand. The scale for this descriptor was derived from the CIP, which references the different education levels. Our findings on this descriptor include

- descriptive statistics in line with expectations;
- high reliability;
- logical correlations with other education, training, experience, and licensure/certification descriptors;
- prominence in defining the factor of Education (factor analytic results); and
- usefulness in differentiating occupations.

These findings provide generally positive evidence for retaining the item as written. Note, however, that this conclusion is based on the premise that the level of education required is the relevant level of analysis.

If it is determined that users may be more interested in the relevance of each of the levels of education, then a change in the item might be warranted. This change would amount to splitting the item into 11 different descriptors, each of which evaluates the importance of obtaining education at the given level. This will naturally provide more information and thus increase overall reliability and validity, but it would come at the cost of adding items to an already lengthy survey.

### Educational Subject Area

These descriptors were meant to determine the amount of formal education required in each of 15 different subject areas. The scale for these items was also developed from the CIP. Our findings on this set of descriptors include

- descriptive statistics in line with expectations;
- generally adequate reliability, with a few exceptions;
- logical correlations with other education, training, experience, and licensure/certification descriptors;
- particularly high intercorrelations;
- some loadings on the factor of Education (D2l) (factor analytic results); and
- some usefulness collectively in differentiating occupations.

These findings provide mixed evidence for retaining the descriptors as measured in this study. The descriptors appear to have reasonable internal validity; however, the information they provide is somewhat redundant with General Education Level (D1).

To determine whether the same information could be obtained with fewer items, we conducted a principal-components factor analysis of these descriptors alone. We discovered five factors (Technical Vocational, Business Vocational, English/Language Arts, Foreign Language, and Math/Science). Thus, items could be constructed that tap these broader coursework areas. Use of these revised items would reduce the overall length of the survey while still providing essentially the same information to users. However, as mentioned previously, these findings are somewhat limited by the occupations included in this sample. Thus, we suggest further study of these descriptors with other samples of occupations. If these findings persist, we recommend reducing the descriptors down to a smaller set based on factor analysis and the needs of users.

### Instructional Program

As previously noted, Instructional Program (D2) was intended as a single descriptor with the purpose of indicating the major field of study required to perform the job. However, as 26% of the respondents to the item indicated that more than one instructional program was required, we decided it may be useful to evaluate Instructional Program (D2) as 42 separate

descriptors, each corresponding to a different instructional program.

Our findings on Instructional Program (D2), examined as 42 separate descriptors, include

- descriptive statistics in line with expectations, with many instructional programs being endorsed by less than 1% of the sample;
- great variance in reliability when viewed as 42 separate descriptors, with those programs receiving little endorsement having unacceptable reliabilities; and
- generally uninterpretable correlations with other descriptors.

Our findings on Instructional Program (D2), examined as a single descriptor, include

- a profile of endorsement for the sample as a whole consistent with expectations;
- acceptable reliability; and
- a logical profile of endorsement for six example occupations.

Given these findings, it seems clear that Instructional Program (D2) provides more than adequate information for its intended purpose of describing and differentiating among occupations in terms of the instructional program or programs reported by incumbents as being required. However, given that many incumbents endorsed more than one instructional program, it may be prudent to reword the item to explicitly allow respondents to check more than one. Even with this refinement, however, the item will provide limited information in that it does not allow for the evaluation of the relevance of individual instructional programs.

Information on the relevance of individual instructional programs may be valued by certain users. For example, a job seeker with a degree in Computer Sciences (D3i) might want to examine the data on occupations to see whether or not a degree in Computer Sciences is relevant. To serve the purpose of providing information on the relevance of individual instructional programs, 42 separate items would have to be created, with a separate rating for each one. This treatment of Instructional Program (D2) would require more effort on the part of the respondents, but it may be warranted, depending on the needs of the users. It is of note that the relevance of individual instructional programs could likely also be assessed by users through an examination of occupation scores within the knowledge domain.

Our recommendations on this descriptor are to (a) reword the item to make it clear that more than one instructional program can be endorsed and (b) determine whether the needs of the users to have information on the relevance of individual instructional programs warrants the costs of expanding the item to 42 separate items.

### *Licensure/Certification*

These descriptors were meant to determine (a) whether or not licensure/certification/registration is required, (b) the type of license/certification/registration required, (c) the requirements for obtaining licensure/certification/registration, and (d) the entities requiring the licensure/certification/registration. There are 12 items, 11 with a response scale of "yes/no" and 1 "fill in the blank." Our findings on this set of descriptors include

- descriptive statistics in line with expectations;
- generally high reliability;
- logical correlations with other education, training, experience, and licensure/certification descriptors;
- some variables with particularly high intercorrelations;
- loadings on the factor of Licensure (factor analytic results); and
- some usefulness in differentiating occupations.

These findings provide evidence for retaining the descriptors as measured in this study. The descriptors appear to have reasonable internal validity, and they are useful for differentiating among occupations.

However, some of the descriptors provide statistically redundant information. With the occupations in our sample, some of the requirements to obtain and retain licensure/certification/registration have intercorrelations of .90 or higher (i.e., On-the-Job Training Experience [D5c], Examination [D5d], Character References [D5e], and Coursework [D5f]). In addition, when a nonvehicle license was reported as required, it also was usually reported as required by both the employer and the law; thus, the three descriptors relevant to these issues had intercorrelations of .90 or higher.

Given these statistical redundancies, the items might be collapsed so that, at least in theory, the same amount of information could be gathered with fewer items. However, we advise caution before taking this step. The items are generally distinct in terms of content, and additional samples including other occupations may reveal less statistical redundancy.

### *Training/Experience*

These descriptors were meant to determine the amount of training/experience required for the given occupation. There are four items with a response scale of "years of experience" based on an expanded version of the scale used to assign Specific Vocational Preparation in the current DOT (U.S. DOL, 1991). Our findings on this set of descriptors include

- descriptive statistics in line with expectations;
- adequate reliability;
- logical correlations with other education, training, experience, and licensure/certification descriptors;
- loadings on the factor of Training (factor analytic results); and
- some usefulness in differentiating occupations.

These findings provide evidence for retaining the descriptors as measured in this study. The descriptors appear to have reasonable internal validity, and they are useful for differentiating among occupations.

### Summary

We found that the education, training, experience, and licensure/certification descriptors have acceptable reliability and validity. Thus, in general, we recommend that the descriptor measures be retained as used in the prototype. A refinement to one descriptor is strongly recommended (i.e., Instructional Program Requirements [D2]). Other refinements to reduce redundancies in the measures should be considered if the data in additional samples indicate the stability of these findings.

# Generalized Work Activities

P. RICHARD JEANNERET, WALTER C. BORMAN, U. CHRISTEAN KUBISIAK,
AND MARY ANN HANSON

Ernest J. McCormick made one of the most important contributions to job analysis research when he observed that descriptors of job content can be classified as either job-oriented or worker-oriented (McCormick, 1979). This distinction is now especially important when considering how job analysis information will be used to document the activities of tomorrow's workforce. Traditionally, most job analysis approaches have focused on identifying job tasks (i.e., a job-oriented perspective) and used the resulting information to prepare job descriptions, develop content-specific selection measures, design training curricula, and occasionally build job hierarchies. However, when comparing or combining job analysis information across differing job content domains, the task-oriented information is not amenable to such analyses.

One of the key considerations that led to the development of the Occupational Information Network (O*NET) was the realization that today's national compendium of job information, *The Dictionary of Occupational Titles* (DOT; U.S. Department of Labor [U.S. DOL], 1991a), was a system that could not respond to user needs for analysis across occupations and was limited by the task specificity inherent to its design and implementation (Advisory Panel for the Dictionary of Occupational Titles [APDOT], 1993). McCormick's vision of worker-oriented or behaviorally based job descriptors was a very viable solution to the problems inherent in the current DOT and other systems that rely on task-based information as primary descriptors. Work behaviors are not specific to tasks or technologies. Rather, work behaviors reflect the human attributes that underlie the accomplishment of tasks. In addition, we can measure work behaviors as accurately as task activities so that information obtained from worker-oriented instrumentation can be quantified and analyzed with the same level of rigor and confidence as job-oriented data. Now widely divergent occupations or jobs can be studied from a common frame of reference, and analytical techniques can be used to understand relevant similarities and differences. Furthermore, as the structure of work changes (fewer concrete tasks, less-

well-defined boundaries), there will be a significant need to measure work activities at more broadly defined levels that still have meaningful utility for multiple human resource management purposes. This chapter will first discuss how generalized work activities have been defined. Then we will discuss how we developed measures for collecting this information, before providing a review of our results.

## DEFINITION OF A GENERALIZED WORK ACTIVITY

Athough there has been considerable research associated with the identification and use of generalized work activities (GWAs), the term itself has not acquired an explicit definition that is widely acknowledged. McCormick, Cunningham, and Gordon (1967) initially coined the term *job dimension* and described the dimensions of work as combinations of worker-oriented elements. In follow-on research, Jeanneret (1969) investigated the hypothesis that "there is some structure underlying the domain of human work, and that this structure can be identified in terms of one or more sets of job dimensions" (p. viii). Again, these dimensions were characterized as composites of worker-oriented job analysis elements that applied to a wide range of work activities, generally established using factor analytic techniques. Furthermore, it was reasoned that if jobs were characterized by these dimensions, "they would be of considerable importance to both the theoretical and practical developments of the study of the world of work" (Jeanneret, 1969, p. 2).

Cunningham (1971) had a similar perspective. His vision was expressed by the term *ergometrics*, the integration of principles from the study of human behavior with the rigor of psychometrics and job analysis procedures. Furthermore, Cunningham (1971) viewed the use of a structured job analysis process that was not task-specific as being a nomothetic (as opposed to an ideographic) methodology, "an approach emphasizing the common dimensions rather than the unique characteristics of tasks, jobs, and occupations" (p. 8). Cunningham (1996) has re-emphasized his vision of 25 years ago and forecasts that some form of generic job descriptors that have meaning across the occupational spectrum will have a significant influence on the design and implementation of new job analysis and classification systems.

Similarly, Harvey (1991a) has concluded that the principal proposition of research focused on worker-oriented job analysis is to describe the general dimensions (found through factor analytic procedures) that underlie all jobs. Harvey (1991a) stated that "the issue of defining the dimensionality of work centers on the question of identifying general job behavior constructs" (p. 146).

Thus, research that has focused on identifying the dimensionality or structure of work using behavioral elements is viewed as a fundamental approach to defining GWAs. Furthermore, within the O*NET content model, GWAs represent a crucial component needed to develop a comprehensive framework for describing the similarities and differences between jobs. Any job description must consider the work to be done and the tasks people do. However, specific job tasks lack the generality needed to formulate a viable set of cross-job descriptors. GWAs, therefore, provide a plausible basis for describing work activities in a way that promotes cross-job comparisons. Using this perspective as a framework, the criteria for determining whether a construct would qualify as a GWA include

- being broad in scope and having applicability to a wide range of occupations,
- being based on job-analytic research, and
- being characteristic of the underlying structure of work.

A simple definition has evolved from these criteria: A GWA is an aggregation of similar job activities/behaviors that underlie the accomplishment of major work functions.

This definition is consistent with the concept set forth by Outerbridge (1981), who identified "generalized work behaviors" (GWBs) by examining cluster analysis results for a set of job analyses. In effect, her operational definition of a GWB was a final cluster that had "sufficient homogeneity to be descriptive of work behaviors yet possess[ed] enough heterogeneity to cover more than occupation-specific duties" (p. 7).

Finally, it should be noted that during the last 20 years several researchers have identified sets of GWAs. Some of their analyses have been based on behaviorally oriented job analysis data, and other analyses have been based on task-oriented job information. (See McCormick, 1979, or Harvey, 1991a, for a discussion of these two types of job analysis data.) A review of these research efforts will be presented in subsequent subsections of this chapter because they have been influential in the final selection and definition of the GWAs proposed for the O*NET.

## ORIGIN OF THE GWA CONCEPT

A review of the literature focused on identifying GWAs clearly indicated that the intention of several researchers was to identify constructs to support the synthetic validation of job requirement predictors. Jeanneret (1992a) and Mossholder and Arvey (1984) have traced the history of synthetic validation, and Lawshe (1952), Lawshe and Steinberg (1955), Balma (1959), and McCormick (1959) discussed how results from empirical validation studies could be generalized to situations where sample sizes were small or other validation strategies were not feasible. McCormick's research went further. He and several associates documented how GWAs (job dimensions) could serve as the linking pins between two kinds of jobs: (a) those for which there was empirical-validity evidence for a particular predictor and (b) other jobs for which validity evidence could not be obtained that were otherwise similar (on the basis of their job dimensions) to the jobs with the necessary validation support (Cunningham & McCormick, 1964a; Gordon, 1963; Gordon & McCormick, 1963; Jeanneret & McCormick, 1969; Marquandt & McCormick, 1974; McCormick, DeNisi, & Shaw, 1979; McCormick & Jeanneret, 1988; McCormick, Jeanneret, & Mecham, 1972; McCormick, Mecham, & Jeanneret, 1977, 1989; Mecham, 1985; Mecham & McCormick, 1969a; Sparrow, Patrick, Spurgeon, & Barwell, 1982).

The primary requirement of the synthetic validity concept is the analysis of job information according to a set of common dimensions that classify jobs into groups or families on the basis of their overall similarities. Then it may be possible to infer that a predictor that has been validated for certain jobs within a particular family (i.e., having a certain profile on a specified set of job dimensions) would be valid for other jobs in the same family (i.e., having the same profile on the same specified set of job dimensions). The job dimensions themselves were also found to be specifically related to certain basic aptitude measures (such as those included in the General Aptitude Test Battery [GATB]), as reported by Cunningham (1964), Jeanneret (1972, 1985), and McCormick et al. (1972).

Outerbridge (1981) had a similar perspective when she examined the viability of using GWBs in a modified application of Primoff's J-coefficient technique (Primoff, 1955a, 1955b). This modification, according to Outerbridge, was proposed by Trattner in an unpublished and undated manuscript and served as another model of synthetic validation. Specifically, Outerbridge proposed that GWBs would be the performance elements (appropriately weighted for importance) in a synthetic validation study.

A somewhat related reason for identifying GWBs was described by O'Leary, Rheinstein, and McCauley (1989), who argued that a work behavior taxonomy would group together (using cluster analysis) job duties across positions for a large number of federal government professional and administrative positions. Such an argument is very reasonable in light of the prior research efforts on the development of job families using job dimensions from various job analysis questionnaires. Success in defining families on the basis of similarity in job dimensions, for example, has been reported by Arvey, Maxwell, Gutenberg, and Camp (1981); Cornelius, Carron, and Collins (1979); DeNisi and McCormick (1974); McCormick, DeNisi, and Shaw (1977); Pass and Cunningham (1975a) and Sackett, Cornelius, and Carron (1981). In some instances, the specific purpose for forming families has been to support validity generalization efforts (Colbert & Taylor, 1978; Taylor, 1978; and Taylor & Colbert, 1978) or the transport of validity (Hoffman & Lamartine, 1995.) In other instances, the examination has focused on other personnel-related issues, such as classification, job evaluation, occupational guidance, or performance appraisal (see, e.g., Ballentine, Cunningham, & Wimpee, 1992; Champagne & McCormick, 1964a; Cornelius et al., 1979; Cunningham & Scott, 1988; Dickinson, 1977; Harvey, Friedman, Hakel, & Cornelius, 1988; Jeanneret, 1988; McCormick, DeNisi, & Marquardt, 1974; McCormick & Jeanneret, 1988; Mecham & McCormick, 1969b; Pass & Cunningham, 1975a; Scott, Cunningham, & Pass, 1989; Talbert, Carroll, & Ronan, 1976).

## THE GWA TAXONOMIC STRUCTURE

The taxonomic paradigm that underlies the structure of the GWA constructs is rooted in the primary foundation of modern psychology. As postulated by Watson (1913, 1919, 1925), behavior in any setting is a function of stimuli (S) and responses (R). Subsequently, both Hull (1943) and Skinner (1938) argued that the S–R formula also was the foundation for understanding all forms of learning, including the type of "learning" that takes place as an individual performs some activity in a work setting. The S–R theorem has been expanded in the applications of psychology to include the organism (O). In the case of analyzing the behavior of individuals at work, the O represents the worker who is the receptor of the stimuli (S) and, after processing of those stimuli, provides one or more responses (R). Miller (1953) was the first to apply the S–O–R model to the study of work, and he did so in performing what he referred to as a *task-equipment analysis* (TEA). With the emergence of the cognitive paradigm, these operations-oriented variables have become even more important.

McCormick (1964a), in developing the *Worker Activity Profile*, and McCormick, Jeanneret, and Mecham (1969a), in designing the *Position Analysis Questionnaire* (PAQ), used the S–O–R paradigm in an information-theory context to organize their structured worker-oriented job analysis questionnaires. In this context, the S–O–R model is directly representative of three primary components of work behavior:

- S: represents the information that is received by the worker (i.e., the stimulus),
- O: represents the mediation process as performed by the worker, and
- R: represents the action performed by the worker in response to the "processed stimulus."

Additional support for the above model comes from Berliner, Angell, and Shearer (1964), who proposed a taxonomy to classify the behavior of the "universal operator." The model postulated four primary operator "processes": perceptual, mediational, communication, and motor.

McCormick, Jeanneret, and Mecham (1969b, 1972) reasoned that the S–O–R model was limited when describing behavior in a work setting because it omitted two important considerations: (a) work behavior typically involves interactions and relationships with individuals, and (b) work behavior occurs within a physical and social context that typically is described in terms of working conditions, interpersonal relationships, and structured job characteristics. Interactions with others, such as communications and supervision, are included within the development of our GWAs, whereas the environmental influences will be considered in greater detail in chapter 9, which is devoted to work context.

The highest order GWA taxonomy is presented in the form of a diagrammatic model in Figure 8-1. The intent of this model is to communicate that the interactive components (i.e., the S–O–R), or information input, mental processes, and work output components, occur (a) while interactions with other people take place and (b) within a worker's and an organization's work context. This is not a level, however, at which occupations, jobs, or work functions could be meaningfully described for analytical purposes. At this level, the model simply states that the accomplishment of any

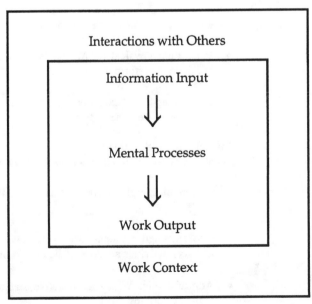

**FIGURE 8-1.** Highest order generalized work activities taxonomy.

form of work activity requires the worker to receive some information, process that information, and then make some response, and that work accomplishment often involves interactions with others and occurs within a defined context. There is little meaningful differentiation that can be made among jobs at such a broadly defined level of description.

Because the structured interpersonal, social, physical, and environmental contexts of work (i.e., the components of the work context dimension set forth in Figure 8-1) are themselves extensive and comprehensive in scope, a decision was made at the outset to provide descriptors of these work characteristics in a separate questionnaire from the one designed for the other GWAs that fall within the highest order taxonomic model. Chapters 9 and 10 describe the measurement of work context variables.

A second-order taxonomy was also identified for the GWA constructs and is presented in Figure 8-2. Brief definitions of the constructs set forth in this second-order taxonomy delineate the relationships between the highest order and second-order dimensions. This taxonomy was primarily derived on a rational rather than an empirical basis, after examining all of the constructs that were considered relevant for the GWA domain. This is not to say, however, that there is not some precedent and even empirical evidence to support a second-order taxonomic structure. We now review that evidence.

## RESEARCH RELEVANT TO THE LOWER ORDER GWAs

In the preceding section we proposed a broad, general structure based on an "S–O–R" model for or-

**Information Input**
Where and how are the information and data gained that are needed to perform this job?

- Looking For and Receiving Job-Related Information: How is the information obtained to perform this job?

- Identifying/Evaluating Job-Relevant Information: How is information interpreted to perform this job?

**Mental Processes**
What processing, planning, problem-solving, decision-making, and innovating activities are performed with job-relevant information?

- Information/Data Processing: How is information processed to perform this job?

- Reasoning/Decision Making: What decisions are made and problems solved in performing this job?

**Work Output**
What physical activities are performed, what equipment and vehicles are operated/controlled, and what complex/technical activities are accomplished as job outputs?

- Performing Physical and Manual Work Activities: What activities using the body and hands are done to perform this job?

- Performing Complex/Technical Activities: What skilled activities using coordinated movements are done to perform this job?

**Interactions with Others**
What interactions with other persons or supervisory activities occur while performing this job?

- Communicating/Interacting: What interactions with other people occur while performing this job?

- Coordinating/Developing/Managing/Advising Others: What coordinating, managerial, or advisory activities are done while performing this job?

- Administering: What administrative, staffing, monitoring, or controlling activities are done while performing this job?

**FIGURE 8-2.** Second-order generalized work activities taxonomy embedded in highest order taxonomy.

ganizing dimensions describing GWAs. This broad organizing structure clearly finds some support in the research literature. However, as mentioned, the global, higher order dimensions lack the specificity needed to describe in depth the similarities and differences among jobs or to support the identification of specific job families. Nonetheless, because a number of earlier factor analytic studies sought to identify dimensions of people's work activities at a more narrowly focused level, these studies provided a useful starting point for the development of our GWA taxonomy. In the following section of this chapter, we will briefly review the literature that was particularly influential in taxonomy development.

Three primary research sources were examined to identify and define the GWAs selected for inclusion in the O*NET: (a) the factor analytic results derived from the application of nomothetic job analysis inventories that contain general descriptors of work activity and have been applied to a wide range of jobs, (b) supervisory or management taxonomies intended to describe the dimensions underlying managerial work, and (c) factor or cluster analyses of widely relevant behavioral dimensions and models of generalized activities that cut across all or at least many types of jobs.

## Nomothetic Job Analysis Inventories

The nomothetic questionnaires that have been used to collect and measure the content of a wide spectrum of jobs across the domain of work include the Position Analysis Questionnaire (PAQ; McCormick, Jeanneret, & Mecham, 1969a, 1972); the OAI (Occupational Analysis Inventory; Cunningham, 1988), the GWI (General Work Inventory; Cunningham, Wimpee, & Ballantine, 1990); and the JEI (Job Element Inventory; Cornelius, Hakel, & Sackett, 1979).

### The PAQ

As previously mentioned, McCormick (1959) was the first to clarify the distinction between job-oriented and worker-oriented job analysis approaches from a theoretical perspective. Furthermore, with students at the Occupational Research Center of Purdue University, McCormick was able to establish (a) that job analysis terminology could be classified as either "worker-oriented" or "job-oriented" and (b) that the use of worker-oriented variables led to the identification of the structure underlying the domain of work. (See the research of Chalupsky, 1962; Cunningham, 1964; Cunningham & McCormick, 1964a, 1964b; Gordon, 1963; Gordon & McCormick, 1963; McCormick, Cunningham, & Gordon, 1967; Palmer & McCormick, 1961; and Peters & McCormick, 1962.) The ideas and early work of McCormick and his students came to fruition with the publication of the *Position Analysis Questionnaire Form A* (McCormick, Jeanneret, & Mecham, 1967) and then Forms B and C (McCor-

mick et al., 1989). The PAQ is composed of 187 items (elements) that are organized into six divisions: Information Input, Mental Processes, Work Output, Relationships with Other Persons, Job Context, and Other Job Characteristics (primarily job demands and responsibilities). Each PAQ element describes a general work behavior/activity, work condition, or job characteristic. The relevance of a PAQ item to the job being analyzed is determined by a rating scale. The rating scales measure extent of use, importance, length of time, possibility of occurrence, applicability, and particular elements (e.g., level of math used on the job).

Much research has been completed during the development and use of the PAQ that is useful for identifying meaningful GWAs for the O*NET. Regarding the underlying structure of work, Jeanneret (1969) identified five overall dimensions and 27 lower order, divisional dimensions on the basis of factor analyses of PAQ item responses. Although this original work used a relatively small sample of jobs, later work (Marquardt & McCormick, 1974; McCormick, Mecham, & Jeanneret, 1977, 1989; Harvey, 1987; Jeanneret, 1987, 1990), using larger, more representative samples and different analytic techniques, confirmed and extended these results.

Another line of research examined the structure of the PAQ by factor analyzing PAQ elements that had been rated in terms of attribute requirements (i.e., ratings of the relevance of each of 71 cognitive, perceptual, psychomotor, temperament, or interest variables for each PAQ element). The results of these factor analyses produced findings that were often very similar to those found for actual job data (Marquardt & McCormick, 1972), supporting the notion that work could be characterized in essentially the same structure using either worker behaviors (PAQ elements) or worker requirements (the attributes). Recent work by Cunningham, Powell, Wimpee, Wilson, and Ballentine (1996) on factor analyzing attribute ratings for three job analysis instruments produced several factors that are similar to the second order GWA taxonomic structure we have used for O*NET.

Finally, research completed by Jeanneret (1987, 1990) and McCormick, Mecham, and Jeanneret (1977, 1989) showed that the underlying structure of the PAQ was stable across large samples of jobs representative of the 1970 and 1980 labor force composition as determined by the census.

### The OAI and GWI

These two questionnaires are interrelated in that the GWI (Cunningham & Ballantine, 1982) is a 268-item questionnaire derived from the longer (617-item) OAI (Cunningham, 1988). Furthermore, the GWI is considered to be a less technically difficult questionnaire and is based on certain factors derived from the OAI and modifications to some of the OAI items (Cunningham et al., 1990). Both questionnaires contain worker-oriented and job-oriented items; however, the GWI is considered to be more worker oriented (Cunningham et al., 1990).

A research program that was parallel to the one focused on the PAQ was begun by Cunningham and his associates in the early 1970s. Data collected with both the OAI and its companion, the GWI, have been analyzed with factor analytic procedures similar to those used for the PAQ, and similar results have been observed. Boese and Cunningham (1975) conducted the first major factor analyses of the 602 work elements of the OAI. The analyses produced 132 first-order factors and 28 higher order dimensions that were found to be highly stable. Cunningham and Scott (1988) subjected the worker-oriented variables of the OAI to factor- and cluster-analytic procedures ($N$ = 1,343 job analyses) and found 47 "sectional" factors that could be grouped into 11 clusters. Many of these clusters are comparable to the "overall" dimensions of the PAQ database. Cunningham and Scott (1988) also analyzed 34 of the U.S. Employment Service (USES) Worker Functions and Characteristics ratings for 12,375 jobs and then used a multitrait, multimethod analysis to relate the USES clusters to those of the OAI across 1,034 jobs that had been rated with both procedures. They concluded that seven general factors underlie the USES and OAI worker-oriented variables. Conceptually, these OAI general factors match many of the overall PAQ dimensions.

Finally, the GWI was used to obtain data on 164 U.S. Air Force enlisted specialties, and a factor analysis of these data resulted in 62 first-order factors, which were subjected to higher order factor analysis (Cunningham et al., 1990). Of 15 second-order factors, 14 were interpreted; because of the nature of the sample of jobs analyzed, these factors are much more specific than those previously identified for the PAQ and OAI.

### The JEI

This questionnaire was developed by Cornelius and Hakel (1978) by editing the PAQ to make it easier to read and more meaningful to Coast Guard incumbents. The result was a 153-item questionnaire that used only one rating scale (a 6-point scale measuring Relative Time Spent) for all items. The JEI retained the same divisional format for the revised items as is found in the PAQ, and the underlying content of the JEI items is the same as that of the corresponding items in the PAQ.

Two factor analytic studies of the JEI, following procedures similar to those applied to the PAQ, led another group of researchers to conclude that there were consistent subjective and quantitative similarities in the factor structures that resulted after the two questionnaires were used to analyze the work activities of very different samples of jobs (Harvey et al., 1988). They also concluded that correlations ranging from the .80s and .90s between PAQ and JEI factors when the data were collected under very different administrative circumstances make "a strong statement

regarding the robustness of the job dimensions measured by these instruments" (Harvey et al., 1988, p. 646). Finally, these researchers pointed out that such a finding is "consistent with the basic worker-oriented premise that there is an underlying structure of work that can be assessed through standardized job analysis methods (Jeanneret, 1969; McCormick, 1959)" (Harvey et al., 1988, p. 646).

### Summary of Taxonomic Research Using Nomothetic Questionnaires

Clearly, the factor analysis of data collected with worker-oriented job analysis questionnaires has provided considerable insight into the structure that underlies the domain of human work. Because the worker-oriented approach is not specific to technology or tasks, it permits an understanding of the general, cross-job structure that is not possible with a job-oriented job analysis methodology. Furthermore, the stability of the factor structure found using a worker-oriented questionnaire when the databases change is satisfying evidence that the worker-oriented approach can withstand the changes of time as the mechanics and tasks of jobs evolve with technology and innovation. And finally, the fact that there is a degree of convergence, albeit often subjectively assessed, across the various factor structures that have been obtained using different worker-oriented questionnaires and very diverse samples of jobs is sufficient to encourage the use of GWAs based on such research to study jobs in the future.

## Managerial Taxonomies

Much of the foregoing discussion has focused on taxonomies of GWAs derived using global task questionnaires. One characteristic of many of these questionnaires is that the tasks under consideration are somewhat slanted toward hands-on and production-type jobs. Thus, in developing a truly general, cross-job taxonomy, it was important to consider the results obtained in efforts intended to capture the dimensions that are useful in summarizing managerial work.

The following empirically derived managerial taxonomies were used to guide selection of dimensions for the supervisory portion of the GWA descriptors: Flanagan's (1951) six summary dimensions from his critical incident study of Air Force officers; Williams' (1956) taxonomy of executive performance, also derived from critical incident research, which included six general requirement categories and 82 specific performance dimensions; Hemphill's (1960) 10 job dimensions, derived from a factor analysis of executives' responses to a job analysis questionnaire; the Tornow and Pinto (1976) 13-dimension managerial taxonomy, also based on factor analyses of responses by 500 managers to a 197-item job analysis questionnaire; Mitchell's (1978) dimension system for professional and managerial jobs, resulting from factor analyses of managerial responses to the *Professional and Managerial Position Questionnaire* (PMPQ); Yukl's (1987) integrating taxonomy of 13 "mid-range" dimensions of managerial behavior; and the Borman and Brush (1993) taxonomy of managerial "mega-dimensions" developed by summarizing all of the above dimensions, as well as other statistically derived dimensions, using an empirical clustering of expert judgments regarding the structure of these dimensions.

All of these dimension systems and taxonomies were seen as very useful in contributing to the supervisory/managerial part of the GWAs. The Borman and Brush dimension system was especially appealing as a source of GWAs because it represents a summary of all of the other managerial taxonomies in addition to other empirical studies of managerial performance across a variety of managerial levels and types of organizations.

## Other Work Activity Dimensions

The following additional dimension sets were reviewed as potential sources of GWAs: The Dowell and Wexley (1978) taxonomy of first-line supervisor job attributes, based on factor analyses of supervisors' responses to a 100-item work activity survey; Outerbridge's (1981) summary clusters of activities related to professional-level government employees, based on a similarity sorting of 223 U.S. DOT duty statements; O'Leary et al.'s (1989) updated categorization of these professional jobs' activity dimensions, resulting in 57 dimensions; the Campbell, McCloy, Oppler, and Sager (1993) set of eight categories from their comprehensive model of job performance, resulting in large part from Project A work (Campbell, 1990a); a summary list of 12 dimensions from a study intended to identify and summarize general performance requirements for all nonmanagerial jobs in the U.S. economy (Borman, Ackerman, Kubisiak, & Quigley, 1994); competency dimension systems developed by the U.S. Office of Personnel Management (1991) for managerial, professional, and administrative occupations (the *Multipurpose Occupational Systems Analysis Inventory—Close Ended*); activities from the National Job Analysis survey (American College Testing, 1993); and work on the Secretary's Commission for Achieving Necessary Skills (SCANS; Peterson, 1994), an effort to summarize job activities across a wide variety of jobs in the U.S.

It should be observed that the Campbell et al. (1993) and Borman et al. (1994) taxonomies are not necessarily intended to reflect GWAs. They represent *performance requirements*, dimensions that should differentiate between effective and ineffective performance. Accordingly, some of these dimensions are not appropriate for a GWA taxonomy (e.g., Initiative, Cooperation). Nevertheless, some of the other dimensions in these systems were thought to be more useful for a GWA taxonomy (e.g., Communication, Organization, and Judgment/Problem Solving).

## THE LOWER ORDER GWA TAXONOMIC STRUCTURE

We believe that selecting a lower order GWA taxonomic structure to guide the development of the GWA questionnaire is consistent with the principles expressed by Cappelli (1995) in his discussion of the conceptual issues underlying a system for classifying occupations. He stated that the choice of a classification scheme should consider the number and importance of propositions that can be made. Cappelli also contended that the classification system selected should reflect some underlying theory and demonstrate stability and robustness. We have carefully reviewed the theoretical and taxonomic arguments set forth by the prominent job analysis researchers of the last three decades and have extensively relied on their findings to create our GWAs. A comprehensive discussion of the research findings and interpretations underlying our GWAs as well as a cross-walk portraying the relationship between our 42-dimension taxonomy and each of the other taxonomic systems just discussed is given by Jeanneret and Borman (1995).

### Overview of GWA Development Strategy

In the preceding sections we have reviewed a variety of taxonomies of GWAs. Some of these taxonomies represent rather broad organizing frameworks, as in the higher order taxonomies. Others represent more narrow, but nonetheless cross-job, variables that might be used to describe people's work activities. The question that arises at this juncture is rather straightforward: How might we synthesize these dimensions to create a comprehensive taxonomy of people's work activities? In this section we use extant literature to develop such a taxonomy and link the resulting lower order GWAs to a broader set of higher order variables.

As indicated previously, a number of taxonomic structures and job analysis research efforts were examined to develop both a model for the GWA constructs as well as the definitions and rating scale levels for each individual GWA to be included in the O*NET. The researchers began by selecting the GWA constructs, using several criteria:

- The construct should have a foundation in one or more research efforts;
- The construct should have definitive underlying content that, for GWAs derived from factor analyses of job analysis data, was determined by examining the content of individual items with significant factor loadings on the factor of interest;
- The constructs as a set should be comprehensive,

as much as possible reflecting work activities of all jobs in the U.S. economy; and

- The constructs should provide unique descriptive information.

By following such a strategy, we also addressed the matter of specificity. The taxonomic structures presented earlier indicate that GWAs could be expressed at a very broad level of generality or at successively narrower levels across the specificity–generality continuum. Clearly, the analysis of work at a more specific level will yield occupational information at a finer level of differentiation. Because we intend for the GWAs to act as stand-alone sources of occupational information that can be used to derive meaningful outputs for human resource management, we have selected a level of specificity that is consistent with the research findings for comparable sets of GWAs.

After an initial set of GWAs was developed, we expanded our search to be sure that we had captured constructs that were included in other job analysis systems, or ones that we believed would be relevant to understanding work as it is expected to evolve in the next century. Consequently, there are a few GWAs that are not well grounded in past research but seem to have strong likelihood for measuring work content that is more often found in high-performance organizations or will become more prevalent in the future.

The following procedures were used to complete the definitions for the GWAs. Initially, working definitions for items were prepared by the researchers, and after refinement these became the operational definitions for each GWA construct. A GWA's definition evolved from the titles and definitions given to the factors or dimensions by their original researchers/authors. Furthermore, the content of the factors/dimensions was considered by examining the items with high factor loadings, when factor analysis data were available, to give further clarity to the definition. Finally, after a pilot trial of the GWAs, the construct labels and definitions were simplified so that they could be understood by most job incumbents throughout the world of work. Each of the 42 GWAs is identified in Table 8-1, which presents an operational definition for each construct and examples of high and low points on the Level scale designed to measure the construct. A brief summary of the 42 GWAs, organized in terms of the four highest order taxonomic categories, is presented below.

### Information Input

Within this domain we identified two second-order factors: Looking For and Receiving Job-Related Information and Identifying/Evaluating Job-Relevant Information. Research that used data obtained from the PAQ, JEI, and GWI was the dominant source for defining the GWA constructs that are necessary to describe the scope of the Information Input domain.

Getting Information Needed to Do the Job (D1)[1] and Monitoring Processes, Materials, and Surroundings (D2) were the two GWAs that describe activities of a worker when looking for and receiving job-related information. Once information is received, it must then be identified or evaluated. Three GWAs consistently emerged in the research literature that describe identifying/evaluating job-relevant information: Identifying Objects, Actions, and Events (D3); Inspecting Equipment, Structures, or Materials (D4); and Estimating the Characteristics of Materials, Products, Events, or Information (D5).

### Mental Processes

Once job-relevant input has been received, the worker's mental capabilities are involved and can be categorized as two second-order factors: Processing Information or Data, and Reasoning/Making Decisions. Four GWAs were identified from the research literature that were descriptive of Information/Data Processing activities: Judging the Qualities of Objects, Services, or Persons (D6); Evaluating Information for Compliance to Standards (D7); Processing Information (D8); and Analyzing Data or Information (D9). These GWAs emerged from the analysis of all levels of work. On the other hand, when examining the Reasoning/Making Decisions second-order factor, the research literature indicated that many of the relevant constructs were derived from studies of supervisory, managerial, or professional work. More specifically, two GWAs—Making Decisions and Solving Problems (D10) and Updating and Using Job-Relevant Knowledge (D12)—emerged from studies of all types and levels of jobs. Alternatively, three other GWAs are more specific to managerial/professional work. These GWAs include Thinking Creatively (D11); Developing Objectives and Strategies (D13); and Scheduling Work and Activities (D14). Because of the distinction that is made in the literature between organizing one's own work versus the activities of others, (D15) Organizing, Planning, and Prioritizing Work is intended to include personal time management; therefore it is likely to be relevant at some level to virtually all jobs.

Work output. Given that job-relevant information has been received and processed and decisions have been made, the worker responds with some type of output. Two second-order factors were identified that segment the work output into either physical or technical activities. The first second-order factor, Performing Physical and Manual Work Activities, includes four GWAs: Performing General Physical Activities (D16); Handling and Moving Objects (D17); Controlling Machines and Processes (D18); and Operating Vehicles and Mechanized Devices or Equipment (D19). The other second-order factor was labeled *Performing Complex/Technical Activities*. Al-

---

[1]Each GWA was given an identification that begins with "D" followed by a sequential number that ranged from 1 to 42.

**TABLE 8-1**
**Descriptions and Definitions of Generalized Work Activities**

| Construct label | Operational definition | Level scale |
|---|---|---|
| *Looking For and Receiving Job-Related Information* | | |
| 1. Getting information needed to do the job. | Observing, receiving, and otherwise obtaining information from all relevant sources. | High—Getting new information from many sources, often by actively interacting with the sources. Low—Making regular use of the same types of information from a single source. |
| 2. Monitoring processes, materials, or surroundings. | Monitoring and reviewing information from materials, events, or the environment, often to detect problems or to find out when things are finished. | High—Monitoring very complex processes, events, or circumstances. Low—Monitoring processes, events, or circumstances that are not complex. |
| *Identifying and Evaluating Job-Related Information* | | |
| 3. Identifying objects, actions, and events. | Identifying information received by making estimates or categorizations, recognizing differences or similarities, or sensing changes in circumstances or events. | High—Making extremely difficult identifications based on very complex information. Low—Making easy identifications based on information that is not complex. |
| 4. Inspecting equipment, structures, or materials. | Inspecting or diagnosing equipment, structures, or materials to identify the causes of errors or other problems or defects. | High—Making inspections or diagnoses of a complex system that may have many interrelated parts and determining whether conditions exist within a range of acceptable limits. Low—Making easy judgments about the quality or importance of things or people when there are many guidelines. |
| 5. Estimating the characteristics of materials, products, events, or information. | Estimating sizes, distances, and quantities, or determining time, costs, resources, or materials needed to perform a work activity. | High—Making very difficult estimates of characteristics, time, or resources where there is limited guidance or supporting information. Low—Making straightforward estimates of characteristics, time, or resources where there is considerable guidance and supporting information. |
| *Information/Data Processing* | | |
| 6. Judging the qualities of objects, services, or persons. | Making judgments about or assessing the value, importance, or quality of things or people. | High—Making very difficult judgments about the quality or importance of things or people for which there is limited guidance or supporting information. Low—Evaluating information against a simple criterion. |
| 7. Evaluating information for compliance to standards. | Evaluating information against a set of standards and verifying that it is correct. | High—Evaluating complex information for compliance with regulations, laws, or technical criteria, where compliance decisions require significant interpretation or judgment. Low—Evaluating information against a simple criterion. |
| 8. Processing information. | Compiling, coding, categorizing, calculating, tabulating, auditing, verifying, or processing information or data. | High—Processing very different and complicated data or information, where there are several ways in which the information can be processed. Low—Processing data or information that is standardized and easy to understand, where there is only one way to process the information. |
| 9. Analyzing data or information. | Identifying underlying principles, reasons, or facts by breaking down information or data into separate parts. | High—Analyzing very different and complicated data or information that can be used for making critical decisions. Low—Analyzing data or information that is easy to understand. |
| *Reasoning/Decisions Making* | | |
| 10. Making decisions and solving problems. | Combining, evaluating, and reasoning with information and data to make decisions and solve problems. These processes involve making decisions about the relative importance of information and choosing the best solution. | High—Reaching conclusions after considering a large number of choices that are often ambiguous or abstract, where there are competing viewpoints and alternatives that must be considered before reaching final decisions and the solutions decided upon will have very significant impact. Low—Reaching conclusions after considering a few choices that are usually well defined, where there are a limited number of possible actions, and the decisions or solutions will have minor impact. |

*Table 8-1 continues*

**TABLE 8-1** (*Continued*)

| Construct label | Operational definition | Level scale |
|---|---|---|
| 11. Thinking creatively. | Originating, inventing, designing, or creating new applications, ideas, relationships, systems, or products, including artistic contributions. | High—Creating or inventing new and yet-to-be-proven practices, technologies, materials, products, or strategies, where the creative effort will have widespread impact and will result in substantial improvements for both an organization and its customers.<br>Low—Offering suggestions for some change or improvement to immediate work functions or products. |
| 12. Updating and using job-relevant knowledge. | Keeping up-to-date technically and knowing one's own job's and related jobs' functions. | High—Learning, retaining, and staying current with complex, often highly technical information.<br>Low—Learning, retaining, and staying current with relatively easy-to-master information. |
| 13. Developing objectives and strategies. | Establishing long-range objectives and specifying the strategies and actions to achieve these objectives. | High—Doing complex, future-oriented strategic planning.<br>Low—Doing strategic or long-term planning that is not complex. |
| 14. Scheduling work and activities. | Scheduling events, programs, activities, as well as the work of others. | High—Engaging in complex and difficult scheduling activities.<br>Low—Engaging in simple or straightforward scheduling activities. |
| 15. Organizing, planning, and prioritizing work. | Developing plans to accomplish work, and prioritizing and organizing one's own work. | High—Doing a high degree of complex planning, organizing, and prioritizing of one's own work.<br>Low—Doing uncomplicated planning, organizing, or prioritizing of one's own work. |

Performing Physical and Manual Work Activities

| Construct label | Operational definition | Level scale |
|---|---|---|
| 16. Performing general physical activities. | Performing physical activities that require moving one's whole body, such as in climbing, lifting, balancing, walking, stooping, where the activities often also require considerable use of the arms and legs, such as in the physical handling of materials. | High—Making repetitive and often fatiguing extensive use of the whole body in completing work activities that are done with or without the use of tools.<br>Low—Making nonfatiguing use of the whole body in completing work activities that are done with or without the use of tools. |
| 17. Handling and moving objects. | Using one's own hands and arms in handling, installing, forming, positioning, and moving materials, or in manipulating things, including the use of keyboards. | High—Using one's hands and arms to do the same functions almost continually.<br>Low—Making little use of one's hands and arms. |
| 18. Controlling machines and processes. | Using either control mechanisms or direct physical activity to operate machines or processes (not including computers of vehicles). | High—Controlling machines or processes that are very difficult to operate.<br>Low—Controlling machines or processes that are easy to operate. |
| 19. Operating vehicles, mechanized devices, or equipment. | Running, maneuvering, navigating, or driving vehicles or mechanized equipment, such as forklifts, passenger vehicles, aircraft, or water craft. | High—Operating equipment or vehicles that are very difficult to run.<br>Low—Operating equipment or vehicles that are easy to run. |

Performing Complex/Technical Activities

| Construct label | Operational definition | Level scale |
|---|---|---|
| 20. Interacting with computers. | Controlling computer functions by using programs, setting up functions, writing software, or otherwise communicating with computer systems. | High—Using computers to develop very complex, high speed data linkages and operating systems.<br>Low—Using computers to produce standard correspondence, graphic materials, and business-related information. |
| 21. Drafting, laying-out, and specifying technical devices, parts, and equipment. | Providing documentation, detailed instructions, drawings, or specifications to inform others about how devices, parts, equipment, or structures are to be fabricated, constructed, assembled, modified, maintained, or used. | High—Drafting and specifying the components or technical relationships for complicated devices, parts, or equipment.<br>Low—Drafting or specifying the components or technical relationships for devices, parts, or equipment that are easily understood. |
| 22. Implementing ideas, programs, systems, or products. | Conducting or carrying out work procedures and activities in accord with one's own ideas or information provided through directions/ instructions for purposes of installing, modifying, preparing, delivering, constructing, integrating, finishing, or completing programs, systems, structures, or products. | High—Performing highly complex and very difficult work activities with very limited guidelines to follow.<br>Low—Performing activities that have clear-cut directions and are easy to carry out. |

*Table 8.1 continues*

**TABLE 8-1** (*Continued*)

| Construct label | Operational definition | Level scale |
|---|---|---|
| 23. Repairing and maintaining mechanical equipment. | Fixing, servicing, aligning, setting up, adjusting, and testing machines, devices, moving parts, and equipment that operate primarily on the basis of mechanical (not electronic) principles. | High—Performing complex or nonroutine repair, maintenance, or adjustment of mechanical equipment, often involving overhauls or rebuilding.<br>Low—Performing straightforward repair, maintenance, or adjustment of mechanical equipment using established, easy to understand procedures. |
| 24. Repairing and maintaining electronic equipment. | Fixing, servicing, adjusting, regulating, calibrating, fine-tuning, or testing machines, devices, and equipment that operate primarily on the basis of electrical or electronic (not mechanical) principles. | High—Performing complex or nonroutine repair, maintenance, or adjustment of electronic equipment, where repairs are often made to complex internal components or circuitry.<br>Low—Performing straightforward repair, maintenance, or adjustment of electronic devices or equipment using established, easy to understand procedures. |
| 25. Documenting and recording information. | Entering, transcribing, recording, storing, or maintaining information in either written form or by electronic/magnetic recording. | High—Documenting or recording very complex information using new, unstandardized procedures.<br>Low—Documenting or recording straightforward information using predetermined forms and procedures. |

Communicating/Interacting

| | | |
|---|---|---|
| 26. Interpreting the meaning of information for others. | Translating or explaining what information means and how it can be understood or used to support responses or feedback to others. | High—Making very difficult interpretations of information with limited, if any, guidance to follow.<br>Low—Making easy interpretations of information with a high degree of guidance to follow. |
| 27. Communicating with supervisors, peers, or subordinates. | Providing information to supervisors, fellow workers, and subordinates. This information can be exchanged face-to-face, in writing, or via telephone/electronic transfer. | High—Providing complex oral and written communications to others in the organization.<br>Low—Providing straightforward oral or written communications to others in the organization. |
| 28. Communicating with persons outside the organization. | Communicating with persons outside the organization, representing the organization to customers, the public, government, and other external sources. This information can be exchanged face-to-face, in writing, or via telephone/electronic transfer. | High—Presenting complex oral and written communications to persons outside the organization.<br>Low—Presenting routine and simple oral and written communications to persons outside the organization. |
| 29. Establishing and maintaining interpersonal relationships. | Developing constructive and cooperative working relationships with others. | High—Developing very good interpersonal relationships with highly diverse individuals or stakeholders in difficult situations.<br>Low—Developing very few working relationships with others. |
| 30. Assisting and caring for others. | Providing assistance or personal care to others. | High—Providing care or assistance to others in highly stressful or difficult situations.<br>Low—Needing to provide minimal help or assistance to others. |
| 31. Selling or influencing others. | Convincing others to buy merchandise/goods, or otherwise changing their minds or actions. | High—Doing a lot of high-level persuading to accomplish work objectives, involving persuading a very difficult to convince audience.<br>Low—Doing little persuading to accomplish work objectives, because there is little need to convince others in any area. |
| 32. Resolving conflicts and negotiating with others. | Handling complaints, arbitrating disputes, and resolving grievances, or otherwise negotiating with others. | High—Handling complaints and negotiations in very challenging situations, involving complex matters and significant conflict and pressure.<br>Low—Handling negotiations that involve very simple matters that are easily resolved or involve complaint-handling or negotiation. |
| 33. Performing for or working directly with the public. | Performing for people or dealing directly with the public, including serving persons in restaurants and stores, and receiving clients or guests. | High—Handling interactions with the public, where the audience is hard to please or other conflict is involved.<br>Low—Having little interaction with the public, or needing to have only brief interactions. |

Coordinating/Developing/Managing/Advising Others

| | | |
|---|---|---|
| 34. Coordinating the work and activities of others. | Coordinating members of a work group to accomplish tasks. | High—Coordinating the work of many employees, where a complex sequencing of others' tasks is required.<br>Low—Needing to do little coordinating of others. |

*Table 8-1 continues*

**TABLE 8-1** (*Continued*)

| Construct label | Operational definition | Level scale |
|---|---|---|
| 35. Developing and building teams. | Encouraging and building mutual trust, respect, and cooperation among team members. | High—Managing large teams and building cooperation among diverse team members toward accomplishment of highly complex or poorly defined activities/projects.<br>Low—Doing little team building. |
| 36. Teaching others. | Identifying educational needs, developing formal training programs or classes, and teaching or instructing others. | High—Teaching and explaining difficult tasks, concepts, or material and conducting complex training.<br>Low—Doing little training or educating of others. |
| 37. Guiding, directing, and motivating subordinates. | Providing guidance and direction to subordinates, including setting performance standards and monitoring subordinates. | High—Directing and motivating several organization members and building and maintaining morale in difficult or unpleasant work settings.<br>Low—Doing little directing or motivating of subordinates. |
| 38. Coaching and developing others. | Identifying developmental needs of others and coaching or otherwise helping others to improve their knowledge or skills. | High—Identifying effective ways of developing others to perform highly complex or difficult tasks and coaching them under these difficult conditions.<br>Low—Doing little coaching or developing of others. |
| 39. Providing consultation and advice to others. | Providing consultation and expert advice to management or other groups on technical, systems-related, or process-related topics. | High—Providing expert guidance on complex matters regarding the design, development, or implementation of major programs.<br>Low—Providing little advice or consultation to others. |
| | Administering | |
| 40. Performing administrative activities. | Approving requests, handling paperwork, and performing day-to-day administrative tasks. | High—Overseeing administrative activities for a large workforce, with a complex set of administrative procedures.<br>Low—Doing very straightforward administrative activities. |
| 41. Staffing organizational units. | Recruiting, interviewing, selecting, hiring, and promoting persons for an organization. | High—Overseeing the staff of a large and diverse workforce, with complex staffing needs.<br>Low—Doing very straightforward staffing activities. |
| 42. Monitoring and controlling resources. | Monitoring and controlling resources and overseeing the spending of money. | High—Monitoring and controlling a large number of resources, including managing a large budget.<br>Low—Needing to do little monitoring or controlling of resources or money. |

though certain physical movements are necessarily involved in the accomplishment of the specific GWAs subsumed under this factor, they are characterized more by the skill demands required for successful performance. These six GWAs are Interacting with Computers (D20); Drafting, Laying-Out and Specifying Technical Devices, Parts, and Equipment (D21); Implementing Ideas, Programs, Systems or Products (D22); Repairing and Maintaining Mechanical Equipment (D23); Repairing and Maintaining Electronic Equipment (D24); and Documenting and Recording Information (D25).

### Interacting With Others

Communication is, of course, a critical activity in organizational life, and we found Communicating/ Interacting to be a useful second-order factor that is descriptive of a critical component of interpersonal relationships. One important element of any communication is making sure that the intended audience understands the content of the communication. (D26) Interpreting the Meaning of Information for Others, addresses this aspect of communication.

The GWA taxonomy draws a distinction between communicating inside an organization and communicating to customers and others outside the organization, including the public. Communicating With Supervisors, Peers, or Subordinates (D27) is concerned with the internal communication activity; Communicating With Persons Outside the Organization (D28) relates to external communication activities. A related activity is establishing good working relations with others, which is especially relevant in a team setting but more generally important for contributing to a smooth-running organization. The dimension covering this activity is labeled Establishing and Maintaining Interpersonal Relationships (D29). An activity that is especially relevant to the health care industry and to elder-care operations is (D30) Assisting and Caring for Others.

Still another interpersonal activity, but of a very different type, is Selling or Influencing Others (D31). This GWA includes persuading others to buy products or otherwise influencing others to change their behavior. Similar in some ways is (D32) Resolving Conflicts and Negotiating With Others. However, this GWA involves handling complaints and arbitrating disputes. A GWA that at first appears related to the external communication dimension is Performing or Working Directly With the Public (D33). Actually, this activity is intended to represent important dimensions of certain high-population occupations such as police officers, restaurant servers, and government employees dealing directly with the public. Another second-order factor underlying interaction with others was Coordinating/Developing/Managing/Advising Others. There are six GWAs that we believe describe these types of interrelationships. D36 is similar to D33 in that it is targeted toward a particularly large population set of occupations. Teaching Others (D36) involves both the development of training programs and the delivery of training or instruction to others. Presumably, this dimension is at the core of school teaching jobs as well as trainer positions in corporate or other types of organizations.

GWAs D34 and D35, as well as D37–D39, are supervisory or management dimensions. They are intended to cover, in a comprehensive yet parsimonious fashion, work activities required in a supervisory/managerial setting. (D34) Coordinating the Work and Activities of Others, involves overseeing the coordination of a team's or a large group's work activities. A similar GWA, but with a more direct team focus, is Developing and Building Teams (D35). The increasing emphasis in U.S. organizations on team-based structures motivated this dimension.

A broader GWA, Guiding, Directing, and Motivating Subordinates (D37), is concerned with setting standards for performance and monitoring employee performance against those standards. (D38) Coaching and Developing Others has overlap with the teaching dimension but is more focused on providing developmental opportunities for subordinates as a supervisor working directly with them on a full-time basis. Providing Consultation and Advice to Others (D39) is not necessarily a management dimension. It may involve external consulting on technical or management matters.

The third second-order factor involving relationships with others we labeled *Administering*, and the last three GWAs relate more to administrative than hands-on management or supervision dimensions. Performing Administrative Activities (D40) describes the paperwork, recordkeeping, and similar activities in management jobs. Staffing Organizational Units (D41) refers to the recruiting, selecting, and hiring functions in an organization. Finally, Monitoring and Controlling Resources (D42) involves overseeing non-personnel-related resources such as budgets, materials, and other assets.

## SAMPLE AND MEASURES

Chapter 4 describes the target sample of occupations for job analysis and the subset of these occupations that have actually been sufficiently analyzed to date. Briefly, the data analyses to be reported involve 35

**TABLE 8-2**
**Thirty-Five Occupations With Four or More Incumbents Completing the Generalized Work Activities Questionnaire**

| Occupation code | Occupation title | Number of respondents |
|---|---|---|
| 15005 | Education Administrators | 11 |
| 19005 | General Managers & Top Executives | 43 |
| 21108 | Loan Officers & Counselors | 6 |
| 22135 | Mechanical Engineers | 11 |
| 25105 | Computer Programmers | 7 |
| 31302 | Teachers, Preschool | 6 |
| 31305 | Teachers, Elementary School | 13 |
| 32502 | Registered Nurses | 25 |
| 32902 | Medical & Clinical Laboratory Technologists | 8 |
| 49008 | Salespersons, Except Scientific & Retail | 13 |
| 49011 | Salespersons, Retail | 18 |
| 49021 | Stock Clerks, Sales Floor | 13 |
| 49023 | Cashiers | 22 |
| 51002 | First Line Supervisors, Clerical/Administrative | 59 |
| 53102 | Tellers | 4 |
| 53311 | Insurance Claims Clerks | 7 |
| 53905 | Teachers' Aides & Assistants, Clerical | 8 |
| 55108 | Secretaries, Except Legal & Medical | 65 |
| 55305 | Receptionists & Information Clerks | 5 |
| 55338 | Bookkeeping, Accounting & Auditing Clerks | 25 |
| 55347 | General Office Clerks | 88 |
| 61005 | Police & Detective Supervisors | 13 |
| 63014 | Police Patrol Officers | 24 |
| 65008 | Waiters & Waitresses | 10 |
| 65026 | Cooks, Restaurant | 4 |
| 65038 | Food Preparation Workers | 27 |
| 66008 | Nursing Aides, Orderlies & Attendants | 22 |
| 67005 | Janitors & Cleaners | 30 |
| 85119 | Other Machinery Maintenance Mechanics | 4 |
| 85132 | Maintenance Repairers, General Utility | 27 |
| 87902 | Earth Drillers, Except Oil & Gas | 4 |
| 89108 | Machinists | 4 |
| 92974 | Packaging & Filling Machine Operators | 16 |
| 97102 | Truck Drivers, Heavy or Tractor Trailer | 9 |
| 97111 | Bus Drivers, Schools | 11 |

occupations with a minimum of four incumbents per occupation (see Table 8-2). The number of incumbents varies from 4 to 88, with a harmonic mean of 9.68 per occupation. Occupational Analysis Field Center (OAFC) job analysts also provided ratings on the GWAs. At least six analyst ratings were generated for each GWA on each of the 80 occupations in the entire sample.

## THE GWA RATING SCALES

Level, Importance, and Frequency scales were developed for the GWA questionnaire, and each GWA has a unique Level scale definition. As in several other domains, the Level scales can be characterized as measuring complexity. As pointed out by Cain and

Treiman (1981), as well as Hunter (1983, 1986), complexity is a major influence on job performance and clearly delineates one type of job from another within the same occupational domain. In many instances, the research studies we consulted reported on specific jobs that were high, medium, or low with respect to the degree of complexity of that construct or the extent to which the construct was required of job incumbents. In most cases, the intent has been to demonstrate the complexity of a GWA as it occurs *across* the domain of work. Hence, the Level scale is a rating that reflects "across-jobs" rather than "within-a-job" complexity. The Level scales are 7-point scales (1–7) with an additional *not relevant* option. Three behavioral statements were also developed for each GWA Level scale to anchor the high, mid-range, and low levels. Where possible, we identified statements from research on the PAQ or OAI that had been previously scaled according to level or complexity. The remaining anchors were prepared by us specifically for this study.

The Importance scale has 5 points (1–5), with the verbal anchors *not important, somewhat unimportant, important, very important,* and *extremely important.* The Frequency scale is a 7-point scale with the verbal anchors *once per year or less, more than once per year, more than once per month, more than once per week, daily, several times per day,* and *hourly or more often.* Both the Importance and Frequency scales are "within-job" ratings. For each descriptor, the respondent to the survey was asked to read the descriptor label and definition and then answer the Level scale question, the Importance scale question next, and then the Frequency question. Figure 8-3 contains an example GWA descriptor and the rating scales.

# RESULTS

## Descriptive Statistics

Table 8-3 contains the GWA overall means across all 35 occupations and the standard deviations associated with those means. Also appearing in Table 8-3 are the interrater agreement coefficients for each descriptor along with the standard error of measurement. Examined together, these statistical indices imply that job incumbents can use the GWAs to describe their jobs and that they can do so in a consistent manner.

Focusing first on the Level scale data, there is considerable variation in the means across the 42 descriptors. The specifying equipment and repair dimensions and some of the managerial dimensions have quite low means, reflecting the fact that most jobs in the economy (and in our sample of 35 occupations) do not involve any lay out, repairing, or managing. The highest means are for descriptors such as Establishing Relationships (D29) and Communicating, Internal (D27)—activities that apply to most occupations. Even with the latter dimensions, how-

ever, the means are only slightly above the scale midpoint, with considerable variation across occupations. This suggests that range restriction is not a problem with these GWA Level scales. A similar pattern of means and standard deviations is evident for the Importance scales. The Frequency scale means are almost uniformly higher than the Level scale means, where this comparison is appropriate (i.e., they both have 7-point scales). The standard deviations are in general lower, indicating a relative restriction-in-range for the frequency ratings.

## Reliability

The *k*-rater interrater agreement coefficients are for the most part quite impressive, especially for the Level scales. Most of the coefficients are in the .70s and .80s for the Level scales, with the range from .51 to .92 and a median of .82; for the Importance scale, these coefficients are usually slightly lower (*Mdn* = .78). Finally, interrater agreement is lower still for the Frequency scale (*Mdn* = .68). Nonetheless, overall reliability for the GWA descriptor scales is acceptable. Of course, once the target of 30 incumbents per occupation is achieved, interrater agreement should be outstanding.

Along these lines, we computed estimates of the interrater reliabilities to be expected, from 30 raters and from a single rater. For the Level scales, 35 of the 42 descriptors have coefficients of .90 or higher at the 30-rater level. As expected, the Importance scale provides somewhat lower reliabilities, but 33 of the 42 dimensions have 30-rater interrater agreement coefficients at .90 or higher. Again, the Frequency scale interrater agreement coefficients are somewhat lower, but at the 30-rater level, these scale ratings are also quite reliable as well. In summary, these analyses demonstrate that the GWA requirements of occupations can be reliably evaluated by incumbents in those occupations. As a benchmark, the reader is referred to the work of Geyer, Hice, Hawk, Boese, and Brannon (1989), who analyzed the reliabilities of four experienced occupational analysts across 20 diverse occupations using the standard United States Employment Services job analysis procedures. For work functions (data, people, things), the reported reliabilities ranged from .77 (one rater) to .95 (four raters), using coefficient alpha and a variance ratio procedure to measure analyst consistency.

As discussed in chapter 5, it might be argued that including *not relevant* (i.e., zero) scores when computing interrater agreement provides higher estimates of reliability than if these zeros were not included. This argument could be extended to the Importance and Frequency scales in that when *not relevant* was indicated, a rating of 1 (*not important* or *once per year or less*) was used in computing the interrater agreement for the Importance and Frequency scales. To address the possibility of different reliability estimates for these different scoring procedures, we recalculated the reliabilities with *not relevant* responses removed. Finally, for the Level scales only, reliabili-

### 23. Repairing and Maintaining Mechanical Equipment

Fixing, servicing, aligning, setting up, adjusting, and testing machines, devices, moving parts, and equipment that operate primarily on the basis of mechanical (not electronic) principles.

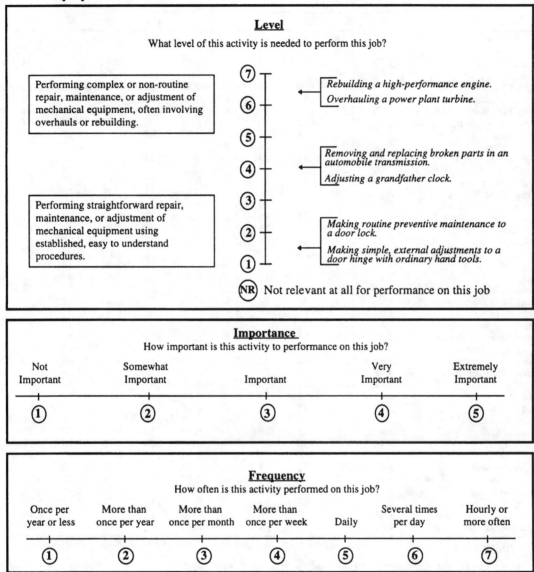

**FIGURE 8-3.** Example page from the Generalized Work Activities Questionnaire.

ties were computed using a simple relevant/not relevant coding scheme.

For the Level and Frequency scales, the interrater agreement coefficients are not affected when the *not relevant* option is eliminated. They are virtually the same as when *not relevant* is scored as zero. For importance, the changes in reliabilities are very small; in several cases, interrater agreement actually improves slightly when the not relevant response on the Level scale is ignored. When the Level scales are scored dichotomously, as relevant or not relevant, some of the descriptors suffer a substantial loss of reliability, but others lose very little; and in four cases reliabilities actually improve.

From both a reliability and a conceptual perspective, the full scale scoring method using the *not relevant* response seems preferable. Interrater agreement is somewhat higher for the Importance ratings when the not relevant (zero) scale point is included. In addition, the case certainly can be made that a *not relevant* rating for a GWA is conceptually quite different from a low level requirement for that GWA.

### Descriptor and Scale Relationships

As with other domains in the content model, we investigated redundancies among the Level, Impor-

**TABLE 8-3**

**Descriptive Statistics Across All Occupations and Reliability Estimates for Rated Differences Between Occupations: Generalized Work Activities**

| | Variable | | | | | | | | | | | |
|---|---|---|---|---|---|---|---|---|---|---|---|---|
| | Level | | | | Importance | | | | Frequency | | | |
| Descriptor | M | SD | SEM[a] | $r_k$[b] | M | SD | SEM | $r_k$ | M | SD | SEM | $r_k$ |
| 1. Getting Information | 3.47 | 1.35 | .55 | .83 | 3.15 | 0.70 | .35 | 0.75 | 4.06 | 0.88 | .53 | .64 |
| 2. Identifying Objects | 2.92 | 1.28 | .57 | .80 | 2.75 | 0.73 | .37 | 0.75 | 3.79 | 0.87 | .58 | .56 |
| 3. Monitoring Processes | 2.77 | 1.23 | .56 | .79 | 2.65 | 0.71 | .36 | 0.75 | 3.79 | 1.04 | .60 | .67 |
| 4. Inspecting Equipment | 1.91 | 1.10 | .52 | .77 | 2.31 | 0.69 | .32 | 0.78 | 2.99 | 0.82 | .47 | .67 |
| 5. Estimating Characteristics | 1.76 | 0.83 | .50 | .64 | 2.09 | 0.50 | .33 | 0.57 | 2.73 | 0.72 | .50 | .53 |
| 6. Judging the Qualities | 2.58 | 1.30 | .55 | .82 | 2.47 | 0.72 | .34 | 0.78 | 3.26 | 0.96 | .54 | .68 |
| 7. Evaluating Information | 2.72 | 1.27 | .52 | .83 | 2.82 | 0.72 | .35 | 0.77 | 3.63 | 0.98 | .50 | .74 |
| 8. Processing Information | 2.54 | 1.27 | .62 | .76 | 2.54 | 0.74 | .36 | 0.77 | 3.36 | 1.07 | .58 | .71 |
| 9. Analyzing Data | 2.37 | 1.54 | .58 | .86 | 2.41 | 0.77 | .33 | 0.82 | 2.98 | 0.90 | .44 | .76 |
| 10. Making Decisions | 3.12 | 1.34 | .54 | .84 | 2.90 | 0.73 | .32 | 0.80 | 3.79 | 0.88 | .48 | .70 |
| 11. Thinking Creatively | 2.78 | 1.33 | .61 | .79 | 2.51 | 0.72 | .33 | 0.78 | 3.17 | 0.92 | .48 | .73 |
| 12. Using Job Knowledge | 3.80 | 1.22 | .61 | .75 | 3.19 | 0.68 | .36 | 0.72 | 3.59 | 0.70 | .51 | .47 |
| 13. Developing Objectives | 2.19 | 1.28 | .48 | .86 | 2.26 | 0.75 | .27 | 0.87 | 2.37 | 0.62 | .36 | .65 |
| 14. Scheduling Work | 2.44 | 1.18 | .52 | .81 | 2.46 | 0.67 | .31 | 0.79 | 3.06 | 1.00 | .46 | .79 |
| 15. Organizing and Planning | 3.80 | 1.18 | .52 | .80 | 3.26 | 0.73 | .32 | 0.80 | 4.30 | 0.86 | .46 | .72 |
| 16. Performing Physical Work Tasks | 2.70 | 1.35 | .54 | .84 | 2.51 | 0.76 | .32 | 0.82 | 4.26 | 1.11 | .68 | .62 |
| 17. Handling Objects | 3.40 | 0.91 | .64 | .51 | 2.86 | 0.54 | .36 | 0.56 | 4.50 | 0.84 | .62 | .46 |
| 18. Controlling Machines | 1.70 | 1.54 | .62 | .84 | 2.17 | 0.83 | .37 | 0.80 | 3.07 | 1.39 | .66 | .77 |
| 19. Interacting With Computers | 2.01 | 1.39 | .54 | .85 | 2.50 | 0.86 | .31 | 0.87 | 3.48 | 1.47 | .50 | .89 |
| 20. Operating Vehicles | 1.53 | 1.54 | .44 | .92 | 1.96 | 0.95 | .26 | 0.92 | 2.54 | 1.51 | .41 | .92 |
| 21. Specifying Equipment | 0.87 | 0.92 | .40 | .81 | 1.48 | 0.55 | .24 | 0.81 | 1.59 | 0.65 | .30 | .78 |
| 22. Implementing Ideas | 2.02 | 1.00 | .54 | .71 | 2.25 | 0.62 | .33 | 0.71 | 2.82 | 0.78 | .49 | .61 |
| 23. Repairing, Mechanical | 1.11 | 1.25 | .47 | .86 | 1.63 | 0.74 | .27 | 0.86 | 1.85 | 0.93 | .39 | .82 |
| 24. Repairing, Electronic | 1.04 | 1.25 | .55 | .80 | 1.62 | 0.69 | .32 | 0.78 | 1.91 | 0.82 | .46 | .68 |
| 25. Documenting Information | 2.45 | 1.05 | .61 | .67 | 2.67 | 0.65 | .38 | 0.65 | 3.63 | 0.93 | .57 | .63 |
| 26. Interpreting Information | 2.32 | 0.93 | .54 | .66 | 2.48 | 0.57 | .35 | 0.63 | 3.40 | 0.92 | .56 | .64 |
| 27. Communicating, Internal | 4.14 | 1.14 | .51 | .80 | 3.54 | 0.57 | .30 | 0.73 | 4.78 | 0.66 | .51 | .41 |
| 28. Communicating, External | 3.09 | 1.35 | .56 | .83 | 2.88 | 0.83 | .34 | 0.84 | 3.62 | 1.13 | .54 | .77 |
| 29. Establishing Relationships | 4.48 | 0.93 | .48 | .73 | 3.76 | 0.63 | .33 | 0.73 | 5.18 | 0.78 | .44 | .68 |
| 30. Assisting Others | 3.08 | 1.05 | .56 | .72 | 3.11 | 0.58 | .37 | 0.59 | 4.16 | 0.86 | .53 | .63 |
| 31. Selling or Influencing | 2.07 | 1.18 | .52 | .81 | 2.31 | 0.69 | .32 | 0.79 | 2.94 | 0.92 | .49 | .71 |
| 32. Resolving Conflicts | 2.82 | 1.25 | .48 | .85 | 2.77 | 0.75 | .33 | 0.81 | 3.19 | 0.86 | .42 | .77 |
| 33. Working with the Public | 2.58 | 1.49 | .65 | .81 | 2.65 | 0.90 | .43 | 0.77 | 3.41 | 1.35 | .65 | .77 |
| 34. Coordinating Others' Work | 2.43 | 1.24 | .47 | .86 | 2.57 | 0.65 | .30 | 0.78 | 3.31 | 0.77 | .47 | .63 |
| 35. Developing Teams | 2.46 | 1.09 | .49 | .80 | 2.56 | 0.60 | .29 | 0.76 | 3.18 | 0.67 | .43 | .60 |
| 36. Teaching Others | 2.48 | 0.97 | .48 | .76 | 2.70 | 0.55 | .33 | 0.64 | 3.11 | 0.83 | .45 | .70 |
| 37. Directing Subordinates | 2.01 | 1.34 | .41 | .91 | 2.30 | 0.73 | .26 | 0.87 | 2.69 | 0.89 | .36 | .84 |
| 38. Developing Others | 2.58 | 1.07 | .45 | .82 | 2.66 | 0.61 | .31 | .74 | 3.15 | 0.73 | .39 | .71 |
| 39. Providing Consultation | 2.17 | 1.15 | .49 | .82 | 2.28 | 0.61 | .29 | .78 | 2.71 | 0.69 | .40 | .65 |
| 40. Performing Administrative Tasks | 2.38 | 1.18 | .53 | .80 | 2.59 | 0.64 | .31 | .77 | 3.52 | 1.00 | .49 | .76 |
| 41. Staffing Organizational Units | 1.19 | 1.12 | .39 | .88 | 1.73 | 0.66 | .22 | .89 | 1.57 | 0.46 | .29 | .61 |
| 42. Monitoring Resources | 1.41 | 1.17 | .47 | .84 | 1.85 | 0.72 | .29 | .84 | 2.13 | 0.71 | .41 | .67 |

*Note.* Statistics are based on 35 occupations with responses from at least four incumbents (mean number of incumbents = 18.91, *Mdn* = 13, harmonic mean = 9.68).
[a]This estimate of the standard error of measurement was calculated as $SEM = SD * \sqrt{(1 - rk)}$. [b]This estimate of reliability was obtained by calculating the intraclass correlation for *k* ratings across occupations: $ICC(1, k) = [BMS - WMS]/BMS$ (Shrout & Fleiss, 1979), where *k* is the harmonic mean of the number of ratings provided on each occupation.

tance, and Frequency scales. Although there are clear conceptual distinctions among the scales, empirical redundancies certainly are possible. Table 8-4 summarizes correlations among the three types of scales computed in two different ways. First, a mean correlation among each pair of scale types was computed for each dimension (at the 42-dimension level) across the 35 occupations and then averaged over the 42 dimensions. A second mean correlation was derived by computing a between-scale correlation for each occupation across the 42 dimensions and averaging over the 35 occupations. Correlations are high between the Level and Importance scales— .92 and .93 for the two approaches to data averag-

ing. The standard deviations for these mean correlations are higher when the correlations are computed across the 42 descriptors within occupation and averaged across the 35 occupations. Apparently, for some occupations, the level–importance relationship is lower. The corresponding importance–frequency mean correlations are somewhat lower than the level–importance ratings (.89 and .91), but still very high. The level–frequency mean correlations are definitely lower (.82 and .88). Overall, Table 8-4 suggests considerable redundancy for the Level and Importance scales. The Frequency scale demonstrated less redundancy, particularly with the Level scale.

**TABLE 8-4**

**Means and Standard Deviations of Correlations Between Level, Importance, and Frequency Scales Across Occupations and Descriptors: Generalized Work Activities**

| Scale | Level | | | Importance | | | Frequency | | |
|---|---|---|---|---|---|---|---|---|---|
| | *n* | *M* | *SD* | *n* | *M* | *SD* | *n* | *M* | *SD* |
| Level | — | — | — | 35 | .93 | .11 | 35 | .88 | .08 |
| Importance | 42[a] | .92 | .05 | — | — | — | 35 | .91 | .06 |
| Frequency | 42[a] | .82 | .07 | 42[a] | .89 | .06 | — | — | — |

*Note.* All correlations were calculated from the mean of ratings assigned by raters for a given occupation, descriptor, and scale. Level–Importance means above the diagonal were calculated by taking the Level scale means on a given occupation for all descriptors, correlating them with Importance scale means for that occupation, and then averaging them with the correlations for other occupations. Level–Importance means below the diagonal were calculated by taking the Level scale means on a given descriptor for all occupations, correlating them with Importance scale means for that descriptor, and averaging them with correlations for other descriptors. Other means in the table were calculated in a similar manner.
[a]Number of correlations averaged, not number of observations on which correlations were calculated.

We also calculated correlations *between dimensions* for the Level scale ratings. The correlations are at the occupation level, with the N for each correlation equal to 35. For the most part, these correlations make good intuitive sense. Perhaps most impressive, as with several other O*NET domains, the mean correlations between descriptors *within* higher order constructs is .61, whereas the mean between-descriptor *across* higher order construct correlation is .43. As an example, for the Administering higher level composite, the three GWAs in this composite (Performing Administrative Tasks [D40], Staffing Organizational Units [D41], and Monitoring Resources [D42]) intercorrelate .55, .55, and .77 on the basis of the occupation-level data. The negative correlations between descriptors are also intuitively appealing. For example, Controlling Machines (D18) and Performing Administrative Tasks (D40) correlate −.50; Performing Physical Work Tasks (D16) and Processing Information (D8) correlate −.60. The sense of these negative relationships is that for several of these pairs of dimensions, occupations require either one of the dimensions or the other, but seldom both. Overall, the GWA scales provide a coherent and meaningful pattern of correlations.

### Factor Structure

Examining the patterns of correlations among descriptors is useful for evaluating the rationality of the relationships among the GWAs. However, a more comprehensive and efficient approach is to conduct an exploratory factor analysis of the correlation matrix. Accordingly, we conducted a principal-components analysis with an orthogonal rotation of the correlations between the Level scales. A three-factor solution proved to be the most interpretable, and this solution is presented in Table 8-5. The three factors accounted for 71% of the total variance for ratings on the Level scale. Also, the communalities suggested that for the most part the GWA dimensions are well-represented in this solution.

The first factor we called *Working With Information*. It accounts for 48% of the total variance. The second factor has many of the supervisory and working with others GWAs loading on it; the factor is

labeled *Working With and Directing the Activities of Others* and accounts for 14% of the variance. The third factor was named *Manual and Physical Activities: Performing Repair and Other Physical Work*, and it accounts for 8% of the variance.

The three-factor solution is reasonably consistent with the highest order four-dimension system in the Jeanneret and Borman (1995) hierarchical taxonomy (see Figure 8-1). The Working With Others factor overlaps considerably with the Interacting With Others dimension, and the Manual and Physical Activities factor contains many of the work output GWAs. Factor 1, Working With Information, overlaps with much of the information-input and mental-processes part of the GWA model. Overall, this three-factor system summarizes well the GWA domain. The factors are highly interpretable, and almost all of the GWAs are represented in the solution.

As mentioned in previous chapters, we must remember that the factor analysis is based on a small sample size (N = 35 in this domain). This may create less than a stable solution. However, the interpretability of these results argues against this conclusion. Also, a factor analysis of the analyst data on the same 35 jobs revealed a three-factor solution very similar to the solution from the incumbent data.

### Job Profiles

An important application of the O*NET data will be to provide profiles of occupational requirements on the O*NET descriptors. Accordingly, we present the GWA profiles for six different occupations selected to be representative of very different types of employment. This should provide an initial view as to what the profiles might look like in the GWA domain. Table 8-6 displays the means and standard deviations for the Level scales relative to these six occupations. A summary observation is that the GWAs appear to describe these occupations quite accurately. The similarities and especially the differences between occupations seem appropriate, given the nature of these occupations. For example, for Performing Physical Work Tasks (D16) means for the General Managers and Computer Programmers are very low; substantially higher means are evident for Patrol Of-

**TABLE 8-5**
**Principal-Components Analysis Pattern Matrix for the Level Scale: Generalized Work Activities**

| | Component | | | |
|---|---|---|---|---|
| Descriptor | F1 | F2 | F3 | Communality |
| 1. Getting Information | .82 | .30 | −.17 | .78 |
| 2. Identifying Objects | .81 | .44 | .05 | .85 |
| 3. Monitoring Processes | .69 | .47 | .33 | .81 |
| 4. Inspecting Equipment | .24 | .00 | .90 | .86 |
| 5. Estimating Characteristics | .70 | .23 | .46 | .76 |
| 6. Judging the Qualities | .65 | .61 | −.12 | .81 |
| 7. Evaluating Information | .84 | .40 | .02 | .87 |
| 8. Processing Information | .78 | .12 | −.40 | .79 |
| 9. Analyzing Data | .87 | .21 | .20 | .83 |
| 10. Making Decisions | .82 | .50 | .06 | .94 |
| 11. Thinking Creatively | .86 | .20 | .14 | .80 |
| 12. Using Job Knowledge | .80 | .33 | .15 | .76 |
| 13. Developing Objectives | .61 | .65 | −.16 | .82 |
| 14. Scheduling Work | .49 | .54 | −.11 | .55 |
| 15. Organizing and Planning | .73 | .45 | −.15 | .75 |
| 16. Performing Physical Work Tasks | −.39 | .22 | .68 | .67 |
| 17. Handling Objects | −.06 | −.35 | .51 | .38 |
| 18. Controlling Machines | −.15 | −.21 | .82 | .75 |
| 19. Interacting With Computers | .82 | −.27 | −.05 | .75 |
| 20. Operating Vehicles | −.24 | .14 | .63 | .48 |
| 21. Specifying Equipment | .41 | −.12 | .56 | .49 |
| 22. Implementing Ideas | .81 | .14 | .28 | .75 |
| 23. Repairing, Mechanical | .15 | −.18 | .89 | .85 |
| 24. Repairing, Electronic | .27 | −.21 | .82 | .80 |
| 25. Documenting Information | .52 | .32 | −.15 | .40 |
| 26. Interpreting Information | .75 | .40 | −.14 | .75 |
| 27. Communicating, Internal | .75 | .43 | −.05 | .75 |
| 28. Communicating, External | .57 | .53 | −.31 | .70 |
| 29. Establishing Relationships | .35 | .63 | −.10 | .53 |
| 30. Assisting Others | −.13 | .74 | −.06 | .57 |
| 31. Selling or Influencing | .35 | .57 | −.17 | .47 |
| 32. Resolving Conflicts | .29 | .78 | −.12 | .70 |
| 33. Working With the Public | −.15 | .66 | −.22 | .50 |
| 34. Coordinating Others' Work | .44 | .80 | −.01 | .84 |
| 35. Developing Teams | .50 | .74 | −.09 | .80 |
| 36. Teaching Others | .42 | .61 | .10 | .56 |
| 37. Directing Subordinates | .34 | .88 | .01 | .89 |
| 38. Developing Others | .36 | .85 | −.01 | .84 |
| 39. Providing Consultation | .73 | .54 | .02 | .83 |
| 40. Performing Administration Tasks | .47 | .61 | −.35 | .72 |
| 41. Staffing Organizational Units | .42 | .54 | .13 | .48 |
| 42. Monitoring Resources | .50 | .48 | .16 | .51 |
| % of variance | 48 | 14 | 8 | |
| Eigenvalue | 20.23 | 6.08 | 3.41 | |

*Note.* N = The correlation matrix was based on means calculated at the occupation level. F1 = Working With Information, F2 = Working With and Directing the Activities of Others, and F3 = Manual and Physical Activities: Performing Repair and Other Physical Work. These loadings are based on an orthogonal varimax rotation.

ficers, Janitors, and Repairers. For Operating Vehicles (D20), as would be expected, the highest mean value is for Patrol Officers, whereas the Computer Programmer mean is literally zero (not relevant). Also, as expected, General Managers have the highest mean score on Directing Subordinates (D37), and Managers and Patrol Officers are highest on Resolving Conflict (D32). The profiles, for both occupations (across GWAs) and GWAs (across these occupations), seem to offer an appropriate and useful picture of the GWA requirements for occupations.

Some of the standard deviations are instructive as well. For example, one of the highest standard deviations is for Providing Consultation (D39) relative to Computer Programmers. It is quite possible this re-

flects actual differences in the respondents' jobs, such that some Programmers work alone and others consult. Thus, in some cases, the standard deviations may be interpretable and provide useful additional occupational information.

### Analyst Comparisons

As mentioned previously, OAFC occupational analysts provided ratings on GWAs and several other content model domains for all 80 occupations in the target sample. In this section, we compare their GWA ratings with the incumbent ratings on the 35 occupations evaluated by both the incumbents and the analysts. Table 8-7 presents these comparisons for the

**TABLE 8-6**
**Descriptor Means and Standard Deviations on the Level Scale on Six Example Occupations: Generalized Work Activities**

| Descriptor | General Managers & Top Executives (n = 43) | | Computer Programmers (n = 7) | | Registered Nurses (n = 25) | | Police Patrol Officers (n = 24) | | Janitors & Cleaners[a] (n = 30) | | Maintenance Repairers, General Utility (n = 27) | |
|---|---|---|---|---|---|---|---|---|---|---|---|---|
| | M | SD | M | SD | M | SD | M | SD | M | SD | M | SD |
| 1. Getting Information | 5.48 | 0.93 | 6.00 | 1.15 | 3.56 | 2.41 | 4.00 | 1.88 | 2.20 | 2.29 | 3.40 | 2.09 |
| 2. Identifying Objects | 4.23 | 1.91 | 4.57 | 2.50 | 3.84 | 2.49 | 3.87 | 2.36 | 0.80 | 1.32 | 3.00 | 1.88 |
| 3. Monitoring Processes | 4.37 | 2.03 | 2.71 | 2.62 | 4.00 | 2.54 | 3.29 | 2.42 | 1.50 | 1.92 | 3.48 | 1.80 |
| 4. Inspecting Equipment | 2.32 | 2.39 | 1.85 | 2.47 | 2.56 | 2.20 | 1.62 | 1.68 | 2.76 | 2.14 | 3.77 | 2.15 |
| 5. Estimating Characteristics | 2.79 | 2.08 | 2.71 | 2.05 | 2.04 | 1.98 | 1.33 | 1.73 | 1.10 | 1.37 | 2.33 | 2.43 |
| 6. Judging the Qualities | 4.39 | 2.19 | 3.28 | 2.49 | 4.00 | 2.54 | 3.62 | 2.31 | 1.73 | 2.14 | 2.85 | 2.16 |
| 7. Evaluating Information | 4.13 | 2.04 | 4.71 | 1.88 | 3.84 | 2.33 | 3.54 | 2.08 | 0.70 | 1.31 | 2.92 | 2.18 |
| 8. Processing Information | 3.58 | 2.14 | 5.00 | 1.41 | 2.84 | 2.33 | 1.91 | 2.48 | 0.90 | 1.70 | 2.18 | 2.25 |
| 9. Analyzing Data | 4.13 | 1.71 | 4.71 | 2.42 | 3.12 | 2.27 | 2.70 | 2.21 | 0.36 | 0.88 | 2.25 | 2.41 |
| 10. Making Decisions | 5.16 | 1.47 | 4.85 | 1.77 | 3.52 | 2.45 | 4.08 | 2.50 | 1.53 | 2.02 | 3.44 | 2.20 |
| 11. Thinking Creatively | 3.90 | 1.99 | 6.71 | 0.75 | 2.92 | 2.05 | 2.62 | 2.12 | 2.13 | 2.37 | 2.81 | 2.16 |
| 12. Using Job Knowledge | 4.95 | 1.77 | 5.71 | 1.70 | 5.12 | 2.22 | 4.29 | 2.29 | 2.66 | 2.49 | 4.22 | 1.86 |
| 13. Developing Objectives | 4.04 | 1.87 | 2.85 | 2.47 | 3.56 | 2.38 | 1.83 | 1.83 | 1.16 | 1.68 | 2.25 | 2.34 |
| 14. Scheduling Work | 4.09 | 1.90 | 3.14 | 1.67 | 3.64 | 2.25 | 1.33 | 1.73 | 2.10 | 2.52 | 2.59 | 2.20 |
| 15. Organizing and Planning | 5.32 | 1.20 | 5.28 | 1.25 | 4.76 | 1.92 | 3.83 | 2.18 | 2.86 | 2.25 | 3.88 | 2.06 |
| 16. Performing Physical Work Tasks | 1.60 | 1.49 | 0.42 | 1.13 | 3.48 | 1.93 | 4.50 | 2.50 | 4.26 | 2.65 | 4.00 | 2.51 |
| 17. Handling Objects | 1.67 | 1.91 | 3.71 | 2.69 | 2.60 | 2.46 | 3.29 | 2.44 | 4.03 | 2.79 | 4.29 | 2.23 |
| 18. Controlling Machines | 0.41 | 0.98 | 0.00 | 0.00 | 1.52 | 2.08 | 1.62 | 1.90 | 2.53 | 2.38 | 3.18 | 2.45 |
| 19. Interacting With Computers | 2.27 | 1.99 | 6.71 | 0.48 | 1.12 | 1.90 | 2.08 | 1.95 | 0.60 | 1.54 | 1.55 | 1.98 |
| 20. Operating Vehicles | 0.74 | 1.41 | 0.00 | 0.00 | 1.24 | 2.18 | 4.50 | 2.10 | 1.60 | 2.04 | 3.44 | 1.84 |
| 21. Specifying Equipment | 0.81 | 1.40 | 0.85 | 2.26 | 0.56 | 1.55 | 0.75 | 1.72 | 0.50 | 1.43 | 2.25 | 2.36 |
| 22. Implementing Ideas | 2.69 | 2.34 | 4.28 | 2.56 | 1.68 | 2.05 | 1.04 | 1.45 | 1.23 | 1.54 | 2.51 | 2.24 |
| 23. Repairing, Mechanical | 0.46 | 1.33 | 0.42 | 1.13 | 0.64 | 1.15 | 0.58 | 1.31 | 2.00 | 2.40 | 3.81 | 2.88 |
| 24. Repairing, Electronic | 0.32 | 0.99 | 0.85 | 1.21 | 0.88 | 1.64 | 0.91 | 1.79 | 1.00 | 1.57 | 2.37 | 2.69 |
| 25. Documenting Information | 2.25 | 2.01 | 3.28 | 2.75 | 4.04 | 2.35 | 4.25 | 2.04 | 1.43 | 2.44 | 2.66 | 2.27 |
| 26. Interpreting Information | 3.20 | 1.90 | 4.00 | 2.30 | 3.28 | 2.09 | 2.41 | 2.39 | 1.36 | 1.82 | 2.37 | 2.07 |
| 27. Communicating, Internal | 5.55 | 1.05 | 5.57 | 1.27 | 4.96 | 1.67 | 4.58 | 2.06 | 3.00 | 1.78 | 4.50 | 2.06 |
| 28. Communicating, External | 4.30 | 1.76 | 3.57 | 2.14 | 3.52 | 1.98 | 4.70 | 2.27 | 1.83 | 2.29 | 2.70 | 2.43 |
| 29. Establishing Relationships | 5.26 | 1.09 | 4.42 | 1.27 | 5.40 | 1.22 | 5.29 | 1.42 | 3.60 | 1.81 | 4.44 | 1.69 |
| 30. Assisting Others | 3.23 | 2.14 | 1.85 | 1.77 | 5.24 | 2.00 | 5.04 | 1.85 | 3.10 | 1.76 | 2.55 | 2.10 |
| 31. Selling or Influencing | 3.20 | 2.27 | 1.71 | 1.49 | 2.60 | 2.23 | 2.25 | 2.50 | 2.03 | 2.02 | 1.51 | 1.69 |
| 32. Resolving Conflicts | 4.51 | 1.86 | 1.28 | 1.60 | 3.92 | 1.99 | 5.00 | 2.26 | 1.68 | 2.30 | 1.77 | 1.92 |
| 33. Working With the Public | 2.76 | 2.36 | 0.14 | 0.37 | 3.52 | 2.51 | 5.29 | 1.96 | 1.60 | 2.02 | 1.66 | 1.98 |
| 34. Coordinating Others' Work | 4.58 | 1.77 | 2.57 | 1.90 | 3.96 | 2.11 | 2.29 | 1.62 | 2.72 | 2.09 | 2.40 | 2.04 |
| 35. Developing Teams | 4.44 | 1.60 | 2.00 | 1.52 | 3.36 | 2.27 | 2.37 | 2.14 | 1.83 | 1.72 | 2.00 | 2.07 |
| 36. Teaching Others | 3.34 | 1.78 | 3.14 | 1.46 | 4.24 | 2.20 | 2.65 | 2.49 | 1.86 | 1.87 | 2.59 | 1.82 |
| 37. Directing Subordinates | 4.88 | 1.89 | 1.14 | 1.46 | 3.44 | 2.36 | 2.45 | 2.41 | 1.96 | 2.05 | 2.00 | 1.77 |
| 38. Developing Others | 3.88 | 2.06 | 1.85 | 2.03 | 4.12 | 1.92 | 3.37 | 2.08 | 2.23 | 2.04 | 2.22 | 1.80 |
| 39. Providing Consultation | 4.32 | 2.03 | 3.42 | 2.63 | 3.28 | 2.47 | 2.25 | 2.34 | 1.34 | 1.84 | 2.29 | 2.33 |
| 40. Performing Administrative Tasks | 4.18 | 1.94 | 1.57 | 1.90 | 3.00 | 2.08 | 2.83 | 1.94 | 1.33 | 1.86 | 2.37 | 2.63 |
| 41. Staffing Organizational Units | 3.46 | 2.27 | 1.71 | 1.70 | 2.20 | 2.19 | 0.70 | 1.57 | 1.66 | 2.13 | 0.77 | 1.84 |
| 42. Monitoring Resources | 4.07 | 2.17 | 0.85 | 1.46 | 1.56 | 2.10 | 0.66 | 1.60 | 2.00 | 2.25 | 1.37 | 2.32 |

[a]The full title for this occupation is "Janitors and Cleaners, except Maids and Housekeeping."

**TABLE 8-7**

**Comparison Between Incumbent and Analyst Descriptive Statistics Across All Occupations and Reliability Estimates for Rated Differences Between Occupations for the Level Scale: Generalized Work Activities**

| Descriptor | Incumbent | | | Analyst | | | $t$ | $F$ | $r_{ia}$ | $d^2$ |
|---|---|---|---|---|---|---|---|---|---|---|
| | M | SD | $r_k$ | M | SD | $r_k$ | | | | |
| 1. Getting Information | 3.47 | 1.35 | .83 | 3.55 | 1.14 | .95 | −0.57 | 1.40 | .79 | 0.67 |
| 2. Identifying Objects | 2.92 | 1.28 | .80 | 3.21 | 1.01 | .89 | −1.80 | 1.60 | .68 | 0.95 |
| 3. Monitoring Processes | 2.77 | 1.23 | .79 | 2.95 | 0.91 | .90 | −1.41 | 1.85 | .77 | 0.64 |
| 4. Inspecting Equipment | 1.91 | 1.10 | .77 | 2.05 | 0.99 | .92 | −1.12 | 1.22 | .76 | 0.54 |
| 5. Estimating Characteristics | 1.76 | 0.83 | .64 | 2.32 | 0.86 | .90 | −4.87* | 1.09 | .68 | 0.76 |
| 6. Judging the Qualities | 2.58 | 1.30 | .82 | 2.75 | 1.01 | .92 | −1.27 | 1.68 | .80 | 0.63 |
| 7. Evaluating Information | 2.72 | 1.27 | .83 | 2.89 | 0.87 | .91 | −1.07 | 2.15* | .69 | 0.84 |
| 8. Processing Information | 2.54 | 1.27 | .76 | 2.89 | 1.12 | .94 | −2.83* | 1.29 | .82 | 0.65 |
| 9. Analyzing Data | 2.37 | 1.54 | .86 | 2.90 | 1.20 | .96 | −2.67* | 1.67 | .68 | 1.57 |
| 10. Making Decisions | 3.12 | 1.34 | .84 | 2.76 | 1.17 | .95 | 2.65* | 1.31 | .80 | 0.78 |
| 11. Thinking Creatively | 2.78 | 1.33 | .79 | 2.28 | 1.27 | .94 | 3.18* | 1.09 | .74 | 1.10 |
| 12. Using Job Knowledge | 3.80 | 1.22 | .75 | 2.96 | 1.21 | .94 | 4.86* | 1.01 | .64 | 1.74 |
| 13. Developing Objectives | 2.19 | 1.28 | .86 | 1.58 | 1.37 | .94 | 5.52* | 1.15 | .88 | 0.79 |
| 14. Scheduling Work | 2.44 | 1.18 | .81 | 1.91 | 1.36 | .92 | 3.30* | 1.34 | .73 | 1.17 |
| 15. Organizing and Planning | 3.80 | 1.18 | .80 | 2.73 | 1.16 | .93 | 6.58* | 1.02 | .66 | 2.04 |
| 16. Perform. Physical Work Tasks | 2.70 | 1.35 | .84 | 2.82 | 1.21 | .93 | −0.75 | 1.25 | .72 | 0.93 |
| 17. Handling Objects | 3.40 | 0.91 | .51 | 3.32 | 0.89 | .87 | 0.53 | 1.04 | .47 | 0.85 |
| 18. Controlling Machines | 1.70 | 1.54 | .84 | 1.95 | 1.15 | .92 | −1.78 | 1.80 | .85 | 0.74 |
| 19. Interacting With Computers | 2.01 | 1.39 | .85 | 1.89 | 1.13 | .94 | 0.76 | 1.50 | .76 | 0.82 |
| 20. Operating Vehicles | 1.53 | 1.54 | .92 | 1.01 | 1.24 | .95 | 4.13* | 1.54 | .87 | 0.82 |
| 21. Specifying Equipment | 0.87 | 0.92 | .81 | 0.84 | 1.19 | .95 | 0.15 | 1.69 | .63 | 0.86 |
| 22. Implementing Ideas | 2.02 | 1.00 | .71 | 2.37 | 1.09 | .89 | −2.54* | 1.18 | .68 | 0.80 |
| 23. Repairing, Mechanical | 1.11 | 1.25 | .86 | 1.44 | 1.33 | .95 | −2.42* | 1.13 | .80 | 0.76 |
| 24. Repairing, Electronic | 1.04 | 1.25 | .80 | 1.19 | 0.64 | .75 | −0.85 | 3.76* | .58 | 1.03 |
| 25. Documenting Information | 2.45 | 1.05 | .67 | 2.80 | 0.89 | .88 | −2.34* | 1.40 | .59 | 0.88 |
| 26. Interpreting Information | 2.32 | 0.93 | .66 | 2.29 | 1.01 | .91 | 0.17 | 1.20 | .55 | 0.84 |
| 27. Communicating, Internal | 4.14 | 1.14 | .80 | 3.24 | 1.20 | .94 | 5.74* | 1.10 | .69 | 1.64 |
| 28. Communicating, External | 3.09 | 1.35 | .83 | 3.01 | 1.37 | .93 | 0.39 | 1.03 | .68 | 1.16 |
| 29. Establishing Relationships | 4.48 | 0.93 | .73 | 3.44 | 1.01 | .93 | 6.21* | 1.17 | .47 | 2.06 |
| 30. Assisting Others | 3.08 | 1.05 | .72 | 2.18 | 1.29 | .94 | 5.35* | 1.51 | .65 | 1.79 |
| 31. Selling or Influencing | 2.07 | 1.18 | .81 | 1.90 | 1.32 | .93 | 1.22 | 1.25 | .79 | 0.68 |
| 32. Resolving Conflicts | 2.82 | 1.25 | .85 | 2.44 | 1.41 | .95 | 2.38* | 1.26 | .75 | 1.02 |
| 33. Working With the Public | 2.58 | 1.49 | .81 | 2.28 | 1.41 | .91 | 2.20* | 1.12 | .85 | 0.73 |
| 34. Coordinating Others' Work | 2.43 | 1.24 | .86 | 2.31 | 1.31 | .93 | 0.68 | 1.11 | .67 | 1.05 |
| 35. Developing Teams | 2.46 | 1.09 | .80 | 1.63 | 1.44 | .93 | 4.51* | 1.75 | .66 | 1.83 |
| 36. Teaching Others | 2.48 | 0.97 | .76 | 1.94 | 1.32 | .93 | 3.04* | 1.86 | .62 | 1.34 |
| 37. Directing Subordinates | 2.01 | 1.34 | .91 | 1.49 | 1.68 | .96 | 2.57* | 1.58 | .72 | 1.61 |
| 38. Developing Others | 2.58 | 1.07 | .82 | 1.89 | 1.38 | .93 | 3.88* | 1.68 | .66 | 1.55 |
| 39. Providing Consultation | 2.17 | 1.15 | .82 | 2.40 | 1.47 | .95 | −1.26 | 1.64 | .69 | 1.16 |
| 40. Performing Administrative Tasks | 2.38 | 1.18 | .80 | 2.55 | 1.12 | .93 | −1.13 | 1.10 | .70 | 0.79 |
| 41. Staffing Organizational Units | 1.19 | 1.12 | .88 | 0.96 | 1.52 | .97 | 1.41 | 1.83 | .76 | 1.00 |
| 42. Monitoring Resources | 1.41 | 1.17 | .84 | 2.56 | 1.06 | .87 | −7.54* | 1.21 | .67 | 2.12 |

*Note.* Incumbent statistics are based on 35 occupations with GWA Questionnaire responses from at least 4 incumbents (mean number of incumbents = 18.91, *Mdn* = 13, harmonic mean = 9.68). Analyst statistics are based on the same 35 occupations with GWA Questionnaire responses from at least 6 analysts (mean number of analysts = 10.11, *Mdn* = 12, harmonic mean = 8.37). The estimate of reliability was obtained by calculating the intraclass correction for *k* ratings across occupations: $ICC(1, k) = [BMS − WMS]/BMS$ (Shrout & Fleiss, 1979), where *k* is the harmonic mean of the number of ratings provided on each occupation. The *t* statistic tests for differences between the incumbent and analyst group means. The *F* statistic tests for differences between the incumbent and analyst group standard deviations. The $r_{ia}$ correlation indicates the degree of relationship between incumbent and analyst mean occupations ratings. The $d^2$ statistic indicates the squared differences between incumbent and analyst mean occupations ratings.
*$p < .05$.

Level scale. The table provides means, standard deviations, and *k*-level reliabilities for both incumbent and analyst ratings. Also provided are *t* and *F* tests comparing the means and standard deviations of incumbent and analyst data, as well as the correlation between the two sets of ratings for each GWA and a $d^2$ statistic indicating the average squared difference between analyst and incumbent mean ratings.

The interrater agreement within-source findings indicate that analyst ratings are about .10 points higher than those for the incumbents (median $r_s = .93$ and .82). The analyst GWA level ratings are highly reliable, with no need to have additional analysts provide these ratings. Reliability results for the PAQ job dimensions provide benchmark data for analyst ratings that are relevant to many of our GWAs. McCormick et al. (1989) reported the reliability of job dimension scores calculated from 43 studies that involved 19,961 analyst pairs. The median of the median reliability coefficients across all 45 PAQ dimensions was .91. If we examine just the reliabilities for those PAQ dimensions that are "matched" to the GWAs, there are 20 such dimensions with median reliabilities that range from .84 to .97 and an overall median of .92. Correlations *between* the two sources (i.e., incumbents and analysts) are reasonably high. The median correlation between the mean level ratings is .70. Looking at agreement in a correlational sense, the lowest agreement between analysts and incumbents is on the Handling Objects (D17) and Establishing Relationships (D29) GWAs. The latter case is curious because the reliabilities *within* source are reasonably high; incumbents and analysts are in good agreement among themselves on how to order occupations on this dimension, but these views are fairly idiosyncratic to their own source. More broadly, however, the correlational results for the Level scales suggest substantial agreement across the two sources in the rated patterns of occupational GWA requirements for this sample of occupations.

Although correlational agreement is high, many significant level differences were found between incumbents' and analysts' ratings. The *t* tests indicate that a little more than half of the GWAs (23) show significant differences between the two sources' ratings. In seven cases, the analysts' means are significantly higher than the incumbents' means. However, for 16 of the GWAs, the incumbent means are higher, with some substantial differences. For example, the Using Job Knowledge (D12) means for the incumbent and analyst groups are 3.80 and 2.96. For Organizing and Planning (D15), the corresponding means are 3.80 and 2.73. Thus, on several GWAs, the incumbents believe that the GWA requirements are at a higher level than do the analysts. Essentially, incumbents are reporting that their job is more complex than is seen by the analysts. Overall, the correlational results show reasonable convergent validity for the incumbent and analyst ratings. However, significant, and in some cases substantial, differences in means are evident between the two sources.

## CONCLUSIONS

Research reported in this chapter indicates that job incumbents using the GWA descriptors can reliably describe their jobs. Interrater agreement is quite high, even for the *k*-level reliabilities, where *k* fell considerably short of the target 30 incumbents per occupation. For GWAs, at least, this target might be reduced somewhat on the basis of these results. Of the three types of rating scales, the behaviorally anchored Level scales showed the highest reliabilities, slightly higher than for an Importance scale, and substantially higher than those obtained with a Frequency scale. Relationships between the Level and Importance scales were high (above .90). The Level scales did not correlate as highly with the Frequency scales.

The present research provides substantive support for the proposed taxonomy. Evidence that supports the hierarchical nature of the structure was developed by comparing the intercorrelations of GWA descriptors within their second order taxonomic level to their correlations with other GWA descriptors outside their second order level. For example, we compared the intercorrelations between the GWAs that are within the Information/Data Processing category with the correlations between these GWAs and other GWAs that are in the other second order levels (i.e., Information Input, Work Output, etc.; see Figure 8-2). Data from the Level Scale ratings indicate that the mean correlation between GWA descriptors within a second order taxonomic level is substantially higher than the mean correlation between GWA descriptors across the second order taxonomic levels (r = .61 vs. 43). This provides support for the particular hierarchical system proposed for the GWAs. Also, a factor analysis of the between-descriptor correlations yielded a readily interpretable three-factor solution, further evidence for the coherence of this GWA taxonomy.

Especially important for evaluating the usefulness of O*NET with respect to the GWAs is the fact that the GWA descriptors accomplished what was intended by describing activity requirements that differentiate occupations. The GWA profiles for the six example occupations demonstrated in a concrete way how useful these profiles can be for documenting differences between occupations.

In sum, the proposed GWA taxonomy received considerable support in this research. The scales measuring dimensions of the taxonomy provided reliable, coherent, and useful occupational information. The GWA taxonomy and measures of its dimensions present a viable system for describing similarities and differences between occupations. Accordingly, the vision of the pioneers advocating the study of jobs from the perspective of worker-oriented dimensions, or what we now call GWAs, has become a well established and useful process and a significant component of the O*NET system.

# Work Context: Taxonomy and Measurement of the Work Environment

MARK H. STRONG, P. RICHARD JEANNERET, S. MORTON McPHAIL,
BARRY R. BLAKLEY, AND ERIKA L. D'EGIDIO

A full understanding of how work gets accomplished requires consideration of the environment in which it occurs. Social, physical, and organizational contexts can serve as the impetuses for tasks and activities and can greatly affect the worker, job performance, and work outcomes. Often focusing on specific job tasks, duties, or activities, job analysis efforts commonly fail to assess adequately the physical, social, and structural contexts in which those tasks or activities occur.

Significant changes are occurring in the world of work. Advances in technology, a shift toward a more service-oriented economy, changing demographics of the workforce, and the globalization of business have all affected the ways work is performed. Job duties and activities have changed (and continue to change) to reflect these factors. Changes in the nature of work influence the way work is performed and the environments in which it is accomplished.

As an example, the transition from a manufacturing-oriented economy to a more service-oriented economy affects many aspects of the work context, including the degree of social contact required and the level of automation or structure of tasks and activities. Additionally, changes in technology have generally reduced the number of employees working in physically demanding or dangerous work environments. Thus, although the effect of the physical environment may have become less significant for certain occupations, the social and structural environments now have an increased impact on many jobs.

A more subtle (but potentially more far-reaching) example of a change in the work context involves the use of work teams. Working as part of a group significantly alters the social work environment. Even if the tasks performed are similar to those performed by individuals, working as part of a team adds dimensions to the work that will affect the employees, work activities, and job requirements.

It is clear that employees adapt to their environment (Cunningham, 1988; Kochhar & Armstrong, 1988; Lopez, 1988; McCormick, Jeanneret, & Mecham, 1969a, 1969b, 1972; Rohmert, 1988); work context may be conceptualized as a set of moderator variables affecting or altering worker behavior as part of the adaptation. The physical, structural, and social environments represent pervading contexts in which workers must perform, and it is in these contexts that workers respond, interact, and have relationships with other individuals. (See Figure 9-1, which portrays the relationship between work processes and the context within which they occur; Boese & Cunningham, 1975.) This chapter describes the development of the work context component of the O*NET taxonomy and provides the results of the study used to test the accuracy of this taxonomy.

## THE IMPORTANCE OF WORK CONTEXT

It is well documented that working conditions can contribute to occupational diseases and injuries (e.g., carpal tunnel syndrome, back injuries, etc.) and can otherwise influence employee health (Cooper & Payne, 1979; Parker & West, 1973; Poulton, 1970; Selye, 1980). In addition to having an effect on physical health, many work context factors, such as exposure to hazards and types of role relationships, have been linked to a variety of work outcomes, including job performance, satisfaction, group formation, group cohesion, organizational effectiveness, and psychological health (see Cooper, 1987; Evans, Johansson, & Carrere, 1994; Ivancevich & Matteson, 1980; Kahn & Byosiere, 1992; Shaw & Riskind, 1983; Sundstrom & Sundstrom, 1986).

Employee health and well-being are sufficient reasons to study and evaluate environmental factors. In fact, the study of work context has allowed identification and correction of job hazards and development of appropriate guidelines for worker safety, but assessment of the complete work context is important for a number of other reasons as well. The design of selection systems can be improved by using information concerning the types of interpersonal relationships required by a job. Compensation systems often include some components of work context

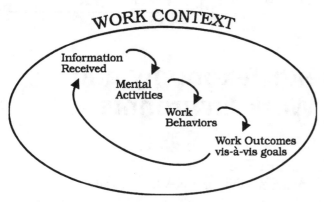

**FIGURE 9-1.** Work context and work processes (Figure from Boese & Cunningham, 1975)

(e.g., working in hazardous conditions or having a high level of responsibility for the work or safety of others often results in higher pay). Work context information also can be used by job designers to facilitate communication among workers and reduce hazards and work interruptions. Furthermore, employment agencies and job seekers can use such information to gain better understanding of work requirements through more realistic and comprehensive job previews.

Although work context variables can be among the most salient aspects of a person's job and can greatly influence how jobs are performed and perceived, the study of these constructs has often been only a supplemental component of job analysis procedures that focus mainly on work tasks and behaviors. Almost all job analysis instruments assess some aspect of the work environment (Gael, 1988; Ghorpade, 1988), but investigation of these variables has been very fragmented. Without a framework for contextual work characteristics, job analysis instruments have lacked structure and consistency in the evaluation of the full range of work environment factors.

## CONSIDERATIONS IN THE DEVELOPMENT OF THE WORK CONTEXT TAXONOMY

The research examining variables that we classify as work context, or the psychosocial aspects and physical conditions of work, is extensive and transcends many disciplines. Medical researchers, industrial engineers, psychologists, workplace designers, and architects have all studied work context factors and their effects on individuals, groups, and organizations. These disciplines have different objectives and use different labels when discussing work context factors, and no well-defined area of study specifically addressing contextual factors has emerged. To develop a theoretical model of the physical and psychosocial aspects of work, information from clinical, industrial/organizational, and social psychology; human factors; medicine; and ergonomics was in-

corporated into a general framework of variables thought to provide valuable job information. The variables included in the model are believed to differentiate between jobs and provide important job information to O*NET users.

Our efforts have focused on developing a taxonomic structure specifically addressing work context variables. *Work context* is defined here as non-task-related factors of work that affect intrapersonal, interpersonal, or work outcomes or activities. The taxonomy uses a broad definition of work context and is similar to McGrath's (1976) global division of organizational factors into tasks, roles, and settings. From previous job analysis work, research literature, and earlier taxonomic efforts, three broad categories of variables were identified that can be said to affect the worker in the immediate work environment: people, physical conditions, and structure of the work. Thus, work context was initially divided into three higher order dimensions: (a) Interpersonal Relationships, (b) Physical Work Conditions, and (c) Structural Job Characteristics.

Several models were used in the development of the work context taxonomy, including an information-processing model and several psychosocial models of organizations. These models of human and organizational performance were referenced because of their emphasis on work context variables.

## Information-Processing Model

The objective for the taxonomy was to integrate the existing body of research regarding contextual variables into an organized structure that would provide a systematic approach for examining work context constructs. The constructs included in the taxonomy were compiled using an information-processing or systems approach to studying jobs and work. The information-processing paradigm views work as a process in which inputs are transformed into outputs through a worker's mental activities and behaviors. As depicted in Figure 9-2, the process of work occurs within a context, defined here by a hierarchical structure that includes the three higher order dimensions and a number of second-order dimensions. This paradigm is based on the idea that a worker serves as an agent who transforms materials and information into work outcomes, but it acknowledges that the context in which this occurs can influence various steps of the process.

The importance of this paradigm and the inclusion of the work context is evident in the organization of the *Position Analysis Questionnaire* (PAQ; McCormick et al., 1972). The PAQ job elements are organized into six divisions: (a) Information Input, (b) Mental Processes, (c) Work Output, (d) Relationships With Others, (e) Job Context, and (f) Other Job Characteristics. The first three divisions encompass the information-processing model of receiving information, performing mental processes, and producing an output or action—which occur in virtually all jobs (Mc-

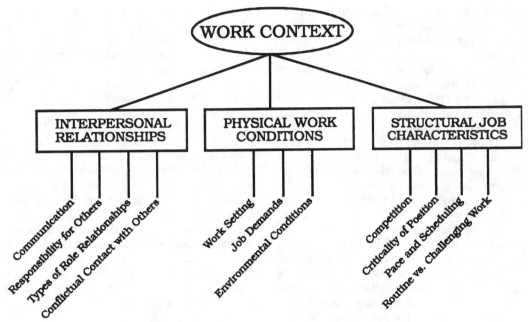

**FIGURE 9-2.** Work context taxonomy: Higher order factors

Cormick & Jeanneret, 1988). However, this input–process–output occurs within the framework of work relationships, job context (i.e., physical conditions), and other job characteristics. Job elements within these latter three divisions were used as a source of constructs for the proposed O*NET work context taxonomy. Conceptually, our three higher order dimensions are closely related to divisions in the PAQ.

## Psychosocial Models

Katz and Kahn (1978) view organizations as sets of subsystems and discuss integrating the technological and social subsystems in the workplace. When this systems approach is applied at the job level, the social, structural, and technological elements of jobs may be seen as highly integrated. Aspects of both the social and technological subsystems can be labeled as work context according to the definition above. The social subsystem includes contextual factors such as the roles that workers must assume. The technological subsystem includes factors that can affect worker behavior (e.g., use of computer communications). Constructs that correspond to elements of these subsystems were considered in the development of the O*NET work context taxonomy, focusing on identifying environmental or contextual constructs that have been found to affect worker behavior.

Psychosocial factors and physical work conditions have been addressed under various construct labels, and numerous classification schemas have been used in the literature to organize the large number of work-related characteristics that affect performance, health, and well-being. Neff (1987) described work behavior as the product of characteristics of the worker and characteristics of the work situation.

Cooper (1987), in discussing occupational stress, differentiated between six contextual aspects of the work environment: (a) factors intrinsic to the job, (b) role in the organization, (c) career development, (d) relationships at work, (e) organizational structure and climate, and (f) home–work interface.

McGrath (1976) conceptualized an organization as a combination of behavioral settings, tasks, and roles. In addition, Evans and his colleagues (Evans et al., 1994) extensively discussed the psychosocial and physical factors of the workplace. They classified these characteristics as structural, organizational, interpersonal, task parameters, ambient conditions, layout and arrangement of space, architectural design, and ergonomic factors. Excluding the variables that relate to the organization or external environment, the proposed taxonomy includes the aspects of the psychosocial and physical work environment discussed by Evans et al. (1994).

## WORK CONTEXT TAXONOMY

As noted above, most job analysis instruments assess at least some component of work context (e.g., Department of Labor's [DOL] *Revised Handbook for Analyzing Jobs* [U.S. DOL, 1991b]; Occupational Analysis Inventory [OAI; Cunningham, 1988], PAQ, etc.). Even variables we have included to reflect current technology (such as the use of interactive computer communication or the amount of electronic mail a worker receives) have, in some cases, been assessed elsewhere. This work of other job analysis researchers was used in the development of the O*NET work context taxonomy described below.

There are many variables that could fall under the rubric of work environment. Factors such as the color of walls, the layout of furniture, and even the number of restrooms available to employees have been shown to affect workers (Sundstrom & Sundstrom, 1986). Because a goal of a broad-based job analysis system includes the ability to identify differences and similarities between jobs, we attempted to identify only those variables along which jobs could be expected to differ consistently. Thus, for instance, the color of paint may be idiosyncratic to either the job incumbent or the organization or equivocal across jobs in an organization. In either case, paint color would be unlikely to provide meaningful or consistent information about differences between, for example, supervising and clerical positions.

In cases where it was concluded that particular contextual characteristics did not differentiate meaningfully between occupations for any of a variety of reasons (e.g., overlap with other characteristics, difficulty in operationalization, inappropriate level of detail, etc.), the variable was combined with other factors or removed from the taxonomy. Accordingly, we acknowledge that our taxonomy is not an exhaustive listing of variables that could be classified as part of the work context; rather the taxonomy consists of those variables in the work environment that are likely to affect workers and that will provide information about the differences and similarities between jobs.

On the basis of a review of the relevant literature, work context was divided into three higher order dimensions: (a) Interpersonal Relationships, (b) Physical Work Conditions, and (c) Structural Job Characteristics. These dimensions were further divided into lower order dimensions from which specific item-level constructs were generated. Table 9-1 presents the 3 higher order dimensions, 10 second-order dimensions, and the item-level constructs. The three higher order constructs are described below, together with the second-order dimensions they subsume.

## Interpersonal Relationships

This dimension describes the context of the job in terms of human interaction processes. Evans et al. (1994) discussed the psychosocial environment as the social climate of the workplace, the settings produced by the activities of the organization, and the people in those settings. This definition includes the types of social relationships and roles the job holder must assume as part of the job, including communication and accountability for others' performance. The Interpersonal Relationships dimension is divided into four second-order factors: (a) Communication, (b) Types of Role Relationships, (c) Responsibility for Others, and (d) Conflictual Contact With Others.

## Physical Work Conditions

The actual physical conditions under which an employee is asked to perform a job are arguably the most obvious aspects of a taxonomy of work context. There are few, if any, job analysis instruments that do not consider the tangible aspects of the work environment. Physical Work Conditions are considered to be the relationships or interactions between the worker and the physical job environment. Evans et al. (1994) defined physical characteristics of work as the inanimate facets of the work environment. For the proposed taxonomy, Physical Work Conditions include (a) the Work Setting; (b) the Environmental Conditions that may pose a hazard to the worker; and (c) Job Demands, including body positions and work attire, that are part of the work environment. Aspects of these factors are measured by the frequency with which a job exposes employees to various work settings, conditions, and hazards, as well as the possibility and impact of injuries. The specific facets of Physical Work Conditions included in the taxonomy were obtained mainly through review of the human factors literature, as well as an examination of existing job analysis instruments.

## Structural Job Characteristics

Many structural job characteristics are assessed by job analysis instruments (e.g., Generalized Work Inventory [Cunningham & Ballentine, 1982]; Job Diagnostic Survey [Hackman & Oldham, 1980], PAQ; Professional and Managerial Position Questionnaire [Yukl, 1987]). The second-order dimensions within Structural Job Characteristics are Criticality of Position, Routine Versus Challenging Work, Pace and Scheduling of work, and Competition required by the job. Specific characteristics within these second-order dimensions including frustrating circumstances, degree of automation, responsibility level, and decision latitude. Research has shown that incumbents' reports of these types of job characteristics are related to job satisfaction, work frustrations, anxiety on the job, turnover intentions, number of physician visits, and other work outcomes (Spector & Jex, 1991). The specific facets of the Structural Job Characteristics dimension were obtained both through a review of job analysis instruments and relevant literature, as well as by rationally identifying the aspects of job structure on which occupations may differ.

## Measurement of the Taxonomic Variables

Important constructs within the three higher order dimensions were identified, and these preliminary second-order factors were refined, and in some cases redefined, on the basis of an examination of research literature and items from existing job analysis instruments. This review was used both to assess the specific individual factors that fell within the domains of the three higher order dimensions and to "validate" the higher order dimensions as factors that can be researched and used to differentiate between occupations. Specific item-level constructs were generated from the second-order factors. A schematic of the

**TABLE 9-1**
**Descriptions and Definitions of Work Context Variables**

| Second order factor | Item-level constructs | Technical definition |
|---|---|---|
| | | Interpersonal Relationships |
| Communication | Formality of Communication | Extent to which communication is informal and personal (such as words spoken face to face, touching, eye contact) or formal and impersonal (such as telephone calls, letters, reports, memoranda, electronic mail, or facsimile). |
| | Communication Method | Extent to which the job requires a variety of communication methods, including face-to-face, public speaking, video conferencing, voice mail, telephone, interactive computer communication, electronic mail, handwritten notes or messages, letters or memos, and written reports. |
| | Objectivity of Information Communicated | Extent to which the job requires the communication of emotionally/psychologically valued subjective information, feelings, thoughts, and ideas versus the communication of objective and verifiable data-based information. |
| | Frequency of Job-Required Social Interaction | Extent to which the worker is required to have interpersonal contact with others, including customers, trainees, supervisors, phone callers, etc. |
| | Privacy of Communication | Extent to which an individual's work materials and communications (face-to-face, phone, fax, e-mail, etc.) can be monitored by others. |
| Types of Role Relationships | Supervisory Roles | Importance of interactions requiring the worker to assume a role of trainer, coach, leader, supervisor, manager, etc., with respect to other workers. |
| | Sales Roles | Importance of interpersonal contacts requiring the worker to engage in persuasion or influence. |
| | Service Roles | Importance of interpersonal interactions requiring the worker to provide others with needed services or to assist others to accomplish an objective, including customer service and advisor-client/patient relationships. |
| | Adversarial Roles | Importance of interpersonal contacts requiring the worker to state, defend, or advocate some goal or objective in opposition to others'. Job activities may involve negotiation to a compromise, but the emphasis is on the taking of a position opposed to that taken by others of equal or similar power. |
| | Team Participant Roles | Importance of job activities requiring the worker to contribute to group accomplishment of goals or objectives, to work closely with others, to be supportive and cooperative, and to place group accomplishment ahead of individual aspirations. |
| Responsibility for Others | Responsibility for the Safety of Others | Extent to which the job requires the worker to be particularly careful not to cause harm or injury to others, including the responsibility to establish policies and programs to protect others. |
| | Responsibility for Work Outcomes and Results | Extent to which the job requires the worker to assume responsibility for the results of the work of others, including being responsible for the errors or failures of others. |
| Conflictual Contact With Others | Interpersonal Conflict | Extent to which the job structure itself creates a role for the worker that inevitably places him/her in conflict with others (e.g., police officer making an arrest, utility worker collecting overdue bills, labor relations manager dealing with grievances). |
| | Strained Interpersonal Relations | Extent to which the worker must from time to time deal with others who are discourteous, angry, hostile, or otherwise unpleasant even when the job structure does not make such encounters inevitable (e.g., food servers, customer service representatives, postal counter workers). |
| | | Physical Work Conditions |
| Work Setting | Types of Work Settings | Extent to which the work is performed in a variety of settings, including indoors (environmentally or not environmentally controlled), outdoors (exposed to weather conditions or under cover), in a vehicle or operating equipment (open or enclosed). |
| | Privacy of Work Area | Extent to which the work area is private. |
| | Physical Proximity | Extent to which the job requires the worker to perform job tasks in close physical proximity to other people. |
| Environmental Conditions | Exposure to Extreme Environmental Conditions | Extent to which the work is performed under extreme temperatures, noise levels, lighting, air contaminants, or in a confined space. |
| | Exposure to Job Hazards | Extent to which the work is performed under hazardous conditions (e.g., radiation, disease/infection, high places, equipment). |
| | Possibility of Injury From Job Hazards | The likelihood the worker will be injured while working under hazardous conditions. |
| | Impact of Injury | The likely extent, duration, and seriousness of injuries possible on the job. |
| Job Demands | Body Positioning | Extent to which the worker sits, stands, walks, climbs, etc. |
| | Work Attire | Extent to which the worker must wear various types of clothing and equipment. |

*Table 9-1 continues*

**TABLE 9-1 (*Continued*)**

| Second order factor | Item-level constructs | Technical definition |
|---|---|---|
| | | Structural Job Characteristics |
| Criticality of Position | Consequence of Error | Breadth and severity of outcomes resulting from errors made by the worker. |
| | Impact of Decisions | Breadth and impact of results of the decisions required of a worker. |
| | Responsibility/ Accountability | Extent to which the worker's performance is judged from the ultimate outcome of work activities and/or results of errors and mistakes. |
| | Decision Latitude | Level of responsibility assigned to the job to be exercised by the worker, including the level of decision making that must be approved by others before action can proceed. |
| Routine Versus Challenging Work | Frustrating Circumstances | Extent to which the worker's goal-oriented behavior is blocked by impediments over which the worker has little or no control. |
| | Degree of Automation | Degree to which significant job functions are automated and require little input from the worker beyond monitoring. |
| | Task Clarity | Extent to which tasks or objectives are not clearly defined or communicated. |
| | Required Precision | Extent to which the job requires the worker to maintain a high level of accuracy and precision including both manual and mental precision. |
| | Required Attention to Detail | Extent to which a job requires a high level of thoroughness to ensure that nothing is left undone or that steps are not taken out of order, including attending to the details of a set of procedures, checking the completion of a series of tasks, auditing the correctness and documentation of activities or financial results. |
| | Required Maintenance of Vigilance | Extent to which the job requires the worker to maintain attention or alertness, either for events or circumstances that do not occur often or for those that are subject to continual change. |
| | Monotony/Repetitive Activities | Extent to which the worker is required to perform the same physical and/or mental activities repeatedly, in a relatively short period of time, usually less than 1 hour. |
| | Structured vs. Unstructured Work | The degree to which job activities are at the discretion of the worker rather than being predetermined and requiring following directions and carrying out orders. |
| | Level of Competition | Extent job requires the worker to compete or be aware of competitive pressures. |
| Pace and Scheduling | Frequency and Stringency of Deadlines | Extent that the job imposes frequent strict deadlines. |
| | Distractions and Interruptions | Extent to which the worker cannot expect to start and complete a task without interruptions, including the extent to which the worker has control over the interruptions. |
| | Machine Driven Work Pace | Extent to which the work pace is machine driven or controlled by the speed of process, such as assembly lines, leaving the worker little control over it. |

taxonomic structure, including item-level constructs and measurement scale types, is presented in Table 9-2.

Although all of the second-order dimensions are assessed by multiple questions, most of the item-level constructs for work context are measured by a single item or scale. For instance, Communication is a second-order dimension under Interpersonal Relationships, and there are five items assessing Communication. However, each of these five items measures a different type or aspect of Communication. Also, because of the type of information being collected, some of the Physical Work Conditions constructs involved multiple ratings (e.g., level, frequency, etc.), but these also are arguably different aspects of the conditions being assessed.

Multiple items for all work context constructs would require an extremely large set of questions. Increasing the length of the instrument was not practical, and it was judged that additional items would not provide incremental utility. Because of the relative objectivity of most of the constructs and the existing research evidence, multiple items for each construct have not been developed. Research suggests that many of the work context variables proposed can be rated quite reliably with single-item scales. A number of the item-level constructs are similar to PAQ job elements, OAI work elements, or ratings from the Dictionary of Occupational Titles (DOT; U.S. DOL, 1991a), and single-item scales from these instruments produced acceptable to high reliabilities. As reviewed by McPhail et al. (1995), the dimensions of the PAQ that correspond to the work context dimensions have very high interrater and rate–rerate reliabilities (.85–.95), and the job elements within these dimensions are assessed with single-item scales (McCormick, Mecham, & Jeanneret, 1989). Reliability estimates for OAI items with content similar to that of work context taxonomy items are moderate to high (.62–.93) and certainly within acceptable standards (Boese & Cunningham, 1975). Furthermore, the results of an analysis of ratings from the DOT indicate that many work context constructs can be rated very reliably (.63–.94) without multiple items for each construct (Geyer, Hice, Hawk, Boese, & Brannon, 1989).

**TABLE 9-2**
**Work Context Taxonomic Structure**

| Second order factor | Item-level constructs | Scale |
|---|---|---|
| | Interpersonal Relationships | |
| Communication | Formality of Communication | Level |
| | Communication Method | Frequency |
| | Objectivity of Information Communicated | Level |
| | Frequency of Job-Required Social Interaction | Frequency |
| | Privacy of Communication | Level |
| Types of Role Relationships | Supervisory Roles | Importance |
| | Sales Roles | Importance |
| | Service Roles | Importance |
| | Adversarial Roles | Importance |
| | Team Participant Roles | Importance |
| Responsibility for Others | Responsibility for the Safety of Others | Level |
| | Responsibility for Work Outcomes and Results | Level |
| Conflictual Contact With Others | Interpersonal Conflict | Frequency |
| | Strained Interpersonal Relations | Frequency |
| | Physical Work Setting | |
| Work Setting | Types of Work Settings | Frequency |
| | Privacy of Work Areas | Level |
| | Physical Proximity | Level |
| Environmental Conditions | Exposure to Extreme Environmental Conditions | Frequency |
| | Exposure to Job Hazards | Frequency |
| | Possibility of Injury From Job Hazards | Likelihood of Occurrence |
| | Impact of Injury | Seriousness of Injury |
| Job Demands | Body Positioning | Time Spent |
| | Work Attire | Frequency |
| | Structural Job Characteristics | |
| Criticality of Position | Consequence of Error | Level |
| | Impact of Decisions | Level |
| | Responsibility/ Accountability | Level |
| | Decision Latitude | Level |
| Routine Versus Challenging Work | Frustrating Circumstances | Level |
| | Degree of Automation | Level |
| | Task Clarity | Level |
| | Required Precision | Importance |
| | Required Attention to Detail | Importance |
| | Required Maintenance of Vigilance | Importance |
| | Monotony/Repetitive Activities | Importance |
| | Structured vs. Unstructured Work | Level |
| | Level of Competition | Level |
| Pace and Scheduling | Frequency and Stringency of Deadlines | Frequency |
| | Distractions and Interruptions | Importance |
| | Machine Driven Work Pace | Importance |

## SUMMARY OF TAXONOMIC DEVELOPMENT

The contextual factors of work clearly are important features on which occupations may differ. These factors, along with organizational variables and Generalized Work Activities (GWAs), may affect workers and work outcomes (see Figure 9-3). Contextual factors have been linked to such outcome variables as job performance, satisfaction, compensation, group formation, group cohesion, organizational effectiveness, and physical and psychological health. However, attempts to assess these factors have been unstructured and have lacked a systematic approach. Although many job analysis instruments tap various aspects of the physical and psychosocial work environment, none individually captures or assesses individually the broad range of work context factors.

The proposed taxonomy builds on research literature and existing job analysis instruments to organize relevant work context factors into a coherent structure for job-analytic purposes. The assessment of these contextual factors is supported by numerous job analysis studies and will provide valuable information for a variety of human resource management functions. However, the development of a taxonomy is of little utility if the results are not reliable or do not provide meaningful information regarding differences and similarities between jobs. Thus, the next phase in the development of the taxonomy involved an evaluation of job incumbents' and analysts' ratings of work context variables, and the remainder of this chapter involves analyses and interpretations of this information.

## SAMPLES

Job incumbents from a wide range of occupations and organizations completed the work context survey. (See chap. 4 for a detailed description of the sampling procedures.) Although work context information was collected from 80 occupations, data from only the 37 occupations for which at least four incumbent respondents completed the Work Context Questionnaire are included in these analyses. A list of the 37 occupations and the number of incumbent respondents within each is provided in Table 9-3.

In addition to the job incumbent sample, ratings from six occupational analysts were collected. Experienced analysts from the North Carolina Occupational Analysis Field Center (OAFC) reviewed commonly performed tasks from the DOT for each of the occupations, then rated the occupations on selected work context variables. A review of the DOT job tasks without actually observing the job being performed did not provide sufficient information regarding several of the work context variables, and these variables were not rated by the analysts. For instance, the Formality of Communication

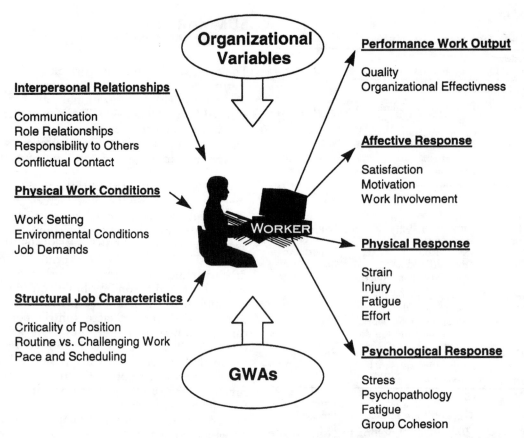

**FIGURE 9-3.** Impact of work context variables

(D1),[1] Communication Methods (D2), and Privacy of Communication (D5) are difficult to evaluate from only a list of job tasks and would require observation before accurate assessments could be performed. Although the six analysts rated all 80 occupations, only those 37 occupations noted above were used in the data analyses.

## RESULTS

### Descriptive Statistics

The rating scale for each variable, together with the mean, standard deviation, standard error of measurement, and interrater agreement coefficient, are provided in Table 9-4. Unlike the descriptors in many of the other domains, the work context variables are not measured on common rating scales, rendering a comparison of means across all items inappropriate. However, comparisons of subitems under several categories bear closer examination.

A review of the mean values for each descriptor indicated that the most commonly used communication method across the occupations was Face-to-

Face Interactions with other individuals (D2a), followed closely by use of a Telephone (D2f). Even with current innovations in computer technology, the use of Electronic Mail (D2h) and Interactive Computer (D2g) communication was rated relatively low for the occupations in this sample.

The types of job interaction rated most important were Working With or Contributing To a Team (D6e) and Providing a Service to Others (D6c). With the proliferation of team-based work practices and the shift toward a service economy, this finding is not surprising. The ratings reflect the fact that these types of interactions can be found in almost all occupations, ranging from janitors to managers. Persuading or Influencing (D6b) and Taking an Opposing Position (D6d), however, are important for a much more limited subset of jobs.

The type of Work Setting (D12) in which workers from this sample spent the most time was Indoors (D12a) in a climate-controlled environment. Distracting Noise (D15a) was the highest-rated environmental condition. Alternatively, exposure to various job hazards received relatively low ratings, with Exposure to Hazardous Situations (D21a) (those likely to involve cuts, bites, or minor burns) receiving the highest mean rating of this group of items.

The general findings reflect what is commonly known about how and where work is performed. A majority of jobs are performed Indoors (D12a), in

---

[1]Notation within parentheses represents the item number on the Work Context survey (e.g., D1 indicates Item 1 on the survey instrument, D2 indicates Item 2, etc.).

**TABLE 9-3**
**Thirty-Seven Occupations With Four or More Incumbents Included in Data Analysis**

| Occupation code | Occupation title | Incumbent sample size |
|---|---|---|
| 15005 | Education Administrators | 9 |
| 19005 | General Managers & Top Executives | 55 |
| 22114 | Chemical Engineers | 5 |
| 22135 | Mechanical Engineers | 5 |
| 25105 | Computer Programmers | 9 |
| 31303 | Teachers, Preschool | 4 |
| 31305 | Teachers, Elementary School | 13 |
| 32502 | Registered Nurses | 30 |
| 32902 | Medical & Clinical Laboratory Technologists | 5 |
| 32905 | Medical & Clinical Laboratory Technicians | 6 |
| 49008 | Salespersons, Except Scientific & Retail | 7 |
| 49011 | Salespersons, Retail | 21 |
| 49021 | Stock Clerks, Sales Floor | 15 |
| 49023 | Cashiers | 28 |
| 51002 | First Line Supervisors, Clerical/Administrative | 57 |
| 53102 | Tellers | 4 |
| 53121 | Loan & Credit Clerks | 5 |
| 53311 | Insurance Claims Clerks | 10 |
| 53905 | Teachers' Aids & Assistants, Clerical | 4 |
| 55108 | Secretaries, Except Legal & Medical | 78 |
| 55305 | Receptionists & Information Clerks | 7 |
| 55338 | Bookkeeping, Accounting & Auditing Clerks | 38 |
| 55347 | General Office Clerks | 78 |
| 61005 | Police & Detective Supervisors | 11 |
| 63014 | Police Patrol Officers | 25 |
| 65008 | Waiters & Waitresses | 22 |
| 65026 | Cooks, Restaurant | 6 |
| 65038 | Food Preparation Workers | 25 |
| 66005 | Medical Assistants | 6 |
| 66008 | Nursing Aides, Orderlies & Attendants | 17 |
| 67005 | Janitors & Cleaners | 30 |
| 85132 | Maintenance Repairers, General Utility | 37 |
| 87902 | Earth Drillers, Except Oil & Gas | 8 |
| 89108 | Machinists | 4 |
| 92974 | Packaging & Filling Machine Operations | 12 |
| 97102 | Truck Drivers, Heavy or Tractor Trailer | 16 |
| 97111 | Bus Drivers, School | 16 |

relatively safe conditions. Individual communication, either Face-to-Face (D2a) or via Telephone (D2f), remains the most frequently used technique to convey information. One finding that may reflect somewhat recent changes in the way work is structured is the high mean rating for working with and contributing to a team (Work/Contribute to Team, D6e). Employees at all levels of organizations find it relatively important to work with or contribute to the work of teams in order to perform their work activities.

### Interrater Agreement

As reported in Table 9-4, based on a harmonic mean of 9.44 respondents per occupation, most variables had an acceptable level of interrater agreement. The median interrater agreement coefficient was .83, with a range from .20 to .97. Given the relatively small number of raters per occupation, the agreement co-

efficients are acceptable for most items. Only four items had an agreement coefficient of .50 or less (Descriptors 2a, 2d, 3, 30).

We also computed estimates of single-rater reliability and of the reliability that would have resulted if the initial sampling plan of 30 raters per occupation had been obtained. Obviously, the single-rater estimates were lower than those found using either the harmonic mean number of raters or the estimate found for 30 raters. With only three exceptions—(D2d) Video Conferencing, .44; (D3) Communication Subjectivity, .69; and (D30) Task Performance Clarity, .62)—the estimates for 30 raters provide very high levels of reliability (ranging from .44 to .99).

When comparing these results with the median reliabilities reported for work context variables obtained using other procedures, we find the present results to be very satisfactory. Specifically, the median reliability for PAQ dimensions that reflect the work context range from .86 to .99 ($n = 19,961$ analyzed pairs) (McCormick et al., 1989). Reliability estimates based on use of the OAI to analyze work context range from .62 to .93 (Boese & Cunningham, 1975), and ratings of DOT work context items by four trained analysts range from .63 to .94 (Geyer et al., 1989). The reliabilities found for the variables in the work context taxonomy typically fall within the ranges found for other measures of work context variables.

The evaluation of the more salient or tangible aspects of people's jobs resulted in the most consistently high levels of agreement, including responses to items regarding Work Setting (D12), Work Attire (D23), Body Positioning (D22), and Environmental Conditions (D15). Only three items have estimated reliability coefficients for 30 raters below .70, and very few are below .70 using the harmonic mean of 9.44 raters. Thus, even with small samples, an acceptable level of interrater agreement was found for the work context variables, and samples of 10 to 30 raters should provide very satisfactory levels of reliability.

The descriptor with the lowest agreement estimate is the use of video conferencing as a communication method (Video Conference, D2d). The infrequent use of this method may account for the low level of agreement. It also is possible that some incumbents did not understand the term "video conferencing." Janitors rated the item almost as high as did executives. It is possible that some incumbents interpreted the question to include videotaped addresses by managers and executives.

In general, the results of the various interrater agreement analyses lead to the conclusion that the work context descriptors can be assessed with sufficient levels of agreement by job incumbents. As always, a large sample of respondents per occupation is recommended. There was a raw average of approximately 20 incumbents per occupation in the current sample (harmonic mean = 9.44), and it appears that a sample of that size, and certainly a sample of 30 raters per occupation, would yield adequate interrater agreement.

**TABLE 9-4**

**Descriptive Statistics Across All Occupations and Reliability Estimates for Rated Differences Between Occupations: Work Context**

| Descriptor | Scale anchors | M | SD | SEM[a] | $r_k$[b] |
|---|---|---|---|---|---|
| 1. Communication Formality | 1 = very informal<br>7 = very formal | 3.94 | 0.86 | 0.49 | 0.68 |
| 2. Communication Methods | | | | | |
|   a. Face-to-Face Individuals | 0 = never or less than once a month | 5.38 | 0.70 | 0.52 | 0.44 |
|   b. Face-to-Face Groups | 1 = once or more per month, but less than weekly | 1.98 | 0.87 | 0.41 | 0.77 |
|   c. Public Speaking | 2 = once or more per week, but less than daily | 0.97 | 1.00 | 0.46 | 0.79 |
|   d. Video Conference | 3 = daily (once or twice a day) | 0.22 | 0.30 | 0.27 | 0.20 |
|   e. Voice Mail | 4 = several times per day | 1.52 | 1.49 | 0.48 | 0.89 |
|   f. Telephone | 5 = hourly | 4.08 | 1.49 | 0.42 | 0.92 |
|   g. Interactive Computer | 6 = more than hourly | 1.49 | 1.16 | 0.60 | 0.73 |
|   h. Electronic Mail | 7 = continually | 1.28 | 1.38 | 0.45 | 0.89 |
|   i. Handwritten Notes | | 3.09 | 0.93 | 0.42 | 0.80 |
|   j. Letters and Memos | | 2.26 | 0.77 | 0.38 | 0.75 |
|   k. Written Reports | | 1.76 | 0.95 | 0.46 | 0.77 |
| 3. Communication Subjectivity | 1 = very objective<br>7 = very subjective | 3.33 | 0.56 | 0.43 | 0.41 |
| 4. Social Interaction | 1 = very little contact<br>7 = very extensive contact | 5.72 | 0.91 | 0.44 | 0.76 |
| 5. Privacy of Communication | 1 = little privacy<br>7 = substantial privacy | 3.66 | 0.70 | 0.36 | 0.73 |
| 6. Job Interactions | | | | | |
|   a. Supervise/Develop Others | 0 = does not apply | 3.03 | 0.76 | 0.32 | 0.83 |
|   b. Persuade or Influence | 5 = extremely important | 1.83 | 1.15 | 0.40 | 0.88 |
|   c. Provide Service to Others | | 3.53 | 1.09 | 0.51 | 0.78 |
|   d. Take Opposing Position | | 1.75 | 0.80 | 0.39 | 0.77 |
|   e. Work/Contribute to Team | | 3.80 | 0.55 | 0.35 | 0.59 |
|   f. Deal With Public | | 2.84 | 1.12 | 0.46 | 0.83 |
|   g. Coordinate/Lead Activity | | 2.99 | 0.75 | 0.41 | 0.70 |
| 7. Health/Safety of Others | 0 = none (no responsibility)<br>7 = very substantial responsibility | 3.95 | 1.84 | 0.47 | 0.94 |
| 8. Responsible for Others' Work | 0 = none (no responsibility)<br>7 = very substantial responsibility | 3.45 | 1.21 | 0.50 | 0.83 |
| 9. Conflict Situations | 0 = never (or does not apply)<br>4 = always | 1.81 | 0.45 | 0.23 | 0.75 |
| 10. Unpleasant Individuals | 0 = never (or does not apply)<br>4 = always | 2.06 | 0.38 | 0.22 | 0.65 |
| 11. Physical Aggression | 0 = never (or does not apply)<br>4 = always | 0.94 | 0.64 | 0.19 | 0.91 |
| 12. Work Settings | | | | | |
|   a. Indoors, Controlled | 0 = never (or does not apply) | 5.71 | 1.35 | 0.54 | 0.84 |
|   b. Indoors, Uncontrolled | 1 = once per year or less | 1.48 | 1.33 | 0.60 | 0.80 |
|   c. Outdoors, Exposed | 2 = more than once per year, but less than monthly | 1.94 | 2.05 | 0.42 | 0.96 |
|   d. Outdoors, Covered | 3 = more than once per month, but less than weekly | 0.91 | 1.21 | 0.35 | 0.92 |
|   e. Open Vehicle/Equip. | 4 = more than once per week, but less than daily | 0.51 | 1.10 | 0.31 | 0.92 |
|   f. Enclosed Vehicle/Equip. | 5 = daily (1 or 2 times/day)<br>6 = several times per day<br>7 = hourly or more often (including continually) | 1.48 | 2.03 | 0.38 | 0.97 |
| 13. Privacy of Work Area | 1 = little privacy<br>7 = substantial privacy | 2.97 | 1.18 | 0.44 | 0.86 |
| 14. Physical Proximity | 1 = not close<br>7 = very close | 4.48 | 0.85 | 0.44 | 0.73 |
| 15. Environmental Conditions | | | | | |
|   a. Distracting Noise | 0 = never (or does not apply) | 3.39 | 1.22 | 0.70 | 0.67 |
|   b. Extreme Temperature | 1 = once per year or less | 2.05 | 1.71 | 0.49 | 0.92 |
|   c. Poor Lighting | 2 = more than once per year, but less than monthly | 1.35 | 1.25 | 0.48 | 0.85 |
|   d. Contaminants | 3 = more than once per month, but less than weekly | 2.52 | 1.73 | 0.62 | 0.87 |
|   e. Cramped Work Space | 4 = more than once per week, but less than daily | 1.38 | 0.98 | 0.44 | 0.80 |
|   f. Whole Body Vibration | 5 = daily (1 or 2 times/day)<br>6 = several times per day<br>7 = hourly or more often (including continually) | 0.46 | 1.18 | 0.30 | 0.94 |
| 16. Radiation | | | | | |
|   a. Exposure | 0 = never (or does not apply)<br>7 = hourly or more often (including continually) | 0.44 | 0.72 | 0.37 | 0.73 |
|   b. Likelihood of Injury | 0 = no possibility<br>7 = very high possibility | 0.43 | 0.47 | 0.30 | 0.59 |
|   c. Extent of Injury | 0 = no treatment required<br>7 = injury resulting in permanent total impairment/death | 0.43 | 0.47 | 0.30 | 0.59 |
| 17. Diseases/Infections | | | | | |
|   a. Exposure | 0 = never (or does not apply)<br>7 = hourly or more often (including continually) | 2.10 | 1.86 | 0.55 | 0.91 |

*Table 9-4 continues*

**TABLE 9-4 (Continued)**

| Descriptor | Scale anchors | M | SD | SEM[a] | $r_k$[b] |
|---|---|---|---|---|---|
| b. Likelihood of Injury | 0 = no possibility<br>7 = very high possibility | 1.64 | 1.32 | 0.42 | 0.90 |
| c. Extent of Injury | 0 = no treatment required<br>7 = injury resulting in permanent total impairment/death | 1.15 | 1.11 | 0.36 | 0.90 |
| 18. High Places | | | | | |
| a. Exposure | 0 = never (or does not apply)<br>7 = hourly or more often (including continually) | 0.77 | 1.00 | 0.26 | 0.93 |
| b. Likelihood of Injury | 0 = no possibility<br>7 = very high possibility | 0.68 | 0.82 | 0.24 | 0.91 |
| c. Extent of Injury | 0 = no treatment required<br>7 = injury resulting in permanent total impairment/death | 0.68 | 0.77 | 0.25 | 0.89 |
| 19. Hazardous Conditions | | | | | |
| a. Exposure | 0 = never (or does not apply)<br>7 = hourly or more often (including continually) | 1.29 | 1.28 | 0.44 | 0.88 |
| b. Likelihood of Injury | 0 = no possibility<br>7 = very high possibility | 1.11 | 1.02 | 0.36 | 0.88 |
| c. Extent of Injury | 0 = no treatment required<br>7 = injury resulting in permanent total impairment/death | 0.86 | 0.89 | 0.31 | 0.88 |
| 20. Hazardous Equipment | | | | | |
| a. Exposure | 0 = never (or does not apply)<br>7 = hourly or more often (including continually) | 1.69 | 1.90 | 0.44 | 0.95 |
| b. Likelihood of Injury | 0 = no possibility<br>7 = very high possibility | 1.28 | 1.43 | 0.33 | 0.95 |
| c. Extent of Injury | 0 = no treatment required<br>7 = injury resulting in permanent total impairment/death | 0.99 | 1.08 | 0.28 | 0.93 |
| 21. Hazardous Situations | | | | | |
| a. Exposure | 0 = never (or does not apply)<br>7 = hourly or more often (including continually) | 2.25 | 1.57 | 0.48 | 0.91 |
| b. Likelihood of Injury | 0 = no possibility<br>7 = very high possibility | 1.93 | 1.34 | 0.41 | 0.91 |
| c. Extent of Injury | 0 = no treatment required<br>7 = injury resulting in permanent total impairment/death | 1.01 | 0.69 | 0.26 | 0.86 |
| 22. Body Positioning | | | | | |
| a. Sitting | 0 = never (or does not apply) | 2.59 | 1.28 | 0.23 | 0.97 |
| b. Standing | 1 = under 10% of the time | 2.96 | 1.21 | 0.23 | 0.96 |
| c. Climbing Ladders, etc. | 2 = between 1/10 and 1/3 of the time | 0.39 | 0.52 | 0.14 | 0.93 |
| d. Walking or Running | 3 = between 1/3 and 2/3 of the time | 2.28 | 1.05 | 0.28 | 0.93 |
| e. Kneeling or Crouching | 4 = over 2/3 of the time | 1.04 | 0.70 | 0.26 | 0.87 |
| f. Keeping/Regaining Balance | 5 = almost continually | 0.76 | 0.62 | 0.30 | 0.77 |
| g. Handling Tools, Objects | | 2.57 | 1.00 | 0.49 | 0.76 |
| h. Bending/Twisting Body | | 1.70 | 0.99 | 0.31 | 0.90 |
| i. Making Repetitive Motions | | 2.70 | 0.91 | 0.42 | 0.78 |
| 23. Work Attire | 0 = never (or does not apply) | 2.20 | 1.66 | 0.37 | 0.95 |
| a. Business/Office Clothes | 1 = once per year or less | 1.21 | 1.47 | 0.41 | 0.92 |
| b. Special Uniform | 2 = more than once per year, but less than monthly | 1.15 | 1.44 | 0.35 | 0.94 |
| c. Maintenance Clothes | 3 = more than once per month, but less than weekly | 2.78 | 2.48 | 0.53 | 0.95 |
| d. Common Safety Attire | 4 = more than once a week, but not daily | 0.67 | 0.96 | 0.32 | 0.89 |
| e. Special Safety Attire | 5 = daily | | | | |
| 24. Consequence of Error | 1 = mildly serious<br>7 = extremely serious | 3.54 | 1.32 | 0.45 | 0.88 |
| 25. Impact of Decisions | | | | | |
| a. Level of Decisions | 1 = very minor results<br>7 = extreme results | 4.28 | 0.90 | 0.37 | 0.83 |
| b. Frequency of Decisions | 0 = never (or does not apply)<br>7 = hourly or more often (including continually) | 3.57 | 1.32 | 0.56 | 0.82 |
| 26. Accountable for Results | 1 = very limited<br>7 = very substantial | 4.86 | 1.03 | 0.49 | 0.78 |
| 27. Decision Latitude | 1 = very little freedom<br>7 = extensive freedom | 4.26 | 0.74 | 0.34 | 0.79 |
| 28. Frustrating Circumstances | 1 = low extent<br>7 = high extent | 3.41 | 0.96 | 0.54 | 0.68 |
| 29. Level of Automation | 1 = low automation<br>7 = high automation | 3.13 | 0.90 | 0.48 | 0.72 |
| 30. Task/Performance Clarity | 1 = low clarity<br>7 = high clarity | 5.64 | 0.53 | 0.43 | 0.34 |
| 31. Accuracy/Exactness | 0 = does not apply<br>7 = extremely important | 4.10 | 0.43 | 0.23 | 0.72 |
| 32. Details and Completeness | 0 = does not apply<br>7 = extremely important | 4.22 | 0.37 | 0.23 | 0.60 |
| 33. Constant Awareness | 0 = does not apply<br>7 = extremely important | 2.47 | 0.85 | 0.44 | 0.73 |

*Table 9-4 continues*

**TABLE 9-4 (Continued)**

| Descriptor | Scale anchors | M | SD | SEM[a] | $r_k$[b] |
|---|---|---|---|---|---|
| 34. Repetitive Activities | 0 = does not apply<br>7 = extremely important | 2.52 | 0.82 | 0.43 | 0.72 |
| 35. Unstructured Tasks/Goals | 1 = very structured<br>7 = very unstructured | 4.37 | 0.78 | 0.40 | 0.74 |
| 36. Level of Competition | 1 = low competition<br>7 = high competition | 3.32 | 0.74 | 0.48 | 0.57 |
| 37. Deadlines/Time Pressure | 0 = never (or does not apply)<br>7 = hourly or more often (including continually) | 4.32 | 0.84 | 0.50 | 0.65 |
| 38. Work With Distractions | 0 = does not apply<br>5 = extremely important | 3.29 | 0.64 | 0.40 | 0.61 |
| 39. Machine Driven Pace | 0 = does not apply<br>5 = extremely important | 1.75 | 0.98 | 0.46 | 0.78 |

*Note.* Statistics are based on 37 occupations with Work Context Questionnaire responses from at least 4 incumbents (mean number of incumbents = 19.68; *Mdn* = 12.5; harmonic mean = 9.44). [a]This estimate of the standard error of measurement was calculated as $SEM = SD^* \sqrt{1 - r_k}$. [b]This estimate of reliability was obtained by calculating the intraclass correlation for $k$ ratings across occupations: $ICC(1, k) = [BMS - WMS]/BMS$ (Shrout & Fleiss, 1979), where $k$ is the harmonic mean of the number of ratings provided on each occupation.

## Descriptor Relationships

Intercorrelations between work context variables were computed from the mean item ratings for each occupation. The intercorrelations were interpreted within each of the three higher order work context dimensions (Interpersonal Relationships, Physical Work Conditions, and Structural Job Characteristics) and not across dimensions. The intercorrelations within the Interpersonal Relationship dimension yield meaningful patterns of relationships. For instance, Responsibility for Others' Work (D8) is strongly related to Supervising and Developing Others (D6a; $r = .66$) and to Coordinating and Leading Others (D6g; $r = .72$). Dealing With the Public (D6f) is strongly related to Social Interaction (D4; $r = .60$), Persuading and Influencing Others (D6b; $r = .62$), Public Speaking (D2c; $r = .57$), and interacting with Unpleasant Individuals (D10; $r = .53$).

Intercorrelations within the Physical Work Conditions dimension also display expected patterns of relationships. Work Setting: Indoors, Controlled (D12a) has negative correlations with descriptors measuring uncomfortable working conditions (Descriptors 15a to 15f; $r = -.43$ through $-.79$) and has a positive relationship with Business or Office Attire (D23a; $r = .47$). Privacy of Work Area (D13), which should be associated with office jobs, was positively related to the Sitting (D22a; $r = .49$) body position but negatively related to all other Body Positioning variables (D22b to 22i; $r = -.23$ through $-.71$). Exposure to Diseases and Infections (D17) is positively related to wearing a Special Uniform (D23b; $r = .72$) and Physical Proximity (D14; $r = .56$), which may reflect duties found in jobs such as nursing and public safety.

Rational patterns of intercorrelations are also found within the Structural Job Characteristics dimension. Machine Driven Pace (D39) is negatively correlated with Unstructured Tasks (D35; $r = -.63$) but positively correlated with Repetitive Activities (D34; $r = .59$) and working under Time Pressure or Deadlines (D37; $r = .66$). Level of Automation (D29) on the job is positively related to the necessity of be-

ing Accurate and Exact (D31; $r = .55$) and Attention to Details (D32; $r = .55$). Dealing With Frustrating Circumstances (D28) is negatively related to Clarity of Tasks or Performance goals (D30; $r = .37$) and positively related to Accountability for Results (D26; $r = .70$) and Decision Latitude (D27; $r = .77$).

## Factor Structure

An exploratory factor analysis was conducted on the data in order to elaborate on the rational patterns of intercorrelations between variables. A review of factor solutions from principal-components factor analyses with varimax rotation indicated that a seven-factor solution (reported in Table 9-5) allowed for the most meaningful interpretations. The first factor was labeled *Environmental Conditions*, and it accounted for 23.5% of the total variance. Items associated with Work Setting (D12) and Environmental Conditions (D15) produced strong loadings on this factor. The second factor accounted for 16.1% of the variance and was labeled *Physical Activity and Manual Work*. This factor consisted mostly of Body Positioning (D22) variables. The use of Voice Mail (D2e) and Electronic Mail (D2h) also loaded on this factor, but the loadings were negative. The patterns of positive and negative loadings on this factor were consistent with aspects of manual labor and physical tasks versus those work activities that do not require extensive physical effort.

*Managerial and Interpersonal Relations* was the label assigned to the third factor extracted from the analysis, and it accounted for 10.3% of the variance. The variables within this factor were common to supervisory or management positions and positions requiring the worker to interact with and relate to others on an individual basis. The fourth factor accounted for 8.5% of the total variance and was labeled *Structured and Machine Operations*. This factor was characterized by variables associated with performing automated or strictly defined tasks. For example, performing Repetitive Activities (D34), Level of Automation (D29), Unstructured Tasks and

**TABLE 9-5**
**Principal-Components Analysis Pattern Matrix for the Level Scale: Work Context**

| Descriptor | Factor | | | | | | | Communality |
|---|---|---|---|---|---|---|---|---|
| | F1 | F2 | F3 | F4 | F5 | F6 | F7 | |
| 1. Communication Formality | −.02 | −.23 | .28 | −.10 | .51 | .45 | −.15 | .63 |
| 2. Communication Methods | | | | | | | | |
| a. Face-to-Face Individuals | −.03 | .33 | .33 | .22 | .35 | .18 | .19 | .46 |
| b. Face-to-Face Groups | .15 | .01 | .73 | −.14 | .27 | .16 | .09 | .68 |
| c. Public Speaking | −.05 | .13 | .30 | −.01 | .15 | .01 | .71 | .63 |
| d. Video Conference | −.09 | .10 | .26 | −.15 | −.03 | .13 | .53 | .41 |
| e. Voice Mail | .02 | −.64 | .46 | −.14 | .37 | −.19 | .04 | .81 |
| f. Telephone | −.11 | −.41 | .20 | .07 | .59 | −.02 | .24 | .63 |
| g. Interactive Computer | −.27 | −.28 | .10 | .35 | .29 | .06 | .10 | .38 |
| h. Electronic Mail | −.18 | −.56 | .35 | −.06 | .27 | −.20 | −.09 | .59 |
| i. Handwritten Notes | −.07 | −.47 | −.11 | −.16 | .56 | .12 | .28 | .67 |
| j. Letters and Memos | −.23 | −.42 | −.02 | −.22 | .58 | −.08 | .13 | .64 |
| k. Written Reports | .35 | −.20 | .24 | .14 | .18 | .67 | .16 | .74 |
| 3. Communication Subjectivity | −.04 | .29 | .20 | −.57 | .17 | .07 | .20 | .53 |
| 4. Social Interaction | −.05 | .16 | .06 | .00 | .52 | .22 | .55 | .65 |
| 5. Privacy of Communication | .21 | .22 | .66 | −.03 | −.19 | .20 | .13 | .62 |
| 6. Job Interactions | | | | | | | | |
| a. Supervise/Develop Others | .09 | .12 | .68 | −.09 | .04 | .20 | .07 | .55 |
| b. Persuade or Influence | .03 | −.11 | .76 | −.08 | .06 | −.17 | .46 | .84 |
| c. Provide Service to Others | .05 | .01 | .41 | .51 | .25 | −.01 | .43 | .67 |
| d. Take Opposing Position | .05 | −.12 | .78 | −.27 | −.11 | −.07 | .04 | .72 |
| e. Work/Contribute To Team | −.05 | .42 | .46 | .18 | .20 | .20 | .00 | .50 |
| f. Deal With Public | .07 | −.04 | .20 | .09 | .26 | .08 | .81 | .79 |
| g. Coordinate/Lead Activity | .13 | .12 | .71 | −.22 | .09 | .18 | .22 | .67 |
| 7. Health/Safety of Others | .43 | .45 | .10 | −.33 | −.36 | .50 | .02 | .88 |
| 8. Responsible for Others' Work | .21 | .22 | .66 | −.03 | −.19 | .20 | .13 | .62 |
| 9. Conflict Situations | .51 | −.16 | .33 | −.21 | .23 | .30 | .30 | .67 |
| 10. Unpleasant Individuals | .34 | −.07 | −.08 | −.15 | .31 | .45 | .53 | .73 |
| 11. Physical Aggression | .43 | .13 | .04 | −.27 | .05 | .70 | .13 | .79 |
| 12. Work Settings | | | | | | | | |
| a. Indoors, Controlled | −.79 | −.09 | .06 | .00 | .02 | −.21 | −.09 | .69 |
| b. Indoors, Uncontrolled | .36 | −.02 | .30 | −.22 | −.48 | −.17 | −.10 | .54 |
| c. Outdoors, Exposed | .86 | .06 | .01 | −.21 | −.04 | .27 | .20 | .91 |
| d. Outdoors, Covered | .72 | −.07 | .13 | −.11 | −.22 | .09 | .26 | .67 |
| e. Open Vehicle/Equipment | .87 | .22 | .17 | .08 | .10 | .00 | −.16 | .88 |
| f. Enclosed Vehicle/Equipment | .77 | −.27 | .09 | −.11 | −.08 | .26 | .37 | .90 |
| 13. Privacy of Work Area | −.23 | −.53 | .49 | −.28 | .25 | .04 | −.02 | .72 |
| 14. Physical Proximity | .12 | .52 | .06 | .20 | .14 | .53 | .03 | .63 |
| 15. Environmental Conditions | | | | | | | | |
| a. Distracting Noise | .72 | .00 | −.08 | −.02 | −.21 | −.12 | −.09 | .59 |
| b. Extreme Temperature | .91 | .10 | −.01 | −.05 | −.26 | .01 | .10 | .91 |
| c. Poor Lighting | .91 | −.02 | −.02 | .10 | −.08 | .18 | .18 | .91 |
| d. Contaminants | .59 | .16 | .10 | .17 | −.52 | .12 | −.23 | .74 |
| e. Cramped Work Space | .79 | .26 | .16 | .16 | −.25 | .15 | −.05 | .83 |
| f. Whole Body Vibration | .84 | .15 | .01 | .16 | .05 | .03 | −.06 | .75 |
| 16a. Radiation—Exposure | .22 | −.03 | .35 | .25 | .07 | −.01 | −.45 | .44 |
| 17a. Diseases/Infections—Exposure | −.21 | .30 | −.01 | .17 | −.12 | .81 | .02 | .84 |
| 18a. High Places—Exposure | .80 | .27 | .25 | −.04 | .05 | −.22 | −.10 | .84 |
| 19a. Hazardous Conditions—Exposure | .62 | .14 | .20 | .38 | −.35 | .20 | −.35 | .87 |
| 20a. Hazardous Equipment—Exposure | .77 | .09 | .15 | .03 | −.42 | −.05 | −.19 | .84 |
| 21a. Hazardous Situations—Exposure | .55 | .41 | .03 | −.05 | −.53 | .08 | −.08 | .77 |
| 22. Body Positioning | | | | | | | | |
| a. Sitting | −.09 | −.93 | −.08 | .09 | .15 | .07 | −.11 | .93 |
| b. Standing | .04 | .93 | .04 | −.03 | −.21 | −.01 | .05 | .92 |
| c. Climbing Ladders, etc. | .71 | .35 | .25 | −.09 | −.06 | −.32 | −.27 | .87 |
| d. Walking or Running | .14 | .83 | .01 | −.24 | −.11 | .06 | .02 | .78 |
| e. Kneeling or Crouching | .19 | .83 | .00 | −.20 | .01 | .07 | .02 | .76 |
| f. Keeping/Regain Balance | .47 | .79 | .13 | −.06 | .07 | .05 | −.02 | .88 |
| g. Handling Tools, Objects | .40 | .50 | −.27 | .47 | −.38 | −.17 | .06 | .88 |
| h. Bending/Twisting Body | .34 | .82 | −.09 | −.08 | −.12 | −.03 | .21 | .87 |
| i. Making Repetitive Motions | .07 | .45 | −.37 | .60 | −.16 | −.17 | −.04 | .76 |
| 23. Work Attire | | | | | | | | |
| a. Business/Office Clothes | −.32 | −.47 | .13 | .02 | .61 | −.16 | .17 | .77 |
| b. Special Uniform | .06 | .19 | .10 | .25 | −.33 | .62 | .37 | .75 |
| c. Maintenance Clothes | .55 | .30 | −.12 | .00 | −.58 | −.27 | −.12 | .84 |
| d. Common Safety Attire | .48 | .19 | .32 | .14 | −.55 | .26 | −.28 | .83 |
| e. Special Safety Attire | .72 | −.21 | .28 | .00 | −.06 | .17 | −.18 | .72 |
| 24. Consequence of Error | .36 | −.24 | .42 | .31 | −.15 | .55 | −.17 | .81 |

*Table 9-5 continues*

**TABLE 9-5 (Continued)**

| Descriptor | F1 | F2 | F3 | F4 | F5 | F6 | F7 | Communality |
|---|---|---|---|---|---|---|---|---|
| 25. Level of Decisions | | | | | | | | |
|    a. Impact of Decisions | .18 | −.32 | .56 | .25 | .15 | .54 | .08 | .82 |
|    b. Frequency of Decisions | .26 | −.30 | .40 | .35 | .24 | .38 | .32 | .75 |
| 26. Accountable for Results | .20 | −.31 | .62 | .36 | −.22 | .27 | .24 | .83 |
| 27. Decision Latitude | .31 | −.46 | .67 | .16 | −.12 | .05 | .03 | .79 |
| 28. Frustrating Circumstances | .40 | −.48 | .55 | .12 | −.19 | −.01 | −.11 | .75 |
| 29. Level of Automation | −.22 | −.25 | .20 | .72 | .02 | .03 | −.27 | .74 |
| 30. Task/Performance Clarity | −.12 | .20 | −.47 | .27 | .09 | .27 | −.05 | .44 |
| 31. Accuracy/Exactness | −.18 | −.25 | −.02 | .68 | −.03 | .33 | −.05 | .67 |
| 32. Details and Completeness | −.14 | −.13 | .01 | .76 | .02 | .32 | −.05 | .67 |
| 33. Constant Awareness | .43 | .11 | .17 | .41 | .00 | .47 | .27 | .69 |
| 34. Repetitive Activities | .10 | .13 | −.40 | .80 | .13 | .10 | −.02 | .85 |
| 35. Unstructured Tasks/Goals | −.05 | −.12 | .37 | −.70 | .30 | .08 | .02 | .75 |
| 36. Level of Competition | .25 | .17 | .52 | .16 | −.25 | −.18 | .24 | .54 |
| 37. Deadlines/Time Pressure | .25 | −.17 | −.02 | .37 | −.59 | .20 | .11 | .63 |
| 38. Work with Distractions | .10 | −.54 | .14 | .41 | .09 | .09 | .14 | .53 |
| 39. Machine Driven Pace | .32 | −.09 | −.14 | .69 | −.36 | −.11 | −.11 | .76 |
|    % of Variance | 23.50 | 16.10 | 10.30 | 8.50 | 6.00 | 4.00 | 3.00 | — |
|    Eigenvalue | 18.37 | 12.55 | 8.05 | 6.65 | 4.84 | 3.25 | 2.68 | — |

*Note.* $N = 37$. The correlation matrix was based on means calculated at the occupation level. F1 = Environmental Conditions, F2 = Physical Activity and Manual Work, F3 = Managerial/Interpersonal Relations, F4 = Structured/Machine Operations, F5 = Business/Office Environment, F6 = Health and Safety Conditions, F7 = Interacting With Public. These headings are based on an orthogonal varimax rotation.

Goals (D35), and Machine Driven Pace (D39) had strong loadings on this factor.

The fifth factor extracted from the analyses included variables found in *Business or Office Environments*. This factor accounted for 6% of the total variance. Communicating via the Telephone (D2f), with Letters and Memos (D2j), and Wearing Business Clothes (D23a) produced positive loadings on this factor, and Wearing Safety Equipment (D23e) and Maintenance Clothing (D23c) yielded negative loadings.

Although the sixth and seventh factors account for only 4% and 3% of the total variance, respectively, they represent meaningful groupings of variables. The sixth factor, labeled *Health and Safety Conditions*, was defined by variables that can be associated with tasks found in health care and public safety jobs, such as Exposure to Diseases (D17), Wearing a Special Uniform (D23b), and being responsible for the Health and Safety of Others (D7). The final factor extracted from the analysis was labeled *Interacting With the Public*. Obviously, Dealing With the Public (D6f), Public Speaking (D2c), and Social Interaction (D4) strongly loaded on this factor. Apparently, encountering Unpleasant Individuals (D10) also is associated with public interactions, and it produced a strong loading on this factor.

Overall, the variable loadings can be interpreted as meaningful work context factors. We also examined our original three-dimension taxonomy by limiting the principal-components analysis to the extraction of three factors. The results were surprisingly similar to our initial taxonomy given the very small sample size and restricted set of occupations. The first factor was the Physical Work Conditions dimension from the original taxonomy, and only two extraneous items loaded on this factor that were not readily explained (Deadline and Time Pressure [D37] and Level

of Competition [D36]). The second factor was the original Interpersonal Relationships dimension. This factor was also extremely clear and had only one extraneous item, namely that of Unstructured Tasks and Goals (D35). The final component matched the structural job characteristics dimension from the initial taxonomy. This factor was the most confounded in that it included all of the physical body position items (e.g., Sitting [D22a], Standing [D22b]), as well as interpersonal items associated with using computers, writing reports, and providing service. It is interesting to speculate that all of these activities, especially the use of a computer, add more structure to a job as opposed to facilitating interpersonal relationships. Perhaps this confirmatory analysis is more accurate than our rational taxonomy in describing the structure of work context as it is experienced.

## Occupation Differences

Six occupations (General Managers and Top Executives, Computer Programmers, Registered Nurses, Police Patrol Officers, Janitors and Cleaners, and Maintenance Repairers and General Utility Workers) were selected to represent distinct and diverse jobs in the overall economy. The mean ratings of the work context variables for each of the six occupations are presented in Table 9-6.

An examination of the patterns of mean ratings reveals meaningful differences between the occupations. For instance, Computer Programmers reported the lowest level of Social Interaction (D4) and the highest level of Making Repetitive Motions (D22i). Managers and Top Executives yielded the highest levels of Supervising and Developing Others (D6a), Accountability for Results (D26), and wearing Business or Office Clothing (D23). The two occupations that

**TABLE 9-6**
**Descriptor Means and Standard Deviations on the Level Scale on Six Example Occupations: Work Context**

| | Occupations | | | | | | | | | | | |
|---|---|---|---|---|---|---|---|---|---|---|---|---|
| | General Managers & Top Executives (n = 55) | | Computer Programmers (n = 9) | | Registered Nurses (n = 30) | | Police Patrol Officers (n = 25) | | Janitors & Cleaners[a] (n = 30) | | Maintenance Repairers, General Utility (n = 37) | |
| Descriptor | M | SD | M | SD | M | SD | M | SD | M | SD | M | SD |
| 1. Communication Formality | 4.29 | 1.54 | 3.67 | 2.00 | 3.64 | 1.64 | 5.24 | 1.81 | 3.14 | 1.80 | 3.78 | 1.87 |
| 2. Communication Methods | | | | | | | | | | | | |
|   a. Face-to-Face Individuals | 5.36 | 1.70 | 5.00 | 1.66 | 5.63 | 1.65 | 5.80 | 1.47 | 4.27 | 2.07 | 4.62 | 1.96 |
|   b. Face-to-Face Groups | 2.31 | 1.20 | 2.75 | 1.64 | 2.73 | 1.01 | 2.48 | 1.56 | 1.03 | 1.25 | 1.68 | 1.33 |
|   c. Public Speaking | 0.85 | 1.53 | 0.63 | 0.70 | 0.70 | 1.09 | 2.08 | 2.36 | 0.33 | 0.80 | 0.43 | 0.96 |
|   d. Video Conference | 0.22 | 0.53 | 0.22 | 0.44 | 0.20 | 0.61 | 0.56 | 1.45 | 0.27 | 0.52 | 0.27 | 0.51 |
|   e. Voice Mail | 3.05 | 2.25 | 2.22 | 1.39 | 0.90 | 1.58 | 2.24 | 2.24 | 0.27 | 1.14 | 0.76 | 1.61 |
|   f. Telephone | 5.53 | 1.54 | 2.33 | 1.58 | 5.00 | 1.39 | 4.56 | 1.58 | 2.17 | 1.84 | 3.19 | 2.09 |
|   g. Interactive Computer | 1.43 | 1.74 | 0.78 | 1.56 | 1.47 | 2.34 | 2.00 | 2.40 | 0.23 | 0.77 | 0.65 | 0.98 |
|   h. Electronic Mail | 1.91 | 1.98 | 4.67 | 1.50 | 1.30 | 1.68 | 1.64 | 1.91 | 0.31 | 0.83 | 0.51 | 0.96 |
|   i. Handwritten Notes | 3.80 | 1.69 | 1.78 | 0.97 | 3.73 | 1.55 | 3.32 | 1.93 | 2.03 | 1.69 | 2.62 | 1.48 |
|   j. Letters and Memos | 2.91 | 1.68 | 1.33 | 1.32 | 1.93 | 1.62 | 1.92 | 1.12 | 2.20 | 1.83 | 1.73 | 1.24 |
|   k. Written Reports | 1.96 | 1.71 | 1.33 | 0.87 | 2.63 | 2.36 | 5.04 | 1.74 | 1.03 | 1.59 | 1.92 | 1.50 |
| 3. Communication Subjectivity | 3.36 | 1.13 | 2.89 | 1.17 | 3.30 | 1.49 | 3.24 | 1.64 | 3.87 | 1.98 | 3.41 | 1.54 |
| 4. Social Interaction | 6.00 | 1.26 | 3.67 | 1.22 | 6.53 | 0.90 | 6.52 | 0.82 | 3.97 | 2.20 | 5.16 | 1.94 |
| 5. Privacy of Communication | 5.22 | 1.29 | 3.78 | 1.20 | 3.86 | 1.48 | 3.08 | 1.89 | 3.62 | 2.11 | 3.22 | 1.46 |
| 6. Job Interactions | | | | | | | | | | | | |
|   a. Supervise/Develop Others | 4.22 | 0.71 | 2.44 | 1.33 | 3.77 | 1.28 | 3.44 | 1.36 | 2.73 | 1.48 | 2.46 | 1.56 |
|   b. Persuade or Influence | 3.43 | 1.26 | 2.78 | 1.48 | 1.83 | 1.80 | 1.92 | 1.96 | 1.13 | 1.59 | 1.16 | 1.32 |
|   c. Provide Service to Others | 4.09 | 1.09 | 3.33 | 1.58 | 4.13 | 1.53 | 4.08 | 1.35 | 2.83 | 1.93 | 2.50 | 1.86 |
|   d. Take Opposing Position | 2.67 | 1.44 | 2.78 | 1.48 | 1.97 | 1.54 | 2.08 | 1.85 | 1.33 | 1.60 | 1.57 | 1.41 |
|   e. Work/Contribute To Team | 3.91 | 0.97 | 3.89 | 0.93 | 4.37 | 0.76 | 3.60 | 1.26 | 3.30 | 1.37 | 3.30 | 1.37 |
|   f. Deal With Public | 3.19 | 1.68 | 2.33 | 1.58 | 3.70 | 1.68 | 4.80 | 0.41 | 1.93 | 1.82 | 1.33 | 1.67 |
|   g. Coordinate/Lead Activity | 3.81 | 0.94 | 2.33 | 1.58 | 3.27 | 1.60 | 3.28 | 1.40 | 2.57 | 1.33 | 2.86 | 1.58 |
| 7. Health/Safety of Others | 4.18 | 2.04 | 0.22 | 0.44 | 5.60 | 1.79 | 5.96 | 1.46 | 5.00 | 2.03 | 5.19 | 1.94 |
| 8. Responsible for Others' Work | 5.53 | 1.61 | 3.11 | 2.67 | 4.40 | 2.21 | 3.68 | 2.21 | 3.40 | 2.37 | 3.68 | 2.43 |
| 9. Conflict Situations | 2.31 | 0.66 | 1.78 | 0.97 | 2.37 | 0.61 | 2.88 | 0.53 | 1.57 | 1.10 | 1.83 | 0.96 |
| 10. Unpleasant Individuals | 2.18 | 0.75 | 1.56 | 0.88 | 2.40 | 0.72 | 3.16 | 0.62 | 2.07 | 1.11 | 1.97 | 0.90 |
| 11. Physical Aggression | 0.95 | 0.85 | 0.00 | 0.00 | 1.83 | 0.91 | 2.80 | 0.76 | 1.10 | 1.12 | 0.78 | 0.85 |
| 12. Work Settings | | | | | | | | | | | | |
|   a. Indoors, Controlled | 6.42 | 1.67 | 6.22 | 2.33 | 6.57 | 1.33 | 3.84 | 2.44 | 5.10 | 2.76 | 5.06 | 1.94 |
|   b. Indoors, Uncontrolled | 1.58 | 2.23 | 0.11 | 0.33 | 1.07 | 2.32 | 1.52 | 1.94 | 2.17 | 2.69 | 3.81 | 2.49 |
|   c. Outdoors, Exposed | 1.40 | 1.90 | 0.00 | 0.00 | 1.13 | 2.13 | 6.52 | 0.87 | 2.50 | 2.32 | 4.41 | 1.94 |
|   d. Outdoors, Covered | 0.71 | 1.40 | 0.00 | 0.00 | 0.73 | 1.60 | 3.24 | 2.71 | 1.07 | 1.87 | 2.89 | 2.00 |
|   e. Open Vehicle/Equip. | 0.09 | 0.35 | 0.00 | 0.00 | 0.17 | 0.91 | 2.08 | 3.04 | 0.53 | 1.14 | 2.43 | 2.06 |
|   f. Enclosed Vehicle/Equip. | 1.82 | 2.23 | 0.00 | 0.00 | 1.30 | 2.20 | 6.40 | 0.91 | 0.37 | 0.89 | 3.22 | 1.99 |
| 13. Privacy of Work Area | 5.38 | 2.05 | 3.89 | 1.27 | 3.87 | 2.29 | 2.88 | 2.17 | 1.96 | 1.73 | 2.22 | 1.78 |
| 14. Physical Proximity | 3.98 | 1.52 | 3.00 | 1.22 | 5.83 | 1.21 | 4.48 | 1.92 | 3.80 | 2.17 | 5.05 | 1.58 |
| 15. Environmental Conditions | | | | | | | | | | | | |
|   a. Distracting Noise | 2.58 | 2.12 | 1.33 | 1.66 | 4.07 | 2.38 | 3.80 | 2.24 | 2.40 | 2.55 | 4.97 | 2.11 |
|   b. Extreme Temperature | 0.96 | 1.47 | 0.00 | 0.00 | 0.90 | 1.45 | 5.08 | 1.68 | 3.13 | 2.40 | 4.19 | 2.03 |
|   c. Poor Lighting | 0.45 | 1.00 | 0.33 | 1.00 | 1.10 | 2.12 | 4.68 | 2.72 | 0.76 | 1.55 | 3.11 | 2.20 |
|   d. Contaminants | 1.65 | 2.30 | 0.11 | 0.33 | 4.03 | 2.46 | 3.96 | 2.24 | 5.27 | 1.98 | 4.11 | 1.73 |
|   e. Cramped Work Space | 0.51 | 0.94 | 0.22 | 0.44 | 2.00 | 2.33 | 2.88 | 2.44 | 1.97 | 2.08 | 3.58 | 1.86 |
|   f. Whole Body Vibration | 0.00 | 0.00 | 0.00 | 0.00 | 0.00 | 0.00 | 1.28 | 2.46 | 0.43 | 1.19 | 1.53 | 1.61 |
| 16. Radiation | | | | | | | | | | | | |
|   a. Exposure | 0.38 | 1.43 | 1.44 | 2.65 | 0.73 | 1.26 | 0.92 | 2.1 | 0.47 | 1.25 | 1.65 | 2.36 |
|   b. Likelihood of Injury | 0.22 | 0.50 | 0.33 | 0.50 | 0.33 | 0.61 | 1.16 | 2.08 | 0.57 | 1.48 | 0.89 | 1.51 |
|   c. Extent of Injury | 0.07 | 0.26 | 0.44 | 1.33 | 0.00 | 0.00 | 1.12 | 1.96 | 0.40 | 0.10 | 0.57 | 1.37 |
| 17. Diseases/Infections | | | | | | | | | | | | |
|   a. Exposure | 1.69 | 2.24 | 0.00 | 0.00 | 5.63 | 1.71 | 4.64 | 1.70 | 4.30 | 2.14 | 2.11 | 2.38 |
|   b. Likelihood of Injury | 1.31 | 1.71 | 0.00 | 0.00 | 4.07 | 1.68 | 4.52 | 1.56 | 3.30 | 1.93 | 1.54 | 1.79 |
|   c. Extent of Injury | 1.04 | 1.44 | 0.00 | 0.00 | 2.80 | 1.54 | 3.00 | 1.63 | 2.37 | 1.85 | 1.16 | 1.52 |
| 18. High Places | | | | | | | | | | | | |
|   a. Exposure | 0.53 | 1.05 | 0.00 | 0.00 | 0.03 | 0.18 | 2.08 | 1.78 | 1.70 | 1.64 | 3.57 | 1.52 |
|   b. Likelihood of Injury | 0.53 | 1.07 | 0.00 | 0.00 | 0.10 | 0.31 | 2.28 | 1.99 | 2.03 | 1.99 | 2.73 | 1.35 |
|   c. Extent of Injury | 0.71 | 1.42 | 0.00 | 0.00 | 0.07 | 0.25 | 2.24 | 1.92 | 1.67 | 1.69 | 2.41 | 1.38 |
| 19. Hazardous Conditions | | | | | | | | | | | | |
|   a. Exposure | 1.11 | 1.91 | 0.33 | 0.71 | 1.57 | 2.22 | 2.48 | 1.90 | 2.67 | 2.45 | 3.27 | 2.10 |
|   b. Likelihood of Injury | 0.89 | 1.34 | 0.22 | 0.67 | 1.03 | 1.40 | 2.80 | 2.31 | 2.33 | 2.23 | 2.73 | 1.63 |
|   c. Extent of Injury | 0.73 | 1.19 | 0.11 | 0.33 | 0.93 | 1.28 | 2.52 | 1.92 | 1.57 | 1.61 | 1.95 | 1.65 |

*Table 9-6 continues*

**TABLE 9-6 (Continued)**

| | General Managers & Top Executives (n = 55) | | Computer Programmers (n = 9) | | Registered Nurses (n = 30) | | Police Patrol Officers (n = 25) | | Janitors & Cleaners* (n = 30) | | Maintenance Repairers, General Utility (n = 37) | |
|---|---|---|---|---|---|---|---|---|---|---|---|---|
| Descriptor | M | SD | M | SD | M | SD | M | SD | M | SD | M | SD |
| 20. Hazardous Equipment | | | | | | | | | | | | |
|   a. Exposure | 0.84 | 1.34 | 0.00 | 0.00 | 0.83 | 1.82 | 0.76 | 1.71 | 1.37 | 1.88 | 4.65 | 1.83 |
|   b. Likelihood of Injury | 0.62 | 0.91 | 0.00 | 0.00 | 0.53 | 1.17 | 4.68 | 1.80 | 1.20 | 1.73 | 2.81 | 1.41 |
|   c. Extent of Injury | 0.60 | 1.05 | 0.00 | 0.00 | 0.33 | 0.71 | 3.84 | 1.28 | 0.97 | 1.52 | 2.14 | 1.49 |
| 21. Hazardous Situations | | | | | | | | | | | | |
|   a. Exposure | 1.16 | 1.78 | 0.22 | 0.67 | 3.07 | 2.18 | 4.16 | 1.65 | 2.25 | 1.94 | 3.97 | 1.83 |
|   b. Likelihood of Injury | 1.05 | 1.51 | 0.22 | 0.67 | 2.70 | 1.73 | 4.24 | 1.42 | 2.17 | 1.91 | 3.05 | 1.47 |
|   c. Extent of Injury | 0.69 | 0.98 | 0.11 | 0.33 | 1.53 | 1.33 | 2.68 | 1.49 | 1.20 | 1.30 | 1.35 | 1.01 |
| 22. Body Positioning | | | | | | | | | | | | |
|   a. Sitting | 3.47 | 0.96 | 4.44 | 0.73 | 2.37 | 0.89 | 3.17 | 0.90 | 0.97 | 0.96 | 1.43 | 0.90 |
|   b. Standing | 2.05 | 0.95 | 1.67 | 0.71 | 3.13 | 1.04 | 2.52 | 0.77 | 4.50 | 0.82 | 3.84 | 1.07 |
|   c. Climbing Ladders, etc. | 0.24 | 0.43 | 0.00 | 0.00 | 0.00 | 0.00 | 0.40 | 0.58 | 0.97 | 0.85 | 1.92 | 1.09 |
|   d. Walking or Running | 1.58 | 0.90 | 0.78 | 0.67 | 3.10 | 1.09 | 2.16 | 0.99 | 4.27 | 1.14 | 3.00 | 1.11 |
|   e. Kneeling or Crouching | 0.51 | 0.74 | 0.33 | 0.50 | 1.13 | 1.07 | 1.00 | 0.71 | 2.40 | 1.71 | 2.14 | 1.18 |
|   f. Keeping/Regaining Balance | 0.48 | 1.07 | 0.11 | 0.33 | 1.20 | 1.32 | 0.96 | 0.98 | 1.67 | 1.92 | 1.57 | 1.39 |
|   g. Handling Tools, Objects | 1.07 | 1.57 | 2.22 | 2.22 | 2.33 | 1.63 | 2.40 | 1.50 | 3.57 | 1.45 | 3.46 | 1.30 |
|   h. Bending/Twisting Body | 0.75 | 1.04 | 0.33 | 0.50 | 2.00 | 1.49 | 1.92 | 1.41 | 3.63 | 1.52 | 2.70 | 1.43 |
|   i. Making Repetitive Motions | 1.36 | 1.38 | 2.89 | 2.09 | 1.93 | 1.31 | 2.56 | 1.42 | 3.20 | 1.58 | 2.65 | 1.34 |
| 23. Work Attire | | | | | | | | | | | | |
|   a. Business/Office Clothes | 4.18 | 1.39 | 1.67 | 1.80 | 1.90 | 2.17 | 2.36 | 1.38 | 0.24 | 0.68 | 0.41 | 1.17 |
|   b. Special Uniform | 0.49 | 1.35 | 0.00 | 0.00 | 3.07 | 2.30 | 4.72 | 0.98 | 1.33 | 2.25 | 0.41 | 1.38 |
|   c. Maintenance Clothes | 0.15 | 0.56 | 0.56 | 1.67 | 0.13 | 0.57 | 0.52 | 1.23 | 3.93 | 2.03 | 4.50 | 1.44 |
|   d. Common Safety Attire | 1.51 | 2.00 | 0.00 | 0.00 | 4.73 | 2.42 | 5.32 | 2.67 | 4.31 | 2.39 | 4.92 | 2.30 |
|   e. Special Safety Attire | 0.51 | 1.27 | 0.22 | 0.67 | 1.33 | 2.06 | 3.48 | 3.28 | 1.52 | 2.25 | 2.49 | 2.14 |
| 24. Consequences of Error | 4.24 | 1.86 | 3.33 | 1.12 | 5.79 | 1.69 | 5.48 | 1.90 | 2.30 | 1.73 | 4.11 | 1.95 |
| 25. Decision Making | | | | | | | | | | | | |
|   a. Impact of Decisions | 5.80 | 0.97 | 3.89 | 1.27 | 5.20 | 1.42 | 6.12 | 1.51 | 3.37 | 1.96 | 3.78 | 1.64 |
|   b. Frequency of Decisions | 5.04 | 1.40 | 3.11 | 1.76 | 5.07 | 1.51 | 5.76 | 1.94 | 2.53 | 2.54 | 2.14 | 1.93 |
| 26. Accountable for Results | 6.13 | 0.96 | 5.33 | 1.41 | 5.73 | 1.46 | 5.92 | 1.58 | 4.24 | 2.08 | 4.76 | 1.75 |
| 27. Decision Latitude | 5.55 | 0.94 | 4.22 | 1.39 | 4.77 | 0.94 | 5.28 | 1.06 | 3.67 | 1.65 | 4.19 | 1.51 |
| 28. Frustrating Circumstances | 4.15 | 1.52 | 4.56 | 1.88 | 3.93 | 1.48 | 3.96 | 2.09 | 3.03 | 1.97 | 4.38 | 1.66 |
| 29. Level of Automation | 3.47 | 1.72 | 2.78 | 1.39 | 2.77 | 1.43 | 2.48 | 1.76 | 3.14 | 1.68 | 2.81 | 1.73 |
| 30. Task/Performance Clarity | 5.38 | 1.06 | 4.56 | 1.42 | 5.63 | 1.00 | 5.60 | 1.15 | 5.28 | 1.82 | 5.27 | 1.45 |
| 31. Accuracy/Exactness | 4.07 | 0.81 | 3.88 | 0.93 | 4.53 | 0.57 | 4.36 | 0.81 | 2.93 | 1.44 | 3.89 | 0.99 |
| 32. Details and Completeness | 4.15 | 0.65 | 4.43 | 0.68 | 4.50 | 0.57 | 4.36 | 0.76 | 3.47 | 1.14 | 4.05 | 0.91 |
| 33. Constant Awareness | 2.67 | 1.48 | 1.11 | 1.27 | 3.53 | 1.59 | 4.48 | 0.65 | 2.07 | 1.74 | 2.41 | 1.57 |
| 34. Repetitive Activities | 1.60 | 1.51 | 1.78 | 1.86 | 2.27 | 1.68 | 2.72 | 1.62 | 2.17 | 1.97 | 2.00 | 1.37 |
| 35. Unstructured Tasks/Goals | 5.67 | 1.37 | 4.67 | 1.94 | 4.93 | 1.28 | 4.88 | 1.39 | 4.67 | 1.69 | 4.30 | 1.79 |
| 36. Level of Competition | 3.98 | 1.89 | 3.44 | 1.51 | 3.40 | 1.54 | 3.16 | 1.72 | 3.07 | 1.74 | 3.24 | 1.95 |
| 37. Deadlines/Time Pressure | 3.93 | 1.49 | 3.11 | 0.78 | 4.86 | 1.68 | 4.64 | 1.29 | 3.60 | 2.39 | 4.16 | 1.62 |
| 38. Work With Distractions | 3.56 | 1.23 | 3.44 | 1.51 | 3.90 | 0.76 | 3.56 | 1.50 | 2.43 | 1.65 | 2.89 | 1.20 |
| 39. Machine Driven Pace | 0.82 | 1.19 | 1.44 | 2.01 | 0.72 | 1.11 | 1.36 | 1.63 | 1.53 | 1.61 | 1.54 | 1.52 |

*The full title for this occupation is "Janitors and Cleaners, Except Maids and Housekeeping."

most directly involve decisions affecting the Health and Safety of Others (D7)—Registered Nurses and Police Patrol Officers—reported the highest levels of Consequence of Error (D24) and Impact of Decisions (D25). Police Patrol Officers also reported more Interacting With the Public (D6f) and handling Physical Aggression (D11) than did other occupations.

Teamwork was reasonably important to all six occupations, but it had greater variability among the Janitor and Maintenance Repairer categories. Communicating Face-to-Face With Other Individuals (D2a) was the most common communication method across all six occupations. Computer Programmers and Janitors consistently used all communication methods less frequently than did the other occupations. However, Computer Programmer is apparently the only occupation from this group using Electronic Mail (D2h) to any significant degree. Not surprisingly, Police Patrol Officers, Janitors and Cleaners, and Maintenance Repairers reported working more frequently under unpleasant Environmental Conditions (D15) than did workers in the other occupations, and they were less likely to work in an Indoor Temperature-Controlled area (D12a).

## Convergence of Incumbents' and Analysts' Ratings

Table 9-7 provides the mean ratings from both the incumbent and analyst samples. As stated earlier, analysts made ratings on the basis of a reading of tasks from the DOT for each of the occupations in the

**TABLE 9-7**

**Comparison Between Incumbent and Analyst Descriptive Statistics Across All Occupations and Reliability Estimates for Rated Differences Between Occupations: Work Context**

| Descriptor | Incumbent | | | Analyst | | | $t$ | $F$ | $r_{ia}$ | $d^2$ |
|---|---|---|---|---|---|---|---|---|---|---|
| | $M$ | $SD$ | $r_k$ | $M$ | $SD$ | $r_k$ | | | | |
| 3. Communication Subjectivity | 3.33 | 0.56 | 0.41 | 2.75 | 1.04 | 0.90 | 3.02* | 3.45* | 0.30 | 0.34 |
| 4. Social Interaction | 5.72 | 0.91 | 0.76 | 4.56 | 1.53 | 0.96 | 3.98* | 2.83* | 0.56 | 1.35 |
| 6. Job Interactions | | | | | | | | | | |
|   a. Supervise/Develop Others | 3.03 | 0.76 | 0.83 | 1.19 | 1.45 | 0.95 | 6.82* | 3.64* | 0.45 | 3.39 |
|   b. Persuade or Influence | 1.83 | 1.15 | 0.88 | 1.49 | 1.22 | 0.93 | 1.25 | 1.13 | 0.71 | 0.12 |
|   c. Provide Service to Others | 3.53 | 1.09 | 0.78 | 2.91 | 1.29 | 0.89 | 2.27* | 1.40 | 0.32 | 0.38 |
|   d. Take Opposing Position | 1.75 | 0.80 | 0.77 | 0.86 | 0.57 | 0.83 | 5.48* | 1.97 | 0.57 | 0.79 |
|   f. Deal With Public | 2.84 | 1.12 | 0.83 | 2.64 | 1.50 | 0.94 | 0.66 | 1.79 | 0.71 | 0.04 |
|   g. Coordinate/Lead Activity | 2.99 | 0.75 | 0.70 | 1.50 | 1.12 | 0.90 | 6.75* | 2.23* | 0.56 | 2.22 |
| 7. Health/Safety of Others | 3.95 | 1.84 | 0.94 | 2.33 | 1.74 | 0.92 | 3.90* | 1.12 | 0.75 | 2.62 |
| 8. Responsible for Others' Work | 3.45 | 1.21 | 0.83 | 1.68 | 1.49 | 0.92 | 5.60* | 1.52 | 0.41 | 3.13 |
| 9. Conflict Situations | 1.81 | 0.45 | 0.75 | 1.31 | 0.57 | 0.84 | 4.18* | 1.60 | 0.52 | 0.25 |
| 10. Unpleasant Individuals | 2.06 | 0.38 | 0.65 | 1.37 | 0.58 | 0.88 | 6.00* | 2.33* | 0.60 | 0.48 |
| 11. Physical Aggression | 0.94 | 0.64 | 0.91 | 0.44 | 0.54 | 0.90 | 3.66* | 1.40 | 0.80 | 0.25 |
| 12. Work Settings | | | | | | | | | | |
|   a. Indoors, Controlled[a] | 5.71 | 1.35 | 0.84 | 3.39 | 0.69 | 0.91 | | | 0.75 | |
|   c. Outdoors, Exposed[a] | 1.94 | 2.05 | 0.96 | 1.18 | 0.85 | 0.92 | | | 0.89 | |
| 15. Environmental Conditions | | | | | | | | | | |
|   a. Distracting Noise[a] | 3.39 | 1.22 | 0.67 | 1.16 | 0.74 | 0.89 | | | 0.74 | |
|   b. Extreme Temperature[a] | 2.05 | 1.71 | 0.92 | 0.84 | 0.63 | 0.89 | | | 0.78 | |
|   c. Poor Lighting[a] | 1.35 | 1.25 | 0.85 | 0.89 | 0.43 | 0.77 | | | 0.71 | |
|   d. Contaminants[a] | 2.52 | 1.73 | 0.87 | 1.15 | 0.64 | 0.78 | | | 0.78 | |
|   e. Cramped Work Space[a] | 1.38 | 0.98 | 0.80 | 0.51 | 0.44 | 0.81 | | | 0.70 | |
|   f. Whole Body Vibration[a] | 0.46 | 1.18 | 0.94 | 0.18 | 0.41 | 0.88 | | | 0.91 | |
| 16. Radiation | | | | | | | | | | |
|   a. Exposure[a] | 0.44 | 0.72 | 0.73 | 0.23 | 0.36 | 0.79 | | | 0.08 | |
|   b. Likelihood of Injury | 0.43 | 0.47 | 0.59 | 0.20 | 0.31 | 0.77 | 2.42* | 2.30* | 0.02 | 0.05 |
|   c. Extent of Injury | 0.23 | 0.29 | 0.50 | 0.13 | 0.22 | 0.59 | 1.72 | 1.74 | 0.05 | 0.01 |
| 17. Diseases/Infections | | | | | | | | | | |
|   a. Exposure[a] | 2.10 | 1.86 | 0.91 | 0.62 | 0.99 | 0.96 | | | 0.77 | |
|   b. Likelihood of Injury | 1.64 | 1.32 | 0.90 | 0.64 | 1.01 | 0.95 | 3.67* | 1.71 | 0.72 | 1.00 |
|   c. Extent of Injury | 1.15 | 1.11 | 0.90 | 0.56 | 0.92 | 0.96 | 2.49* | 1.46 | 0.71 | 0.35 |
| 18. High Places | | | | | | | | | | |
|   a. Exposure[a] | 0.77 | 1.00 | 0.93 | 0.26 | 0.35 | 0.73 | | | 0.69 | |
|   b. Likelihood of Injury | 0.68 | 0.82 | 0.91 | 0.32 | 0.52 | 0.80 | 2.22* | 2.49* | 0.78 | 0.13 |
|   c. Extent of Injury | 0.68 | 0.77 | 0.89 | 0.28 | 0.47 | 0.79 | 2.67* | 2.68* | 0.75 | 0.16 |
| 19. Hazardous Conditions | | | | | | | | | | |
|   a. Exposure[a] | 1.29 | 1.29 | 0.88 | 0.60 | 0.61 | 0.84 | | | 0.67 | |
|   b. Likelihood of Injury | 1.11 | 1.02 | 0.88 | 0.69 | 0.76 | 0.85 | 2.00* | 1.80 | 0.61 | 0.18 |
|   c. Extent of Injury | 0.86 | 0.89 | 0.88 | 0.62 | 0.75 | 0.86 | 1.27 | 1.41 | 0.59 | 0.06 |
| 20. Hazardous Equipment | | | | | | | | | | |
|   a. Exposure[a] | 1.69 | 1.90 | 0.95 | 0.84 | 0.91 | 0.92 | | | 0.91 | |
|   b. Likelihood of Injury | 1.28 | 1.43 | 0.95 | 0.95 | 1.00 | 0.90 | 1.13 | 2.04 | 0.82 | 0.11 |
|   c. Extent of Injury | 0.99 | 1.08 | 0.93 | 0.81 | 0.92 | 0.93 | 0.76 | 1.38 | 0.82 | 0.03 |
| 21. Hazardous Situations | | | | | | | | | | |
|   a. Exposure[a] | 2.25 | 1.57 | 0.91 | 1.08 | 0.60 | 0.84 | | | 0.76 | |
|   b. Likelihood of Injury | 1.93 | 1.34 | 0.91 | 1.24 | 0.75 | 0.82 | 2.71* | 3.19* | 0.74 | 0.48 |
|   c. Extent of Injury | 1.01 | 0.69 | 0.86 | 0.76 | 0.42 | 0.75 | 1.89 | 2.70* | 0.60 | 0.06 |
| 22. Body Positioning | | | | | | | | | | |
|   a. Sitting[b] | 2.59 | 1.28 | 0.97 | 2.43 | 0.72 | 0.94 | | | 0.91 | |
|   b. Standing[b] | 2.96 | 1.21 | 0.96 | 0.41 | 0.60 | 0.92 | | | 0.90 | |
|   c. Climbing Ladders, etc.[b] | 0.39 | 0.52 | 0.93 | 0.35 | 0.43 | 0.79 | | | 0.76 | |
|   d. Walking or Running[b] | 2.28 | 1.05 | 0.93 | 1.85 | 0.42 | 0.85 | | | 0.69 | |
|   e. Kneeling or Crouching[b] | 1.04 | 0.70 | 0.87 | 1.18 | 0.45 | 0.77 | | | 0.64 | |
|   f. Keeping/Regaining Balance[b] | 0.76 | 0.62 | 0.77 | 0.46 | 0.34 | 0.56 | | | 0.47 | |
|   g. Handling Tools, Objects[b] | 2.57 | 1.00 | 0.76 | 2.13 | 0.62 | 0.77 | | | 0.64 | |
|   h. Bending/Twisting Body[b] | 1.70 | 0.99 | 0.90 | 1.20 | 0.43 | 0.65 | | | 0.72 | |
|   i. Making Repetitive Motions[b] | 2.70 | 0.91 | 0.78 | 1.60 | 0.44 | 0.66 | | | 0.66 | |
| 23. Work Attire | | | | | | | | | | |
|   b. Special Uniform[b] | 1.21 | 1.47 | 0.92 | 1.49 | 1.21 | 0.94 | | | 0.85 | |
|   d. Common Safety Attire[b] | 2.78 | 2.48 | 0.95 | 1.26 | 1.25 | 0.97 | | | 0.88 | |
|   e. Special Safety Attire[b] | 0.67 | 0.96 | 0.89 | 0.30 | 0.42 | 0.87 | | | 0.62 | |
| 24. Consequence of Error | 3.54 | 1.32 | 0.88 | 3.84 | 1.11 | 0.86 | 1.07 | 1.41 | 0.57 | 0.09 |
| 28. Frustrating Circumstances | 3.41 | 0.96 | 0.68 | 3.03 | 0.66 | 0.73 | 1.99* | 2.12* | 0.61 | 0.14 |
| 29. Level of Automation | 3.13 | 0.90 | 0.72 | 3.19 | 0.85 | 0.78 | 0.28 | 1.12 | 0.52 | 0.00 |
| 31. Accuracy/Exactness | 4.10 | 0.43 | 0.72 | 3.54 | 0.70 | 0.77 | 4.20* | 2.65* | 0.56 | 0.31 |

*Table 9-7 continues*

**TABLE 9-7 (Continued)**

| | Incumbent | | | Analyst | | | | | | |
|---|---|---|---|---|---|---|---|---|---|---|
| Descriptor | M | SD | $r_k$ | M | SD | $r_k$ | t | F | $r_{ia}$ | $d^2$ |
| 32. Details and Completeness | 4.22 | 0.37 | 0.60 | 3.70 | 0.53 | 0.71 | 4.84* | 2.05 | 0.35 | 0.27 |
| 33. Constant Awareness | 2.47 | 0.85 | 0.73 | 2.04 | 0.72 | 0.73 | 2.36* | 1.39 | 0.41 | 0.18 |
| 34. Repetitive Activities | 2.52 | 0.82 | 0.72 | 1.46 | 0.56 | 0.62 | 6.55* | 2.14* | 0.46 | 1.12 |
| 39. Machine Driven Pace | 1.75 | 0.98 | 0.78 | 1.16 | 0.72 | 0.81 | 2.97* | 1.85 | 0.69 | 0.35 |

*Note.* Incumbent statistics are based on 37 occupations with Work Context Questionnaire responses from at least 4 incumbents (mean number of incumbents = 19.68, *Mdn* = 12.5, harmonic mean = 9.44). Analyst statistics are based on the same 37 occupations with Work Context Questionnaire responses from at least 6 analysts (mean number of analysts = 9.73, *Mdn* = 6.00, harmonic mean = 8.00). The estimate of reliability was obtained by calculating the intraclass correlation for *k* ratings across occupations: $ICC(1, k) = [BMS - WMS]/BMS$ (Shrout & Fleiss, 1979), where *k* is the harmonic mean of the number of ratings provided on each occupation. The *t* statistic tests for differences in the incumbent and analyst group means. The *F* statistic tests for differences in the incumbent and analyst group standard deviations. The $r_{ia}$ correlation indicates the degree of relationship between incumbent and analyst mean occupations ratings. The $d^2$ statistic indicates the squared differences between incumbent and analyst mean occupations ratings.
*$p < .05$.
[a]Analysts used a 1 to 4 rating scale (*never* to *always*) and incumbents used a 0 to 7 rating scale (*never* to *hourly*) for this item.   [b]Analysts used a 1 to 4 rating scale (*never* to *always*) and incumbents used a 0 to 5 rating scale (*never* to *almost continually*) for this item.

sample. Many work context variables cannot be accurately assessed from this information, and thus Table 9-7 includes data for only those variables that analysts were capable of rating. Also presented are *t* and *F*-max tests comparing the analyst and incumbent ratings, as well as the correlation coefficient and $d^2$ index. Analysts utilized a modified frequency scale for some items, thus comparisons between incumbent and analyst frequency ratings are not reported for those items.

Analysts' and incumbents' ratings have a moderate level of agreement, with the median correlation between the incumbent and analyst mean ratings being .58. There were statistically significant differences in the mean ratings provided by the two samples, with incumbents consistently providing higher ratings. Of the 33 items with comparable scales, 24 were rated significantly higher by incumbents. Given the nature of the work context items, this result may not be surprising. The physical and structural components of an occupation are much more salient or apparent to incumbents than they are likely to be for analysts reading a list of tasks.

Although the median reliabilities for incumbents and analysts are not substantially different (.83 and .86, respectively), the analysts have fewer items with significantly low reliabilities. Although incumbents used their own idiosyncratic experiences with a job to make ratings, analysts were presented with exactly the same stimuli (DOT task lists) for a job, and it is not surprising that there was less disagreement in the analysts' ratings.

A principal-components factor analysis with varimax rotation was conducted on the analysts' data in an attempt to compare the factor structures from analysts and incumbents. The most appropriate factor solution for the incumbent ratings was a seven-factor structure of the variables. Although the analysts rated only a subset of the work context items, the resulting factor structure was very similar to that found for the incumbent data. The factors from the analyst data—(a) Managerial Relations, (b) Environmental Conditions, (c) Health and Safety Conditions, (d) Interacting With the Public, (e) Physical Activity, (f) Body Movement, and (g) Structured/Machine Operations—were quite similar to the seven factors identified from the incumbent data presented in Table 9-5. Generally, items loaded on the same factors within each data set. The only substantive difference between the two data sets was that the incumbent data yielded a factor related to a business/office environment whereas the analyst data yielded a Body Movement factor. Many of the variables that loaded on the Business or Office Environments factor in the incumbent data were not rated by analysts; thus is it not surprising that this factor was not present. The variables in the Body Movement factor in the analyst data loaded on the Physical Activity and Manual Work factor in the incumbent data.

## LIMITATIONS OF THE RESEARCH

Before discussing the conclusions derived from this part of the study, it is important to note the limitations associated with the current research. One concern is the somewhat marginal results for interrater agreement with as many as eight descriptors. Further review of these items is needed to evaluate their utility in the taxonomy. Using the average number of raters across occupations, there were four items with interrater agreement coefficients below .50. When the agreement is estimated for 30 raters, obviously these coefficients increase, but a few items continue to have inadequate interrater agreement. Although we believe these items can provide valuable job information, revision of the items may be warranted if raters are unable to provide reliable results.

Overall, most the work context variables can be reliably assessed by job incumbents and analysts. However, the nature of some work context variables may make it difficult, if not impossible, to make accurate ratings solely on the basis of task lists. Actual job performance, or at least visual observation of the job being performed, would be required to respond to many descriptors. The moderate levels of agreement for the mean ratings between incumbents and occupational analysts may be due to how salient and pervasive the work context variables are to job incumbents. It is likely to be difficult to discern an accurate assessment of these variables simply by reading task lists. In terms of describing occupations, incumbent data are more likely to provide appropriate work context information.

## CONCLUSION

The world of work is changing, not only in the way we define jobs but also in how the work environment is configured. These changes have implications for the methods and constructs used to analyze work. Because job analysis is an essential component of a majority of personnel or human resources activities (i.e., developing selection, performance appraisal, compensation, and training programs), our methods must adapt to the changing nature of work. As the organization of work shifts from a task-based to more process-based systems, environmental, contextual, and social dimensions of work seem likely to become more important (Cascio, 1995).

The patterns of results across occupations provide evidence that the work context variables included in this taxonomy can be used to differentiate between occupations. Comparisons of variables across the six example occupations provided evidence that these occupations differed in rational, predictable, and measurable ways.

An interesting outcome of the analyses is the prospect of reevaluating the structure of the taxonomy on the basis of the results of the factor analyses. The item loadings on the factors were highly consistent with the grouping in the original taxonomy, but there were several items that loaded with descriptors from other higher order factors. For instance, the factor associated with managerial activities is made up of variables from both the interpersonal and structural components of the taxonomy. Findings such as these are not particularly surprising given the nature of the items, but future research will need to investigate reconfigurations of the taxonomy that may better reflect the observed realities of the workplace.

Information collected on work context has broader implications in terms of several human resource functions. Evaluation of the contextual aspects of jobs and differentiation of jobs on the basis of these factors is likely to be useful in (a) formation of job families or groupings, (b) job evaluation and classification, (c) development of selection instruments to identify individuals best suited to particular jobs, and (d) preparing realistic job previews to allow individuals opportunities for self-selection based on adequate information. For example, for jobs performed in a team environment, selection systems may need to include components to identify individuals likely to be successful in interpersonally demanding jobs. Knowing the communication patterns of jobs may allow organizations to identify additional skills necessary for job performance.

Additionally, identifying work context variables facilitates person–job matching, counseling, development of realistic simulations and training for specific work environments, and the preparation of appropriate equipment and materials. For example, identifying negatively perceived work conditions (i.e., exposure to hazardous conditions) or interpersonal variables (i.e. conflictual contact) encountered on the job would provide an opportunity to offer more realistic previews of work conditions that may increase job survival (Premack & Wanous, 1985). In designing task simulations, specification of the work context contributes to the fidelity of the simulation and potentially increases its validity.

The work context also has implications for work and organization design. For example, determining the type of body positions required to perform a job may have implications for complying with the Americans with Disabilities Act. Once an organization has identified jobs that require certain body positions (i.e., climbing ladders, bending, stooping, bending, and twisting), they can assess whether they represent essential functions and whether reasonable accommodation is possible.

Given the potential effects of work context variables on workers and job performance, a job analysis that focuses only on tasks, work requirements, and worker characteristics is not sufficient. Work context must be examined and integrated with other job analysis information to provide a more complete understanding of a job. Previous attempts to assess the aspects of work context have been fragmented and lacked standardization, primarily because of the extremely broad range of constructs that may be considered under the rubric of work context.

The taxonomy described in this chapter provides a systematic method to examine the work context in order to contribute to a better understanding of work and provide a framework for further study of the structure, reliability, and validity of work context measures. In conjunction with organizational variables and GWAs, contextual factors affect many important work outcomes, including performance, satisfaction, work involvement, effort, injury, stress, and group cohesion. Including work context constructs in job analysis procedures provides insights into more than just the tasks and skills needed to perform a job, these variables contribute to a better understanding of work, provide a clearer picture of the environment in which the jobs are performed, and provide valuable information essential for a comprehensive Occupational Information System.

# Organizational Context

SHARON ARAD, MARY ANN HANSON, AND ROBERT J. SCHNEIDER

Recent changes in the workplace, including rapid technological advances, highly competitive international markets, and an increasingly diverse workforce, have led to changes in how businesses function and adapt. To survive in a highly competitive marketplace, many companies have downsized, restructured, and streamlined their workforces. Such changes typically occur at the organization level, but they are likely to have substantial implications for the nature and scope of individual jobs.

It is likely that the nature of jobs will vary as a function of characteristics of the organizations in which they occur. Organizational characteristics could thus aid in classification analyses aimed at clustering jobs that are similar in specified ways. Aspects of an organization's structure such as degree of centralization and the use of work teams have substantial implications for the nature of jobs. These organization-level variables can affect the design of a job, the tasks associated with it, and the level and importance of skills (e.g., interpersonal, decision making, and management) required for performing that job (Child, 1972; Katz & Kahn, 1978; Lawler, 1992). It is even possible that jobs that have the same title but occur in very different organizations will be classified, on the basis of the tasks included or skills and abilities needed, as different occupations. In fact, the industry designations included in the current *Dictionary of Occupational Titles* (DOT; U.S. Department of Labor, 1991a) are used to distinguish between different occupations that have the same titles but occur in different industries. Descriptive information about the organizations in which jobs occur also is likely to be of more direct interest to job seekers. For example, job seekers will likely benefit from information concerning certain organizational characteristics, such as human resources practices and organizational values, when they are making career and employment decisions.

Finally, information about organizations in the United States should be inherently interesting to many O*NET users, as well. Potential users of organizational context information include a variety of government and Department of Labor (U.S. DOL)

programs, such as the Office of the American Workplace, a relatively recent initiative undertaken to integrate state-of-the-art technology and human resources policies to promote "high-performance" workplaces. Available research on relationships between certain business practices and effectiveness, along with case studies of companies that are successfully using these state-of-the-art practices, has been used to develop a profile of the practices that high-performance organizations use and a checklist of these practices (U.S. DOL, 1994). National and state-level award programs, such as the Malcolm Baldrige National Quality Award, have also been established to reward businesses for quality and for high-performance business practices. Westat (1994) reviewed all of this information, along with popular business literature on the nature of high-performance workplaces (e.g., Lawler, 1993), and identified a set of characteristics commonly associated with high-performance workplaces. High-performance organizations are typically described as using state-of-the-art personnel and management practices and having organizational structures that facilitate flexibility and employee involvement.

The concept of high-performance workplaces is new, and only a limited amount of information is available concerning the effectiveness of high-performance business practices and the extent to which U.S. businesses actually use these practices. The O*NET, as a database system, provides an opportunity to collect information about the use of high-performance practices by organizations and integrate this information with descriptions of work activities and worker requirements. Thus, the identification and measurement of business practices associated with high-performance workplaces were high priorities in the development of the content model underlying O*NET.

Organizational context descriptors are expected to fulfill three key purposes in the O*NET: (a) describing jobs; (b) describing organizations, especially those characteristics associated with high-performance workplaces; and (c) providing useful information for job seekers. This chapter describes the development of the organizational context component of the O*NET taxonomy and reports the results of the prototype study conducted to assess the usefulness of this taxonomy. We first describe the approach taken in developing the organizational context taxonomy and discuss the measurement issues involved in developing such an organization-level taxonomy. We then present the resulting hierarchical taxonomy of organizational context constructs and briefly summarize the relevant literature. The last part of this chapter is devoted to description of the prototype study and discussion of the theoretical and practical implications of our findings.

## DEVELOPMENT OF THE ORGANIZATIONAL CONTEXT TAXONOMY AND DESCRIPTORS

### Approach

One primary objective in developing the organizational context descriptors for O*NET was to measure, as comprehensively as possible, those organizational characteristics thought to differentiate high-performance organizations from more traditional or less effective organizations. However, we chose not to focus exclusively on the high-performance concept because it is relatively new, and there always is the possibility that it will not withstand the test of time. In addition, we found the available high-performance checklists were not sufficiently comprehensive for our purposes; additional organizational characteristics and business practices, beyond those typically associated with high-performance organizations, also are likely to be critical to the effectiveness and adaptability of U.S. businesses. Finally, we wanted to be able to understand the high-performance concept in the context of available research and theory concerning organizations.

Thus, the primary source of input for our taxonomy was the rich, well-established, and extensive literature that is available concerning organizations. We reviewed and integrated the major theoretical and empirical writings on organizations from diverse disciplines, including organizational theory (Blau, 1974; Child, 1972; Hall, 1982; Katz & Kahn, 1978; Mintzberg, 1979; Pugh, Hickson, Hinings, & Turner, 1968); organizational development (Lawler, 1991, 1992, 1993; Limerick & Cunnington, 1993); industrial and organizational psychology (Cascio, 1987; Goldstein, 1993; Hackman & Oldham, 1976, 1980); and social psychology (McGrath, 1994). The extensive literature we reviewed came from numerous approaches, schools, and models—each of which emphasized different aspects and components of organizations. When integrated, this literature offers a comprehensive view and description of organizations.

On the basis of this literature review, we identified a variety of relatively specific organizational context constructs. The selection of these lower order constructs was based on the following criteria. First, constructs were included if they had been measured with reasonable levels of reliability and validity in past research, or if measures could be relatively easily developed that had good potential for being reliable and valid. Second, we tried to include constructs for which the measures could be generalized to different types of organizations without losing their meaning. Third, constructs were included if they were expected, on the basis of theory or past research, to be useful in describing or classifying jobs, or in describing important features of organizations that would be of interest to one or more O*NET users. We also reviewed several sources of information concerning high-performance workplaces, including the Malcolm Baldrige Award criteria, the DOL high-performance checklist (U.S. DOL, 1994), and the popular literature on high-performance organizations (e.g., Lawler, 1993), to determine whether any high-performance constructs had not already emerged in our review of the organizational literature. A few such constructs were identified and included. We then organized all of these constructs according to a hierarchical taxonomy. Finally, because some of the constructs included in our taxonomy had not been previously measured and thus were quite experimental, we obtained a preliminary assessment of the questions we had developed to measure these new constructs from two subject matter experts who had extensive applied experience in the human resources domain. On the basis of their feedback, we revised some measures, dropped others, and added items to assess several additional organizational characteristics.

### Issues in Identifying Constructs and Developing Descriptors

Before we discuss our proposed taxonomy of organizational context, we highlight some issues encountered in taxonomy development that affected the outcome. First, the development of organization-level descriptors was somewhat guided by sampling and other data collection constraints. One goal in developing measures of organizational context constructs was to measure as many of the constructs as possible with questions that could be answered by a single personnel department representative (or an individual with access to similar information) from each participating organization. We made every effort to keep the questions that would be asked of only one organizational representative as objective and concrete as possible because of reliability concerns. In fact, 84% of the questions that were ultimately included in the survey for these individuals asked for concrete, verifiable information. Any questions that could not be answered by such an individual were included only if they could be answered by job incumbents themselves.

Second, the level of analysis used by the operational definitions, and thus the most appropriate source of data, varied across constructs. Each construct in our model was examined and operationalized at a level that we thought would yield the most accurate data. For example, organizational structure constructs such as size, formalization, and decentralization could best be measured and observed at the organization level (i.e., answered by the organizational representative). However, role characteristics and processes in an organization are individual psychological experiences. Hence, the appropriate level of analysis for roles is the individual job incumbent.

Another principle guiding our selection of a particular level of analysis for a construct was the underlying purposes and potential uses of the organizational context descriptors as part of O*NET. The main purpose of this occupational database is to provide information about occupations, so we found it necessary to measure many of the variables at the job level. This allows the O*NET to provide information to users concerning the manifestations of various organizational systems (e.g., selection and training systems) at the job level. Some questions (e.g., about rewards) were included to provide information both about a particular job and to identify high-performance organizations. Therefore, these questions had to be asked twice: once of the job incumbents concerning their particular jobs and once of the organizational representative concerning the organization as a whole.

## PROPOSED HIERARCHICAL TAXONOMY OF ORGANIZATIONAL CONTEXT

The sociotechnical systems approach provided the basic classification of the organizational context domain into two main components: Structural Characteristics and Social Processes. This approach to the study and analysis of organizations suggests that or-

ganizations can be viewed as composed of two main subsystems: technical and social. The technical subsystem involves the process of transforming raw materials into output, and it includes elements such as technology and structure. The social subsystem links human operators both to technology and to each other and includes elements such as values, goals, leadership, and roles (Fuqua & Kurpius, 1993; Katz & Kahn, 1978). The sociotechnical approach proposes that technology, structure, and social processes in an organization are interrelated and interdependent. Furthermore, organizational or unit performance can be maximized by joint optimization of the technical and social subsystems (Katz & Kahn, 1978). The type of industry in which jobs occur is not clearly a part of the structure or the social process subsystem, and thus it was included as a third category at this broadest level. Therefore, the highest level of the organizational context taxonomy is made up of three categories: Structural Characteristics, Social Processes, and Type of Industry.

The constructs of organizational context we selected for the Structural Characteristics portion of the taxonomy can be further grouped according to two second-order constructs or topic areas: Organizational Structure and Human Resources (HR) Systems and Practices. We included four second-order constructs in the Social Processes section: Organizational Culture, Goals, Roles, and Leadership. These six second-order constructs are general categories that correspond to relatively distinct areas of theory and research in the literature. They provide a useful heuristic for categorizing the lower order constructs but do not themselves represent actual, measurable characteristics of organizations or jobs. Figures 10-1 through 10-3 show the hierarchical taxonomy of the organizational context domain. The lower order constructs included in the taxonomy (shown at the bottom of each hierarchy) are the measurable characteristics of organizations or jobs, and they will be discussed within this general framework. A few additional constructs related to high-performance workplaces do not fit well in this taxonomy and are included in a Miscellaneous category.

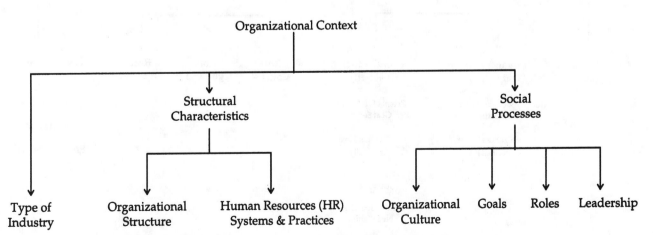

**FIGURE 10-1.** Higher order taxonomy of organizational context constructs.

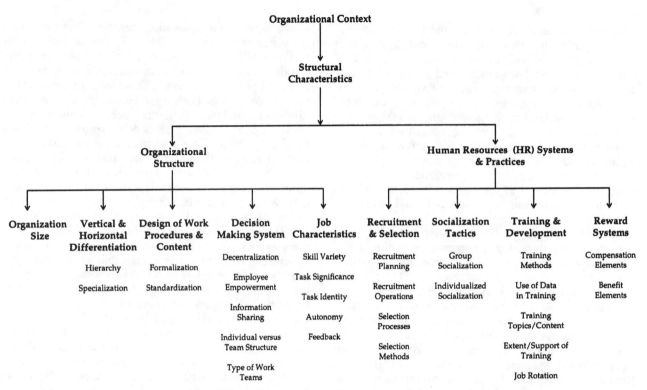

**FIGURE 10-2.** Lower order taxonomy of structural characteristics.

## Type of Industry

The first construct, Type of Industry, is regarded by most organizational theorists and researchers as an important element in understanding and studying organizations (Hall, 1982; Katz & Kahn, 1978; Thompson, 1967). Industry types are identified on the basis of organizational output. This information will be very useful for identifying jobs that occur in growing and declining industries and may be useful in classifying jobs. Industry information may also be useful in interpreting the structural variables.

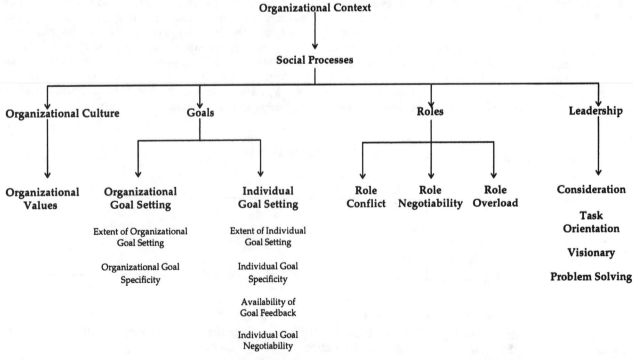

**FIGURE 10-3.** Lower order taxonomy of social processes.

## Structural Characteristics

### Organizational Structure

Organizational Structure may be considered the architecture or the anatomy of an organization. One would be hard pressed to uncover any theories or models of organizations that do not regard organizational structure as a critical element of organizations. It can affect the ability of organizations to adapt effectively to their environments as well as determine the degree to which incumbents will experience autonomy, social interaction, and flexibility in their jobs (e.g., Child, 1972; Dalton, Todor, Spendolini, Fielding, & Porter, 1980; Duncan, 1979; Hall, 1982; Katz & Kahn, 1978; Lawler, 1992).

We found a great deal of overlap among theories and taxonomies of organizational structure and an ample amount of research available documenting relationships between these structural dimensions and organizational behavior and effectiveness (Blau, 1974; Blau & Schoenherr, 1971; Hall, 1982; Lawler, 1992; Mintzberg, 1979; Pugh et al., 1968). We selected lower order constructs reflecting five important dimensions of organizational structure that consistently appear in the literature and have been judged to be relevant to organizational success: Organizational Size, Vertical and Horizontal Differentiation, Design of Work Procedures and Content, Decision Making System, and Job Characteristics.

**Organizational size.** Size is simply the scope of human and capital resources. Size has been found to be related to other structural characteristics of organizations (Pugh et al., 1968) and also certain outcomes, such as performance and turnover (see Dalton et al., 1980). Size can be operationalized as the number of employees in an organization or establishment, the number of different locations, and financial measures of operation scope.

**Vertical and horizontal differentiation.** Vertical and Horizontal Differentiation includes two constructs: Specialization and Hierarchy (Pugh et al., 1968). Specialization refers to the form of division of labor. Hierarchy reflects the vertical structure of an organization (e.g., number of management levels). Two other aspects of differentiation, Administrative Intensity and Span of Control, were included in earlier versions of the taxonomy but were dropped because of problems in developing reliable, meaningful measures.

**Design of work procedures and content.** This area includes two constructs: Formalization and Standardization (Pugh et al., 1968). Formalization refers to the extent to which rules, procedures, and instructions are written. Standardization is the extent to which organizational behavior is controlled by procedures and regulations.

**Decision making system.** The literature on high performance emphasizes a team orientation and empowering employees. The O*NET organizational context taxonomy thus includes several aspects of the Decision Making System relevant to these high-performance concepts. Decentralization (Arthur, 1994) and Employee Empowerment (Spreitzer, 1992) refer to the degree of influence incumbents have on organizational decision making. Information Sharing is the extent to which the organization shares different kinds of information with employees (Lawler, Mohrman, & Ledford, 1992). Individual Versus Team Structure reflects the extent to which teams are used to accomplish organizational goals. The use of work teams is also reflected in the Type of Work Teams used.

**Job characteristics.** Job Characteristics are aspects of employees' jobs that are associated with job enrichment (Hackman & Oldham, 1980). Five core job characteristics were included in the taxonomy: Skill Variety, Task Significance, Task Identity, Autonomy, and Feedback. Skill Variety refers to the extent to which one's job requires the use of multiple skills. Task Significance indicates the importance of one's job to society. Task Identity refers to the extent to which one's job involves doing a whole and identifiable piece of work. Autonomy reflects the degree of independence one has on his or her job. Finally, Feedback refers to the amount of feedback one can get from doing the job.

### HR Systems and Practices

HR Systems and Practices exist to ensure that an organization has employees who are capable of meeting its goals. The management of employees clearly is important to organizations, and, to the extent that HR practices become systematized, they are an unmistakable part of the organizational context within which employees work. The HR Systems and Practices identified as most relevant for O*NET were Recruitment and Selection practices (Cascio, 1987; Rynes, 1991), Socialization Tactics (e.g., Van Maanen & Schein, 1979), Training and Development (Campbell, 1988; Goldstein, 1991, 1993), and Reward Systems (Gerhart & Milkovich, 1992; Lawler & Jenkins, 1992).

**Recruitment and selection.** Recruitment refers to organizational practices and decisions that affect either the number or types of individuals who are willing to apply for, or accept, a given vacancy (Rynes, 1991). Consistent with Cascio (1987), we included two constructs in our taxonomy that correspond to the two main phases of recruitment: Recruitment Planning and Recruitment Operations. Recruitment Planning involves specifying staffing goals and calculating and recording statistics that provide information regarding the time, money, and recruiting staff necessary to generate a specified number of hires within a specified period of time (e.g., time lapse data and yield ratios). Recruitment Operations involve using various sources (e.g., employment agencies, newspaper advertising) to generate leads and tracking prospects administratively as they go through the recruitment process.

Intimately related to the recruitment process is the area of personnel selection. Selection refers to the processes by which an organization identifies individuals for hiring, promotion, and other personnel decisions (Cascio, 1987; Guion, 1991). We broke the selection domain into two lower order constructs: (a) Selection Processes (i.e., the procedures used by an organization to develop its selection systems) and (b) Selection Methods (the actual methods used to assess and select individuals). Information about selection is relevant to the description of high-performance organizations. According to the high-performance literature (e.g., Westat, 1994), high-performance organizations make decisions on the basis of data. Performing job analyses and validating predictor measures provide data that facilitate decision making in the selection domain, so there is reason to expect they are more often used by high-performance organizations.

**Socialization tactics.** Organizational Socialization is the process by which individuals acquire the knowledge, skills, abilities, and other characteristics necessary for them to successfully perform an organizational role (Van Maanen & Schein, 1979). The organizational socialization research most relevant to our purposes deals with the tactics and strategies that organizations use to socialize their employees. Two organizational socialization constructs, derived from Van Maanen's (1978; Van Maanen & Schein, 1979) dimensions of socialization tactics, were included in the organizational context taxonomy: Group Socialization and Individualized Socialization. Group Socialization refers to whether an organization has a formal socialization process targeted toward groups of people. Individualized Socialization refers to whether an organization has a formal one-on-one socialization process in place (e.g., a mentoring program).

**Training and development.** A fair amount of literature is available concerning the design, implementation, and evaluation of training programs (e.g., Campbell, 1988; Goldstein, 1991, 1993; Noe, 1986). However, some of the steps involved in the training process either did not appear to be particularly relevant to O*NET or were unlikely to be endorsed by any organization. The following constructs, however, showed some promise for describing organizations (including high-performance organizations) and are thus included in the taxonomy: Needs Assessment, Training Methods and Topics, and Evaluating the Training Program.

Several additional training and development constructs were suggested by the literature on high performance (Lawler, 1993; U.S. DOL, 1994). This literature indicates that high-performance organizations emphasize the importance of training by requiring that their employees spend a certain amount of time each year in training activities and supporting continuous learning through programs such as job rotation. Lawler (1993) also argued that high-performance organizations often provide training in areas such as team skills, problem solving, quality control, and economic and business literacy.

We ultimately selected five lower order training and development constructs: (a) Training Methods refers to whether an organization uses various available training methods; (b) Use of Data in Training reflects the extent to which an organization uses quantitative data to design and evaluate its training and development programs; (c) Training Topics/Content refers to whether or not an organization offers training programs in various high-performance domains; (d) Extent/Support of Training by the organization is the extent to which an organization provides, or financially supports, training; and (e) Job Rotation practices refers to the extent to which organizations use job rotation to facilitate learning.

**Reward systems.** Rewards, in this context, refers to both monetary compensation and monetary and nonmonetary benefits. Most employees engage in role behaviors primarily in exchange for rewards that the organization provides (Gerhart & Milkovich, 1992). Rewards are, therefore, of great interest to both job seekers and job incumbents. Organizational reward systems also figure prominently in the high-performance organization literature (e.g., Lawler, 1987, 1993). According to that literature, high-performance organizations pay the person, rather than the job, through knowledge-, skill-, and merit-based pay systems. In addition, they often reward team performance as well as individual performance, as a means of supporting a team-based organizational culture. Finally, they provide benefits that help to accommodate the needs of their employees, such as flexible working hours and paid leave.

From our review of the literature, we identified a variety of types of formal compensation and benefit elements. Compensation Elements include skill and knowledge-based pay (Luthans & Fox, 1989), merit pay (Lawler & Jenkins, 1992), incentive-based pay (Brown, 1990), gainsharing (Lawler, 1983), profit-sharing (Smith, 1989), external comparisons (Ellig, 1985), seniority/job experience-based pay (Wallace & Fay, 1983), and salary (Lawler, 1983). A few additional reward-related constructs were included because they were identified in the high-performance literature. For example, high-performance organizations are more likely to use rewards based on group rather than individual performance. Benefit elements included employee ownership programs/stock options (Hammer, 1988) and nonobligatory benefits such as pensions, health insurance, life insurance, disability insurance, paid vacation, and family leave (Gerhart & Milkovich, 1992). Other benefits thought to be used frequently in high-performance organizations include flexible working hours and day care.

## Social Processes

### Organizational Culture

Organizational Culture often is regarded as a general label for social and behavioral patterns observed in organizations. Culture typically is thought to be composed of shared assumptions, values, norms, and artifacts, and it is described as important by most organizational theorists and writers (e.g., Katz & Kahn, 1978; Lawler, 1992; Limerick & Cunnington, 1993; Mintzberg, 1979; Perrow, 1961; Schein, 1992). A well-developed and business-specific culture has been thought to underpin stronger organizational commitment, higher morale, more efficient performance, and generally higher productivity (Deal & Kennedy, 1982; Furnham & Gunter, 1993; Graves, 1986; Peters & Waterman, 1982).

Many if not all researchers in the area of organizational culture would argue that organizational values are a core and defining element of any organization's culture (Katz & Kahn, 1978; Lawler, 1991; Perrow, 1970). Organizational values convey to organization members the choices and priorities of the organization in terms of its mode of functioning. In high-performance organizations, values should be consistent with participative approaches to organizing and managing people.

From the available literature, we concluded that assessment of organizational values would be the most practical approach to measuring culture. General/universal values and work-related values have a long tradition of research, but values more specifically targeted toward organizations appeared much more relevant for assessing values likely to be related to organizational culture. Moreover, Quinn (1988) proposed a model of organizational values that are related to different aspects of organizational effectiveness. He distinguished among different organizational value systems and suggested that each value system is associated with different elements of performance. For example, organizations that try to be adaptive, effective, and innovative should emphasize innovation, human resource, and rational goal values, while de-emphasizing hierarchical values. The high-performance literature supports this notion. Typically, high-performance organizations are associated with values such as innovation, employee involvement, goal achievement, vision, growth, and flexibility (Lawler, 1992; Peters & Waterman, 1982).

### Goals

Few organizational theorists exclude goal constructs from their models and discussions. Goal setting, both organizational and individual, is central to the functioning of modern organizations. Aspects of both types of goal setting are relevant to O*NET users, and thus they were included in the taxonomy.

**Organizational goal setting.** Organizational goal setting permeates the literature on organizational theory and behavior (e.g., Cyert & March, 1963; Et-zioni, 1964; Hall, 1982; Perrow, 1961, 1970; Porras & Robertson, 1992). One organizational goal-setting construct relevant for the O*NET is simply the extent to which an organization systematically engages in Goal-Setting Behavior (Campbell, 1977). In Campbell's (1977) review, this construct was conceptually associated with organizational effectiveness, and systematic goal-setting behavior has also been associated with high-performance organizations (Lawler, 1993; Limerick & Cunnington, 1993). Another construct, Goal Specificity, was adapted from the individual goal-setting literature (e.g., Kanfer, 1990; Locke, 1968; Locke, Shaw, Saari, & Latham, 1981). Support for the importance of this construct at the organizational level has been reported by Smith, Locke, and Barry (1990), who showed that organizations simulated in a university laboratory tended to do better if they were given specific and difficult collective goals.

**Individual goal setting.** As to individual goal setting, the literature in industrial/organizational psychology suggests that people who are given difficult and specific goals perform better than people not given such goals (e.g., Kanfer, 1990; Locke, 1968; Locke et al., 1981), and people who receive goal-relevant feedback perform better than those who merely have goals (Bandura & Cervone, 1983; Erez, 1977; Komaki, Collins, & Penn, 1982). Thus, Individual Goal Specificity and Availability of Goal Feedback are important individual goal-setting constructs, and we have incorporated them into the content model. To parallel the organization level, we also included the Extent of Individual Goal Setting in our proposed taxonomy.

Another individual goal-setting construct included in the content model is the method used to assign individual-level goals. This refers to whether employees are allowed to have input into the nature of the goals they set. Participation in goal setting is also prominently represented in the literature on high-performance organizations (e.g., Lawler, 1993). Thus, we included Goal Negotiability in our taxonomy as well.

### Roles

Roles are sets of behaviors expected of role incumbents (Ilgen & Hollenbeck, 1991). The literature suggests several aspects of roles that are likely to be relevant to O*NET: Role Conflict, Role Overload, and Role Negotiability. Role Conflict refers to incompatible role expectations (e.g., Kahn, Wolf, Quinn, Snoek, & Rosenthal, 1964; Katz & Kahn, 1978; King & King, 1990). Role Overload was originally conceptualized as a variant of Role Conflict, but it recently has been studied independently (Beehr, Walsh, & Taber, 1976; Kahn & Byosiere, 1992). It refers to a discrepancy between the demands of one's role set and one's ability to meet those demands.

Role Negotiability refers to the extent to which an incumbent is able to negotiate his or her role as opposed to simply being given one (Graen, 1976; Graen & Scandura, 1987). It reflects the adaptability of the organization to individual needs and organizational environments that are increasingly characterized by a need for fast and flexible behavior (Lawler, 1993). Of the role constructs suggested by the literature, Role Negotiability is the one that appears most likely to be an indicator of high-performance organizations. We have encountered no data indicating that jobs differ systematically on these role constructs, although occupations are often selected for investigation on the basis of their hypothesized level of Role Conflict (Katz & Kahn, 1978). It therefore seems plausible to suggest that some of the variance in these role constructs will be tied to jobs as well as to organizations.

### Leadership

Another important aspect of the work environment is supervision or leadership. For example, characteristics of the manager or supervisor have been shown to affect employees' satisfaction (see Yukl, 1989, for a review of relevant research). Early research on leadership identified two relatively independent characteristics of leaders that have important implications for their effectiveness. One has been called leader Consideration (Fleishman, 1953a), or relationship-oriented behavior (Likert, 1961). This leadership dimension is defined as the degree to which a leader acts in a friendly and supportive manner, shows concern for subordinates, and looks out for their welfare. The second characteristic is known as initiating structure (Fleishman, 1953a), or task-oriented behavior (Likert, 1961). Task Orientation refers to the degree to which a leader defines his or her role and the roles of subordinates in terms of attainment of the group's formal goals. These two constructs are well accepted, and there is a large body of research that supports their usefulness for describing managers and supervisors (see Yukl, 1989).

Other theorists, however, have argued that these two dimensions are deficient for describing managers and supervisors and have posited more detailed, multidimensional views of leader behaviors and characteristics (e.g., Van Fleet & Yukl, 1986). To better cover the breadth of the leadership domain while keeping the number of scales included to a minimum, we chose to include two additional characteristics of managers or supervisors: visionary and problem solving leadership. The concept of Visionary Leadership comes from leadership research that has focused on leaders' roles in championing and leading major changes necessary for their organizations' survival and success. "Transformational" or "charismatic" are the terms often used to describe leaders' abilities to influence changes in members' attitudes and commitment to the organization. One of the central propositions of this type of leadership is that leaders appeal to the ideas and hopes of followers through the communication of inspiring values, beliefs, and visions (Bass, 1985; Conger & Kanungo, 1987; House,

1977). Finally, recent research has also identified the importance of creative problem solving for effective leadership (see Mumford & Connelly, 1991). Problem Solving in social and task domains is a critical capability for managers; therefore, this dimension was also included in the measurement of leadership.

## Miscellaneous High-Performance Constructs

Finally, from the high-performance literature and checklists and the review of our taxonomy by industry representatives, we identified several organizational characteristics that do not fit well in the O*NET organizational context taxonomy but are thought to be characteristics of high-performance organizations. First, as more and more companies move toward "outsourcing" work, the Use of Contractors to accomplish work tasks has become a noticeable characteristic of many organizations. Second, to respond flexibly to a rapidly changing international market, many organizations are also making frequent, sometimes drastic, changes to their organizational structures. These changes range from simple reorganizations to downsizing or "rightsizing" the workforce. Finally, organizations that are coping effectively with the changing workplace are thought to use data extensively to make organizational decisions. Use of data in HR Systems and Practices has been discussed elsewhere, but we also included a more general construct regarding the Use of Data to make organizational decisions in our taxonomy.

## PROCEDURES, MEASURES, AND SAMPLES

The O*NET prototype data were collected to assess the reliability and validity of the descriptors in the taxonomy. This section describes the procedures used to collect these data, the measures developed to assess each of the lower order organizational context constructs, and the samples of incumbents and organizational representatives who were surveyed.

## Data Collection Procedures

Details concerning the incumbent data collection procedures can be found in chapter 4. For the organizational representative data, we asked for a single organizational representative in each sampled organization who was either a representative of the HR function or management. Data were collected from these individuals, using a computer-assisted telephone interview (CATI). The CATI comprised 70 questions, which generally asked respondents to rate the extent, frequency, or existence of each of the organizational characteristics, using Likert-type rating scales, check lists, or simple yes/no questions. These CATIs, each lasting approximately one half hour, were conducted by professional interviewers. The computer-assisted nature of the CATI allowed the interviewers to skip irrelevant or unnecessary questions on the basis of the interviewees' responses to previous items. It also systematically prompted interviewers to ask follow-up questions or provide clarification when interviewees had trouble with particular questions.

## Measures

The general approach taken in measuring organizational context characteristics was to obtain as much of the information as possible from a single organizational representative. This was done for two reasons. First, incumbent time was at a premium in the O*NET data collection. Virtually all of the other areas in the content model rely heavily on incumbent data and require a fair amount of incumbent time. Second, incumbent data concerning organizational descriptors is confounded because incumbents necessarily answer from the perspective of their job or occupation. Unless we could sample a large number of representative occupations from a single organization, it would be impossible to assess even the extent to which this confound affects the data at the organizational level.

Even so, some of the organizational context constructs could not be measured appropriately at the organizational level and were therefore included in the incumbent questionnaire. Constructs such as Job Characteristics, Employee Empowerment, and Roles, traditionally measured at the individual level, seemed more appropriately asked of job incumbents and were included in the incumbent questionnaire. The Leadership variables were also deemed more appropriate at the incumbent level for the present research. Information concerning Recruitment Sources and Selection Methods used is likely to be of most interest to O*NET users as it relates to particular occupations, so data concerning these descriptors also were collected only from incumbents.

For still other organizational context constructs, the organizational and incumbent perspectives were expected to provide different but relevant information (e.g., Goals and Decentralization). We therefore measured the following variables at both the organization and incumbent levels: Decentralization, Training Topics/Programs and Training Methods used, Job Rotation policies, Individual Versus Team Structure, Benefit and Compensation Elements, Goals, and Organizational Values. Questions concerning these variables in the incumbent questionnaire generally asked respondents to focus on their specific jobs. Questions in the organizational representative survey asked about the organization as a whole. Data concerning all of the remaining organizational context constructs in the content model were collected from the organizational representative only.

Existing measures were used where available. For those constructs for which measures were not available, the authors developed items or scales. Table 10-1 summarizes the organizational context constructs and the measures developed for each of them. This table also indicates which constructs were measured at the organizational representative level, at the incumbent level, or at both levels. The incumbent questionnaire itself can be found in Arad, Schneider, and Hanson (1995). The interview protocol used to collect data from the organizational representatives, with the exact wording of the questions included, is provided in Arad, Hanson, and Schneider (1996).

We adapted existing measures to assess the following constructs: Formalization and Standardization (Pugh et al., 1968), Information Sharing (Lawler et al., 1992), Decentralization (Arthur, 1994), Employee Empowerment (Spreitzer, 1992), Job Characteristics (Hackman & Oldham, 1980), Organizational Values (O'Reilly, Chatman, & Caldwell, 1991), and Role Conflict and Role Overload (King & King, 1990; Rizzo, House, & Lirtzman, 1970; Schuler, Aldag, & Brief, 1977). We also used the Standard Industrial Classification (SIC) codes (U.S. Office of Management and Budget, 1987) to classify organizations into types of industry. For all other constructs, we wrote items to reflect each construct.

## Samples

### Incumbents

A total of 733 respondents, representing 53 different occupations, completed the job incumbent survey. The sampled occupations ranged from General Managers and Top Executives to Janitors. (See chap. 4 for a detailed description of the sampling procedures.) The incumbents also represented a broad and diverse cross-section of the workforce in terms of age, sex, ethnic status, and education. The sample included both job holders (71%) and supervisors (29%). To compute meaningful descriptive statistics and reliabilities across occupations and across organizations, we included occupations and organizations in our sample only if responses were available from four or more incumbents. As a result, the sample used in the analyses reported here included 554 incumbents who represented 30 occupations and 70 establishments. Table 10-2 lists these occupations and the numbers of incumbents in each occupation who completed the organizational context questionnaire.

### Organizational Representatives

A total of 661 organizational representatives were interviewed; the majority worked in personnel or HR (61%), and virtually all of the others were managers or representatives of higher management. The 661 sampled establishments represented almost every type of industry as well as private, government, profit, and nonprofit organizations. The size of these establishments ranged from 5 employees to 6,000 employees (including both full- and part-time). Seventy of the sampled establishments were also represented in the incumbent sample. The remaining

**TABLE 10-1**

**Descriptions and Definitions of Organizational Context Constructs and Relevant Items in Incumbent and Organizational Representative Surveys**

| Construct label | Operational definition | Descriptor/scale in incumbent questionnaire (# of items) | Item number(s) in organizational representative CATI |
|---|---|---|---|
| | Type of Industry | | |
| Type of Industry (i.e., Organizational Output) | The organizational output or the class of industry to which the organization belongs. | | (derived from the SIC Codes) |
| | Structural Characteristics | | |
| Organizational Structure | | | |
| Organization and Establishment Size | The scope and the amount of growth and decline in human and capital resources. | | 6, 7, 8, 9, 10, 11, 12 |
| Hierarchy | The vertical structure of an organization (e.g., number of management levels) and changes in this structure. | | 18 |
| Specialization | The form of division of labor (e.g., the number of different occupation titles, the different functional activities pursued within an organization) and changes in these variables (e.g., the number of new jobs created). | | 22, 24, 28 |
| Formalization | The extent to which rules, procedures instructions, and communication are written (e.g., the number of written documents prescribing behavior). | | 20, 21 a–e |
| Standardization | The extent to which organizational behavior is controlled by procedures and regulations (i.e., the number of behavior-control procedures). | | 29 a–n |
| Decentralization | The extent to which nonsupervisory employees monitor data, determine work flow, etc. | 13 (4) | 30 a–e |
| Employee Empowerment | The degree to which employees participate in decision-making, and the level of autonomy and influence employees experience in their jobs. | 1 | |
| Information Sharing | The degree to which employees are provided with different types of organizational information. | | 31 a–e |
| Individual Versus Team Structure | The extent to which work is being performed by groups of employees versus individual employees (e.g., the number of employees working in permanent intact teams). | 23, 26 | 32, 33, 34 |
| Type of Work Teams | The use of difference types of work teams (e.g., functional work teams, cross-functional work teams, quality teams, project teams, and management teams). | | 35 a–e |
| Job Characteristics | Aspects of employees' jobs associated with job enrichment. That is, the level of skill variety, task significance, task identity, autonomy, and feedback. | 4 (3), 5 (3), 3 (3), 2 (3), 6 (3) | |
| Human Resources (HR) Systems & Practices | | | |
| Recruitment Planning | Determining staffing needs and collecting information to help ensure that those needs are met on a timely basis. | | 56, 57 |
| Recruitment Operations | Activities involved in implementing recruitment plans (e.g., selecting sources, realistic job previews). | 30 | 58 |
| Selection Processes | The extent to which selection systems are based on formal job analysis and predictors are validated against criteria. | | 61, 62, 63 |
| Selection Methods | The methods used for selection or promotion of employees. | 29 | |
| Group Socialization | The extent to which formal programs exist that involve socializing employees in groups. | | 59 |

*Table 10-1 continues*

**TABLE 10-1 (Continued)**

| Construct label | Operational definition | Descriptor/scale in incumbent questionnaire (# of items) | Item number(s) in organizational representative CATI |
|---|---|---|---|
| Individualized Socialization | The extent to which formal programs exist that involve socializing employees individually. | | 60 |
| Training Methods | The methods used in training programs. | 27 | |
| Use of Data in Training | The use of quantitative methods to identify training needs and evaluate training programs. | | 46, 47 |
| Training Topics/Content | What trainers intend to teach trainees through training programs. | 28 | 45 a–k, 48 a–j, 50a |
| Extent/Support of Training | The extent to which an organization makes training available to its employees and provides financial support for training activities. | | 44, 49 a–c, 54 |
| Job Rotation | The extent to which an organization uses job rotation to develop employee skills. | 33 | 53, 55 |
| Compensation Elements | The extent to which organizations reward individuals based on certain criteria such as: (a) knowledge, skills, and performance, (b) seniority, (c) team performance, (d) organizational performance, and (e) job attributes. | 31 | 66, 67, 68 a–h |
| Benefit Elements | The extent to which employees' compensation includes benefits such as pensions, insurance, paid leave, awards and bonuses, pay for time not worked. | 32 | 69 a–h |

Social Processes

| Construct label | Operational definition | Descriptor/scale in incumbent questionnaire (# of items) | Item number(s) in organizational representative CATI |
|---|---|---|---|
| Organizational Culture | | | |
| Organizational Values | The hierarchy of values that guide an organization. The importance of certain values such as tradition, stability, innovation, and collaboration. | 14 (3), 15 (6), 16 (2), 17 | 70a–70bb |
| Goals | | | |
| Extent of Individual Goal Setting | The extent to which an organization requires its members to periodically set goals. | | 39, 41 |
| Individual Goal Specificity | The extent to which an individual's goals are made explicit. | 11 (2) | |
| Availability of Goal Feedback | The extent to which an individual is given periodic feedback regarding his or her progress toward goals. | 12 (3) | 43 |
| Individual Goal Negotiability | The extent to which employees are allowed to participate in setting their own goals. | | 40, 42 |
| Extent of Organizational Goal Setting | The extent to which an organization systematically sets organizational goals. | | 37 |
| Organizational Goal Specificity | The extent to which an organization's goals are made explicit. | | 38 |
| Roles | | | |
| Role Conflict | The extent to which an individual has to deal with conflicting demands. | 7 (4) | |
| Role Negotiability | The extent to which an individual can negotiate his/her role in an organization. | 10 (2) | |
| Role Overload | A discrepancy between the demands of others and one's ability to meet those demands. | 8 (2), 9 | |
| Leadership | | | |
| Consideration | The extent to which the immediate supervisor acts in a friendly and supportive manner. | 18 | |
| Task-Orientation | The extent to which the immediate supervisor sets goals and assigns tasks for the work group. | 19 | |

*Table 10-1 continues*

**TABLE 10-1 (Continued)**

| Construct label | Operational definition | Descriptor/scale in incumbent questionnaire (# of items) | Item number(s) in organizational representative CATI |
|---|---|---|---|
| Visionary | The extent to which the immediate supervisor provides a clear vision for the work group and inspires commitment. | 20 | |
| Problem Solving | The extent to which the immediate supervisor solves difficult problems quickly and effectively. | 21 | |
| | Miscellaneous High-Performance Constructs | | |
| Use of Independent Contractors | The extent to which the organization uses external consultants and contractors to accomplish work tasks. | | 14, 15 |
| Change in Organizational Structure | The frequency with which the organizational structure and related documents (e.g., the organizational chart) are revised. | 22, 24, 25 | 13, 23, 25, 27 |
| Use of Data | The extent to which the organization uses quantitative data to make organizational decisions and invests in collecting such data. | | 64, 65 |

*Note.* CATI = computer-assisted telephone interview. See Appendix F of *Development of Prototype Occupational Information Network (O\*NET) Content Model* (Peterson, Mumford, Borman, Jeanneret, & Fleishman, 1995) for the exact wording of the incumbent questionnaire items. See Appendix of O\*NET *Final Technical Report* (Peterson, Mumford, Borman, Jeanneret, Fleishman, & Levin, 1996) for the exact wording of the organizational representative CATI items. The constructs in the above taxonomy differ slightly from those in the original taxonomy proposed by Arad, Schneider, and Hanson (1995); the taxonomy has been modified, based in part on feedback from organizational representatives.

establishments had no incumbents selected to complete the organizational context questionnaire, opted not to participate in incumbent surveying after completing the CATI survey, or did not return completed incumbent surveys. The entire CATI sample was used for the analyses presented here.

## Overview of Organizational Context Analyses

Analyses for the organizational context descriptors are necessarily somewhat different from those for the other O\*NET content domains, in part because data were collected from both incumbents and organizational representatives and in part because the focus is on describing organizations in addition to occupations. The analyses of the organizational context data fall into three general categories: analyses of the incumbent data, analyses of the organizational representative (i.e., CATI) data, and analyses aimed at understanding the commonalities and differences between these two sources of data.

For both the incumbent and the organizational representative data analyses, descriptive statistics and reliability estimates were computed. For the incumbent data, this included estimating interrater reliabilities. For both incumbent and organizational representative descriptors, data sets were intercorrelated and factor analyzed to assess the underlying structure. Comparisons of occupational means in the incumbent data were used to assess the potential usefulness of these descriptors in describing and classifying occupations. For the organizational representative data,

comparisons of mean scores obtained by organizations representing different types of industries were conducted to provide a preliminary assessment of the usefulness of these descriptors for describing and classifying organizations. Finally, comparisons between the incumbent and organizational representative data sets involved comparing the underlying structure (i.e., factor analyses). Each of these analyses is described in more detail in the following section.

## RESULTS

### Incumbent Data Analysis Results

It is important to keep in mind that even the incumbent-level descriptors in this domain were developed, at least in part, for the purpose of describing organizations, whereas descriptors in other domains were developed for the purpose of describing jobs and occupations. Data collected from job incumbents concerning these organizational context descriptors can be viewed as containing variance due to the organizations in which they work, but also variance attributable to the way in which these organizations affect individual job holders. It is also likely that, for at least some of the descriptors, a portion of the variance is directly due to the respondents' occupations. For example, one would expect managers to, on average, report more Empowerment (D1) than janitors, even if there also were systematic differences in the overall degree of employee empowerment across organizations. Thus, these data were examined from three perspectives: (a) their usefulness in describing

**TABLE 10-2**
**Thirty Occupations With Four or More Incumbents Completing the Organizational Context Questionnaire**

| Occupation code | Occupation title | Number of respondents |
|---|---|---|
| 15005 | Education Administrators | 8 |
| 19005 | General Managers & Top Executives | 40 |
| 22114 | Chemical Engineers | 4 |
| 25105 | Computer Programmers | 9 |
| 27311 | Recreation Workers | 6 |
| 31302 | Teachers, Preschool | 5 |
| 31305 | Teachers, Elementary School | 5 |
| 32502 | Registered Nurses | 27 |
| 32902 | Medical & Clinical Laboratory Technologists | 4 |
| 49008 | Salespersons, Except Scientific & Retail | 11 |
| 49011 | Salespersons, Retail | 15 |
| 49021 | Stock Clerks, Sales Floor | 7 |
| 49023 | Cashiers | 15 |
| 51002 | First Line Supervisors, Clerical/Administrative | 50 |
| 55108 | Secretaries, Except Legal & Medical | 64 |
| 55305 | Receptionists & Information Clerks | 12 |
| 55338 | Bookkeeping, Accounting, & Auditing Clerks | 20 |
| 55347 | General Office Clerks | 68 |
| 61005 | Police & Detective Supervisors | 12 |
| 63014 | Police Patrol Officers | 20 |
| 65008 | Waiters & Waitresses | 12 |
| 65038 | Food Preparation Workers | 29 |
| 66008 | Nursing Aides, Orderlies, & Attendants | 17 |
| 67005 | Janitors & Cleaners | 21 |
| 85119 | Other Machinery Maintenance Mechanics | 5 |
| 85132 | Maintenance Repairer, General Utility | 30 |
| 87902 | Earth Drillers, Except Oil & Gas | 6 |
| 92974 | Packaging & Filling Machine Operators | 12 |
| 97102 | Truck Drivers, Heavy or Tractor Trailers | 9 |
| 97111 | Bus Drivers, School | 11 |

organizations, (b) their usefulness in describing occupations, and (c) their usefulness in describing occupations within organization "cells" (i.e., incumbents working in the same occupation *and* the same organization).

### Reliability

For each of the a priori scales (i.e., scales adapted from the literature), we computed an estimate of internal consistency reliability (coefficient alpha), and these estimates are presented in Table 10-3. For Organizational Values, the a priori scales were based on the factor analysis of the organizational representative data (described later), which partially replicated past research (O'Reilly et al., 1991). For most scales, the internal consistency reliability estimates were above .70. For one scale, Role Overload, the internal consistency was unacceptably low. One of the three items on this scale, the availability of Adequate Resources (D9), had low correlations with the other two items, and it was thus treated as a separate descriptor for the remaining analyses. With this item removed, the Role Overload (D8) internal consistency was .61. Several other two-item scales—Role

Negotiability (D10), Goal Specificity (D11), and Attention to Detail Values (D16)—also have relatively low internal consistency (.31, .44, and .45, respectively).

Interrater reliability for these descriptors can be viewed in three ways: (a) agreement between incumbents who are in the same occupation; (b) agreement between incumbents who are in the same organization, regardless of their occupation; (c) and agreement between incumbents who are in the same occupation and the same organization. For descriptors that vary systematically across both occupations and organizations, the latter type of reliability, across occupation within organization "cells," was expected to be the highest. Table 10-3 presents interrater reliabilities computed across occupations (based on a harmonic mean of 10.14 judges per occupation) and across organizations (based on a harmonic mean of 6.51 judges per organization), along with the associated standard errors of measurement. In general, reliabilities across occupations were higher than those across organizations, but the number of raters per occupation is higher than the number of raters per organization.

**TABLE 10-3**

**Descriptive Statistics Across All Occupations and Organizations and Reliability Estimates for Rated Differences Between Occupations and Organizations: Organizational Context**

| Descriptor/scale (# items) | Scale anchors | Across occupations[a] | | | | | Across organizations[b] | | | |
|---|---|---|---|---|---|---|---|---|---|---|
| | | $\alpha$ | $M$ | $SD$ | $SEM$[c] | $r_k$[d] | $M$ | $SD$ | $SEM$[c] | $r_k$ |
| 1. Empowerment (2) | 1 = strongly disagree<br>5 = strongly agree | .91 | 3.17 | 0.49 | .23 | .77 | 3.16 | 0.46 | .40 | .27 |
| 2. Autonomy (3) | 1 = very little autonomy<br>5 = very much autonomy | .77 | 3.90 | 0.34 | .21 | .59 | 3.91 | 0.29 | .27 | .13 |
| 3. Task Identity (3) | 1 = my job is only part of the work<br>5 = my job involved doing a whole piece of work | .71 | 3.79 | 0.32 | .28 | .26 | 3.79 | 0.31 | .34 | .00 |
| 4. Skill Variety (3) | 1 = very little variety<br>5 = very much variety | .71 | 3.97 | 0.48 | .24 | .76 | 3.98 | 0.45 | .27 | .62 |
| 5. Task Significance (3) | 1 = not very significant<br>5 = highly significant | .74 | 4.17 | 0.41 | .23 | .67 | 4.23 | 0.35 | .24 | .51 |
| 6. Feedback (3) | 1 = very little feedback<br>5 = very much feedback | .77 | 3.89 | 0.30 | .27 | .23 | 3.95 | 0.24 | .24 | .00 |
| 7. Role Conflict (4) | 1 = strongly disagree<br>5 = strongly agree | .70 | 2.74 | 0.34 | .27 | .42 | 2.80 | 0.25 | .21 | .32 |
| 8. Role Overload (2) | 1 = strongly disagree<br>5 = strongly agree | .61 | 2.93 | 0.34 | .26 | .40 | 2.94 | 0.44 | .32 | .46 |
| 9. Adequate Resources | 1 = strongly disagree<br>5 = strongly agree | | 3.09 | 0.44 | .32 | .46 | 3.24 | 0.48 | .42 | .24 |
| 10. Role Negotiability (2) | 1 = strongly disagree<br>5 = strongly agree | .31 | 3.36 | 0.31 | .21 | .54 | 3.33 | 0.32 | .28 | .23 |
| 11. Goal Specificity (2) | 1 = none; 2 = few;<br>3 = some; 4 = most;<br>5 = all goals specific | .44 | 1.91 | .078 | .36 | .79 | 1.96 | 0.70 | .50 | .49 |
| 12. Goal Feedback (3) | 1 = never; 2 = once a year;<br>3 = twice a year;<br>4 = 3 times a year;<br>5 = 4 times a year | .59 | 2.38 | 0.47 | .28 | .64 | 2.40 | 0.45 | .36 | .35 |
| 13. Decentralization (4) | 1 = not at all<br>5 = to a great extent | .76 | 2.32 | 0.47 | .20 | .83 | 2.33 | 0.51 | .40 | .37 |
| 14. People-Oriented Values (3) | 1 = not important<br>5 = extremely important | .74 | 3.41 | 0.45 | .45 | .00 | 3.34 | 0.29 | .27 | .15 |
| 15. Risk-Taking Values (6) | 1 = not important<br>5 = extremely important | .80 | 3.30 | 0.32 | .32 | .00 | 3.31 | 0.24 | .21 | .24 |
| 16. Attention to Detail Values (2) | 1 = not important<br>5 = extremely important | .45 | 3.84 | 0.34 | .31 | .19 | 3.82 | 0.27 | .25 | .12 |
| 17. Stability Value | 1 = not important<br>5 = extremely important | | 3.41 | 0.50 | .50 | .00 | 3.37 | 0.36 | .31 | .26 |
| 18. Leader: Consideration | 1 = not at all<br>5 = to a great extent | | 3.84 | 0.34 | .28 | .28 | 3.93 | 0.45 | .42 | .10 |
| 19. Leader: Task Orientation | 1 = not at all<br>5 = to a great extent | | 3.62 | 0.37 | .30 | .41 | 3.56 | 0.49 | .41 | .30 |
| 20. Leader: Visionary | 1 = not at all<br>5 = to a great extent | | 3.45 | 0.40 | .36 | .20 | 3.45 | 0.42 | .42 | .00 |
| 21. Leader: Problem Solving | 1 = not at all<br>5 = to a great extent | | 3.58 | 0.38 | .27 | .48 | 3.57 | 0.46 | .45 | .04 |
| 22. No. of Supervisors | 1 = only 1; 2 = 2; 3 = 3;<br>4 = 4 or more | | 1.80 | 0.58 | .31 | .72 | 1.72 | 0.49 | .36 | .45 |
| 23. No. of Teams | 1 = none; 2 = 1, 3 = 2–3;<br>4 = 4–6; 5 = 7–10;<br>6 = 11 or more | | 2.63 | 0.67 | .31 | .79 | 2.40 | 0.46 | .41 | .23 |
| 24. No. of Reorganizations | 1 = never; 2 = once;<br>3 = twice; 4 = 3–5 times;<br>5 = 6 times or more | | 2.12 | 0.32 | .27 | .27 | 2.02 | 0.45 | .38 | .28 |
| 25. No. of Changes in Job Duties | 1 = never; 2 = once;<br>3 = twice; 4 = 3–5 times;<br>5 = 6 times or more | | 1.84 | 0.39 | .36 | .16 | 1.75 | 0.48 | .39 | .38 |
| 26. % Time Spent in Teams | 1 = none;<br>2 = less than 25%;<br>3 = 25–50%;<br>4 = 51–75%;<br>5 = more than 75% | | 2.91 | 0.82 | .40 | .76 | 2.72 | 0.78 | .59 | .42 |
| 27. No. of Training Methods | # items checked out of 12 | | 2.73 | 0.86 | .49 | .68 | 2.72 | 1.17 | .76 | .57 |
| 28. No. of Training Topics | # items checked out of 7 | | 1.45 | 0.72 | .39 | .71 | 1.52 | 0.87 | .59 | .55 |

*Table 10-3 continues*

**TABLE 10-3** (*Continued*)

| Descriptor/scale (# items) | Scale anchors | Across occupations[a] | | | | | Across organizations[b] | | | |
|---|---|---|---|---|---|---|---|---|---|---|
| | | $\alpha$ | M | SD | SEM[c] | $r_k$[d] | M | SD | SEM[c] | $r_k$ |
| 29. No. of Selection Methods | # items checked out of 13 | | 4.11 | 1.21 | .70 | .67 | 4.21 | 1.22 | .95 | .39 |
| 30. No. of Recruitment Sources | # items checked out of 16 | | 3.42 | 0.61 | .34 | .34 | 3.51 | 0.82 | .62 | .44 |
| 31. No. of Comp. Elements | # items checked out of 8 | | 1.20 | 0.61 | .50 | .70 | 1.19 | 0.70 | .46 | .57 |
| 32. No. of Benefit Elements | # items checked out of 8 | | 4.13 | 1.03 | .33 | .61 | 4.25 | 1.19 | .46 | .70 |
| 33. Job Rotation Practices | 1 = no job rotation | | 2.08 | 0.56 | .35 | .60 | 1.91 | 0.52 | .44 | .28 |
| | 2 = rotate within work-group | | | | | | | | | |
| | 3 = rotate across work-groups | | | | | | | | | |
| | 4 = rotate across departments | | | | | | | | | |

[a]Statistics across occupations are based on 30 occupations with Organizational Context Questionnaire responses from at least 4 incumbents (mean number of incumbents = 18.47, Mdn = 12, harmonic mean = 10.14).    [b]Statistics are across organizations, based on 70 organizations with Organizational Context Questionnaire responses from at least 4 incumbents (mean number of incumbents = 7.91, median = 7.00, harmonic mean = 6.51).    [c]This estimate of the standard error of measurement was calculated as $SEM = SD*\sqrt{1 - r_k}$.    [d]This estimate of reliability was obtained by calculating the intraclass correlation for the mean of k ratings across occupations: $ICC(1, k) = [BMS - WMS]/BMS$ (Shrout & Fleiss, 1979), where k is the harmonic mean of the number of ratings provided on each organization.

Table 10-4 shows estimates of the interrater reliability that would have been obtained if 30 judges had been available for each occupation and also the reliability of ratings provided by a single rater. This table also shows the 1-rater and 30-rater reliability estimates across organizations and across the occupation within organization cells. Table 10-4 shows that, in general, reliabilities across occupations are higher than those across organizations, even when the number of raters is the same. On average, however, reliabilities across the occupation within organization cells were the highest. Table 10-4 shows that for several variables—Task Identity (D3), Feedback (D6), the four Organizational Values scales (Descriptors 14–17), and two of the Leadership variables: Consideration (D18) and Visionary (D20)—these estimates are all quite low (all across-occupation $r_1$ estimates < .05). These descriptors would have low reliabilities even if 30 judges were available for each occupation. Consequently, these descriptors were not included in subsequent advanced analyses (e.g., factor and discriminant analyses).

### Intercorrelations

Another way of obtaining evidence for the meaningfulness of the incumbent-level measures of organizational context is by examining the nature of the relationships among the organizational context descriptors. For this purpose, we computed the correlations among organizational context descriptor ratings at the job, organization, and individual levels. Individual-level correlations were computed by randomly selecting only four individuals from each job to control for differences in the number of incumbents drawn from the different jobs. These latter correlations were virtually identical to those computed using job-level data and are not discussed here (see Arad et al., 1996). The intercorrelations at the job and organization levels are discussed.

Not surprisingly, the magnitude and direction of these two sets of correlations appear similar. However, some differences are worth noting. First, the organizational change descriptors (i.e., Number of Reorganizations [D24] and Number of Changes in Job Duties [D25]) were negatively correlated with Role Negotiability (D10), Goal Specificity (D11), and Goal Feedback (D12; correlations ranging from −.04 to −.22) at the occupation level, whereas positive correlations were observed at the organization level (correlations ranging from .16 to .30). Second, the Job Rotation Practices (D33) descriptor was negatively correlated with Empowerment (D1) and Autonomy (D2; −.22 and −.25, respectively) at the occupation level but showed no significant correlations at the organization level. Third, the correlations between the team descriptors (i.e., Number of Teams [D23] and % Time Spent in Teams [D26]) and Decentralization (D13) were substantially higher at the occupation level (.62 and .34, compared with .14 and .19). The correlations between the team descriptors and Empowerment (D1) and Autonomy (D2) were also substantially higher at the occupation level.

### Factor Analysis

We used principal-components analysis with a varimax rotation to examine the underlying structure of the incumbent data. Occupation means were used in this analysis, in part because the organizational context descriptors appear most reliable across occupations and in part because occupation means were used for factor analyses in the other content model domains. Several different solutions with different numbers of factors were examined, and the four-factor solution was chosen on the basis of a scree plot of the eigenvalues and the interpretability of the various solutions; this rotated factor pattern matrix is shown in Table 10-5. These four factors were labeled (a) Decentralization and Employee Empowerment,

**TABLE 10-4**

**Reliability of Rated Differences Between Occupations and Organizations Considering Varying Numbers of Raters: Organizational Context**

| | Number of raters for each level of analysis | | | | | |
| --- | --- | --- | --- | --- | --- | --- |
| | Across occupations[a] | | Across organizations[b] | | Within organization cells[c] | |
| Descriptor/scale | $r_1$[d] | $r_{30}$[e] | $r_1$ | $r_{30}$ | $r_1$ | $r_{30}$ |
| 1. Empowerment | 25 | 91 | 05 | 63 | 23 | 90 |
| 2. Autonomy | 12 | 81 | 02 | 42 | 21 | 89 |
| 3. Task Identity | 03 | 51 | 00 | 00 | 04 | 57 |
| 4. Skill Variety | 24 | 91 | 20 | 88 | 21 | 89 |
| 5. Task Significance | 17 | 86 | 14 | 82 | 13 | 82 |
| 6. Feedback | 03 | 46 | 00 | 00 | 01 | 30 |
| 7. Role Conflict | 07 | 68 | 07 | 69 | 06 | 64 |
| 8. Role Overload | 06 | 66 | 11 | 80 | 14 | 82 |
| 9. Adequate Resources | 08 | 71 | 05 | 59 | 11 | 79 |
| 10. Role Negotiability | 11 | 78 | 04 | 58 | 07 | 68 |
| 11. Goal Specificity | 27 | 92 | 13 | 82 | 30 | 93 |
| 12. Goal Feedback | 15 | 84 | 08 | 72 | 21 | 89 |
| 13. Decentralization | 32 | 93 | 08 | 73 | 23 | 90 |
| 14. People-Oriented Values | 00 | 00 | 03 | 44 | 06 | 67 |
| 15. Risk-Taking Values | 00 | 00 | 05 | 60 | 08 | 72 |
| 16. Attention to Detail Values | 02 | 41 | 02 | 38 | 11 | 78 |
| 17. Stability Value | 00 | 00 | 05 | 62 | 05 | 63 |
| 18. Leader: Consideration | 04 | 54 | 02 | 33 | 03 | 52 |
| 19. Leader: Task Orientation | 06 | 67 | 06 | 66 | 21 | 89 |
| 20. Leader: Visionary | 02 | 43 | 00 | 00 | 03 | 49 |
| 21. Leader: Problem Solving | 08 | 73 | 01 | 18 | 18 | 87 |
| 22. No. of Supervisors | 20 | 88 | 11 | 79 | 30 | 93 |
| 23. No. of Teams | 28 | 92 | 04 | 58 | 15 | 84 |
| 24. No. of Reorganizations | 04 | 52 | 06 | 64 | 21 | 89 |
| 25. No. of Changes in Job Duties | 02 | 37 | 09 | 74 | 16 | 85 |
| 26. % Time Spent in Teams | 23 | 90 | 10 | 77 | 16 | 85 |
| 27. No. of Training Methods | 17 | 86 | 17 | 86 | 37 | 95 |
| 28. No. of Training Topics | 20 | 88 | 16 | 85 | 39 | 95 |
| 29. No. of Selection Methods | 17 | 86 | 09 | 75 | 27 | 92 |
| 30. No. of Recruitment Sources | 05 | 61 | 11 | 78 | 12 | 80 |
| 31. No. of Comp. Elements | 19 | 87 | 17 | 86 | 28 | 92 |
| 32. No. of Benefit Elements | 22 | 89 | 15 | 84 | 39 | 95 |
| 33. Job Rotation Practices | 13 | 82 | 06 | 65 | 13 | 82 |

[a]Reliability estimates across occupations are based on 30 occupations with Organizational Context Questionnaire responses from at least 4 incumbents (mean number of incumbents = 18.47, $Mdn$ = 12, harmonic mean = 10.14). Decimals are omitted.
[b]Reliability estimates across organizations are based on 70 organizations with Organizational Context Questionnaire responses from at least 4 incumbents (mean number of incumbents = 7.91, $Mdn$ = 7.00, harmonic mean = 6.51). Decimals are omitted.
[c]Statistics are based on 50 cells where a cell is defined as incumbents in the same occupation and the same organization with Organizational Context Questionnaire responses from at least 4 incumbents per cell (mean number of incumbents = 4.85, $Mdn$ = 4.00, harmonic mean = 4.72).
[d]Single rater estimates of reliability were obtained by calculating the intraclass correlation for single judge ratings across occupations: $ICC(1, 1) = [BMS - WMS]/[BMS + (k\text{-}1)WMS]$ (Shrout & Fleiss, 1979), where $k$ is the harmonic mean of the number of ratings provided on each occupation.
[e]Estimates of reliability for 30 raters were obtained by applying the Spearman-Brown correction formula to the single rater reliability estimates.

(b) Work in Teams, (c) Task-Oriented Leadership, and (d) Skill Variety.

## Job Differences

One of the key pieces of evidence for the external validity of our descriptive systems is its ability to capture the similarities and differences among jobs (Fleishman & Mumford, 1991). To assess the ability of our taxonomy to differentiate among jobs, we conducted job profile analyses.

A presentation of how the patterns of organizational characteristics are related to jobs is provided in Table 10-6. This table presents the means and

standard deviations of the organizational context measures for six sample occupations: (a) General Managers and Top Executives, (b) Computer Programmers, (c) Registered Nurses, (d) Police Patrol Officers, (e) Janitors and Cleaners, and (f) Maintenance Repairers, General Utility.

As expected, some organizational characteristics were found to differ systematically across occupations. For example, General Managers and Top Executives showed the highest levels of Empowerment (D1), Autonomy (D2), Role Conflict (D7), and Decentralization (D13), and the largest Number of Training Topics (D28). Computer Programmers in-

**TABLE 10-5**
**Principal-Components Analysis Pattern Matrix: Organizational Context**

| Descriptor | Factor | | | | Communality |
|---|---|---|---|---|---|
| | F1 | F2 | F3 | F4 | |
| 1. Empowerment | .80 | .07 | −.12 | .18 | .69 |
| 2. Autonomy | .72 | −.15 | −.21 | .30 | .68 |
| 3. Skill Variety | .38 | .12 | −.16 | .78 | .80 |
| 4. Task Significance | −.02 | −.02 | .05 | .74 | .55 |
| 5. Role Conflict | .26 | .64 | .00 | .27 | .54 |
| 6. Role Overload | .41 | .17 | −.57 | −.07 | .53 |
| 7. Adequate Resources | −.47 | −.33 | −.02 | −.14 | .35 |
| 8. Role Negotiability | .44 | −.17 | −.11 | −.16 | .26 |
| 9. Goal Specificity | .74 | −.03 | −.17 | −.06 | .58 |
| 10. Goal Feedback | .80 | −.16 | −.01 | −.05 | .66 |
| 11. Decentralization | .67 | .44 | −.32 | .08 | .75 |
| 12. Leader: Task Orientation | .01 | −.26 | .68 | −.08 | .53 |
| 13. Leader: Problem Solving | −.12 | .06 | .65 | −.26 | .51 |
| 14. No. of Supervisors | −.24 | .44 | .71 | −.20 | .79 |
| 15. No. of Teams | .46 | .63 | .00 | .16 | .64 |
| 16. No. of Reorganizations | −.14 | .76 | .07 | −.08 | .62 |
| 17. No. of Changes in Job Duties | −.21 | .70 | .22 | −.09 | .58 |
| 18. % Time Spent in Teams | −.02 | .74 | −.09 | .01 | .56 |
| 19. No. of Training Topics | .48 | .15 | −.22 | .29 | .39 |
| 20. No. of Training Methods | .05 | .14 | −.50 | .45 | .48 |
| 21. No. of Selection Methods | −.02 | .01 | −.26 | .87 | .82 |
| 22. No. of Comp. Elements | .43 | .03 | −.57 | −.42 | .68 |
| 23. No. of Benefits Elements | .24 | −.34 | −.64 | .04 | .59 |
| 24. Job Rotation Practices | −.37 | .57 | −.44 | −.16 | .69 |
| % of variance | 18 | 15 | 13 | 11 | |
| Eigenvalue | 4.60 | 3.80 | 3.36 | 2.85 | |

*Note.* N = 30. The correlation matrix was based on means calculated at the occupation level. F1 = Decentralization/Employee Empowerment; F2 = Work in Teams; F3 = Task-Oriented Leadership; F4 = Skill Variety. These loadings are based on an orthogonal varimax rotation.

dicated they spent the greatest percentage of their time working in teams (D26). Police Patrol Officers experienced the least Empowerment (D1), Role Negotiability (D10), and Decentralization (D13).

## Organizational Representative Data Analysis Results

In general, the CATI data from the organizational representatives were very complete, with two exceptions. First, financial information (i.e., establishment and organization annual revenue) was missing for 37% of the establishments, mainly because respondents were unable or refused to provide the information. None of the financial variables is included in the present results. Second, organizational change (i.e., rightsizing and reorganization) descriptors had, on average, 26% missing data. The change items asked about the rate of organizational changes over the previous 5 years, and therefore respondents were asked only if the establishment had been in existence for at least 5 years. Consequently, 13% of the establishments in the sample did not answer the change questions simply because they were not asked. These latter descriptors were excluded from some of the present analyses (e.g., the factor analyses) in order to maximize sample size.

For the continuous items, we computed means and standard deviations. Table 10-7 presents these descriptive statistics for the organizational context CATI questions for which the rating scale is obvious (e.g., Number of Organization Locations; CATI Item 6). Table 10-8 presents the descriptive statistics for those questions for which the rating scale used is needed to interpret the results (e.g., Use of Contractors: Extent; CATI Item 14). For the yes/no items, we computed the percentage of the sample endorsing each response. Table 10-9 presents descriptive statistics for these dichotomous questions. Finally, we calculated the mean and standard deviation of ratings for how characteristic each of the Organizational Values is of the respondents' organizations, and these are presented in Table 10-10.

As Table 10-10 shows, the organizations represented in this survey comprise a broad range of sizes. There also is a great deal of variability in the Number of Job Titles (CATI Item 22) and the Number of Management Levels (CATI Item 18) across these companies. On average, more than 30% of employees work in some sort of team, and it appears that the majority of them work in Functional Teams. On average, about 50% of employees in the organizations sampled are salaried (CATI Item 68a), and the most common Compensation Element is, not surprisingly, Individual Performance (CATI Item 68d), although other Compensation Elements also appear

**TABLE 10-6**
**Descriptor Means and Standard Deviations on Six Example Occupations: Organizational Context**

| Descriptor | General Managers & Top Executives (n = 40) | | Computer Programmers (n = 9) | | Registered Nurses (n = 27) | | Police Patrol Officers (n = 20) | | Janitors & Cleaners[a] (n = 21) | | Maintenance Repairers, General Utility (n = 30) | |
|---|---|---|---|---|---|---|---|---|---|---|---|---|
| | M | SD | M | SD | M | SD | M | SD | M | SD | M | SD |
| 1. Empowerment | 4.15 | 1.03 | 3.33 | .75 | 3.50 | .91 | 2.35 | .89 | 2.95 | 1.00 | 3.27 | 1.07 |
| 2. Autonomy | 4.30 | .60 | 4.19 | .60 | 4.10 | .66 | 4.15 | .59 | 3.89 | .65 | 3.99 | 1.03 |
| 3. Task Identity | 3.60 | .98 | 3.48 | 1.11 | 3.73 | .86 | 3.40 | .96 | 4.03 | .64 | 4.03 | .99 |
| 4. Skill Variety | 4.39 | .62 | 4.33 | .44 | 4.48 | .53 | 4.42 | .48 | 3.56 | .95 | 4.30 | .86 |
| 5. Task Significance | 4.44 | .62 | 3.52 | .56 | 4.60 | .38 | 4.47 | .69 | 4.27 | .77 | 4.19 | .89 |
| 6. Feedback | 3.79 | .82 | 3.59 | .64 | 3.99 | .58 | 3.72 | .73 | 4.13 | .65 | 3.93 | 1.08 |
| 7. Role Conflict | 3.10 | .62 | 2.75 | .73 | 2.77 | .70 | 2.71 | .64 | 2.65 | .71 | 2.88 | .80 |
| 8. Role Overload | 3.18 | .63 | 3.50 | 1.00 | 3.26 | .94 | 2.48 | .59 | 2.79 | .96 | 2.87 | .86 |
| 9. Adequate Resources | 2.88 | .99 | 2.78 | .83 | 3.52 | 1.19 | 3.35 | 1.04 | 2.90 | 1.00 | 3.20 | 1.30 |
| 10. Role Negotiability | 3.71 | .53 | 3.56 | .30 | 3.57 | .66 | 3.00 | .78 | 3.29 | .89 | 3.38 | .76 |
| 11. Goal Specificity | 2.98 | 1.04 | 2.28 | 1.42 | 2.46 | 1.42 | 1.73 | 1.25 | 1.74 | 1.33 | 1.92 | 1.37 |
| 12. Goal Feedback | 2.90 | 1.05 | 2.41 | .70 | 2.68 | .97 | 2.27 | .82 | 2.24 | .96 | 2.28 | .93 |
| 13. Decentralization | 3.34 | .68 | 2.75 | .78 | 2.52 | .89 | 1.50 | .61 | 1.93 | 1.03 | 2.59 | 1.04 |
| 14. People-Oriented Values | 3.58 | .92 | 3.00 | .88 | 3.88 | .82 | 3.68 | 1.06 | 3.32 | .99 | 3.48 | .91 |
| 15. Risk-Taking Values | 3.25 | .76 | 3.46 | .60 | 3.46 | .60 | 3.27 | .86 | 3.11 | .80 | 3.26 | .84 |
| 16. Attention to Detail Values | 3.58 | .68 | 4.06 | .63 | 4.04 | .71 | 3.72 | .97 | 3.40 | .83 | 3.55 | .93 |
| 17. Stability Values | 3.28 | 1.11 | 2.78 | .97 | 3.67 | .92 | 3.60 | 1.05 | 3.45 | .97 | 3.13 | 1.17 |
| 18. Leader: Consideration | 3.92 | 1.19 | 4.22 | .83 | 4.44 | .97 | 3.90 | .97 | 3.43 | 1.25 | 4.36 | .93 |
| 19. Leader: Task Orientation | 2.94 | 1.05 | 3.67 | 1.22 | 3.63 | 1.11 | 3.85 | .99 | 3.55 | 1.12 | 3.75 | 1.07 |
| 20. Leader: Visionary | 3.16 | 1.10 | 3.56 | .73 | 4.04 | 1.02 | 3.50 | .89 | 3.38 | 1.20 | 3.78 | 1.24 |
| 21. Leader: Problem Solving | 2.90 | 1.13 | 3.44 | 1.01 | 4.11 | 1.01 | 3.85 | .88 | 3.33 | 1.11 | 3.72 | 1.17 |
| 22. No. of Supervisors | 1.58 | 1.13 | 1.22 | .44 | 1.59 | .84 | 2.35 | 1.23 | 2.05 | 1.16 | 1.63 | 1.10 |
| 23. No. of Teams | 2.90 | 1.10 | 2.22 | .83 | 2.67 | 1.04 | 2.80 | .83 | 1.86 | .91 | 2.20 | 1.03 |
| 24. No. of Reorganizations | 2.20 | .91 | 2.00 | .87 | 2.04 | .98 | 2.40 | 1.14 | 1.76 | .89 | 1.57 | .73 |
| 25. No. of Changes in Job Duties | 1.80 | .99 | 1.33 | .50 | 1.78 | 1.05 | 1.55 | .83 | 1.71 | .96 | 1.73 | 1.26 |
| 26. % Time Spent in Teams | 3.05 | 1.38 | 3.89 | 1.54 | 3.33 | 1.69 | 2.15 | 1.31 | 2.00 | 1.10 | 2.17 | 1.18 |
| 27. No. of Training Topics | 2.78 | 1.87 | 1.22 | 1.48 | 2.17 | 2.17 | 1.65 | 1.57 | 1.24 | 1.64 | 1.57 | 1.65 |
| 28. No. of Training Methods | 3.92 | 2.37 | 2.78 | 2.44 | 4.14 | 1.98 | 4.15 | 2.35 | 1.81 | 1.86 | 2.40 | 2.31 |
| 29. No. of Selection Methods | 5.13 | 2.16 | 3.11 | 1.45 | 5.07 | 2.99 | 7.45 | 2.86 | 3.24 | 2.83 | 4.23 | 2.88 |
| 30. No. of Recruitment Sources | 3.37 | 1.79 | 4.60 | 1.55 | 3.96 | 2.15 | 3.34 | 2.20 | 2.95 | 1.51 | 3.15 | 1.53 |
| 31. No. of Comp. Elements | 1.85 | 1.48 | 2.78 | 1.64 | 1.85 | 1.26 | 1.05 | 1.15 | .67 | .97 | .84 | .95 |
| 32. No. of Benefits Elements | 4.95 | 1.06 | 6.78 | 0.44 | 4.15 | 1.43 | 4.10 | 1.33 | 4.33 | 1.59 | 4.20 | 1.67 |
| 33. Job Rotation Practices | 1.90 | 1.30 | 1.89 | 1.27 | 2.26 | 1.16 | 2.15 | 1.35 | 1.66 | .65 | 2.03 | 1.19 |

[a]The full title for this occupation is "Janitors and Cleaners, except Maids and Housekeeping."

to be widely used. Benefits such as a Retirement Plan (CATI Item 69b) and Paid Vacation (CATI Item 69h) are very common, whereas Day Care (CATI Item 69g) is relatively uncommon.

Table 10-12 shows that the majority of organizations in our sample had downsized in the last 5 years. Training in Team Skills (CATI Item 48b), Quality Control (CATI Item 48c), Problem Solving (CATI Item 48e), Leadership (CATI Item 48f), and Customer Service (CATI Item 48g) were conducted by more than half of these organizations as well. Formal Orientation programs (CATI Item 59) were used frequently, and Formal Mentoring programs (CATI Item 60) were far less common. Finally, Table 10-10 shows that, on average, respondents thought that Quality (CATI Item 70m) values were most characteristic of their organizations. Other values that received high average ratings included Customer Oriented (CATI Item 70a) and Fairness (CATI Item 70f). Risk Taking (CATI Item 70b) and Analytically Ori-

ented (CATI Item 70d) values had among the lowest average ratings but the highest standard deviations. Apparently there is more variability among the organizations in our sample concerning the extent to which these latter values are important.

### Reliability

For the organizational representative data, only one respondent was available for each organization (i.e., the organizational representative), so interrater reliability could not be assessed. We therefore computed internal consistency reliability coefficients. All of the a priori scales included in the CATI had high internal consistency reliabilities: Formalization (5 items [CATI Items 21a–e], $\alpha = .69$); Standardization (14 items [CATI Items 29a–n], $\alpha = .88$); Specialization (15 items [CATI Items 28a–o], $\alpha = .67$); Decentralization (5 items [CATI Items 30a–e], $\alpha = .79$); Information Sharing (5 items [CATI Items 31a–e], $\alpha =$

**TABLE 10-7**
**Descriptive Statistics for Organizational Representative (CATI) Data: Organizational Context**

| Item # | Item/scale label | N | M | SD |
|---|---|---|---|---|
| 6 | No. of Organization Locations | 661 | 177.24 | 527.88 |
| 7 | No. of Countries Do Business | 661 | 12.37 | 40.17 |
| 8 | Full-Time Organization Employees | 661 | 13703.37 | 51304.79 |
| 9 & 10 | Total Employees (Establishment) | 661 | 322.71 | 659.21 |
| 11 | No. of New Employees Joined Last Year | 620 | 55.77 | 120.25 |
| 12 | No. of Employees Last Year | 630 | 298.58 | 601.02 |
| 18 | No. of Management Levels | 605 | 10.18 | 38.50 |
| 22 | No. of Job Titles | 661 | 57.55 | 117.37 |
| 24 | No. of New Jobs Created (Last 5 Yrs) | 553 | 10.04 | 25.15 |
| 31 | Information Sharing (% Informed, 5 items) | 659 | 49.69 | 29.52 |
| 34 | % Working in Teams | 661 | 31.78 | 36.57 |
| 35a | % in Functional Teams | 661 | 29.25 | 34.71 |
| 35b | % in Cross-Functional Teams | 661 | 19.21 | 28.40 |
| 35c | % in Management Teams | 661 | 8.41 | 17.59 |
| 35d | % in Project Teams | 661 | 7.37 | 16.86 |
| 35e | % in Quality Improvement Teams | 661 | 12.90 | 24.22 |
| 39 | % Managers Set Goals | 649 | 70.05 | 41.60 |
| 40 | % Managers Negotiate Goals | 640 | 64.97 | 44.02 |
| 41 | % Non-Managers Set Goals | 650 | 56.79 | 44.58 |
| 42 | % Non-Managers Negotiate Goals | 647 | 44.09 | 45.28 |
| 43 | No. of Performance Reviews in Last 2 Yrs | 652 | 2.17 | 1.50 |
| 49a | % Attend No Training | 523 | 20.59 | 29.71 |
| 49b | % Attend One Training Course | 522 | 24.47 | 28.75 |
| 49c | % Attend Two+ Training Courses | 640 | 40.16 | 38.17 |
| 50a | % Get Quality Control Training | 642 | 25.06 | 38.33 |
| 66 | % Pay Adjusted on Evaluated Studies | 638 | 50.18 | 44.97 |
| 67 | % Pay Adjusted on Comparisons | 642 | 54.93 | 43.53 |
| 68a | % w/ Salary | 650 | 52.17 | 40.16 |
| 68b | % w/ Profit-Sharing | 655 | 25.57 | 40.34 |
| 68c | % w/ Skill-Based Pay | 642 | 26.62 | 38.70 |
| 68d | % w/Individual Performance-Based Pay | 650 | 52.29 | 44.46 |
| 68e | % w/ Team Performance-Based Pay | 649 | 12.50 | 29.10 |
| 68f | % w/Cust. Satisfaction-Based Pay | 647 | 17.45 | 34.70 |
| 68g | % w/ Seniority-Based Pay | 646 | 31.08 | 41.45 |
| 68h | % w/ Hay Points | 638 | 13.91 | 30.51 |
| 69a | % w/ Stocks | 654 | 13.97 | 31.36 |
| 69b | % w/ Retirement Plan | 657 | 73.99 | 39.46 |
| 69c | % w/ Medical Insurance | 659 | 81.00 | 32.06 |
| 69d | % w/ Life Insurance | 656 | 76.18 | 37.16 |
| 69e | % w/ Disability Insurance | 653 | 70.21 | 41.48 |
| 69f | % w/ Flex Hours | 651 | 35.44 | 41.28 |
| 69g | % w/ Daycare | 659 | 7.77 | 25.88 |
| 69h | % w/ Paid Vacation | 660 | 84.90 | 28.93 |

*Note.* CATI = computer-assisted telephone interview.

.73); Use of Contractors (2 items [CATI Items 14–15], α = .79); and Use of Data in organizational decision making (7 items [CATI Items 46, 47, 57, 62, 63, 64, 65], α = .80). Note that the items involving Use of Data actually come from several different parts of the taxonomy, but they intercorrelate quite highly. The items that measured changes in organizational structure were divided into two scales, representing two types of change: Rightsizing (e.g., downsizing and removing layers of managers; 2 items [CATI Items 13 & 19]) and Reorganization (e.g., Number of Reorganizations, Number of Organizational Chart Revisions; 4 items [CATI Items 23, 25, 26, & 27]). Coefficient alpha was .68 for the Rightsizing scale and .56 for the Reorganization scale.

## Factor Structure

The five categories that represent the highest level of the content model for organizational context (Organizational Structure, Organizational Values, HR Systems and Practices, Goal Setting, and Roles) might best be viewed as a useful heuristic for organizing the constructs in the content model, but they were not necessarily expected to describe the empirical structure of the data. Constructs in the various categories come from different literatures and even, in some cases, different disciplines, so there is no readily available theory to predict or explain the relationships among them. However, *within* each of these broad domains there is a good deal of information in the literature concerning the expected structure. Roles were measured only in the incumbent questionnaire, and only a few questions concerning Goals were included in the organizational representative questionnaire. Therefore, three separate factor analyses were conducted: (a) HR Systems and Practices and the Goal items, (b) Organizational Structure, and (c) Organizational Values.

Only half of the organizational representative sample (*n* = 326) was used to conduct these exploratory

**TABLE 10-8**
**Descriptive Statistics and Rating Scales Used for Organizational Representative (CATI) Data: Organizational Context**

| Item # | Item/scale label (# items) | Scale anchors | N | M | SD |
|---|---|---|---|---|---|
| 14 | Use of Contractors: Extent | 1 = not at all<br>5 = to a great extent | 658 | 2.25 | 1.10 |
| 15 | Use of Contractors: Frequency | 1 = never<br>5 = always | 657 | 2.66 | 1.19 |
| 20 | No. of Formal Documents | # checked out of 7 | 661 | 5.72 | 1.34 |
| 21 | Document Relate to Perform (5) | 1 = not at all<br>5 = to a great extent | 585 | 3.81 | 0.88 |
| 23 | Changes in Job Duties: Frequency | 1 = never<br>5 = always | 656 | 2.69 | 0.90 |
| 25 | No. of Reorganizations | 0 = never, 1 = 1, 2 = 2,<br>3 = 3, 4 = 4, 5 = 5,<br>6 = 6 or more | 562 | 0.91 | 1.26 |
| 27 | No. of Organization Chart Revisions | 0 = never, 1 = 1, 2 = 2,<br>3 = 3, 4 = 4, 5 = 5 or more | 266 | 2.96 | 1.88 |
| 28 | No. of Specializations | # checked out of 15 | 661 | 10.76 | 3.02 |
| 29 | Standardization (14) | 1 = not standardized<br>5 = completely standardized | 661 | 3.84 | 0.68 |
| 30 | Decentralization (5) | 1 = not at all<br>5 = to a great extent | 658 | 2.33 | 0.84 |
| 32 | Extent Use of Teams | 1 = not at all<br>5 = to a great extent | 661 | 3.03 | 1.49 |
| 33 | Team Accountability | 1 = not at all<br>5 = to a great extent | 661 | 3.03 | 1.50 |
| 37 | Dept. Heads Set Quant Goals | 1 = none<br>5 = all | 655 | 3.29 | 1.63 |
| 45 | No. of Training Methods | # checked out of 11 | 659 | 6.56 | 2.61 |
| 46 | Training Based on Needs Analysis | 1 = few<br>5 = all | 648 | 2.76 | 1.42 |
| 47 | Frequency of Training Evaluation | 1 = never<br>5 = always | 650 | 3.04 | 1.38 |
| 48 | No. of Training Topics | # checked out of 7 | 658 | 4.47 | 1.92 |
| 55 | Job Rotation Policies | 1 = no job rotation<br>2 = rotate within workgroup<br>3 = rotate across workgroups<br>4 = rotate across departments | 654 | 2.48 | 1.20 |
| 57 | Types of Recruit Data Collected | # checked out of 6 | 654 | 1.13 | 1.82 |
| 62 | Select Systems Based on Job Analysis | 1 = none<br>5 = all | 653 | 2.94 | 1.49 |
| 63 | Select Systems Validated | 1 = none<br>5 = all | 649 | 2.86 | 1.43 |
| 64 | Spend Money on Data | 1 = not at all<br>5 = to a great extent | 634 | 2.36 | 1.18 |
| 65 | Use Data for Organizational Decisions | 1 = not at all<br>5 = to a great extent | 642 | 2.93 | 1.21 |

*Note.* CATI = computer-assisted telephone interview.

factor analyses. The remainder of the sample was held out for use in confirmatory analyses. We used principal-factor analysis with a varimax rotation to examine the underlying structure of each of these three broad domains. Only cases with complete data could be included, so sample sizes were slightly different for the three factor analyses. Several solutions with different numbers of factors were examined, and one solution was chosen for each category on the basis of a scree plot of the eigenvalues, results of a parallel analysis, and the interpretability of the various solutions.

A six-factor solution was selected for Organizational Structure, and the factor pattern is shown on Table 10-11. These factors were labeled (a) Use of Teams, (b) Formalization/Standardization, (c) Information Sharing, (d) Decentralization, (e) Establishment Size/Specialization, and (f) Organization Size.

Most of the structure descriptors load on at least one of these factors, with the exception of Number of Management Levels (CATI Item 18, a measure of hierarchy), which does not correlate with any of the other structure variables. The six factors account for 40% of the total variance in these data and are highly interpretable; most of the variables load cleanly on only one factor.

Table 10-12 shows the results of the analysis of the domain of HR Systems and Practices (along with the few Goal items). The four-factor solution was selected. These factors were labeled (a) Multiple Skill Training, (b) Employee Benefits, (c) Goal Setting, and (d) High-Performance HR Practices. Table 10-13 shows the results for Organizational Values. The four-factor solution was selected, and the factors were labeled (a) People Orientation, (b) Risk Taking, (c) Attention to Detail, and (d) Stability.

**TABLE 10-9**
**Descriptive Statistics for Organizational Representative (CATI) Data: Dichotomous Organizational Context Variables**

| Item # | Item label | N | % Yes | No |
|--------|-----------|---|-------|-----|
| 13 | Downsized in Last 5 Years | 567 | 74.5 | 25.5 |
| 38 | Publicize One Quantitative Goal | 645 | 65.4 | 34.6 |
| 44 | Formal Training | 660 | 82.1 | 17.9 |
| 45a | Training Method 1: Case Studies | 528 | 52.1 | 47.9 |
| 45b | Training Method 2: Conference/Discuss | 537 | 90.1 | 9.9 |
| 45c | Training Method 3: Lectures | 537 | 84.4 | 15.6 |
| 45d | Training Method 4: Business Games | 527 | 30.6 | 69.4 |
| 45e | Training Method 5: Simulators | 537 | 20.3 | 79.7 |
| 45f | Training Method 6: Films | 540 | 88.7 | 11.3 |
| 45g | Training Method 7: Interact Videos | 530 | 40.2 | 59.8 |
| 45h | Training Method 8: Workbooks | 538 | 74.9 | 25.1 |
| 45i | Training Method 9: Role-Play | 536 | 67.4 | 32.6 |
| 45j | Training Method 10: Comput Inst | 537 | 61.5 | 38.5 |
| 45k | Training Method 11: Audio Cassettes | 534 | 53.0 | 47.0 |
| 48a | Diversity Training | 532 | 54.9 | 45.1 |
| 48b | Team Skills Training | 536 | 70.3 | 29.7 |
| 48c | Quality Control Training | 530 | 68.7 | 31.3 |
| 48d | Basic Business Training | 535 | 32.5 | 67.5 |
| 48e | Problem Solving Training | 534 | 70.6 | 29.4 |
| 48f | Leadership Training | 538 | 75.5 | 24.5 |
| 48g | Customer Service Training | 538 | 78.4 | 21.6 |
| 53 | Continuous Learning Programs | 657 | 67.1 | 32.9 |
| 54 | Financial Assist for Training | 660 | 70.0 | 30.0 |
| 56 | Formal Recruitment Plan | 656 | 43.0 | 57.0 |
| 58 | Realistic Job Previews | 654 | 39.1 | 60.9 |
| 59 | Formal Orientation Programs | 659 | 64.8 | 35.2 |
| 60 | Formal Mentoring Programs | 655 | 28.8 | 74.2 |
| 61 | Formal Selection Systems | 657 | 83.7 | 16.3 |

*Note.* CATI = computer-assisted telephone interview. Comput inst = computer-assisted instruction.

To examine relationships across these three broad domains and to determine whether the items and factors thought to be high-performance do, in fact, tend to coexist, we developed a set of unit-weighted composites based on these three within-domain factor solutions. For each factor, a composite was identified that included all variables loading .30 or greater on that factor. The few items that loaded .30 or greater on more than one factor were assigned to the factor on which the loading was the highest. Variables assigned to each composite were then standardized and summed to form composite scores. We then examined the intercorrelations among scores on these factor-based composites *across* domains. Table 10-14 presents these factor-based composite intercorrelations.

Contrary to our expectations (based on the literature), size was not strongly related to any other organizational characteristic. Measures of Establishment Size/Specialization had small correlations with the Formalization/Standardization composite ($r$ = .20), Multiple Skill Training ($r$ = .26), Employee Benefits ($r$ = .18), and Goal Setting ($r$ = .17). Organization Size correlated .20 or greater with only one other organizational context variable, Information Sharing ($r$ = .20). The factor-based composites that included variables considered high-performance did, in fact, show moderate intercorrelations. For example, Use of Teams was correlated with Information Sharing ($r$ = .34), Decentralization ($r$ = .33), Multiple Skill

Training ($r$ = .33), and Goal Setting ($r$ = .37). Also, Information Sharing was correlated with Decentralization ($r$ = .46), Multiple Skill Training ($r$ = .36), Goal Setting ($r$ = .43), and Risk Taking values ($r$ = .30).

To further assess the interrelationships among these three content domains, explore the overall structure of these data, and perhaps identify a high-performance factor across the domains, we factor analyzed the data in Table 10-14. The three-factor solution is presented in Table 10-15, and these factors were labeled (a) Organizational Values, (b) High-Performance Practices, and (c) Establishment Size.

As mentioned previously, the measures of Change in Organizational Structure were not included in the factor analyses because of missing data, so relationships between these variables and the factor-based composites were examined separately. The correlation between the two organizational change scales (Rightsizing and Reorganization) was .57. Of interest is that even though these two scales were fairly highly correlated, when correlated with the factor-based composites measuring other aspects of organizational context, the two scales showed different correlation patterns. Reorganization was positively related to Establishment Size/Specialization ($r$ = .22) and Employee Benefits ($r$ = .21). Rightsizing, however, was positively related to Decentralization ($r$ = .22), Multiple Skill Training ($r$ = .21), and Employee Benefits

**TABLE 10-10**
**Descriptive Statistics for Organizational Representative (CATI) Data: Organizational Values**

| Item # | Organizational value | N | M | SD |
|---|---|---|---|---|
| 70a | Employment Security | 653 | 5.43 | 1.47 |
| 70b | Risk Taking | 645 | 3.42 | 1.75 |
| 70c | Flexibility | 654 | 5.06 | 1.52 |
| 70d | Analytical Oriented | 646 | 4.05 | 1.75 |
| 70e | People Oriented | 657 | 5.87 | 1.32 |
| 70f | Fairness | 656 | 6.10 | 1.07 |
| 70g | Competitiveness | 656 | 5.07 | 1.69 |
| 70h | Collaboration | 650 | 5.28 | 1.44 |
| 70i | Adaptability | 656 | 5.52 | 1.26 |
| 70j | Predictability | 653 | 4.87 | 1.44 |
| 70k | Innovation | 656 | 4.95 | 1.45 |
| 70l | Social responsibility | 653 | 5.41 | 1.52 |
| 70m | Quality | 657 | 6.23 | 0.99 |
| 70n | Results Oriented | 653 | 5.76 | 1.29 |
| 70o | Tolerance | 654 | 5.52 | 1.24 |
| 70p | Taking Advantage of Opportunity | 655 | 5.42 | 1.28 |
| 70q | Customer Oriented | 655 | 6.06 | 1.37 |
| 70r | Action Oriented | 648 | 5.47 | 1.32 |
| 70s | Stability | 655 | 5.52 | 1.36 |
| 70t | Autonomy | 646 | 4.75 | 1.49 |
| 70u | Attention to Details | 656 | 5.68 | 1.15 |
| 70v | Team Oriented | 657 | 5.27 | 1.51 |
| 70w | Sharing Information Freely | 656 | 5.33 | 1.41 |
| 70x | Willing to Experiment | 655 | 4.64 | 1.52 |
| 70y | Aggressiveness | 654 | 4.90 | 1.43 |
| 70z | Precision | 653 | 5.37 | 1.22 |
| 70aa | Achievement Oriented | 656 | 5.53 | 1.30 |
| 70bb | Supportiveness | 657 | 5.73 | 1.17 |

*Note.* CATI = computer-assisted telephone interview. The values were rated on a 7-point Likert-type scale where 1 = *least characteristic* and 7 = *most characteristic.*

($r$ = .24) and negatively related to Formalization/Standardization ($r$ = −.21).

**Confirmatory factor analysis.** Using the remainder of the organizational representative sample, which was held out from the exploratory factor analyses ($n$ = 335), we conducted a second-order confirmatory factor analysis to test the hypothesis that a single higher order construct, which might be labeled "High-Performance Business Practices," could explain the relationships between several hypothesized lower order factors: Decentralization, Information Sharing, Use of Teams, Use of Data in decision making, Risk Taking values, and Multiple Skill Training. We used *LISREL VIII* (Jöreskog & Sörbom, 1993) to test this model. This model was selected in part on the basis of the exploratory factor analysis and in part on the literature and theory concerning high-performance organizations. The indicators for each of these latent variables and the factor loadings obtained in the confirmatory factor analysis are shown in Table 10-16. Figure 10-4 presents structural coefficients and fit indices for the second-order factor analysis. All structural coefficients were significant, and a relatively good fit was obtained (GFI = .92, AGFI = .90, RMSR = .06). Use of Teams had the largest loading on the higher order High-Performance factor (.60), whereas *Risk-Taking* values had the smallest loading (.37).

We also developed a "High-Performance Business Practices" factor score by first multiplying each of the six lower order factors in the above confirmatory model by its loading and then computing the mean for each factor. We then examined correlations between this composite and other more traditional organizational characteristics. The High-Performance composite did not correlate significantly with Establishment Size. However, it showed small positive relationships with the items from the CATI that measure Formalization and Standardization ($r$ = .16 and $r$ = .30, respectively) and somewhat larger relationships with Extent of Organizational Goal Setting ($r$ = .46), Goal Negotiability ($r$ = .40), and Compensation Elements and Benefits ($r$ = .31 and $r$ = .32, respectively). Of interest is that High-Performance Business Practices showed small but positive correlations with Rightsizing and Reorganization ($r$ = .11 and $r$ = .19, respectively).

## Industry Type Comparisons

Type of Industry was included in the O*NET organizational context taxonomy in part because the literature suggested that organizations from different industries differ systematically in terms of certain organizational characteristics. Thus, to obtain a preliminary assessment of the usefulness of the variables measured in the CATI for describing organizations, we compared scores on the 14 organizational-context factor-based composites for organizations from different types of industries. We used multivariate analysis of variance (MANOVA), analysis of variance, and $t$ tests to determine whether scores on the 14 factor-based organizational context composites differed significantly for organizations from eight major industries: construction, manufacturing, service, finance, retail and wholesale trade, transportation and public utilities, public administration, and high technology (U.S. Office of Management and Budget, 1987).

The MANOVA for industry type was significant, and 6 of the 14 factor-based organizational characteristics significantly differentiated among different industries. Formalization/Standardization was the highest for organizations in public administration and the lowest in wholesale and retail organizations. High-technology and finance establishments indicated the highest levels of Information Sharing, whereas construction companies showed the lowest levels. Establishment Size/Specialization was the highest for high-technology establishments and lowest for public administration and construction establishments. High technology and public administration organizations scored the highest on Employee Benefits, whereas those involved in construction scored the lowest. High-technology and finance establishments scored the highest on High-Performance HR Practices, whereas public administration establishments scored the lowest. Finally, People-Oriented Values were the most important in service and finance establishments and the least important in

**TABLE 10-11**
**Principal Factor Analysis Pattern Matrix for Organizational Representative (CATI) Data:**
**Organizational Structure**

| Item # | Item label | Factor | | | | | | Communality |
| | | F1 | F2 | F3 | F4 | F5 | F6 | |
|---|---|---|---|---|---|---|---|---|
| 6 | No. of Locations | −.01 | .03 | .00 | .03 | .73 | .09 | .54 |
| 7 | No. of Countries Do Business | .12 | −.10 | .04 | .01 | .26 | .24 | .15 |
| 8 | Full Time Organization Employees | .01 | .02 | .04 | .13 | .73 | .07 | .55 |
| 9 & 10 | Total Employees (Establishment) | −.08 | .16 | .05 | .05 | .05 | .62 | .42 |
| 18 | No. of Management Levels | .05 | .14 | −.03 | .07 | .24 | −.05 | .09 |
| 20 | No. of Formal Documents | .12 | .68 | .12 | .01 | −.01 | .28 | .57 |
| 21a | Formal 1: Employment Contracts | .17 | .20 | .19 | −.05 | −.07 | .12 | .12 |
| 21b | Formal 2: Organizational Chart | .06 | .43 | .07 | .07 | −.04 | .15 | .22 |
| 21c | Formal 3: Job Descriptions | .04 | .56 | .05 | .07 | .04 | −.03 | .33 |
| 21d | Formal 4: Procedure Manuals | .10 | .78 | .02 | .05 | .06 | −.01 | .62 |
| 21e | Formal 5: Policy Manuals | .02 | .81 | .00 | .03 | .10 | .08 | .67 |
| 22 | No. of Job Titles (Establishment) | −.11 | .12 | .05 | .06 | .07 | .59 | .38 |
| 28 | No. of Specializations (Establishment) | .08 | .10 | .23 | −.10 | −.04 | .27 | .16 |
| 29 | Standardization | .19 | .29 | .19 | .09 | .06 | −.02 | .17 |
| 30a | Decentral 1: Monitor Quality | .09 | .06 | .63 | .07 | .10 | .20 | .46 |
| 30b | Decentral 2: Work Flow | .05 | .11 | .66 | .11 | .08 | −.03 | .46 |
| 30c | Decentral 3: New Equipment | .13 | .06 | .45 | .16 | −.07 | .00 | .25 |
| 30d | Decentral 4: New Products | .16 | .09 | .57 | .21 | −.08 | .03 | .42 |
| 30e | Decentral 5: New Members | .20 | −.01 | .46 | .12 | .04 | .07 | .28 |
| 31a | Information Sharing 1: Finance | .17 | .13 | .00 | .69 | .10 | .26 | .60 |
| 31b | Information Sharing 2: Unit Finance | .20 | .07 | .04 | .68 | .07 | .23 | .57 |
| 31c | Information Sharing 3: New Tech. | .12 | .06 | .21 | .46 | .05 | −.11 | .29 |
| 31d | Information Sharing 4: Bus. Plans | .03 | .13 | .26 | .60 | .03 | −.12 | .46 |
| 31e | Information Sharing 5: Competitors | .08 | −.05 | .25 | .48 | .11 | −.07 | .32 |
| 32 | Extent Use of Teams | .76 | .15 | .22 | .06 | .07 | −.14 | .67 |
| 33 | Team Accountability | .73 | .20 | .19 | .09 | .10 | .05 | .64 |
| 34 | % Working in Teams | .76 | .07 | .08 | .05 | .10 | −.13 | .62 |
| 35a | % in Functional Teams | .73 | .03 | .08 | .07 | .14 | −.13 | .58 |
| 35b | % in Cross-Functional Teams | .62 | .09 | .12 | .07 | .01 | −.09 | .42 |
| 35c | % in Management Teams | .40 | .07 | −.03 | .14 | −.15 | .04 | .21 |
| 35d | % in Project Teams | .38 | .01 | .28 | .22 | .02 | .11 | .28 |
| 35e | % in Quality Improve Teams | .38 | .00 | .24 | .08 | −.01 | .03 | .21 |
| | % of variance | 11 | 8 | 7 | 6 | 4 | 4 | |
| | Eigenvalue | 3.38 | 2.58 | 2.15 | 2.01 | 1.34 | 1.27 | |

*Note.* N = 245. CATI = computer-assisted telephone interview. F1 = Use of Teams, F2 = Formalization/Standardization, F3 = Information Sharing, F4 = Decentralization, F5 = Establishment Size/Specialization, F6 = Organization Size.

manufacturing and public administration establishments.

# DISCUSSION

This chapter describes the taxonomy of organizational context descriptors included in the O*NET content model and presents the justification for the constructs and measures included. Analyses of the prototype data, conducted to evaluate the usefulness of these descriptors for describing jobs and organizations, generally support the reliability and validity of the organizational context descriptors.

## Limitations

Before discussing the main conclusions of our results, however, the limitations of the incumbent sample used in this study should be noted. Most of the analyses reported here assess the internal validity of the descriptors and scales. The findings provide preliminary evidence for the reliability and meaningfulness of the descriptive organizational context information. However, cross-domain and other external analyses are needed to provide evidence for the external validity of the measures.

## Reliability of the Organizational Context Descriptors

Data concerning several of the organizational context descriptors in the O*NET content model have traditionally been collected using scales. The internal consistency reliability of the scales included in both the incumbent and organizational representative surveys was generally quite good and comparable to that obtained using similar scales in previous research (see Table 10-3).

Interrater reliability could be assessed only for the data collected from incumbents, and these data were assessed in terms of reliability for describing occupations, reliability for describing organizations, and reliability for describing occupation within organization cells. As expected, individual descriptor reliabilities were generally highest for describing occu-

**TABLE 10-12**
**Principal Factor Analysis Pattern Matrix for Organizational Representative (CATI) Data:**
**Human Resources Practices**

| Item # | Item label | Factor | | | | Communality |
|---|---|---|---|---|---|---|
| | | F1 | F2 | F3 | F4 | |
| 36 | Formal mission statement | .46 | .37 | .17 | .05 | .37 |
| 37 | Dept heads set quantitative goals | .29 | .21 | .52 | .05 | .40 |
| 38 | Publicize one quantitative goal | .23 | .22 | .53 | .19 | .42 |
| 39 | % managers set goals | .17 | .11 | .72 | .17 | .59 |
| 40 | % managers negotiate goals | .08 | .14 | .74 | .06 | .58 |
| 41 | % nonmanagers set goals | .23 | .10 | .58 | .34 | .51 |
| 42 | % nonmanagers negotiate goals | .13 | .01 | .62 | .13 | .42 |
| 43 | No. of performance reviews in 2 years | .17 | −.01 | .21 | .14 | .09 |
| 45a | Training method 1: Case studies | .56 | .27 | .13 | −.02 | .41 |
| 45b | Training method 2: Conf/group | .78 | .12 | .18 | −.01 | .66 |
| 45c | Training method 3: Lectures | .76 | .14 | .17 | −.05 | .64 |
| 45d | Training method 4: Business games | .41 | .04 | .06 | .28 | .25 |
| 45e | Training method 5: Simulators | .26 | .05 | .04 | .11 | .08 |
| 45f | Training method 6: Film/video | .79 | .21 | .09 | −.01 | .68 |
| 45g | Training method 7: Interact videos | .49 | .14 | .07 | .10 | .28 |
| 45h | Training method 8: Workbooks | .66 | .16 | .12 | .10 | .48 |
| 45i | Training method 9: Role-play | .73 | .10 | .17 | .01 | .57 |
| 45j | Training method 10: Comput Inst | .53 | .19 | .20 | .12 | .38 |
| 45k | Training method 11: Audio Cassettes | .49 | .25 | .15 | −.07 | .33 |
| 46 | Training based on needs analysis | .73 | .02 | .20 | .09 | .57 |
| 47 | Frequency of training evaluation | .79 | .10 | .15 | .00 | .66 |
| 48a | Diversity training | .57 | .18 | .18 | .06 | .39 |
| 48b | Team training | .71 | .08 | .19 | .11 | .56 |
| 48c | Quality control training | .64 | .01 | .10 | .07 | .43 |
| 48d | Basic business training | .38 | .04 | .08 | .19 | .19 |
| 48e | Problem solving training | .75 | .09 | .11 | .04 | .59 |
| 48f | Leadership training | .79 | .15 | .11 | −.03 | .66 |
| 48g | Customer service training | .64 | −.02 | .14 | .12 | .44 |
| 49b | % attend one training course | .24 | .22 | .21 | .04 | .15 |
| 49c | % attend two+ training courses | .66 | .02 | .00 | −.08 | .44 |
| 50a | % get quality control training | .42 | .22 | .06 | .16 | .26 |
| 53 | Continuous learning programs | .26 | .12 | .12 | .31 | .19 |
| 54 | Financial assist for training | .24 | .38 | .16 | −.02 | .23 |
| 55 | Job rotation policies | .27 | .06 | .14 | .43 | .28 |
| 57 | Types of recruit data collected | .41 | .13 | .14 | .30 | .30 |
| 58 | Realistic job previews | .50 | .11 | .13 | .21 | .32 |
| 62 | Select systems based on job analysis | .43 | .10 | .06 | .25 | .26 |
| 63 | Select systems validated | .45 | .01 | .09 | .28 | .29 |
| 66 | % pay adjusted on evaluate studies | .16 | .11 | .10 | .46 | .26 |
| 67 | % Pay Adjusted on Comparisons | .27 | .25 | .08 | .29 | .23 |
| 68a | % w/ Salary | .05 | .41 | .05 | .00 | .18 |
| 68b | % w/ Profit Sharing | .02 | .31 | .07 | .36 | .23 |
| 68c | % w/ Skill-Based Pay | .03 | .01 | .05 | .40 | .16 |
| 68d | % w/Indiv Perform-Based Pay | −.05 | .11 | .00 | .52 | .28 |
| 68e | % w/ Team Perform-Based Pay | −.04 | .03 | .08 | .46 | .22 |
| 68f | % w/Custm Satis-Based Pay | −.02 | −.15 | .10 | .58 | .37 |
| 68g | % w/ Seniority-Based Pay | .08 | −.01 | .07 | −.05 | .01 |
| 68h | % w/ Hay Points | .07 | .22 | .07 | .17 | .08 |
| 69a | % w/ Stock Options | .11 | .18 | .04 | .25 | .11 |
| 69b | % w/ Retirement Plan | .16 | .76 | .11 | .01 | .62 |
| 69c | % w/ Medical Insurance | .10 | .83 | .03 | .04 | .69 |
| 69d | % w/ Life Insurance | .11 | .84 | −.01 | .06 | .73 |
| 69e | % w/ Disability Insurance | .19 | .64 | .07 | .09 | .46 |
| 69f | % w/ Flex Time | .02 | −.22 | −.02 | .33 | .16 |
| 69g | % w/ Day Care | .14 | .03 | .16 | .01 | .04 |
| 69h | % w/ Paid Vacation | .11 | .61 | .08 | .08 | .39 |
| | % of variance | 19 | 8 | 6 | 5 | |
| | Eigenvalue | 10.63 | 4.22 | 3.06 | 2.66 | |

*Note.* $N = 256$. CATI = computer-assisted telephone interview. F1 = Multiple Skill Training, F2 = Employee Benefits, F3 = Goal Setting, F4 = High Performance Human Resources Practices.

pation within organization cells, suggesting that most descriptors capture both organizational and occupational differences. In addition, the majority of the descriptors showed better reliability for describing occupations than for describing organizations. Only a few elements of organizational context, as rated by job incumbents, were affected more by the incumbents' organizational affiliation than by their occupation (e.g., Number of Reorganizations [D24], Number of Changes in Job Duties [D25]).

The majority of the descriptors included in the incumbent questionnaire showed adequate interrater

**TABLE 10-13**
**Principal Factor Analysis Pattern Matrix for Organizational Representative (CATI) Data: Organizational Values**

| Item # | Item label | Factor | | | | Communality |
|--------|-----------|--------|--------|--------|--------|-------------|
| | | F1 | F2 | F3 | F4 | |
| 70a | Security of Employment | .07 | .05 | .08 | .54 | .31 |
| 70b | Risk-Taking | .04 | −.10 | .42 | −.05 | .19 |
| 70c | Flexibility | .56 | −.07 | .20 | .10 | .37 |
| 70d | Analytical Orientation | .08 | .22 | .47 | .02 | .27 |
| 70e | People Orientation | .61 | .18 | .11 | .04 | .42 |
| 70f | Fairness | .49 | .30 | .11 | .25 | .40 |
| 70g | Competitiveness | .05 | .16 | .51 | −.03 | .29 |
| 70h | Collaboration | .54 | .16 | .18 | .09 | .36 |
| 70i | Adaptability | .60 | .18 | .16 | .18 | .45 |
| 70j | Predictability | .09 | .19 | .00 | .54 | .34 |
| 70k | Innovation | .34 | .26 | .47 | .11 | .42 |
| 70l | Social Responsibility | .40 | .31 | .14 | .27 | .35 |
| 70m | Quality | .44 | .53 | .09 | .21 | .53 |
| 70n | Results Orientation | .25 | .57 | .32 | .14 | .51 |
| 70o | Tolerance | .56 | .32 | −.04 | .22 | .47 |
| 70p | Taking Advantage of Opportunity | .30 | .39 | .52 | .07 | .52 |
| 70q | Customer Service Orientation | .43 | .19 | .12 | −.12 | .25 |
| 70r | Action Orientation | .32 | .53 | .33 | −.01 | .48 |
| 70s | Stability | .29 | .20 | −.02 | .66 | .56 |
| 70t | Autonomy | .25 | .18 | .34 | .36 | .34 |
| 70u | Attention to Detail | .25 | .63 | .06 | .28 | .54 |
| 70v | Team Orientation | .50 | .30 | .13 | .22 | .41 |
| 70w | Sharing Information Freely | .54 | .16 | .15 | .31 | .44 |
| 70x | Willing to Experiment | .37 | .01 | .49 | .17 | .41 |
| 70y | Aggressiveness | .09 | .17 | .59 | .16 | .40 |
| 70z | Precision | .20 | .60 | .14 | .35 | .55 |
| 70aa | Achievement Orientation | .17 | .59 | .38 | .25 | .59 |
| 70bb | Supportiveness | .60 | .34 | −.02 | .43 | .66 |
| | % of variance | 15 | 11 | 9 | 8 | |
| | Eigenvalue | 4.15 | 3.07 | 2.45 | 2.14 | |

*Note.* N = 295. F1 = People Orientation, F2 = Risk Taking, F3 = Attention to Detail, F4 = Stability.

reliability for describing occupations (16 above .80 for 30 raters, 19 above .70). The fact that the reliabilities were not higher may be because organizational context was not as immediate a part of incumbents' day-to-day working environments, or perhaps it was because many of the descriptors in this domain are quite abstract. Only a few of the organizational context characteristics in the incumbent questionnaire had generally poor interrater reliability (i.e., Task Identity [D3], Feedback [D6], Organizational Values [D14–17], leader Consideration [D18], and Visionary Leadership [D20]). It is interesting to note that Task Identity and Feedback both had good internal consistency reliability. Perhaps levels of identity and feedback are specific to individual positions rather than generalizable within occupations.

In general, these findings suggest that the manifestations of organizational context characteristics vary across occupations. The same organizational structure, for example, may be experienced differently by a secretary, an engineer, or a top executive. It seems reasonable to hypothesize that the immediate work context of job incumbents (i.e., their job demands, requirements, characteristics) has a large impact on their experience of most organizational context characteristics. The sample available for the analyses described here did not allow us to systematically assess the extent to which respondents' occupations affected their perceptions of organizational characteristics, because, at best, data from incumbents in only a few occupations were available for any given organization.

The theoretical implications of these findings are even more far-reaching. The observed interactions between organizational and occupational effects highlight the shortcomings of most organizational and occupational theories. Traditionally, organizational theories do not include occupational variables, nor do they propose how organizational variables will affect individuals who are working in different jobs. Similarly, occupational theories typically ignore the effects of organizational context on job requirements and characteristics. The findings in the present research highlight the need for more integration between these two disciplines.

## Differentiating Among Organizations and Occupations

In general, the organizational context descriptors showed sensible differences between organizations as well as between occupations. In terms of organization differences, we found expected differences between organizations representing different types of industries. For example, the results indicated that some of the organizational context descriptors show systematic differences between high-technology and low-technology (e.g., manufacturing, transportation, construction, retail) establishments. Specifically, high-

**TABLE 10-14**

**Factor-Based Composite Intercorrelations for Organizational Representative (CATI) Data: Organizational Context**

| Composite label | 1 | 2 | 3 | 4 | 5 | 6 | 7 | 8 | 9 | 10 | 11 | 12 | 13 | 14 |
|---|---|---|---|---|---|---|---|---|---|---|---|---|---|---|
| 1. Use of Teams | — | | | | | | | | | | | | | |
| 2. Formalization/Standardization | .15 | — | | | | | | | | | | | | |
| 3. Info. Sharing | .34 | .12 | — | | | | | | | | | | | |
| 4. Decentralization | .33 | .16 | .46 | — | | | | | | | | | | |
| 5. Establishment Size | .08 | .20 | .08 | .04 | — | | | | | | | | | |
| 6. Organization Size | .10 | .10 | .20 | .14 | .05 | — | | | | | | | | |
| 7. Skill Training | .33 | .38 | .36 | .34 | .26 | .13 | — | | | | | | | |
| 8. Employee Benefits | .17 | .12 | .28 | .28 | .18 | .10 | .37 | — | | | | | | |
| 9. Goal Setting | .37 | .17 | .43 | .31 | .17 | .06 | .39 | .25 | — | | | | | |
| 10. High Performance HR | .26 | .00 | .27 | .20 | .02 | .01 | .14 | .14 | .28 | — | | | | |
| 11. People Orientation | .35 | .10 | .30 | .19 | −.05 | .08 | .21 | .07 | .34 | .24 | — | | | |
| 12. Risk Taking | .22 | .05 | .30 | .24 | .05 | .10 | .22 | .17 | .30 | .31 | .66 | — | | |
| 13. Attention to Detail | .26 | .09 | .30 | .22 | .05 | .05 | .27 | .30 | .35 | .26 | .69 | .73 | — | |
| 14. Stability | .17 | .05 | .06 | .02 | .00 | .01 | .09 | .05 | .18 | .11 | .59 | .39 | .57 | — |

*Note.* $N = 288$. CATI = computer-assisted telephone interview. Correlation coefficients greater than .08 are significant at the $p < .05$ level.

technology establishments reported more Information Sharing, Specialization, Benefit Elements, and High-Performance HR practices than did low-technology establishments.

The organizational context data collected from incumbents showed a systematic and sensible pattern of mean differences across jobs. For example, workers in professional and managerial jobs (e.g., General Managers and Top Executives, Computer Programmers) reported, on average, more Empowerment (D1), Autonomy (D2), Role Conflict (D7), Decentralization (D13), and a larger number of Training Topics (D28) than did those in more traditionally blue collar jobs (e.g., Janitors and Cleaners, Maintenance Repairers). Also, Police Patrol Officers reported the lowest average levels of Empowerment (D1), Role Negotiability (D10), and Decentralization (D13). These results could be viewed as reflecting two patterns of relationships between occupations and organizational context: Occupation level exhibits

a positive relationship with some of the organizational context descriptors and, as suggested before, job demands/activities/characteristics often overpower or limit the impact of the organizational context.

## Describing High-Performance Organizations

The growing interest in high-performance organizations was at the core of the development of the O*NET content model for the organizational context domain. One of the goals in this area was to describe this high-performance phenomenon and collect information concerning the business practices of these high-performance organizations. Indeed, the exploratory and confirmatory analyses of the organizational representative data provide evidence for the existence of a high-performance syndrome or phenomenon. Many of the characteristics of high-performance organizations identified in the literature

**TABLE 10-15**

**Principal Factor Analysis Pattern Matrix for Organizational Representative (CATI) Data: Factor-Based Composites**

| Composite label | Factor | | | Communality |
|---|---|---|---|---|
| | F1 | F2 | F3 | |
| People Orientation | .74 | .25 | .00 | .61 |
| Attention to Detail | .73 | .19 | .15 | .59 |
| Risk-Taking | .62 | .36 | .06 | .51 |
| Stability | .55 | −.06 | −.03 | .31 |
| Goal Setting | .15 | .54 | .27 | .39 |
| Information Sharing | .09 | .51 | .32 | .37 |
| Use of Teams | .22 | .46 | .22 | .31 |
| High Performance HR Practices | .15 | .46 | −.07 | .23 |
| Multiple Skill Training | .20 | .19 | .58 | .41 |
| Formalization/Standardization | .06 | .11 | .50 | .27 |
| Employee Benefits | .01 | .24 | .43 | .25 |
| Establishment Size | −.05 | −.08 | .41 | .18 |
| Decentralization | .06 | .33 | .38 | .26 |
| Organization Size | −.04 | .15 | .19 | .06 |
| % of variance | 13.71 | 10.36 | 9.79 | |
| Eigenvalue | 1.92 | 1.45 | 1.37 | |

*Note.* $N = 288$. F1 = Organizational Values, F2 = High-Performance Practices, F3 = Establishment Size. CATI = computer-assisted telephone interview.

**TABLE 10-16**
**Factor Loadings for Second-Order Confirmatory Factor Analysis: Organizational Context**

| | | Factor | | | | | |
|---|---|---|---|---|---|---|---|
| Item # | Indicator label | F1 | F2 | F3 | F4 | F5 | F6 |
| 32 | Extent Use of Teams | .96 | | | | | |
| 33 | Team Accountability | 1.00 | | | | | |
| 34 | % Working in Teams | .85 | | | | | |
| 30a | Decentral 1: Monitor Quality | | .89 | | | | |
| 30b | Decentral 2: Work Flow | | 1.00 | | | | |
| 30c | Decentral 3: New Equipment | | .90 | | | | |
| 30d | Decentral 4: New Products | | .95 | | | | |
| 31a, 31b | Information Sharing 1: Finance | | | | | | |
| 31c | Information Sharing 3: New Tech | | | .71 | | | |
| 31d | Information Sharing 4: Bus. Plans | | | .68 | | | |
| 31e | Information Sharing 5: Competitors | | | .68 | | | |
| 70b, 70k, 70x | Risk-Taking Values 1: Innovation | | | | 1.00 | | |
| 70g, 70p, 70q, 70r, 70y, 70aa | Risk-Taking Values 2: Competitiveness | | | | .70 | | |
| 70c, 70t | Risk-Taking Values 1: Autonomy | | | | .59 | | |
| 46, 47 | Use Data to Develop & Evaluate Training | | | | | 1.00 | |
| 62, 63 | Use Data to Develop Selection Sys | | | | | .87 | |
| 64, 65 | Collect/Use Data for Org Decisions | | | | | .67 | |
| 55 | Job Rotation Policies | | | | | | .95 |
| 48 | No. of Training Topics | | | | | | 1.00 |

*Note.* N = 326. F1 = Use of Teams, F2 = Decentralization, F3 = Information Sharing, F4 = Risk-taking Values, F5 = Use Data in Decision Making, F6 = Multiple Skill Training.

on high performance (Galbraith, Lawler, et al., 1993; Lawler, 1992; U.S. DOL, 1994) appear to be captured by the descriptors in this domain, and the covariance in these descriptors can be accounted for by a single higher order factor that might be labeled "High-Performance Practices."

The confirmatory analyses supported the hypothesis that the high-performance phenomenon includes six organizational elements: Decentralization, Information Sharing, Use of Teams, Use of Data in decision making, Risk-Taking values, and Multiple Skill Training, which are consistent with Westat's literature-based list of high-performance charac-

teristics (Westat, 1994). This constellation of high-performance practices also had positive relationships with other more traditional organizational constructs such as Standardization, numbers of Benefit and Compensation Elements, Extent of Goal Setting, and Goal Negotiability.

## Structure of the Organizational Context Data

The organizational representative data provided strong support for the O*NET organizational con-

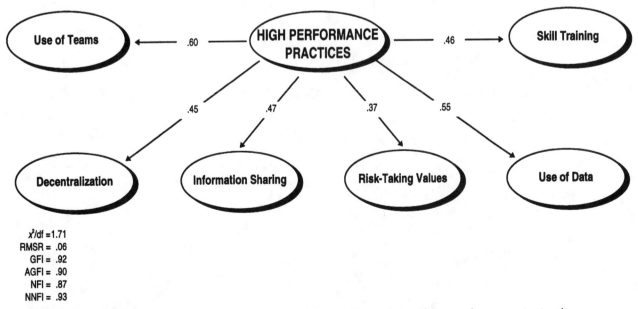

**FIGURE 10-4.** Model and structural coefficients for second-order confirmatory factor analysis: organizational context.

text taxonomy. Within the HR Practices and Structure categories, the factors that were identified resemble the constructs included in the O*NET organizational context taxonomy (Arad et al., 1995). The four Organizational Values factors identified (i.e., People Oriented, Risk Taking, Attention to Detail, and Stability) make a great deal of sense and partially replicate previous findings (e.g., O'Reilly et al., 1991). Factor analysis results for the incumbent data were also consistent with the O*NET organizational context taxonomy. When occupational-level data were used, four meaningful factors were identified: Employee Empowerment, Team Structure, Task-Oriented Leadership, and Skill Variety; and there is a great deal of overlap between these factors and the categories included in the taxonomy.

## Summary

The O*NET organizational context descriptors and taxonomy can be used to describe organizations and differentiate between high-performance organizations and more traditional organizations. This tax-onomy also provides information that is likely to be of interest to job seekers and may be useful in enhancing the quality and accuracy of any occupational classification system that is developed from the data collected for the entire content model. The organizational context provides information necessary to understand variations in jobs across organizations.

Results of the prototype analyses show that the O*NET organizational-context descriptors yield data that are adequately reliable, have an empirical structure that supports the O*NET content model, and appear to have potential for describing both occupations and organizations. Future research aimed at better understanding relationships between organizational and occupational variables would be extremely useful. This could be done by comparing either the same occupations across organizations or different occupations within the same organization. The survey developed to measure organizational context in the O*NET also provides an excellent starting point for future research aimed at understanding the relationships between high-performance business practices and other organizational characteristics and organizational effectiveness and success.

# Abilities

EDWIN A. FLEISHMAN, DAVID P. COSTANZA, AND
JOANNE MARSHALL-MIES

This chapter describes a comprehensive taxonomic system for describing and classifying jobs in terms of the abilities required to perform these jobs effectively. The taxonomic system provided is comprehensive in its coverage of the cognitive, psychomotor, physical, and sensory–perceptual domains of human abilities and is applicable to the full range of jobs found in the world economy. Specifically, the chapter provides the conceptual background of the taxonomic system, the developmental background of this taxonomy, and the development of the measurement system that uses the taxonomy in assessing the ability requirements of jobs. The system is evaluated in terms of its reliability, validity, and utility.

## DEFINITIONS

### Ability

The term *ability* is commonly used in everyday language as well as in discussions among psychologists, educators, vocational counselors, human resource managers and planners, and other specialists. However, its exact meaning is seldom explicated. Most recently, Carroll (1993, pp. 1–9) has discussed the issues with regard to defining the term *ability*. These issues include, In what sense does ability imply "potential?" Is ability a matter of degree? To what extent may ability vary within an individual and across different individuals? How general is ability (does it apply only to single performances, to some class of performances, or to all possible performances)? To what extent is an ability to be construed as a "trait" of an individual. Many of these conceptual issues were dealt with in earlier work on taxonomic issues in describing human abilities (see, e.g., Fleishman, 1967a, 1972a, 1975c, 1982).

Both Carroll and Fleishman define abilities as relatively enduring attributes of an individual's capability for performing a particular range of different tasks. Abilities are regarded as traits in that they exhibit some degree of stability over relatively long periods of time. It is recognized, however, that abilities

may develop over time and with exposure to multiple situations (Snow & Lohman, 1984).

### Competency

Recently, the term *competencies* has come into use to describe individual attributes related to quality of work performance (see e.g., Corts & Gowing, 1992; McClelland, 1973; Spencer, McClelland, & Spencer, 1994). A competency has been defined as "an underlying characteristic of an individual which is causally related to effective or superior performance in a job" (Boyatzis, 1982). This definition is, of course, consistent with our definition of ability. However, lists of competencies often contain a mixture of knowledges, skills, abilities, motivation, beliefs, values, and interests. In the extensive work supported by the Secretary's Commission on Achieving Necessary Skills (SCANS, 1991; Peterson 1992a), the term *competencies* was ultimately used to refer to "functional skills," which reflect what people in a wide range of jobs actually do at work (Peterson, 1992a).

### Skill

The distinction between abilities and skills is often made (see, e.g., Bilodeau, 1966; Fleishman, 1966, 1967b, 1972a). An ability is a general trait of an individual that is inferred from the relationships among performances of individuals observed across a range of different tasks. Skills are more dependent on learning and represent the product of training in particular tasks. Skills are more situational and tend to improve. The development of a given skill (e.g., airplane piloting) is predicated, in part, on the individual's possession of relevant underlying abilities (e.g., spatial orientation, multilimb coordination). These underlying abilities are related to the rate of acquisition and final levels of performance that a person can achieve in particular skills (see Ackerman, 1988; Fleishman, 1966, 1967a, 1972a).

## Task

Tasks have been defined in many ways. Elsewhere, Fleishman (1982) and Fleishman and Quaintance (1984) have described the different conceptual bases for defining tasks. Thus, R. B. Miller (1967) stated, "A task is any set of activities, occurring at the same time, sharing some common purpose that is recognized by the task performer" (p. 11). Wheaton (1973) proposed that a task reflects an organized set of responses to a specified stimulus situation intended to bring about the attainment of a goal state. This definition of a task is similar to one proposed by Hackman (1968) and McCormick (1979) and, more recently, by Carroll (1993), who defined a task as an activity in which a person engages in order to achieve a specifiable objective or result. Thus, there is a convergence among this set of definitions.

Of particular interest in the present project is the relation between tasks and abilities. Tasks can be described in terms of the abilities required to perform them. The performance of any task requires certain abilities, if performance is to be maximized. Tasks requiring the same ability or a similar group of abilities would be placed in the same category. The use of empirical information on the relationships among performances of individuals performing different tasks allows us to capitalize on knowledge we already possess concerning the basic underlying abilities (Carroll, 1993).

## STRUCTURE OF HUMAN ABILITIES

Much of our knowledge about the identification of human abilities comes from programmatic factor analysis research. Critical questions have concerned the *generality* of the constructs used to describe individual differences in human abilities. As has been discussed elsewhere, constructs such as "mental abilities," "motor abilities," "problem solving ability," "decision making ability," and "agility" have turned out to be too broad; the tasks required by such broad categories are too diverse to yield high correlations between performances of these tasks. Factor analyses of the correlations among performances within these domains typically yield somewhat more narrowly defined abilities (see e.g., Carroll, 1993; Ekstrom, French, & Harmon, 1976; Guilford & Hoepfner, 1971; Fleishman, 1964, 1972a). Similarly, expressions like "athletic ability" and "musical ability" are often used, but it is known that there are a number of separate constructs that better define several different abilities involved in the tasks that make up these broad activities. However, characterizing an individual as having the ability to "lift barbells of a given weight" or to "solve quadratic equations of a given complexity" yields information that is too specific and not very descriptive of an ability trait that extends to performance in a variety of tasks requiring the same underlying ability.

The ability categories used in the present project largely come from factor analyses of the intercorrelations among performances on tasks within several broad domains of human performance (e.g., cognitive, psychomotor, physical, sensory-perceptual). The emphasis in this project is on abilities identified in programmatic research and on abilities replicated in many different studies. It is recognized that the study of human abilities has a long history and that a number of alternative factor analytic models and theories regarding the structure of human abilities have been proposed (e.g., Cattell, 1971; Gustafsson, 1988; Guilford, 1985; Holzinger & Swineford, 1939; Horn, 1988; Spearman, 1923; Thurstone, 1938; Vernon, 1961).

Carroll (1993) has recently reviewed these programs and other historical developments in the factor analysis of human cognitive abilities. Structural issues often involve the presence and nature of a "general cognitive ability," the importance of ability factors found among subgroups of performances relative to such a general ability, and the existence and nature of hierarchical structures that relate general and more narrow ability categories. Thus, Spearman's hierarchy (Spearman, 1931) emphasized a general factor ("g"); Cattell and Horn's (1978) work stressed broader group factors (e.g., fluid and crystallized intelligence); and the work of Thurstone (1938) and Guilford (1985) emphasized a larger number of more narrowly defined abilities spanning a more limited range of performances (e.g., numerical and verbal abilities, inductive reasoning).

It should be pointed out that hierarchical models investigated in previous work have been largely confined to performance in the cognitive areas of human performance. Carroll's (1993) recent review has proposed a hierarchical theory of cognitive abilities, recognizing abilities classified at three strata: (a) numerous, narrow first-stratum factors; (b) a smaller number of broader, second-order factors; and (c) a single general factor at the third stratum. He has also shown the difficulties and limitations in designing and carrying out hierarchical factor analysis studies to adequately name and define general and second-order factors and in matching these factors across studies.

In this chapter, the ability taxonomy adopted falls into the first stratum of Carroll's system. The abilities in the taxonomy cover a broad spectrum of performances likely to be found in the world of work and include cognitive, psychomotor, physical, and sensory-perceptual abilities. Most of the abilities at this level have been identified in programmatic research and replicated across many studies. Furthermore, operational definitions of each of these abilities have been developed, linkages of job tasks with each ability have been established, and a methodology has been developed for evaluating jobs in terms of their requirements for these abilities. And, for the most part, measures to assess each of these abilities have been developed and specified (see Fleishman & Reilly, 1992b).

## CRITERIA FOR AN ABILITY REQUIREMENTS TAXONOMY

Earlier, in their book *Taxonomies of Human Performance: The Description of Human Tasks,* Fleishman and Quaintance (1984) reviewed the conceptual and methodological issues in developing taxonomies of human performance. Criteria for evaluating such systems were identified, with an emphasis on the utility of alternative classifications for describing human task performance for a variety of purposes. More recently, Fleishman and Mumford (1991) described the relevance of these issues to problems of describing and classifying jobs and evaluated the ability requirements approach and measurement system (Fleishman, 1975a, 1975b, 1975c) by applying the evaluative criteria previously developed. The present chapter reviews the ability requirements approach in the context of developing O*NET.

To be optimally effective, any classification of descriptors must meet several criteria. The descriptors should be composed of constructs linking job task characteristics with the abilities required for effective task performance. The system for describing jobs should also be grounded in a programmatic research base and include a reliable measurement system demonstrating internal and external validity. The system should have demonstrated utility for integrating eclectic information into a useful database. Use of the database should improve predictions about human performance. Additionally, the system must be user-friendly in terms of format, accessibility, terminology, and time and effort requirements.

These criteria for a classification system describing ability requirements were originally proposed by Fleishman and Quaintance (1984). Although it is most likely true that no one system for describing abilities will meet all of the requirements for O*NET, the ability-requirements taxonomy developed by Fleishman and his colleagues provides a foundation that meets several of the outlined criteria. The taxonomy has a research base spanning nearly 40 years and includes psychomotor, physical, cognitive, and sensory–perceptual constructs. The job analysis measurement system based on this taxonomy, called the Fleishman-Job Analysis Scales (F-JAS; Fleishman, 1975b, 1992a), now has a long history of use and evaluation for jobs in industry, state and federal government agencies, and military occupational specialties (for one review, see Fleishman, 1988). The system has been successfully used in nationwide job analysis studies (e.g., Landy, 1992). To further facilitate their use in large-scale administration, these scales have undergone some modifications to suit the specific purposes of O*NET.

## DEVELOPMENT OF THE ABILITY REQUIREMENTS TAXONOMY

Ability identification within a subarea of human task performance usually begins by administering representative tasks to a sample of subjects. The tasks are not chosen haphazardly but rather are specifically designed to address certain inferences about the hypothesized ability categories underlying performance on these tasks. The correlations among the tasks are then computed and subsequently factor-analyzed to identify clusters of tasks requiring common abilities. This information then serves as a basis for additional hypothesis generation, and further studies are conducted to sharpen the categories' definitions and boundaries, as well as to identify the range of tasks encompassed by the category definitions.

Later studies often impose variations in the tasks to explore the relationships among the tasks and ability categories. Marker tests or reference measures are included to help identify task and ability parameters. The ultimate objective is to identify the most comprehensive but parsimonious set of relatively independent ability categories that are the most useful and meaningful for describing human performance on the widest range of tasks within an ability domain. This approach is illustrated by Fleishman's programmatic work in the areas of physical and psychomotor task performance (for reviews, see Fleishman, 1964, 1972b). The initial steps involved detailed reviews of the relevant factor analytic literature for empirically derived ability categories that might be very useful in describing human task performance (see, e.g., Fleishman, 1953a; Nicks & Fleishman, 1962). Subsequent research programs within each area involved a series of interlocking experimental and factor analytic studies involving hundreds of tasks. Particular task batteries were administered to 200–400 participants for factor analytic study. Experimental-correlational studies were designed to introduce variations in the task requirements aimed at sharpening, limiting, or broadening initial factor definitions.

Experimental studies of the type described above have been conducted over many years, and this work has been described elsewhere in great detail (see, e.g., Fleishman, 1954, 1957, 1958, 1964, 1966, 1967a, 1967b, 1972b; Fleishman & Ellison, 1962; Fleishman & Hempel, 1956; Hempel & Fleishman, 1955; Myers, Gebhardt, Crump, & Fleishman, 1993; Parker & Fleishman, 1960). In short, a total of 10 psychomotor and 9 physical abilities were found to account for the preponderance of variance in performance on several hundred different kinds of tasks.

Under a project supported by the U.S. Defense Advanced Research Projects Agency, the taxonomy was expanded to include cognitive and sensory–perceptual categories (Fleishman, 1975b; Theologus & Fleishman, 1973; Theologus, Romashko, & Fleishman, 1973). The fundamental sources for these abilities were Thurstone's work in primary abilities (Thurstone, 1947), Guilford's structure of intellect model (Guilford, 1967), work being conducted at the Educational Testing Service (French, 1951; French, Ekstrom, & Price, 1963), research in the Air Force aptitude research program (Guilford, 1947), and more recent work (see later discussion). Nineteen additional abilities were added, based on the criterion that each category had been identified in at least 10 studies.

Subsequently, the taxonomy was reviewed and refined to ensure comprehensive coverage of all ability domains. The physical, psychomotor, cognitive, and sensory–perceptual abilities were combined into a single list, and definitions were written for each. This provisional list was reviewed by psychologists in a series of discussions and interviews. Feedback from the reviewers identified three areas needing further improvement: (a) some definitions were too vague; (b) additional examples of the ability categories were needed; and (c) the ability list was not comprehensive enough. Hence, an effort was made to clarify the definitions and include more task examples for each category. An expanded review of the experimental and measurement fields, together with more recent reviews (Carroll, 1976; Ekstrom, French & Harman, 1976, 1979; Harman, 1975; Horn, 1976; Peterson & Bownas, 1982), led to the inclusion of additional categories that seemed applicable to human task performance. Some of these, such as time sharing and selective attention, had not yet been widely studied. The resulting list of 52 abilities composed the Ability Requirements Taxonomy (Fleishman, 1975c) that was incorporated into the *Manual for Ability Requirements Scales (MARS;* Fleishman, 1975a, 1975b) and in a later version called the Fleishman Job Analysis Survey (*F-JAS*) Fleishman, 1992a, 1992b. Table 11-1 provides a list of these abilities. Complete definitions are provided in the *Handbook of Human Abilities: Definitions, Measurements, and Job Task Requirements* (Fleishman & Reilly, 1992b) and the *Administrator's Guide for the Fleishman Job Analysis Survey (F-JAS;* Fleishman & Reilly, 1992a). Table 11-1 also provides adaptations of these ability definitions for use in the present O*NET effort.

Table 11-1 has arranged these ability constructs into a three-level hierarchical system. At the most general level, we have clustered the abilities into the four general categories represented: cognitive (21 abilities), psychomotor (10 abilities), physical (9 abilities), and sensory (12 abilities). Within each of these four categories, we have identified intermediate levels.

The hierarchy is mainly provided as an aid in conceptualizing the 52 different abilities represented in the ability requirements taxonomy. This hierarchy is not meant to conform to the results of any particular hierarchical factor analysis. However, the hierarchy of cognitive abilities is consistent with some previous hierarchical models developed in the cognitive domain (see Carroll, 1993). The hierarchy within the physical ability category is consistent with the conceptualization of J. Hogan (1991), although she eventually prefers to use the more analytical first-level physical abilities (Fleishman, 1964) in the description of jobs. The psychomotor hierarchy is based on correlational information from Fleishman's studies (see 1972b), although no factor analysis of the correlations between primary ability factors has been carried

out. Under the sensory category, the cluster of visual abilities is separate from a cluster of auditory and speech abilities, which is consistent with recent reviews of these areas (Carroll, 1993, chaps. 8 and 9).

# DEVELOPMENT OF THE ABILITY REQUIREMENTS MEASUREMENT SYSTEM

The next phase of the programmatic effort entailed developing a measurement system for evaluating the ability requirement levels of various jobs and job tasks using this ability taxonomy. Procedures that were followed in constructing the measurement rating format are described in detail in Fleishman (1975b), Fleishman and Mumford (1988, 1991), and Fleishman and Quaintance (1984). Initially, descriptions of three laboratory tasks and tasks from three jobs were presented to a panel of 18 psychologists specializing in human performance, psychometrics, and industrial psychology (Theologus & Fleishman, 1973; Theologus, Romashko, & Fleishman, 1973). Using the ability definitions and a rating scale format, the raters were asked to evaluate the level of each ability required for adequate task performance. Task ratings, when compared with task factor loadings on the ability categories from previous factor analytic studies, supported the feasibility of this procedure. Furthermore, relatively high interrater reliabilities were found. Follow-up interviews with the raters suggested that clearer instructions and more precise ability definitions might be further sources of improvement.

The appropriate revisions were made, and 57 psychologists (32 psychometricians and 25 psychologists from varying specialties) were presented with the tasks and ability category definitions. These judges were asked to rate each task with respect to 37 ability dimensions. Intraclass correlations were obtained from groups of 25, 15, and 5 raters, as well as from a single rater. It was found that 15 raters were needed to obtain reliability coefficients exceeding .70, when agreement for each task was assessed across raters. However, the raters again suggested the need for refinement to more behaviorally oriented definitions of the abilities.

Hence, behaviorally anchored rating scales were developed using the following procedures. Psychologists familiar with the abilities generated detailed behavioral descriptions for the high and low ends of each scale. These descriptions, along with the ability definitions, were presented to panels. Panel members generated examples of common familiar tasks requiring high, medium, and low levels of each ability. More than 1,000 task examples were created. Next, these tasks were presented to groups that were asked to rate, on a 7-point scale, the level of each ability required to perform each task. Means and standard deviations of the ratings were calculated; then, tasks

**TABLE 11-1**
**Definitions of Abilities in the Taxonomy With Task Examples**

| Construct label | Operational definition | Level rating | Example |
|---|---|---|---|
| | | | Level scale |
| | Cognitive Abilities | | |
| **Verbal Abilities** | | | |
| 1. Oral Comprehension | The ability to listen to and understand information and ideas presented through spoken words and sentences. | High | Understanding a lecture on advanced physics. |
| | | Low | Understanding a television commercial. |
| 2. Written Comprehension | The ability to read and understand information and ideas presented in writing. | High | Understanding an instruction book on repairing a missile guidance system. |
| | | Low | Understanding signs on the highway. |
| 3. Oral Expression | The ability to communicate information and ideas in speaking so others will understand. | High | Explaining advanced principles of genetics to college freshmen. |
| | | Low | Canceling newspaper delivery by phone. |
| 4. Written Expression | The ability to communicate information and ideas in writing so others will understand. | High | Writing an advanced economics textbook. |
| | | Low | Writing a note to remind someone to take something out of the freezer to thaw. |
| **Idea Generation and Reasoning Abilities** | | | |
| 5. Fluency of Ideas | The ability to come up with a number of ideas about a given topic. It concerns the number of ideas produced and *not* the quality, correctness, or creativity of the ideas. | High | Naming all the possible strategies for a particular military battle. |
| | | Low | Naming four different uses for a screwdriver. |
| 6. Originality | The ability to come up with unusual or clever ideas about a given topic or situation, or to develop creative ways to solve a problem. | High | Inventing a new type of human-made fiber. |
| | | Low | Using a credit card to open a locked door. |
| 8. Problem Sensitivity | The ability to tell when something is wrong or is likely to go wrong. It does *not* involve solving the problem, only recognizing that there is a problem. | High | Recognizing an illness at an early stage of a disease when there are only a few symptoms. |
| | | Low | Recognizing that an unplugged lamp does not work. |
| 11. Deductive Reasoning | The ability to apply general rules to specific problems to come up with logical answers. It involves deciding if an answer makes sense. | High | Designing an aircraft wing using the principles of aerodynamics. |
| | | Low | Knowing that, because of the law of gravity, a stalled car can coast down the hill. |
| 12. Inductive Reasoning | The ability to combine separate pieces of information, or specific answers to problems, to form general rules or conclusions. It includes coming up with a logical explanation for why a series of seemingly unrelated events occur together. | High | Diagnosing a disease using the results of many different lab tests. |
| | | Low | Determining clothing to wear on the basis of the weather report. |
| 13. Information Ordering | The ability to correctly follow a given rule or set of rules in order to arrange things or actions in a certain order. The things or actions can include numbers, letters, words, pictures, procedures, sentences, and mathematical or logical operations. | High | Assembling a nuclear warhead. |
| | | Low | Putting things in numerical order. |
| 14. Category Flexibility | The ability to produce many rules so that each rule tells how to group (or combine) a set of things in a different way. | High | Classifying man-made fibers in terms of their strength, cost, flexibility, melting points, etc. |
| | | Low | Sorting nails in a toolbox on the basis of length. |
| **Quantitative Abilities** | | | |
| 9. Mathematical Reasoning | The ability to understand and organize a problem and then to select a mathematical method or formula to solve the problem. | High | Determining the mathematics required to simulate a space craft landing on the moon. |
| | | Low | Determining how much 10 oranges will cost when they are priced at 2 for 29 cents. |
| 10. Number Facility | The ability to add, subtract, multiply, or divide quickly and correctly. | High | Manually calculating the flight path of an aircraft, taking into account speed, fuel, wind, and altitude. |
| | | Low | Adding 2 and 7. |

*Table 11-1 continues*

**TABLE 11-1** (*Continued*)

| Construct label | Operational definition | Level rating | Example |
|---|---|---|---|
| **Memory** | | | |
| 7. Memorization | The ability to remember information such as words, numbers, pictures, and procedures. | High | Reciting the Gettysburg Address after studying it for 15 minutes. |
| | | Low | Remembering the number on your bus to be sure you get back on the right one. |
| **Perceptual Abilities** | | | |
| 15. Speed of Closure | The ability to quickly make sense of information that seems to be without meaning or organization. It involves quickly combining and organizing different pieces of information into a meaningful pattern. | High | Interpreting the patterns on a weather radarscope to decide if the weather is changing. |
| | | Low | Recognizing a song after hearing only the first few notes. |
| 16. Flexibility of Closure | The ability to identify or detect a known pattern (a figure, object, word, or sound) that is hidden in other distracting material. | High | Identifying camouflaged tanks while flying in a high speed airplane. |
| | | Low | Tuning in a radio weather station in a noisy truck. |
| 19. Perceptual Speed | The ability to quickly and accurately compare letters, numbers, objects, pictures, or patterns. The things to be compared may be presented at the same time or one after the other. This ability also includes comparing a presented object with a remembered object. | High | Inspecting electrical parts for defects as they flow by on a fast-moving assembly line. |
| | | Low | Sorting mail according to zip codes with no time pressure. |
| **Spatial Abilities** | | | |
| 17. Spatial Organization | The ability to know one's location in relation to the environment, or to know whether other objects are in relation to one's self. | High | Navigating an ocean voyage using only the positions of the sun and stars. |
| | | Low | Using the floor plan to locate a store in a shopping mall. |
| 18. Visualization | The ability to imagine how something will look after it is moved around or when its parts are moved or rearranged. | High | Anticipating opponent's as well as your own future moves in a chess game. |
| | | Low | Imagining how to put paper in the typewriter so the letterhead comes out at the top. |
| **Attentiveness** | | | |
| 20. Selective Attention | The ability to concentrate and not be distracted while performing a task over a period of time. | High | Studying a technical manual in a noisy boiler room. |
| | | Low | Answering a business call with coworkers talking nearby. |
| 21. Time Sharing | The ability to efficiently shift back and forth between two or more activities or sources of information (such as speech, sounds, touch, or other sources). | High | Monitoring radar and radio transmission to keep track of aircraft during periods of heavy traffic. |
| | | Low | Listening to music while filing papers. |

**Psychomotor Abilities**

| Construct label | Operational definition | Level rating | Example |
|---|---|---|---|
| **Fine Manipulative Abilities** | | | |
| 27. Arm-Hand Steadiness | The ability to keep the hand and arm steady while making an arm movement or while holding the arm and hand in one position. | High | Cutting facets in diamonds. |
| | | Low | Lighting a candle. |
| 28. Manual Dexterity | The ability to quickly make coordinated movements of one hand, a hand together with the arm, or two hands to grasp, manipulate, or assemble objects. | High | Performing open-heart surgery using surgical instruments. |
| | | Low | Screwing a light bulb into a lamp socket. |
| 29. Finger Dexterity | The ability to make precisely coordinated movements of the fingers of one or both hands to grasp, manipulate, or assemble very small objects. | High | Putting together the inner workings of a small wrist watch. |
| | | Low | Putting coins in a parking meter. |
| **Control Movement Abilities** | | | |
| 22. Control Precision | The ability to quickly and repeatedly make precise adjustments in moving the controls of a machine or vehicle to exact positions. | High | Drilling a tooth. |
| | | Low | Adjusting a room light with a dimmer switch. |
| 23. Multilimb Coordination | The ability to coordinate movements of two or more limbs together (for example, two arms, two legs, or one leg and one arm) while sitting, standing, or lying down. It does not involve performing the activities while the body is in motion. | High | Playing the drum set in a jazz band. |
| | | Low | Rowing a boat. |

*Table 11-1 continues*

**TABLE 11-1 (*Continued*)**

| Construct label | Operational definition | Level rating | Example |
|---|---|---|---|
| | | **Level scale** | |
| 24. Response Orientation | The ability to choose quickly and correctly between two or more movements in response to two or more different signals (lights, sounds, pictures, etc.). It includes the speed with which the correct response is started with the hand, foot, or other body parts. | High | In a spacecraft that is out of control, reacting quickly to each malfunction with the correct control movements. |
| | | Low | When the doorbell and telephone ring at the same time, quickly selecting which to answer first. |
| 25. Rate Control | The ability to time the adjustments of a movement or equipment control in anticipation of changes in the speed and/or direction of a continuously moving object or scene. | High | Operating aircraft controls used to land a jet on an aircraft carrier in rough weather. |
| | | Low | Riding a bicycle alongside a jogger. |
| **Reaction Time and Speed Abilities** | | | |
| 26. Reaction Time | The ability to quickly respond (with the hand, finger, or foot) to one signal (sound, light, picture, etc.) when it appears. | High | Hitting the brake when a pedestrian steps in front of the car. |
| | | Low | Starting to slow down the car when a traffic light turns yellow. |
| 30. Wrist-Finger Speed | The ability to make fast, simple, repeated movements of the fingers, hands, and wrists. | High | Typing a document at the speed of 90 words per minute. |
| | | Low | Using a manual pencil sharpener. |
| 31. Speed of Limb Movement | The ability to quickly move the arms or legs. | High | Throwing punches in a boxing match. |
| | | Low | Sawing through a thin piece of wood. |

Physical Abilities

| Construct label | Operational definition | Level rating | Example |
|---|---|---|---|
| **Physical Strength Abilities** | | | |
| 32. Static Strength | The ability to exert maximum muscle force to lift, push, pull, or carry objects. | High | Lifting 75-pound bags of cement onto a truck. |
| | | Low | Pushing an empty shopping cart. |
| 33. Explosive Strength | The ability to use short bursts of muscle force to propel oneself (as in jumping or sprinting), or to throw an object. | High | Propelling (throwing) a shot-put in a track meet. |
| | | Low | Hitting a nail with a hammer. |
| 34. Dynamic Strength | The ability to exert muscle force repeatedly or continuously over time. This involves muscular endurance and resistance to muscle fatigue. | High | Performing a gymnastics routine using the rings. |
| | | Low | Using pruning shears to trim a bush. |
| 35. Trunk Strength | The ability to use one's abdominal and lower back muscles to support part of the body repeatedly or continuously over time without "giving out" or fatiguing. | High | Doing 100 sit-ups. |
| | | Low | Sitting up in an office chair. |
| **Endurance** | | | |
| 40. Stamina | The ability to exert one's self physically over long periods of time without getting winded or out of breath. | High | Running a 10 mile race. |
| | | Low | Walking a quarter of a mile to deliver a letter. |
| **Flexibility, Balance, and Coordination** | | | |
| 36. Extent Flexibility | The ability to bend, stretch, twist, or reach out with the body, arms, and/or legs. | High | Working under a car dashboard to repair the heater. |
| | | Low | Reaching for a microphone in a patrol car. |
| 37. Dynamic Flexibility | The ability to quickly and repeatedly bend, stretch, twist, or reach out with the body, arms, and/or legs. | High | Maneuvering a kayak through swift rapids. |
| | | Low | Hand picking a bushel of apples from a tree. |
| 38. Gross Body Coordination | The ability to coordinate the movement of the arms, legs, and torso together in activities where the whole body is in motion. | High | Performing a ballet dance. |
| | | Low | Getting in and out of a truck. |
| 39. Gross Body Equilibrium | The ability to keep or regain one's body balance to stay upright when in an unstable position. | High | Walking on narrow beams in high-rise construction. |
| | | Low | Standing on a ladder. |

Sensory Abilities

| Construct label | Operational definition | Level rating | Example |
|---|---|---|---|
| **Visual Abilities** | | | |
| 41. Near Vision | The ability to see details of objects at a close range (within a few feet of the observer). | High | Detecting minor defects in a diamond. |
| | | Low | Reading dials on the car dashboard. |

*Table 11-1 continues*

**TABLE 11-1 (Continued)**

| Construct label | Operational definition | Level rating | Example |
|---|---|---|---|
| 42. Far Vision | The ability to see details at a distance. | High | Detecting differences in ocean vessels on the horizon. |
| | | Low | Reading a roadside billboard. |
| 43. Visual Color Discrimination | The ability to match or detect differences between colors, including shades of color and brightness. | High | Painting a color portrait from a living subject. |
| | | Low | Separating laundry into colors and whites. |
| 44. Night Vision | The ability to see under low light conditions. | High | Finding one's way through the woods on a moonless night. |
| | | Low | Reading street signs when driving at dusk (just after the sun sets). |
| 45. Peripheral Vision | The ability to see objects or movement of objects to one's side when the eyes are focused forward. | High | When piloting a plane in air combat, distinguishing friendly and enemy aircraft. |
| | | Low | Keeping in step while marching in a military formation. |
| 46. Depth Perception | The ability to judge which of several objects is closer or farther away from the observer, or to judge the distance between an object and the observer. | High | Throwing a long pass to a teammate who is surrounded by opponents. |
| | | Low | Merging a car into traffic on a city street. |
| 47. Glare Sensitivity | The ability to see objects in the presence of glare or bright lighting. | High | Snow skiing in bright sunlight. |
| | | Low | Driving on a familiar roadway on a cloudy day. |
| **Auditory and Speech Abilities** | | | |
| 48. Hearing Sensitivity | The ability to detect or tell the difference between sounds that vary over broad ranges of pitch and loudness. | High | Tuning an orchestra. |
| | | Low | Noticing when the hourly watch alarm goes off. |
| 49. Auditory Attention | The ability to focus on a single source of auditory (hearing) information in the presence of other distracting sounds. | High | Listening to instructions from a coworker in a noisy saw mill. |
| | | Low | Listening to a lecture while people are whispering nearby. |
| 50. Sound Localization | The ability to tell the direction from which a sound originated. | High | Determining the direction of an emergency vehicle from the sound of its siren. |
| | | Low | Listening to a stereo to determine which speaker is working. |
| 51. Speech Recognition | The ability to identify and understand the speech of another person. | High | Understanding a speech presented by someone with a strong foreign accent. |
| | | Low | Recognizing the voice of a coworker. |
| 52. Speech Clarity | The ability to speak clearly so that it is understandable to a listener. | High | Giving a lecture to a large audience. |
| | | Low | Calling the numbers in a bingo game. |

*Note.* Adapted from Fleischman (1975a, 1992a) with permission of the publisher.

were selected as anchors for the high, medium, and low points of each scale on the basis of their means and their low standard deviations about each mean.

The format of the ability-requirements scales, for application to new jobs and tasks, involves presenting raters with a 7-point rating scale for each of the taxonomy's abilities. Above each scale is a definition of the ability; as noted previously, these definitions are the end product of numerous iterative changes and refinements based on research and rater feedback. The definition may include a table distinguishing the particular ability from other similar abilities. To further guide the rater, each scale contains "ability-level requirements" explaining what is meant by high and low ratings. Finally, each scale contains

empirically derived behavioral anchors at high, intermediate, and low positions on the scale. It is important to stress that these anchors were empirically derived in prior studies. They were chosen because of the high interrater agreement (low standard deviations) about their mean scale position and because they represent activities familiar to all raters. The rater's instruction is to evaluate the level of the ability requirement of the new job or task being rated on that ability scale. The rater proceeds from one ability to the next, using this procedure. Figure 11-1 provides an example of a scale as it appears in the F-JAS (Fleishman, 1975a, 1992a). The entire job's profile is obtained by averaging the ratings obtained on each ability across raters.

## 1. Oral Comprehension

This is the ability to listen and understand spoken words and sentences.

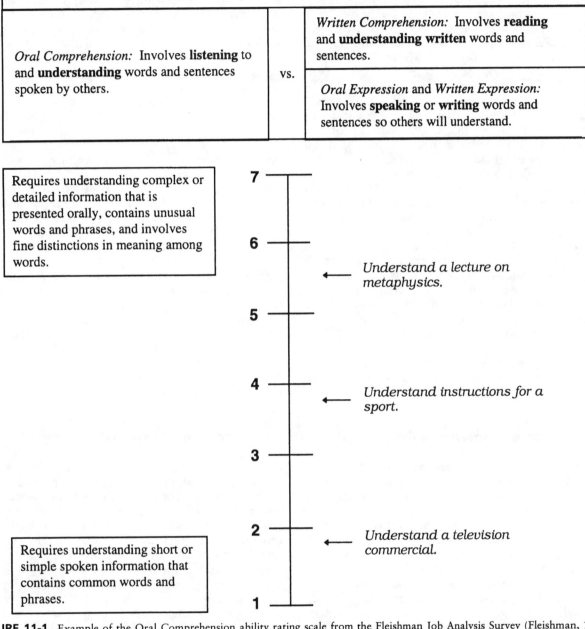

| How Oral Comprehension Is Different From Other Abilities | |
|---|---|
| *Oral Comprehension:* Involves **listening** to and **understanding** words and sentences spoken by others. | vs. | *Written Comprehension:* Involves **reading** and **understanding written** words and sentences. |
| | | *Oral Expression* and *Written Expression:* Involves **speaking** or **writing** words and sentences so others will understand. |

Requires understanding complex or detailed information that is presented orally, contains unusual words and phrases, and involves fine distinctions in meaning among words.

7 —

6 —

← *Understand a lecture on metaphysics.*

5 —

4 —

← *Understand instructions for a sport.*

3 —

2 —

← *Understand a television commercial.*

1 —

Requires understanding short or simple spoken information that contains common words and phrases.

**FIGURE 11-1.** Example of the Oral Comprehension ability rating scale from the Fleishman Job Analysis Survey (Fleishman, 1975a; Fleishman, 1992a). Reproduced with permission of the publisher.

## PREVIOUS EVALUATIONS OF THE ABILITY REQUIREMENTS TAXONOMY AND MEASUREMENT SYSTEM

The F-JAS ability requirements scales have been extensively evaluated prior to their inclusion in the present study (see, e.g., Fleishman & Mumford, 1988, 1991).

## Prior Evidence of Reliability

Reliability analyses have included (a) degree of agreement among different raters on the level of a particular ability required for a given job or task, (b) agreement among raters with respect to the profile of different abilities required for particular jobs or tasks, and (c) agreement between different kinds of rater groups (e.g., incumbents, supervisors, job analysts).

The studies demonstrated that job incumbents' ratings of abilities typically yield reliability coefficients of .80–.97 when 15 or more judges are used. Occupations studied include 15 civil service jobs (J. Hogan, Ogden, & Fleishman, 1978), court security officers (Myers, Jennings, & Fleishman, 1981), assorted Army military jobs (Myers, Gebhardt, Price, & Fleishman, 1981), electric power industry jobs (Cooper, Schemmer, Gebhardt, Marshall-Mies, & Fleishman, 1982), Navy and Marine Corps jobs (Cooper et al., 1987), and managers (Driskill & Dittmar, 1993; Friedman, Fleishman, & Fletcher, 1992).

J. Hogan, Ogden, and Fleishman (1978) investigated whether raters drawn from different backgrounds would evaluate the abilities required for task performance in a similar manner. Profiles of mean ability ratings obtained from job incumbents, supervisors, and job analysts who rated warehouse jobs were found to correlate from the .70s to the .90s. Similarly, Romashko, Brumbach, Fleishman, and Hahn (1974) and Romashko, Hahn, and Brumbach (1976) found correlations of .66 to .81 between ability profiles obtained from supervisors and job analysts in fire, police, and sanitation jobs. Zedeck (1975) found comparable correlations for ability ratings of telephone company jobs. Reilly and Zink (1980) found substantial agreement between ability ratings obtained from supervisors and incumbents using F scales with communication technical jobs. Similarly, Fogli (1988) found that ability requirements ratings made by supermarket clerks did not vary significantly by rater characteristics like gender, age, job tenure, and educational level.

## Prior Evidence of Internal Validity

Evidence of the ability taxonomy's internal validity comes from a number of sources. This evidence includes both the relationships between categories and among behaviors within a category. A necessary starting point is the system's comprehensiveness. J. Hogan, Ogden, and Fleishman (1979) found that 80% of the tasks performed by warehouse workers could be assigned to one or more of the ability categories. Similar findings were obtained for Army officers (Mumford, Yarkin-Levin, Korothkin, Wallis, & Marshall-Mies, 1985), FBI special agents (Cooper et al., 1983) and New York City police officers (Landy, 1988).

More evidence for the ability requirements taxonomy's parsimony is found in the diverse range of jobs for which it has been used successfully to describe job tasks. Examples include attorneys, accountants, mechanics, and equipment operators (J. Hogan et al., 1978); military pilots, cryptographers, and maintenance personnel (Cooper et al., 1987); military officers at various levels (Mumford et al., 1985); industrial managers (Fleishman & Friedman, 1990; Fleishman, Buffardi, Morath, McCarthy, & Friedman, 1994), and craft and technical jobs (Reilly & Zink, 1980).

Internal validity implies that raters should be able to agree on the abilities that best summarize a particular kind of performance. Even within narrower performance domains, raters should still agree on the tasks requiring different abilities. Several previous studies have focused on physically demanding jobs like those of corrections officers (Gebhardt & Weldon, 1982; Myers, Jennings, & Fleishman, 1981), various Army occupational specialties (Myers, Gebhardt, Price, & Fleishman, 1981), court security officers (Myers et al., 1981), telecommunications workers (Inn, Schulman, Ogden, & Sample, 1982), and pipeline repair and maintenance crews (Gebhardt, Cooper, Jennings, Crump, & Sample, 1983). Fleishman and Mumford (1988) noted that for samples of 20 subject matter experts (SMEs) in these studies, interrater agreement coefficients typically exceeded .80 and rarely fell below .70.

Other investigators have also proposed taxonomies containing abilities intended to summarize task performance (e.g., Cunningham, 1988; Drauden, 1988; Lopez, 1988; Primoff & Eyde, 1988) Because these different worker-oriented classification schemes were built using different assumptions and different methodologies, the convergence in category content adds additional meaningfulness to the ability requirements taxonomy (Cunningham, 1996; Cunningham, Powell, Wimpee, Wilson, & Ballentine, 1996). In this connection, McCormick (1976) explicitly stated that the worker-oriented attributes of the Position Analysis Questionnaire (PAQ; McCormick, Jeanneret, & Mecham, 1972) drew on Fleishman's earlier ability taxonomy for ability categories.

## Prior Evidence of External Validity

External validity addresses the issue of how well a classification system can be used to understand, describe, or predict forms of behavior outside the original classification scheme. Attempts to estimate external validity of a taxonomy are likely to begin with generality tests extending the classification to new populations and situations (Cronbach, 1971; Fleishman & Mumford, 1991).

For example, in separate studies with repairmen (Zedeck, 1975), warehouse jobs (J. Hogan et al., 1978), and electric power maintenance workers (Cooper, Schemmer, Gebhardt, Marshall-Mies, & Fleishman, 1982), similar ability profiles were obtained for the same jobs in different plants or cities, or both. Fleishman and Friedman (1990) demonstrated that ability requirement profiles changed in a meaningful way across different managerial jobs (see Friedman, Fleishman, & Fletcher, 1992).

A second category of external validity evidence examined relationships between the ability-requirements taxonomy of F-JAS and empirically derived dimensions of task performance. Thus, J. Hogan and Fleishman (1979) and J. Hogan, Ogden, Gebhardt, and Fleishman (1980) found high positive correlations (.85) between independent ratings of the tasks' ability requirements and independently determined metabolic requirements of these tasks (Fleishman, Gebhardt, & Hogan, 1986; J. Hogan & Fleishman, 1979; J. Hogan et al., 1980). In another study, J. Hogan, Ogden, Gebhardt, and Fleishman (1979) reported a correlation of .88 between foot-pounds of work required by various material-handling tasks and the tasks' physical ability requirements ratings. Fleishman and Buffardi (1998) used the ability-requirement scales to describe the tasks in maintenance and operator jobs in the Air Force and in nuclear power plants. These studies showed that ability requirements, as measured by the F-JAS scales, were highly related to objective error rates in the Air Force jobs and to independently derived human error probability ratings on nuclear plant tasks. Cross-validated multiple correlations of .60 and above were obtained between combinations of ability ratings and the error rate criteria. These studies provide additional evidence of the external validity of the F-JAS scales in predicting performance requirements.

A third body of external validity evidence involves the use of the ability-requirements taxonomy in F-JAS to predict task performance. Thus, Theologus and Fleishman (1973) obtained a multiple correlation of .64 between ratings of ability requirements on 27 laboratory tasks and actual task performance of 400 participants. Myers, Gebhardt, Price, and Fleishman (1981) developed job sample tests representing Army job tasks based on ability requirements identified by F-JAS. They found that performance on these job-sample tests correlated with performance on generic marker tests of these abilities. Additionally, J. Hogan et al. (1978) used a job sample to simulate the operations in a large warehouse and found that generic ability tests, selected on the basis of the F-JAS ability requirements, yielded an $R$ of .45 in predicting performance on the job sample. Similarly, Gebhardt and Schemmer (1985) found validities in the .80s for generic tests of abilities in the taxonomy against job samples of tasks performed by dock workers. A major source of evidence regarding external validity, as well as utility, is the achievement of job–person matches and test validity studies conducted on the basis of this job analysis system. Fleishman (1988) and Fleishman and Mumford (1988) reviewed the diverse jobs in the private and public sector for which tests developed on the basis of ability profiles derived from the F-JAS have resulted in highly valid selection tests.

Another issue related to predictive applications of the ability-requirements taxonomy is test transportability. Schemmer and Cooper (1986), using craft occupations in the telecommunications industry, identified several clusters of jobs requiring the same abilities drawn from Fleishman's (1975b) taxonomy. An analysis of test transportability found that the same ability measures were likely to predict job performance across jobs within a cluster. Likewise, when there was a shift in task demands, different tests predicted performance in different job clusters. A recent study (Hauke et al., 1995) confirmed the utility of the F-JAS ability-requirement scales in the clustering

of approximately 150 jobs in a large government agency into *job families* based on their common ability and knowledge requirements as derived from job incumbents. These clusters formed the basis of a test validation project, relating test scores to employee performance in the core jobs within each job family.

Two additional developments are relevant to the subsequent use of the ability-requirements taxonomy and measurement system for the present O*NET project. Bayer (1992) examined the effect of SME experience, scale rating format (task anchors vs. no anchors), job-level ratings (task, dimension, total job), and their interactions, on rating reliability and validity using the F-JAS system. Results indicated that reliabilities were high for all groups, but the use of task anchors produced superior reliabilities and the highest validities (predictions of experts' ratings). Overall, the results supported the use of whole-job ratings rather than the more time-consuming task ratings. A major finding was the high correlation between whole-job ratings and a composite of the task ratings. The study also showed that the experience of SMEs, within the range of experience studied (all SMEs had at least 1 year of experience), was not a major factor in the reliability, validity, or profile of requirements obtained. However, anchors were especially important in improving reliabilities and validities obtained using less experienced SMEs.

A current feature of the system is the availability of a publication that links the ability definitions to representative examples of tasks and jobs requiring these abilities as well as to tests for assessing these abilities (Fleishman & Reilly, 1992b).

## ADAPTATION OF THE ABILITY REQUIREMENT SCALES FOR O*NET

We now turn to some more recent developments in the present project. These developments were undertaken to further ensure the utility of the F-JAS measurement approach for large-scale administration, for which less time may be available for completing the survey and reading levels of job incumbents are of particular concern. Consequently, some ability definitions were revised to further reduce readability requirements. Additionally, a number of the task examples used to anchor the rating scales were revised to include more occupationally oriented tasks as well as tasks more likely to be familiar to raters regardless of their job.

New anchors were also developed to replace anchors that may seem offensive or insensitive to certain cultural groups and those anchors that may appear to require specialized experiences or knowledge. These revisions included replacing proper names that may be unfamiliar to certain cultural groups or to incumbents with less education. It is important to note that these new anchors were empirically rescaled and placed on each scale in accordance with their empirically determined positions (from low to high levels of each ability requirement).

Attention was given to the few instances in the taxonomy where ability levels may not be in the vocabulary of lay persons. Thus, project personnel attempted to come up with alternatives for terms like "flexibility of closure." It was found that alternatives tried were misleading or no improvement (e.g., "pattern recognition" or "pattern completion" for "flexibility of closure" are misleading substitutes). The conclusion was that the definitions provided were clear enough and that it was unwise and misleading to use labels that provide the respondents with the wrong "set." There are many terms used by laymen (e.g., "agility") that have no construct validity and no basis in research. An objective is to have the respondent go beyond the label and actually read the definition provided without assuming too much from a familiar label.

Finally, the original F-JAS (Fleishman, 1992b) ability scales were edited. The new format dropped the tables that show how a particular ability is different from other abilities with which it might be confused. These tables were removed from the current scales to further reduce the reading time and reading level required to complete this section of the ratings. Despite these modifications, the essential characteristics of the scales were retained. These characteristics include (a) the operational definitions of each ability; (b) clarifying definitions of high and low levels of each ability; and (c) generally recognizable task anchor examples located at different points on each scale using their empirically derived positions. Figure 11-2 provides an example of a current version of an ability rating scale for the ability of static strength.

In accomplishing these adaptations of the F-JAS system, the comments of Occupational Analysis Field Center (OAFC) personnel during an initial pilot study with job incumbents were particularly helpful, as were preliminary data received from this administration. Comments from various user groups and from the Technical Review Committee were also helpful in adapting the materials. Particularly encouraging were the analyses of preliminary data from early field try-outs showing that the ability scales used had the highest interrater reliabilities (in the .70s) of any other section of the survey, despite the small samples of incumbent raters. Use of more raters in operational administrations, as has been amply demonstrated, should raise these reliabilities into the .80-.90 range. The additional adaptations made to these scales should also raise reliability levels.

It is important to note that the procedures used to adapt the F-JAS scales were consistent with the scaling methodology and the methods for deriving scale anchors developed originally by Fleishman and his associates (see, e.g., Fleishman, 1975b; Fleishman & Quaintance 1984; Theologus et al. 1973). Thus, the body of literature documenting the reliability and validity of this system remains applicable to the revised F-JAS ability-requirements taxonomy and measurement system as adapted for the O*NET.

## SAMPLE AND MEASURES

### Sample

In the data collection effort, two groups of judges provided ratings on the abilities required to perform the target occupations. (See chap. 4 for a detailed description of the sampling procedures.) This initial data collection included job incumbents from 80 jobs. For the analyses, only jobs for which at least four incumbents provided ratings were used in order to ensure the reliability and stability of the ratings. Application of this criterion resulted in a sample of incumbents from 32 occupations (see Table 11-2). The demographics of this subsample were similar to the employed population as a whole, and a sufficiently diverse group of occupations remained among the 32 (janitors to managers).

The second group of raters included job analysts provided by the OAFCs. In this sample, a minimum of six analysts rated the ability requirements for each of the 80 target occupations. Because incumbent ratings for only 32 occupations were available, only the analyst ratings on the same 32 jobs were used for comparison purposes.

### Measures

The incumbents and analysts rated each of the 52 abilities on two scales. First, they rated the level of the ability required for the job on a point scale of 1 to 7. This scale also included a "Not relevant" option to allow for abilities that were not at all required for the target occupation. Second, the incumbents and analysts rated the *importance* of the ability to job performance, this time on a point scale of 1 to 5. If respondents rated the level "zero," they were instructed to skip the importance rating.

## RESULTS

### Descriptive Statistics

Table 11-3 presents the means, standard deviations, standard errors of measurement, and interclass correlations obtained for the Level and Importance scales for each of the 52 abilities. These results are averaged across the 32 occupations for which there were at least four respondents per occupation. As these are averaged, only broad-level interpretations of these results are possible. In terms of the Level scale, what emerges is a general trend for the more cognitive abilities to be rated higher than the more physical ones. For example, the abilities rated highest (on the 7-point Level scale) across jobs include Oral Expression (D3), ($M = 4.58$), Written Comprehension (D2; $M = 4.29$), and Problem Sensitivity (D7; $M = 4.21$), whereas those rated lowest include Explosive Strength (D33; $M = 1.52$), Dynamic Strength (D34;

## 32. Static Strength

The ability to exert maximum muscle force to lift, push, pull, or carry objects.

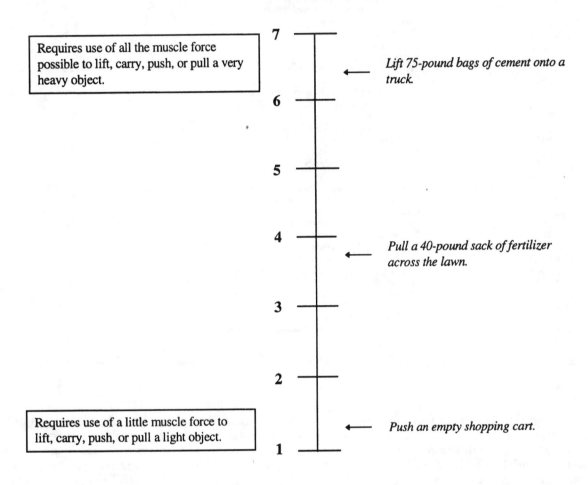

**Level**

What level of this ability is needed to perform this job?

Requires use of all the muscle force possible to lift, carry, push, or pull a very heavy object.

7 ──
      *Lift 75-pound bags of cement onto a truck.*

6 ──

5 ──

4 ──
      *Pull a 40-pound sack of fertilizer across the lawn.*

3 ──

2 ──

Requires use of a little muscle force to lift, carry, push, or pull a light object.

1 ──
      *Push an empty shopping cart.*

**NR** Not relevant at all for performance on this job.

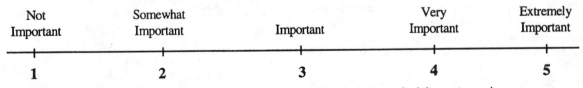

**Importance**

How important is this ability to performance on this job?

| Not Important | Somewhat Important | Important | Very Important | Extremely Important |
|:---:|:---:|:---:|:---:|:---:|
| 1 | 2 | 3 | 4 | 5 |

**FIGURE 11-2.** Example of a current version of the Static Strength ability rating scale.

$M = 1.61$), and Gross Body Equilibrium (D40; $M = 1.68$). This suggests that most of the occupations included were more office-type or administrative rather than physical, outdoor occupations. The standard deviations were relatively consistent across all the abilities, with most being at or around 2.0. The exceptions were the more highly rated cognitive abilities, which had standard deviations of approximately 1.75.

Among the importance ratings (using a 5-point scale), a similar pattern emerges, with the cognitive abilities, such as Oral Comprehension (D1; $M = 3.70$) and Written Expression (D4; $M = 3.40$) rated higher than most of the physical abilities, including

**TABLE 11-2**
**Thirty-Two Occupations With Four or More Incumbents Completing the Abilities Questionnaire**

| Occupation code | Occupation title | Number of respondents |
|---|---|---|
| 15005 | Education Administrators | 8 |
| 19005 | General Managers and Top Executives | 43 |
| 21108 | Loan Officers and Counselors | 5 |
| 22135 | Mechanical Engineers | 13 |
| 25105 | Computer Programmers | 6 |
| 27311 | Recreation Workers | 4 |
| 31303 | Teachers, Preschool | 6 |
| 31305 | Teachers, Elementary School | 13 |
| 32502 | Registered Nurses | 30 |
| 32902 | Medical and Clinical Laboratory Technologists | 8 |
| 49008 | Salespersons, Except Scientific and Retail | 7 |
| 49011 | Salespersons, Retail | 21 |
| 49021 | Stock Clerks, Sales Floor | 8 |
| 49023 | Cashiers | 16 |
| 51002 | First Line Supervisors, Clerical/Administrative | 47 |
| 53311 | Insurance Claims Clerks | 7 |
| 55108 | Secretaries | 63 |
| 55305 | Receptionists and Information Clerks | 5 |
| 55338 | Bookkeeping, Accounting, and Auditing Clerks | 28 |
| 55347 | General Office Clerks | 76 |
| 61005 | Police and Detective Supervisors | 13 |
| 63014 | Police Patrol Officers | 23 |
| 65008 | Waiters and Waitresses | 19 |
| 65038 | Food Preparation Workers | 16 |
| 66008 | Nursing Aides, Orderlies, and Attendants | 12 |
| 67005 | Janitors & Cleaners | 27 |
| 85132 | Maintenance Repairers, General Utility | 38 |
| 87902 | Earth Drillers | 4 |
| 89108 | Machinists | 4 |
| 92974 | Packaging and Filling Machine Operators | 11 |
| 97102 | Truck Drivers | 16 |
| 97111 | Bus Drivers, Schools | 12 |

Dynamic Strength (D34; $M = 1.81$) and Stamina (D36; $M = 2.01$). Again, the standard deviations were generally around 1.20, with the cognitive abilities a little lower (around 1.1) and the physical abilities a little higher (approximately 1.2 to 1.3). These findings also support the less physically active, "indoor worker" conclusion above.

## Reliability

Table 11-3 also presents the intraclass correlations (reliabilities) of the ability ratings. Overall, these reliabilities reflect general agreement among the job incumbents across jobs. Most of the reliabilities for both the Level and Importance scales were sufficiently high, generally above .80. These high overall reliabilities led to relatively low standard error of measurement (SEM) results, with almost all being below 1.0 for level and .75 for importance. From these findings, we can conclude that the ability ratings showed acceptably high reliabilities across occupations and that there is at least some variation between the occupations as to the level and importance of these human abilities.

To assess both the lower limits and optimal reliabilities, the reliability for a single rater was estimated,

as was the reliability for 30 raters. The single rater reliability estimates are, for the most part, quite good. The Spearman-Brown corrected reliabilities for 30 raters are, as might be expected, substantial, with almost all coefficients for both level and importance in the upper .90s. The few exceptions were for those abilities that initially had generally low reliability estimates. We also compared the reliabilities of the Level and Importance scales obtained with the various recoding schemes (0 to 7, 1 to 7, and 0–1). In each case, the reliabilities were sufficiently high and in fact did not differ substantially regardless of the recoding scheme used.

The reliabilities across all jobs and abilities for the incumbents were computed. These estimates were very high across the board, with the actual rater results for level ($r_k = .82$) and importance ($r_k = .81$) being substantial. Again, Spearman-Brown was used to calculate reliability estimates for 1 and 30 raters. The findings here echo those above, as the single rater estimates for level and importance are .32 and .31, respectively, and the 30-rater estimates are both at .99. These results lead to the conclusion that if there are a sufficient number of incumbents rating a given occupation for the abilities, they can be reliably rated by individuals in a variety of jobs.

**TABLE 11-3**

**Descriptive Statistics Across All Occupations and Reliability Estimates for Rated Differences Between Occupations: Abilities**

| | Variable | | | | | | | |
|---|---|---|---|---|---|---|---|---|
| | Level | | | | Importance | | | |
| Descriptor | M | SD | SEM[a] | $r_k$[b] | M | SD | SEM | $r_k$ |
| 1. Oral Comprehension | 4.31 | 1.66 | .82 | .75 | 3.70 | 1.06 | .61 | .66 |
| 2. Written Comprehension | 4.29 | 1.73 | .70 | .83 | 3.59 | 1.06 | .52 | .75 |
| 3. Oral Expression | 4.58 | 1.69 | .83 | .73 | 3.71 | 1.06 | .56 | .71 |
| 4. Written Expression | 3.98 | 1.85 | .65 | .87 | 3.40 | 1.11 | .42 | .85 |
| 5. Fluency of Ideas | 2.77 | 1.97 | .79 | .84 | 2.51 | 1.18 | .51 | .81 |
| 6. Originality | 3.34 | 1.99 | .82 | .83 | 2.72 | 1.18 | .52 | .81 |
| 7. Problem Sensitivity | 4.21 | 1.86 | .71 | .85 | 3.41 | 1.16 | .50 | .81 |
| 8. Deductive Reasoning | 3.64 | 1.96 | .80 | .83 | 3.01 | 1.17 | .55 | .78 |
| 9. Inductive Reasoning | 3.37 | 2.08 | .73 | .88 | 2.79 | 1.23 | .44 | .87 |
| 10. Information Ordering | 3.75 | 1.87 | 1.00 | .70 | 3.19 | 1.17 | .82 | .50 |
| 11. Category Flexibility | 2.46 | 2.17 | 1.10 | .74 | 2.28 | 1.23 | .69 | .68 |
| 12. Math Reasoning | 2.74 | 2.01 | .86 | .82 | 2.57 | 1.23 | .58 | .78 |
| 13. Number Facility | 3.61 | 1.86 | .79 | .82 | 3.08 | 1.19 | .60 | .74 |
| 14. Memorization | 4.06 | 1.66 | 1.15 | .52 | 3.25 | 1.05 | .85 | .33 |
| 15. Speed of Closure | 3.27 | 1.92 | .91 | .77 | 2.71 | 1.15 | .60 | .73 |
| 16. Flexibility of Closure | 2.45 | 2.22 | 1.22 | .69 | 2.25 | 1.25 | .78 | .61 |
| 17. Perceptual Speed | 2.76 | 2.08 | 1.54 | .45 | 2.46 | 1.22 | .99 | .34 |
| 18. Spatial Orientation | 2.68 | 2.25 | 1.27 | .68 | 2.36 | 1.27 | .68 | .71 |
| 19. Visualization | 2.79 | 2.11 | 1.16 | .69 | 2.42 | 1.22 | .79 | .58 |
| 20. Selective Attention | 3.98 | 1.88 | 1.51 | .63 | 3.23 | 1.13 | .69 | .62 |
| 21. Time Sharing | 4.10 | 1.95 | 1.13 | .66 | 3.16 | 1.17 | .77 | .57 |
| 22. Arm–Hand Steadiness | 2.26 | 2.32 | .94 | .83 | 2.12 | 1.28 | .47 | .86 |
| 23. Manual Dexterity | 2.63 | 2.29 | .98 | .82 | 2.31 | 1.33 | .54 | .83 |
| 24. Finger Dexterity | 2.41 | 2.20 | 1.27 | .66 | 2.21 | 1.22 | .70 | .67 |
| 25. Control Precision | 2.13 | 2.18 | .81 | .86 | 2.07 | 1.21 | .45 | .86 |
| 26. Multilimb Coordination | 2.14 | 2.25 | .87 | .85 | 2.05 | 1.23 | .45 | .86 |
| 27. Response Orientation | 2.50 | 2.28 | .85 | .86 | 2.29 | 1.32 | .49 | .86 |
| 28. Rate Control | 1.75 | 2.26 | .69 | .90 | 1.83 | 1.19 | .34 | .92 |
| 29. Reaction Time | 2.63 | 2.63 | .92 | .88 | 2.37 | 1.48 | .57 | .87 |
| 30. Wrist–Finger Speed | 3.50 | 2.25 | 1.01 | .80 | 2.78 | 1.34 | .55 | .83 |
| 31. Speed of Limb Movement | 2.45 | 2.43 | .95 | .84 | 2.17 | 1.31 | .50 | .85 |
| 32. Static Strength | 2.38 | 2.32 | .70 | .91 | 2.14 | 1.25 | .37 | .91 |
| 33. Explosive Strength | 1.52 | 2.15 | .69 | .90 | 1.70 | 1.13 | .37 | .89 |
| 34. Dynamic Strength | 1.61 | 2.13 | .76 | .87 | 1.81 | 1.16 | .44 | .85 |
| 35. Trunk Strength | 2.14 | 2.05 | .87 | .82 | 2.15 | 1.20 | .57 | .77 |
| 36. Stamina | 1.90 | 2.03 | .79 | .85 | 2.01 | 1.19 | .47 | .85 |
| 37. Extent of Flexibility | 2.52 | 2.10 | .81 | .85 | 2.25 | 1.20 | .47 | .85 |
| 38. Dynamic Flexibility | 1.80 | 2.01 | .83 | .83 | 1.90 | 1.13 | .48 | .82 |
| 39. Gross Body Coordination | 2.01 | 2.03 | .77 | .86 | 2.04 | 1.17 | .47 | .84 |
| 40. Gross Body Equilibrium | 1.68 | 2.09 | .75 | .87 | 1.89 | 1.19 | .43 | .87 |
| 41. Near Vision | 3.63 | 1.92 | 1.15 | .66 | 2.90 | 1.16 | .80 | .51 |
| 42. Far Vision | 2.52 | 2.16 | .91 | .82 | 2.26 | 1.19 | .52 | .81 |
| 43. Visual Color Discrimination | 2.21 | 2.20 | .88 | .84 | 2.16 | 1.26 | .50 | .84 |
| 44. Night Vision | 1.88 | 2.23 | .77 | .88 | 1.93 | 1.22 | .36 | .92 |
| 45. Peripheral Vision | 2.02 | 2.24 | .70 | .90 | 2.03 | 1.28 | .38 | .91 |
| 46. Depth Perception | 1.73 | 2.13 | .67 | .90 | 1.91 | 1.21 | .38 | .90 |
| 47. Glare Sensitivity | 1.72 | 2.07 | .74 | .87 | 1.87 | 1.13 | .42 | .86 |
| 48. Hearing Sensitivity | 2.25 | 2.14 | .91 | .82 | 2.14 | 1.21 | .56 | .78 |
| 49. Auditory Attention | 3.17 | 2.20 | 1.39 | .60 | 2.63 | 1.24 | .81 | .57 |
| 50. Sound Localization | 2.56 | 2.34 | .88 | .86 | 2.26 | 1.25 | .48 | .85 |
| 51. Speech Recognition | 4.10 | 2.04 | 1.46 | .49 | 3.12 | 1.21 | .88 | .47 |
| 52. Speech Clarity | 4.34 | 1.81 | 1.21 | .57 | 3.45 | 1.12 | .08 | .46 |

*Note.* Statistics are based on 32 occupations with Abilities Questionnaire responses from at least 4 incumbents (mean number of incumbents = 18.57, *Mdn* = 13.0, harmonic mean = 9.65).
[a]This estimate of the standard error of measurement was calculated as $SEM = SD * \sqrt{(1 - r_k)}$. [b]This estimate of reliability was obtained by calculating the intraclass correlation for $k$ ratings across occupations: $ICC(1, k) = [BMS - WMS]/BMS$ (Shrout & Fleiss, 1979), where $k$ is the harmonic mean of the number of ratings provided on each occupation.

Another way of looking at the reliability of the ratings is to assess the amount of variance that the abilities and the jobs being rated account for in an analysis of variance (ANOVA) framework. Accordingly, ANOVAs run for the abilities across jobs showed that the ability ratings did significantly differentiate the jobs for both level ($F = 5.84$, $p < .05$) and importance ($F = 4.99$, $p < .05$). Furthermore, there were both significant differences within jobs across abilities (as might be expected) as well as interactions between jobs and abilities for both scales. When the abilities were grouped into their higher order taxonomy, these trends continued, with jobs, the aggregated abilities, and the interaction between them all significant for level and importance. What can be concluded from these analyses is that the abilities—individually, incrementally aggregated, and as a whole—were able to reliably account for a significant amount of the variance both within and across jobs. Additionally, these results are consistent with the previously established reliability and validity of the ability requirements scales (Fleishman, 1992a).

## Scale Relationships

Table 11-3 presented the results using both the Level scales and Importance scales with each of the 52 ability descriptors. From these results it appears that the information provided by the two scales is largely redundant. The scales were found to correlate .92 across descriptors within jobs and .82 across jobs within descriptors, indeed indicating considerable redundancy across these two scales. Interrater agreement coefficients for Level and Importance scales were shown to be high (.82 and .81), based on 32 occupations with at least four incumbent respondents. No clear superiority for one type of scale over the other emerged from these data. However, the Level scale was linked to previous work with these scales and is preferred for future use with the ability descriptors.

## Correlations Between the Descriptors

Intercorrelations among the abilities were calculated for the Level scale. The primary conclusion from these correlational analyses is that they further support the meaningfulness and coherence of the ability scales as job descriptors. For example, for the ratings of ability levels, we again see that abilities tend to "cluster" together as expected, with groups of highly correlated cognitive abilities (e.g., Oral Expression [D3] and Written Expression [D4], $r = .80$); psychomotor (e.g., Perceptual Speed [D17] and Selective Attention [D20], $r = .68$); and physical (e.g., Static Strength [D31] and Dynamic Strength [D34], $r = .93$) abilities all in evidence. Although other examples could be cited, these results, in general, provide evidence for the meaningfulness of the abilities as they relate to each other and as they work together to describe occupational requirements.

## Factor Analysis

The next step was to conduct a factor analysis of the ability level ratings. The ability ratings were entered into a principal-components analysis. The results, shown in Table 11–4, suggested that seven components/factors should be retained. The first factor was a broad Psychomotor/Perceptual factor and included

a number of the physical abilities as well. Several of the abilities loaded above .90 on this factor, including Depth Perception (D46; $r = .95$) and Rate Control (D28; $r = .92$), along with Dynamic Strength (D34; $r = .88$) and Explosive Strength (D33; $r = .86$). Given that there were 27 abilities loading above .60 on this factor, it clearly is a kind of "g" ability factor covering the basic physical and psychomotor areas. The second factor was a relatively broad Cognitive factor, with high loadings on Deductive Reasoning (D8; $r = .95$), Written Expression (D4; $r = .93$), and Written Comprehension (D2; $r = .89$), along with the other cognitive abilities. Once again, this general factor had a large number (18) of abilities loading above .50. The third factor was marked by high Visualization (D19; $r = .71$), Finger Dexterity (D24; $r = .60$), and Perceptual Speed (D17; $r = .60$), and it was termed Visualization. Given the nature of the occupations sampled, this group probably represents a cluster of particular jobs in the study. Factor 4, Time Sharing, was characterized primarily by the loading on Time Sharing (D21; $r = .57$), along with Memorization (D14; $r = .52$) and Selective Attention (D20; $r = .52$). Because the two abilities marking Factor 5 were Speech Recognition (D51; $r = .87$) and Speech Clarity (D52; $M = .73$), this factor was clearly a Speech factor. The last interpretable factor was termed Wrist-finger Speed, from the loadings of abilities such as Wrist-finger Speed (D30; $r = .84$) as well as Near Vision (D41; $r = .59$) and Perceptual Speed (D17; $r = .48$). The last factor appeared to be a noninterpretable, residual factor. Overall, these seven factors accounted for 59.72% of the variance and were, for the most part, interpretable.

It should be stressed that these factors are based on incumbents' ratings of ability requirements for a limited number of jobs. As has been pointed out recently (Cunningham et al., 1996), such factors do not necessarily reflect factor structures underlying tested abilities of people. These results are consistent with other findings (e.g., Cunningham & Scott, 1988) that ability requirement estimates may produce less differentiated factors than those developed from test scores.

## OCCUPATION PROFILES

Having derived the average responses across occupations, the next step was to examine the descriptive statistics (means and standard deviations) for a sample of specific jobs for which the abilities might prove useful. As with other descriptors, the representative occupations included General Managers, Computer Programmers, Nurses, Police Patrol Officers, Janitors/Cleaners, and Maintenance Repairers. The results for the Level and Importance scales appear in Tables 11-5 and 11-6. From these results, several broad trends emerge. First, as noted above, the more cognitive abilities were rated higher on level for most of the representative occupations. For example, Written Comprehension (D2) was rated high by General

**TABLE 11-4**
**Principal-Components Analysis Pattern Matrix for the Level Scale: Abilities (loadings over .30)**

| Descriptor | F1 | F2 | F3 | F4 | F5 | F6 | F7 | Communality |
|---|---|---|---|---|---|---|---|---|
| 1. Oral Comprehension | −.10 | .80 | .10 | −.30 | .27 | .08 | −.14 | .85 |
| 2. Written Comprehension | −.13 | .89 | −.06 | .18 | −.05 | −.00 | −.09 | .86 |
| 3. Oral Expression | −.07 | .78 | .06 | .31 | .25 | −.17 | .06 | .80 |
| 4. Written Expression | −.14 | .93 | −.18 | .09 | .06 | −.05 | −.06 | .93 |
| 5. Fluency of Ideas | −.14 | .79 | .11 | −.12 | .35 | −.22 | .16 | .86 |
| 6. Originality | .03 | .86 | .09 | .04 | .02 | −.27 | .23 | .87 |
| 7. Problem Sensitivity | .16 | .79 | .09 | −.01 | .41 | −.00 | −.10 | .83 |
| 8. Deductive Reasoning | −.06 | .95 | .03 | .12 | −.11 | −.01 | −.08 | .94 |
| 9. Inductive Reasoning | .15 | .89 | −.00 | .07 | .09 | .06 | .04 | .84 |
| 10. Information Ordering | −.10 | .87 | .15 | .14 | −.15 | .23 | .12 | .89 |
| 11. Category Flexibility | −.17 | .58 | .18 | .04 | .06 | −.02 | .58 | .73 |
| 12. Math Reasoning | −.22 | .76 | .30 | −.31 | −.21 | −.00 | −.14 | .87 |
| 13. Number Facility | −.32 | .66 | .35 | −.28 | −.13 | .11 | −.27 | .83 |
| 14. Memorization | −.06 | .63 | .10 | .52 | .20 | −.08 | −.16 | .75 |
| 15. Speed of Closure | −.17 | .87 | −.04 | .02 | .13 | .24 | −.02 | .85 |
| 16. Flexibility of Closure | .21 | .64 | .40 | .12 | .18 | .12 | .31 | .77 |
| 17. Perceptual Speed | .23 | .37 | .60 | .29 | −.13 | .48 | .23 | .93 |
| 18. Spatial Orientation | .86 | .09 | −.13 | .12 | −.07 | −.01 | .24 | .83 |
| 19. Visualization | .24 | .38 | .71 | .06 | −.11 | −.17 | .10 | .77 |
| 20. Selective Attention | .16 | .54 | .14 | .52 | −.16 | .38 | .13 | .79 |
| 21. Time Sharing | .03 | .68 | .05 | .57 | .08 | .15 | .06 | .82 |
| 22. Arm-Hand Steadiness | .76 | .02 | .32 | .15 | .16 | .22 | −.08 | .78 |
| 23. Manual Dexterity | .81 | −.03 | .41 | .04 | −.02 | .26 | −.03 | .89 |
| 24. Finger Dexterity | .60 | .04 | .60 | −.26 | −.00 | .29 | −.14 | .89 |
| 25. Control Precision | .79 | .15 | .22 | −.10 | −.29 | .19 | −.27 | .90 |
| 26. Multilimb Coordination | .88 | −.15 | .03 | −.01 | −.09 | .18 | .11 | .85 |
| 27. Response Orientation | .94 | .08 | .05 | .02 | .09 | .11 | −.11 | .91 |
| 28. Rate Control | .92 | .04 | −.02 | .02 | −.16 | .02 | −.16 | .90 |
| 29. Reaction Time | .92 | .05 | .04 | .02 | −.20 | .11 | −.15 | .93 |
| 30. Wrist-Finger Speed | .06 | −.13 | −.04 | −.02 | .01 | .84 | .01 | .73 |
| 31. Speed of Limb Movement | .86 | −.27 | .01 | −.12 | .20 | .20 | −.05 | .90 |
| 32. Static Strength | .88 | −.22 | .04 | −.05 | −.16 | −.06 | .16 | .89 |
| 33. Explosive Strength | .86 | −.09 | .16 | −.15 | −.04 | −.07 | .30 | .88 |
| 34. Dynamic Strength | .88 | −.09 | .10 | −.13 | −.17 | −.07 | .31 | .94 |
| 35. Trunk Strength | .83 | −.29 | .17 | −.23 | .01 | .10 | .31 | .95 |
| 36. Stamina | .83 | −.23 | .14 | −.25 | .02 | −.06 | .28 | .90 |
| 37. Extent Flexibility | .82 | −.38 | .26 | −.18 | −.05 | .13 | .09 | .93 |
| 38. Dynamic Flexibility | .84 | −.40 | .11 | −.18 | .04 | .00 | .17 | .93 |
| 39. Gross Body Coordination | .85 | −.32 | .24 | −.17 | .10 | −.02 | .17 | .95 |
| 40. Gross-Body Equilibrium | .83 | −.22 | .10 | −.42 | −.06 | −.14 | .13 | .95 |
| 41. Near Vision | .40 | .36 | .31 | .14 | .05 | .59 | −.15 | .79 |
| 42. Far Vision | .75 | .11 | −.17 | .35 | .13 | −.12 | −.15 | .78 |
| 43. Visual Color Discrimination | .66 | .12 | .18 | .23 | .21 | .26 | −.04 | .64 |
| 44. Night Vision | .91 | −.02 | −.12 | .19 | .09 | .03 | −.04 | .89 |
| 45. Peripheral Vision | .90 | −.08 | −.03 | .28 | .08 | −.08 | −.02 | .90 |
| 46. Depth Perception | .95 | .10 | −.01 | .03 | −.14 | −.02 | −.11 | .94 |
| 47. Glare Sensitivity | .85 | .10 | −.22 | .09 | −.04 | .18 | −.31 | .92 |
| 48. Hearing Sensitivity | .84 | .05 | .23 | .25 | −.09 | −.07 | −.24 | .90 |
| 49. Auditory Attention | .74 | .13 | .28 | .29 | .11 | .04 | .06 | .74 |
| 50. Sound Localization | .89 | −.03 | .17 | .08 | .19 | −.01 | −.20 | .89 |
| 51. Speech Recognition | −.03 | .21 | −.03 | .02 | .87 | .03 | −.03 | .80 |
| 52. Speech Clarity | −.10 | .56 | −.15 | .08 | .73 | −.04 | .13 | .89 |
| % of variance | 41 | 25 | 6 | 5 | 4 | 3 | 2 | |
| Eigenvalue | 21.41 | 13.20 | 2.95 | 2.45 | 2.01 | 1.69 | 1.19 | |

*Note.* N = 32. The correlation matrix was based on means calculated at the occupation level. F1 = Psychomotor/Perceptual, F2 = Cognitive, F3 = Visualization, F4 = Time Sharing, F5 = Speech, F6 = Wrist-Finger Speed, F7 = Noninterpretable. These loadings are based on an orthogonal varimax rotation.

Managers and Top Executives ($M$ = 5.21), Police Patrol Officers ($M$ = 4.70), and Maintenance Repairers ($M$ = 4.26) alike. The only occupation not rated above the scale mean (i.e., 4.0) on this and other cognitive abilities (Oral Expression [D3], Problem Sensitivity [D7], etc.) was Janitors. However, the physical and psychomotor abilities were generally rated low by several of these occupations, with Computer Programmer ratings of Gross-Body Equilibrium (D40; $M$ = .50) and Nurse ratings of Rate Control (D28; $M$ = 1.43) almost negligible. As expected in the more physical jobs, such as Police Patrol Officers and Maintenance Repairers, there were, of course, higher ratings on these abilities. Among them, Police

**TABLE 11-5**
**Descriptor Means and Standard Deviations on the Level Scale on Six Example Occupations: Abilities**

| Descriptor | General Managers and Top Executives (n = 6) | | Computer Programmers (n = 30) | | Registered Nurses (n = 23) | | Police Patrol Officers (n = 27) | | Janitors and Cleaners[a] (n = 38) | | Maintenance Repairers, General Utility (n = 43) | |
|---|---|---|---|---|---|---|---|---|---|---|---|---|
| | M | SD | M | SD | M | SD | M | SD | M | SD | M | SD |
| 1. Oral Comprehension | 5.10 | 1.13 | 5.67 | .82 | 5.03 | 1.85 | 4.57 | 1.44 | 2.67 | 2.29 | 4.29 | 1.71 |
| 2. Written Comprehension | 5.21 | 1.39 | 6.00 | .89 | 5.33 | 1.56 | 4.70 | 1.11 | 2.74 | 2.43 | 4.26 | 1.84 |
| 3. Oral Expression | 5.35 | 1.45 | 5.83 | .98 | 5.23 | 1.79 | 5.30 | .76 | 3.00 | 2.47 | 4.68 | 1.58 |
| 4. Written Expression | 5.36 | .78 | 6.17 | .98 | 5.23 | 1.17 | 4.91 | 1.31 | 2.48 | 2.34 | 4.00 | 1.83 |
| 5. Fluency of Ideas | 4.62 | 1.21 | 4.33 | 1.97 | 3.67 | 1.73 | 2.70 | 2.10 | 1.63 | 1.92 | 2.92 | 2.08 |
| 6. Originality | 5.07 | .80 | 5.17 | 1.47 | 4.13 | 1.76 | 3.61 | 1.53 | 2.22 | 2.42 | 3.71 | 2.08 |
| 7. Problem Sensitivity | 5.49 | 1.16 | 4.33 | 2.42 | 6.23 | .94 | 4.83 | 1.37 | 2.48 | 2.14 | 4.32 | 1.76 |
| 8. Deductive Reasoning | 4.95 | 1.53 | 5.50 | 1.22 | 4.67 | 1.77 | 4.09 | 1.70 | 1.81 | 2.27 | 3.92 | 1.71 |
| 9. Inductive Reasoning | 4.95 | 1.15 | 4.50 | 2.43 | 5.27 | 1.62 | 4.65 | 1.15 | 2.22 | 2.24 | 3.54 | 1.84 |
| 10. Information Ordering | 4.44 | 1.67 | 5.17 | 1.60 | 4.52 | 2.06 | 4.13 | 1.39 | 2.37 | 2.20 | 3.89 | 1.77 |
| 11. Category Flexibility | 4.21 | 1.85 | 3.50 | 2.26 | 2.55 | 2.42 | .87 | 1.58 | 1.59 | 2.22 | 2.58 | 2.16 |
| 12. Math Reasoning | 3.90 | 1.57 | 4.83 | 1.17 | 3.57 | 1.76 | 1.65 | 1.53 | 1.70 | 1.96 | 3.08 | 2.08 |
| 13. Number Facility | 4.45 | 1.52 | 4.50 | 1.38 | 3.90 | 2.09 | 2.61 | 1.59 | 1.88 | 1.80 | 4.00 | 1.68 |
| 14. Memorization | 4.72 | 1.32 | 5.17 | 1.72 | 4.70 | 1.86 | 4.27 | 1.39 | 2.63 | 2.44 | 4.11 | 1.61 |
| 15. Speed of Closure | 4.35 | 1.43 | 4.17 | 2.48 | 4.30 | 1.29 | 4.22 | 1.00 | 1.78 | 1.89 | 3.65 | 1.71 |
| 16. Flexibility of Closure | 3.63 | 2.17 | 3.50 | 2.74 | 3.30 | 2.38 | 2.96 | 2.12 | 1.33 | 2.02 | 3.32 | 2.27 |
| 17. Perceptual Speed | 3.44 | 1.98 | 2.50 | 2.95 | 2.70 | 2.37 | 2.57 | 2.09 | 2.22 | 2.42 | 3.11 | 2.05 |
| 18. Spatial Orientation | 2.86 | 2.17 | 1.00 | 2.45 | 2.97 | 2.31 | 4.73 | 1.86 | 2.54 | 2.41 | 3.50 | 2.20 |
| 19. Visualization | 3.67 | 2.20 | 1.50 | 2.81 | 2.47 | 2.26 | 2.68 | 2.12 | 2.30 | 2.15 | 4.11 | 1.77 |
| 20. Selective Attention | 4.47 | 1.55 | 3.50 | 2.88 | 4.53 | 1.94 | 4.22 | 1.44 | 3.11 | 2.56 | 4.53 | 1.74 |
| 21. Time Sharing | 4.74 | 1.65 | 4.00 | 2.83 | 5.03 | 1.65 | 4.57 | .79 | 2.11 | 2.17 | 4.16 | 1.98 |
| 22. Arm–Hand Steadiness | 1.36 | 2.01 | 1.17 | 1.94 | 4.17 | 2.42 | 4.04 | 2.25 | 1.81 | 2.37 | 3.53 | 2.41 |
| 23. Manual Dexterity | 1.98 | 2.18 | 1.33 | 1.97 | 4.03 | 2.46 | 3.70 | 1.72 | 2.26 | 2.14 | 4.00 | 2.00 |
| 24. Finger Dexterity | 1.74 | 1.99 | 1.50 | 1.52 | 3.60 | 2.40 | 2.61 | 2.13 | 2.11 | 2.17 | 3.52 | 2.41 |
| 25. Control Precision | 1.81 | 2.01 | 1.00 | 1.26 | 2.37 | 2.19 | 3.09 | 1.86 | 2.44 | 2.47 | 4.26 | 1.94 |
| 26. Multilimb Coordination | 1.91 | 2.21 | .83 | 1.17 | 2.57 | 2.19 | 3.17 | 1.80 | 2.04 | 2.10 | 3.76 | 2.14 |
| 27. Response Orientation | 2.26 | 2.33 | 1.00 | 2.00 | 3.33 | 2.23 | 5.00 | 1.24 | 2.30 | 2.55 | 3.58 | 2.27 |
| 28. Rate Control | 1.37 | 1.99 | .67 | 1.21 | 1.43 | 2.01 | 4.39 | 1.16 | 2.33 | 2.57 | 3.71 | 2.13 |
| 29. Reaction Time | 2.37 | 2.65 | .50 | .84 | 3.40 | 2.49 | 6.00 | 1.17 | 3.07 | 2.85 | 3.74 | 2.30 |
| 30. Wrist-Finger Speed | 2.19 | 2.14 | 2.83 | 2.23 | 2.83 | 2.21 | 3.91 | 1.86 | 2.33 | 2.25 | 3.45 | 1.97 |
| 31. Speed of Limb Movement | 1.65 | 2.25 | .67 | 1.21 | 3.37 | 2.43 | 4.74 | 2.09 | 2.93 | 2.60 | 3.63 | 1.88 |
| 32. Static Strength | 1.56 | 2.07 | .67 | 1.03 | 3.53 | 2.26 | 4.65 | 2.17 | 3.33 | 2.53 | 4.87 | 2.15 |
| 33. Explosive Strength | 1.05 | 1.89 | .33 | .82 | 1.70 | 2.15 | 4.83 | 1.59 | 2.93 | 2.64 | 2.82 | 2.37 |
| 34. Dynamic Strength | 1.02 | 1.81 | .33 | .82 | 1.80 | 2.06 | 3.91 | 1.86 | 2.96 | 2.46 | 3.18 | 2.39 |
| 35. Trunk Strength | 1.23 | 1.86 | .33 | .82 | 2.80 | 2.07 | 3.61 | 1.78 | 3.35 | 2.25 | 3.55 | 2.13 |
| 36. Stamina | 1.23 | 1.80 | .17 | .41 | 2.66 | 2.02 | 3.96 | 1.43 | 3.22 | 2.21 | 3.13 | 2.23 |
| 37. Extent Flexibility | 1.72 | 2.07 | .50 | .84 | 3.17 | 1.89 | 3.74 | 1.51 | 3.19 | 2.20 | 4.29 | 2.09 |
| 38. Dynamic Flexibility | 1.12 | 1.79 | .17 | .41 | 2.13 | 2.06 | 3.17 | 1.67 | 2.59 | 2.04 | 3.34 | 2.22 |
| 39. Gross Body Coordination | 1.74 | 2.22 | .17 | .41 | 2.37 | 1.90 | 3.61 | 1.67 | 2.85 | 2.27 | 3.39 | 1.92 |
| 40. Gross-Body Equilibrium | 1.40 | 2.09 | .50 | .84 | 1.97 | 2.28 | 3.48 | 1.65 | 3.11 | 2.06 | 3.71 | 2.07 |
| 41. Near Vision | 3.81 | 2.04 | 2.83 | 2.56 | 4.27 | 2.08 | 4.57 | .84 | 2.56 | 2.21 | 4.37 | 1.76 |
| 42. Far Vision | 2.91 | 2.17 | 1.00 | 1.67 | 2.76 | 2.27 | 4.74 | 1.48 | 2.30 | 2.27 | 3.97 | 2.11 |
| 43. Visual Color Discrimination | 2.12 | 2.26 | 1.67 | 1.86 | 3.24 | 2.70 | 3.82 | 1.75 | 2.22 | 2.17 | 3.84 | 2.07 |
| 44. Night Vision | 1.95 | 2.16 | .33 | .52 | 2.13 | 2.18 | 5.09 | 1.31 | 2.22 | 2.52 | 3.24 | 2.20 |
| 45. Peripheral Vision | 1.77 | 2.13 | .33 | .52 | 2.00 | 2.08 | 5.04 | 1.61 | 1.81 | 2.43 | 3.50 | 1.87 |
| 46. Depth Perception | 1.58 | 2.05 | .50 | .84 | 2.37 | 2.19 | 4.43 | 1.47 | 1.88 | 2.29 | 3.63 | 1.95 |
| 47. Glare Sensitivity | 1.42 | 1.94 | .67 | .82 | 1.73 | 2.12 | 3.83 | 1.23 | 1.38 | 2.02 | 3.50 | 2.14 |
| 48. Hearing Sensitivity | 2.02 | 1.97 | .83 | .98 | 3.27 | 2.35 | 3.52 | 1.50 | 2.22 | 2.45 | 3.53 | 2.04 |
| 49. Auditory Attention | 3.19 | 2.10 | 1.83 | 1.94 | 3.87 | 2.27 | 4.57 | 1.83 | 2.30 | 2.45 | 3.47 | 2.17 |
| 50. Sound Localization | 1.98 | 2.18 | .50 | 1.22 | 3.45 | 2.14 | 4.70 | 1.46 | 2.63 | 2.68 | 3.87 | 1.98 |
| 51. Speech Recognition | 4.12 | 2.14 | 3.33 | 2.94 | 5.79 | 1.13 | 3.78 | 1.51 | 2.74 | 2.35 | 4.16 | 2.11 |
| 52. Speech Clarity | 5.35 | 1.17 | 5.00 | 1.55 | 5.40 | 1.87 | 4.61 | 1.78 | 3.04 | 2.39 | 4.16 | 1.87 |

[a]The full title for this occupation is "Janitors and Cleaners, Except Maids and Housekeeping."

Patrol Officers rated abilities like Reaction Time (D29; M = 6.00), Response Orientation (D27; M = 5.00), and Night Vision (D44; M = 5.09) very high, as did Maintenance Repairers on Static Strength (D32; M = 4.87) and Control Precision (D25; M = 4.26).

The second interesting finding is that the pattern of responses within occupations was effective in describing those jobs. This is to be expected given the long history and evidence for the validity of the abilities taxonomy in describing jobs (for a review, see Fleishman & Mumford, 1991). For example, Com-

**TABLE 11-6**
**Descriptor Means and Standard Deviations on the Importance Scale on Six Example Occupations: Abilities**

| Descriptor | General Managers and Top Executives (n = 6) | | Computer Programmers (n = 30) | | Registered Nurses (n = 23) | | Police Patrol Officers (n = 27) | | Janitors and Cleaners[a] (n = 38) | | Maintenance Repairers, General Utility (n = 43) | |
|---|---|---|---|---|---|---|---|---|---|---|---|---|
| | M | SD | M | SD | M | SD | M | SD | M | SD | M | SD |
| 1. Oral Comprehension | 4.00 | .79 | 3.83 | .75 | 4.23 | 1.07 | 3.91 | .90 | 2.67 | 1.33 | 3.66 | 1.07 |
| 2. Written Comprehension | 4.02 | .94 | 4.17 | .75 | 4.27 | .94 | 3.78 | .74 | 2.59 | 1.37 | 3.55 | 1.06 |
| 3. Oral Expression | 4.23 | .95 | 3.83 | .75 | 4.13 | 1.11 | 4.09 | .60 | 2.74 | 1.35 | 3.76 | 1.02 |
| 4. Written Expression | 4.02 | .71 | 4.33 | .52 | 4.07 | .94 | 4.04 | .93 | 2.22 | 1.12 | 3.45 | 1.16 |
| 5. Fluency of Ideas | 3.42 | .88 | 3.33 | 1.03 | 3.03 | 1.03 | 2.35 | 1.11 | 1.85 | 1.10 | 2.71 | 1.31 |
| 6. Originality | 3.57 | .66 | 3.67 | 1.37 | 3.20 | 1.19 | 2.78 | .85 | 2.15 | 1.26 | 3.05 | 1.33 |
| 7. Problem Sensitivity | 3.93 | .88 | 3.33 | 1.37 | 4.43 | .82 | 4.04 | 1.07 | 2.48 | 1.34 | 3.61 | 1.05 |
| 8. Deductive Reasoning | 3.70 | .99 | 3.67 | 1.21 | 3.47 | 1.07 | 3.30 | 1.02 | 2.07 | 1.36 | 3.14 | 1.04 |
| 9. Inductive Reasoning | 3.67 | .94 | 3.50 | 1.38 | 3.87 | 1.07 | 3.83 | .98 | 2.11 | 1.25 | 2.87 | 1.14 |
| 10. Information Ordering | 3.43 | 1.12 | 3.83 | 1.17 | 3.45 | 1.38 | 3.26 | .96 | 2.44 | 1.42 | 3.26 | 1.13 |
| 11. Category Flexibility | 3.00 | 1.15 | 2.83 | 1.33 | 2.41 | 1.40 | 1.35 | .71 | 1.89 | 1.28 | 2.42 | 1.39 |
| 12. Math Reasoning | 3.12 | 1.07 | 3.50 | .84 | 3.17 | 1.12 | 1.87 | .92 | 1.85 | 1.10 | 2.65 | 1.28 |
| 13. Number Facility | 3.24 | 1.06 | 3.00 | 1.10 | 3.43 | 1.36 | 2.39 | .99 | 2.22 | 1.22 | 3.16 | 1.03 |
| 14. Memorization | 3.44 | .96 | 3.33 | 1.21 | 3.50 | 1.11 | 3.27 | .86 | 2.26 | 1.20 | 3.19 | .98 |
| 15. Speed of Closure | 3.09 | .92 | 2.83 | 1.47 | 3.37 | .81 | 3.13 | .63 | 1.78 | 1.01 | 2.95 | 1.09 |
| 16. Flexibility of Closure | 2.63 | 1.22 | 2.67 | 1.37 | 2.70 | 1.39 | 2.65 | 1.19 | 1.70 | 1.14 | 2.84 | 1.31 |
| 17. Perpetual Speed | 2.44 | 1.22 | 2.00 | 1.55 | 2.47 | 1.36 | 2.43 | 1.16 | 2.11 | 1.28 | 2.63 | 1.28 |
| 18. Spatial Orientation | 2.21 | 1.25 | 1.50 | 1.22 | 2.37 | 1.22 | 3.64 | 1.11 | 2.19 | 1.21 | 2.92 | 1.24 |
| 19. Visualization | 2.88 | 1.31 | 1.83 | 1.60 | 2.23 | 1.17 | 2.36 | 1.23 | 2.33 | 1.33 | 3.13 | 1.04 |
| 20. Selective Attention | 3.14 | .99 | 3.00 | 1.90 | 3.47 | 1.07 | 3.13 | .92 | 2.52 | 1.22 | 3.34 | 1.05 |
| 21. Time Sharing | 3.30 | 1.10 | 3.17 | 1.60 | 3.67 | 1.03 | 3.22 | .80 | 2.07 | 1.17 | 3.11 | 1.09 |
| 22. Arm–Hand Steadiness | 1.57 | 1.12 | 1.33 | .82 | 3.23 | 1.36 | 3.17 | 1.34 | 1.81 | 1.14 | 2.82 | 1.35 |
| 23. Manual Dexterity | 1.81 | 1.20 | 1.33 | .82 | 3.27 | 1.39 | 2.74 | 1.05 | 2.19 | 1.18 | 3.16 | 1.24 |
| 24. Finger Dexterity | 1.71 | .93 | 1.67 | 1.03 | 2.97 | 1.35 | 2.09 | 1.08 | 1.96 | 1.06 | 2.93 | 1.38 |
| 25. Control Precision | 1.71 | .98 | 1.17 | .41 | 2.17 | 1.12 | 2.70 | 1.11 | 2.22 | 1.25 | 3.37 | 1.20 |
| 26. Multilimb Coordination | 1.60 | .98 | 1.17 | .41 | 2.27 | 1.23 | 2.52 | 1.12 | 2.00 | 1.11 | 3.10 | 1.25 |
| 27. Response Orientation | 1.79 | 1.17 | 1.17 | .41 | 2.83 | 1.32 | 3.70 | .93 | 2.19 | 1.33 | 2.87 | 1.38 |
| 28. Rate Control | 1.53 | .98 | 1.17 | .41 | 1.63 | .93 | 3.39 | .66 | 2.04 | 1.22 | 2.87 | 1.23 |
| 29. Reaction Time | 2.05 | 1.31 | 1.17 | .41 | 2.77 | 1.45 | 4.26 | .96 | 2.56 | 1.50 | 2.95 | 1.37 |
| 30. Wrist–Finger Speed | 1.79 | .91 | 2.67 | 1.97 | 2.27 | 1.28 | 2.91 | 1.20 | 2.11 | 1.12 | 2.72 | 1.24 |
| 31. Speed of Limb Movement | 1.53 | .96 | 1.17 | .41 | 2.60 | 1.40 | 3.30 | 1.18 | 2.33 | 1.30 | 2.87 | 1.26 |
| 32. Static Strength | 1.60 | 1.03 | 1.33 | .52 | 2.63 | 1.19 | 3.17 | 1.15 | 2.70 | 1.30 | 3.26 | 1.33 |
| 33. Explosive Strength | 1.37 | .87 | 1.17 | .41 | 1.80 | 1.16 | 3.35 | 1.07 | 2.44 | 1.34 | 2.45 | 1.43 |
| 34. Dynamic Strength | 1.45 | .91 | 1.17 | .41 | 2.00 | 1.23 | 3.00 | 1.13 | 2.38 | 1.27 | 2.68 | 1.40 |
| 35. Trunk Strength | 1.56 | .98 | 1.17 | .41 | 2.37 | 1.25 | 3.00 | 1.09 | 2.73 | 1.23 | 2.87 | 1.26 |
| 36. Stamina | 1.63 | .98 | 1.17 | .41 | 2.41 | 1.30 | 3.35 | .93 | 2.59 | 1.15 | 2.61 | 1.39 |
| 37. Extent Flexibility | 1.60 | .93 | 1.33 | .52 | 2.52 | 1.07 | 3.13 | .97 | 2.54 | 1.15 | 3.16 | 1.26 |
| 38. Dynamic Flexibility | 1.42 | .85 | 1.17 | .41 | 2.13 | 1.25 | 2.61 | 1.08 | 2.33 | 1.11 | 2.66 | 1.30 |
| 39. Gross Body Coordination | 1.65 | 1.15 | 1.17 | .41 | 2.23 | 1.10 | 3.09 | 1.08 | 2.48 | 1.22 | 2.68 | 1.25 |
| 40. Gross-Body Equilibrium | 1.53 | 1.01 | 1.33 | .52 | 1.87 | 1.25 | 2.70 | .88 | 2.74 | 1.32 | 3.08 | 1.22 |
| 41. Near Vision | 2.67 | 1.08 | 2.50 | 1.38 | 3.03 | 1.19 | 3.26 | .75 | 2.37 | 1.21 | 3.29 | 1.09 |
| 42. Far Vision | 2.14 | 1.04 | 1.67 | 1.21 | 2.45 | 1.19 | 3.39 | .78 | 2.19 | 1.14 | 2.89 | 1.29 |
| 43. Visual Color Discrimination | 1.91 | 1.15 | 1.67 | 1.21 | 2.72 | 1.41 | 2.86 | 1.10 | 2.26 | 1.13 | 3.21 | 1.14 |
| 44. Night Vision | 1.67 | .94 | 1.17 | .41 | 2.00 | 1.11 | 3.87 | .81 | 2.00 | 1.21 | 2.61 | 1.22 |
| 45. Peripheral Vision | 1.70 | 1.01 | 1.17 | .41 | 1.90 | 1.09 | 3.86 | 1.01 | 1.96 | 1.32 | 2.71 | 1.14 |
| 46. Depth Perception | 1.67 | 1.02 | 1.17 | .41 | 2.10 | 1.16 | 3.52 | .90 | 1.92 | 1.21 | 2.89 | 1.11 |
| 47. Glare Sensitivity | 1.56 | .83 | 1.33 | .52 | 1.83 | 1.05 | 2.96 | .77 | 1.69 | .99 | 2.63 | 1.15 |
| 48. Hearing Sensitivity | 1.86 | .91 | 1.17 | .41 | 2.67 | 1.37 | 2.65 | 1.07 | 2.04 | 1.19 | 2.92 | 1.30 |
| 49. Auditory Attention | 2.35 | .92 | 1.67 | 1.21 | 2.97 | 1.33 | 3.13 | 1.10 | 2.11 | 1.25 | 2.74 | 1.27 |
| 50. Sound Localization | 1.77 | .95 | 1.17 | .41 | 2.76 | 1.28 | 3.04 | 1.07 | 2.26 | 1.38 | 2.89 | 1.16 |
| 51. Speech Recognition | 2.93 | 1.20 | 2.17 | 1.60 | 4.00 | .98 | 2.96 | .93 | 2.44 | 1.19 | 3.00 | 1.14 |
| 52. Speech Clarity | 3.63 | .93 | 2.67 | 1.21 | 3.93 | 1.11 | 3.74 | 1.14 | 2.77 | 1.28 | 3.24 | 1.13 |

[a]The full title for this occupation is "Janitors and Cleaners, Except Maids and Housekeeping."

puter Programmers rated the levels of the more cognitive abilities all above average, with most in the upper 4s and 5s. Conversely, almost all of the physical abilities they rated near 1, reflecting the sedentary nature of their work. Police Patrol Officers, on the other hand, displayed a more stable, even distribution across the abilities, with many of the cognitive, psychomotor, and physical ability groups evidencing level ratings above 4. The only abilities rated exceptionally low by Police Patrol Officers were several very specific cognitive abilities, such as Category Flexibility (D11; $M = .87$) and Math Reasoning

(D12; $M = 1.65$). Janitors showed a pattern of response similar to that of the Police Patrol Officers but at a lower mean level. Their responses were relatively similar across all the abilities, but in only a few cases did any of the level ratings exceed 3.0, and none exceeded 3.5.

The results for the importance ratings on the abilities for these six jobs appear in Table 11-6, and these are generally similar to those for the Level scale. Once again, General Managers and Top Executives and Computer Programmers rated the cognitive abilities as more important and the physical ones less so, whereas Police Patrol Officers rated most of them across the board as at least somewhat important. Registered Nurses, Police Patrol Officers, Janitors, and Maintenance Repairers evidenced similar response patterns as for the Level scale results.

### Incumbent/Analyst Comparisons

The fact that we were able to collect ratings from both job incumbents and job analysts allowed for some comparisons between these two groups' views of the target occupations. These comparisons were made for both the Level and Importance scales, including means, standard deviations, $t$, and $F$ tests, along with correlations and $d^2$. Overall, both the analysts and the incumbents were generally in agreement regarding the ratings they assigned to the abilities. The overall correlation between the ratings furnished by these two groups was .88 for their level ratings and .84 for their importance ratings. Thus, there was high agreement between incumbents and analysts in the profiles of ability requirements determined for the same set of jobs. For the specific abilities, the correlations ranged from .37 to .88 for level, with most of the correlations in the .70s and .80s, and from .14 to .88 for importance, with most correlations again in the .70s and .80s.

Furthermore, although the reliability of ratings from both groups was high, the job analysts' level ratings were somewhat more reliable than those of the incumbents ($M_{analysts} = .87$ vs. $M_{incum.} = .79$), even considering that there were fewer analysts rating these occupations ($M_{analysts} = 10.51$ vs. $M_{incum.} = 18.57$). The Importance scale showed a similar pattern, with analyst reliabilities slightly higher than those for incumbents.

There were some significant differences between analysts and incumbents in the mean level ratings of certain individual abilities, as evidenced by the significant $t$ test results and significant $F$ tests for variance differences. What these differences show is that for level, the incumbents in the samples rated more abilities higher than did the analysts. Of interest is that this pattern reversed itself for the importance ratings, with the analysts rating the abilities as more important than did the incumbents. However, the major finding was the high correlations between the mean ratings of analysts and those received from incumbents across different jobs.

## CONCLUSIONS

This chapter has described the development of the ability taxonomy and associated measurement system for determining the ability requirements of jobs. The taxonomy, which spans the cognitive, psychomotor, physical, and sensory–perceptual domains of human performance capabilities, is based on earlier work of Fleishman and associates and has been adapted to the requirements of the O*NET system. For the present effort, special attention was given to making the measures more readable, understandable, and user friendly so that they would be as applicable as possible across the wide range of target occupations.

To achieve the reductions in reading and administration time, modifications in the *Fleishman Job Analysis Survey* format included a) exclusion of the table accompanying each ability definition showing its distinctions from certain other abilities, and b) addition of a "not relevant" option on each level scale. It is at least possible that these modifications may have resulted in some decrease in differentiation among ability requirement ratings by respondents.

The results of this study confirm the findings from earlier work with this taxonomy and measurement system. They indicate that the ability-requirements approach provides useful descriptive and interpretative information that contributes to the understanding and measurement of the kinds and levels of human abilities required in a wide range of occupations. The fact that the profiles of ability ratings were equally interpretable for both top managers and janitors is but one piece of evidence supporting this conclusion. Furthermore, despite the fact that only 33 occupations were represented in these analyses, the clarity of the results for the occupations represented makes it reasonable to conclude that the abilities taxonomy would prove useful for other jobs not included. Also, the taxonomy of abilities was shown to be comprehensive in spanning the range of abilities required in the diverse jobs studied.

The data collection and rating methodology for determining both the level and importance of these abilities in performing these jobs was shown to have high reliability and internal validity. Missing from the present effort is additional evidence for the criterion-related validity of the ratings. Certainly, one avenue for future research would be to gather job performance criteria and demonstrate the predictive power derived from the ability ratings as well as from the other descriptive systems developed in this project. However, we do know that earlier studies have shown that tests and assessments developed on the basis of ability requirements derived from this system have high criterion-related validity. Thus, we can be reasonably confident that additional criterion studies will further support the body of research demonstrating the overall validity of the abilities taxonomy.

With respect to the reliability of the ratings, it was shown that job incumbents and job analysts demonstrated a high degree of agreement in the profiles of abilities derived to describe the ability requirements of different jobs. Although there were some differences in mean scores in particular abilities, the reliabilities of ratings of individual ability requirements were mostly high. The factor analyses supported the internal validity of the system, but interpretations were limited by the particular mix of jobs in the sample.

With respect to the rating-scale formats evaluated, there was high agreement between use of Level and Importance scales and comparable reliabilities. Furthermore, regardless of the scoring scheme used, these reliabilities remained reasonably high, and there was little difference between the ratings of analysts and incumbents across coding approaches. Given the high correlations across jobs and individuals between the level and importance ratings, the utility of using both scales in data collection is a

question that is worthy of further attention. On balance, however, it appears that the Level scale conceptually has more advantages for future use.

In summary, the content, structure, and scaling methodology developed should be useful in areas such as job analysis, person–job matching, occupational and career counseling, and the development of job families having similar ability requirements. The diversity of the included occupations along with the opportunity to compare the ratings of incumbents and analysts provide some assurance that the results just presented are both representative and generalizable to the larger population of occupations. That said, we think it is safe to conclude that the ability taxonomy and scaling methodology should assist in the overall effort to develop a more complete understanding of the requirements of human work.

# Occupational Interests and Values

CHRISTOPHER E. SAGER

The measurement of occupational interests and values is grounded in the effort to match people to jobs. It is an enduring proposition that performance is a function of ability and motivation. As pointed out by Hakel (1986) and Dawis (1991), understanding interests and values is part of understanding motivation. The idea is that individuals who are motivated will perform well and that interests and values are important parts of motivation. Maximizing performance, however, is not the only reason for trying to achieve good matches between people and jobs. Borgen, Weiss, Tinsley, Dawis, and Lofquist (1968) pointed to the theory that satisfaction is dependent on the agreement between individual needs and environmental characteristics. This all leads to the hypothesis that job performance and job satisfaction are at least partially dependent on the extent to which the job matches a person's interests and values. Because the goals of the Occupational Information Network (O*NET) include the description of occupations for the purpose of person–job matching, occupational interests and values are an important part of the content model.

What are occupational interests and values? For the purposes of this chapter, they will be defined as a collection of constructs including occupational interests, values, and preferences that are relatively stable characteristics based on affective judgments about life events (Dawis, 1991). Dawis pointed out that the differences among these constructs are subtle and that the definitions of the constructs themselves are not firmly delineated. However, generally speaking, interests are tendencies that vary in strength and duration and are related to attention, experience, and satisfaction. Values and interests differ in that interests tend to refer to the like or dislike of activities, whereas values refer to an evaluation of the importance of activities and other characteristics of work environments. However, this is not a clear distinction, because likes and dislikes could be evaluated in terms of importance, and evaluations of importance could be made relative to likes and dislikes (Dawis, 1991). Finally, preference deals with choices among options. For example, choosing one job over another is the expression of an occupational preference.

Dawis (1991) also reviewed the evidence relating to the validity of measures of interests and values. This review reinforces the assertion that measures of values discriminate among occupations. However, there are more data supporting the inference that measures of interest predict later occupational membership than there are data supporting this inference for measures of values. In terms of predicting future job satisfaction, the evidence for interests is mixed, whereas the evidence linking measures of occupational values to job satisfaction is stronger.

This chapter explores the possibility of including measures of occupational interests and values in O*NET's content model. Some prominent measures in these domains are reviewed. Next, methods of assessing occupational interests and values within the context of O*NET are proposed. Finally, evidence regarding the reliability and validity of these methods is reviewed in terms of their ability to address the goals of O*NET.

## INTERESTS

It is important to note that the initial goal of O*NET is to describe occupations, not people. That is, we are currently on the job side of the person–job matching effort. The focus is on measuring occupations in terms of their potential to satisfy people's occupational interests and values. However, the discussion of interests will begin with a review of two person measures, because taxonomies of interests primarily stem from the analysis of responses to empirically developed interest measures that focus on the measurement of people. Two commonly used self-report instruments have been the Strong Interest Inventory (SII; Hansen & Campbell, 1985) and the Kuder Occupational Interest Survey (KOIS; Dawis, 1991).

### The Strong Interest Inventory (SII)

The SII includes 325 items, most of which include three response options: "like," "indifferent," and "dislike." The items cover seven areas: (a) occupations; (b) school subjects; (c) activities (e.g., repairing electrical wiring, making statistical charts, and interviewing clients); (d) leisure activities; (e) types of people (e.g., highway construction workers, high school students, and babies); (f) preference between two activities (the response is on the "attractiveness" scale); and (g) the respondents characteristics (the response is on an "extent to which the statement describes me" scale).

The items contribute to three sets of scores. The first set of scores is based on Holland's six-factor taxonomy of occupational interests; the SII refers to them as "General Occupational Themes." The other two sets of scores are on the "Basic Interest" and "Occupational" scales. The former refers to particular domains (e.g., agriculture, science, teaching, etc.) and the latter refers to 207 particular occupations (e.g., Army Officer, Nurse, Travel Agent, etc.). The Occupational scale scores are relative to male or female respondents in those occupations. The General Occupational Theme, Basic Interest, and Occupational scales are arranged in a hierarchy with Themes at the top and occupations at the bottom. Table 12-1 contains titles of the six themes and a brief description of each; the descriptions are based on selected language from the *Manual for the Strong Interest Inventory* (Hansen & Campbell, 1985). (The latest version of the SII contains 317 items. The accompanying manual is the *Strong Interest Inventory Applications and Technical Guide* [Harmon, Hansen, Borgen, & Hammer, 1994]). It is important to note that (a) the SII has a long empirical tradition that began in 1927 with the development of the Strong Vocational Interest Inventory (Dawis, 1991), and (b) the SII compares respondents' scores to the responses made by incumbents in each of a large number of occupations. It is equally important to note, however, that the method by which scores are obtained involves a 325-item instrument that focuses on person measurement. Basically, the method used by the developers of the SII to describe an occupation is to administer the whole SII to a large number of incumbents in that occupation.

Other instruments produce scores on the six Holland factors (Dawis, 1991). The Self-Directed Search (SDS Form R) is a prominent example (Holland, 1994).

Examination of Holland's factors suggests that, to some extent, they may be measuring personality-based constructs. For example, individuals scoring high on Investigative are described as not being particularly social, and individuals scoring high on Social are described as people who like to be in the middle of social situations (Hansen & Campbell, 1985). Tokar and Swanson (1995) addressed this issue by comparing responses to Holland's SDS instrument and Costa and McCrae's (1992a) measure of the Big-Five personality factors (i.e., NEO Five-Factor Inventory [Form S]). From this investigation, Tokar and Swanson concluded that the Big Five dimensions of Openness and Extraversion reasonably discriminated among the Holland types for males and that the personality dimensions of Openness, Extraversion, and Agreeableness did the same for females.

Other researchers have categorized the Holland types into the personality domain (e.g., R. Hogan, 1991). Personality constructs are covered by the work styles domain in the O*NET content model (see chap. 13); therefore, including Holland's six types in the content model raises the question of redundancy across domains. However, researchers point out that conventional personality measures do not completely account for the Holland taxonomy (e.g., Dawis, 1991; Tokar & Swanson, 1995). Therefore, describing occupations according to Holland's types is likely to provide information about occupations beyond that provided by the descriptors in the portion on work styles (see chap. 13) of O*NET's content model.

It also is important to note that (a) Holland's types are prominent in the theoretical and applied vocational and career counseling literatures, and (b) there is favorable evidence concerning the validity of the Holland taxonomy (e.g., G. Gottfredson & Holland, 1989; Prediger & Vansickle, 1992; Tokar & Swanson, 1995; Tracey & Rounds, 1992). For example, the General Occupational Theme scale scores for an

**TABLE 12-1**

**Titles and Descriptions of the Strong Interest Inventory General Occupational Themes (i.e., Holland Taxonomy of Interests)**

| Theme | Description |
|---|---|
| Realistic | People scoring high here usually are rugged, robust, practical, and physically strong; they usually have good physical skills but sometimes have trouble expressing themselves or in communicating their feelings to others. |
| Investigative | This theme centers around science and scientific activities. Extremes of this type are task-oriented; they are not particularly interested in working around other people. |
| Artistic | The extreme type here is artistically oriented and likes to work in artistic settings that offer many opportunities for self-expression. |
| Social | The pure type here is sociable, responsible, humanistic, and concerned with the welfare of others. |
| Enterprising | The extreme type of this theme has a great facility with words, especially in selling, dominating, and leading; frequently these people are in sales work. |
| Conventional | Extremes of this type prefer the highly ordered activities, both verbal and numerical, that characterize office work. |

*Note.* This table contains the titles of the General Themes from the SII that are based on Holland's taxonomy and a brief description of each. Modified and reproduced by special permission of the publisher, Consulting Psychologists Press, Inc., Palo Alto, CA 94303 from *Manual for the Strong Interest Inventory* by J. C. Hansen and D. P. Campbell. Copyright 1985 by The Board of Trustees of the Leland Stanford Junior University. All rights reserved. Printed under license from Stanford University Press, Stanford, California 94305. Further reproduction is prohibited without the Publisher's written consent. Strong Interest Inventory is a trademark of the Stanford University Press.

earlier version of the SII showed 2-week, 30-day, and 3-year test–retest reliabilities in the .85 to .93, .84 to .91, and .78 to .87 ranges, respectively (Hansen & Campbell, 1985). The same authors reviewed studies that showed strong convergent validity between the General Occupational Theme scores from earlier versions of the SII and other interest measures. Additionally, Varca and Shaffer (1982; as cited by Hansen & Campbell, 1985) showed that adolescents and adults picked avocational activities that were congruent with their General Occupational Theme types.

## The Kuder Occupational Interest Survey (KOIS)

Another commonly used measure of interests is the KOIS; it includes 100 items (Dawis, 1991). Each item presents three activities that are known to sixth graders. The respondent is required to indicate the most and least preferred activity. Responses to this survey are scored in terms of the similarity of an individual's responses to the responses of members of a number of criterion groups. Respondents receive scores indicating the similarity of their responses to the responses of individuals in a number of groups (i.e., 40 occupations for females, 79 occupations for males, 19 college majors for females, and 29 college majors for males). The KOIS is similar to the SII in that the instrument (a) includes a large number of items, (b) focuses on person measurement, and (c) bases descriptions of occupations on responses to the instrument from a large number of respondents. Factor analyses of the KOIS items have been performed (Kuder, 1977; Zytowski, 1976); the resulting factors/ dimensions are shown by Dawis (1991) to overlap considerably with the dimensions resulting from factor analyses of an earlier version of the SII. The dimensions include areas such as Mechanical, Persuasive, Outdoor, Mathematic–Numeric, and Art.

## Summary

Certain characteristics of the SII, the KOIS, and other similar interest measures make them unattractive for use in O*NET. First, the instruments are person based; they are designed to measure people not occupations. Another problematic characteristic is that their method of job description depends on administering large numbers of items to large numbers of incumbents in each occupation being described. But still, the description is not a description of the occupation; it is a description of a sample of individuals in that occupation. Furthermore, the process of measuring interests and generating occupational descriptions in this manner is a very resource-intensive undertaking. Finally, the approach taken in developing these instruments and their associated taxonomies assumes a fixed occupational structure; this assumption may be problematic in a rapidly changing labor mar-

ket. That is, if a new occupation emerges, a large number of individuals with a reasonable amount of tenure in that occupation need to be sampled to discover which items differentiate the occupation from other occupations.

## Describing Occupations

Holland's six-factor taxonomy is used to describe people and occupations (G. Gottfredson & Holland, 1996; Holland, 1976). Table 12-1 contains the titles and descriptions of the Strong Interest Inventory General Occupational Themes (i.e., Holland's six types) that are used to describe people. Research on the description of occupations has produced evidence that occupations can also be meaningfully described according to the Holland types (G. Gottfredson & Holland, 1996; Prediger & Vansickle 1992; Tracey & Rounds, 1992). Holland "codes" can be used to describe an occupation in terms of one, two, or three Holland types that fit the occupation. An occupation's three-point code consists of the first letter of each of the three relevant types (i.e., R = Realistic; I = Investigative; A = Artistic; S = Social; E = Enterprising; and C = Conventional) presented in order of importance. For example, Prediger and Vansickle (1992) assigned the occupation Natural Resources Manager a three-letter Holland code of *CER*. This means that Natural Resources Manager is primarily described as a Conventional occupation, secondarily as an Enterprising occupation, and as having some Realistic aspects.

The challenge for the O*NET project was to find an efficient way to describe occupations in terms of a taxonomy of interests. Holland's six types were selected to represent the interest domain because of the extensive literature supporting this taxonomy and its ubiquitousness in applied career and vocational counseling. The challenge was addressed by G. Gottfredson and Holland (1996).

### Procedures

The Holland codes for six of the occupations sampled during development of the O*NET prototype are presented in Table 12-2 with their O*NET occupation codes and titles: (a) General Managers and Top Executives, (b) Computer Programmers, (c) Registered Nurses, (d) Police Patrol Officers, (e) Janitors and Cleaners, and (f) Maintenance Repairers, General Utility.

The codes are reproduced here with permission from Psychological Assessment Resources, Incorporated from the third edition of the *Dictionary of Holland Occupational Codes (DHOC)* (G. Gottfredson & Holland, 1996). The Holland codes for 80 of the O*NET occupations were derived from Holland codes generated for their related *Dictionary of Occupational Titles* (DOT; U.S. Department of Labor,

**TABLE 12-2**
**O*NET Codes, Titles, and Holland Codes for Six Occupations**

| O*NET occupation code | Occupation title | Holland code[a] |
|---|---|---|
| 19005 | General Manager and Top Executives | ESR |
| 25105 | Computer Programmers | IRE |
| 32502 | Registered Nurses | SIE |
| 63014 | Police Patrol Officers | SER |
| 67005 | Janitors and Cleaners[b] | REC |
| 85132 | Maintenance Repairers, General Utility | RIS |

*Note.* Holland occupational codes in Column 3 are from the *Dictionary of Holland Occupational Codes, Third Edition,* by Gary D. Gottfredson and John L. Holland, 1996, Odessa, FL: Psychological Assessment Resources, Inc. Copyright 1982, 1989, and 1996 by Psychological Assessment Resources, Inc. Reprinted with permission.
[a]R = Realistic; I = Investigative; A = Artistic; S = Social; E = Enterprising; C = Conventional.   [b]The full title for this job is "Janitors and Cleaners, Except Maids and Housekeeping."

1991a) occupations.[1] The process is briefly summarized here.

First, multiple discriminant analysis was used to develop classification functions based on 193 DOT occupations for which there was confidence regarding their Holland codes. These functions used DOT job analysis data to estimate the probability of assignment of each occupation to each Holland type. Each occupation was assigned a three-letter code such that the letters represented the most probable types in descending order. The functions were then used to generate codes for 12,741 DOT occupations. The new codes for these occupations were reviewed for consistency with other job analysis information, including their associated codes from the second edition of the DHOC (G. Gottfredson & Holland, 1996). This review resulted in some adjustments; however, there were very few changes in Holland codes for DOT occupations between the second and third editions of the DHOC (i.e., only 3% of these DOT occupations were affected).

In the third edition of the DHOC (G. Gottfredson & Holland, 1996), the Holland codes for the O*NET occupations were derived from the codes for their associated DOT occupations. As indicated earlier, the O*NET occupational structure is based on the Occupational Employment Statistics (OES) structure, and the DOT occupations have been linked to OES occupations (National Crosswalk Services Center, 1993). Because there are many more occupations in the DOT structure than the OES/O*NET structure, the linkages are generally multiple DOT occupations to one OES/O*NET occupation. Within each OES/O*NET occupation, scores were assigned to the Holland types for each DOT occupation; a score of 3 was assigned to the type if it was the first in the occupation's code, 2 if it was the second, 1 if it was the third, and 0 if it was not in the top three. The scores for each type were summed across the DOT

occupations linked to each OES/O*NET occupation. The three Holland types that scored highest on the associated DOT occupations, taken in descending order, were combined to generate the Holland code for each OES/O*NET occupation. The Holland codes for the OES/O*NET codes were reviewed along with the codes for their associated DOT occupations. In some instances, this review suggested that a DOT occupation had been linked to the wrong OES/O*NET occupation. In these cases, OES/O*NET Holland codes were recalculated across the corrected set of DOT occupations.

G. Gottfredson and Holland (1996) presented evidence supporting the validity of the DOT Holland codes. One example is a comparison between the Holland codes and the *Guide for Occupational Exploration* (GOE; U.S. Department of Labor [DOL], 1979) categories. Employment Service occupational analysts assigned the DOT occupations to 12 GOE categories. These categories represent 11 interest dimensions and 1 category for occupations that require physical performance. DOL mapped the 12 GOE categories onto the six Holland types. This allowed an examination of the extent to which occupations assigned by classificatory function to a particular Holland category were assigned by occupational analysts to the associated GOE category. The occupational analysts assigned 76.8% of the DOT occupations into the predicted categories. This comparison was based on Holland codes from the first edition of the DHOC (G. Gottfredson, Holland, & Ogawa, 1982). Finally, it is important to note that although G. Gottfredson and Holland (1996) supported the validity of the Holland codes associated with O*NET occupations, they indicated that there are times when users should consider these codes in the context of direct assessments of occupations (e.g., important individual decisions).

### Results

The Holland codes that are part of the O*NET prototype were not collected via incumbent/supervisor or analyst questionnaires; therefore, the reliability and validity analyses associated with the other O*NET domains are not possible. However, the Holland codes shown in Table 12-2 provide information that allows profile comparisons across occupations in a manner similar to the information presented for the Occupational Values Questionnaire and for the other domain questionnaires in other chapters.

Examination of the Holland codes for the six occupations in Table 12-2 provides preliminary evidence that the codes do reflect differences and similarities among occupations. For example, Janitors and Cleaners, and Maintenance Repairers, General Utility are the most "blue collar" of the six occupations, and the first letter of their code is *R* for Realistic. This makes sense because occupations primarily classified as this type "tend to involve concrete and practical activity involving machines, tools, and materials" (G. Gottfredson & Holland, 1989, p. 6).

---

[1]Holland codes were derived for the 80 occupations included in the initial O*NET sample. See chapter 4 for the rationale for the selection of the 80 occupations.

However, the second and third letters in the codes for these two occupations do not match, distinguishing these two primarily Realistic occupations in a way that makes sense. The remaining part of the code for Janitors and Cleaners is E for Enterprising and then C for Conventional. Enterprising occupations, "tend to involve working with people in a supervisory or persuasive way to achieve some organizational goal." (G. Gottfredson & Holland, 1989, p. 6). Members of this occupation often need to persuade people to comply with standard rules associated with the orderly functioning of a facility, such as walking around barriers that indicate a wet floor or keeping food and drink out of some parts of a building. Conventional occupations "tend to involve working with things, numbers, or machines in an orderly way to meet the regular and predictable needs of an organization or to meet specified standards" (G. Gottfredson & Holland, 1989, p. 6). Janitors and Cleaners generally have a relatively fixed set of tools and responsibilities.

The second and third letters of the Holland code for Maintenance Repairers, General Utility are I for Investigative and S for Social. Occupations in the investigative category "tend to involve analytical or intellectual activity aimed at problem-solving, trouble-shooting, or the creation and use of knowledge." (G. Gottfredson & Holland, 1989, p. 6). Repair involves finding and correcting the causes of equipment malfunctions. Social occupations "typically involve working with people in a helpful or facilitative way." (G. Gottfredson & Holland, 1989, p. 6). This occupation often involves direct interaction with the individuals who use the equipment being repaired.

The Holland codes for the other occupations are also logically consistent. The first letter of the code for General Managers and Top Executives is E for Enterprising. Supervising people is part of the definition of this Holland type. The code for Computer Programmers indicates that it primarily is an Investigative occupation. Debugging programs and the application of knowledge of computer languages are central parts of this occupation. Finally, the first letter of codes for Registered Nurses and Police Patrol officers is S for Social, correctly reflecting the fact that working with and helping people are important activities in these occupations.

## VALUES

There are a number of measures of occupational values that are person based; that is, the instruments are designed to identify the characteristics of work environments that are important to the individual. An example of such an instrument is the Minnesota Importance Questionnaire (MIQ; Dawis & Lofquist, 1984). The difficulty again is that, like most interest measures, this instrument is designed to measure people, not occupations.

An exception is the Minnesota Job Description Questionnaire (MJDQ; Borgen et al., 1968, Dawis, 1991, Dawis & Lofquist, 1984). This instrument is designed to describe occupations in terms of their occupational reinforcer patterns (ORPs). Respondents are required to describe their jobs in terms of 21 need-reinforcers that occupations can potentially offer. These reinforcers are listed in Table 12-3. The MJDQ presents the respondent with a reinforcer statement associated with each need-reinforcer. Table 12-3 also presents the statements used in O*NET's Occupational Values Questionnaire, some of which are modifications of the original MJDQ statements. Each statement begins, "Workers on this job . . . ." For example, "Workers on this job are busy all the time," is the statement representing the need reinforcer "Activity." There are two forms of the MJDQ. In one form the statements are presented to respondents five at a time, in a multiple rank-order format; the other form follows a paired comparison format. After this instrument is administered to a number of individuals in an occupation, an ORP can be generated for that occupation that describes it in terms of the relative existence of the reinforcers in the occupation (Dawis & Lofquist, 1984). That is, the ORP is the occupation's profile of scores on the 21 reinforcers.

The MJDQ is an attractive measure for a number of reasons. One reason is that this instrument is specifically designed to measure occupations. The MJDQ literally asks the respondents to make judgments relative to their jobs. This keeps the instrument in the realm of measuring characteristics of occupations that people may value and away from the indirect situation of measuring the interests or values of people who are in the occupations.

Another attractive characteristic of this instrument is that it is well suited to the purpose of matching people to jobs and occupations. This point is convincingly made by the Minnesota Information Questionnaire (MIQ). The ranked form of the MIQ asks the respondent to rank order sets of five statements in terms of the relative importance of the statements in an "ideal" job. The statements are the same as those used for describing jobs in the MJDQ. This situation allows for the comparison of an occupation's ORP to an individual's responses to the MIQ. A final attractive characteristic of the MJDQ and the MIQ is that this matching system is not as tied to existing occupations as are the matching systems associated with other instruments.

Constructs measured by the MJDQ are worth including in O*NET because they provide reasonable coverage of the work values domain. Dawis (1991) compared these 21 reinforcers measured by the MJDQ/MIQ to the constructs measured by four other instruments that measure work-related values. This comparison showed that the 21 reinforcers addressed all of the content areas covered by the other instruments and that none of the other instruments covered all of the content areas addressed by the MJDQ/MIQ. In addition, comparison of these constructs with those measured by the other O*NET instruments suggests that the 21 reinforcers constitute

**TABLE 12-3**

**Minnesota Job Description Questionnaire's 21 Reinforcers and Their Associated Statements in the Occupational Values Questionnaire**

| Reinforcer | Reinforcer statement (Each statement begins with "Workers on this job . . . ") |
|---|---|
| 1. Ability Utilization | make use of their individual abilities. |
| 2. Achievement | get a feeling of accomplishment. |
| 3. Activity | are busy all the time. |
| 4. Advancement | have opportunities for advancement. |
| 5. Authority | give directions and instructions to others. |
| 6. Company Policies | are treated fairly by the company. |
| 7. Compensation | are well paid in comparison with other workers. |
| 8. Coworkers | have coworkers who are easy to get along with. |
| 9. Creativity | try out their own ideas. |
| 10. Independence | do their work alone. |
| 11. Moral Values | are never pressured to do things that go against their sense of right and wrong. |
| 12. Recognition | receive recognition for the work they do. |
| 13. Responsibility | make decisions on their own. |
| 14. Security | have steady employment. |
| 15. Social Service | have work where they do things for other people. |
| 16. Social Status | are looked up to by others in their company and their community. |
| 17. Supervision—Human Relations | have supervisors who back up their workers with management. |
| 18. Supervision—Technical | have supervisors who train their workers well. |
| 19. Variety | have something different to do every day. |
| 20. Working Conditions | have good working conditions. |
| 21. Autonomy | plan their work with little supervision. |

*Note.* The reinforcers and their associated statements are from the Minnesota Job Description Questionnaire (MJDQ). However, Statements 5, 6, 8, 11, 16, 17, and 18 were modified in the Occupational Values Questionnaire to modernize the language. From *A Psychological Theory of Work Adjustment*, pp. 41 & 195, by R. V. Dawis & L. H. Lofquist, 1984, Minneapolis, MN: University of Minnesota Press. Copyright 1984 by the University of Minnesota. Adapted with permission.

a conceptually unique contribution to the description of occupations.

The 21 reinforcers have also been organized into a higher order taxonomy of work values. The reinforcers represent the first level of the taxonomy. The titles and definitions of the factors representing a hypothesized second level of the taxonomy and the reinforcers (i.e., descriptors) associated with each of these higher level factors are presented in Table 12-4. This structure came from Dawis's (1991) review of studies

**TABLE 12-4**

**The 21 Reinforcers From the Minnesota Information Questionnaire and the Titles and Descriptions of Their Associated Factors**

| Factor | Description | Defining MIQ scales |
|---|---|---|
| Achievement | The importance of an environment that encourages accomplishment | Ability Utilization<br>Achievement |
| Comfort | The importance of an environment that is comfortable and not stressful | Activity<br>Independence<br>Variety<br>Compensation<br>Security<br>Working Conditions |
| Status | The importance of an environment that provides recognition and prestige | Advancement<br>Recognition<br>Authority<br>Social Status |
| Altruism | The importance of an environment that fosters harmony and service to others | Coworkers<br>Social Service<br>Moral Values |
| Safety | The importance of an environment that is predicable and stable | Company Policies<br>Supervision, Human Relations<br>Supervision, Technical |
| Autonomy | The importance of an environment that stimulates initiative | Creativity<br>Responsibility<br>Autonomy |

*Note.* Modified and reproduced by special permission of the publisher, Consulting Psychologists Press, Inc., Palo Alto, CA 94303. From *Handbook of Industrial and Organizational Psychology* (2nd ed.) Volume 2, by Marvin D. Dunnette & Leatta M. Hough (Eds). Copyright 1991 by Consulting Psychologist Press, Inc. All rights reserved. Further reproduction is prohibited without the publisher's written consent.

that factor analyzed responses to the MIQ. As indicated previously, it consists of the same need-reinforcer statements as the MJDQ. The results of these factor analyses represent the higher level of the taxonomy for the importance of reinforcers in people's ideal occupations. Therefore, it is a working hypothesis that this structure applies equally well as the higher level of the taxonomy for ratings of the presence of reinforcers in actual occupations.

Borgen et al. (1968) investigated the reliability and validity of the ranked version of the MJDQ. Their study included 81 occupations. For each occupation, two ORPs were created, each based on half of the respondents completing the questionnaire for that particular occupation. The within-occupation correlations between the groups ranged from $r = .78$ to $r = .98$, with a median correlation of $r = .91$. The median correlation between profiles from different occupations was $r = .55$. This result provided evidence that the MJDQ could reliably differentiate among occupations because the correlations between profiles were on average higher within occupations than between occupations. The authors concluded that for sufficiently stable results, a minimum of 20 respondents per occupation is required. The authors also made a strong concurrent-validity argument. First, they showed that each reinforcer scale score shows significant mean differences across the 81 occupations. That is, each of the individual scales shows variation across occupations. Second, a cluster analysis was performed on the ORPs for each occupation. The resulting clusters differed considerably in terms of their patterns of scores, and the clusters were judged to represent meaningful groups of occupations.

In the research presented by Borgen et al. (1968), the respondents were supervisors. Can entry-level workers understand the items in the MJDQ? Weiss, Dawis, England, and Lofquist (1964) showed that the statements in the MIQ are at a fifth grade readability level. Furthermore, the manual for the MIQ discusses the successful use of this instrument with a number of populations that include vocational/technical school students, high school students, and eighth graders (Gay, Weiss, Hendel, Dawis, & Lofquist, 1971). Recall that the MIQ uses the same set of 21 statements as the MJDQ.

## Measure

The MJDQ matched O*NET's need; however, one difficulty remained. Both the paired comparison form and the multiple rank-order form of the MJDQ require the respondent to make a large number of judgments. One reason for requiring a respondent to make judgments about reinforcers in comparison to other reinforcers is to prevent a positive response bias. That is, without forced comparisons there is the possibility that respondents would indicate that all of the reinforcers are present in their occupation. Another reason for forced comparisons is the fear of a halo effect associated with job satisfaction. For ex-

ample, if the respondents are not forced to favor some reinforcers over others, respondents who are satisfied with their jobs might indicate that all of the reinforcers are present, whereas respondents who are not satisfied with their jobs might indicate that none of the reinforcers is present. However, because of the large number of questionnaires and items included in the O*NET data collection, the judgment was made that there was not enough time or space available to use MJDQ in either of its existing formats (i.e., paired comparison or multiple rank order).

For the purpose of a pre-data collection try-out study of the draft questionnaires, the 21 "Workers on this job . . ." statements from the MJDQ were presented to respondents in a format that required them to rate the extent to which they agreed that each statement described their job. The statements were taken directly from the version of the MJDQ that is presented in Dawis and Lofquist (1984). The ratings were made on a 7-point Amount of Agreement scale. In the try-out study, the overall interrater agreement value was $r_k = .36$, based on two respondents per occupation across eight occupations. This was considered a satisfactory level of interrater agreement, especially considering that it was based on only two raters per occupation.

The try-out results were also examined to address the possibility of a positive response bias or a halo effect associated with job satisfaction. The mean ratings on the 21 scales across all respondents ranged from $M = 4.12$ to $M = 6.06$. This suggested that the responses were negatively skewed. However, the standard deviations ranged from $SD = 0.90$ to $SD = 1.96$. The mean ratings were high, and raters did not make extensive use of the whole 7-point scale; however, there was a fair amount of variation in the ratings. To address the possibility of a halo effect associated with job satisfaction, the responses to the 21 items were examined within each respondent. Evidence in support of such a general satisfaction effect would consist of individual respondents showing a lack of variation in their responses across the 21 ratings. Such an effect was not observed.

From the results of the try-out study, an O*NET questionnaire was developed that differs from the MJDQ in two significant ways. First, respondents are required to rate each statement on a 5-point Amount of Agreement scale. The scale anchors are 1 = *strongly disagree* to 5 = *strongly agree*. Second, the statements from the MJDQ for the reinforcers Authority (D5), Company Policies (D6), Co-workers (D8), Moral Values (D11), Social Status (D16), Supervision-Human Relations (D17), and Supervision-Technical (D18) were modified to modernize and simplify language. The 21 reinforcers and the statements used in O*NET's Occupational Values Questionnaire are presented in Table 12–3.

## Sample

The sampling and data collection procedures used to obtain the O*NET prototype incumbent/supervisor sample are described in chapter 4. Of the 80 occupations targeted, 36 yielded four or more completed Occupational Values Questionnaires.[2] Only respondents in those 36 occupations were included in the analyses, for a total of 681 respondents. For each occupation, Table 12-5 lists the O*NET occupation code, occupation title, and the number of respondents. The 36 occupations represent a broad range of occupations in terms of level and industry.

## Results

### Descriptive Statistics

Table 12-6 presents some descriptive statistics for each of the items on the Occupational Values Questionnaire. Consistent with the description above, each item is a statement that carries the descriptor label of its associated need-reinforcer, and responses to the items were ratings on a 5-point agreement scale. The second column of Table 12-6 shows the mean of the mean ratings for each occupation on each descriptor. These means show that overall the ratings are concentrated in the top part of the 5-point scale. However, the standard deviations of the mean ratings show that there is some variation across occupations in terms of agreement about the presence of reinforcers. The fourth and fifth columns of Table 12-6 show the standard error of estimate and reliability of the mean occupation rating for each descriptor.

### Reliability

The standard deviations in Table 12-6 suggest that occupations do vary on the reinforcers and that they might be useful for discriminating among occupations. To what extent does this variation represent reliable differences among occupations? The results presented in Tables 12-6 and 12-7 address the reliability of the mean occupation ratings on the Occupational Values Questionnaire.

The standard error of measurement (SEM) and reliability estimates in Table 12-6 provide a mixed picture. The SEMs are generally not small relative to the standard deviations, indicating that a substantial part of the variation in mean ratings across occupations is due to unreliability. The reliabilities, based on a harmonic mean of $k = 9.69$ raters per occupation, also are not generally high; the reliabilities for eight descriptors are below $r_k = .50$. However, the reliabilities for five of the descriptors are above $r_k = .70$. The mean reliability is .53; the median is .55. It is relevant to note that reliabilities depend on the number of raters per occupation. Table 12-7 provides estimates of what the reliabilities for the mean occupation ratings would be if they were based on 1 and 30 raters

per occupation. The single rater reliabilities are all low; the highest is $r_1 = .28$. Predictably, the 30-rater reliabilities are substantially higher than the $k$ rater reliabilities. For 14 of the descriptors, they are $r_{30} = .75$ or greater; however, some are low. For example, the 30-rater reliability for Moral Values (D11) still is only $r_{30} = .26$. These results indicate that reliable occupation mean ratings on individual Occupational Values Questionnaire descriptors require at least 30 raters per occupation.

Analysis of variance (ANOVA) was used to separately calculate the effects of occupations, raters within occupations, descriptors, descriptor × occupation interactions, and descriptor × raters within occupation interactions on the variation in ratings. An interrater agreement coefficient was calculated for the questionnaire as a whole. It is based on the 36 occupations shown in Table 12-5, having questionnaire responses from at least four incumbents (mean number of incumbents = 18.92, $Mdn = 12$, harmonic mean = 9.69). A full sample interrater agreement coefficient ($r_k$) was obtained by considering the "Descriptor × Occupations" term from the ANOVA as true variance; error variance was defined as the "Descriptor × S(Occupations)" term. Estimates of this interrater agreement coefficient were also calculated for 1 and 30 raters by applying the Spearman-Brown correction formula to the $k$ rater reliability estimates, where $k$ is the harmonic mean of the number of raters for each occupation. The overall interrater agreement for the questionnaire, based on $k$ raters per occupation, is not high ($r_k = .60$), and the interrater agreement for one rater per occupation is low ($r_1 = .13$). However, the overall interrater agreement for 30 raters per occupation is fairly strong ($r_{30} = .82$). This result suggests that, with 30 raters per occupation, the pattern of scores on the descriptors in the Occupational Values Questionnaire could reliably discriminate among occupations.

### Relationships Among Reinforcers

We also examined correlations among the ratings at the occupation level. This analysis indicates that the relationships among the reinforcer ratings are generally positive, with two notable exceptions: (a) Independence (D10) is negatively correlated with almost all of the other ratings, and (b) there is a relatively high negative correlation between Social Service (D15) and Compensation (D7; $r = -.48$). Examination of the correlations relative to the hypothesized higher level structure, shown in Table 12-4, shows that the correlations are not particularly consistent with this structure, with the exception of the first hypothesized aggregate "Achievement"; its two constituent reinforcers (i.e., Ability Utilization [D1] and Achievement [D2]) show a relatively high correlation ($r = .77$). The highest mean correlation for any of the other aggregates is .45 for Safety. Comfort is a mixture of positive and negative correlations, with a mean of .04.

---

[2]Occupational analysts completed ratings using a modified version of the Occupational Values Questionnaire as part of a related project, but those results are not discussed here.

**TABLE 12-5**
**Thirty-Six Occupations With Four or More Incumbents Completing the Occupational Values Questionnaire**

| Occupation code | Occupation title | Number of respondents |
|---|---|---|
| 15005 | Education Administrators | 11 |
| 19005 | General Managers and Top Executives | 43 |
| 21108 | Loan Officers and Counselors | 6 |
| 22135 | Mechanical Engineers | 11 |
| 25105 | Computer Programmers | 7 |
| 31303 | Teachers, Preschool | 6 |
| 31305 | Teachers, Elementary School | 13 |
| 32502 | Registered Nurses | 26 |
| 32902 | Medical and Clinical Laboratory Technologists | 7 |
| 49008 | Salespersons, Except Scientific and Retail | 14 |
| 49011 | Salespersons, Retail | 21 |
| 49021 | Stock Clerks, Sales Floor | 13 |
| 49023 | Cashiers | 20 |
| 51002 | First Line Supervisors, Clerical/Administrative | 59 |
| 53102 | Tellers | 4 |
| 53311 | Insurance Claims Clerks | 7 |
| 53905 | Teachers' Aides and Assistants, Clerical | 9 |
| 55108 | Secretaries, Except Legal and Medical | 67 |
| 55305 | Receptionists and Information Clerks | 6 |
| 55338 | Bookkeeping, Accounting, and Auditing Clerks | 27 |
| 55347 | General Office Clerks | 92 |
| 61005 | Police and Detective Supervisors | 13 |
| 63014 | Police Patrol Officers | 24 |
| 65008 | Waiters and Waitresses | 11 |
| 65026 | Cooks, Restaurant | 5 |
| 65038 | Food Preparation Workers | 31 |
| 66005 | Medical Assistants | 4 |
| 66008 | Nursing Aides, Orderlies, and Attendants | 21 |
| 67005 | Janitors and Cleaners[a] | 29 |
| 85119 | All Other Machinery Maintenance Mechanics | 4 |
| 85132 | Maintenance Repairers, General Utility | 26 |
| 87902 | Earth Drillers, Except Oil and Gas | 5 |
| 89108 | Machinists | 4 |
| 92974 | Packaging and Filing Machine Operators | 15 |
| 97102 | Truck Drivers, Heavy or Tractor-Trailer | 9 |
| 97111 | Bus Drivers, Schools | 11 |

[a]The full title for this occupation is "Janitors and Cleaners, Except Maids and Housekeeping."

## Factor Structure

Table 12-8 presents the pattern matrix from a principal-components analysis of the occupation-level correlation matrix after an orthogonal varimax rotation. Examination of eigenvalues and interpretability of the solutions favor a five-factor solution that accounts for 71% of the variance in mean ratings. The communalities indicate that five factors generally account for a substantial amount of the variance in mean occupation ratings, with the exception of Working Conditions (D20), whose communality is only .39.

Factor 1 is labeled *Individual Accomplishment* and accounts for 25% of the variance in mean occupation ratings. This factor subsumes the hypothesized aggregates Achievement and Autonomy, shown in Table 12-4, because the highest loadings for the reinforcers Ability Utilization (D1; .87), Achievement (D2; .87), Creativity (D9; .88), Responsibility (D13; .77), and Autonomy (D21; .71) are on this factor. The highest loadings for Authority (D5; .79) and Variety (D19; .78) also are on Factor 1.

Factor 2 accounts for 12% of the variance in mean occupation ratings and is labeled *Structure*. This factor shares some of the reinforcers associated with the hypothesized aggregates of Comfort and Safety. The highest loadings for four reinforcers are on this factor: (a) Activity (D3; .61), (b) Independence (D10; −.78), (c) Supervision—Human Relations (D17; .71), and (d) Supervision—Technical (D18; .60). Company Policies (D6; .46) also shows a relatively high loading on this factor.

Factor 3 is labeled *Social Comfort* and accounts for 12% of the variance in mean occupation ratings. This factor shares some of the reinforcers associated with the hypothesized aggregates of Altruism and Safety. However, the reinforcers with high loadings on Factor 3 together appear to describe the extent to which occupations are socially comfortable. Reinforcers with high loadings on this factor include Company Policies (D6; .48), Coworkers (D8; .76), Moral Values (D11; .66), Recognition (D12; .62), Supervision—Human Relations (D17; .41), and Working Conditions (D20; .61).

**TABLE 12-6**

**Descriptive Statistics Across All Occupations and Reliability Estimates for Rated Differences Between Occupations: Occupational Values Agreement Ratings**

| | Agreement ratings | | | |
|---|---|---|---|---|
| Descriptor | M | SD | SEM[a] | $r_k$[b] |
| 1. Ability Utilization | 4.04 | 0.35 | 0.20 | 0.67 |
| 2. Achievement | 3.81 | 0.34 | 0.24 | 0.49 |
| 3. Activity | 4.00 | 0.54 | 0.25 | 0.79 |
| 4. Advancement | 3.17 | 0.54 | 0.33 | 0.63 |
| 5. Authority | 3.86 | 0.52 | 0.24 | 0.78 |
| 6. Company Policies | 3.47 | 0.37 | 0.29 | 0.38 |
| 7. Compensation | 3.11 | 0.47 | 0.31 | 0.55 |
| 8. Co-workers | 3.76 | 0.31 | 0.26 | 0.31 |
| 9. Creativity | 3.53 | 0.47 | 0.24 | 0.73 |
| 10. Independence | 3.10 | 0.47 | 0.28 | 0.65 |
| 11. Moral Values | 3.32 | 0.34 | 0.32 | 0.10 |
| 12. Recognition | 3.18 | 0.33 | 0.28 | 0.28 |
| 13. Responsibility | 3.62 | 0.36 | 0.24 | 0.55 |
| 14. Security | 4.03 | 0.33 | 0.21 | 0.59 |
| 15. Social Service | 4.12 | 0.37 | 0.21 | 0.67 |
| 16. Social Status | 3.23 | 0.44 | 0.21 | 0.77 |
| 17. Supervision—Human Relations | 4.48 | 0.37 | 0.31 | 0.31 |
| 18. Supervision—Technical | 3.17 | 0.32 | 0.29 | 0.19 |
| 19. Variety | 3.46 | 0.50 | 0.27 | 0.72 |
| 20. Working Conditions | 3.71 | 0.31 | 0.22 | 0.48 |
| 21. Autonomy | 3.81 | 0.38 | 0.25 | 0.55 |

*Note.* Statistics are based on 36 occupations with Occupational Values Questionnaire responses from at least 4 incumbents (mean number of incumbents = 18.92, *Mdn* = 12, harmonic mean = 9.69).
[a]This estimate of the standard error of measurement was calculated as $SEM = SD*\sqrt{(1 - r_k)}$. [b]This estimate of reliability was obtained by calculating the intraclass correlation for *k* ratings across occupations: $ICC(1, k) = [BMS - WMS]/BMS$ (Shrout & Fleiss, 1979), where *k* is the harmonic mean of the number of ratings provided on each occupation.

Factor 4 accounts for 12% of the variance in mean occupation ratings and is labeled *Career Advancement*. This factor is not strongly related to any of the hypothesized aggregates in terms of shared reinforcers. The reinforcers Advancement (D4; .73) and Compensation (D7; .83) show the highest loadings on this factor. Company Policies (D6; .40) and Recognition (D12; .41) also show high loadings on this factor. Social Service (D15; −.69) loads negatively on Factor 4, suggesting that, in this sample, occupations that pay well and provide opportunities for Advancement (D4) do not emphasize Social Service (D15) and vice versa.

Factor 5, labeled *Stability*, accounts for 11% of the variance in mean occupation ratings. This factor also is not strongly related to any of the hypothesized aggregates. Loadings for two reinforcers are highest on this factor: Security (D14; .77) and Social Status (D16; .77). Social Service (D15; .45) also has a high loading on Factor 5. This factor seems to capture the degree of stability in the organization and community that the occupation offers.

Overall the results of the principal-components analysis are interpretable. They suggest that meaningful constructs are being assessed by the Occupational Values Questionnaire and that the mean ratings on the reinforcers can discriminate among occupations in meaningful ways. However, the empirically discovered structure of the occupation mean

ratings is different from the hypothesized structure. There are three salient possible reasons for this difference. First, the hypothesized structure is based on factor analyses of the MIQ, an instrument designed to measure the importance of reinforcers in people's ideal occupations, not the presence of reinforcers in actual occupations. Second, as previously stated in this chapter, some of the statements (i.e., items) in the Occupational Values Questionnaire are modifications of those in the MJDQ; changes in wordings may have affected the relationships among some of the reinforcers. Finally, the sample of 681 respondents in 36 occupations may be somewhat idiosyncratic.

## Occupation Differences

Table 12-9 offers a demonstration of the extent to which ratings on the Occupational Values Questionnaire can capture the similarities and differences among occupations according to its 21 reinforcers. This table presents the mean ratings and standard deviations for six distinct occupations: (a) General Managers and Top Executives, (b) Computer Programmers, (c) Registered Nurses, (d) Police Patrol Officers, (e) Janitors and Cleaners, and (f) Maintenance Repairers, General Utility.

**TABLE 12-7**

**Reliability of Rated Differences Between Occupations Considering Varying Numbers of Raters: Occupational Values**

| | Number of raters on each descriptor | |
|---|---|---|
| Descriptor | $r_1$[a] | $r_{30}$[b] |
| 1. Ability Utilization | 18 | 86 |
| 2. Achievement | 09 | 75 |
| 3. Activity | 28 | 92 |
| 4. Advancement | 15 | 84 |
| 5. Authority | 27 | 92 |
| 6. Company Policies | 06 | 65 |
| 7. Compensation | 11 | 79 |
| 8. Coworkers | 04 | 59 |
| 9. Creativity | 22 | 89 |
| 10. Independence | 16 | 85 |
| 11. Moral Values | 01 | 26 |
| 12. Recognition | 04 | 54 |
| 13. Responsibility | 11 | 79 |
| 14. Security | 13 | 82 |
| 15. Social Service | 17 | 86 |
| 16. Social Status | 25 | 91 |
| 17. Supervision—Human Relations | 04 | 58 |
| 18. Supervision—Technical | 02 | 42 |
| 19. Variety | 21 | 89 |
| 20. Working Conditions | 09 | 74 |
| 21. Autonomy | 11 | 79 |

*Note.* Reliability estimates are based on 36 occupations with Occupational Values Questionnaire responses from at least 4 incumbents (mean number of incumbents = 18.92, *Mdn* = 12, harmonic mean = 9.69). Decimals have been omitted.
[a]Single rater estimates of reliability were obtained by calculating the intraclass correlation for single judge rating across occupations: $ICC(1, 1) = [BMS - WMS]/[BMS + (k - 1)WMS]$ (Shrout & Fleiss, 1979), where *k* is the harmonic mean of the number of ratings provided on each occupation. [b]Estimates of reliability for 30 raters were obtained by applying the Spearman-Brown correction formula to the single rater reliability estimates.

**TABLE 12-8**
**Principal-Components Analysis Pattern Matrix for Agreement Scale: Occupational Values**

| Descriptor | Factor | | | | | Communality |
| | F1 | F2 | F3 | F4 | F5 | |
|---|---|---|---|---|---|---|
| 1. Ability Utilization | .87 | .01 | .20 | .01 | −.05 | .81 |
| 2. Achievement | .84 | .25 | .05 | .17 | −.08 | .81 |
| 3. Activity | .20 | .61 | .13 | −.21 | −.32 | .58 |
| 4. Advancement | .09 | .34 | .04 | .73 | .36 | .78 |
| 5. Authority | .79 | .30 | .09 | −.08 | .26 | .79 |
| 6. Company Policies | .28 | .46 | .48 | .40 | .15 | .70 |
| 7. Compensation | .05 | −.02 | .05 | .83 | −.10 | .71 |
| 8. Co-workers | −.05 | .13 | .76 | −.04 | .07 | .61 |
| 9. Creativity | .88 | .09 | .02 | −.02 | .11 | .79 |
| 10. Independence | −.16 | −.78 | .16 | −.10 | −.02 | .67 |
| 11. Moral Values | .06 | −.03 | .66 | −.31 | −.27 | .60 |
| 12. Recognition | .38 | .15 | .62 | .41 | .15 | .74 |
| 13. Responsibility | .77 | −.11 | −.08 | −.02 | .26 | .68 |
| 14. Security | .19 | −.18 | −.11 | −.16 | .77 | .70 |
| 15. Social Service | .15 | .21 | .19 | −.69 | .45 | .77 |
| 16. Social Status | .37 | .17 | .14 | .17 | .77 | .81 |
| 17. Supervision—Human Relations | .27 | .71 | .41 | .24 | .04 | .81 |
| 18. Supervision—Technical | −.35 | .60 | .22 | −.12 | .40 | .71 |
| 19. Variety | .78 | .15 | .11 | −.11 | .36 | .79 |
| 20. Working Conditions | .12 | .00 | .61 | .07 | .04 | .39 |
| 21. Autonomy | .71 | .05 | .30 | .29 | −.03 | .68 |
| % of variance | 25 | 12 | 12 | 12 | 10 | |
| Eigenvalue | 5.27 | 2.52 | 2.48 | 2.44 | 2.20 | |

*Note.* N = 36. The correlation matrix was based on means calculated at the occupational level. F1 = Individual Accomplishment, F2 = Structure, F3 = Social Comfort, F4 = Career Advancement, F5 = Stability. These loadings are based on an orthogonal varimax rotation.

Table 12-9 shows that mean ratings of a number of the reinforcers vary little across the six occupations. For example, the range of mean ratings for four reinforcers on the 5-point agreement scale is .50 or less across these occupations: Ability Utilization (D1), Coworkers (D8), Supervision—Human Relations (D17), and Autonomy (D21). This result suggests that these six occupations are generally similar with regard to the presence of these reinforcers and that they do not discriminate well among these occupations.

However, some of the reinforcers do vary across these six occupations. For example, the range of mean ratings of Social Service (D15) across the six occupations is 1.83. The mean Social Service (D15) rating is near $M = 4.00$ for five of the occupations; however, it is relatively low for Computer Programmers ($M = 2.86$, $SD = .90$). Likewise, the range of mean ratings on Social Status (D16) is 1.39. The mean ratings on this reinforcer are lower for Computer Programmers ($M = 2.86$, $SD = .90$) and Janitors and Cleaners ($M = 2.93$, $SD = 1.07$) than for Police Patrol Officers ($M = 4.25$, $SD = .68$) or General Managers and Top Executives ($M = 3.93$, $SD = .70$). Finally, the range of mean ratings on Activity (D3) is 1.19. General Managers and Top Executives show the highest mean rating on Activity (D3; $M = 4.44$, $SD = .70$), whereas Police Patrol Officers show the lowest ($M = 3.25$, $SD = .90$). On Advancement (D4), there is a difference of 1.27 between the mean ratings for Computer Programmers (higher) and Janitors and Cleaners. These comparisons of mean ratings on occupation reinforcers are consistent with expected similarities and differences among the six occupations included in Table 12-9.

### Additional Validity Evidence

As noted previously, the Occupational Values Questionnaire is a modification of the MJDQ. There are two important characteristics of the MJDQ to note: (a) Occupations are primarily compared by occupational reinforcer profile, not by individual reinforcers (e.g., Borgen et al., 1968; Dawis & Lofquist, 1984) and (b) researchers suggest that stable results depend on a minimum of 20 raters per occupation (e.g., Borgen et al., 1968). As indicated previously, the results presented in this chapter are based on 36 occupations, with a median of only 12 raters per occupation. This small sample does not provide strong evidence in support of the reliability of the Occupational Values Questionnaire. However, analyses discussed in the *Reliability* section of this chapter show that the estimated overall interrater agreement for the questionnaire would be $r_{30} = .82$ if there were 30 raters per occupation. This estimated reliability considered along with these two characteristics of the MJDQ suggest an alternative method of examining the reliability and validity of the Occupational Values Questionnaire.

Table 12-10 summarizes the results of a method of examining the reliability and validity of the Occupational Values Questionnaire that was not used in the examination of most of the other O*NET questionnaires. It compares mean group profiles within and across occupations. Three of the 36 occupations

**TABLE 12-9**
**Descriptor Means and Standard Deviations on the Agreement Scale on Six Example Occupations: Occupational Values**

| Descriptor | General Managers and Top Executives ($n = 43$) | | Computer Programmers ($n = 7$) | | Registered Nurses ($n = 26$) | | Police Patrol Officers ($n = 24$) | | Janitors and Cleaners[a] ($n = 29$) | | Maintenance Repairers, General Utility ($n = 26$) | |
|---|---|---|---|---|---|---|---|---|---|---|---|---|
| | M | SD | M | SD | M | SD | M | SD | M | SD | M | SD |
| 1. Ability Utilization | 4.51 | 0.55 | 4.57 | 0.53 | 4.08 | 0.69 | 4.13 | 0.68 | 4.07 | 0.53 | 4.08 | 0.80 |
| 2. Achievement | 4.23 | 0.57 | 4.29 | 0.49 | 4.12 | 0.82 | 3.83 | 0.87 | 3.66 | 0.97 | 3.62 | 0.75 |
| 3. Activity | 4.44 | 0.70 | 4.00 | 1.41 | 4.04 | 0.87 | 3.25 | 0.90 | 3.96 | 0.78 | 3.92 | 0.89 |
| 4. Advancement | 3.58 | 1.18 | 3.86 | 0.38 | 3.19 | 1.06 | 3.29 | 1.08 | 2.59 | 1.30 | 3.04 | 1.28 |
| 5. Authority | 4.60 | 0.49 | 3.86 | 0.38 | 4.20 | 0.80 | 4.33 | 0.96 | 3.78 | 0.82 | 3.62 | 0.98 |
| 6. Company Policies | 3.98 | 0.77 | 3.43 | 0.53 | 3.27 | 1.00 | 2.96 | 1.33 | 3.48 | 0.95 | 3.58 | 1.06 |
| 7. Compensation | 3.81 | 1.03 | 3.71 | 0.49 | 3.15 | 1.26 | 2.67 | 1.20 | 2.72 | 1.13 | 3.00 | 1.17 |
| 8. Coworkers | 3.60 | 0.90 | 3.71 | 0.76 | 3.65 | 0.94 | 3.75 | 0.79 | 3.83 | 0.71 | 3.77 | 0.91 |
| 9. Creativity | 4.12 | 0.73 | 3.71 | 0.49 | 3.77 | 0.82 | 3.42 | 0.78 | 3.46 | 0.91 | 3.73 | 0.83 |
| 10. Independence | 2.60 | 0.98 | 3.00 | 1.00 | 3.04 | 0.92 | 3.63 | 0.92 | 3.45 | 0.91 | 3.04 | 1.04 |
| 11. Moral Values | 3.16 | 1.15 | 3.00 | 0.82 | 3.38 | 1.20 | 3.42 | 1.25 | 3.24 | 1.21 | 3.50 | 1.17 |
| 12. Recognition | 3.60 | 0.76 | 3.14 | 0.90 | 2.85 | 1.22 | 2.83 | 0.92 | 3.34 | 1.08 | 3.50 | 0.81 |
| 13. Responsibility | 3.84 | 0.81 | 3.71 | 0.76 | 3.81 | 0.85 | 4.33 | 0.76 | 3.59 | 0.95 | 3.73 | 0.87 |
| 14. Security | 3.93 | 0.77 | 3.71 | 0.76 | 4.35 | 0.56 | 4.67 | 0.48 | 4.31 | 0.54 | 4.08 | 1.02 |
| 15. Social Service | 4.12 | 0.73 | 2.86 | 0.90 | 4.69 | 0.55 | 4.42 | 0.65 | 4.17 | 0.47 | 3.96 | 0.87 |
| 16. Social Status | 3.93 | 0.70 | 2.86 | 0.90 | 3.58 | 1.06 | 4.25 | 0.68 | 2.93 | 1.07 | 3.15 | 1.05 |
| 17. Supervision—Human Relations | 3.74 | 0.88 | 3.57 | 1.13 | 3.31 | 1.16 | 3.25 | 1.11 | 3.57 | 0.86 | 3.58 | 1.03 |
| 18. Supervision—Technical | 3.30 | 0.83 | 2.57 | 0.79 | 3.42 | 0.86 | 3.08 | 1.14 | 3.79 | 0.77 | 3.19 | 1.10 |
| 19. Variety | 3.91 | 0.95 | 3.14 | 0.90 | 3.58 | 1.10 | 4.13 | 0.95 | 3.31 | 1.14 | 4.00 | 0.57 |
| 20. Working Conditions | 4.07 | 0.63 | 4.00 | 0.00 | 3.76 | 0.86 | 3.42 | 0.97 | 3.69 | 0.81 | 3.81 | 0.98 |
| 21. Autonomy | 4.12 | 0.88 | 4.14 | 0.69 | 3.84 | 0.88 | 3.92 | 0.83 | 3.79 | 0.82 | 3.77 | 1.14 |

[a]The full title for this occupation is "Janitors and Cleaners, Except Maids and Housekeeping."

included in the sample were rated by close to or more than 60 raters. The occupations are (a) First Line Supervisors, Clerical/Administrative ($n = 59$), (b) Secretaries, Except Legal and Medical ($n = 67$), and (c) General Office Clerks ($n = 92$). Within each occupation, respondents were randomly assigned to two groups of 30 each, except that the first group of First Line Supervisors, Clerical/Administrative contained only 29 raters. Profiles were calculated for each of the six groups (i.e., two groups for each of three occupations). Each profile consists of the mean ratings for that group on each of the 21 reinforcers. A matrix containing the correlations among the six group profiles was then calculated.

To achieve more stable estimates of these correlations, the process of assigning raters randomly to one of two groups within each occupation was performed 10 times, resulting in 10 different randomly assigned sets of six groups. A correlation matrix was calculated for each set of six-group profiles. Table 12-10 presents the median correlations across the 10 correlation matrices.

The within-occupation median correlations between group profiles are $r_{30} = .86$, $r_{30} = .87$, and $r_{30} = .91$, respectively. These correlations are estimates of the overall reliability of the Occupational Values Questionnaire for these occupations when there are 30 raters per occupation. These reliabilities are good and similar to the projected interrater agreement discussed in the *Reliability* section of this chapter ($r_{30} = .82$).

The question remains, however, Can profiles on this questionnaire capture similarities and differences between occupations? The remaining off-diagonal median correlations in Table 12-10 address this question. They are correlations between group profiles across occupations. There are four such correlations for each pair of occupations. For example, the between-group and across-occupation median profile correlations for Occupations 1 and 2 (i.e., First Line Supervisors, Clerical/Administrative, and Secretaries Except Legal and Medical, respectively) are $r = .69$, $r = .64$, $r = .74$, and $r = .70$. These values are lower than the within-occupation median correlations for these two occupations ($r_{30} = .86$ and $r_{30} = .87$, respectively). This result is evidence that this questionnaire recognizes differences between these two occupations, even though they tend to occur in the same environment and involve many of the same tasks. The between-occupation median correlations comparing Occupation 1 profiles with Occupation 3 (i.e., General Office Clerks) profiles are also somewhat lower than the relevant within-occupation median correlations, suggesting that this questionnaire can differentiate between these two occupations.

However, the median correlations comparing Occupation 2 profiles with Occupation 3 profiles are high relative to their respective within-occupation median correlations. This result suggests that this questionnaire does not differentiate Occupation 2 from Occupation 3 in terms of reinforcers. This is not surprising given the similarities in these occupa-

**TABLE 12-10**
**Correlations Among Group Mean Ratings Profiles Between and Within Three Example Occupations: Occupational Values**

| | Occupation 1 | | Occupation 2 | | Occupation 3 | |
|---|---|---|---|---|---|---|
| | Group 1[a] | Group 2 | Group 1 | Group 2 | Group 1 | Group 2 |
| Occupation 1 | | | | | | |
| Group 1 | — | | | | | |
| Group 2 | 86 | — | | | | |
| Occupation 2 | | | | | | |
| Group 1 | 69 | 74 | — | | | |
| Group 2 | 64 | 70 | 87 | — | | |
| Occupation 3 | | | | | | |
| Group 1 | 77 | 84 | 87 | 84 | — | |
| Group 2 | 74 | 75 | 85 | 86 | 91 | — |

*Note.* Within each occupation $n = 60$ raters, randomly divided in half; therefore each group's profile of mean ratings is based on 30 raters. This process was performed 10 times, resulting in 10 different randomly assigned sets of six groups (i.e., 2 groups per occupation). A correlation matrix was calculated for each set of six group profiles. Each element of this table contains the median of its associated elements across all 10 correlation matrices. Occupation 1 = First-Line Supervisors and Managers/ Supervisors; Clerical and Administrative Support Workers; Occupation 2 = Secretaries Except Legal and Medical; Occupation 3 = General Office Clerks. Decimals have been omitted.
[a]The mean profile for this group is based on only 29 raters because the sample available for analysis included only 59 raters of this occupation.

tions; Occupation 2 is regular Secretaries, and Occupation 3 is Office Clerks.

Taken as a whole, the results presented in Table 12-10 provide evidence that the Occupational Values Questionnaire can reliably describe occupations in terms of reinforcers if it is supported by 30 raters per occupation. It also is interesting that the questionnaire was able to partially differentiate among three occupations that take place in the same environment and involve very similar tasks; all three are clerical office occupations. Smaller between-occupation profile correlations would be likely if less similar occupations were considered.

## DISCUSSION

The primary motivation for describing occupations in terms of the constructs discussed in this chapter is to facilitate the match between the interests and values of people and occupations that are likely to satisfy those interests and values. That is, occupations vary according to the activities they involve and the potential reinforcers that they offer incumbents. Two taxonomies and their associated indicators are discussed in this chapter: (a) Holland codes that denote the three Holland types most closely associated with each occupation and (b) mean occupation ratings on the 21 need-reinforcers presented in the Occupational Values Questionnaire. The goal was to assess the feasibility of including these constructs and their indicators in O*NET's content model. In this context there are three parts to the feasibility question. First, do research and theory support the selected occupational interest and value taxonomies? Second, are the procedures for assessing occupations according to the selected interest and value taxonomies practically usable in the context of O*NET? Finally, are the assessments of the occupations according to the selected interest and value taxonomies reliable and valid?

## Interests

The six Holland types are a significant part of the vocational and career counseling literature, and there is evidence supporting the reliability and validity of various assessments of occupations according to the Holland types (e.g., Dawis 1991; Hansen & Campbell, 1985). A good deal of this research depends on large numbers of individuals completing long instruments for each occupation in question. The alternative procedure that G. Gottfredson and Holland (1996) used for developing Holland codes for OES/O*NET occupations is relatively efficient and has already generated Holland codes for every occupation in this structure.

Holland and G. Gottfredson review evidence supporting the validity of the Holland codes for DOT occupations (1989, 1996). We have examined the validity of the Holland codes for O*NET occupations by reviewing the codes for six occupations that vary across industry and level (see Table 12-2). The codes describe and differentiate among the occupations in a manner that is logically consistent with definitions of each of the Holland types and with what is known about these occupations.

The evidence supporting the validity of the Holland codes developed by G. Gottfredson and Holland (1996) is positive, yet preliminary. There is a fair amount of evidence supporting the validity of these codes for DOT occupations, but more evidence is needed to support their validity for the O*NET occupations. Analyses comparing these Holland codes with other parts of the O*NET content model could substantially increase confidence in the validity of the Holland codes. However, given the positive preliminary evidence, the substantial literature behind the

Holland types, and the wide use of the Holland taxonomy in vocational and career counseling, it is recommended that the Holland codes remain part of O*NET's content model.

## Values

The literature supports the need to describe occupations in terms of values (i.e., the importance of particular work activities and other characteristics of the work environments, Dawis, 1991). The MJDQ is an instrument designed to describe occupations according to the relative presence of 21 need-reinforcers (i.e., work values). Dawis (1991) provided evidence that these 21 reinforcers address the work values assessed by other instruments. Borgen et al. (1968), Dawis and Lofquist (1984), and (Dawis, 1991) described and summarized evidence supporting the reliability and validity of the MJDQ. Finally, Weiss et al. (1964) and Gay et al. (1971) provided evidence that the statements presented in the MJDQ to assess the reinforcers are easy to read and understand. Clearly, the Occupational Values Questionnaire is based on sound theoretical ground and a very practical and usable occupation assessment instrument (i.e., the MJDQ).

There are, however, some concerns about the Occupational Values Questionnaire and the nature of the sample of occupations and respondents included in the O*NET prototype data collection effort. First, as previously mentioned, the Occupational Values Questionnaire is based on the MJDQ, with two substantial modifications: (a) the MJDQ requires forced choices between or among statements that represent each of the 21 reinforcers, whereas the Occupational Values Questionnaire requires that each statement be individually rated, and (b) in the Occupational Values Questionnaire, the wording of some of the 21 MJDQ statements was modified. These modifications have implications for consideration of the results of the analyses. As discussed earlier in this chapter, if respondents are not forced to make choices about reinforcers relative to each other, they may display (a) a positive bias and rate every reinforcer as present in their occupation or (b) a job satisfaction bias and rate every reinforcer according to their overall level of job satisfaction. The concern was that this would result in mean occupation ratings that were uniformly high or showed little variation across occupations and reinforcers. Such a result could reduce the effectiveness of the ratings on the Occupational Values Questionnaire in terms of its ability to differentiate among occupations. Additionally, there is some concern that modifications to the wording of the reinforcer statements may affect the construct that each assesses and thus change the structure of the taxonomy.

It is in the context of these strengths and weaknesses that the evidence regarding the reliability and the validity of the Occupational Values Questionnaire should be considered. The results discussed in this chapter present evidence regarding the extent to which the occupation mean ratings on the questionnaire can reliably differentiate among occupations. The *Reliability* section of this chapter presents reliability evidence in terms of the extent to which there is more variation in respondent ratings across occupations than within occupations. This method of considering reliability, referred to as interrater agreement, assumes that occupations vary on the constructs being assessed. Therefore, these indices of interrater agreement provide relatively direct evidence about the extent to which the reinforcers assessed by the Occupational Values Questionnaire can differentiate among occupations. The results suggest that in the current sample the reliability of occupation mean ratings of individual reinforcers is low and that reasonably reliable ratings at the level of individual reinforcers would require at least 30 respondents per occupation. However, the evidence considering the reliability of the questionnaire as a whole is more optimistic. The results show an interrater agreement of $r_k = .60$ for the questionnaire as a whole, with a harmonic mean of $k = 9.69$ respondents per occupation and a very respectable estimate of what the interrater agreement would be if there were 30 respondents per occupation ($r_{30} = .82$). This, by itself, is evidence that if the Occupational Values Questionnaire were supported by 30 respondents per occupation, it could reliably differentiate among occupations.

Some of the analyses address the validity of the Occupational Values Questionnaire in terms of the similarities and differences among occupations. Examination of the occupation means on the 21 reinforcers across six varied occupations (see Table 12-9) indicates that some reinforcers show little variation across the six occupations; however, others do vary in a manner consistent with expected similarities and differences among the examined occupations.

Table 12-10 represents an alternative method of examining the reliability and validity of the Occupational Values Questionnaire. Reliability in this context is defined as the extent to which the mean ratings for one group of respondents from a particular occupation are related to the mean ratings for another group of respondents from the same occupation. Here the reliability of the Occupational Values Questionnaire, supported by 30 respondents per occupation, is strong. The results presented in Table 12-10 also support the hypothesis that when this questionnaire is completed by 30 respondents per occupation, it can recognize differences and similarities in occupational reinforcer profiles across occupations.

Research and theory support the hypothesis that the constructs measured by the Occupational Values Questionnaire are relevant to the description of occupations. Furthermore, this questionnaire is practical and usable in the context of O*NET. It is simple and short relative to the other questionnaires. The results of this study also provide favorable evidence for the ability of the questionnaire as a whole to reliably differentiate among occupations when there are 30 respondents per occupation. This successful differentiation among occupations minimizes the concern that not using a forced-choice rating format would result in too little variation in ratings across occupations.

As was true for the measurement of interests using the Holland codes, the current evidence supports the inclusion of the Occupational Values Questionnaire in the O*NET content model. This questionnaire should be maintained as part of the system. However, additional studies with larger numbers of occupations and respondents per occupation would allow a more definitive evaluation of the extent to which the questionnaire can reliably differentiate among occupations. Additionally, comparison of these ratings with ratings in other domains of the content model

would enhance the evaluation of the Occupational Values Questionnaire.

The results suggest that some of the individual items (i.e., reinforcer statements) could not reliably differentiate among occupations, even if there were 30 respondents per occupation. This could be interpreted as suggesting that individual items showing low reliabilities should be eliminated from the questionnaire. However, it is recommended that all 21 items be retained in the questionnaire because further studies including more occupations and more respondents per occupation will likely provide more favorable item-level reliability evidence. Additionally, the Occupational Values Questionnaire would no longer represent a complete taxonomy of occupational values if items were removed.

# Work Styles

WALTER C. BORMAN, U. CHRISTEAN KUBISIAK,
AND ROBERT J. SCHNEIDER

This chapter is about work style requirements for occupations and jobs. The term *work styles* is used purposefully; the domain could have been called personality, but we wanted to emphasize personal characteristics that are work- and job-related and to avoid clinically oriented personality constructs. Accordingly, it seemed most appropriate to refer to this domain as work styles.

Work style requirements in occupations are becoming more important as occupations and organizations undergo what is proving to be considerable change. Changes include organizations' increasing use of teams to do work (e.g., Guzzo & Salas, 1995); organizational citizenship or contextual performance being more often considered important (e.g., Borman & Motowidlo, 1993; Landy, Shankster, & Kohler, 1994); service jobs becoming more numerous (e.g., Schneider, 1990); and person–organization fit between employees and the values and "personality" of the organization increasingly being a focus of study (e.g., Borman, Hanson, & Hedge, 1997; Schneider, Goldstein, & Smith, 1996). Each of these trends is associated with increased importance for work styles. To be successful, teams require that their members have certain interpersonal and consensus-building skills. Contextual performance has personality constructs as antecedents or predictors. Most service jobs require strong interpersonal skills, and person–organization fit generally focuses on the personality, motivational, and values areas. Accordingly, the work style domain is an important part of the Occupational Information Network (O*NET) content model.

Below we review several personality taxonomies. After reviewing these existing taxonomies, we describe the methodology used to develop a taxonomy of work styles to be used in the O*NET; then we explain and justify the content of that taxonomy. The general goal of this effort was to identify a comprehensive yet reasonably small number of personal characteristics that describe the important interpersonal and work style requirements in jobs and occupations in the U.S. economy. Finally, the chapter describes an initial empirical investigation of the descriptors associated with the taxonomy.

## REVIEW OF EXISTING TAXONOMIES

We first reviewed several taxonomies that have been used in an industrial/organizational psychology context, mostly in the area of personnel selection. The point of departure for building our taxonomy was the five-factor model (FFM; e.g., Barrick & Mount, 1991; Goldberg, 1993). Factor analyses of self-ratings (e.g., Goldberg, 1981) and peer-ratings under several conditions (Goldberg, 1990; Norman, 1963; Tupes & Christal, 1961/1992) have often resulted in a five-factor solution, usually characterized by these or similar construct labels: Surgency, Agreeableness, Emotional Stability, Conscientiousness, and Intellectance. The weight of evidence supporting the existence of these five factors strongly argued for considering them when developing our taxonomy.

A second personality taxonomy we paid considerable attention to was that of R. Hogan (e.g., R. Hogan, 1982). This is because the Hogan Personality Inventory (HPI; R. Hogan & J. Hogan, 1992), which measures the constructs in R. Hogan's taxonomy, was explicitly developed to predict job performance. R. Hogan (1982) has suggested that Surgency contains two elements that are sufficiently independent to warrant separate measurement. He calls these elements Ascendance and Sociability. His other dimensions correspond reasonably well to the FFM: Adjustment, Likability, Self-Control, and Intellectance.

Third, work on the Assessment of Background and Life Experiences (ABLE; see Hough, 1997) in the U.S. Army's Project A was considered in developing our dimensions for the work styles domain. That research was also focused on the prediction of job performance. The ABLE constructs are Achievement, Physical Condition, Cooperativeness, Adjustment, Potency, Dependability, and Locus of Control. These dimensions correspond in part to the Big Five, but Surgency is subdivided into Potency and Achievement, Intellectance is not represented in the ABLE, and two additional dimensions outside of the FFM are evident (Physical Condition and Locus of Control).

Fourth, we referred to the constructs measured in the Occupational Personality Questionnaire (OPQ;

Saville & Holdsworth, 1990). The OPQ scales were not derived from the FFM. Instead, they were deductively developed to operationalize constructs directly relevant to the working population. The constructs are grouped into three broad areas: Relationships with People, Thinking Style, and Feelings/Emotions.

Finally, a fifth category system that guided our efforts deserves a more complete description. Guion and his colleagues (Guion, 1992; Raymark, Schmit, & Guion, 1997) developed a job analysis questionnaire specifically intended to measure personality requirements of jobs. Part of their research in this domain involved identifying constructs that differentiate personality requirements across jobs.

In our judgment, this is exactly what the work styles taxonomy in the O*NET content model should reflect. That is, what are the work style constructs that differentiate among jobs? The goal of the research by Raymark et al. was to evaluate the validity of the inventory by first using it to identify work style requirements in several jobs and then determining how well work style test scores corresponding to the required traits predict job performance. If the job analysis inventory is to be useful for selection, it should identify as work style requirements traits that prove to be good predictors of performance.

As mentioned, because our objectives are very similar to some of the objectives in the research program conducted by Guion and colleagues (Raymark et al., 1997), we considered this work very carefully in building our *taxonomy* of work styles. Their analyses to date have resulted in a 12-dimension system: General Leadership, Interest in Negotiation, Achievement Striving, Friendly Disposition, Sensitivity to Interests of Others, Cooperative or Collaborative Work Tendency, General Trustworthiness, Adherence to a Work Ethic, Thoroughness and Attentiveness to Detail, Emotional Stability, Desire to Generate Ideas, and Tendency to Think Things Through.

## REVIEW OF FACTOR ANALYTIC AND OTHER CORRELATIONAL DATA RELATING TO PERSONALITY STRUCTURE

In addition to our review of the taxonomies discussed above, we examined factor analytic and correlational data that provided evidence for the structure of work styles by indicating the relationships among work style constructs. Such data, together with consideration of taxonomic work, helped us to (a) decide on an appropriate number of first-level constructs; (b) place second-level constructs under the appropriate first-level constructs; (c) assess the relative independence of various constructs; and (d) better understand the nature of the constructs in our taxonomy.

We drew on a variety of research studies to help determine an appropriate number of first-level constructs. Research on the FFM (e.g., Goldberg, 1990; McCrae, & Costa, 1987; Tupes & Christal, 1961/

1992) provided strong indications regarding higher order constructs that should be included in our taxonomy. R. Hogan's (1982; see also R. Hogan & J. Hogan, 1992) six-factor taxonomy and Hough's (1992) nine-factor taxonomy also were useful.

We were able to draw on a variety of work to assist us in defining second-level constructs. This work included FFM facet-level research (Costa, McCrae, & Dye, 1991); R. Hogan and J. Hogan's (1992) homogeneous item composites (HICs), which are facets of their six broad constructs; the second-level personality constructs in Tellegen's (1982) taxonomy; certain constructs in Gough's (1987) California Psychological Inventory; and the constructs measured by the OPQ. The job-requirements-based facets of the Big Five suggested by Guion (1992) also informed our selection of second-level constructs, as did Fleishman and Gilbert's (1994) social/interpersonal characteristics taxonomy and Mumford's (1994) social skills taxonomy, which he prepared in connection with the O*NET content model.

Work by Mumford (1994) is important for our taxonomy for an additional reason. He has argued that his personality factors include concepts related to learning. More specifically, some of Mumford's constructs address motivation and other concepts facilitating learning and adaptability to a changing environment. Because learning and adaptability are becoming more and more critical for employees in modern organizations operating in a rapidly changing global environment, it was important for us to attend to Mumford's (1994) personality constructs.

We also relied on factor analytic and other correlational research to verify that certain constructs we believed were distinct were, in fact, relatively independent. For example, we confirmed the relative independence of Achievement and Social Influence by referring to Tellegen and Waller (in press) and established the relative independence of our Practical Intelligence construct from mental ability by attending to McCrae and Costa (1987).

Finally, we clarified the content of the constructs in our taxonomy by reviewing a variety of work. This review included examination of definitions of closely related constructs included in various other taxonomies (e.g., Costa, McCrae, & Dye, 1991; Gough, 1987; R. Hogan & J. Hogan, 1992; Hough, 1992; Tellegen, 1982; Tellegen & Waller, in press; Wiggins, Trapnell, & Phillips, 1988); examination of factor solutions relating to personality structure (e.g., Goldberg, 1990; McCrae & Costa, 1987); and review of critical discussions regarding the nature of certain constructs (e.g., Barrick & Mount, 1991; Goldberg, 1993; McCrae & Costa, 1987).

## ESTABLISHMENT OF JOB-RELATEDNESS

In developing our taxonomy of work styles, we also emphasized constructs that have been empirically shown to correlate with important job behaviors or related criteria. Accordingly, we examined literature reviews, meta-analyses, and relevant criterion-related validity evidence to identify work style constructs that relate to job behaviors. This work is discussed next.

In an early paper, Ghiselli (1973) suggested that the reason why personality tests did not seem to predict job performance very well was that correlations between performance and personality scales that had no conceptual relation to criteria were often included in evaluating average personality–job-performance relationships. An example is when correlations between scores on each scale of an inventory and performance on the job are examined even when some of the scales would not be expected to have any relationship to performance. This often was the case, for example, with studies reviewed by Guion and Gottier (1965) in their influential review. Thus, Ghiselli first reviewed literature and identified those personality–performance links where a reasonable conceptual argument could be made for a correlation between the two. Then he averaged those correlations, ignoring all of the other personality–performance correlations he hypothesized would not yield significant relations. Results of this review were more positive than previous reviews and the prevailing opinion about personality in a personnel selection context. A median correlation of .26 was found across the seven occupational categories he included.

The use of personality and criterion taxonomies to summarize criterion-related validity studies has resulted in a steady accumulation of findings clearly indicating the relevance of personality constructs to job-related criteria. For example, Kamp and Hough (1986) summarized studies that related the ABLE constructs described earlier to a variety of organizationally relevant criteria, including training, job proficiency, job involvement/withdrawal, and delinquency (e.g., substance abuse). Kamp and Hough (1986) reported reasonably good validities against these criteria for several of the personality constructs they studied.

Barrick and Mount (1991), using the FFM to categorize personality constructs, and Hough (1992), using her nine-construct expansion of the FFM, reported meta-analytic findings that further support the relevance of personality to the workplace. Barrick and Mount's (1991) paper was noteworthy for its identification of Conscientiousness as a consistent correlate of important work-related criteria across a variety of occupations (estimated true validity = .22). In their meta-analysis, other relationships between Big Five personality constructs and performance were considerably lower. By contrast, Hough's (1992) results showed the relevance of each of the nine personality variables in her taxonomy to at least one criterion construct.

R. Hogan (1991) conducted a broad review of the role of personality in industrial/organizational psychology. Part of this review included a summary of a major research program studying personality in a personnel selection context. Bentz (1985) studied the performance of thousands of managers and executives in a large retail company over a 20-year period. Among the predictor measures was the Guilford-Zimmerman Temperament Survey (GZTS). Bentz found that several scales from the GZTS were moderately but consistently related to several important performance criteria, including performance ratings, compensation, and promotability. He concluded that personality is an important predictor of both managerial performance and advancement.

Finally, R. Hogan (1991) pointed to his own research with the HPI (R. Hogan, 1986). R. Hogan, J. Hogan, and colleagues have successfully used the HPI to predict performance in numerous samples and in many different jobs. More recent research involving the HPI summarized in R. Hogan and J. Hogan (1992) has indicated that HPI scales corresponding to each of the Big Five correlated significantly and meaningfully with a variety of job-related criteria. These and other results were carefully examined as we attempted to identify appropriate constructs for our taxonomy of work styles.

## EXPLANATION AND JUSTIFICATION OF TAXONOMY CONTENT

The work style taxonomy comprises seven first-level constructs and 17 second-level constructs. The taxonomy is arranged hierarchically, with the second-level constructs reflecting a finer grained definition of the first-level constructs. For example, Conscientiousness (first-level) has as its second-level constructs Dependability, Attention to Detail, and Integrity. Table 13-1 presents the seven first-level constructs, including construct labels and definitions, the most relevant citations, and Level scale anchors describing high, medium, and low work style requirements for each construct. Table 13-2 presents the same kind of information for the 17 lower order constructs.

### Achievement Orientation

Achievement Orientation has been a core construct in personality theory and research for many years. It is perhaps the most intensively studied of Murray's (1938) needs, and it is also included in the California Psychological Inventory, the OPQ, the Multidimensional Personality Questionnaire (Tellegen, 1982), and the ABLE (Hough, 1992), among other questionnaires. Achievement Orientation is also represented in Fleishman and Gilbert's (1994) taxonomy of social/interpersonal characteristics.

In the FFM, Achievement Orientation is included in the Conscientiousness factor (e.g., Costa, McCrae, & Dye, 1991; Goldberg, 1990; McCrae & Costa, 1987). In the Digman and Takemoto-Chock (1981) FFM, the factor is even labeled *Will to Achieve*, reflecting the importance of the achievement element. Hough's (1992) view is that Achievement and De-

**TABLE 13-1**
**Descriptions and Definitions of Higher Order Work Style Descriptors**

| Operational definition | Citations | Level scale | |
|---|---|---|---|
| | | Level | Anchors |
| **I. Achievement Orientation** | | | |
| Job requires personal goal setting, trying to succeed at those goals, and striving to be competent in own work. | Digman & Takemoto-Chock (1981) Fleishman & Gilbert (1994) Gough (1987) Guion (1992) R. Hogan & J. Hogan (1992) Hough (1992) Saville & Holdsworth (1990) Tellegen (1982) | High | Requires setting very high standards, concentrating on and persisting in challenging tasks, and being driven by a need for success. |
| | | Medium | Requires setting high standards, trying to do a good job, concentrating on and persisting in routine tasks, and a moderate level of need for success. |
| | | Low | Does not necessarily require high standards in work or an undue amount of effort or persistence. |
| **II. Social Influence** | | | |
| Job requires having an impact on others in the organization and displaying energy and leadership. | Fleishman & Gilbert (1994) Gough (1987) Guion (1992) R. Hogan & J. Hogan (1992) Hough (1992) Mumford (1994) Saville & Holdsworth (1990) Tellegen (1982) Wiggins, Trapnell, & Phillips (1988) | High | Requires being very energetic and strongly preferring to lead and influence others. |
| | | Medium | Requires being moderately outgoing and energetic and having some preference to lead and influence others. |
| | | Low | Rarely requires outgoing, energetic, or influential behavior. |
| **III. Interpersonal Orientation** | | | |
| Job requires being pleasant, cooperative, sensitive to others, easy to get along with, and having a preference for associating with other organization members. | Fleishman & Gilbert (1994) Guion (1992) R. Hogan & J. Hogan (1992) Hough (1992) McCrae & Costa (1987) Mumford (1994) Tellegen (1982) Wiggins, Trapnell, & Phillips (1988) | High | Requires very friendly, helpful, and nonconfrontational behavior. |
| | | Medium | Requires moderately friendly, helpful, and nonconfrontational behavior. |
| | | Low | Requires comparatively little friendly, helpful, or nonconfrontational behavior. |
| **IV. Adjustment** | | | |
| Job requires maturity, poise, flexibility, and restraint to cope with pressure, stress, criticism, setbacks, personal and work-related problems, etc. | Fleishman & Gilbert (1994) Goldberg (1990) Gough (1987) Guion (1992) R. Hogan & J. Hogan (1992) Hough (1992) McCrae & Costa (1987) Mumford (1994) Saville & Holdsworth (1990) Tellegen (1982) | High | Requires being very calm and adaptable, maintaining composure, and avoiding overly emotional behavior. |
| | | Medium | Requires being generally calm and adaptable, attempting to maintain composure, and avoiding overly emotional behavior. |
| | | Low | Does not necessarily require being calm or maintaining composure. |
| **V. Conscientiousness** | | | |
| Job requires dependability, commitment to doing the job correctly and carefully, and being trustworthy, accountable, and attentive to details. | Goldberg (1990) R. Hogan & J. Hogan (1992) Hough (1992) McCrae & Costa (1987) Saville & Holdsworth (1990) | High | Requires being highly responsible, dependable, and trustworthy on the job. |
| | | Medium | Requires being moderately responsible, dependable, and trustworthy on the job. |
| | | Low | Does not necessarily require much dependability on the job. |
| **VI. Independence** | | | |
| Job requires being autonomous, following own way of doing things, guiding oneself with little or no supervision, and depending mainly on oneself to get things done. | Fleishman & Gilbert (1994) Gough (1987) Hough (1992) Kamp & Gough (1986) | High | Requires a very high level of autonomy, with little or no dependence on others, to get job done. |
| | | Medium | Requires a moderate level of autonomy, with some dependence on others, to get job done. |
| | | Low | Does not require working on own to get job done. |

*Table 13-1 continues*

**TABLE 13-1** *(Continued)*

| Operational definition | Citations | Level scale | |
|---|---|---|---|
| | | Level | Anchors |
| VII. Practical Intelligence | | | |
| Job requires generating useful ideas and thinking things through logically. | Goldberg (1990)<br>R. Hogan & J. Hogan (1992)<br>Hough (1992)<br>McCrae & Costa (1987)<br>Norman (1963)<br>Tupes & Christal (1961/1992) | High | Requires consistently generating high-quality, very useful, work-related ideas and being very logical and effective in thinking through job and work issues and problems. |
| | | Medium | Requires generally coming up with useful, work-related ideas and usually being logical and effective in thinking through job and work issues and problems. |
| | | Low | Does not necessarily require generating useful, work-related ideas or having to logically think through job and work issues and problems. |

pendability are confounded in the FFM, and she explicitly differentiated those constructs in her taxonomy. Within R. Hogan and J. Hogan's (1992) taxonomy, aspects of Achievement Orientation can be found in the Competitive homogeneous item composite (HIC), in their Ambition factor, and in the Mastery HIC within the Prudence factor. Guion's (1992) work with the personality-related job analysis questionnaire identified an Achievement Striving factor, as did Fleishman and Gilbert's (1994) social/interpersonal characteristics taxonomy. In sum, Achievement Orientation is prominently reflected in personality taxonomies and inventories.

The construct involves striving for competence in one's work, working hard and valuing hard work, persisting in the face of obstacles, setting high standards, and wanting to get ahead (e.g., Costa, McCrae, & Dye, 1991; R. Hogan & J. Hogan, 1992; Hough, 1992; Tellegen & Waller, in press). Thus, in our judgment, Achievement Orientation might be decomposed into three subconstructs for the second-level taxonomy: Achievement/Effort, Persistence, and Initiative. *Achievement/Effort* reflects setting high standards, establishing tough goals, and expending considerable effort. *Persistence* refers to the element of not giving up and overcoming even formidable obstacles in getting the job done. *Initiative* represents the notion of a willingness to take on new or additional work responsibilities and challenges.

## Social Influence

The second first-level construct, Social Influence, closely corresponds to one of the two dimensions of the interpersonal circumplex, which has a long history in personality psychology (Kiesler, 1983; Leary, 1957; Wiggins, 1979; Wiggins et al., 1988). It is represented in R. Hogan and J. Hogan's (1992) taxonomy as part of Ambition; in Hough's (1992) taxonomy as Potency; in Fleishman and Gilbert's (1994) taxonomy as Persuasion and Energy/Assertiveness; in Mumford's (1994) taxonomy as Persuasion; and in Tellegen's (1982) taxonomy as Social Potency. In addition, it is reflected in Gough's (1987) Dominance

scale and the Persuasive scale of the OPQ. The Social Influence construct is also partly reflected in Guion's (1992) Leadership Orientation facet.

Despite past theoretical linkages between Achievement and Social Influence (e.g., Murray, 1938), the two constructs correlate only about .20 to .30 (Tellegen & Waller, in press). Similarly, Social Influence is distinct from, though moderately related to, Affiliation (R. Hogan & J. Hogan, 1992), which is represented in this taxonomy as part of a construct labeled *Interpersonal Orientation*. Our feeling is that there are elements of striving and wanting to lead inherent in Social Influence that are not present in Affiliation (Tellegen & Waller, in press; Wiggins, 1991). Affiliation is more inherently communal, involving working well with other people.

The way our taxonomy is configured, Social Influence contains components of interpersonal impact, persuasiveness, and energy. Individuals with high scores for Social Influence enjoy leadership roles and are correspondingly forceful and decisive. Accordingly, Energy and Leadership Orientation were identified as second-level constructs in this domain. Although it seems reasonable to suggest that Energy facilitates Leadership Orientation, the two subconstructs are also distinct. Leadership Orientation is an inherently social construct, whereas Energy is a temperament construct.

## Interpersonal Orientation

The third construct, Interpersonal Orientation, has elements of Agreeableness and Sociability. Regarding the FFM, this construct aligns well with Sociability. Abod, Gilbert, and Fleishman (1996), Fleishman and Gilbert (1994), and Mumford (1994) offered several constructs related to Interpersonal Orientation and its second-level constructs, Cooperative, Caring, and Social. Fleishman and Gilbert suggested Agreeableness, Social Sensitivity, and Sociability, which correspond closely to the meanings of our subconstructs. Also related to our subconstructs are Coordination, Social Perceptiveness, and Engagement, which appear in Mumford's taxonomy.

**TABLE 13-2**
**Descriptions and Definitions of Lower Order Work-Style Descriptors**

| Construct label | Operational definition | Citations | Level scale | |
|---|---|---|---|---|
| | | | Level | Anchor |
| I. Achievement Orientation | | | | |
| A. Achievement/ Effort | Job requires establishing and maintaining personally challenging achievement goals and exerting effort toward task mastery. | Costa, McCrae, & Dye (1991) Guion (1992) R. Hogan & J. Hogan (1992) | High | Requires continual extensive effort toward achievement of work goals. |
| | | | Medium | Requires sustained effort toward achievement of work goals. |
| | | | Low | Requires only moderate levels of effort toward achievement of work goals. |
| B. Persistence | Job requires persistence in the face of obstacles on the job. | Costa, McCrae, & Dye (1991) R. Hogan & J. Hogan (1992) | High | Requires high levels of persistence when work becomes difficult. |
| | | | Medium | Requires moderate levels of persistence on the job. |
| | | | Low | Requires little persistence on the job; few obstacles are encountered. |
| C. Initiative | Job requires being willing to take on job responsibilities and challenges. | Robertson & Kinder (1993) | High | Requires volunteering to take on new or additional work responsibilities and challenges. |
| | | | Medium | Requires some willingness to take on new work responsibilities and challenges. |
| | | | Low | Requires little interest in new work responsibilities or challenges; responsibilities are structured and stable. |
| II. Social Influence | | | | |
| A. Energy | Job requires the energy and stamina to accomplish work tasks. | Costa, McCrae, & Dye (1991) | High | Requires very high levels of energy to get tasks done. |
| | | | Medium | Requires moderate levels of energy to get tasks done. |
| | | | Low | Requires little energy to get tasks done; job is not very physically or mentally demanding. |
| B. Leadership Orientation | Job requires a willingness to lead, take charge, and offer opinions and direction. | Costa, McCrae, & Dye (1991) Guion (1992) R. Hogan & J. Hogan (1992) Tellegen (1982) | High | Requires a strong preference for making decisions and leading or directing other organization members. |
| | | | Medium | Requires some preference for making decisions and leading or directing other organization members. |
| | | | Low | Requires little or no leader decision making. |
| III. Interpersonal Orientation | | | | |
| A. Cooperation | Job requires being pleasant with others on the job and displaying a good-natured, cooperative attitude encourages people to work together. | Costa, McCrae, & Dye (1991) Fleishman & Gilbert (1994) Guion (1992) R. Hogan & J. Hogan (1992) Hough (1992) Mumford (1994) | High | Requires working very smoothly and cooperatively with others on the job. |
| | | | Medium | Requires generally working smoothly and cooperatively with others on the job. |
| | | | Low | Requires little interaction with others. |
| B. Concern for Others | Job requires being sensitive to others' needs and feelings and being understanding and helpful on the job. | Costa, McCrae, & Dye (1991) Fleishman & Gilbert (1994) Gough (1987) Guion (1992) R. Hogan & J. Hogan (1992) Mumford (1994) Saville & Holdsworth (1990) | High | Requires very high levels of sensitivity to others' needs and feelings and consistent caring and support for others on the job. |
| | | | Medium | Requires high levels of sensitivity, caring, and support toward others on the job. |
| | | | Low | Requires sensitivity, caring, and support toward others on the job, but this is not a highly important trait for this job. |

*Table 13-2 continues*

**TABLE 13-2 (*Continued*)**

| Construct label | Operational definition | Citations | Level scale | |
|---|---|---|---|---|
| | | | Level | Anchor |
| C. Social Orientation | Job requires preferring to work with others rather than alone and being personally connected with others on the job. | Costa, McCrae, & Dye (1991)<br>Fleishman & Gilbert (1994)<br>Gough (1987)<br>Guion (1992)<br>R. Hogan & J. Hogan (1992)<br>Hough (1992)<br>Mumford (1994)<br>Saville & Holdsworth (1990) | High<br><br><br>Medium<br><br><br><br>Low | Requires a high degree of participation and working closely with other organization members.<br>Requires a moderate degree of participation and, at times, working closely with other organization members.<br>Requires little participation with other organization members; usually works alone. |
| | | **IV. Adjustment** | | |
| A. Self-Control | Job requires maintaining composure, keeping emotions in check even in very difficult situations, controlling anger, and avoiding aggressive behavior. | Costa, McCrae, & Dye (1991)<br>Gough (1987)<br>R. Hogan & J. Hogan (1992)<br>McCrae & Costa (1987)<br>Saville & Holdsworth (1990)<br>Tellegen (1982) | High<br><br><br>Medium<br>Low | Requires a very high degree of self-control and behaving in a nonthreatening manner.<br>Requires a high degree of self-control.<br>This job does not usually involve situations that challenge self-control. |
| B. Stress Tolerance | Job requires accepting criticism, and dealing calmly and effectively with high stress situations. | Costa, McCrae, & Dye (1991)<br>Fleishman & Gilbert (1994)<br>R. Hogan & J. Hogan (1992)<br>Saville & Holdsworth (1990)<br>Tellegen (1982) | High<br><br><br>Medium<br><br><br>Low | Requires being extremely calm and tolerant of stress imposed by other people or by circumstances.<br>Requires being moderately calm and tolerant of stress imposed by other people or by circumstances.<br>This job does not involve much stress. |
| C. Adaptability/ Flexibility | Job requires being open to change (positive or negative) and to considerable variety in the workplace. | Costa, McCrae, & Dye (1991)<br>Fleishman & Gilbert (1994)<br>Gough (1987)<br>R. Hogan & J. Hogan (1992)<br>Mumford (1994)<br>Saville & Holdsworth (1990) | High<br><br><br>Medium<br><br><br>Low | Requires being highly flexible and adaptable, even to rapidly changing work situations.<br>Requires being moderately flexible and adaptable to changing work situations.<br>Rarely requires being flexible to changing work situations; this job and work setting are usually stable. |
| | | **V. Conscientiousness** | | |
| A. Dependability | Job requires being reliable, responsible, and dependable, and fulfilling obligations. | Costa, McCrae, & Dye (1991)<br>Fleishman & Gilbert (1994)<br>Gough (1987)<br>Guion (1992)<br>R. Hogan & J. Hogan (1992) | High<br><br><br>Medium<br><br><br>Low | Requires the highest levels of responsibility and dependability in fulfilling job and work obligations.<br>Requires considerable responsibility and dependability in fulfilling job and work obligations.<br>Requires responsibility and dependability, but if work is not done, it can be transferred to others. |
| B. Attention to Detail | Job requires being careful about detail and thorough in completing work tasks. | Costa, McCrae, & Dye (1991)<br>Guion (1992)<br>Saville & Holdsworth (1990) | High<br><br><br>Medium<br><br><br>Low | Requires a very high degree of care and thoroughness in handling details on the job.<br>Requires a high degree of care and attention to detail in handling job duties.<br>Requires attention to detail in handling job duties, but this is not a highly important trait for this job. |

*Table 13-2 continues*

**TABLE 13-2 (Continued)**

| Construct label | Operational definition | Citations | Level scale | |
|---|---|---|---|---|
| | | | Level | Anchor |
| C. Integrity | Job requires being honest and avoiding unethical behavior. | Costa, McCrae, & Dye (1991) Fleishman & Gilbert (1994) Guion (1992) R. Hogan & J. Hogan (1992) | High | Requires the highest levels of integrity and a willingness to abide by a strict code of ethics or behavior. |
| | | | Medium | Requires a great deal of integrity and abiding by a standard code of ethics and behavior. |
| | | | Low | Job does not generally require ethical choices or abiding by a code of ethics. |
| | | VI. Independence | | |
| Independence | Job requires developing own ways of doing things, guiding oneself with little or no supervision, and depending mainly on oneself to get things done. | Fleishman & Gilbert (1994) Gough (1987) Hough (1992) Kamp & Gough (1986) | High | Requires a very high level of autonomy, with little or no dependence on others, to get job done. |
| | | | Medium | Requires a moderate level of autonomy, with some dependence on others, to get job done. |
| | | | Low | Does not work alone; requires working with others to get the job done. |
| | | VII. Practical Intelligence | | |
| A. Innovation | Job requires creativity and alternative thinking to come up with new ideas for and answers to work-related problems. | Fleishman & Gilbert (1994) Guion (1992) R. Hogan & J. Hogan (1992) Saville & Holdsworth (1990) | High | Requires a lot of creative thinking and coming up with new ideas related to work, addressing job and work issues and problems, etc. |
| | | | Medium | Requires moderate levels of creative thinking and coming up with ideas related to work, addressing job and work issues and problems, etc. |
| | | | Low | Work requires little or no creative thinking. |
| B. Analytical Thinking | Job requires analyzing information and using logic to address work or job issues and problems. | Costa, McCrae, & Dye (1991) Guion (1992) Saville & Holdsworth (1990) | High | Requires being very good at analyzing complex issues, data, or problems related to work and consistently coming up with high quality, useful information. |
| | | | Medium | Requires being generally good at analyzing complex issues, data, or problems related to work and coming up with high quality, useful information. |
| | | | Low | Job does not require analyzing complex information. |

Hough's (1992) taxonomy includes two personality constructs that suggested the Interpersonal Orientation construct: Affiliation and Agreeableness/Likeability. Tellegen's (1982) Social Closeness scale captures aspects of both Affiliation and Agreeableness, and thus is quite similar to our Interpersonal Orientation construct. Guion (1992) offered the general dimensions Friendly Disposition, Sensitivity to Others, and Cooperative Work Tendency. These dimensions correspond very closely to the Interpersonal Orientation second-level constructs in the present taxonomy. Our second-level constructs are similarly reflected in several HICs in the HPI (Easy to Live With, Caring, Sensitive, and Likes People) and in several facets of the Big Five measured by the NEO-Personality Inventory—Revised (Costa & McCrae, 1992a): Compliance, Altruism, Warmth, and Gregarious.

Thus, the Interpersonal Orientation construct, as we have configured it, contains elements of display-ing a cooperative attitude toward others on the job, being sensitive to coworkers' needs, and preferring to work with others rather than alone. Our three second-level constructs, Cooperative, Caring, and Social, respectively represent these facets of Interpersonal Orientation. Interpersonal Orientation will be very important to the increasing numbers of individuals who work on teams. Uncooperative, insensitive people who prefer to work alone will have a difficult time in a workplace that, more and more, spawns tasks and projects requiring interdependent work.

## Adjustment

An Adjustment construct appears in virtually every major personality taxonomy. The FFM includes a factor usually labeled Neuroticism (e.g., McCrae & Costa, 1987) or Emotional Stability (e.g., Goldberg, 1990). Both Hough's (1992) and R. Hogan and J.

Hogan's (1992) taxonomies include a construct called Adjustment, and Tellegen's (1982) taxonomy includes a construct closely related to Neuroticism that he has labeled Negative Emotionality.

Adjustment involves being calm, composed, and rational even when confronted with stressful situations. The well-adjusted individual also displays an evenness of mood and is adaptable to even rapidly changing work situations. The three second-level constructs—Self-Control, Stress Tolerance, and Adaptability/Flexibility—reflect these elements of Adjustment.

Self-Control involves restraining the social expression of negative emotion. It corresponds fairly closely with Tellegen's (1982) Aggression construct; R. Hogan and J. Hogan's (1992) Even-Tempered HIC; Costa, McCrae, and Dye's (1991) Hostility facet of Big Five Neuroticism; Gough's (1987) Self Control scale; and the Emotional Control scale from the OPQ. Stress Tolerance is defined as the ability to control negative emotion when exposed to stressors, which, in turn, affects people's ability to function effectively. This second-level construct is closely related to Tellegen's (1982) Stress Reaction construct; R. Hogan and J. Hogan's (1992) Calmness HIC; Costa, McCrae, & Dye's (1991) Vulnerability facet of Big Five Neuroticism; and the Worrying and Relaxed scales from the OPQ. In addition, Fleishman and Gilbert (1994) described a Self Control construct that involves the degree to which self-control, composure, and rationality are maintained in the presence of irritating or stressful stimuli. Despite its label, Fleishman and Gilbert's (1994) Self-Control construct corresponds closely to the Stress Tolerance construct in our taxonomy.

Adaptability/Flexibility was suggested by the Change Orientated scale of the OPQ; R. Hogan and J. Hogan's (1992) Experience Seeking HIC; Costa, McCrae, & Dye's (1991) Actions facet of Big Five Openness to Experience; Fleishman and Gilbert's (1994) and Mumford's (1994) Behavioral Flexibility constructs; and Gough's (1987) Flexibility scale. Adaptability/Flexibility is not usually included in the description of Adjustment and related constructs. Nevertheless, it seems most appropriately included there. In our taxonomy, Adaptability/Flexibility less involves the curiosity, broad interests, love of novelty, and open-mindedness that characterize the FFM Openness to Experience/Intellectance factor (McCrae & Costa, 1987; Goldberg, 1990) than the capacity to cope with stress that is inherent in exposure to a frequently changing work environment. This construct is related to Stress Tolerance; however, it involves tolerating a special kind of stress: the stress caused by exposure to change. It therefore seemed reasonable to distinguish the two constructs. This distinction also makes sense in light of the increasingly dynamic nature of the workplace that external business conditions and rapidly advancing technology are causing. The work environments of the immediate future are clearly going to favor workers who are adaptable.

## Conscientiousness

Although the label Conscientiousness is taken from the FFM, we exclude Achievement-related content from our Conscientiousness construct. Therefore, Conscientiousness, as defined in this taxonomy, corresponds more closely to Hough's (1992) Dependability construct than to FFM Conscientiousness. Our Conscientiousness construct also is similar to R. Hogan and J. Hogan's Prudence construct, although Prudence also contains some Achievement-related content. Thus, our definition of Conscientiousness includes the elements of being careful, planful, dependable, and disciplined, as well as honest, trustworthy, and accepting of authority. Out of this definition emerge our three second-level constructs: Dependability, Attention to Detail, and Integrity.

Several researchers have proposed second-level dimensions relevant to our Conscientiousness construct (Costa, McCrae, & Dye, 1991; Fleishman & Gilbert, 1994; Gough, 1987; Guion, 1992; R. Hogan & J. Hogan, 1992; Saville & Holdsworth, 1990). For example, Costa, McCrae, and Dye (1991) proposed the following dimensions: *Dutifulness*, defined as strict adherence to standards of conduct; *Order*, defined as the tendency to keep one's environment tidy and well organized; and *Deliberation*, defined as being cautious, planful, and thoughtful. These correspond reasonably closely, respectively, with our Integrity, Attention to Detail, and Dependability second-level constructs. R. Hogan and J. Hogan (1992) included the following HICs under their Prudence dimension: *Moralistic*, defined as adhering strictly to conventional values (our Dependability); and *Impulse Control*, defined as a tendency to avoid negative behavior (our Integrity, although there are aspects of our Self-Control here, as well). Furthermore, our second-level constructs map almost perfectly onto three of Guion's (1992) dimensions identified by their research team in developing their job analysis questionnaire: General Trustworthiness (Integrity), Adherence to a Work Ethic (Dependability), and Thoroughness and Attentiveness to Details (Attention to Detail).

All of these facets of Conscientiousness are important to many jobs. Employee Integrity (which includes, but is not limited to, our Integrity subconstruct; see Ones, Schmidt, & Viswesvaran, 1994) has become especially important in light of the billions of dollars that American businesses annually lose to employee theft (Camara & Schneider, 1994). Concern about theft and other dishonest behavior is particularly great in workplaces "in which employees have access to cash or merchandise or perform security functions" (Camara & Schneider, 1994, p. 112).

## Independence

Independence is represented in the personality taxonomies of Gough (1987), Hough (1992), and Fleishman and Gilbert (1994). Gough (1987; see also Kamp & Hough, 1986) calls the construct *Masculinity* and Hough (1992) referred to it as *Rugged Individualism*. Hough's (1992) Rugged Individualism refers to "decisive, action-oriented, independent, and rather unsentimental" behavior, and this is the essence of our definition of the construct. Fleishman and Gilbert (1994) proposed a construct of Self-Sufficiency, which is also related to Independence. The construct seems sufficiently focused that we elected not to define any second-level constructs.

It should be noted that Independence can be approximated by a combination of FFM Neuroticism and Agreeableness, which are represented in our taxonomy as Adjustment and Interpersonal Orientation (Hofstee, de Raad, & Goldberg, 1992; McCrae, Costa, & Piedmont, 1993). We chose, however, to include Independence as a separate construct. It has good face validity as an important work style requirement for some jobs.

There appears to be a trend toward individualism in organizational life, or at least "collaborative individualism" (Limerick & Cunnington, 1993). As this trend continues, Independence should become increasingly relevant to success in the workplace. It seems reasonable, however, to suggest that extreme levels of Independence may be counterproductive, particularly in large organizations, where the ability to fit into teams and groups is also increasingly crucial (e.g., Lawler, 1993).

## Practical Intelligence

Our Practical Intelligence construct has its roots in the FFM construct that has been variously labeled *Openness to Experience* (McCrae & Costa, 1987); *Culture* (Norman, 1963; Tupes & Christal, 1961/1992); *Intellect* (Goldberg, 1990); and *Intellectance* (R. Hogan & J. Hogan, 1992; Hough, 1992). There has been more disagreement over the appropriate interpretation of this factor than over any of the other FFM constructs. The crux of the disagreement has been whether the construct should be primarily defined by characteristics such as originality, imagination, breadth of interests, and daring (McCrae & Costa, 1987), which is an Openness to Experience/Culture interpretation, or by intelligence and intellectuality (e.g., Goldberg, 1990). Goldberg (1993) suggested that the Intellect interpretation of the factor is more appropriate. He pointed out that Cattell, whose early work is largely responsible for our current understanding of the FFM (e.g., Cattell, 1943, 1945, 1946, 1947), omitted variables relating to Intellect in his early research in favor of using an intelligence test. This, according to Goldberg (1993), directly led to subsequent interpretations of the factor as Culture (e.g., Norman, 1963; Tupes & Christal, 1961/1992). In Goldberg's research, the Intellect factor is defined by variables such as intellectuality, depth, insight, intelligence, and creativity.

Our Practical Intelligence construct is closer to Goldberg's (1990) Intellect construct than to other researchers' versions of this elusive factor. We acknowledge that the construct also contains some content related to Culture, but these elements have been deemphasized, primarily because they seem less relevant to jobs and the workplace.

It is important to note that our Practical Intelligence factor is distinct from cognitive ability. McCrae and Costa (1987) reported correlations of approximately .30 between Openness to Experience and intelligence. It is possible that the more Intellect-based versions of the factor overlap with intelligence to a somewhat greater extent than the Culture/Openness to Experience versions, but the discriminant validity of Practical Intelligence is unlikely to be a problem.

The second-level constructs associated with Practical Intelligence are Innovative and Analytical. In selecting these subconstructs, we were influenced by Guion's (1992) constructs of Desire to Generate Ideas and Tendency to Think Things Through. The OPQ constructs Innovative and Critical and Fleishman and Gilbert's (1994) Openness to Experience also suggested these second-level constructs.

Practical Intelligence is another construct that should become increasingly important in the workplace. To remain competitive in today's business environment, organizations often encourage employees at all levels to question the status quo and to propose and implement innovations derived from such questioning. Practical Intelligence, and especially the Innovative second-level construct, is far more important now than it was in the era of the conforming organization man (Whyte, 1956).

## Summary

In this section, we have described and provided literature support for the two-level taxonomy of work style variables developed for the content model. We have firmly embedded the majority of our constructs in existing, well-respected work style taxonomies. Constructs at both levels are intended to be relevant to jobs and the workplace. They are work-style-related job-performance requirements. We believe that the taxonomy is comprehensive, within the constraints of parsimony and job-relatedness. The constructs should be useful in describing important work style requirements in jobs.

## SAMPLE AND MEASURES

### Sample

As mentioned in chapter 4, the target number of occupations for the initial data collection was 80. However, the analyses to be described involve 35 occupations with a minimum of four incumbents per occupation (see Table 13-3). The number of incum-

## TABLE 13-3
**Thirty-Five Occupations With Four or More Incumbents Completing the Work Styles Questionnaire**

| Occupation code | Occupation Title | Number of respondents |
|---|---|---|
| 15005 | Education Administrators | 11 |
| 19005 | General Managers and Top Executives | 44 |
| 22135 | Mechanical Engineers | 6 |
| 25105 | Computer Programmers | 8 |
| 31305 | Teachers, Elementary School | 8 |
| 31502 | Librarians, Professional | 4 |
| 32502 | Registered Nurses | 34 |
| 32902 | Medical and Clinical Laboratory Technologists | 9 |
| 32905 | Medical and Clinical Laboratory Technicians | 5 |
| 49008 | Salespersons, Except Scientific and Retail | 7 |
| 49011 | Salespersons, Retail | 24 |
| 49017 | Counter and Rental Clerks | 5 |
| 49021 | Stock Clerks, Sales Floor | 8 |
| 49023 | Cashiers | 29 |
| 51002 | First Line Supervisors, Clerical/Administrative | 65 |
| 53102 | Tellers | 5 |
| 53311 | Insurance Claims Clerks | 5 |
| 53905 | Teachers' Aides and Assistants, Clerical | 11 |
| 55108 | Secretaries, Except Legal and Medical | 75 |
| 55305 | Receptionists and Information Clerks | 6 |
| 55338 | Bookkeeping, Accounting, and Auditing Clerks | 27 |
| 55347 | General Office Clerks | 78 |
| 61005 | Police and Detective Supervisors | 14 |
| 63014 | Police Patrol Officers | 19 |
| 65008 | Waiters and Waitresses | 18 |
| 65026 | Cooks, Restaurant | 6 |
| 65038 | Food Preparation Workers | 18 |
| 66008 | Nursing Aides, Orderlies, and Attendants | 17 |
| 67005 | Janitors and Cleaners | 34 |
| 85119 | Other Machinery Maintenance Mechanics | 4 |
| 85132 | Maintenance Repairers, General Utility | 39 |
| 87902 | Earth Drillers, Except Oil and Gas | 8 |
| 92974 | Packaging and Filling Machine Operators | 13 |
| 97102 | Truck Drivers, Heavy or Tractor Trailer | 10 |
| 97111 | Bus Drivers, Schools | 10 |

bents actually ranged from 4 to 40, with a harmonic mean of 9.81 per occupation. Occupational Analysis Field Center (OAFC) analysts did not provide work style ratings.

## Measures

Regarding the work style survey instrument, Level and Importance scales were developed. The Level scales are 7-point scales (1–7) with an additional *not-relevant* option. Three behavioral anchors were

also developed, at the high, midrange, and low levels. These anchors were reviewed by the project staff, OAFC staff, and persons in our pilot sample. Revisions were made on the basis of their comments, and the anchors were placed opposite the 6–7, 4, and 1–2 scale points, respectively. The Level scales can best be characterized as measuring complexity. The Importance scales are 5-point (1–5) scales with the anchors *not important*, *somewhat important*, *important*, *very important*, and *extremely important*, respectively, for the 1 to 5 scale points. As with other domains, for each descriptor, the level question was asked first, followed by the importance question.

## RESULTS

### Descriptive Statistics

Table 13-4 contains the overall means across the 35 occupations. Also shown are the standard deviations and interrater agreement indices based on 9.81 raters per occupation, and the standard errors of measurement. For the level ratings, the means are high and the range is quite restricted for some of the descriptors. Dependability (D12) is most noteworthy in this regard, with a mean of 6.30 and a standard deviation of only .36. Attention to Detail (D13), Cooperation (D6), Stress Tolerance (D10), and, to a lesser extent, Adaptability/Flexibility (D11) also have high means and standard deviations that are somewhat restricted.

The pattern of means and standard deviations for the importance ratings is similar to that experienced with the level ratings. Means for Dependability (D12), Attention to Detail (D13), and Cooperation (D6) are high, and their standard deviations are restricted. The mean for Integrity (D14) is also high, but its standard deviation is not so restricted.

### Reliability

For the level ratings, the median $k$-rater reliability is .66, with Dependability (D12) the lowest at .15. The reliability for this descriptor is probably that low because of the serious restriction in range. Interrater agreement for the importance ratings are comparable but slightly lower than those for the level ratings. The median $k$-rater reliability is .64. Again, Dependability (D12) has the lowest reliability ($r = .26$).

We also estimated single-rater and 30-rater reliabilities, using the Spearman-Brown formula to make the estimates. The single-rater reliabilities are indeed quite low for both the level and the importance ratings. However, the 30-rater reliabilities are almost all above .75, and many are above .85. If we were to attain our goal of obtaining 30 incumbents per occupation, the reliabilities for work styles would be very acceptable, with the exception of the Dependability (D12) descriptor. It may be necessary to have

**TABLE 13-4**

**Descriptive Statistics Across All Occupations and Reliability Estimates for Rated Differences Between Occupations: Work Styles**

| | Variable | | | | | | | |
| | Level | | | | Importance | | | |
| Descriptor | M | SD | SEM[a] | $r_k$[b] | M | SD | SEM | $r_k$ |
|---|---|---|---|---|---|---|---|---|
| 1. Achievement/Effort | 4.69 | 0.88 | .52 | .64 | 3.58 | 0.45 | .31 | .52 |
| 2. Persistence | 5.20 | 0.77 | .44 | .67 | 3.68 | 0.47 | .26 | .69 |
| 3. Initiative | 5.32 | 0.70 | .40 | .67 | 3.83 | 0.41 | .26 | .59 |
| 4. Energy | 4.97 | 0.81 | .53 | .58 | 3.56 | 0.48 | .33 | .52 |
| 5. Leadership Orientation | 4.65 | 1.05 | .42 | .84 | 3.42 | 0.63 | .25 | .84 |
| 6. Cooperation | 5.98 | 0.52 | .33 | .59 | 4.16 | 0.38 | .25 | .57 |
| 7. Concern for Others | 5.20 | 0.85 | .51 | .64 | 3.79 | 0.49 | .31 | .60 |
| 8. Social Orientation | 5.05 | 0.89 | .48 | .71 | 3.58 | 0.53 | .32 | .63 |
| 9. Self-Control | 5.62 | 0.82 | .45 | .70 | 4.05 | 0.45 | .26 | .66 |
| 10. Stress Tolerance | 5.61 | 0.54 | .36 | .55 | 3.98 | 0.38 | .23 | .64 |
| 11. Adaptability/Flexibility | 5.43 | 0.52 | .37 | .50 | 3.82 | 0.34 | .24 | .51 |
| 12. Dependability | 6.30 | 0.36 | .33 | .15 | 4.40 | 0.25 | .22 | .26 |
| 13. Attention to Detail | 5.99 | 0.48 | .32 | .55 | 4.18 | 0.34 | .22 | .57 |
| 14. Integrity | 5.74 | 0.73 | .44 | .63 | 4.11 | 0.47 | .27 | .66 |
| 15. Independence | 5.25 | 0.69 | .49 | .50 | 3.77 | 0.40 | .29 | .46 |
| 16. Innovation | 4.54 | 1.08 | .52 | .77 | 3.25 | 0.61 | .32 | .73 |
| 17. Analytical Thinking | 4.64 | 1.12 | .48 | .82 | 3.39 | 0.64 | .31 | .78 |

*Note.* Statistics are based on 35 occupations with Work Styles Questionnaire responses from at least 4 incumbents (mean number of incumbents = 19.5, *Mdn* = 11, harmonic mean = 9.81). [a]This estimate of the standard error of measurement was calculated as $SEM = SD * \sqrt{(1 - r_k)}$. [b]This estimate of reliability was obtained by calculating the intraclass correlation for *k* ratings across occupations: $ICC(1, k) = [BMS - WMS]/BMS$ (Shrout & Fleiss, 1979), where *k* is the harmonic mean of the number of ratings provided on each occupation.

somewhat higher numbers of incumbents completing the work styles scales compared with the scales in some of the other domains, such as skills and abilities. Nonetheless, we have demonstrated that it is possible to obtain reasonably reliable incumbent ratings of the work-style requirements for their jobs. To our knowledge, incumbents have not heretofore been asked to make judgments about the work style requirements for jobs and occupations. This study indicates that it is feasible to gather this kind of information.

As mentioned in previous chapters, it might be argued that including *not relevant* (i.e., zero) scores in the computation of Level scale reliabilities is inappropriate. A similar argument could be made for the Importance scales in that when *not relevant* was indicated on the Level scale, a 1 (*not important*) rating was used in computing the interrater agreement of the Importance scales. To address this possibility, we recalculated reliabilities, omitting the *not relevant* responses. Additionally, the Level scale reliabilities were recomputed using a simple *relevant/not relevant* coding scheme.

First, the coefficients are virtually unchanged for the Level scales, when ignoring the *not relevant* response. For the Importance scales, interrater agreement drops considerably for one scale (Independence [D15]), a small amount for eight of the scales, and actually improves for six of the scales. In two cases the coefficients did not change. In summary, reliability suffered only minimally or not at all when the *not relevant* rescaling was used for the work-styles descriptors. Except for one case (Independence [D15]), interrater agreement was considerably lower when Level scales were scored *relevant/not relevant*. Ac-

cordingly, this simple scoring method does not appear to be prudent.

Overall, the full scale scoring method including *not relevant* appears preferable and was used for subsequent analyses. Considering *not relevant* in the Level scale scoring adds information that for the most part enhances the reliability of the Importance scales. This has intuitive appeal in that a *not relevant* rating for a work style seems conceptually quite different from a level requirement that is low for that work style; in parallel, being of no importance is different from being of low importance.

## Descriptor and Scale Relationships

One might question whether data from the two scales, Level and Importance, are largely redundant. We computed the correlations between the Level and Importance scales in two different ways: (a) for each dimension across the 35 occupations and averaged over the 17 dimensions and (b) for each occupation across the 17 dimensions and averaged over the 35 occupations. The correlations are high (.90 and .93), and the low standard deviations indicate that they are uniformly high, especially by occupation across the 17 dimensions. These results suggest that indeed there is considerable redundancy across the Level and Importance scales.

We also computed the correlations among dimensions for the Level scales. As with other domains, for occupations that had more than four incumbents providing ratings, we randomly selected four to include in this analysis. Because our primary concern in the research is to identify differences between occupations, we focus our discussion on the occupation-level data.

The correlations among dimensions make good intuitive sense. For example, correlations among the three descriptors that make up the higher level Achievement construct (Achievement/Effort [D1], Persistence [D2], and Initiative [D3]) are .78, .65, and .79, respectively. Similarly, the Innovation (D16) and Analytical Thinking (D17) descriptors that together form the Practical Intelligence higher order factor correlate .81. In fact, the mean between-descriptor correlation for within the higher order construct is .69; the mean between-descriptor correlation for across the higher order construct is .42. Negative correlations also were obtained and are of the amount that we would expect. Independence (D15) correlates −.35 with Social Orientation (D8) and −.18 with Cooperation (D6), as examples. Thus, the work style scales seem to provide a meaningful pattern of relationships.

## Factor Structure

Another way to evaluate the patterns of relationships between work style dimensions is to factor analyze the correlation matrix. Accordingly, we conducted a principal-components factor analysis with varimax rotation. The 2–7 factor solutions were examined, and the pattern of eigenvalues along with interpretability of the solutions suggested that the three-factor solution best summarized the correlation matrix. This solution is depicted in Table 13-5. The three factors accounted for 75% of the total variance for ratings on the Level scale. Also, the communalities suggested that, with two exceptions, the dimensions were well represented in the solution.

The first factor is a strong one, with 8 of the 17 dimensions loading substantially on it and 35% of the variance accounted for. We labeled the factor *Surgency, Achievement, High-Activity-Level Orientation*. Referring to the higher order seven-dimension set, Factor 1 combines four of these dimensions: Achievement Orientation, Social Influence, Independence, and Practical Intelligence. Factor 2 was called *People Orientation* and accounted for 29% of the total variance. Again, focusing on the higher order dimension structure to aid in interpretation, this factor includes all of the Interpersonal Orientation descriptors and two of the three Adjustment descriptors. The third factor, accounting for 12% of the variance, only has a single high-loading descriptor, Attention to Detail (D13). We labeled this factor *Detail Orientation*. Two of the Conscientiousness descriptors (Dependability [D12] and Integrity [D14]) and one of the Adjustment descriptors (Adaptability/Flexibility [D11]) are not represented in the three-factor system. However, at least one descriptor from each of the seven higher order dimensions loads substantially on one of the factors. So, from that perspective, the three factors reflect well the entire scope of the work styles domain.

Of course, it must be remembered that this factor analysis was conducted on data representing 35 occupations. The stability of the solution, therefore, may not be high. Nonetheless, the three factors make reasonably good conceptual sense.

## Occupation Differences

One of the ways O*NET will be of use in actual practice is to generate profiles of occupational requirements on the O*NET descriptors. To provide an initial idea of the usefulness of profile data in the work styles domain, Table 13-6 contains the means and standard deviations for each of the 17 work style dimensions on the Level scale for six different occupations selected to reflect very different types of employment: (a) General Managers and Top Executives, (b) Computer Programmers, (c) Registered Nurses, (d) Police Patrol Officers, (e) Janitors and Cleaners, and (f) Maintenance Repairers, General Utility.

Examining the level means indicates that some descriptors have relatively high means for all of the occupations. For example, Dependability (D12) and Attention to Detail (D13) show no mean ratings below 5 on the 7-point Level scales. However, even for these descriptors that have relatively restricted ranges of means, there is some differentiation that makes good conceptual sense. For example, the two occupations with the highest Dependability (D12) ratings are Patrol Officers and Nurses. These same two occupations plus Computer Programmers have the highest Attention to Detail (D13) mean ratings. For the remaining descriptors, the differentiation between occupations is more evident. As examples, Computer

**TABLE 13-5**
**Principal-Components Analysis Pattern Matrix for the Level Scale: Work Styles**

| Descriptor | Factor F1 | F2 | F3 | Communality |
|---|---|---|---|---|
| 1. Achievement/Effort | .85 | .07 | .22 | .78 |
| 2. Persistence | .87 | .01 | .19 | .79 |
| 3. Initiative | .83 | .19 | −.00 | .73 |
| 4. Energy | .69 | .37 | −.15 | .64 |
| 5. Leadership Orientation | .85 | .32 | −.07 | .83 |
| 6. Cooperation | −.19 | .84 | .08 | .75 |
| 7. Concern for Others | .09 | .90 | −.11 | .83 |
| 8. Social Orientation | .05 | .84 | .22 | .76 |
| 9. Self-Control | .00 | .92 | −.02 | .84 |
| 10. Stress Tolerance | .20 | .75 | .29 | .69 |
| 11. Adaptability/Flexibility | .53 | .53 | .56 | .87 |
| 12. Dependability | .30 | .58 | .64 | .84 |
| 13. Attention to Detail | .02 | .07 | .92 | .85 |
| 14. Integrity | .37 | .52 | .21 | .46 |
| 15. Independence | .64 | −.23 | −.04 | .46 |
| 16. Innovation | .86 | .06 | .17 | .78 |
| 17. Analytical Thinking | .86 | −.10 | .31 | .84 |
| % of Variance | 35 | 29 | 12 | |
| Eigenvalue | 7.30 | 3.96 | 1.48 | |

*Note.* N = 35. The correlation matrix was based on means calculated at the occupation level. F1 = Surgency, Achievement, High Activity Level Orientation, F2 = People Orientation, and F3 = Detail Orientation. These loadings are based on an orthogonal varimax rotation.

**TABLE 13-6**
**Descriptor Means and Standard Deviations on the Level Scale on Six Example Occupations: Work Styles**

| Descriptor | General Managers and Top Executives (*n* = 43) | | Computer Programmers (*n* = 7) | | Registered Nurses (*n* = 25) | | Police Patrol Officers (*n* = 24) | | Janitors and Cleaners[a] (*n* = 30) | | Maintenance Repairers, General Utility (*n* = 27) | |
|---|---|---|---|---|---|---|---|---|---|---|---|---|
| | M | SD | M | SD | M | SD | M | SD | M | SD | M | SD |
| 1. Achievement/Effort | 5.54 | 1.06 | 4.62 | 1.18 | 5.08 | 1.21 | 4.84 | 1.30 | 4.14 | 2.04 | 4.23 | 2.00 |
| 2. Persistence | 5.90 | 0.83 | 5.50 | 1.60 | 5.91 | 0.93 | 5.73 | 0.99 | 4.58 | 1.82 | 4.61 | 1.75 |
| 3. Initiative | 6.27 | 0.75 | 5.37 | 0.74 | 5.97 | 1.24 | 5.47 | 1.12 | 4.61 | 1.66 | 5.35 | 1.56 |
| 4. Energy | 5.18 | 1.36 | 4.12 | 1.24 | 5.32 | 1.42 | 5.42 | 1.12 | 5.26 | 1.58 | 4.87 | 1.62 |
| 5. Leadership Orientation | 6.13 | 1.21 | 4.25 | 1.03 | 5.50 | 1.30 | 5.68 | 1.15 | 3.79 | 2.01 | 4.61 | 1.82 |
| 6. Cooperation | 5.86 | 1.32 | 4.75 | 1.38 | 6.35 | 0.98 | 5.84 | 1.06 | 5.58 | 1.76 | 5.71 | 1.27 |
| 7. Concern for Others | 5.13 | 1.45 | 3.62 | 1.30 | 6.58 | 0.74 | 5.63 | 1.46 | 4.58 | 1.95 | 4.66 | 1.64 |
| 8. Social Orientation | 5.31 | 1.27 | 2.87 | 1.12 | 5.82 | 1.21 | 5.00 | 1.10 | 3.67 | 2.09 | 4.38 | 1.74 |
| 9. Self-Control | 5.47 | 1.45 | 3.50 | 1.41 | 6.38 | 1.07 | 6.68 | 0.67 | 4.61 | 2.16 | 5.23 | 1.54 |
| 10. Stress Tolerance | 5.63 | 1.38 | 5.25 | 1.03 | 6.11 | 1.09 | 6.68 | 0.58 | 4.64 | 1.96 | 5.12 | 1.30 |
| 11. Adaptability/Flexibility | 5.75 | 1.29 | 5.25 | 0.70 | 6.11 | 0.97 | 5.89 | 0.73 | 4.58 | 1.94 | 4.82 | 1.83 |
| 12. Dependabiity | 6.15 | 1.31 | 5.62 | 1.50 | 6.58 | 0.65 | 6.57 | 0.60 | 5.82 | 1.76 | 6.00 | 1.16 |
| 13. Attention to Detail | 5.47 | 1.26 | 6.12 | 0.83 | 6.29 | 0.90 | 6.31 | 0.82 | 5.35 | 1.55 | 5.69 | 1.17 |
| 14. Integrity | 6.04 | 1.19 | 4.62 | 1.68 | 6.50 | 0.74 | 6.89 | 0.31 | 4.97 | 1.97 | 5.25 | 1.40 |
| 15. Independence | 5.50 | 1.15 | 5.75 | 0.70 | 5.70 | 1.19 | 5.26 | 0.87 | 5.50 | 1.61 | 5.61 | 1.28 |
| 16. Innovation | 5.36 | 1.27 | 5.87 | 1.12 | 5.17 | 1.33 | 5.00 | 1.05 | 3.67 | 2.01 | 5.02 | 1.26 |
| 17. Analytical Thinking | 5.84 | 0.96 | 6.62 | 0.74 | 5.29 | 1.58 | 5.21 | 1.27 | 3.47 | 2.23 | 5.17 | 1.25 |

[a]The full title for this occupation is "Janitors and Cleaners, Except Maids and Housekeeping."

Programmers have the highest rating on the Analytical Thinking (D17) level descriptor; Janitors have the lowest rating on this descriptor. On the other hand, Janitors have a relatively high mean rating on Energy (D4). General Managers have the highest ratings on Initiative (D3) and Leadership Orientation (D5); Nurses have the highest ratings on Cooperation (D6), Concern for Others (D7), Social Orientation (D8), Adaptability, and (as mentioned) Attention to Detail (D13); and Computer Programmers have the highest ratings on Independence (D15) and Analytical Thinking (D17) and the lowest ratings on the Cooperation (D6), Concern for Others (D7), and Social Orientation (D8) descriptors. In summary, the mean level ratings are consistent with the nature of these occupations. The work style Level scales appear to provide a meaningful description of the similarities and differences between occupations.

Some of the standard deviations are of interest, as well. Several of the highest standard deviations are evident with the Janitors and Cleaners. For example, Leadership Orientation (D5) and Analytical Thinking (D17) have high standard deviations for this group. This may reflect more heterogeneity in the jobs within occupation. Some of the Janitors sampled may have supervisory responsibilities, for example.

## CONCLUSIONS

We should remind the reader of significant limitations to the research conducted to date. First, the sample size is small at this point. Second, correlations between the two scales were high, suggesting considerable redundancy in level and importance information. However, it should be remembered that even with a high correlation, there may be some occupations for which legitimate and substantial differences exist between level and importance on certain work-style descriptors.

Overall, this research lends support for the work styles taxonomy, including the proposed hierarchical structure. The mean correlation between-descriptor, within-higher-order construct is .69; the mean between-descriptor, across-higher-order construct correlation is .42. Furthermore, other between-descriptor relationships made intuitive sense, and a factor analysis of the correlations between descriptors yielded a readily interpretable three-factor solution.

Perhaps most important for the purposes of this effort, the work style descriptors successfully differentiated among the six exemplar occupations. The taxonomy is primarily designed to describe occupational requirements and how these differ across occupations. The work styles Level scales seem useful in this role.

In summary, the proposed work styles taxonomy received considerable support from this research. The descriptor scales measuring the taxonomy's constructs yielded reliable, coherent, and useful data. The scales appear to provide an adequate basis for identifying and describing the similarities and differences across occupations in the domain of work style requirements.

# Occupation-Specific Descriptors: Approaches, Procedures, and Findings

CHRISTOPHER E. SAGER, MICHAEL D. MUMFORD, WAYNE A. BAUGHMAN, AND RUTH A. CHILDS

The intent of this chapter is to describe a set of procedures that might be used to gather occupation-specific information and organize this kind of descriptive data in terms of the broader cross-occupation variables described in chapters 5 through 13. We will briefly review some literature related to occupation-specific information, present some alternative approaches to data collection, and review the results obtained in a series of pilot studies intended to assess the feasibility of using some of these approaches. We emphasize what is perhaps the most commonly used kind of occupation-specific descriptor—job tasks (McCormick, 1979).

Virtually all of the foregoing chapters have focused on analyses of measures that might be used to describe most occupations. This kind of cross-occupation description provides the foundation for a system intended to answer questions about many occupations. These cross-occupation descriptors, however, do not and cannot address all of the types of variables used to describe jobs. More specifically, these taxonomies of cross-occupation descriptors do not provide occupation-specific information—such as the tasks—that only applies to a single occupation or to a narrowly defined group of occupations.

Many questions about occupations can be answered without referring to occupation-specific information (Pearlman, 1993). But as McCage (1993) pointed out, occupation-specific information may be required to answer other important questions. For example, occupation-specific information may be necessary to specify training requirements, develop position descriptions, and undertake the redesign of jobs.

The various applications of occupation-specific information clearly argue for the inclusion of occupation-specific descriptors in a comprehensive occupational information system such as the O*NET. The inclusion of occupation-specific information, however, raises a host of issues. As illustrated in the history of the *Dictionary of Occupational Titles* (DOT; U.S. Department of Labor, 1991a) and the concerns voiced by the Advisory Panel for the DOT (APDOT, 1993), occupation-specific informa-

tion often is collected in an unsystematic fashion. Furthermore, by its very nature, this kind of descriptive information is difficult to embed within a broader organizing structure. Finally, collection of occupation-specific descriptive information can be extremely resource intensive.

These and other considerations suggest that it may be difficult and perhaps not especially useful to include occupation-specific information in the O*NET, at least in the short term. An important advantage of the cross-occupation descriptors described in the previous chapters is that together they constitute a comprehensive structure into which occupation-specific information can be organized. For example, as is discussed later in this chapter, occupation-specific tasks can be organized by generalized work activities (GWAs; see chap. 8). It may be most sensible to defer extensive collection of occupation-specific information until procedures have been developed and refined that allow the embedding of such information into the cross-occupation descriptor structure.

## OCCUPATION-SPECIFIC TASKS

### Background

As Fleishman and Quaintance (1984) pointed out, a variety of techniques might be used to generate descriptive information about the activities being performed in a particular occupation. One might, for example, describe occupations in terms of performance errors. Alternatively, the work people do in their occupations could be described through qualitative ethnographic procedures. Still another approach to the description of occupational activities flows from recent work on the role of cognition in performance. In this instance, activities are described in terms of the differences observed in the knowledge structures characterizing experts and novices in a particular field of endeavor (Camara, 1992).

Each of these techniques used to describe the requirements of a given occupation has unique strengths and weaknesses. Furthermore, it should be apparent that these techniques all provide somewhat different information about the nature of performance in a particular occupation. By the same token, however, these techniques all attempt to define the nature of the activities people are performing in their occupations.

As a result, the definition and description of work activities provides a basis for virtually all job analysis efforts. The procedure most commonly used to define and describe these activities is task analysis. At a general level, task analysis represents a way of framing or organizing job activities. As McCormick (1979) pointed out, fundamentally, a task is an action applied to some object under certain conditions. The starting point for attempts to describe a specific occupation is, therefore, the definition of the tasks to be performed in the occupation.

Task analysis is a part of most job analysis efforts because tasks are markers of important constructs that are used to describe occupations. Just as multiple-choice items in a vocabulary test are considered markers of verbal ability, tasks performed in an occupation are considered markers of the knowledge and skills required for performance in an occupation. It is common for job analysts or occupation subject matter experts (SMEs) to be presented with a list of tasks performed in an occupation and to be required to use this list to evaluate the extent to which particular domains of knowledge and skill are required of incumbents in that occupation (e.g., Harvey, 1991a). Tasks are the behaviors of job incumbents that we observe, from which we can make inferences about an occupation's requirements. For example, if we observe that an occupation includes a number of tasks relating to the conceptualization, drafting, and editing of marketing reports, we can infer that incumbents in this occupation should have fairly high levels of reading and writing skills and knowledge of marketing.

A variety of procedures have been used to identify the tasks performed in an occupation and to obtain descriptive information about the nature of requisite job tasks. Tasks are sometimes identified by having occupational analysts watch people perform the work. At other times, individual interviews or panel meetings with incumbents or supervisors are used to define tasks. A third approach is to use existing task inventories (McCormick, Jeanneret, & Mecham, 1972) that have usually themselves been developed through one of the two just-mentioned methods. Generally, these task lists are used to identify the more important or frequently performed tasks (Friedman, 1990; Harvey & Lozada-Larsen, 1988). Often, however, these task lists, inventories, and questionnaires request other types of information about the nature of task performance, such as learning difficulty, criticality, or degree of discretion (e.g., Mumford, Weeks, Harding, & Fleishman, 1987).

Although a variety of procedures may be used to identify requisite tasks in an occupation, a common procedure is to convene a meeting of SMEs. In SME meetings, a group of five to seven incumbents, or their supervisors, are called together. These SMEs are then asked to describe the activities performed on the job at hand. This unstructured-recall approach will elicit usable task statements. However, to attain comprehensive coverage of the tasks performed in an occupation, it often is necessary to conduct a number of meetings. As a result, this technique can become unduly time consuming and expensive. Alternatives such as critical incident analysis or observation of job performance also, unfortunately, suffer from the same kind of problem.

This task identification problem has important implications for the development of an occupational information system. Even with a well-developed classification system, there still are likely to be a relatively large number of occupations for which detailed information will be needed concerning the underlying work activities. In the following section, we review four potential techniques for collecting occupation-specific information about the tasks that are performed, all of which might provide an economical and efficient basis for the collection of this descriptive information.

## Approaches

### General Task Inventories

One approach to efficient collection of task data is the general, cross-occupation task inventory. Two advantages of this approach are that it is relatively fast and inexpensive. Perhaps the most frequently used general job analysis inventory of this sort is the Position Analysis Questionnaire (PAQ; McCormick et al., 1972). Cunningham (1988) and Harvey (1991b) have also contributed general inventories. More recently, the American College Testing Program has developed a general task survey under the auspices of the U.S. Department of Labor (American College Testing, 1994).

There is evidence that these kinds of general cross-occupation task surveys can provide meaningful descriptions of activities performed in a number of occupations (McCormick et al., 1972). However, by virtue of their focus (i.e., tasks appearing in multiple occupations), they necessarily give less attention to the specific activities occurring in a given occupation (Levine, 1983). As a result, it is questionable whether this approach will provide a truly comprehensive description of the tasks that make occupations different from each other. This potential shortcoming of generic surveys in turn limits their value in defining occupation-specific skills and knowledges. They may have greater value, however, in identifying intermediate work activities of the sort described by Cunningham, Drewes, and Powell (1995).

### Available Task Inventories

A second technique that could be used to obtain information about tasks relies on the use of existing, occupation-specific, job analysis inventories. Earlier efforts have provided task analysis data for a number of occupations. Conceivably, an effort might be initiated in which a library is built up over time that describes the tasks identified in earlier job analysis efforts. When attempting to describe a particular occupation, relevant task inventories would be drawn from this library. These task lists would be reviewed and then used as the basis for developing task inventories tailored to the job at hand that would presumably extend across locations and establishments.

This approach clearly would reduce the amount of effort needed to generate an initial set of task statements. However, a substantial amount of work would be required to develop the kind of library needed to make this approach feasible. Available task analysis inventories would have to be edited so that task statements would be written at a common level of detail in order to permit generalization across establishments. Furthermore, arrangements would have to be made to obtain what in many areas would be proprietary data. Finally, such task inventories would be likely to be available for only a relatively select sample of occupations, typically occupations in which performance is of sufficient importance to organizations to warrant expensive and time-consuming job analysis efforts. As a result, other techniques would still be required for identifying the tasks occurring in other occupations not covered by the available task inventories.

Even if these difficulties could be overcome, one problem would remain. The lists of tasks would probably be deficient. There are at least three reasons for this potential deficiency: (a) some of the inventories would be based on relatively old job analyses, and important changes in the occupations may have occurred since the inventories were developed; (b) some of the inventories would be based on job analyses that were performed for specific purposes, resulting in inventories focusing only on some parts of the examined occupations; and (c) the inventories would be based on job analyses that vary greatly in quality and comprehensiveness.

### Activity Analysis

A third approach for generating occupation-specific tasks in a time- and cost-efficient fashion has been suggested by Prien (1994). This approach is based on the notion that all occupations involve a limited set of common activities, such as installing, repairing, writing, tracking, or supervising. These common activities, or action verbs, might be used as a basis for generating tasks by applying the following procedures. First, a general taxonomy of action verbs would be identified, such as those proposed by Prien (1994). Second, a group of SMEs would be asked to review this activity list and to indicate which activities they perform in their occupation. Third, a second group of SMEs would be presented with each of these activities, and for each activity they would be asked to list all objects of the activity, providing modifications as necessary. Thus, in the case of electricians,

incumbents might list "install switches," "install wiring," and "install control boxes."

The procedures described above would, at least in theory, result in a set of task statements consistent with the first two elements of McCormick's (1979) definition of a task as an activity occurring in relation to some object in a particular context. Furthermore, it is possible that this procedure, if coupled with an expert system, might be used to generate tasks "on-line" or through telephone interviews. Thus, an activity-based approach to task generation would seem to warrant further consideration.

We use the word *consideration* quite intentionally. Although this activity-based approach to task generation has some attractive features, it has not been widely applied. Moreover, it may prove difficult to obtain a comprehensive list of activity statements and create procedures for identifying synonyms within a list of activity statements. Additionally, any activity-based approach may implicitly downplay the specific objects and unique behavioral demands associated with a given occupation.

### GWAs

A fourth approach that might be used to generate task statements has been suggested by Mumford and his colleagues (Clifton, Connelly, Reiter-Palmon, & Mumford, 1991; Connelly, Reiter-Palmon, Clifton, & Mumford, 1991; Gilbert, Connelly, Clifton, Reiter-Palmon, & Mumford, 1992; Mumford, Threlfall, Costanza, Baughman, & Smart, 1992; Reiter-Palmon et al., 1990). This approach depends on GWAs (see chap. 8) to help elicit and organize tasks. A GWA "is an aggregation of similar job activities/behaviors that underlies the accomplishment of major work functions" (chap. 8). GWAs can therefore be viewed as a higher order structure under which tasks can be organized. They also provide a method for structuring task generation exercises; asking respondents to generate tasks within a single GWA can cue their recall within a domain that is more cognitively manageable than the "whole occupation."

In this approach, a panel of SMEs is presented with a list of GWAs and asked to reach a consensus regarding the GWAs relevant for their occupation. Then, within each of the retained GWAs, panel members are asked to list the specific tasks occurring in their occupation.

This approach differs from more traditional approaches in the process used to elicit tasks. Rather than being asked a global question, "What do you do on your job?," panel members are asked a series of more specific questions referring to the tasks performed under a given dimension or GWA. By using recall in relation to GWAs, tasks can be generated far more rapidly. Typically, the research cited above showed that a 1-day panel meeting with five or six SMEs is sufficient to obtain 90% to 95% coverage of the occupation's relevant tasks.

Perhaps the most important advantage of this approach is that it allows tasks to be generated quickly with good coverage of the relevant domains, but it has the additional advantage of allowing tasks to be generated and organized within broader GWAs, thereby providing a system for identifying tasks that explicitly integrates these tasks into a broader taxonomic structure.

## Procedures and Findings

The relative advantages and disadvantages of job analysis procedures discussed so far led us to pursue a two-step approach to the development of a task database for inclusion in O*NET. For the purposes of the prototype, a variant of the available task inventories approach described above was used as an interim solution. However, a version of the GWA approach might provide a more satisfactory long-term solution. Both approaches are described below.

### Modified Available Task Inventories Approach

**Development of measures.**  A variation of this approach was used for the O*NET prototype. The current DOT provides definitions that include major tasks to be performed in each DOT occupation. Thus, it is possible to identify a set of tasks for particular Occupational Employment Statistics (OES)/O*NET occupations by abstracting core tasks included in those DOT occupations that were subsumed under a given OES/O*NET occupation.

This work was performed by the Occupational Analysis Field Centers (OAFCs). The OAFCs began by using the *National Occupational Information Coordinating Committee (NOICC) Master Crosswalk* (1994) to identify those DOT occupations associated with each of the 80 OES/O*NET occupations targeted in the initial O*NET data collection effort. This initial categorization served to convert DOT occupations into the broader OES/O*NET occupational structure.

Tasks abstracted from the DOT definitions were used to create a list of tasks for each relevant OES/O*NET occupation. Experienced OAFC occupational analysts then edited the tasks to eliminate redundancy. Then a second panel of occupational analysts reviewed the resulting list of task statements for generality and comprehensiveness, adding to or correcting the initial task lists to ensure that each was reasonably comprehensive and that the tasks were written to a common level of specificity.

This procedure resulted in the identification of 7 to 30 relatively broad task statements for each of the 80 targeted occupations. The task lists were then used to create occupation-specific task rating questionnaires. One of these questionnaires is presented in Figure 14-1. As the figure illustrates, incumbents were asked to read each task statement and identify those tasks relevant to the performance of their job.

If incumbents indicated that a task was relevant, they were asked to rate (a) the frequency with which they perform the task and (b) the importance of the task with respect to performance of the job. Importance and frequency ratings are used in part because they have been shown to provide unique descriptive information and in part because the simultaneous collection of multiple ratings contributes to reliability (McCormick, 1976). It is of note that the frequency ratings were collected on an absolute, rather than a relative, scale.

The tasks shown in Figure 14-1 represent a modified version of the available task inventories notion described earlier in this chapter. In a more elaborate version, the initial task lists would come from multiple sources (i.e., not just the DOT task lists). They would stem from a review of prior job analysis programs, including the job analysis work conducted by (a) the Department of Defense, (b) the Office of Personnel Management, and (c) those research institutes, consulting firms, and employers willing to share proprietary data. The process would include a careful review of the quality of each job analysis and its resulting task list. The task lists that were judged of sufficient quality would be edited for clarity and a common level of specificity. It is important to note that this procedure would likely result in occupation-specific task rating questionnaires with a greater number of tasks per occupation (e.g., 100–200) than the present questionnaires. Also, the tasks would probably be at a more specific level than tasks derived from the DOT.

**Sample.**  The sampling and data collection procedures used to obtain the O*NET prototype incumbent/supervisor sample are described in chapter 4. The results that follow are based on the sample of occupations on which the cross-domain analyses were performed (see chap. 16). Of the 80 occupations targeted, 29 yielded four or more complete sets of all nine cross-occupation questionnaires. Only respondents in those 29 occupations were included in the analyses. For each occupation, Table 14-1 lists the O*NET occupation code, the occupation title, and the number of respondents who completed an occupation-specific task questionnaire for each occupation. The 29 occupations represent a broad range in terms of level and industry.

**Results.**  Despite the fact that a limited version of the available task inventories approach was used, the results obtained in the O*NET initial data collection provide support for the potential value of this approach. Table 14-1 presents the interrater agreement coefficients obtained for task frequency and importance ratings. Estimates for 1 and for 30 raters are also presented. The interrater agreement coefficients, which reflect the degree of consistency across respondents in their task ratings within an occupation, are uniformly high. For 30 respondents, they ranged from .80 to .98 for the frequency rating and .77 to

### Instructions for Making Task Ratings

In this questionnaire you will be presented with a list of tasks. A task is an action or set of actions performed together to accomplish an objective. This list of tasks will be specific to the job you are describing.

For each task, please make the following three ratings: **RELEVANCE, FREQUENCY,** and **IMPORTANCE.**

(1) **RELEVANCE.** If the task is NOT RELEVANT at all to performance on the job, mark through the "0" in the NOT RELEVANT column. Carefully read the task before deciding whether it is RELEVANT or NOT RELEVANT to this job. If you select the "0" in the NOT RELEVANT column, however, there is no need to complete the IMPORTANCE and FREQUENCY ratings described below. If the task is part of this job, rate IMPORTANCE and FREQUENCY.

(2) **FREQUENCY.** (Do not complete if NOT RELEVANT was selected.) Ask yourself, "How often is this task performed on this job?" For example, "Interact with potential customers" is a task that an employee in one job might perform only "once per week or less," but an employee in another job might perform "hourly or more often."

Rate the FREQUENCY with which a task is performed by marking through the appropriate number, from 1 (indicating that the task is performed once per year or less often) to 7 (indicating that the task is performed hourly or more often) on the FREQUENCY scale.

(3) **IMPORTANCE.** (Do not complete if NOT RELEVANT was selected.) Ask yourself, "How important is this task to performance on this job?" For example, "Develop objectives and strategies to guide the organization" might be very important for an employee in one job, but less important for another job. For the second job, however, "Provide performance feedback to subordinates" might be very important.

Rate the IMPORTANCE of the task for performance on the job by marking through the appropriate number, from 1 (indicating that the task is of no importance) to 5 (indicating that the task is extremely important) on the IMPORTANCE scale.

The first two tasks show how "Frequency" and Importance" differ. An employee in a particular job indicates that "Land a plane under emergency conditions" occurs only "once per year or less," but, the task is an "extremely important" part of the employee's job. In contrast, the employee indicates that task 2 is performed, "several times per day," but is less important than task 1. Finally, task 3 is not part of this job, so the employee indicates this by selecting the "Not Relevant" circle.

[three completed examples were included here]

Turn the page to begin the Tasks Questionnaire.

**FIGURE 14-1.** An example of an Occupation-Specific Tasks questionnaire (*figure continues*).

.97 for the importance rating. The occupations with the lowest reliabilities—Stock Clerks and Packaging and Filling Machine Operators—may be those with the least consistency in task demands across, or even within, organizations.

We also calculated interrater agreement coefficients where task ratings were coded in three ways: (a) using the full Frequency and Importance scales, as in Table 14-1; (b) using only relevant responses on the Frequency and Importance scales (i.e., *not relevant* responses set to missing); and (c) dichotomously (i.e., *relevant/not relevant*). Predictably, the relevant-only and dichotomous recoding yielded lower reliabilities than the full scale coding; however, the reliabilities for these two recodings were surprisingly high and very similar to reliabilities for full-scale coding. With the exception of incumbents in the Packaging and Filling Machine Operators occupation, a large number of whom indicated that the tasks on the occupation-specific questionnaire were not relevant

to their jobs (the coefficient was .21), the relevant-only reliabilities for the Frequency scale ranged from .74 to .99 and were, on average, about 3 points lower. The relevant/not relevant reliabilities for frequency ranged from .66 to .99 and were, on average, about 2 points lower. The results for importance ratings were very similar.

Additional evidence bearing on the meaningfulness of these descriptions might be obtained by considering the relationships between the frequency and importance ratings. In accordance with the results obtained in earlier studies (Harvey, 1991a), the task frequency and importance ratings yielded the expected positive relationship. Across occupations, the mean correlations between task frequency and importance ratings ranged from .55 to .92, with a median mean correlation of .78. These results suggest that respondents are differentiating between the Frequency and Importance scales. The relatively short length of the Occupation-Specific Task question-

| Task | Not Relevant | Frequency | | | | | | | Importance | | | | |
|---|---|---|---|---|---|---|---|---|---|---|---|---|---|
| | | Once per year or less | More than once per year | More than once per month | More than once per week | Daily | Several times per day | Hourly or more often | Not important | Somewhat important | Important | Very Important | Extremely important |
| 1 Observes, evaluates, and records patient data. | ⓪ | ① | ② | ③ | ④ | ⑤ | ⑥ | ⑦ | ① | ② | ③ | ④ | ⑤ |
| 2 Reviews diagnostic tests. | ⓪ | ① | ② | ③ | ④ | ⑤ | ⑥ | ⑦ | ① | ② | ③ | ④ | ⑤ |
| 3 Conducts laboratory tests. | ⓪ | ① | ② | ③ | ④ | ⑤ | ⑥ | ⑦ | ① | ② | ③ | ④ | ⑤ |
| 4 Aids physician and other health care professionals during treatment and examination of patients. | ⓪ | ① | ② | ③ | ④ | ⑤ | ⑥ | ⑦ | ① | ② | ③ | ④ | ⑤ |
| 5 Performs physical examinations. | ⓪ | ① | ② | ③ | ④ | ⑤ | ⑥ | ⑦ | ① | ② | ③ | ④ | ⑤ |
| 6 Administers injections, medications and treatments. | ⓪ | ① | ② | ③ | ④ | ⑤ | ⑥ | ⑦ | ① | ② | ③ | ④ | ⑤ |
| 7 Cleans and sterilizes instruments and equipment. | ⓪ | ① | ② | ③ | ④ | ⑤ | ⑥ | ⑦ | ① | ② | ③ | ④ | ⑤ |
| 8 Consults with other medical professionals on policy and patient care. | ⓪ | ① | ② | ③ | ④ | ⑤ | ⑥ | ⑦ | ① | ② | ③ | ④ | ⑤ |
| 9 Supervises and coordinates activities of nursing personnel. | ⓪ | ① | ② | ③ | ④ | ⑤ | ⑥ | ⑦ | ① | ② | ③ | ④ | ⑤ |
| 10 Develops standards and procedures for providing nursing care. | ⓪ | ① | ② | ③ | ④ | ⑤ | ⑥ | ⑦ | ① | ② | ③ | ④ | ⑤ |
| 11 Provides nursing orientation, teaching, and guidance to staff. | ⓪ | ① | ② | ③ | ④ | ⑤ | ⑥ | ⑦ | ① | ② | ③ | ④ | ⑤ |
| 12 Identifies problems and instructs and advises personnel in infection control procedures. | ⓪ | ① | ② | ③ | ④ | ⑤ | ⑥ | ⑦ | ① | ② | ③ | ④ | ⑤ |
| 13 Investigates infection control problems and follows up with persons exposed to infection and diseases. | ⓪ | ① | ② | ③ | ④ | ⑤ | ⑥ | ⑦ | ① | ② | ③ | ④ | ⑤ |
| 14 Administers anesthetics. | ⓪ | ① | ② | ③ | ④ | ⑤ | ⑥ | ⑦ | ① | ② | ③ | ④ | ⑤ |
| 15 Provides instruction in health education and disease prevention | ⓪ | ① | ② | ③ | ④ | ⑤ | ⑥ | ⑦ | ① | ② | ③ | ④ | ⑤ |

32502 Registered Nurses

FIGURE 14-1. *Continued (figure continues).*

naires, the job relevance of the questions, and the fact that incumbents may have had prior experience with similar job analysis instruments all may have contributed to increased engagement with the rating tasks on the task questionnaires. This engagement, in turn, may have led to well-differentiated frequency and importance ratings.

These findings provide some evidence for the potential meaningfulness of task statements generated using this modified version of the available task inventories approach. However, the fact that (a) the data are not totally consistent, (b) archival data are likely to grow dated, and (c) the approach may not yield viable data when our concern is new or

| | Not Relevant | Once per year or less | More than once per year | More than once per month | More than once per week | Daily | Several times per day | Hourly or more often | Not important | Somewhat important | Important | Very Important | Extremely important |
|---|---|---|---|---|---|---|---|---|---|---|---|---|---|
| 16 Provides first aid. | ⓪ | ① | ② | ③ | ④ | ⑤ | ⑥ | ⑦ | ① | ② | ③ | ④ | ⑤ |
| 17 Assesses community health care needs. | ⓪ | ① | ② | ③ | ④ | ⑤ | ⑥ | ⑦ | ① | ② | ③ | ④ | ⑤ |
| 18 Provides employee health services within industrial organization. | ⓪ | ① | ② | ③ | ④ | ⑤ | ⑥ | ⑦ | ① | ② | ③ | ④ | ⑤ |
| 19 Plans and participates in school health program. | ⓪ | ① | ② | ③ | ④ | ⑤ | ⑥ | ⑦ | ① | ② | ③ | ④ | ⑤ |
| 20 Participates in surveys and research studies. | ⓪ | ① | ② | ③ | ④ | ⑤ | ⑥ | ⑦ | ① | ② | ③ | ④ | ⑤ |
| 21 Counsels and provides support for patients and families. | ⓪ | ① | ② | ③ | ④ | ⑤ | ⑥ | ⑦ | ① | ② | ③ | ④ | ⑤ |
| **Additional Relevant Tasks** Please write in additional relevant tasks and provide a rating | | | | | | | | | | | | | |
| 22 _____ | ⓪ | ① | ② | ③ | ④ | ⑤ | ⑥ | ⑦ | ① | ② | ③ | ④ | ⑤ |
| 23 _____ | ⓪ | ① | ② | ③ | ④ | ⑤ | ⑥ | ⑦ | ① | ② | ③ | ④ | ⑤ |
| 24 _____ | ⓪ | ① | ② | ③ | ④ | ⑤ | ⑥ | ⑦ | ① | ② | ③ | ④ | ⑤ |
| 25 _____ | ⓪ | ① | ② | ③ | ④ | ⑤ | ⑥ | ⑦ | ① | ② | ③ | ④ | ⑤ |

32502 Registered Nurses

**FIGURE 14-1.** *Continued*

rapidly changing occupations all suggest that alternative strategies might be desirable for generating occupation-specific tasks.

## The GWA Approach

The procedures described above are appropriate when existing task inventories are available. However, a different approach will be needed when up-to-date task lists are not available. We believe that the most attractive approach for generating these new task lists is a cued recall approach in which the GWAs provide a basis for task generation. This approach is based on the earlier work of Mumford and his colleagues (Mumford et al., 1992; Mumford & Supinski, 1995; Reiter-Palmon et al., 1990), although the general techniques (e.g., using SME panels) are broadly applied in job analysis.

The GWA task generation procedure requires a group of five to six SMEs. Typically, these SMEs are incumbents or supervisors who have at least 6 months' experience in an occupation and who have different backgrounds and somewhat different career histories (e.g. Campion, 1992; Landy & Vasey, 1991). Additionally, panel members should be good performers who hold roughly similar positions in the organization (Landy & Vasey, 1991). It may also be desirable to select panel members to represent differ-

**TABLE 14-1**
**Reliability of Task Ratings Considering Varying Numbers of Raters:**
**Occupation-Specific Tasks**

| | | Number of raters on each variable | | | | | |
| | | Frequency | | | Importance | | |
| Occupation | $n$ | $r_k{}^a$ | $r_1{}^b$ | $r_{30}{}^c$ | $r_k$ | $r_1$ | $r_{30}$ |
|---|---|---|---|---|---|---|---|
| 15005 Education Administrators | 39 | .97 | .42 | .96 | .95 | .34 | .94 |
| 19005 General Managers & Top Executives | 135 | .99 | .45 | .96 | .98 | .30 | .93 |
| 25105 Computer Programmers | 18 | .87 | .27 | .92 | .86 | .25 | .91 |
| 31305 Teachers, Elementary School | 79 | .99 | .46 | .96 | .98 | .43 | .96 |
| 32502 Registered Nurses | 93 | .99 | .47 | .96 | .98 | .40 | .95 |
| 32902 Medical & Clinical Laboratory Technologists | 7 | .90 | .58 | .98 | .89 | .53 | .97 |
| 49008 Salespersons, Except Scientific & Retail | 39 | .97 | .43 | .96 | .97 | .43 | .96 |
| 49011 Salespersons, Retail | 58 | .97 | .39 | .95 | .97 | .36 | .94 |
| 49021 Stock Clerks, Sales Floor | 24 | .76 | .12 | .80 | .81 | .15 | .84 |
| 49023 Cashiers | 68 | .97 | .34 | .94 | .97 | .31 | .93 |
| 51002 First Line Supervisors, Clerical/Administrative | 165 | .99 | .32 | .93 | .98 | .27 | .92 |
| 53102 Tellers | 17 | .95 | .55 | .97 | .94 | .49 | .97 |
| 53905 Teachers' Aides & Assistants, Clerical | 23 | .87 | .22 | .89 | .83 | .18 | .87 |
| 55108 Secretaries, Except Legal & Medical | 238 | 1.00 | .51 | .97 | .99 | .32 | .94 |
| 55305 Receptionists & Information Clerks | 29 | .98 | .58 | .98 | .97 | .56 | .97 |
| 55338 Bookkeeping, Accounting, & Auditing Clerks | 87 | .98 | .37 | .95 | .98 | .33 | .94 |
| 55347 General Office Clerks | 237 | 1.00 | .46 | .96 | .99 | .31 | .93 |
| 61005 Police & Detective Supervisors | 38 | .96 | .39 | .95 | .93 | .25 | .91 |
| 63014 Police Patrol Officers | 65 | .99 | .58 | .98 | .98 | .45 | .96 |
| 65008 Waiters & Waitresses | 53 | .98 | .43 | .96 | .97 | .37 | .95 |
| 65026 Cooks, Restaurant | 13 | .89 | .38 | .95 | .87 | .34 | .94 |
| 65038 Food Preparation Workers | 69 | .97 | .30 | .93 | .96 | .27 | .92 |
| 66008 Nursing Aides, Orderlies, & Attendants | 49 | .97 | .44 | .96 | .97 | .40 | .95 |
| 67005 Janitors & Cleaners | 98 | .99 | .48 | .96 | .98 | .32 | .93 |
| 85132 Maintenance Repairers, General Utility | 100 | .96 | .20 | .88 | .96 | .21 | .89 |
| 87902 Earth Drillers, Except Oil & Gas | 16 | .95 | .53 | .97 | .94 | .48 | .97 |
| 92974 Packaging & Filling Machine Operators | 31 | .77 | .10 | .76 | .78 | .10 | .77 |
| 97102 Truck Drivers, Heavy or Tractor Trailer | 36 | .97 | .44 | .96 | .96 | .42 | .96 |
| 97111 Bus Drivers, Schools | 34 | .98 | .66 | .98 | .98 | .56 | .97 |

*Note.* Reliability estimates are based on incumbents' ratings of occupation-specific tasks. [a]Observed reliability estimates were obtained by calculating the interrater reliability across tasks, $r_k = [MS_t - MS_i]/MS_t$ (Crocker & Algina, 1986), where $k$ is the number of judges actually providing ratings. [b]Single rater estimates of reliability were obtained by calculating the interrater reliability for a single judge across tasks: $r_1 = [MS_t - MS_i]/[MS_t + (k - 1)MS_i/1]$. [c]Estimates of reliability for 30 raters were obtained by calculating the interrater reliability for thirty judges across tasks: $r_{30} = [MS_t - MS_i]/[MS_t + (k - 30)MS_i/30]$.

ent organizations when there is a need to obtain task data that extend across organizations.

The procedures used to generate task statements in these meetings are quite straightforward. First, each SME is asked to review the definition of each GWA and determine whether this type of activity is performed on the job. Second, panel members are asked to reach a consensus decision concerning the approximately 10 to 15 GWAs that represent the most important components of job performance. Third, panel members are asked to (a) identify the major subcategories of activities falling under each GWA and (b) describe the specific tasks falling under each subcategory.

After panel members have generated their lists of activities and specific tasks under each GWA, one panel member reads aloud one activity and the associated tasks he or she has generated. Other panel members then review these task statements for relevance, comprehensiveness, and clarity, and recommend any necessary changes. This procedure is repeated round-robin, until panel members think that all the tasks falling under a given GWA have been identified. The group then moves on to the next

GWA. Throughout this process, occupational analysts write down the task statements proposed by panel members and use these notes to develop the final task list.

Typically, these procedures yield 150 to 400 tasks (depending on the complexity of the occupation) and provide a rather detailed occupational description. The interrater agreement coefficients obtained when incumbents were asked to assess the frequency with which these tasks are performed on their job and the importance of these tasks were similar to those obtained for the available task inventory approach described earlier. Applications of this method generally yield importance and frequency rating interrater agreement coefficients in the upper .80s or better (Mumford et al., 1992; Mumford & Supinski, 1995; Reiter-Palmon et al., 1990).

These interrater agreement coefficients are noteworthy for two reasons. First, the tasks resulting from the "top-down" GWA approach apparently provide reasonably reliable descriptions of people's job activities. Second, it appears that this procedure is flexible enough to yield viable task statements across the broad range of occupations examined in these studies, including sales representatives and technicians as well as managers and financial analysts.

These observations about the reliability of task ratings raise a new question: Is there reason to suspect that this procedure yields task ratings that provide a meaningful description of people's jobs? One piece of evidence bearing on the meaningfulness of these task statements has been provided by a series of "comprehensiveness" tests that were part of the studies cited above. In those tests, three to five SMEs were asked to review the lists of tasks obtained using these procedures and identify any additional tasks needed to ensure a comprehensive description of occupations. Although this comprehensiveness test often resulted in the addition of a few tasks, the number of tasks added was relatively small and in no case resulted in more than a 5% increase in the number of tasks identified. Thus, it appears that this procedure in fact yields the sort of tasks that provide a comprehensive description of occupations.

Another way one might assess the meaningfulness of the descriptive information provided by these procedures is by examining the ability of these task ratings to capture cross-position and cross-site differences in the nature of the work being done. For example, in the Reiter-Palmon et al. (1990) study, it was found that the resulting task statements accurately identified changes in work load associated with new shipping and pricing procedures. The Mumford and Supinski (1995) study contrasted the tasks required in emerging and diminishing telecommunications positions. As might be expected from the changes in technology occurring in the telecommunications field, tasks associated with "black box" technology were more important and more frequently performed in emerging as opposed to diminishing positions.

Taken as a whole, these studies provide some compelling evidence for the reliability and validity of task statements formulated using this top-down GWA task generation procedure. As noted earlier, this method of task generation has two other desirable characteristics. First, it appears to provide an efficient basis for task generation, greatly reducing the cost, as well as the time, needed to obtain occupation-specific tasks. Typically, two 1-day meetings are sufficient to obtain a set of comprehensive, detailed task statements. Second, because tasks are generated and organized in terms of the GWAs, it becomes possible to integrate occupation-specific tasks into a larger taxonomy (i.e., the GWA portion of the O*NET taxonomy).

## Summary

Alternative procedures for identifying and describing job tasks were carefully examined. The effort seemed called for, in part, because task data provide the essential information needed to identify and understand other important occupation-specific descriptors. Furthermore, occupation-specific data, particularly task descriptions, represent a cornerstone of many personnel interventions, including training, job redesign, and human factors analysis.

Unfortunately, it has traditionally proven difficult to apply task descriptions in an effective fashion across large numbers of occupations. This problem is most likely attributable to the high cost of obtaining occupation-specific information, particularly task descriptions. Additionally, the number of tasks involved in most jobs and the use of multiple ratings make it difficult to apply this information, because the resulting data cannot be readily organized within a broader structure that facilitates various applications.

The approaches described in this chapter, particularly task generation based on the GWAs, are expressly intended to address these issues, and the results obtained in these initial efforts are promising. Not only can the GWAs be used to organize task data, but the availability of this organizing structure allows us to collect comprehensive and accurate tasks.

# Occupational Descriptor Covariates: Potential Sources of Variance in O*NET Ratings

RUTH A. CHILDS, NORMAN G. PETERSON, AND MICHAEL D. MUMFORD

The Occupational Information Network (O*NET) occupational information system relies on empirical data—ratings provided by job incumbents and occupational analysts—as the basis for its descriptions of occupations. This is one of its strengths, as demonstrated throughout this book. However, the O*NET's reliance on job incumbents' and occupational analysts' ratings—indeed, the reliance of most job analysis efforts on similarly collected data—may be considered problematic by those who question the accuracy of such ratings. Morgeson and Campion (1996), for example, challenged the assumption that job incumbents and occupational analysts can and do provide accurate ratings of occupations in job analysis studies. They describe a myriad of social and cognitive factors that might reduce the accuracy of ratings and, consequently, the accuracy of the resulting occupation descriptions. Among these factors are the cognitive complexity of the judgments requested and the impact of group dynamics, both of which may cause unintentional inaccuracy. Also included are factors that might motivate deliberate inflation of ratings. Other research studies on the accuracy of self-reports (e.g., Menon, 1994; Sudman, Bradburn, & Schwarz, 1996; Turner & Martin, 1985) also raise concerns about the effects of memory and cognitive load on survey data.

Because of the central role of occupational ratings in the O*NET occupational information system, we have given careful consideration to identifying potential sources of variance in the O*NET ratings. In this chapter, we present a model of these occupational descriptor covariates and describe the steps we have taken to minimize or control the effects of each covariate on the O*NET system. We also discuss the implications of our preliminary analyses of the O*NET data for future research on the accuracy of occupational analysis data.

However, we should point out at the outset that the O*NET data collection strategy was not expressly designed to support an investigation of rating accuracy. Rather, it was designed to control some potential sources of variance, to account for others through random sampling at several stages of rater selection, and to allow direct analysis of only a small subset of the possible occupational descriptor covariates. Although the data collection design precludes careful examination of many of the potential sources of error, the coherence and interpretability of the results of the analyses presented throughout this book—particularly the high interrater agreement coefficients and the similarity of the job incumbents' and occupational analysts' ratings—suggest that the ratings largely reflect "true" variance.

## THE MODEL

The potential sources of variance in descriptor ratings discussed in this chapter include a variety of factors, such as the raters' familiarity with the occupations, attributes of the organizations, features of the questionnaires, and a number of other factors that may influence occupational ratings. It is important to bear in mind that although some of these factors may be construed as sources of error, others are generally considered true variance. As Morgeson and Campion (1996) pointed out, some of the sources of variance, including uniformity of data collection media, may actually inflate the observed reliability of the ratings by subtly biasing respondents to provide particular ratings.

The potential sources of variance in occupational ratings that will be considered here are outlined in Figure 15-1. This figure illustrates our model, showing how different factors may contribute to inaccuracies in final occupational ratings. The examples used here apply to the O*NET, but most are relevant for other job analysis efforts.

To the far left of the figure is a box representing the actual job demands. These demands are the reality we would like to reflect in the O*NET occupational information system. However, we recognize that occupations may differ within a given occupation from establishment to establishment, depending on such factors as the industry type (e.g., an electrical engineer for an electronics manufacturing firm might

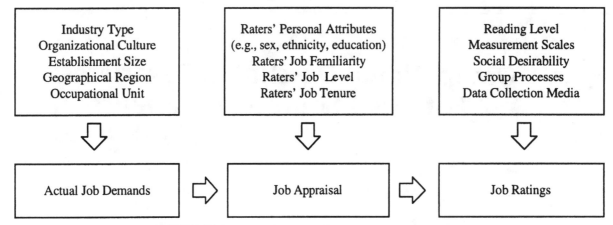

**FIGURE 15-1.** Potential sources of variance in O*NET ratings.

have different responsibilities from an electrical engineer for a broadcasting station); the organizational culture (e.g., the management structure and degree of bureaucratization in a company); the size of the establishment; and the geographic region. We also recognize that the breadth of our occupational analysis unit (e.g., whether we are targeting the general category of mechanic or the more specific subspecialty of aircraft mechanic) will have some impact on how the occupation's features will be summarized and on what activities and requirements will be considered typical.

In addition, as is shown in the center of the figure, the raters' appraisals of the occupation may be influenced by factors such as personal attributes (e.g., sex, ethnicity, education); raters' familiarity with the occupation (e.g., a rater's status as incumbent or occupational analyst); the raters' job level (e.g., incumbent or supervisor); and the raters' tenure on the job. All of these factors may influence an occupation's actual demands as experienced by the raters. The extent to which these factors vary within an occupation in a sample will affect the occupational profile that results.

Finally, even assuming that the particular instance of the occupation is not unusual and the raters appraise the occupation accurately, there are still opportunities for added variance to affect the ratings. This is reflected on the right side of Figure 15-1. For example, the reading level on the questionnaires might be too high for some job incumbents or the terminology might be unfamiliar. The questionnaire scales might lack the categories needed to accurately describe a particular occupation. Incumbent raters may be motivated to provide inaccurately favorable ratings for their occupation. When incumbents generate ratings in focus groups, group processes (e.g., motivational losses or pressures to conform to the group norm) may affect the variance observed in ratings (Morgeson & Campion, 1996). Finally, the data collection medium (e.g., paper-and-pencil administration vs. computer administration) may affect the ratings obtained.

## STRATEGIES

In designing the O*NET data collection, we considered three approaches for addressing each of the possible occupational descriptor covariates in the model just described:

- Controlling the covariate (e.g., in the O*NET questionnaires, we chose to ask raters to judge the level of a particular skill required for an occupation before rating that skill's importance; therefore, this possible source of variance related to the order of the measurement scales was controlled);
- Allowing the covariate to vary (e.g., many of the covariates, such as rater sex and level of job experience, were balanced in the sample through random selection of raters within occupations and establishments; some of these covariates yielded sufficient data for comparison analyses, but such analyses were not a goal of the data collection effort); and
- Purposefully including different values of a covariate and attempting to measure its effects (e.g., both job incumbents and occupational analysts provided ratings; analyses comparing the ratings of these two groups with presumably different levels of job familiarity were explicitly included in the original analysis plan).

Table 15-1 indicates which of these three strategies was selected for addressing each of the occupational descriptor covariates in the O*NET data collection effort. These choices and their implications for future job analysis efforts are discussed in the following sections.

## APPLYING THE STRATEGIES TO THE MODEL

In this section, we describe each occupational descriptor covariate included in the model shown in

**TABLE 15-1**
**Strategies for Addressing Occupational Descriptor Covariates in the O*NET Data Collection**

| | Strategy | | |
|---|---|---|---|
| Covariate | Controlling | Allowing to vary | Measuring and comparing multiple levels |
| Industry type | | | ✓ |
| Organizational culture | | ✓ | |
| Establishment size | | ✓ | |
| Geographical region | | ✓ | |
| Occupational unit | ✓ | | |
| Raters' personal attributes | | ✓ | |
| Rater job familiarity | | | ✓ |
| Raters' job level | | ✓ | |
| Raters' job tenure | | ✓ | |
| Reading level | ✓ | | |
| Measurement scales | ✓ | | |
| Social desirability | ✓ | | |
| Group processes | ✓ | | |
| Data collection media | | | ✓ |

**TABLE 15-2**
**Numbers of Participating Establishments by Standard Industrial Classification Division**

| Standard industrial classification division | Number of establishments |
|---|---|
| Agriculture, Forestry and Fishing | 3 |
| Construction | 2 |
| Manufacturing | 22 |
| Transportation, Communication, Electric, Gas and Sanitary Services | 5 |
| Wholesale Trade | 5 |
| Retail Trade | 15 |
| Finance, Insurance and Real Estate | 17 |
| Services | 98 |
| Public Administration | 10 |

Figure 15-1 as it relates to the O*NET data collection. In addition, we discuss our selection of strategies for addressing these covariates, summarized in Table 15-1.

## Influences on Actual Job Demands

We first consider the factors—industry type, organizational culture, establishment size, geographical region, and occupational unit—that are likely to affect actual job demands.

### Industry Type

Establishments participating in the O*NET prototype data collection were selected from establishments in Standard Industrial Classification (SIC) categories that were identified as likely to employ individuals in the 80 occupations targeted in the initial data collection. The selection of establishments was stratified across 143 selected SICs (grouped into nine divisions) and across four establishment sizes. Table 15-2 shows the numbers of establishments in each SIC Division that contributed data to the initial O*NET data collection database. Additional establishments also contributed data, but for occupations with too few respondents to be included in these analyses. In most occupations, incumbents were sampled from a number of establishments in a variety of SICs. For example, for the occupation Cashiers, questionnaires were completed by 78 job incumbents from 24 establishments in five of the nine SIC Divisions—in this case, Manufacturing, Transportation, Communication, Electric, Gas and Sanitary Services, Retail Trade, Services, and Public Administration.

Clearly, we chose to address this potential source of variance by deliberately sampling establishments

from particular SICs. Eventually, after a large amount of data has been collected, it will be possible to perform comparisons of occupational ratings for individual occupations across industries. Of course, occupations will vary considerably with respect to their occurrence across industries. In this analysis, industry could be analyzed at the level of the nine major SIC groupings into which the establishments are classified. Sufficient data are not yet available to allow this analysis to be performed across most of the occupations. However, an illustrative analysis was performed for the occupation of "Secretary, Except Legal and Medical." In this analysis, for the 46 skills on the Skills Questionnaire, the level ratings provided by 12 incumbents from four establishments in the Manufacturing sector are compared with those from 12 incumbents working at five establishments in the Public Administration sector. No statistically significant differences between the mean skill level ratings across the two sectors were found. In other words, the skills required for Secretaries in the Manufacturing sector are very similar to those required for Secretaries in the Public Administration sector. However, for certain other occupations, in other sectors, differences in ratings might well occur. In particular, organizational context and generalized work activity (GWA) ratings might be expected to differ across types of industry.

### Organizational Culture

By organizational culture, we mean such aspects of an organization as its management structure, the degree of bureaucratization in a company, and the company's emphasis on employee responsibility. Also included are the degree to which an organization is involved in the production or use of new technology and, particularly, whether an organization can be classified as "high performance." In chapter 4 of this book, we discuss common criteria for classification as a high-performance organization: for example, an organizational emphasis on the importance of innovation and technology in the workplace.

As indicated in Table 15-1, we chose to address this covariate by allowing it to vary across raters, assuming that the random selection of establishments within SIC would prevent a preponderance of establishments with particular organizational culture attributes. This decision was influenced by the fact that prescreening establishments for organizational culture variables would have been impractical because, unlike industry type, this information was not readily apparent when establishments were selected. It may be possible to perform post-hoc comparisons of occupational ratings between raters from different organizational cultures, as suggested by some of the analyses of the organizational context variables (reported in chap. 10). However, obtaining sufficient sample sizes within these organizational context types may be difficult.

## Establishment Size

Establishments of widely varying sizes have contributed and will continue to contribute data to the O*NET database. Establishments defined for the purposes of the O*NET data collection as single sites (an organization may consist of multiple sites) must have at least five employees in order to participate, but it may have as many as several thousand employees. Establishments participating in the initial O*NET data collection ranged in size from 0 to 5,000 full-time employees, with a median of 70. The size of the establishment is expected to directly affect the data collected from the establishment (e.g., how many employees are available for the data collection and in how many occupations). It may also have indirect effects (e.g., the duties of a mechanical engineer in a small company may be more varied than the duties of a mechanical engineer in a large, specialized engineering shop).

Although not as difficult to determine in prescreening as organizational culture, establishment size was nevertheless not known with certainty when selecting the establishments for inclusion in the data collection. Therefore, establishments were selected randomly without regard to establishment size. However, the version of the organizational context questionnaire that was administered to organizational representatives does provide information about the size of the establishment. These data can be combined with the incumbent data from those establishments to compare occupational ratings across establishment size. Unfortunately, because small establishments by definition have fewer employees, they can contribute fewer respondents, particularly for some occupations, such as Secretary, that become prevalent only in larger organizations. In addition, smaller establishments may be less willing to allow employees to take time on the job to complete the questionnaires, further decreasing their representation. There currently is an insufficient number of job incumbents from small organizations in the database to permit an analysis comparing incumbent responses by establishment size. A special effort to target smaller organizations would probably be necessary to collect sufficient data for analyses of this factor.

## Geographical Region

The geographical region in which an establishment is located and where an incumbent works may also affect occupational ratings. For example, a lawyer practicing in New York City may experience different job demands than a lawyer in a rural Midwestern community. Organizations that have establishments in several geographical regions and are centrally organized may also have different attributes than organizations that are located in a single region.

Information about the geographical region in which an establishment is located was collected through the Organizational Context Questionnaire administered to organizational representatives. Geographical region is not included in the sampling plan for the data collection, but rather is allowed to vary as establishments are randomly selected nationwide from within SICs. The incumbent data collected within occupations across establishments in the initial O*NET data collection currently is too sparse to permit meaningful analyses by geographical region.

## Occupational Unit

The breadth or specificity of the occupational categories being described in a job analysis may affect the accuracy of the data. For example, use of broader occupational units, such as "mechanic," might require the collection and combination of ratings from incumbents in a variety of occupational subspecialties, including "automobile mechanic" and "aircraft mechanic." This would probably result in some loss of precision in the resulting occupational profiles. On the other hand, occupational analysts might find it easier to provide ratings for these broader categories than for occupation subspecialties.

A set of 1,122 occupational units, developed by the Occupational Analysis Field Centers (OAFCs), was used to collect data for the prototype O*NET. The occupational units represent a taxonomy of occupations that is intermediate in terms of number of categories between the Occupational Employment Statistics (OES) taxonomy and the *Dictionary of Occupational Titles* (DOT; U.S. Department of Labor, 1991a) taxonomy. Some of the OES categories have been subdivided and many of the DOT categories combined.

In the O*NET data collection, this covariate is controlled (i.e., only one system of occupational units is used). However, it may be possible to perform analyses to suggest the impact of this choice of taxonomies. One possible analysis that might suggest the importance of this factor would involve subdividing several of the current occupational units and collecting ratings from occupational analysts on those units. An additional analysis that might be of interest is the comparison of ratings of more homogeneous subgroups of incumbents within a current occupational unit, perhaps grouped on the basis of their indications of occupational knowledge specialties on the Knowledges Questionnaire.

## Influences on Job Appraisal

The next four factors are related to how the rater perceives the job. These factors include the raters' personal attributes, such as sex, ethnicity, and education; the raters' familiarity with the job; the raters' job level; and the raters' time on the job.

### Raters' Personal Attributes

The personal attributes of raters (e.g., sex, ethnicity, and educational achievement) are very likely to differ across occupations. For example, despite efforts to hire women in occupations traditionally dominated by men and, to some extent, men into jobs traditionally held by women, many occupations are still dominated by one sex. For example, of the 95 Registered Nurses who provided ratings in the initial O*NET data collection, 93 were women. Similarly, of the 67 Police Patrol Officers who provided ratings, 64 were men.

Of the 2,197 incumbents who responded to at least one questionnaire in the initial O*NET data collection, 64% were female and 36% were male; 76% selected White/Not of Hispanic Origin for their ethnicity, 8% selected African American/Not of Hispanic Origin, 6% selected Hispanic, 5% selected Native American, and 3% selected Asian/Pacific American (the remaining 2% marked Other or did not respond); and 95% had at least a high school diploma, but only 8% also had a bachelor's degree.

To what extent do these differences in personal attributes contribute to differences in occupational ratings? And, where individuals differ systematically across, but not within, occupations, how do these differences in personal attributes contribute to perceived occupational differences? The O*NET data collection is designed to randomly select respondents across these rater attributes, in order to control for the effects of variations on ratings. However, this method of control requires that we have a large number of respondents if we want to determine the differential effects of various attributes. There are insufficient data in the initial O*NET data collection to permit analyses to determine to what extent ratings made by incumbents within specific occupations differ according to incumbent attributes. It also is conceivable that occupational analysts' ratings may be influenced by rater attributes (e.g., male analysts might tend to rate traditionally female-dominated jobs less highly than would female analysts). An analysis of variance might be performed to address this issue, with sex, race, and educational level as possible sources of variance within and across occupations. An analysis of the effects of one attribute (race, for example) within an occupation should account for the effects of other possible sources of variance, such as differences in job tenure between minority and majority job incumbents in an occupation that until recently was predominately held by individuals of a particular ethnicity. Personal attributes might be expected to affect ratings in all the domains to some degree, perhaps most notably in the work styles and occupational values domains.

### Raters' Job Familiarity: Incumbents' Versus Analysts' Ratings

In five of the domains (basic and cross-functional skills, GWAs, abilities, work context, and knowledges), both job incumbents and occupational analysts provided ratings for some occupations. Job incumbents were individuals with at least 6 months' experience in the occupation and included not only individuals actually performing the occupation but also some supervisors. All of the incumbents completed at least one of the nine questionnaires, and a few completed as many as five.

Occupational analysts were trained raters (employment specialists at the OAFCs and industrial/organizational psychology graduate students) who familiarized themselves with a particular occupation by studying a list of occupation tasks and then provided ratings for that occupation. Each task list was based on occupation descriptions from the DOT. Each occupation was rated by at least five raters independently, to minimize the effects of rater error. During a rating cycle, each rater rated a set of 125 occupational units on one of the O*NET content model domains.

Although job incumbents have the advantage of more detailed knowledge of their particular occupation, it might be argued that occupational analysts have the advantage of perspective—knowledge of a large number of occupations and the ability to compare the particular occupation being rated with the characteristics of other occupations.

Job incumbents' and occupational analysts' ratings were deliberately collected in separate phases of the data collection, with the intention of comparing the ratings and evaluating the effect of job familiarity. For each of the five domains in which both analysts and incumbents provided ratings, analyses comparing these ratings were performed. The results of these analyses are reported in each of the domain chapters. In general, these analyses found the incumbents' and analysts' ratings to be moderately to highly correlated. In the skills domain, for example, the median correlation between incumbents' and analysts' ratings is .73.

Despite these similarities, there are some differences between the two sets of ratings. Again, taking the skills domain as an example, analysts' ratings for the level of skill required for an occupation tend to be lower than incumbents' ratings, with the exception of some of the technical skills, which the analysts rated slightly higher than did the incumbents. Smaller but consistent differences were also found for the importance ratings.

Incumbents' and analysts' ratings are both acceptably reliable, across occupations and across domains. Table 15-3 shows the average interrater agreement for incumbents' ratings for the actual number of rat-

**TABLE 15-3**
**Estimated Reliabilities of Incumbents' Ratings**

| Questionnaire/scale | $r_k$ | $r_{30}$ |
|---|---|---|
| Skills | | |
| Level | .79 | .93 |
| Importance | .79 | .93 |
| Job Entry Requirement | .60 | .83 |
| Knowledges | | |
| Level | .86 | .95 |
| Importance | .85 | .94 |
| Training, education, licensure, & experience | | |
| Instructional Program | .78 | .92 |
| Educational Subject Area | .74 | .90 |
| Licensure | .85 | .95 |
| Experience | .79 | .93 |
| Generalized work activities | | |
| Level | .80 | .92 |
| Importance | .78 | .92 |
| Frequency | .74 | .90 |
| Work context | .87 | .95 |
| Organizational context | | |
| Across Occupations | .64 | .84 |
| Across Organizations | .45 | .79 |
| Abilities | | |
| Level | .82 | .93 |
| Importance | .82 | .93 |
| Occupational values | .60 | .82 |
| Work styles | | |
| Level | .70 | .88 |
| Importance | .67 | .86 |

*Note.* $r_k$ is the observed interrater agreement coefficient; $r_{30}$ is the estimated interrater agreement coefficient for 30 raters.

**TABLE 15-4**
**Estimated Reliabilities of Analysts' Ratings**

| Questionnaire/scale | Average $r_s$ |
|---|---|
| Abilities | |
| Level | .87 |
| Importance | .85 |
| Generalized work activities | |
| Level | .88 |
| Importance | .85 |
| Frequency | .81 |
| Knowledges | |
| Level | .83 |
| Importance | .83 |
| Skills | |
| Level | .87 |
| Importance | .84 |
| Work context | .82 |

*Note.* $r_s$ is the average estimated reliability of anlaysts' ratings for five raters.

ers per occupation in these data ($r_k$) and the predicted agreement for 30 raters per occupation ($r_{30}$).

For analysts' ratings, descriptor category reliabilities were determined by computing the agreement in ratings across five raters. The reliability of a single rater, or $r_1$, was estimated from a sample of five raters and statistically "stepped up" as an estimate of the reliability of five raters ($r_5$). Reliabilities for each descriptor category were then averaged across all 10 cycles of ratings, including all 1,122 occupational units. Reliabilities for the abilities and work context domains are based on 130 occupational units, pending completion of the final rating cycle. Values for the reliability of ratings in the descriptor categories range from .81 for GWA frequency to .88 for GWA level as shown in Table 15-4. Analyses of the ratings confirmed that the descriptors could be reliably rated using the DOT task lists.

In general, both incumbents and analysts provide reliable occupational ratings, and their ratings are moderately to highly correlated. However, for most descriptors, the level of the ratings tends to be lower for the analysts, which indicates a definite effect of rater type that is most likely due to occupational familiarity. This finding guided our decision to report analysts' and incumbents' ratings separately in the initial version of the O*NET database. Both sets of ratings are useful and provide reliable information. The analysts' ratings have the advantage of covering

more occupations (1,122) but on fewer O*NET descriptors, whereas the incumbents' ratings cover fewer occupations (29) but on all the O*NET descriptors.

### Raters' Job Level

Occupational ratings were provided by both job incumbents and their supervisors (both are typically referred to as *incumbents* throughout this book). The job level of the raters selected to participate in the O*NET data collection was not controlled. We might expect job incumbents to be at least as familiar as supervisors—and possibly more familiar—with the particular requirements of their jobs. However, supervisors may be more aware of variations in job requirements across job assignments and how those requirements compare with the requirements of other jobs. We would expect the effect of job level on ratings to extend across the domains.

Of 2,197 incumbents in 29 occupations providing ratings, 70% identified themselves as job incumbents, 7% as supervisors, and 20% said they both worked in the job and supervised others in the job (3% did not respond to the question). The numbers of supervisors may be inflated because many of the individuals in management-related occupations, such as First Line Supervisor and General Manager, reported that they were supervisors of job incumbents in those positions. It is possible that they misunderstood the question, which requested that the rater select "the category that best describes your relationship to this job." Without specifically targeting supervisors, it is unlikely that the O*NET data collection will yield sufficient numbers of supervisors to permit meaningful comparisons of their ratings with incumbents' ratings.

### Raters' Job Tenure

The amount of time a rater has spent in a job might also be expected to influence judgments made about the job. In collecting these data, we requested that job incumbents have at least 6 months of experience on the job. In fact, the data we received in the initial O*NET data collection were provided by incumbents with job experience ranging from less than 1 month to more than 10 years (median job experience was between 6 and 10 years). However, many years of experience do not necessarily lead to better ratings. Individuals with extensive experience in a single job may lack experience in other jobs, and experience in other jobs may provide a perspective for rating the requirements of the current job. This covariate was allowed to vary randomly across raters, but information about job tenure was requested of participants, with the hope that some exploratory analyses might be possible. The interesting comparison in this case may be between incumbents with very little job experience (e.g., less than 1 year) and those with substantial experience (e.g., 6 or more years). To illustrate such an analysis, we performed an analysis comparing the means of the skills level ratings provided by 14 "Secretaries, Not Medical and Legal" with less than 1 year of experience with ratings from 38 Secretaries with 6 or more years of experience. The results strongly support the notion that experience has a relatively minor effect on these ratings: The mean ratings correlate .93, and only 2 of the 46 descriptors have statistically significant mean differences at the .05 level, roughly the number that would be expected by chance.

## Influences on Job Ratings

The factors in the final group do not influence the job itself or the raters' perception of the job but instead directly affect the rating process or method. These factors are reading level, the measurement scales, social desirability, group processes, and the data collection media. With the exception of the data collection media, each of these possible sources of variance was controlled by carefully designing the data collection instruments and procedures to optimize rating accuracy. Two data collection media—paper-and-pencil and computerized questionnaires—were included in the O*NET data collection design so that the effects of that covariate could be investigated.

### Reading Level

In creating the O*NET questionnaires, every effort was made to write the descriptor definitions and anchors at no more than an eighth-grade reading level. It is probable, however, that some portions of the questionnaires may pose reading difficulties for individuals in some jobs, especially those jobs that have very limited requirements for reading comprehension.

In the try-out of the draft questionnaires in the fall of 1994 (Mumford & Sager, 1995), 202 job incumbents from a variety of jobs, ranging from typist to van driver to occupational analyst, completed drafts of the O*NET questionnaires. After completing each questionnaire, these job incumbents were asked (a) Did you find the instructions in this section of the questionnaire easy to understand? and (b) Did you find the questions easy to understand? On a scale of 1 to 5, on which 5 is the most positive rating, average ratings ranged from a low of 3.67 for the instructions and 3.82 for the questions on the Training, Education, Licensure, and Experience Questionnaire to a high of 4.42 and 4.28 for the instructions and questions related to the Occupational Values Questionnaire. On the basis of the tryout results, the questionnaire instructions were revised and simplified. Although the ratings for ease of understanding from the try-out were quite high, because of the subsequent revisions, we would expect ratings of the current questionnaires to be even higher.

This does not mean that the reading difficulty of the questionnaires may not have discouraged some of the job incumbents asked to participate in the initial O*NET data collection from participating or influenced their responses. In fact, some organizational representatives gave as a reason for refusing to continue their establishment's participation in the initial O*NET data collection that the questionnaires appeared to be too complex for their employees to understand. As far as we can determine, this was the organizational representative's judgment and not a report of problems encountered after distribution of the questionnaires to incumbents.

### Measurement Scales

Attributes of the questionnaires used to collect the occupational ratings can, of course, affect the quality of the data collected. For example, if performance of a job's duties involves a task that is not included on the occupation-specific task questionnaire or within one of the categories of activities included on the GWA Questionnaire, no data about that task or GWA will be collected. In creating the questionnaires, the goal was to balance the need for completeness with the equally important needs for parsimony and for practicality in the time required for data collection.

An additional feature of the questionnaires that could directly affect the quality of the data is the rating scales on which job incumbents or occupational analysts were asked to make their ratings. For example, on several of the questionnaires (i.e., skills, abilities, knowledges, work styles, and GWAs), anchors were provided for the level rating scales. Raters were asked to make their ratings in relation to these descriptions of low, medium, and high levels of the descriptor. Although the anchors were provided to aid raters in understanding each descriptor and in placing their ratings on a common scale across occupations, it is possible that the particular examples given may have influenced the ratings in ways not intended. For example, one of the anchors for the Skills Questionnaire descriptor, Reading Comprehension, is "Reading a memo from management describing new personnel policies." It is possible that an individual rater's associations or experience with this kind of activity may adversely affect the accuracy of his or her ratings for this descriptor (e.g., a recent bad experience with organizational personnel representatives). It is difficult, however, for us to believe that the chosen anchors plausibly could have serious, systematic effects.

### Social Desirability

Social psychologists have suggested that respondents may tend to respond to questions in ways they think will cause others to view them in a positive light (e.g., Crowne & Marlowe, 1964). To reduce the impact of this source of variance, the O*NET data in the initial data collection were collected under conditions of anonymity: Job incumbents could mail their questionnaires back or return them, sealed, to coordinators within their establishments. Even so, job incumbents may have experienced some anxiety about their ratings. We would expect incumbents to attempt to give socially desirable responses in such domains as knowledges and work styles more than in other domains, but such effects could occur in almost any domain.

The effect of social desirability is difficult to assess, because it may tend to inflate ratings uniformly across incumbent raters. One would expect occupational analysts, who are presumably rating an occupation objectively, not to be influenced by this factor. However, occupational analysts' and job incumbents' ratings also may differ for reasons having to do with actual or "true" occupational factors, making it difficult to determine what part of the difference might be due to the effect of social desirability pressures on job incumbents.

### Group Processes

The initial O*NET data were collected from job incumbents and occupational analysts who completed the domain questionnaires individually. Therefore, group processes, such as being influenced by the opinions held by others in the group, are likely to be more relevant if, for example, focus groups are used in future data collections. However, the tendency to respond carelessly or thoughtlessly may have had an impact in this data collection as well, particularly if incumbents perceived themselves as being a part of a larger group of raters. Promises of anonymity may have heightened such an effect. One analysis that might shed light on the extent to which incumbents responded thoughtfully in making ratings is an analysis of the *not relevant* responses, because this response option might be seen as an easy response if one were interested in hurrying through the rating process. However, comparisons of the reliabilities of the full-scale ratings with the reliabilities of the same ratings dichotomized into relevant/not relevant (e.g., those reported in chap. 14 for the occupation-specific task ratings) suggest that respondents are making the relevant/not relevant distinction reliably within occupation and descriptor. Additionally, we expected that rater set might lead to random responding.

However, the reliabilities of the full-scale ratings tend to be high (e.g., for the Skills Questionnaire Level scale, they range from .75 to .92) across almost all questionnaires and scales, suggesting that raters are attending to the rating task and that random responding is not a problem.

### Data Collection Media

All the data analyzed in preparing this book were collected using paper-and-pencil versions of the O*NET questionnaires. The versions of the questionnaires used by incumbents to provide ratings and those used by analysts differed slightly (e.g., analysts did not provide ratings of whether particular skills are required at job entry). However, the differences were minor. As Morgeson and Campion (1996) pointed out, using the same medium to collect occupational information across raters may have the paradoxical effect of artificially inflating the reliability of the ratings.

Until comparable data are available from other media, it will be impossible to assess the amount of variance in occupational ratings that is due to the data collection methodology. Electronic versions of the O*NET questionnaires have been prepared and are available to collect data for such a comparison in the future. The electronic versions are intentionally similar in appearance and identical in wording and structure to the paper-and-pencil versions. A more stringent but much less practical demonstration might be comparison of the questionnaire results with information about the same occupation and worker attributes based on job observations, critical incidents analysis, or focus groups. In such a comparison, however, we would introduce other confounding factors, such as whether the definitions of the descriptors were adequately and comparably conveyed.

## DISCUSSION

The O*NET occupational information system is one of the largest occupational analysis efforts ever undertaken, and as such it may afford a valuable opportunity to investigate data accuracy issues that are of concern in the field of job analysis. The O*NET data collection was designed to control most of the potential sources of ratings variance or to account for them by using random sampling at different stages of the rater selection. For practical reasons, only a few of the possible covariates were explicitly varied in the data collection design to allow direct comparisons across levels of covariates. Although the data, consequently, do not lend themselves to analyses of many of the potential sources of rating variance, the evidence is strong that the ratings are accurately describing the targeted jobs. Agreement among raters within job is high, and correlations across incumbents and analysts are moderate to high. Additionally, the results for particular occupations are consistent with our prior knowledge of the jobs.

As additional data for the O*NET occupational information system are collected, it may become possible to investigate more directly the effects of some of the other covariates, including those currently addressed through random selection of raters and establishments. It is our hope that findings based on O*NET data eventually may provide guidance for prioritizing the possible sources of rat-ings variance to be targeted in future studies. This may be an important contribution, given the enor-mous expense and difficulty of designing and con-ducting studies to thoroughly investigate even a few of the possible sources of rating variance. It may also be that information gleaned from large, thoughtfully designed projects such as the O*NET will prove valuable in suggesting the practical impli-cations of choices of strategies in other job analysis studies.

# Cross-Domain Analyses

MARY ANN HANSON, WALTER C. BORMAN, U. CHRISTEAN KUBISIAK,
AND CHRISTOPHER E. SAGER

The content model underlying the Occupational Information Network (O*NET) occupational information system specifies a number of content domains that can be used in describing jobs and occupations. The O*NET's comprehensive system of descriptors includes information about (a) worker requirements (e.g., skills, knowledges, and abilities); (b) experience requirements (e.g., training and licensure); and (c) job requirements (generalized work activities [GWAs], work context, and organizational context). This abundance of information concerning job and worker characteristics provides an ideal opportunity to examine descriptor relationships across the various content domains. The present chapter describes analyses aimed at examining relationships between descriptors from the various content domains, across occupations, and assessing the structure of these cross-domain relationships.

The O*NET prototype database represents substantial progress toward realizing the vision of a comprehensive database that "portrays the parameters of available jobs" (Dunnette & Borman, 1979, p. 485). The O*NET prototype database also contains a great deal of information concerning worker characteristics and requirements, and it can thus provide some preliminary information concerning links between the job and person domains.

The value of linking the taxonomic domains of worker and job attributes has long been recognized. This information could serve a variety of purposes. For example, it has been argued that such linkages would provide a fuller understanding of human task performance (Fleishman & Quaintance, 1984), facilitate performance enhancement and productivity improvement (Peterson & Bownas, 1982), allow for validity generalization (Sparrow, 1989), and facilitate the conservation of human talent (Dunnette & Borman, 1979). The goal of developing a comprehensive database that links job and person characteristics is ambitious, and until now only limited progress has been made toward this goal. In the most recent edition of the *Handbook of Industrial and Organizational Psychology*, Harvey (1990b) lamented that "we must begin in earnest to assemble an empirical

data base that links the domain of human individual differences constructs (e.g., mental abilities, interests, personality traits) with the domain of job behavior constructs (e.g., delegating/coordinating, exchanging information, operating machines)" (p. 155).

Most attempts to link the worker and the work domains have focused on the job as a whole, or on clusters of jobs (e.g., job families). A substantial amount of data have been accumulated concerning the validity of a variety of worker characteristics for predicting performance in jobs or in clusters of jobs, and meta-analyses are available that summarize this information (e.g., Hunter & Hunter, 1984; Schmitt, Gooding, Noe, & Kirsch, 1984). Less information is available concerning relationships between worker characteristics and specific job requirements, tasks, or activities. One notable exception is Project A, a large-scale project to develop improved selection procedures for the U.S. Army. Validity results for Project A are reported according to five distinct performance criteria (e.g., McHenry, Hough, Toquam, Hanson, & Ashworth, 1990). However, even the five Project A criteria are at a fairly broad level (e.g., Technical Proficiency, Effort and Leadership). More specific information concerning links between tasks or work activities and worker requirements is available from only a few sources.

One source of this information comes from application of the job component validity (JCV) strategy proposed by McCormick, DeNisi, and Shaw (1979). In one such application, expert judgments were collected concerning the relevance of 76 worker attributes for individual items from the Position Analysis Questionnaire (PAQ; Marquardt & McCormick, 1972). These ratings, in conjunction with PAQ responses, can be used to generate estimates of the validity of these worker attributes for predicting job performance, and this is especially useful for jobs that are newly created or situations in which empirical validation is not possible (see Jeanneret, 1992a, for an excellent overview). It is worth noting that validity estimates generated in this manner are necessarily based on the assumptions that (a) when different jobs have a given component in common, the attributes needed to fulfill the requirements imposed by that component are the same across the different jobs; and (b) validities of predictors for these requirements are reasonably consistent across jobs. The expert judgments used in the JCV approach provide a wealth of data concerning relationships between individual worker attributes and specific work activities. Similar JCV research has been conducted by using the Occupational Analysis Inventory (OAI), and the expert judgments of attribute importance for work elements have been collected for the OAI as well (Pass & Cunningham, 1975b).

Expert judgments of the validity of a wide variety of predictors for relatively specific tasks were collected as part of the Army's Project A (Wing, Peterson, & Hoffman, 1984). These judgments were collected early in the project and used to guide decisions concerning the predictors to be included in the validation study. Following Project A, another study was undertaken to develop procedures for generalizing the Project A results to other military occupational specialties (MOSs; i.e., military jobs) not included in Project A. This follow-on project took a synthetic validation approach, which is very similar to the JCV approach described previously. This project also included an expert judgment task, to estimate the validity of the Project A predictor constructs (i.e., worker requirements) for several groups of military tasks (Peterson, Rosse, & Owens-Kurtz, 1989).

All of this work provides information concerning the relationships between worker characteristics and work activities that might be expected in the O*NET data, but there are two important differences between these previous studies and the cross-domain relationships in the O*NET data. First, all of these sources of information concerning relationships between worker characteristics and work activities are based on expert judgments of validity and not on empirical data. However, there is evidence that psychologists are, in fact, accurate judges of the empirical validity of tests (Schmidt, Hunter, Croll, & McKenzie, 1983). Second, and more important, these previous studies have focused on directly estimating the validity of worker characteristics for predicting job performance. In the O*NET database, the worker requirements and work activities involved in each job were judged independently. Correlations across domains in the O*NET data will therefore reflect the extent to which ratings on these descriptors covary across jobs. As such, the correlations between worker requirements and work activities do not directly reflect the validity or importance of the worker requirements for the work activities. For example, some worker requirements may be rated uniformly high across all jobs, whereas others may be rated uniformly low. All of these attributes are likely to have near-zero correlations with the work activities, even though some generally are very important or required at a high level for all jobs and others are generally unimportant. Correlations between worker attributes and work activities in the O*NET are more appropriately viewed as reflecting the extent to which the validity of the attribute is likely to vary across jobs according to the importance of a particular work activity in those jobs.

This suggests that cross-domain correlations in the O*NET are actually more relevant to placement or classification decisions than they are to selection decisions. As Dunnette and Borman (1979) have pointed out, locating and selecting the most qualified persons for available jobs will often lead to different classification decisions than locating the most appropriate jobs for particular persons. They argue that the "conservation of human talent requires that this incompatibility be overcome or substantially reduced" (p. 482). Of interest is that vocational/occupational guidance is perhaps the only real-world situation in which classification models are directly relevant (Campbell, 1990b). The relevance of the cross-domain correlations for classification or placement applications is advantageous, because occupational guidance is likely to be an important use of the O*NET data.

In addition to providing valuable information concerning links between the job and worker domains, these O*NET cross-domain relationships also provide useful information concerning the construct validity of the O*NET descriptors. The analyses for descriptors within each of the O*NET content domains, described in previous chapters, show that data collected using the O*NET descriptors are generally very reliable. These analyses also provide a great deal of information concerning the structure of each domain, but most of these analyses are necessarily internal. The within-domain analyses do, however, provide preliminary evidence that the O*NET descriptors discriminate between occupations in a sensible manner. To the extent that the present cross-domain analyses show the expected relationships between descriptors from different content domains, the construct validity of all of the O*NET descriptors will be further supported. Much of the data concerning descriptors from different content domains was actually collected from different incumbents in the same occupations, which provides for an even stronger test of cross-domain relationships.

## SAMPLE

There is a great deal of overlap between the samples used in the within-domain analyses (described in previous chapters) and the sample used in the present cross-domain analyses, but also a few differences. The cross-domain analyses were conducted after the within-domain analyses, and additional data were collected while the within-domain analyses were being conducted. These additional data were included in the cross-domain analyses but not in the within-domain analyses. Thus, the raw data set for these cross-domain analyses (before screening based on missing data and small occupations) contained 2,487 respondents, which is 301 more respondents than were available for the within-domain analyses. However, a stricter screen was also applied to these data:

**TABLE 16-1**

**Twenty-Nine Occupations With Four or More Respondents Across All Nine O*NET Questionnaires**

| Occupation code | Occupation title | Number of respondents | Number of establishments |
|---|---|---|---|
| 15005 | Education Administrators | 43 | 12 |
| 19005 | General Managers & Top Executives | 147 | 52 |
| 25105 | Computer Programmers | 22 | 3 |
| 31305 | Teachers, Elementary School | 84 | 8 |
| 32502 | Registered Nurses | 97 | 19 |
| 32902 | Medical & Clinical Laboratory Technologists | 19 | 5 |
| 49008 | Salespersons, Except Scientific & Retail | 41 | 11 |
| 49011 | Salespersons, Retail | 64 | 12 |
| 49021 | Stock Clerks, Sales Floor | 33 | 7 |
| 49023 | Cashiers | 78 | 24 |
| 51002 | First Line Supervisors, Clerical/Administrative | 174 | 35 |
| 53102 | Tellers | 20 | 7 |
| 53905 | Teachers' Aides & Assistants, Clerical | 39 | 14 |
| 55108 | Secretaries, Except Legal & Medical | 248 | 67 |
| 55305 | Receptionists & Information Clerks | 34 | 14 |
| 55338 | Bookkeeping, Accounting, & Auditing Clerks | 94 | 39 |
| 55347 | General Office Clerks | 264 | 67 |
| 61005 | Police & Detective Supervisors | 39 | 1 |
| 63014 | Police Patrol Officers | 69 | 4 |
| 65008 | Waiters & Waitresses | 60 | 12 |
| 65026 | Cooks, Restaurant | 19 | 7 |
| 65038 | Food Preparation Workers | 89 | 18 |
| 66008 | Nursing Aides, Orderlies, & Attendants | 56 | 9 |
| 67005 | Janitors & Cleaners | 117 | 34 |
| 85132 | Maintenance Repairers, General Utility | 110 | 31 |
| 87902 | Earth Drillers, Except Oil & Gas | 20 | 1 |
| 92974 | Packaging & Filling Machine Operators | 40 | 5 |
| 97102 | Truck Drivers, Heavy or Tractor Trailer | 41 | 6 |
| 97111 | Bus Drivers, Schools | 36 | 4 |

Occupations were included in the cross-domain analyses only if at least four incumbents (i.e., respondents) were available for each of the nine questionnaires (i.e., domains). Recall that occupations were included in the within-domain analyses if at least four incumbents were available for a particular questionnaire. The additional 301 incumbents were included in these cross-domain analyses (in part) to make up for this stricter data screen and provide as many occupations as possible for these analyses.

Questionnaires were excluded if more than 10% of the questions were not answered. Response rates for each questionnaire were examined separately, and individual questionnaires, not entire observations, were dropped. Table 16-1 shows the 29 occupations included in the cross-domain analyses, the number of

incumbents from each occupation represented in this data set, and the number of establishments from which these incumbents were drawn. Although we use the word *incumbent* to describe the respondents in this sample, 7% were actually the supervisors of job incumbents and 20% both supervised and performed the target occupation.

Most respondents completed more than one of the nine questionnaires, and a few completed as many as five. Thus, a certain percentage of the data available for comparing any two content model domains is based on responses from the same incumbents. Table 16-2 shows the percentage of data for any given comparison (i.e., pair of domains) that is based on responses from the same incumbents. Correlations across domains in which most of the data were pro-

**TABLE 16-2**

**Percentage of Data Across Pairs of Domains Collected From Same Incumbents**

| Domain | 1 | 2 | 3 | 4 | 5 | 6 | 7 | 8 | 9 |
|---|---|---|---|---|---|---|---|---|---|
| 1. Abilities | — | | | | | | | | |
| 2. Generalized work activities | 10 | — | | | | | | | |
| 3. Organizational context | 9 | 12 | — | | | | | | |
| 4. Occupational values | 10 | 93 | 12 | — | | | | | |
| 5. Skills | 11 | 11 | 9 | 11 | — | | | | |
| 6. Training, licensure, and experience | 10 | 10 | 12 | 10 | 10 | — | | | |
| 7. Work context | 10 | 10 | 12 | 10 | 12 | 10 | — | | |
| 8. Work styles | 11 | 11 | 12 | 11 | 10 | 88 | 11 | — | |
| 9. Knowledge | 9 | 12 | 91 | 12 | 9 | 12 | 11 | 13 | — |

vided by the same incumbents could be inflated because of uncaptured differences in jobs within an occupation or because of response bias.

## APPROACH

All of the analyses described here were conducted using occupation-level data because the goal of the O*NET is to describe occupations. To provide as much cross-domain information as possible, we took two general approaches in these analyses. First, we developed composites to summarize information concerning the descriptors in each domain, and relationships between these composites were examined across domains. Second, several a priori hypotheses concerning expected relationships between individual descriptors across domains were generated and tested.

## RELATIONSHIPS BETWEEN FACTOR-BASED COMPOSITES

The entire O*NET content model, across all domains, contains more than 300 descriptors, and the sample of occupations available for cross-domain analyses was only 29. To minimize the number of relationships to be assessed, we identified a smaller set of composites to represent the descriptors in each domain. These composites were then intercorrelated across occupations and factor analyzed to assess the overall structure of the O*NET across all domains.

### Identification of Composites

The composites were identified from the solutions selected in the within-domain principal-components analyses and then modified on the basis of rational considerations. First, using the principal-components solution chosen for each domain (presented in the relevant content domain chapters), one preliminary factor-based composite was developed for each principal component extracted. Items were assigned to a composite if they loaded at least .6 on the relevant factor. Items with substantial loadings on other factors (i.e., within .2 of the primary loading) were not included. Because the principal-component analyses were based on limited samples of occupations (between 30 and 37 occupations for each content domain), these factor-based composites were then refined. Changes were made on the basis of the content model itself, results of past research, and other rational considerations. In general, these modifications were minor and involved assigning additional descriptors to some of the composites (e.g., those that loaded less than .60 on the relevant composite). For the Abilities domain, these revisions were somewhat more extensive. Table 16-3 shows the composition of each of the final factor-based composites. For two

domains—training, licensure, and experience; and organizational context—no composites were created, because very little theory is available to interpret the correlations between higher order factors in these two domains and those from the other domains. Composite scores were formed by calculating mean scores across the descriptors included in each of the composites. Level ratings were used to form scores for abilities, skills, knowledges, work styles, and GWAs. Occupational values used an Importance scale, and work context scales were varied.

### Composite Intercorrelations

Table 16-4 shows the intercorrelations of scores on these 38 factor-based composites across the 29 occupations included in the cross-domain analyses. Reliability estimates for the composites are shown on the diagonal of this matrix. These values were calculated by computing the composite scores for each incumbent who provided ratings and then assessing the interrater reliability of these composite ratings across occupations. These reliabilities obviously limit the extent to which the composites can correlate, but generally they are moderately high, with a median reliability coefficient of .87. For five of the composites (Social Comfort, Structure, Detail Orientation, Career Advancement, and Food Production), the interrater reliabilities were .60 or lower.

Here are some highlights of the composite correlations across domains. Two of the GWA composites—Working With Information and Working With and Directing Others—have generally similar patterns of correlations with the skill, ability, and work style composites. For example, they both correlate highly with Cognitive Abilities, Cognitive Skills, and Organizational Skills, but in all three cases the correlation is slightly higher for Working With Information. These two GWA composites also correlate with Speech Ability, but in this case the correlation for Working With and Directing Others is slightly higher. Both of these GWAs also correlate at about the same level with the work style composite labeled Surgency/Achievement Orientation. These similarities are not too surprising in light of the fact that these two GWA composites correlate .72 with each other. Perhaps this reflects the fact that occupations involving working with people very often also involve working with information (e.g., managerial occupations).

In view of the high correlation between these two GWAs, several differences in the obtained patterns of correlations are notable. For example, Technical Skill and Math Ability correlate significantly with Working With Information but not with Working With and Directing Others. In contrast, Working With Others correlates significantly with the work style composite People Orientation, whereas Working With Information does not. The differences and similarities in the patterns of correlations across occupations for these two GWA composites are concep-

**TABLE 16-3**
**Composition of Factor-Based Composites Used in Cross-Domain Analyses**

| Composite labels | Descriptors included |
|---|---|
| | Ability |
| 1. Physical | Static Strength; Dynamic Strength; Explosive Strength; Trunk Strength; Stamina; Gross Body Conditioning; Gross Body Equilibrium; Dynamic Flexibility; Extent Flexibility |
| 2. Psychomotor | Rate Control; Control Precision; Multi-limb Coordination; Reaction Time; Response Orientation; Speed of Limb Movement |
| 3. Dexterity | Manual Dexterity; Finger Dexterity; Arm-Hand Steadiness; Wrist-Finger Speed |
| 4. Vision/Hearing | Depth Perception; Peripheral Vision; Night Vision; Far Vision; Glare Sensitivity; Visual Color Discrimination; Sound Localization; Hearing Sensitivity; Auditory Attention |
| 5. Cognitive | Deductive Reasoning; Originality; Fluency of Ideas; Inductive Reasoning; Problem Sensitivity; Information Ordering; Category Flexibility; Written Expression; Written Comprehension; Oral Expression; Oral Comprehension |
| 6. Math | Math Reasoning; Number Facility |
| 7. Spatial | Visualization; Spatial Orientation; Flexibility of Closure; Speed of Closure |
| 8. Speech | Speech Clarity; Speech Recognition |
| 9. Attention | Perceptual Speed; Near Vision; Selective Attention; Time Sharing |
| 10. Memory | Memorization |
| | Generalized work activities |
| 1. Manual and Physical Activities | Inspecting Equipment; Performing Physical Work Tasks; Controlling Machines; Operating Vehicles; Repairing, Mechanical; Repairing, Electronic; Handling Objects |
| 2. Working With and Directing Others | Establishing Relationships; Assisting Others; Selling or Influencing; Resolving Conflicts; Working With the Public; Coordinating Others Work; Developing Teams; Teaching Others; Directing Subordinates; Developing Others |
| 3. Working With Information | Getting Information; Identifying Objects; Monitoring Processes; Estimating Characteristics; Evaluating Information; Processing Information; Analyzing Data; Making Decisions; Thinking Creatively; Using Job Knowledge; Organizing and Planning; Interacting With Computers; Implementing Ideas; Interpreting Information; Communicating, Internal; Providing Consultation |
| | Work styles |
| 1. Surgency/Achievement Orientation | Achievement/Effort; Persistence; Initiative; Energy; Leadership Orientation; Independence; Innovation; Analytical Thinking |
| 2. Detail Orientation | Attention to Detail |
| 3. People Orientation | Cooperation; Concern for Others; Social Orientation; Self-Control; Stress Tolerance |
| | Knowledges |
| 1. Arts and Humanities | Geography; Therapy and Counseling; Foreign Language; Fine Arts; History and Archeology |
| 2. Science and Technology | Production and Processing; Engineering and Technology; Design; Building and Construction; Mechanical; Physics |
| 3. Law Enforcement | Public Safety and Security; Law, Government, and Jurisprudence |
| 4. Clerical | Clerical |
| 5. Medicine | Chemistry; Biology; Medicine and Dentistry |
| 6. Business Administration | Sales and Marketing; Customer and Personal Service |
| 7. Food Production | Food Production |
| | Occupational values |
| 1. Individual Accomplishment | Ability Utilization; Achievement; Authority; Creativity; Responsibility; Variety; Autonomy |
| 2. Structure | Activity; Independence (negatively weighted); Supervision HR; Supervision Tech |
| 3. Stability | Security; Social Status |
| 4. Social Comfort | Coworkers; Moral Values; Recognition; Working Conditions |
| 5. Career Advancement | Advancement; Compensation; Social Service (negatively weighted) |
| | Skills |
| 1. Cognitive Skills | Reading Comprehension; Active Listening; Writing; Speaking; Critical Thinking; Active Learning; Learning Strategies; Monitoring; Social Perceptiveness; Coordination; Persuasion; Instructing; Problem Identification; Information Gathering; Service Orientation; Information Organization; Synthesis/Reorganization; Idea Generation; Idea Evaluation; Implementation Planning; Solution Appraisal; Time Management; Negotiation; Systems Perceptions |
| 2. Technical Skills | Mathematics; Science; Operations Analysis; Technology Design; Equipment Selection; Installation; Programming; Testing; Operation Monitoring; Operation and Control; Product Inspection; Equipment Maintenance; Troubleshooting; Repairing |
| 3. Organizational Skills | Visioning; Identification of Downstream Consequences; Systems Evaluation; Management of Financial Resources; Management of Material Resources; Management of Personnel Resources; Identification of Key Causes; Judgment and Decision Making |

*Table 16-3 continues*

**TABLE 16-3 (Continued)**

| Composite labels | Descriptors included |
|---|---|
| | Work context |
| 1. Environmental Factors | Indoors, Controlled (negatively weighted); Outdoors, Exposed; Outdoors, Covered; Open Vehicle/Equipment; Enclosed Vehicle/Equipment; Distracting Noise; Extreme Temperatures; Poor Lighting; Cramped Work Space; Whole Body Vibration; High Places; Hazardous Conditions; Hazardous Equipment; Climbing Ladders, etc.; Special Safety Attire |
| 2. Physical Activity | Sitting (negatively weighted); Standing; Walking or Running; Kneeling or Crouching; Keeping/Regaining Balance; Bending/Twisting Body |
| 3. Health and Safety | Written Reports; Physical Aggression; Diseases; Special Uniform |
| 4. Interacting With the Public | Public Speaking; Deal With Public |
| 5. Managerial Relations | Face-to-Face Groups; Communications; Supervise/Develop Others; Persuade or Influence; Take Opposing Position; Coordinate/Lead Activity; Responsible for Others Work; Accountable for Results; Decision Latitude |
| 6. Structured/Machine Operations | Level of Automation; Accuracy/Exactness; Details and Completeness; Repetitive Activities; Structured Tasks/Goals (negatively weighted); Machine Driven Pace |
| 7. Business/Office | Business/Office Clothes; Deadline Time Pressure (negatively weighted) |

*Note.* Nine generalized work activities, 3 work styles, 13 knowledges, 1 occupational value, and 34 work context descriptors are not included in any composite.

tually meaningful and lend a degree of construct validity to these GWA descriptors as well as the skill, ability and work style descriptors with which they correlate.

The pattern of correlations for the third GWA composite—Manual and Physical Activities—is very different, and it lends further support to the construct validity of the descriptors. For example, this composite correlates positively with Physical Ability, Psychomotor Ability, Dexterity, and Vision and Hearing Ability, whereas the other two GWAs have nonsignificant and slightly negative correlations with these four ability composites across occupations. Manual and Physical Activities correlates significantly with only one of the three skill composites: Technical Skill. Again, the pattern of correlations for this GWA composite with the skill and ability composites is intuitively appealing and supports the construct validity of the descriptors.

There is a fair degree of conceptual overlap between the descriptors in the knowledges, skills, and abilities domains, so obtaining the expected correlations between these descriptors across occupations was an important source of construct validity evidence. As expected, Cognitive Ability correlated highly with both Cognitive and Organizational Skills, and it also correlated significantly with Technical Skills. Spatial Ability correlated positively with all three skill composites. Of interest is that the Memory ability composite correlated significantly with the Cognitive Skills composite but not with the other two skill composites. Abilities such as Physical and Psychomotor did not correlate significantly with any of the three skill composites.

The knowledge composites labeled Science and Technology and Medicine correlated significantly with Technical Skill requirements and to a somewhat lesser extent with Organizational Skills. This relationship was not surprising because occupations in science and technology and in medicine often require technical skills. Both the Business Administration and the Art and Humanities knowledge composites cor-

related with Cognitive and Organizational Skills but not with Technical Skills. Clerical and Food Production knowledge, on the other hand, were not significantly correlated with any of the skill composites, perhaps because they are rather specific, lower level knowledges. Finally, Law Enforcement knowledge requirements correlated positively with Cognitive Skill requirements, perhaps reflecting the cognitive demands involved in law enforcement occupations.

Relationships between ability and knowledge requirements are generally along the lines one would expect as well, and some are rather interesting. For example, occupations that require Clerical knowledge tend not to require Physical Abilities ($r = -.56$). This brings to mind someone who spends his or her day in a chair performing rather sedentary tasks. Similarly, the correlation between Business Administration knowledge and Physical Ability requirements, although not significant, is also negative. Not surprisingly, Law Enforcement knowledge requirements are correlated with Psychomotor, Vision and Hearing, Spatial, and Attention Ability requirements. Cognitive Ability requirements are most strongly related to the Arts and Humanities knowledge composite, but also to several other knowledge composites, including Law Enforcement, Medicine, and Business Administration. Another very understandable finding is that Speech Ability is most strongly related to the Business Administration and Arts and Humanities composites. The abilities most strongly related to medical knowledge requirements are Spatial and Attention. The strong correlation between Arts and Humanities knowledges and Spatial Abilities is somewhat surprising, but Spatial Ability seems to correlate with a broader array of other descriptors than most of the other ability composites. Math Ability requirements are related to both Science and Technology and Business Administration knowledge requirements. Finally, Food Production knowledges correlate only with Physical Abilities, perhaps a reflection of the particular nature of the occupations in our sample. Similarly, Dexterity is only correlated with the knowledge composite called Medicine, again probably a function of the occupations in our sample.

Correlations between the Surgency/Achievement Orientation work styles composite and both Cognitive and Organizational Skills are very strong, perhaps suggesting an achievement-related constellation of job requirements that covary across occupations. Technical Skill requirements are negatively related to the work styles composite labeled People Orientation. In our sample, at least, occupations that require technical skills also tend to involve working alone, or perhaps interpersonal interactions are just not a critical aspect of these occupations.

Not surprisingly, there is a strong relationship between the GWA composite labeled Manual and Physical Activities and a work context that involves Environmental Factors. Similarly, Working With Information is negatively related to the work context composite Physical Activity, whereas Manual and Physical Activities are positively related to this latter aspect of work context. Work context involving Business/Office is negatively related to Manual and Physical Activities and positively related to Working With and Directing Others. Finally, it is not too surprising that Managerial Relations is most strongly related to Working With and Directing Others.

As might be expected, occupational values related to Individual Advancement and Career Accomplishment are correlated with the Surgency/Achievement Orientation work styles composite. These two value composites are also fairly strongly related to the GWAs involving Working With Information and Working With and Directing Others (but not Manual and Physical Activities) and also to Cognitive and Organizational Skills and work context involving Managerial Relations. The occupational values involving Structure are positively related to working in a Business/Office context. Finally, it is somewhat surprising that the occupational values related to Stability are quite strongly related to knowledge requirements in the Arts and Humanities and Law Enforcement areas.

It should be kept in mind that these cross-domain comparisons are to some extent dependent on the sample of occupations included in the present analyses. Although the sample does include a range of occupations, there are only 29 occupations available, and it is unlikely that such a small sample is totally representative of occupations in general. For example, this sample includes nurses and other medical professionals, but not medical doctors and some of the other more highly educated medical professionals. It is likely that if a broader sample of medical professionals were available, some of the correlations involving medical knowledge and other descriptors particularly relevant to the medical profession would be different. In addition, a sample of 29 does not provide a great deal of statistical power. It is likely that some of the correlations that were not significantly different from zero in the present research would be significant if a larger sample were available,

because correlations of less than about .37 are not significant at the $p < .05$ level in a sample this small.

Although most of the data used in each comparison (i.e., the individual correlations) were collected from different incumbents, a certain percentage of these data were collected from the same incumbents. As discussed previously, Table 16-2 shows the extent to which this occurred. For several pairs of domains, virtually all of the data came from the same sample of incumbents, and this was primarily because the number of questionnaires and the length of the questionnaires limited how many different combinations of domains could be presented to individual incumbents. There is some reason to expect that data collected from the same incumbents will result in higher correlations, either because of uncaptured differences between jobs within an occupation or because of response bias. The sample available in the present research was not large enough to provide a good test of this conjecture. Thus, correlations between GWAs and occupational values should be interpreted with caution, especially as they compare with correlations between other pairs of domains.

## Factor Analysis of Composites

To provide a summary of the structure of these cross-domain relationships, the intercorrelations of the factor-based composites were factor analyzed using principal-components analysis with a varimax rotation. A four-factor solution was selected on the basis of the eigenvalues and the meaningfulness of the resulting solutions. The factor pattern matrix for this solution is presented in Table 16-5.

The first factor has strongest loadings for composites that involve working with or managing others and achievement or accomplishment. The GWA factor that involves Working With Information loads on this factor, but it also has a fairly high loading on the third factor. Again, the high correlation between this GWA and Working With and Directing Others appears to have affected the relationships obtained. Of interest is that higher levels of Cognitive and Organizational Skills are also strongly related to this factor.

The second factor is primarily defined by Manual and Physical Activities and Vision/Hearing, Physical, and Dexterity Abilities, with Law Enforcement knowledge and Environmental Factors from work context. The third factor might be labeled "General Office," and it has high loadings for Clerical, Speech, and Memory Abilities, as well as Attention and Cognitive Abilities. However, these latter two abilities are split across Factors 2 and 1, respectively. In terms of work context, this third factor has a strong positive loading for Business/Office and Structured/Machine Operations and a substantial negative loading for Physical Activity.

The fourth factor is somewhat difficult to interpret, because it is defined in part by positive loadings and in part by negative loadings. It might be labeled

**TABLE 16-4**
**Intercorrelations of Factor-Based Composites Across Domains**

| Composites by domain | 1 | 2 | 3 | 4 | 5 | 6 | 7 | 8 | 9 | 10 | 11 | 12 | 13 | 14 | 15 | 16 | 17 |
|---|---|---|---|---|---|---|---|---|---|---|---|---|---|---|---|---|---|
| **Generalized work activities** | | | | | | | | | | | | | | | | | |
| 1. Working With Information | (.90) | | | | | | | | | | | | | | | | |
| 2. Working W/ & Directing Others | .72 | (.90) | | | | | | | | | | | | | | | |
| 3. Manual and Physical Activities | −.20 | −.12 | (.87) | | | | | | | | | | | | | | |
| **Work context** | | | | | | | | | | | | | | | | | |
| 4. Environmental Factors | −.20 | .01 | .80 | (.97) | | | | | | | | | | | | | |
| 5. Physical Activity | −.53 | −.22 | .54 | .43 | (.94) | | | | | | | | | | | | |
| 6. Managerial Relations | .66 | .75 | .12 | .20 | −.10 | (.93) | | | | | | | | | | | |
| 7. Structured/Machine Operations | .05 | −.09 | .13 | .07 | −.31 | −.03 | (.80) | | | | | | | | | | |
| 8. Business/Office | .39 | .45 | −.56 | −.37 | −.57 | .10 | .26 | (.90) | | | | | | | | | |
| 9. Health and Safety | .04 | .33 | .35 | .26 | .15 | .18 | .01 | −.15 | (.96) | | | | | | | | |
| 10. Interacting With the Public | .21 | .57 | −.22 | −.04 | −.09 | .23 | −.12 | .41 | .17 | (.89) | | | | | | | |
| **Skills** | | | | | | | | | | | | | | | | | |
| 11. Cognitive Skills | .85 | .75 | −.07 | .04 | −.37 | .72 | .02 | .36 | .21 | .26 | (.94) | | | | | | |
| 12. Technical Skills | .44 | .08 | .52 | .35 | −.04 | .38 | .27 | −.30 | .13 | −.34 | .51 | (.91) | | | | | |
| 13. Organizational Skills | .72 | .68 | .05 | .15 | −.21 | .79 | .07 | .26 | .02 | .06 | .84 | .58 | (.94) | | | | |
| **Knowledges** | | | | | | | | | | | | | | | | | |
| 14. Arts and Humanities | .26 | .52 | .03 | .25 | .03 | .38 | −.04 | .30 | .12 | .25 | .47 | .12 | .40 | (.80) | | | |
| 15. Science and Technology | .08 | .03 | .54 | .53 | .26 | .28 | .31 | −.20 | −.12 | −.26 | .21 | .56 | .39 | .51 | (.79) | | |
| 16. Law Enforcement | .30 | .62 | .22 | .46 | −.05 | .44 | .14 | .22 | .59 | .29 | .42 | .11 | .37 | .60 | .29 | (.89) | |
| 17. Clerical | .32 | .08 | −.47 | −.39 | −.65 | −.15 | .44 | .62 | −.14 | −.11 | .29 | −.06 | .09 | .17 | −.05 | .09 | (.96) |
| 18. Medicine | .20 | .27 | .43 | .16 | .04 | .35 | .39 | −.03 | .47 | −.05 | .35 | .53 | .33 | .44 | .54 | .34 | .00 |
| 19. Business Administration | .43 | .55 | −.33 | −.15 | −.19 | .45 | .09 | .44 | −.13 | .60 | .53 | −.01 | .54 | .17 | .10 | .08 | .08 |
| 20. Food Production | −.28 | −.09 | .31 | .27 | .49 | −.02 | .05 | −.20 | −.17 | −.10 | −.31 | −.06 | −.14 | .41 | .63 | .16 | −.23 |
| **Abilities** | | | | | | | | | | | | | | | | | |
| 21. Physical | −.49 | −.12 | .69 | .80 | .71 | −.03 | −.09 | −.42 | .39 | .02 | −.26 | .06 | −.14 | .27 | .42 | .43 | −.56 |
| 22. Psychomotor | −.33 | −.07 | .65 | .80 | .30 | −.01 | .14 | −.23 | .41 | −.05 | −.14 | .21 | −.04 | .27 | .38 | .51 | −.35 |
| 23. Dexterity | −.32 | −.19 | .65 | .54 | .29 | −.16 | .43 | −.15 | .43 | −.06 | −.22 | .26 | −.18 | .15 | .35 | .33 | −.19 |
| 24. Vision/Hearing | −.23 | .06 | .55 | .69 | .20 | −.03 | .11 | −.11 | .49 | .08 | −.03 | .18 | −.01 | .41 | .36 | .62 | −.26 |
| 25. Cognitive | .72 | .54 | −.17 | −.05 | −.46 | .47 | .30 | .51 | .12 | .25 | .80 | .47 | .66 | .56 | .32 | .43 | .41 |
| 26. Math | .46 | .18 | −.26 | −.19 | −.38 | .21 | .46 | .32 | −.30 | .03 | .46 | .41 | .45 | .34 | .43 | .06 | .35 |
| 27. Spatial | .40 | .46 | .31 | .43 | −.09 | .42 | .36 | .27 | .32 | .25 | .60 | .47 | .55 | .64 | .56 | .66 | .13 |
| 28. Speech | .43 | .54 | −.36 | −.24 | −.31 | .14 | .18 | .57 | .22 | .47 | .50 | .01 | .30 | .49 | .01 | .37 | .38 |
| 29. Attention | .26 | .23 | .19 | .20 | −.28 | .12 | .62 | .41 | .27 | .14 | .39 | .37 | .31 | .42 | .37 | .46 | .35 |
| 30. Memory | .55 | .45 | −.21 | −.09 | −.43 | .21 | .40 | .46 | .12 | .36 | .52 | .26 | .34 | .40 | .13 | .34 | .37 |
| **Work styles** | | | | | | | | | | | | | | | | | |
| 31. Surgency/Achievement Orientation | .68 | .64 | −.02 | .07 | −.14 | .74 | −.14 | .29 | −.04 | .18 | .73 | .28 | .72 | .36 | .21 | .27 | −.07 |
| 32. People Orientation | −.01 | .42 | −.22 | −.20 | −.02 | .23 | −.23 | .23 | .27 | .35 | .10 | −.51 | −.03 | .29 | −.13 | .27 | .00 |
| 33. Detail Orientation | .15 | −.09 | −.06 | −.22 | −.18 | .08 | .22 | .00 | .05 | −.25 | .19 | .09 | −.01 | −.05 | .08 | −.05 | .29 |
| **Occupational values** | | | | | | | | | | | | | | | | | |
| 34. Individual Accomplishment | .65 | .59 | −.06 | .08 | −.19 | .60 | −.26 | .26 | .10 | .19 | .80 | .27 | .63 | .34 | .01 | .19 | .21 |
| 35. Structure | .14 | .08 | −.09 | −.31 | −.09 | .01 | .26 | .46 | −.09 | −.06 | .24 | .10 | .24 | .15 | .08 | −.17 | .33 |
| 36. Social Comfort | .38 | .38 | −.20 | −.22 | −.12 | .12 | .11 | .37 | −.26 | .40 | .37 | .00 | .33 | .24 | .15 | −.02 | .35 |
| 37. Career Advancement | .34 | .55 | −.04 | .24 | .15 | .66 | −.15 | .07 | −.01 | .29 | .55 | .15 | .65 | .40 | .23 | .27 | −.14 |
| 38. Stability | .34 | .55 | .06 | .40 | −.12 | .47 | −.10 | .25 | .41 | .08 | .60 | .15 | .52 | .63 | .23 | .79 | .25 |

*Note.* N = 29. Correlations of .37 or greater are significant at the p < .05 level. Interrater reliability estimates for each composite appear on the diagonal. These values were obtained by calculating the intraclass correlation for k ratings across occupations: $ICC(1, k) = [BMS − WMS]/BMS$ (Shrout & Fleiss, 1979), where k is the harmonic mean of the number of ratings provided on each occupation.

| 18 | 19 | 20 | 21 | 22 | 23 | 24 | 25 | 26 | 27 | 28 | 29 | 30 | 31 | 32 | 33 | 34 | 35 | 36 | 37 | 38 |
|---|---|---|---|---|---|---|---|---|---|---|---|---|---|---|---|---|---|---|---|---|
| (.87) | | | | | | | | | | | | | | | | | | | | |
| .09 | (.89) | | | | | | | | | | | | | | | | | | | |
| .25 | −.10 | (.57) | | | | | | | | | | | | | | | | | | |
| .18 | −.26 | .47 | (.92) | | | | | | | | | | | | | | | | | |
| .24 | −.32 | .26 | .84 | (.92) | | | | | | | | | | | | | | | | |
| .48 | −.36 | .34 | .66 | .78 | (.81) | | | | | | | | | | | | | | | |
| .31 | −.25 | .24 | .77 | .94 | .72 | (.92) | | | | | | | | | | | | | | |
| .43 | .47 | −.19 | −.18 | .01 | .03 | .15 | (.92) | | | | | | | | | | | | | |
| .35 | .42 | .07 | −.32 | −.20 | −.02 | −.12 | .71 | (.85) | | | | | | | | | | | | |
| .58 | .29 | .07 | .32 | .45 | .45 | .54 | .77 | .54 | (.77) | | | | | | | | | | | |
| .23 | .48 | −.10 | −.14 | −.01 | .04 | .21 | .73 | .46 | .53 | (.74) | | | | | | | | | | |
| .53 | .11 | −.03 | .15 | .42 | .61 | .51 | .70 | .54 | .83 | .60 | (.77) | | | | | | | | | |
| .22 | .39 | −.13 | −.18 | .06 | .11 | .24 | .78 | .59 | .60 | .86 | .68 | (.70) | | | | | | | | |
| .20 | .43 | −.02 | −.16 | −.09 | −.23 | −.07 | .47 | .33 | .38 | .17 | .14 | .21 | (.85) | | | | | | | |
| .17 | .21 | .19 | .01 | −.07 | −.13 | .04 | −.04 | −.18 | −.03 | .25 | −.07 | −.09 | .25 | (.79) | | | | | | |
| .26 | −.09 | .07 | −.25 | −.22 | .02 | −.24 | .08 | .24 | −.03 | −.06 | .12 | −.10 | .32 | .37 | (.58) | | | | | |
| .03 | .35 | −.33 | −.24 | −.21 | −.37 | −.15 | .46 | .08 | .27 | .23 | .08 | .25 | .64 | .08 | .09 | (.87) | | | | |
| .31 | .18 | −.11 | −.30 | −.26 | −.02 | −.20 | .30 | .24 | .15 | .23 | .34 | .18 | .23 | −.05 | .14 | .27 | (.42) | | | |
| .00 | .59 | .10 | −.35 | −.46 | −.32 | −.33 | .29 | .29 | .16 | .43 | .13 | .38 | .18 | .04 | −.08 | .37 | .39 | (.20) | | |
| .05 | .60 | .13 | .09 | −.04 | −.23 | −.04 | .29 | .23 | .32 | .25 | −.03 | .17 | .56 | .20 | −.03 | .51 | −.14 | .30 | (.60) | |
| .17 | .09 | −.04 | .25 | .35 | .03 | .40 | .43 | .02 | .50 | .29 | .28 | .18 | .42 | .27 | .09 | .53 | −.05 | −.01 | .43 | (.80) |

**TABLE 16-5**
**Principal-Components Analysis Pattern Matrix: Cross-Domain Factor-Based Composites**

| Domain and composite label | Factor | | | | Communality |
|---|---|---|---|---|---|
| | F1 | F2 | F3 | F4 | |
| WC: Managerial Relations | .88 | .11 | −.03 | .04 | .79 |
| SK: Cognitive Skills | .87 | .05 | .21 | .23 | .92 |
| SK: Organizational Skills | .87 | −.01 | .39 | .05 | .90 |
| WS: Surgency, Achievement Orientation | .83 | −.04 | .05 | .07 | .70 |
| GWA: Working With/Directing Others | .80 | .08 | .25 | −.41 | .86 |
| OV: Individual Accomplishment | .79 | −.15 | .06 | −.05 | .65 |
| OV: Career Advancement | .77 | .06 | −.13 | −.11 | .62 |
| GWA: Working With Information | .75 | −.23 | .41 | .09 | .79 |
| KN: Business Administration | .58 | −.24 | .28 | −.18 | .50 |
| OV: Stability | .57 | .40 | .13 | −.28 | .58 |
| KN: Arts and Humanities | .47 | .44 | .32 | −.18 | .56 |
| OV: Social Comfort | .35 | −.31 | .34 | −.04 | .33 |
| AB: Psychomotor | −.14 | .92 | −.05 | −.03 | .87 |
| AB: Vision/Hearing | −.08 | .91 | .11 | −.16 | .88 |
| AB: Physical | −.10 | .88 | −.35 | −.09 | .91 |
| AB: Dexterity | −.34 | .82 | .19 | .16 | .84 |
| WC: Environmental Factors | .16 | .80 | −.29 | .15 | .78 |
| GWA: Manual and Physical Activities | .01 | .73 | −.33 | .42 | .82 |
| KN: Law Enforcement | .40 | .65 | .26 | −.35 | .77 |
| AB: Spatial | .44 | .61 | .55 | .09 | .88 |
| WC: Health and Safety | .10 | .54 | .04 | −.31 | .40 |
| KN: Medicine | .24 | .48 | .34 | .33 | .51 |
| KN: Food Production | −.07 | .40 | −.17 | .12 | .21 |
| AB: Attention | .08 | .49 | .80 | .13 | .91 |
| AB: Memory | .26 | .12 | .79 | −.09 | .72 |
| AB: Cognitive | .55 | .12 | .75 | .09 | .88 |
| AB: Speech | .27 | .08 | .74 | −.38 | .77 |
| KN: Clerical | −.4 | −.33 | .70 | .00 | .60 |
| WC: Business/Office | .18 | −.26 | .69 | −.38 | .72 |
| AB: Math | .29 | −.09 | .66 | .40 | .68 |
| WC: Structured/Machine Operations | −.22 | .18 | .64 | .38 | .64 |
| OV: Structure | .08 | −.20 | .43 | .22 | .29 |
| WC: Physical Activity | −.09 | .42 | −.62 | .06 | .57 |
| SK: Technical Skills | .39 | .30 | .14 | .75 | .83 |
| KN: Science and Technology | .28 | .54 | .10 | .56 | .68 |
| WS: Detail Orientation | .07 | −.15 | .14 | .26 | .11 |
| WS: People Orientation | .20 | .01 | −.03 | −.60 | .40 |
| WC: Interacting With Public | .28 | .02 | .20 | −.67 | .58 |
| % of variance | 21.00 | 20.00 | 17.00 | 9.00 | |
| Eigenvalues | 10.53 | 7.57 | 4.10 | 3.24 | |

*Note.* N = 29. The correlation matrix was based on means calculated at the occupation level. F1 = Management and Achievement, F2 = Manual and Physical, F3 = General Office, F4 = Technical Versus Interpersonal. These loadings are based on an orthogonal varimax rotation. Domains are abbreviated: WC = work context; SK = skills; WS = work styles; GWA = generalized work activities; OV = occupational values; KN = knowledges; AB = abilities.

"Technical Versus Interpersonal." Technical Skills and Science and Technology knowledges have strong positive loadings on this factor. On the other hand, the work style composite labeled People Orientation and work context involving Interacting With the Public have substantial negative loadings. The GWA composite Working With and Directing Others also has a fairly strong negative secondary loading on this fourth factor.

To compare the structure of the level and importance ratings, which are available for each descriptor in many of the domains, this factor analysis was conducted again using the importance ratings where appropriate. For five of the seven domains included in this factor analysis, both level and importance ratings are available. For the remaining two domains—work context and occupational values—only a single rating was collected for each descriptor. Thus, this second principal-component analysis included the same

data as did the initial analyses for these latter two domains, and factor-based composites were computed using the importance data for the remaining five domains. The results were virtually identical to those obtained using the level ratings, which is not too surprising given the high correlations obtained between the level and importance ratings in all of the within-domain analyses. The same four factors emerged, and the loadings were very similar to those obtained for the level ratings.

## A PRIORI CROSS-DOMAIN RELATIONSHIPS

Analyses using the factor-based composites are necessarily somewhat limited. For most domains, a subset of the descriptors could not be included on any composite. In addition, the composites provide a fairly broad summary of each content domain and lack the detailed information available for the specific descriptors. Therefore a second set of analyses was conducted to provide an additional test of the extent to which cross-domain relationships obtained in these O*NET prototype data are consistent with rational and theoretical expectations. This involved generating and testing a series of hypotheses concerning expected correlations, across domains, between individual descriptors. We began by identifying pairs of domains for which strong hypotheses could be generated concerning expected relationships. There are clear similarities across a subset of the skill and ability descriptors. For example, one of the ability descriptors is Written Comprehension (Ability D2), and one of the skill descriptors is Reading Comprehension (Skill D1). It would be truly surprising if occupations rated as requiring written comprehension were not also rated as requiring reading comprehension. Similarly, there are some strong conceptual similarities between certain work context and organizational context descriptors. Another pair of domains for which strong hypotheses could be generated was skills and GWAs; similarly, knowledges have some seemingly necessary relationships with a subset of the training and education requirements. Finally, evidence from past research is available concerning relationships between GWAs and certain work context descriptors.

Each of these five pairs of domains was examined closely, and those pairs of descriptors expected to correlate across domains were identified. In generating these cross-domain hypotheses, we focused on identifying only those descriptors for which very strong relationships were expected. In other words, we identified those pairs of descriptors for which a finding of no relationship would be very unexpected and cast doubt on the construct validity of the descriptors involved. To provide an overall assessment of the extent to which these analyses support the construct validity of the descriptors for each pair of domains, we compared the mean of these expected correlations to the mean of the correlations between all other pairs of descriptors across the same two domains. Correlations were first converted using Fisher's $r$ to $z$ transformation, then averaged, and the resulting average $z$ scores were converted back to standard correlation coefficients. It is worth noting that the present analyses focused on subsets of the most obvious expected correlations between descriptors, and many other pairs of domains and individual descriptor correlations remain that would be interesting to examine in the context of past research and available theory.

Twelve pairs of ability and skill descriptors were identified as involving very similar content and thus were hypothesized to correlate highly. The average of these 12 correlations was .74, whereas the overall average correlation between all other pairs of descriptors across these two domains was only .19. A couple of examples of these hypothesized relationships between ability and skill descriptors are Written Comprehension (Ability D2) requirements and Reading Comprehension (Skill D1) requirements ($r = .84$); Originality (Ability D6) and Idea Generation (Skill D21; $r = .81$); and Problem Sensitivity (Ability D7) and Problem Identification (Skill D17; $r = .61$).

For the work context and organizational context domains, there were nine pairs of descriptors that appeared to have a great deal of conceptual similarity. Although these two domains are relatively distinct, there is some overlap. For example, Decision Latitude (Work Context D27) is an aspect of an individual employee's work context, but Empowerment (Organizational Context D1) is a construct that is often manipulated and studied at the organizational level. Clearly, incumbents who report a large degree of Decision Latitude would also be expected to rate their jobs high on Empowerment. The average correlation across the nine pairs of work and organizational context descriptors identified as overlapping was .59; the average across the other pairs of descriptors was only .06. The correlation between Empowerment and Decision Latitude was .51. The latter construct correlated .67 with Autonomy (Organizational Context D2) and .47 with a measure of Decentralization (Organizational Context D13). An organizational context variable, Percentage of Time Spent in Teams (reflecting a team approach to organizational structure; Organizational Context D26), correlated .57 with a related work context variable called Work/Contribute to Teams (Work Context D6e).

The conceptual links between skills and GWAs are not quite as strong as those identified between skills and abilities, but 24 pairs of skill and GWA descriptors were identified that were expected to correlate substantially. The average of these 24 expected correlations was .69, whereas the average of all of the remaining skill–GWA correlations was .45. For example, the correlation between the Speaking (Skill D4) skill requirement and Communicating, Internal (GWA D27) was .74. Negotiation Skill requirements (Skill D14) correlated .55 with the GWA Selling or Influencing (GWA D31). The skill requirement labeled Operation and Control (Skill D32) correlated .65 with the GWA called Controlling Machines (GWA D18).

It is reasonable to expect that if an occupation requires a higher level of education in a particular content area, it will generally require a higher level of knowledge in that same content area as well. Thus, we compared the content areas for 15 education requirements with the content of the 33 knowledge descriptors and found 18 matches. The average of these 18 expected correlations was .67, and the average of the remaining correlations was .32. For example, knowledge descriptors labeled English Language (Knowledge D24) correlated .84 with level of education required in English/Language Arts (Education D3c). A few of these correlations are somewhat lower than would be expected. Language (Education D3e) education requirements correlated only .27 (not significant) with Foreign Language knowledge

(Knowledge D25) descriptors. Still, most of the relationships between knowledge and training requirements are as expected.

Finally, past research, especially that involving the PAQ, provides information concerning relationships between certain aspects of work context and work tasks (i.e., the GWAs). For example, work activities involving controlling machines have been found to be related to certain environmental factors. The O*NET content model contains a large number of rather specific aspects of work context, so we used the work context factor-based composites (described previously) to test for the expected relationships with individual GWA descriptors. A total of 15 expected relationships were identified, and the average of these correlations was .64; the average of the remaining correlations between work context composites and GWA descriptors was .11. For example, the correlation between Controlling Machines (GWA D18) and Environmental Factors was .70. The correlation between the Managerial Relations composite and the GWA Directing Subordinates (GWA D37) was .81. In general, hypotheses involving the Business/Office composite were not as strongly supported as those involving the other work context composites. Possible explanations for this latter finding include the composition of this composite (it is made up of only two descriptors) and the characteristics of the occupations in the sample (e.g., the sampling of business occupations may not be representative).

## DISCUSSION AND CONCLUSIONS

Several different analytical approaches were used in these cross-domain analyses, and each provides a somewhat different perspective on the relationships between descriptors from the various O*NET content domains. In general, these results strongly support the construct validity of the O*NET descriptors across all content domains, and they provide some interesting insights concerning the links between a variety of work and worker characteristics. The fact that most of the cross-domain comparisons involved data from different incumbents strengthens the potential generalizability of these findings. All of the tests of a priori cross-domain hypotheses showed that where strong correlations were expected, strong correlations were in fact obtained.

In general, work activities involving information and people had strong correlations with many cognitive ability and skill requirements. The achievement-oriented work styles and those most cognitively ori-

ented were also strongly related to activities involving information and people, as well as to cognitive ability and skill requirements. Work styles involving interpersonal interactions were positively correlated with activities and environments involving working with others. These relationships are summarized in the factor analysis results, where the first factor was defined by descriptors related to interpersonal and managerial activities, cognitive skill requirements, and achievement-related worker characteristics. This factor was labeled Management and Achievement. Although activities involving working with information and working with people had generally similar patterns of correlations with descriptors from other domains, the differences in these patterns of correlations support the construct validity of these composites. For example, the Working With Information composite was more strongly related to technical skills and math ability, whereas Working With and Directing Others was more strongly related to the people-oriented work style.

Manual and physical work activities, on the other hand, were correlated with technical skills and with psychomotor and physical ability requirements. Environmental factors from the work context domain also tended to be positively correlated with manual and physical activities and related worker requirements. In fact, manual and physical activities, physical and psychomotor abilities, and environmental factors defined the second factor in the factor analysis.

In addition to obtaining the expected relationships across domains, the present analyses also generally showed that constructs not conceptually related do not correlate. For example, physical and psychomotor ability requirements were not significantly correlated with work activities involving information or people.

In summary, results of the cross-domain analyses provide good support for the O*NET content model and some interesting information concerning relationships between various occupational requirements, work activities, and other characteristics. Although the results are limited by the fact that the sample contains only 29 occupations, the sample did include a fairly wide variety of occupations (see Table 16-1), and most of the results obtained here are likely to hold up when larger, more representative samples are available. A larger sample will also allow for more detailed analyses concerning the structure of these cross-domain relationships, as well as provide the power to detect relationships that are somewhat weaker but still important.

# Occupation Classification: Using Basic and Cross-Functional Skills and Generalized Work Activities to Create Job Families

WAYNE A. BAUGHMAN, DWAYNE G. NORRIS, ASHLEY E. COOKE,
NORMAN G. PETERSON, AND MICHAEL D. MUMFORD

Within the O*NET content model, there are 46 basic and cross-functional skills (see chap. 5) and 42 generalized work activities (GWAs) (see chap. 8). These descriptors were designed to be broad enough to allow occupations to be compared directly yet specific enough to provide meaningful description and differentiation of individual occupations (Peterson, Mumford, Borman, Jeanneret, & Fleishman, 1995). In this chapter, we present a series of analyses that test how these higher level occupation descriptors perform when used for the important function of grouping occupations into homogeneous clusters. For example, clustering occupations, jobs, or positions is often used to develop compensation (Henderson, 1988), performance appraisal instruments (Cornelius, Hakel, & Sackett, 1979), or selection systems (Cascio, Sacket, & Schmitt, 1991).

## OCCUPATION CLASSIFICATION

Classification involves the ordering or grouping of objects on the basis of their interrelationships (Sokal, 1974). In personnel research, classification is a process by which occupations, jobs, or positions are grouped, or clustered, on the basis of common profiles across a set of descriptor variables (Pearlman, 1980). In the last 35 years, sophisticated methodologies have been advanced or developed for classification, including cluster analysis (Arabie & Hubert, 1992; Mumford, Stokes, & Owens, 1990). In any clustering effort, the clarity, strength, and meaningfulness of the results is largely determined by the capacity of the descriptor variables to differentiate between the objects. Classification provides an organization of the objects—a taxonomy—for which objects within a cluster are more similar to each other than they are to objects in any other cluster. Taxonomies provide economy of description by making it possible to treat objects in a category as being functionally equivalent (Sokal, 1974).

In personnel work, occupations, jobs, or positions are clustered on the basis of such descriptor variables as the number of tasks in common or incumbent rat-

ings on scales of requisite abilities, skills, and knowledge. The obvious advantage of clustering jobs is that the groups may be treated as essentially the same for a variety of personnel functions. For example, it may be legally advisable to place highly related jobs in the same salary range when developing compensation systems. Similarly, jobs shown to be highly related may use the same selection and performance appraisal instruments. Doing so significantly decreases the development and administrative costs associated with these functions. In short, identifying the essential or practical equivalence of jobs allows us to economize on most major functions of personnel administration.

## Basic and Cross-Functional Skills

The 46 basic and cross-functional skills describe occupations in terms of the higher level skills that make it possible for workers to learn and carry out job tasks in many different occupations. Because skills—like knowledge, abilities, and occupational values—are attributes of people, the scales developed for the basic and cross-functional skills represent part of the "person side" of the O*NET content model. That is, these scales represent one important class of variables used for occupational classification: descriptions of occupations or jobs in terms of human attributes required to perform job tasks (e.g., knowledge, skills, abilities, etc.; Fleishman & Quaintance, 1984). Occupational data on the basic and cross-functional skills are collected via electronic or paper-and-pencil surveys. For each skill, people indicate (a) the level, or amount, of skill required; (b) the importance of the skill; and (c) whether the skill is required to begin working on the job or whether it can be learned on the job.

## GWAs

The 42 GWAs describe occupations in terms of broad classes of behaviors that occur across most occupations. Because GWAs—like tasks, duties, and organizational context—are attributes of jobs or positions, the scales developed for the GWAs represent aspects of the "job side" of the O*NET content model. That is, these scales describe occupations or jobs in terms of activities required of workers, a second important class of variables used for occupational classification. As with the skills, occupational data on the GWAs are collected via electronic or paper-and-pencil surveys. For each GWA, people indicate (a) the level of complexity of the GWA required, (b) the importance of the GWA, and (c) how frequently the GWA is carried out (on an absolute frequency scale).

## ANALYSIS OVERVIEW

We set up the analyses to allow us to evaluate the quality and convergence of cluster solutions under different conditions. One set of criteria provided information about the overall quality of the various cluster solutions without regard to the specific assignment of occupations to clusters. These criteria were statistical and pertained to variability within and between clusters and to errors in classifying occupations. A second criterion provided information about the extent to which the occupations were being clustered in the same or different clusters across various conditions. This criterion was an evaluation of the convergence of final cluster solutions.

Before describing the specific evaluation criteria and analysis procedures, however, we need to describe the factors that we varied in the study as a means of evaluating the O*NET broad descriptors. Our purpose for varying these factors was to establish conditions that would provide good tests of the discriminating and descriptive utility of the broad skills and work activities. We selected three specific "analytic factors" that prior research has shown to influence the stability and overall results of clustering analyses: (a) the descriptors (Cornelius, Carron, & Collins, 1979), (b) the clustering method (Milligan, 1981), and (c) the sample (Pearlman, 1980).

### Analytic Factors

#### Descriptors

The literature is replete with research bearing on the issue of the effect of different descriptors on the classification results (Cornelius et al., 1979; Hartmann, Mumford, & Mueller, 1992; Pearlman, 1980; Reynolds, Laabs, & Harris, 1996; Sackett, Cornelius, & Carron, 1981). Some research suggests that different descriptors cluster objects differently. For example, Cornelius et al. (1979) evaluated the classification outcomes of seven foreman jobs using task-oriented, worker-oriented, and abilities-oriented data. Using Ward's minimum variance technique (Ward, 1963; Ward & Hook, 1963) as the clustering algorithm (de-

scribed below), they found the number of viable clusters to vary from a one-cluster solution (based on worker-oriented data) to a five-cluster solution (based on task-oriented data). The evidence for convergence, or overlap, in the cluster solutions based on different descriptors is minimal, although there is some evidence supporting this view (e.g., Hartmann et al., 1992; Hoffman, 1989). Hoffman (1989) reported finding highly similar job family structures, using data from a worker-oriented measure and from a task-based measure. In this study, job incumbents completed both surveys.

In the current analyses, we created occupation clusters using (a) GWAs only, (b) basic and cross-functional skills only, or (c) GWAs and skills combined. Comparisons of the cluster solutions based on these different ways of using the descriptor variables (i.e., descriptor combinations) provide one way of assessing the utility of these O*NET descriptors.

### Clustering Methods

Clustering methods are the set of decision rules for joining or separating clusters. Most clustering methods cluster objects differently because of differences in the criterion used to evaluate the degree of similarity or differences between clusters. For example, Ward's method uses a least-squares criterion for reducing within-cluster variability across the descriptors. The within-groups-average linkage method seeks to minimize the sum of the distances of all objects within a group to the group mean, or centroid (Norusis/SPSS, Inc., 1993). In these analyses, we compared occupation clusters that were created using both Ward's method and the within-group-average linkage method.

### Samples

Finally, different samples may yield different clustering solutions (Pearlman, 1980). The stability of a solution is as much a concern in clustering as in regression, where we hope that a prediction equation developed in one sample will apply equally well to different samples. In these analyses, we created occupation clusters using data from a sample of job incumbents and data from job analysts, in which both incumbents and analysts provided broad skill and work activity ratings for some overlapping occupations. This comparison has obvious implications for future data collection efforts using scales representing the O*NET broad skill and work activities. Using analysts' ratings instead of incumbents' ratings of occupation characteristics is often necessary when data collection using incumbents is too difficult or costly.

### Database Construction

#### 1,122 Analysts Data

Three databases were formed from the O*NET database to carry out the analyses. The first database, called the *1,122 Analysts Data*, contained ratings made by trained occupational analysts. These occupational analysts consisted of both professional occupational analysts and graduate students in industrial/organizational psychology. The analysts rated 1,122 "occupational units," where occupational units represented a taxonomy, or classification, of jobs with a level of specificity lying between the more general Occupational Employment Statistics (OES) taxonomy and the more specific *Dictionary of Occupational Titles* taxonomy (DOT; U.S. Dept. of Labor, 1991a). Analysts rated the occupational units on a subset of the O*NET content model categories, including the basic and cross-functional skills and GWAs. Scores representing the mean on each descriptor served as the rating for each occupational unit. Thus, the 1,122 Analysts Data contained mean ratings for 1,122 occupational units on each of the three dimensions (level, importance, and frequency/job entry requirement) for the selected O*NET content model categories.

### 29 Incumbent Data

The second database, called the *29 Incumbent Data*, contained ratings by approximately 700 incumbents who rated 29 occupational units. The descriptors from the O*NET content model were rated for level, importance, and frequency or job entry requirement. Our estimates show that these 29 occupational units represent about 34% of the employed population in the United States. Job incumbents typically completed more than one and as many as five questionnaires. As with the analysts data, mean incumbents' ratings on level, importance, and frequency/job entry requirement served as the occupational unit scores. Thus, the incumbent database contains mean ratings on 29 occupational units, as opposed to the 1,122 rated occupational units composing the complete analyst database.

### 29 Analysts Data

Finally, a third database contained analysts' ratings of the 29 occupational units corresponding to those rated by incumbent workers. This database was simply abstracted from the 1,122 Analysts Data and was called the *29 Analysts Data*. Because this extracted database is a subset of the 1,122 Analysts Data, it shares all the other properties of that larger database.

### Summary

We carried out identical cluster analyses on three different datasets, using the O*NET broad skill and work activities. Furthermore, these cluster analyses were conducted using two clustering algorithms: Ward's method and the within-groups-average linkage method. It is important to note that the data consisted of mean occupational ratings; the relationship among occupations across variables was the focus of the analyses, as opposed to the relationship among the variables across occupations. Thus, the level of analysis was the occupation and not the individual. Two of the datasets contained mean ratings of occupations by occupational analysts: the 1,122 Analysts Data and 29 Analysts Data. One dataset contained mean ratings of occupations by incumbents: the 29 Incumbents Data.

To carry out all the analyses described in this chapter, we used only the mean ratings based on the Level scale. We made this decision for practical reasons. First, the scales were all highly intercorrelated, particularly level and importance ratings. Given the high level of intercorrelation, we thought that the clustering outcomes would remain fairly consistent across the different scales. Second, it was necessary to use only one scale in order to contain the scope of the analyses.

## Approach to Clustering

Although cluster analysis is conceptually straightforward, applying cluster analytic techniques typically requires far more judgment than is the case for more familiar methodologies, such as regression or even factor analysis. This is due to the iterative nature of cluster analysis and the diversity of cluster analytic tools. Furthermore, clustering approaches require the researcher to make many, often subjective, decisions. Prior research, however, has provided some basic guidelines that we followed to help simplify and structure the analyses.

To the extent possible, we fixed, or standardized, our clustering approach. We made these decisions on the basis of recommendations in the available literature. Once made, we kept these aspects of the analyses constant. For example, we chose Euclidean distance (Norusis/SPSS, Inc., 1993) as the index of dissimilarity between occupations (in lieu of, for example, squared Euclidean or Manhattan distance), and we used this measure exclusively in all analyses.

Besides reducing the number and complexity of evaluations to make in the analyses, a second advantage of standardizing our clustering approach was to reduce the influence of potential methodological confounds; it would be difficult to interpret differences among cluster solutions if the methods used to produce those solutions varied substantially. We believed that the more elements of the analyses we could control, the more interpretable the results would be.

## Analytic Decisions

There were essentially four major analytic decisions we made in conducting these analyses. The decisions concerned score transformations, a profile similarity index, clustering methodology, and criteria for evaluating cluster solutions.

### Score Transformation

Occupations are clustered on the basis of their profile of scores across the descriptors. The first major analytic decision we made was to identify whether the occupational profiles would be based on raw scores or specific score components (Skinner, 1978). We decided to create occupational clusters in which occupations were grouped according to the shape of their profile only, that is, the pattern of high and low scores across the set of descriptor variables. To eliminate the variability ("scatter") and level ("elevation") contained in the raw mean scores, we standardized the mean level ratings for the broad skills and work activities separately *within* each occupation (Cronbach & Gleser, 1953; Skinner, 1978). The effect of this procedure was to give each occupation, or object, a mean of zero and a standard deviation of 1.0 across each set of skill and work activities measures.

Our decision to create occupational families using only the shape component of the raw score profile was based on three considerations. First, we wanted the final clusters to be highly interpretable. A cluster solution based on raw scores confounds the three basic components of a distance measure: elevation, shape, and scatter. This is because an object's Euclidean distance from another object is the square root of the sum of squared differences between all values for those items (Norusis/SPSS, Inc., 1993); thus, its Euclidean distance could represent anything from large differences on only a few descriptors to small differences on many descriptors.

Second, we believed that the shape of the profile most clearly represents the qualitative, as opposed to quantitative, components of a profile. Qualitative differences represent differences in *kind* or *type* (e.g., Mumford, Stokes, & Owens, 1990). We believe that the most intuitively obvious and potentially useful occupational groupings are those that emphasize qualitative differences. Thus, clustering on the shape component of the profile yields clusters of occupations that share the same relative emphasis on particular skills and work activities. Clustering on scores that include the elevation component (i.e., the level, or amount, of the attributes) often results in occupations being assigned to clusters in ways that may be difficult to explain. For example, it is typical for some occupations in the same career field to differ primarily by level of skill required (e.g., entry-, mid-, and expert-level). Here, the career field represents qualitatively similar occupations because they all share a similar shape of skill profile, but they differ with respect to the level of skills required. If differences in skill level dominated the construction of the occupational clusters, then some occupations might be grouped with occupations from different career fields because all required the same overall level of different skills. This often makes the subsequent occupational structure more difficult to interpret and use.

Third, we prefer to differentiate occupations in the level or variability of skills or work activities at a later stage, after initially clustering by shape. For example, differences within a job family on the required

site levels of skills or work activities is simply a matter of ranking the occupations by their mean score across the set or sets of descriptors. In this way, we can distinguish level differences among those occupations already judged as qualitatively equivalent.

There are clear advantages to using the overall level component of the raw score profile after occupational clusters have been constructed on the basis of the shape component of the profile. For example, such postcluster identification of level differences may allow us to define career paths or career development plans, promotion tracks, and training needs. Similarly, postcluster identification of scatter differences might distinguish the more specialized from the more generalized types of occupations. Hence, we do not consider differences between occupations with respect to level or scatter meaningless; instead, we believe all components of the raw score are potentially extremely useful, but we prefer to use any information at a stage of the analysis where it will most effectively describe and differentiate.

## Distance Measure

The second major analytic decision involved selecting a distance measure. In cluster analysis, the grouping of cases proceeds on the basis of their relatedness, as defined by a dissimilarity or similarity measure. As noted above, we selected Euclidean distance, or $D$, for representing the distance between occupations and groups for these analyses. The Euclidean distance between two objects, $x$ and $y$, is the square root of the sum of squared differences between them across all descriptors (Cronbach & Gleser, 1953).

Euclidean distance is used extensively in clustering applications, and its properties are well understood. Unlike squared Euclidean distance, Euclidean distance does not exaggerate larger distances between objects relative to smaller distances (Cronbach & Gleser, 1953). Furthermore, use of Euclidean distances is currently considered the preferred distance metric in occupational clustering (Colihan & Burger, 1995) and for most other applications (Kaufmann & Rousseeuw, 1990).

## Clustering Methodology

The third major analytic decision involved selecting a clustering method. Many clustering methods exist, each of which provides a unique perspective on the structure of, and potentially viable relationships among, the objects contained in a dataset (e.g., divisive hierarchical, $k$-medoid, binary, etc.; see Kaufmann & Rousseeuw, 1990). Personnel psychologists, however, are most familiar with $k$-means (i.e., partitioning) and agglomerative hierarchical methods (Cornelius et al., 1979; Garwood, Anderson, & Greengart, 1991; Harvey, 1986; Milligan, 1981). Furthermore, these methods are most available, albeit with limited variations, in the major computer packages (Everitt, 1993).

We used an agglomerative hierarchical clustering algorithm for creating the initial occupational clusters. All agglomerative hierarchical procedures begin by treating each case as a distinct cluster, then iteratively building increasingly larger clusters until all cases are clustered together. These procedures first identify the two cases with the most similar profiles on the clustering variables by using a procedure-specific criterion (e.g., least-squares, average linkage, etc.). Next, the procedure evaluates the remaining cases and either forms a new, different cluster or assigns cases to existing clusters. As the cases are combined, the distance between the clusters is recalculated. The procedure ends when all the cases are combined into one cluster. It is clear from this description that hierarchical procedures produce groups of increasing levels of generality.

An agglomerative hierarchical algorithm may use any number of clustering methods for combining cases and creating clusters. We used the Ward's method (Ward & Hook, 1963) and the within-groups-average linkage method for two reasons. First, both methods are based on mathematical models that represent the nature of the intended application (Everitt, 1993). That is, both Ward's and within-group-average linkage methods attempt to find clustering solutions that maximize within-group similarity. Ward's method seeks to minimize the within-groups error variance (and thus maximize between-groups variance), whereas the within-group-average linkage method attempts to minimize within-group distance from the group centroid. In the present effort, the result would be an occupational structure in which occupations within each cluster would have the most similar profiles of skills and work activities. The occupational families themselves, however, would tend to have dissimilar average profiles on the skills and work activities scales. Clearly, these models are consistent with the objectives of typical occupational family development efforts.

Second, both the Ward's and within-group-average linkage methods have track records of reliable application both generally (Overall, Gibson, & Novy, 1993) and in developing clusters of people or jobs (Colihan & Burger, 1995; Everitt, 1993). For example, Everitt (1993) recommended Ward's and group-average methods as the most widely applicable of the hierarchical class of techniques (p. 142). Ward's method has been widely adopted by researchers in areas as diverse as botany, archeology, and sociology (Kaufmann & Rousseeuw, 1990). Furthermore, Ward's method is considered by those working in the area of occupation classification to be one of the most commonly used and effective of the available clustering methods (Harvey, 1986, 1990). Finally, average linkage methods were shown in a recent Monte Carlo study to recover clusters as well as Ward's method, particularly when combined with other

methods for defining the number of clusters in the data (Colihan & Burger, 1995; Overall et al., 1993).

## Use of Job Descriptors

Scores representing the basic and cross-functional skills and GWAs can be used in a number of ways when creating occupation clusters. In these analyses, we explored five ways to use this information. Each of these ways involved creating occupation clusters using the broad skills and work activities scores either as separate sets or in combination. We created clusters using only scores for the 46 basic and cross-functional skills as the set of descriptor variables or using only scores for the 42 GWAs. Clearly, using the descriptors separately will result in occupation clusters reflecting occupations with common skills versus occupations with common work activities.

In addition, we used three combinations of the two types of descriptor scores to create clusters. In the most straightforward approach, we created clusters using all skills and GWA descriptors simultaneously. We also created clusters using both sets of descriptors in a two-stage approach. Here, we first clustered the occupations on one set of descriptors or the other (i.e., skills or GWAs). Then, we carried out separate cluster analyses within each initial cluster, but used the alternate set of descriptors. For example, if we created initial clusters using the basic and cross-functional skills, we then clustered occupations within each initial (skill-based) cluster using the GWAs.

Clustering in stages using different descriptors is not often done, although clustering in stages using different score components has been found to yield superior clarity and interpretability of the resulting solution (Skinner, 1978). We believe, however, that clustering in two or more stages has the potential to represent an advance over current standard practice.

First, it is difficult to know a priori if one type of descriptor (e.g., GWAs) will dominate a clustering solution when several types of descriptors are used simultaneously. A multistage approach allows for the nature and influence of the different descriptor types to be evaluated independently. Second, clustering in stages might be useful if there is a rationale for a particular order of clustering. For instance, it might be argued that occupation clusters created first by using the basic and cross-functional skills produces more stable job families, given the more enduring nature of skills relative to work activities. Then, clustering on GWAs within each skills-based occupation family would suggest how similar sets of skills may be applied to different work activities. This approach represents a perspective of work in which people first master basic or less explicitly work-related broad skills (e.g., high school and college education) before applying those skills to specific domains (e.g., on the job).

## CRITERIA

In this section, we describe the set of objective, statistical criteria we used to evaluate the quality of the cluster solutions obtained from our analyses. These objective criteria are different ways to represent the stability and coherence of a cluster solution. Of course, in practice, subjective criteria are equally important in evaluating the viability of particular cluster solutions. Subjective criteria include the cluster solution's apparent utility, acceptability, or parsimony for particular purposes. In these analyses, however, we used objective criteria because of (a) the sheer number of multiple comparisons across multiple clustering solutions and (b) our having no particular real-world context to guide subjective evaluations; rather, we primarily were exploring methodological issues. The specific objective criteria are percentage of cases correctly reclassified, simple structure, mean squared error (MSE), and effect size.

### Percentage (or Number) of Cases Correctly Reclassified

After creating an initial solution using agglomerative hierarchical clustering procedures, a k-means partitioning analysis can be used to reclassify occupations back to their optimal cluster (Baughman et al., 1995; Mumford, Stokes, & Owens, 1990; Zimmerman, Jacobs, & Farr, 1982). When the proportion of cases reclassified back to their original clusters is high, the analysis provides evidence for the reliability of the initial solution. Occupations not classified to their original clusters may be considered to represent correct reallocation of cases misclassified in the agglomerative hierarchical procedures. Cases may become misclassified because hierarchical procedures recalculate cluster centroids at each stage. Hence, cases initially assigned to a particular cluster may later become a poor fit to that cluster, depending on the nature of the centroid changes.

The k-means partitioning analysis, a cluster analysis that is neither hierarchical nor agglomerative (MacQueen, 1967), allows the use of centroids from the hierarchical agglomerative clustering analysis as initial cluster centers. Typically, the partitioning analysis is run several times, called "chaining," with the final cluster centers from one analysis providing the initial cluster centers for the following analysis. These chained analyses end when the number of occupations assigned to each occupational cluster stabilizes.

### Simple Structure

The criteria of simple structure provides an index of the relative "fuzziness" or clarity of the assignment of occupations to clusters and thus an assessment of internal validity (Hartmann et al., 1992; Mumford & Owens, 1984). Specifically, our simple structure index represents the proportion of occupations, across cluster, having at least a .75 probability of being a member of its assigned cluster. For instance, a simple structure of 1.00 indicates that all the occupations have a .75 or greater probability of being assigned to the cluster in which they were ultimately classified. Operationally, we derived these probabilities from a discriminant classification analysis. The discriminant procedure develops optimal linear composites, or classification functions, for each cluster, using the set or sets of descriptors; then it creates scores on classification functions for each occupation. Occupations are then assigned to clusters on the basis of whichever of the functions yields the largest value. These function scores are also used to derive the probabilities of cluster membership for each occupation that we used for this index of simple structure.

## Mean Squared Error

The MSE provides an index of the average homogeneity of the clusters for a given cluster solution, disregarding the separation between clusters. That is, MSE looks at the within-cluster variability. Having homogeneous occupations represented in the same job family is the primary objective of most job classification efforts. Most often, for example, we are interested in knowing which occupations we may treat similarly with respect to personnel administration, such as developing training programs and salary administration.

Operationally, this homogeneity index is the error term derived from a mixed-design multiple analysis of variance (MANOVA), in which the set of descriptors were treated as a set of repeated measures and the occupational clusters (i.e., cluster membership) served as the independent variable. The error term from this MANOVA represents the average variability within the occupational clusters. Given the variable standardization, MSE can be compared across cluster solutions.

## Effect Size

The effect size provides an index of the amount, or size, of the separation between the occupational clusters and is based on the estimate of between-cluster variability to total variability. This index is derived from the same MANOVA that provides the value for MSE, and it represents the proportion of variance between the clusters relative to the total variance. This criterion gives us a complement to MSE. In this sense, we can assess both the within-cluster "tightness" and "separation."

Table 17-1 presents the study design depicting the 30 separate analyses conducted in this investigation. The first column of Table 17-1 lists the five different ways that the two types of descriptors were combined (e.g., GWAs only vs. GWAs and skills). The

**TABLE 17-1**
**Criteria Estimates for Cluster Solutions Across Study Designs**

| | Incumbent ratings, 29 occupations | | Analyst ratings | | | |
| --- | --- | --- | --- | --- | --- | --- |
| | | | 29 occupations | | 1,122 occupations | |
| Variable combinations | Ward's | Avg. linkage | Ward's | Avg. linkage | Ward's | Avg. linkage |
| GWAs | | | | | | |
| No. of clusters | 4 | 3 | 3 | 3 | 41 | 41 |
| % reclassification | 96.60 | 100.00 | 96.60 | 93.10 | 83.10 | 76.60 |
| Simple structure | 100.00 | 100.00 | 100.00 | 100.00 | 93.54 | 93.80 |
| MSE | 10.63 | 17.04 | 12.63 | 8.44 | 5.84 | 6.30 |
| Effect size | 0.58 | 0.29 | 0.60 | 0.74 | 0.77 | 0.75 |
| Skills only | | | | | | |
| No. of clusters | 5 | 6 | 3 | 3 | 45 | 45 |
| % reclassification | 100.00 | 89.70 | 100.00 | 100.00 | 82.70 | 78.40 |
| Simple structure | 100.00 | 100.00 | 100.00 | 100.00 | 93.81 | 92.94 |
| MSE | 25.54 | 35.35 | 9.96 | 15.72 | 7.96 | 8.50 |
| Effect size | 0.49 | 0.32 | 0.76 | 0.62 | 0.73 | 0.71 |
| GWAs & skills | | | | | | |
| No. of clusters | 6 | 9 | 3 | 4 | 66 | 66 |
| % reclassification | 100.00 | 96.60 | 89.70 | 89.70 | 88.40 | 77.50 |
| Simple structure | 100.00 | 100.00 | 100.00 | 100.00 | 97.98 | 98.03 |
| MSE | 28.75 | 12.13 | 18.49 | 17.85 | 9.06 | 10.89 |
| Effect size | 0.59 | 0.85 | 0.74 | 0.76 | 0.83 | 0.79 |
| GWAs, skills (2-stage) | | | | | | |
| No. of clusters | 11 | 9 | 12 | 8 | 176 | 149 |
| % reclassification | 100.00 | 100.00 | 100.00 | 100.00 | 90.10 | 86.40 |
| Simple structure | 100.00 | 100.00 | 100.00 | 100.00 | 99.09 | 99.04 |
| MSE | 19.24 | 21.73 | 16.00 | 13.63 | 8.53 | 9.45 |
| Effect size | 0.79 | 0.73 | 0.85 | 0.85 | 0.86 | 0.84 |
| Skills, GWAs (2-stage) | | | | | | |
| No. of clusters | 11 | 12 | 10 | 12 | 181 | 160 |
| % reclassification | 100.00 | 96.60 | 100.00 | 100.00 | 89.80 | 87.60 |
| Simple structure | 100.00 | 100.00 | 100.00 | 100.00 | 99.13 | 99.27 |
| MSE | 25.56 | 13.85 | 12.81 | 8.27 | 8.69 | 9.33 |
| Effect size | 0.72 | 0.86 | 0.87 | 0.92 | 0.85 | 0.84 |

*Note.* GWAs = generalized work activities; skills = basic and cross-functional skills; avg. linkage = within-groups-average linkage method.

remaining columns display the three samples, each with the Ward's and within-groups-average linkage clustering methods nested under them. Cell entries include both descriptive information (the number of obtained clusters and number of single-occupation clusters) and the values for the four criteria.

## PROCEDURES

This section briefly outlines the steps we carried out for each analysis. We will not provide detailed information about specific procedures. Instead, we have cited relevant works in each section for the interested reader.

### Score Transformation and Distance Computation

The first step of each analysis was to create two matrices. The first matrix was a dissimilarity matrix of Euclidean distances based on within-case $z$ scores (i.e., the shape component of the profile across descriptors) for the skills and work activities. The second matrix was a correlation matrix representing the correlations among the occupations across the scores for the broad skills and work activities. We factor analyzed this matrix to help identify the number of clusters to retain for each solution, as described in the next section.

### Identifying Number of Clusters

Identifying the number of clusters or sets of clusters that might best represent the structure of the data is a crucial step. Currently, this presents one of the problematic features of cluster analysis: there is no clear-cut methodology for making this determination. We determined the number of clusters to extract by using two widely used procedures: $q$-factor analysis and evaluating clustering coefficients.

### Q-factor Analysis

For the 1,122 Analysts Data, we carried out a $q$-factor analysis on the 1,122 x 1,122 correlation matrix of occupations. Q-analysis represents a class of principal-components or factor analyses in which the cases (e.g., the occupational units) are factored, as opposed to the variables (Coombs & Satter, 1949). With $q$-factor analysis, the number of potential groups in the data can be evaluated by using the factor identification methods of traditional factor and principal-components analysis. Here, we used Kaiser's (1960) eigenvalue-greater-than-one rule as the guideline for setting the number of clusters to extract. Recent research supports the viability of this overall approach for determining number of clusters. For example, Monte Carlo results suggest that the use of $q$-factor analysis to identify the number of groups helps to improve classification results, particularly when using Ward's method (Colihan & Burger, 1995).

### Clustering Coefficients

For the 29 Analysts Data and 29 Incumbent Data, we identified the number of clusters by examining dendrograms. *Dendrograms* are "tree-structured" graphic representations of the clustering coefficients that represent the distance between clusters combined at each stage. Using Kaiser's (1960) eigenvalue-greater-than-one rule with a $q$-factor analysis was not viable with these datasets; the small number of occupations ($n = 29$) relative to the number of potential descriptors ($k = 88$) caused the factor analyses to underestimate the number of groups.

Dendrograms may be displayed together with the rescaled clustering coefficients on which they are based. Large increases in clustering coefficients are indicated by wide intervals between levels in the dendrogram, and they show that very dissimilar clusters have been combined. The number of clusters extant prior to these large increases suggests the number of clusters to retain (Everitt, 1993; Kaufmann & Rousseeuw, 1990).

### Agglomerative Hierarchical Clustering

Once we identified the number of clusters by the methods described above, we carried out the 30 analyses that produced the cells of Table 17-1. Each analysis provided initial clusters for the $k$-means reclassification analysis that followed (Baughman et al., 1995; Mumford, Stokes, & Owens, 1990).

### K-Means Reclassification

After identifying the initial occupation clusters, we used the $k$-means procedure to reclassify all occupations. As noted earlier, this procedure may reallocate poorly classified cases because hierarchical agglomerative clustering procedures suffer from the flaw that cases clustered early in the procedure may not end up being optimally classified. Information used to calculate the percentage, or alternatively, the number of cases correctly reclassified, comes from comparing the initial hierarchical cluster solution with the reclassified $k$-means cluster solutions by cross-tabulation.

## MANOVA and Discriminant Analyses

Finally, we applied MANOVA and discriminant function analysis (DFA) to the clusters obtained from the final, postchaining $k$-means reallocation analysis. The MANOVA/DFA analyses yielded the information needed to obtain the remaining three criterion indices for evaluating the clustering results: simple structure of the cluster solution, *MSE*, and effect size.

## RESULTS AND DISCUSSION

The purpose of this study was to test the utility of measures of the O*NET broad skills and work activities for grouping occupations into clusters. Table 17-1 presents the results of this study in terms of the quality of the cluster solutions. In the following sections, we discuss these results in terms of differences in cluster solutions obtained across our analytic factors of interest: descriptor combinations, clustering methods, and samples.

## Different Descriptor Combinations

The first comparison was between cluster solutions based on using the descriptors in different ways. As described earlier, we used the descriptors alone (i.e., skills or GWAs only), combined simultaneously (i.e., skills and GWAs together), or in a two-stage process—clustering first on skills then GWAs, or first on GWAs then skills.

Table 17-1 shows that using the descriptors in a two-stage approach generally provided better scores on the reclassification, effect size, and simple structure criteria, and nearly as good as the GWAs used alone with regard to *MSE*. These results are particularly pronounced with the 1,122 Analysts Data sample, although a similar pattern of results emerges for the smaller 29 Incumbents Data and 29 Analysts Data samples.

### Reclassification Rates

Across samples and clustering methodology, the two-stage approaches had a slightly higher reclassification rate ($M = 99.71$) than the other approaches to using the descriptors ($M = 98.34$). This convergence in means, however, may reflect the uniformly high reclassification rates with the 29 Incumbent and 29 Analysts Data. The reclassification rates were more divergent with the 1,122 Analysts' Data. For this sample, the percentage of correct reclassification for two-stage approaches ranged from 86.4 to 90.1, whereas the range was 77.5 to 88.4 when using GWAs and skills simultaneously, and 76.7 to 83.1 when using the GWAs or skills only. This finding provides some evidence that the two-staged approaches to using sets of descriptors provides a better initial cluster solution, particularly with a large, diverse set of occupations in which to cluster.

### Effect Size

Across all samples, the two-stage approaches had higher estimates of effect size ($M = .83$) than did the other approaches to using the descriptors ($M = .66$). This finding suggests greater cluster differentiation with the two-stage approach when compared with using the descriptors simultaneously or by themselves. Effect sizes ranged from .73 to .92 when using two-staged approaches, .59 to .85 when using the descriptors simultaneously, and .29 to .77 when using the GWAs or skills only.

Although the two-stage approaches provide for better cluster differentiation in comparison to the other approaches to using the descriptors, Table 17-1 illustrates another important feature. Namely, effect size when using the GWAs and skills simultaneously ($M = .76$) was considerably higher than the effect size for using the GWAs or skills only ($M = .62$). Thus, these results show that using both types of descriptors in a clustering effort will produce greater differentiation among clusters, as opposed to using either by itself.

### Mean Squared Error

The results with respect to *MSE* estimates were less clear-cut. On average, the *MSE* estimates for the two-stage approaches were 15.49 for GWAs, then skills, and 13.59 for skills, then GWAs. Each of these means were higher than the *MSE* estimate for the cluster solution based on GWAs only ($M = 10.90$) but lower than the cluster solutions based on skills only ($M = 18.29$) or using the descriptors simultaneously ($M = 16.97$). These results suggest that the clusters based on GWAs only are the "tightest" across the sample and cluster methods conditions. However, as shown just above, using the GWAs only did not yield a lower effect size when compared with the two-stage approaches. These results suggest that the cluster solutions based on using the GWAs only did not increase cluster separation, despite producing low within-cluster variability.

The pattern of results for *MSE* estimates confirms an hypothesis about the use of multiple descriptors for clustering occupations. As demonstrated, the two-staged approaches do provide for tighter, more widely separated clusters when compared with using the GWAs and skills simultaneously.

### Simple Structure

The simple structure estimates across descriptor combinations present a rather clear picture: use of the GWAs or skills produces cluster solutions that have a high degree of stability and clarity. For the 29 Incumbent Data and the 29 Analysts Data, simple structure estimates were 100% across all conditions.

That is, with these samples, the cluster solutions resulted in occupations being assigned to clusters with at least a .75 probability of belonging to that respective cluster. Although not uniformly 100%, the simple structure results for the 1,122 Analysts Data were equally impressive, ranging from 93.7% for clusters based on GWAs only to 99.2% for clusters based on the skills/GWAs two-stage approach.

### Summary

When comparing different ways to use the descriptors, each of the five approaches provided clearly defined job families, when evaluated by purely statistical criteria. Although the two-stage approaches yielded relatively better results across the statistical criteria, the other approaches yielded excellent results in an absolute sense. Thus, if the purpose for forming job families dictated a need to use skills or GWAs alone, the respective O*NET measures would still produce clearly differentiated job families.

For example, Table 17-2 shows five interpretable job clusters obtained from analysis of the 29 Incumbents Data using Ward's method on the 46 basic and cross-functional skills, together with 11 clusters obtained by analyzing GWAs within the five skill-based clusters. The first skill-based cluster, designated *A*, consists of occupations best classified as managerial/supervisory in nature. The second cluster, *B*, contains only computer programmers, an occupation relatively distinct from the remaining occupations. The third cluster, *C*, consists of a variety of public service jobs. The fourth cluster, *D*, consists of occupations involving material handling and transportation. Finally, the fifth cluster, *E*, consists of occupations involving heavy equipment use, maintenance, and repair. From the occupational titles alone,[1] these jobs appear to be appropriately classified, particularly given the analytic constraints we set for these analyses.

As noted, Table 17-2 also shows the results obtained from the two-stage analysis obtained when we clustered occupations on GWAs within each of the five skill-based clusters. As shown, the four skill-based clusters with more than one occupation were further partitioned to yield 11 final clusters. These final clusters represent a differentiation of each original skill-based cluster into groups relatively homogenous with respect to broad work activities. For example, Cluster D in Table 17-2, based on skills only, combined occupations involving material handling and transportation. This suggests that these occupations have similar broad skill requirements. After we clustered these occupations on the GWAs, this cluster yielded two new clusters: one cluster of occupations involving material handling (Cluster 8) and a second cluster of occupations involving transportation (Cluster 9).

---

[1] For these analyses, we did not examine the actual profiles across descriptors of the resultant cluster solutions.

**TABLE 17-2**
**Twenty-Nine Occupations Clustered First on Incumbents' Ratings of 46 Basic and Cross-Functional Skills; Second on 42 Generalized Work Activities (GWAs) (Ward's Method)**

| Occupation code | Occupation title | Skill cluster | GWA cluster |
|---|---|---|---|
| 15005 | Education Administrators | A | 1 |
| 19005 | General Managers and Top Executives | A | 1 |
| 51002 | First-Line Supervisors and Manager/Supervisors, Clerical and Administrative Support Workers | A | 1 |
| 61005 | Police and Detective Supervisors | A | 2 |
| 49008 | Sales Representatives, except Scientific and Related Products or Services and Retail | A | 3 |
| 25105 | Computer Programmers | B | 4 |
| 32502 | Registered Nurses | C | 5 |
| 31305 | Teachers, Elementary School | C | 5 |
| 53905 | Teacher Aides and Educational Assistants, Clerical | C | 5 |
| 55338 | Bookkeeping, Accounting, and Auditing Clerks | C | 5 |
| 55347 | General Office Clerks | C | 5 |
| 55108 | Secretaries, except Legal and Medical | C | 5 |
| 65026 | Cooks, Restaurant | C | 6 |
| 63014 | Police Patrol Officers | C | 7 |
| 65008 | Waiters and Waitresses | C | 7 |
| 49011 | Salespersons, Retail | C | 7 |
| 49021 | Counter and Rental Clerks | C | 7 |
| 53102 | Tellers | C | 7 |
| 66008 | Nursing Aides, Orderlies, and Attendants | C | 7 |
| 55305 | Receptionists and Information Clerks | C | 7 |
| 49023 | Cashiers | C | 7 |
| 32902 | Medical and Clinical Laboratory Technologists | D | 8 |
| 92974 | Packaging and Filling Machine Operators and Tenders | D | 8 |
| 65038 | Food Preparation Workers | D | 8 |
| 97111 | Bus Drivers, School | D | 9 |
| 97102 | Truck Drivers, Heavy or Tractor-Trailer | D | 9 |
| 67005 | Janitors and Cleaners, except Maids and Housekeeping Cleaners | E | 10 |
| 85132 | Maintenance Repairers, General Utility | E | 11 |
| 87902 | Earth Drillers, except Oil and Gas | E | 11 |

## Different Clustering Procedures

The second comparison was between cluster solutions, using different clustering procedures. As shown in Table 17-1, we compared Ward's method to the within-groups-average linkage method across the other analytic factors. As noted earlier, both of these clustering methods share a similar heuristic for forming the clusters; each seeks to ensure within-cluster homogeneity, although each approaches this objective differently. Ward's method is based on minimizing within-cluster variability, whereas the within-groups average linkage method is based on minimizing the Euclidean dis-

tances of all cases from the cluster centroid (Everitt, 1993). In general, both clustering methods adequately differentiated occupations with regard to the statistical criteria used when considering cluster solutions based on the 1,122 Analysts Data.

### Reclassification

From the results shown in Table 17-1, cluster solutions based on Ward's method appear to have required fewer adjustments, as indicated by their generally higher reclassification rates. In 28 of 30 analyses, cluster solutions based on the Ward's method had a reclassification rate that was higher or equivalent to that for cluster solutions based on the within-groups-average linkage method. These findings, however, may be due to the relationship between Ward's method and the $k$-means procedure we used to reclassify cases. Specifically, both procedures use a variance minimization criteria in which occupations are assigned to clusters such that the variability within the cluster is minimized and the variability between clusters is maximized. The nonindependence between these algorithms creates the possibility that mathematical optimization between these methods partly accounts for the better reclassification rates we obtained with Ward's method.

### Effect Size

The effect-size estimates for method comparisons varied, depending on the specific sample being analyzed. Effect sizes across all descriptor variable comparisons were slightly larger for Ward's method than for the within-groups-average linkage method for the 1,122 Analysts Data (Table 17-1, Columns 6 and 7). Ward's-based solutions, therefore, yielded better differentiated occupational clusters with the 1,122 Analysts Data. However, each cluster method produced well-differentiated clusters as judged by the magnitude of the effect sizes. Regardless of clustering method, effect size was at least .71 when using the 1,122 Analysts Data.

For cluster solutions based on the smaller 29 Analysts and Incumbents data sets, Ward's method did not always provide solutions with larger effect sizes (Table 17-1, Columns 2–5). For example, the effect size estimates are larger for only three of the five Ward's solutions, using the 29 Incumbents Data, and two of the five Ward's solutions, using the 29 Analysts Data. Given this pattern, it is difficult to clearly interpret the cluster method effects on cluster differentiation with the 29 occupations.

### MSE

The results of the *MSE* comparisons across cluster methods parallel those for effect size. *MSE* indices for the 1,122 Analysts Data were consistently smaller across descriptor variable comparisons for Ward's method compared with the within-groups-average linkage method. This finding suggests that the occupation clusters obtained in the 1,122 Analysts Data using Ward's method were more homogeneous. As with the effect size results, *MSE* estimates for cluster solutions using the smaller data sets (analyst and incumbents) were not consistently related to clustering method.

### Simple Structure

The simple structure for cluster solutions based on Ward's method were nearly identical to those based on the within-groups-average linkage method. This finding occurred across sample and descriptor combinations. Furthermore, the simple structure estimates were uniformly high, exceeding 92% in all cases. Regardless of cluster method, the final hierarchical agglomerative clustering solutions were quite unambiguous.

### Summary

There appears to be little basis on which to choose between these two methods of forming clusters, although Ward's method may get a slight edge because of marginally better statistics in the larger analyst sample.

## Sample Comparisons

The final comparison was between cluster solutions created using different samples. We made these comparisons using only the 29 Analysts and Incumbents Data, because they contained ratings on the same 29 occupations. Unlike the previous comparisons across descriptor combinations and clustering procedures, the analysts' and incumbents' ratings produced markedly different results in terms of the statistical criteria of the resulting cluster solutions. As shown in Table 17-1, occupation cluster solutions based on analysts' ratings yielded generally better scores on the statistical criteria.

### Reclassification

Reclassification rates varied across clusters based on the incumbent and analysts data. Of 10 comparisons, 5 were identical, 3 showed better rates for analysts, and 2 showed better rates for incumbents.

### MSE

The *MSE* estimates generally were lower for cluster solutions based on the 29 Analysts' Data. For the analyst-based cluster solutions, *MSE* estimates ranged from 10.54 (skills, then GWAs two-stage approach) to 18.17 (GWAs and skills combined) and were lower for 8 of the 10 possible comparisons. This range was considerably lower than that for incumbent-based cluster solutions, which produced *MSE* estimates ranging from 13.84 (skills only) to 30.45 (GWAs only). From these results, it is clear that the cluster solutions based on the 29 Analysts Data exhibited considerably less within-cluster variability,

despite needing slightly more reallocation of the initial cluster solutions in some instances.

### Effect Size

The effect size estimates were higher among analyst-based occupational clusters. Effect size estimates ranged from .53 (skills only) to .90 (skills, then GWAs two-staged approach) for the analyst-based cluster solutions, and .41 (GWAs only) to .79 (skills, then GWAs two-staged approach) for the incumbent-based cluster solutions. Analyst values were higher in 9 of the 10 direct comparisons.

### Simple Structure

With respect to simple structure, estimates were uniformly 100% across all comparisons for the 29 Incumbents and 29 Analysts Data.

### Summary

The comparison of cluster solutions based on analyst versus incumbent data demonstrates that analysts' ratings provided cluster solutions that have less within-cluster variability and greater between-cluster differentiation when compared with cluster solutions based on incumbents' ratings.

## Comparison Using Only Complete Analysts Data

The results of the these analyses are clearest with the full 1,122 occupations representing the U.S. workforce. Furthermore, it is with this full spectrum of occupations that the cluster outcomes are best evaluated across the three major analytic factors under investigation. The last two columns of Table 17-1 show the results from the 10 cluster analyses using the analyst data for the 1,122 occupations. As noted earlier, all descriptor combinations provide good differentiation of the occupations using either Ward's method or the within-groups-average linkage method, but the statistical results are best for the two-stage approaches (i.e., GWAs first, then skills; or skills first, then GWAs) when compared with using any of the three single-stage approaches (i.e., GWAs only, skills only, or combined GWAs and skills).

## Cluster Solution Convergence

From the results described above, all of the various cluster solutions have acceptable statistical properties. In this section, we present information about the extent to which the different solutions converge, that is, produce clusters containing the same occupations. These cluster convergence comparisons parallel those we have presented with respect to solution quality. We examined the convergence of the cluster solutions across descriptor combinations, cluster procedures, and samples. To make these convergence assessments, we used Cramér's $\phi_c$ (phi) statistic, often known as Cramér's *V*, which provides an index of association between nominal variables (Cramér, 1946; Hays, 1988). This statistic ranges from 0 to 1, with 1 indicating maximal convergence between nominal variables and 0 indicating complete independence. In this context, maximal association means the occupations have been assigned consistently in the two-cluster solutions being compared.

### Different Descriptor Combinations

The first set of cluster convergence tests involved comparing cluster solutions based on different combinations of descriptors. First, we compared cluster solutions based only on GWAs and those based only on skills with each other and with the cluster solutions based on combining the skills and GWAs simultaneously. Second, we compared the solutions based on skills and GWAs combined simultaneously to both two-stage solutions.

We did not, however, compare cluster solutions based on using only the GWAs with the two-stage solution that used the GWAs in the first stage; neither did we compare cluster solutions based on using only the skills with the two-stage solution that used the skills in the first stage. These comparisons resulted in inflated Cramér's $\phi_c$ estimates because of the perfect association between the cluster solutions based on a single descriptor type and the cluster solutions representing the first stages of the two-stage solutions that used that same descriptor type.

As shown in Table 17-3, there was moderate to strong association across the cluster solutions based on different descriptor combinations (the $\phi_c$s range from .52 to 1.0, with a mean coefficient of .81). The lowest level of convergence occurred when comparing cluster solutions based on GWAs only to those based on skills only for the 29 Incumbents' Data ($\phi_c$ = .59 and .61) and the 1,122 Analysts Data ($\phi_c$ = .54 and .52), as is shown in the first row of the table.

This lower level of convergence is expected given the real differences between job attributes (i.e., GWAs) and worker attributes (i.e., skills). Inspection of the corresponding cluster solutions pinpoints the nature of these differences. In the GWAs-only-based cluster solution, Computer Programmers were clustered with occupations performing similar work functions, such as Bookkeeping and Auditing Clerks, Police Patrol Officers, and Office Clerks. Some of the shared GWAs among these occupations included processing information, analyzing data or information, and interacting with computers. However, Computer Programmers require a distinct set of skills (e.g., programming) from those required of Bookkeeping and Auditing Clerks, Patrol Officers, or Office Clerks. The skills-only-based cluster solution (see Table 17-2) shows that computer programmers were indeed placed into a cluster by themselves.

Levels of convergence generally were much higher for all other comparisons. When GWAs are compared with combined or staged methods (Rows 2 and 4 in Table 17-3), the $\phi_c$s range from .72 to .97, with a mean of .81. The same comparisons for skills (Rows 3 and 5) range from .68 to .97, with a mean of .85. The combined skills and GWA solutions converge well with both of the two-stage solutions (see Rows 6 and 7), with $\phi_c$s ranging from .76 to 1.00 and a mean of .88.

Of particular interest is the relationship between the two cluster solutions based on the two-stage approaches. As shown in the last row of Table 17-3, there is good convergence between two-stage cluster solutions based on the 29 Incumbents and Analysts Data; however, the two-stage cluster solutions are less associated when based on the 1,122 Analysts Data. For this later sample, the Cramér's $\phi_c$ estimate is only .64 for both Ward's and within-groups-average linkage methods. Thus, although the two-stage solutions provided statistically sound clusters, the composition of these clusters vary, depending on

**TABLE 17-3**

**Convergence (Cramer's *V*) of Cluster Solutions Based on Different Variable Combinations**

| Descriptor comparisons | Incumbent ratings, 29 occupations | | Analyst ratings | | | |
| | | | 29 occupations | | 1,122 occupations | |
| | Ward's | Avg. linkage | Ward's | Avg. linkage | Ward's | Avg. linkage |
|---|---|---|---|---|---|---|
| GWAs vs. skills | .59 | .61 | .75 | .75 | .54 | .52 |
| GWAs vs. combined | .80 | .75 | .75 | .84 | .72 | .72 |
| Skills vs. combined | .81 | .93 | .90 | .96 | .70 | .68 |
| GWAs vs. skills, GWAs (2-stage) | .80 | .88 | .90 | .97 | .78 | .75 |
| Skills vs. GWAs, skills (2-stage) | .97 | .91 | .96 | .96 | .75 | .69 |
| Combined vs. GWAs, skills (2-stage) | .91 | .78 | .96 | 1.00 | .80 | .76 |
| Combined vs. skills, GWAs (2-stage) | .88 | .94 | .97 | 1.00 | .77 | .78 |
| Skills, GWAs (2-stage) vs. GWAs, skills (2-stage) | .86 | .91 | .85 | .96 | .64 | .64 |

*Note.* GWAs = generalized work activities; skills = basic & cross functional skills; combined = skills and GWAs together; avg. linkage = within-groups-average linkage method.

whether the occupations are clustered first on skills or GWAs. This finding is consistent with the lower convergence between cluster solutions using GWAs only with cluster solutions using skills only, because each of these solutions make up the first-stage solution of one of the two-stage approaches.

### Different Clustering Procedures

The second set of cluster convergence analyses involved assessing the extent to which cluster solutions based on the Ward's and within-groups-average linkage methods converged. The cluster solutions did not vary greatly as a function of using either method; all Cramér's $\phi_c$ estimates equaled or exceeded .68, with a mean value of .84, indicating above-average association among the various cluster solution comparisons. The convergence among cluster solutions tends to be larger in the 29-occupation sample (mean $\phi_c$ = .89) than in the 1,122-occupation sample (mean $\phi_c$ = .72). One possible explanation for this difference is that a greater number of clusters are being generated among a more diverse set of occupations in the large data set. This creates the opportunity for more variability in the clustering procedures and final cluster solutions. These results do indicate that choice of clustering procedure is nontrivial; cluster solutions will be similar but not identical across procedures.

### Different Samples

The final set of cluster convergence analyses compared the cluster solutions based on the 29 Incumbents Data and the 29 Analysts Data. As shown in Table 17-4, the Incumbents- and Analysts-based solutions tend to converge more when using skills rather than GWAs and when using both GWAs and skills. The greatest level of convergence occurs when simultaneously using the GWAs and skills. This implies that the use of more and varied descriptors will

**TABLE 17-4**

**Convergence (Cramer's *V*) of Cluster Solutions Based on Ratings From Incumbents and Analysts on the 29 Common Occupations**

| Variable combinations | Ward's | Average linkage |
|---|---|---|
| GWAs only | .64 | .50 |
| Skills only | .79 | .62 |
| GWAs and skills | .91 | .93 |
| GWAs, skills (2-stage) | .77 | .78 |
| Skills, GWAs (2-stage) | .81 | .80 |

*Note.* GWAs = generalized work activities; skills = basic and cross-functional skills; average linkage = within-groups-average linkage method.

lead to cluster solutions more likely to generalize across rater types.

## CONCLUSION

The results of these investigations tell a straightforward and optimistic story: the scales representing the O*NET basic and cross-functional skills and GWAs provide clusters with good statistical properties. Occupation clusters based on these descriptors were coherent and straightforwardly interpretable, though we spent less time on qualitative interpretation of clusters than on comparing their statistical properties. The statistical properties of occupational clusters did not vary substantially across various parameters of clustering known to influence the results of clustering efforts (i.e., descriptor combinations, clustering methods, and samples). We found differences in cluster solutions where there should be (i.e., between clusters based on GWAs only vs. skills only) and found smaller differences in cluster solutions when more and more varied descriptors were used to form clusters. From these results, the O*NET basic and cross-functional skills and GWAs appear to hold considerable promise for forming statistically defensible and practically useful occupational families.

## CHAPTER 18

# Database Design and Development: Designing an Electronic Infrastructure

ANDREW M. ROSE, BRADFORD W. HESSE, PAUL A. SILVER, AND JOSEPH S. DUMAS

We know we can make government work better and cost less. And the great enabler in reinvention success has been information technology. . . . By encountering a new capacity to handle information and do work in new, more efficient ways, information technology has inspired many people to literally reinvent the organizations they are part of. We're seeing this live up to its potential as a tool for revolutionary change.

U.S. Vice President Al Gore
February 13, 1996

There is little doubt that the U.S. economy is undergoing a period of cataclysmic change and that technology has been playing a leading role. As the United States competes in a rapidly changing global market, businesses have found it necessary to streamline their operations and trim back their workforces. New technologies make entire occupations obsolete overnight. Automation, which requires its own new set of skills to manage, makes it possible for one person to do the work of many. All of this has led to massive restructuring of the workforce. Many heretofore successful managers and mid-level workers have been thrust back into the job market, often to find that with changes in technology their skills have become outdated. Workers can no longer expect that dedication and hard work will guarantee them a lifelong position with an organization. Now, more often than not, the norm is to expect a lifetime of changing jobs and shifting occupations (Handy, 1989).

The response to this change, argued Department of Labor (DOL) Secretary Robert Reich, is not to turn back the tides of history, "stopping technological advances or seceding from the global economy" (Reich, 1994, p. 4). The solution lies in equipping workers with the tools they need to participate fully and actively in this new economic age. In part, this means taking the very technology that is enabling changes in business and using it to better the lives of U.S. workers. This means providing citizens with direct access to the information that will help them get ahead: information about what skills are in demand and where to obtain them, information about how to transfer old skills to new jobs, and information about what new jobs are emerging in the labor market. This is the purpose of the Occupational Information Network (O*NET): to be part of that solution by giving workers the tools they need to compete in today's information-intensive job market.

## SHIFTING PARADIGMS

Since the 1930s, the Department of Labor has published the *Dictionary of Occupational Titles* (DOT; U.S. Dept. of Labor, 1991a). The DOT was intended to be an up-to-date and thorough description of jobs as they were represented in the U.S. labor market. But like many paper-based information sources, the DOT has had its limitations. One of its foremost restrictions has been that it is difficult to revise and disseminate. Updating the DOT has meant systematically changing or deleting thousands of entries by hand, republishing the entire document, and then distributing paper-bound copies through traditional government channels. Often the potential beneficiaries of the DOT knew little of its existence or how to obtain it. Over time, many entries have grown out of date or been considered to be too limited or archaic for the user's purposes.

It was for these reasons that DOL appointed the Advisory Panel for the Dictionary of Occupational Titles (APDOT), an advisory panel to review the status of the DOT and to make recommendations for its revision or replacement. (See chap. 2 for a more detailed discussion of APDOT.) Two themes relevant to this chapter were prevalent in the APDOT's final report (U.S. DOL, 1993b).

First, APDOT saw that the old paradigm of reporting information in the form of occupation-based vignettes, largely consisting of specific job tasks, was no longer meeting the needs of the consumers of occupational information. Textual descriptions of occupations were more useful to large industrial organizations, with their layers of hierarchical management and relatively stable and straightforward jobs. In today's economy, organizational hierarchies are becoming flatter and jobs more complex. Furthermore, assembling these occupational descriptions was done by a cadre of occupational analysts who visited job sites and conducted on-site observations and interviews. The process was time consuming and expensive.

To replace the DOT, APDOT recommended the use of a flexible database of empirically derived occupational descriptors. A number of new measures have been emerging in the field of occupational analysis that, if linked, could help portray the complexity of jobs along a broad series of dimensions. Such a content model could articulate these dimensions and serve as the foundation for an occupational database. If the model were comprehensive and reliable, it could become the basis for a common language that employers, educators, and job seekers could use to describe occupations into the future. The prior chapters in this book have described the effort to develop that content model and associated data collection procedures, as well as the collection of data on an initial sample of occupations.

The second pertinent theme articulated by APDOT was that advances in computer technology could be used to make the new content model accessible to students, job seekers, employers, and other possible users. APDOT recognized that with advances in information technology, and with a move to an electronic database of numeric descriptors, it should be possible to meet the needs of the workforce in new and much more effective ways. The electronic database could serve as a foundation, analogous to a new operating system, to enable new and better career information delivery systems (CIDS).

This argument suggested that if application designers had access to an electronic database of occupational information, they could use it to enrich the content and form of their own applications. For example, matching routines could be developed that would give users the ability to enter one occupation, and with a few keystrokes, produce a list of similar occupations defined in terms of quantified proximity to the first occupation. New techniques in artificial intelligence (AI), such as neural network programming or machine learning tools, could be explored to find ways of making the database adapt to user needs. Clustering routines could be embedded in systems to derive job families on line. Hypermedia could be used to overlay images of people working on the job as illustrations of occupational content.

More broadly, by designing the O*NET with new information technologies, such a system could take full advantage of the nation's computer network infrastructure to support better service delivery to a wide variety of potential users, regardless of location or time of day (Huff, Sproull, & Kiesler, 1989, Sproull & Kiesler, 1991).

## LAYING A FOUNDATION FOR ELECTRONIC DISSEMINATION

Although efforts were underway to finalize the O*NET project's content model and survey techniques, a coordinated effort focused on the use of information technology for maintaining and disseminating O*NET information. To steer the effort, the project formed a design committee. Members of the committee were chosen on the basis of their experience in systems analysis, human factors, decision theory, organizational development, and DOL policy. It was the committee's task to consider the potential applications that could be built on a foundation of occupational information and then to create a prototype system to support those applications.

To lay an enabling infrastructure for applications, the design committee recognized that it would have to identify relevant user groups and consider the social and cognitive context or contexts under which users would be expected to operate. Generally, the DOT was designed for an educated audience. Although job seekers and general managers could obtain the DOT from a bookstore or local library, the information in the book was sufficiently specialized that its use was generally limited to those who had some background in interpreting occupational descriptions. Job seekers would be more likely to obtain the services of a vocational counselor who could interpret the DOT than to buy the DOT themselves.

Consider, now, a computer application designed to replace the DOT and intended to fill the same needs. One such application might support the interaction between a vocational counselor and job seeker, as described above. In that scenario, the product would be designed to support the needs of the vocational counselor directly as the end user and the needs of the job seeker indirectly. To build the application, the design committee would conduct user needs analyses of vocational counselors primarily and job seekers secondarily. It would combine that information with extant theories of idealized practice in job counseling (e.g., Sampson, 1994) and would develop an early set of low-fidelity prototypes. The committee would then submit the prototypes to a cycle of user testing designed to improve the software's ability to support the counselor/job seeker interaction.

Consider also an application designed to support job seekers or students. Under this scenario, developers would begin with the assumption that end-users may have little or no knowledge of classification systems and taxonomies and may also have a limited understanding of computer conventions. The goal in this case would be to provide a maximum degree of interpretation for the audience. The application itself might focus on only a small part of the database (e.g., knowledges for students) and might replace codes and ratings with pictures and graphs.

The two applications described above differ dramatically in their design, and there are dozens of such applications that potentially could be built. The question for the O*NET project in general and the design committee in particular was, Which application or applications should the consortium build as part of its core development work with DOL and which applications should be built by states, other agencies, and vendors? This question has had several different answers throughout the course of the project. Ultimately, our answer was based on what we considered to be the three primary project responsibilities:

- to construct and maintain the integrity of the O*NET database;
- to make O*NET data available to the public as part of DOL's mission; and
- to facilitate the development of innovative, effective end-user applications.

These responsibilities are interdependent. The manner in which the data are made available might be expected to influence the ability of third-party developers to create effective solutions for end users. Similarly, decisions made in constructing and maintaining the integrity of the database will influence the process by which new releases of the database are released to the public and the ability of developers to create effective applications.

## REVIEW OF DATABASE DESIGN AND DEVELOPMENT ACTIVITIES

We have discussed the three central responsibilities of the database design team: to construct and maintain the O*NET database, to make O*NET data generally available to the public, and to facilitate the development of innovative applications. With these responsibilities in mind, the design committee set out to establish the short- and long-term scope of specific activities to be conducted in the project. The committee based its vision on recommendations from the APDOT report, on DOL policy, and its own knowledge of plans to infuse technology into the delivery of statistical information at the federal level. The committee's recommendations led us to proceed along several paths simultaneously.

In the following sections, we describe the activities conducted along those several paths of research and development. We begin by describing our efforts to identify the needs and characteristics of the system's likely users. As will be seen from the discussion, the O*NET user base is not expected to be a homogeneous group. Rather, user groups will vary depending on their purpose for interacting with the database and their sophistication in using database management systems (DBMSs). We then describe progress made in database development, including development of the actual relational database, the data dictionary, and the electronic codebook (ECB), or "viewer," as it also came to be called. We also describe the creation of a demonstration aid designed to illustrate the mission and scope of the project.

## Identifying Users and Reviewing Existing Systems

### Interacting With Representatives From Other Projects

In its approach to technology development, the project team began with the assumption that to develop a useful technology it must come to understand the needs and context of the system's expected users, stakeholders, and beneficiaries. To represent the views of these groups, the project team formulated the design committee described at the beginning of this chapter. The committee's membership fluctuated according to the particular objectives of each meeting, but in general it was composed of individuals from the American Institutes for Research (AIR) consortium and from DOL who were skilled at translating the needs of users into effective system design.

One central responsibility of the design committee was to investigate avenues for disseminating the occupational information maintained within the O*NET data system to developers, researchers, and other intermediate and end users. In meeting that responsibility, the team began its efforts by establishing ties with representatives of related projects, attending relevant conferences, and reviewing the state of the art for CIDS. Those efforts led to discussions among project members and representatives from DOL on how to position the database-creation effort for the future. The emphasis was not just on developing a dissemination strategy that might be effective today but also on how to take advantage of forward-looking technology initiatives to make the database useful and adaptive in the future. Those discussions led to the creation of a plan to aggressively infuse information technologies into the creation and delivery of the new occupational database.

Much of the discussion at the federal level has been focused on how wide-area computer networks may be used to deliver information more effectively to consumers. The O*NET team kept those discussions firmly in mind as it established the design for delivering occupational information to stakeholders and beneficiaries. Likewise, recommendations from the APDOT report highlighted ways that an electronic database might enable application developers to create more effective computer programs. The O*NET team attempted to integrate these discussions and recommendations as it developed specifications for an electronic database.

### Identifying Users and Beneficiaries

Once the design committee had a basic understanding of how others were meeting the needs of their constituencies, it sought to gain a firm understanding of who would use an electronic database of occupational information when it was produced. Ultimately, the O*NET beneficiaries will be the students, workers, and employers who must deal with the realities of a rapidly-changing job market. Although these needs were central, the committee also recognized that to produce the kind of information that students, workers, and employers could use in their day-to-day decisions, it must coordinate its development efforts with a large network of other service professionals.

For example, teachers and counselors are invaluable resources for helping individuals formulate the questions and strategies needed to explore careers and to interpret career information. Materials developers—authors of books and developers of CIDS—create the decision-support tools that provide individuals and counselors with the information they need to make effective choices. Employers create the occupational demands that job seekers must fill; their requirements for an occupational database are central in importance. Finally, labor market analysts and other researchers produce complementary information that also serves the information needs of individuals making career decisions. Users would not be well-served if information from the O*NET project were not compatible with the data being produced through labor market initiatives.

To summarize, in all of its development efforts, the design committee took a user-centered approach. It recognized that no matter how elegant the dissemination system's technical design, it will be effective only if it is useful to, and usable by, the people it was developed to serve. Over the course of the project, the team made many contacts and visits. The following were most salient:

- the National Occupation Information Coordinating Committee (NOICC) and State Occupational Information Coordinating Committees (SOICCs);
- the Association of Computer-Based Systems for Career Information (ACSCI);
- CIDS developers;
- corporate human resources psychologists; and
- the Society for Industrial and Organizational Psychology.

From these contacts, we updated our initial typology of users (which had been distilled from prior user surveys, especially those conducted for APDOT) on the basis of their expected interactions with the database. We present the typology in Figure 18-1, in which the O*NET database is at the center of the diagram, with successive layers of consumers and providers to the left and right. Each layer represents the proximity of the user group to the raw data in the O*NET system. In the layer nearest the center is a group of users who are expected to work with the data in its most unedited form (i.e., without the benefit of interpretive applications). The O*NET database is a set of relational computer files containing numeric values for the occupational descriptors in the content model plus textual definitions of the descriptors. The users closest to the database are expected to have the technical skills necessary to access the data electronically and to interpret the data through their own searches, queries, and analyses. These are users who are sophisticated in the use of DBMSs and who understand the assumptions behind interpreting

statistical data. Types of consumers in this center group include CIDS application developers, occupational researchers, policymakers, and program staff from NOICC, state-based SOICCs, and one-stop shop project staff.

Further out from the center is a group of users who might be expected to use O*NET data in a moderated form but who have the technical capacity to understand the form and function of information in the original database. These are consumers who could serve as translators between the technical creators of information and the end users. They include counselors, teachers, curriculum planners, and disability examiners. Furthest out from the center of Figure 18-1 are the end users: the students, workers, and employers. These are people who would not be expected to have the technical skills necessary to manipulate the data in its raw form but who will be expected to benefit directly from the applications and services that are created by other users in the system. Note that we have portrayed employers (human resources staff) at both ends of Figure 18-1, because they would both provide and consume O*NET information.

This multi-tiered view of database usage is typical of most electronic information systems. Electronic data are collected and maintained by specialists who are well versed in the technical aspects of database management. End users gain access to information through the reports and applications that the technical specialists create (Date, 1995). The implication for the O*NET development team was that a special priority would be set on meeting the needs of the users closest to the center of Figure 18-1, because these users will create the applications and reports from which end users will benefit. We could meet the needs of these technical users by providing the utilities and supporting documentation necessary to facilitate analysis and application development.

### Collecting User Input Using Demonstration Software

To help capture the O*NET vision in a way that could be used to elicit feedback from potential users and stakeholders, the design committee and project staff created a computer-based demonstration of the project's principal goals. Initially, the software prototype was intended to be a self-paced application designed to walk users through the details and hierarchical complexities of the fully articulated content model. Over time, however, the software came to be seen more as a presentation aid to help illustrate the technological underpinnings and future orientation of the project, especially concerning the long-range scope and vision. This demonstration aid was useful for communicating with user groups as members of the project team engaged in customer outreach activities throughout the country. Over the course of the project, the presentation was modified and enhanced, ultimately incorporating an audio component as well

| Consumers | | | O*NET Database | Providers | | |
|---|---|---|---|---|---|---|
| **Group** | **Group 2** | **Group 1** | | **Group 1** | **Group 2** | **Group 3** |
| Alien certifiers | Career counselors | CIDS developers and | | Human resources staff | Federal (FOCIS) staff | Federal (FOCIS) staff |
| Community college | CIDS developers & staff | trainers | | Job Bank staff | Human resources staff | Human resources staff |
| students | Curriculum planners | Data administrator | | OAFC staff | Job Bank staff | Job Bank staff |
| Disabled workers | Disability examiners | Database administrator | | OPM staff | OAFC staff | Newspapers |
| Displaced homemakers | DOL technical staff | DOL technical staff | | Researchers | One-stop shop staff | Professional societies |
| Four-year college | Employment placement | NOICC/SOICC staff | | Vendors | OPM staff | |
| students | staff | OAFC staff | | | SESA staff | |
| Released prisoners | Human resources staff | One-stop shop staff | | | | |
| Retired adults | Insurance company staff | Policymakers staff | | | | |
| Secondary school | Job Bank staff | Researchers | | | | |
| students | JPTA staff | SESA counselors | | | | |
| Technical college | NOICC/SOICC staff | Vendors | | | | |
| students | OAFC staff | | | | | |
| Veterans | One-stop shop staff | | | | | |
| Welfare clients | Policymakers | | | | | |
| Working adults | Researchers | | | | | |
| | School counselors | | | | | |
| | SESA counselors | | | | | |
| | Unions | | | | | |
| | Veterans Administration | | | | | |
| | staff | | | | | |
| | Vocational counselors | | | | | |
| | Vocational rehab, | | | | | |
| | counselors | | | | | |

**FIGURE 18-1.** A typology of O*NET user groups.

as functioning mini-applications (e.g., browsing the content model).

## Developing the O*NET Database

Designing a database to meet the technical needs of researchers and application developers presented two opposing challenges. First, the O*NET content model was expansive. Creating a database structure that could accommodate multiple ratings on the more than 450 variables in the content model required a database of more than 1,000 fields in its design. Combine that requirement with an expected data collection on 1,122 occupations and the resulting data matrix would contain over 1,000,000 values when completed. Second, in spite of its relatively large size, application developers expressed a need to deliver PC-based applications that could make use of the database in a way that was fast, flexible, and easy to query. For simplicity and portability, the design team decided to create a database with a relational data structure.

A relational data structure is simply a way of dividing up information into logical subparts for more efficient processing. Each of the subparts is connected to each other through the use of an indexed identifier, and information across the subparts can be displayed together using any one of many widely available DBMSs for personal computers.[1] In a relational design, new datasets, referred to as tables, can be generated quickly from the intersection, union, or subsetting of existing datasets.

In a dataset of occupational information such as O*NET, it was expected that the primary relational identifier for most of the database would be a suitable identification (ID) code for occupations. A critical decision in the project was deciding what ID code to use. Initially, the project team determined that the O*NET database should be organized around the Bureau of Labor Statistics' *Occupational Employment Statistics* (OES) classification system. This system contains approximately 800 occupations and was designed to be the common system used to collect and report labor market information, both nationally and within individual states. Incumbent data for the O*NET database were collected through surveys using OES codes. In working with the OES system, however, state occupational analysts decided that some of the OES codes encompassed too broad a category to give users discriminating information. As a compromise position, analysts suggested using an intermediary code between OES and DOT codes, referred to as an "Occupational Unit (OU)." OU codes would include the six-digit OES code plus a letter at the end to imply a subgrouping. The data-

base delivered at the end of the O*NET development effort included the capability of relating the occupational databases either on OES code or on OU code, depending on the user's needs.

### Structure of the Database

Once a relational identifier had been chosen, the project team began working on developing an O*NET database structure. The team created a structure that was intuitive for developers to use, captured all relevant data, and allowed for efficient data processing. Whenever possible, the team tried to recreate the domain structure of the O*NET content model. Data on worker characteristics generally were stored in the same table or group of tables; data on worker requirements were stored in a separate table or group of tables, and so on. In this way, the physical structure of the database was developed to reflect the same logical partitions and groupings as the logical model on which the data were based.

The primary data tables accommodated numeric values—means and percentages—representing the aggregated responses of participants on the occupational surveys. In addition to those tables, the team created six descriptive files. As will be discussed below, the descriptive files were used to provide thorough documentation of the database in electronic format. These so-called "metafiles" can be used to enhance applications. When shipped with the data files, these metafiles can provide printable documentation on the files' structure, format, and history.

The O*NET database also includes two occupation-related files and two external cross-walk files. The occupation-related files contain specific information at the level of each occupation. Information includes occupation-specific tasks and occupational definitions, and thus it contains elements typical of both a (text-based) data file and a text-intensive descriptive file. The two cross-walk files serve as on-line thesauri connecting occupational information on the O*NET database with occupational informational systems available elsewhere.

Figure 18-2 depicts the overall structure of the O*NET database, the various types of files included, and the relationships between files. The structure yielded four types of relational data files. These files were the primary data files, descriptive (meta) files, occupation-related files, and external cross-walks.

**The primary data files.** Currently, the O*NET database contains two different types of data: (a) occupational data collected from the O*NET questionnaires ("incumbent data") and (b) occupational data that have been converted from the existing DOT ("converted DOT data"). In the O*NET database, occupations with incumbent data are listed by their OES codes, titles, and definitions—a code system that is managed by DOL. The converted DOT data are listed by their OU codes, titles, and definitions—a system developed by the Occupational Analysis

---

[1]An alternative to the relational structure is an object-oriented database. Object-oriented databases were largely experimental at this time, however, and their relative advantage over standard relational models for our purposes was unclear.

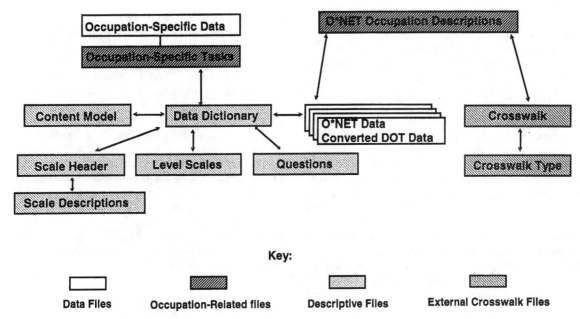

**Key:**

| | | | |
|---|---|---|---|
| Data Files | Occupation-Related files | Descriptive Files | External Crosswalk Files |

**FIGURE 18-2.** Structure of the O*NET database.

Field Centers (OAFCs) that is based on and closely parallels the OES structure.

For the incumbent data, job incumbents and supervisors completed questionnaires rating various aspects of each O*NET content model variable to their jobs. As described in chapter 4 and elsewhere in this book, these questionnaires were administered to workers employed in a number of occupations to collect data for the O*NET prototype database.

The primary data files contain information on all of the content model variables, most including more than one scale (e.g., Level and Importance) for each of these occupations. In addition, incumbents provided frequency and importance ratings for a variety of specific tasks within each occupation. These are contained in the occupation-specific files described below. Between the primary data files and the occupation-specific files, there are a total of 1,221 data fields used to describe the full breadth of content model characteristics on each of the above occupations.

To supplement the incumbent occupational data collected for O*NET, the OAFC network conducted research to convert existing DOT data for use in the O*NET database. Occupational analysts, working from lists of task statements, rated each OU on selected aspects of the content model. (See chaps. 4 and 15 for more details on this process.) The domains covered by these ratings included basic and cross-functional skills, generalized work activities (GWAs), abilities, knowledges, and selected work context variables. Converted DOT data were available for 1,122 occupations in the O*NET database.

From the O*NET questionnaires and analyst ratings, statistics were calculated for each element in the content model, for each occupation (OU). Primarily, these statistics were measures of central tendency—means, medians, and percentages. Other statistics

(e.g., variance estimates, *n*s, covariance matrices) have been calculated through the course of the project but were not included in the primary release of the data sets.

**Descriptive files.** Also included with the numeric data files are descriptive files containing textual descriptions of OUs and OES codes along with a crucial set of metalevel files used to document the database. These metafiles contain the format information necessary (a) to reproduce the hierarchical structure of the content model on a computer screen, (b) to document the purpose and definition of each variable in the database, and (c) to reproduce the survey questions and scale anchors associated with each question in the database.

The utility of the descriptive files can be illustrated with the ECB. This was a sample application developed with the O*NET database. When using the ECB to review the overall list of occupations, users can read the definition of occupations as textual narratives before exploring the numeric details of the means databases. When browsing through items in the content model, users are given reproductions of scales on the screen that essentially reproduce the format of rating scales in the O*NET surveys. Requesting details at this level produces even further documentation on each question to the point of providing the specific behavioral anchors that accompanied each survey in its original form.

These metalevel descriptive files not only serve to produce more complete and informative applications, they also serve to create a fully documented data archive. The creation of fully documented data archives, also referred to as *data warehousing*, has proven to be an essential strategy for large-scale research projects. The development of this type of documentation after the fact can be an expensive proposition, but it is an expense that is often incurred willingly in longitudinal data efforts. The paper version of the data dictionary that accompanies the ECB serves the same purpose and is produced directly from the system-level metafiles.

**Occupation-related files.** The primary data files contain the bulk of the O*NET data matrix (i.e., statistical means and percentages depicting respondent data on the primary domain surveys, e.g., basic and cross-functional skills, generalized work activities, etc.). Separate files are included that contain information collected at the level of each specific occupation. These include definitions of the tasks that are related to occupations as well as a general description of each occupation. In the current database, task definitions were created by occupational analysts from existing DOT descriptions and other sources. Ratings of the importance and frequency of those tasks by job incumbents are available on those occupations included in the initial data collection (see chap. 15). For brevity's sake, general occupational descriptions were derived from extant definitions of OES occupations or were created as brief summaries by occupational analysts during the DOT conversion process. Other types of descriptive information could be included in the database in the future and could include anything from descriptive vignettes to digitized images of individuals working on jobs.

**Cross-walk files.** Finally, the O*NET database incorporates a link between itself and related information from other external systems. These "cross-walk" files include the major occupational and educational classification systems used by the federal government. Files linking OES codes to other federal data sources were obtained from the NOICC. Files linking OUs to the OES and the DOT were created during the project by occupational analysts. O*NET data are associated with these external sources by linking O*NET occupation codes with codes found in the external classification systems. These external systems include the following:

- DOT codes and titles;
- Guide for Occupational Exploration (GOE) codes;
- Standard Occupational Classification (SOC) codes and titles;
- 1990 Census codes and titles;
- Classification of Instructional Programs (CIP) codes and titles;
- Prototype Skills-Based Job Family Matrix codes;
- Military Occupation Codes (MOC); and
- Office of Personnel Management (OPM) codes and titles.

## Documenting the Database: The O*NET Data Dictionary

From the on-line metafiles used to document the structure of the database, the project team created a fully documented, hard-copy data dictionary to be used as a reference guide for system developers. The O*NET data dictionary contains the definition, description, and location of each data element, or variable, within the O*NET database. It is a set of consistent data definitions that helps users better understand and interpret the data within the O*NET database.

The O*NET data dictionary is based on the hierarchical structure of the O*NET content model. It is divided into six main, tabbed sections. Five of the tabs represent one of the five main domains of the content model: worker characteristics, worker requirements, experience requirements, occupational requirements, and occupation-specific tasks. One additional tab contains O*NET system variables (i.e., variables contained in the data dictionary and other non-data files). Figure 18-3 illustrates a sample entry.

## Application Development

Because of its technical complexity, we expect that the O*NET database will be used primarily by researchers, application developers, and database managers. Throughout the project, the design team discussed at length the project's role in developing end-user applications. In those discussions, we recognized the critical role that "vendors" (i.e., non-project-supported applications developers) would eventually play in the acceptance and utilization of O*NET. Nevertheless, the design team argued that a small set of relatively unsophisticated applications ("applets") could be directed to different user groups as a way of demonstrating utility of the system and of "seeding" further development. At one point during the project, we had decided conceptually on a set of four applets, as described briefly in Table 18-1.

After considerable discussion, it was decided that the project team would forgo the development of the first three applets—Assisted Counseling, Self-Directed Counseling, and Employer Restructuring—in favor of more effort at making the fourth application, Research and Analysis, more general and user friendly in its intended applications and audience. This application became the ECB.

## The Electronic Codebook

In determining its relationship to third-party application developers, the design committee returned to the priorities it established at the beginning of the project: (a) to construct and maintain the integrity of the O*NET database, (b) to make data available to the public, and (c) to facilitate the development of innovative, effective end-user applications. To meet the primary objectives associated with these priorities, the design team recognized that its first objective in application development would be to create a delivery system that could be used to put the power of the full O*NET database into the hands of all de-

**Element:**   Written Comprehension
**Description:**   The ability to read and understand information and ideas presented in writing

**Content Model Key: I.A.1.a.2**

I. Worker Characteristics
   A. Abilities
      1. Cognitive Abilities
         a. Verbal Abilities
            2. *Written Comprehension*

| Variable | Variable Description | File Name | Field Values | Ques Code |
|----------|---------------------|-----------|--------------|-----------|
| A02LV00M | Written Comprehension-Level | Means_AB | 1-7, 0(NR) | Level, A |

| Left Label | Value | Right Label |
|------------|-------|-------------|
| Requires understanding complex or detailed written sentences that contain unusual words and phrases. | 7.00 | |
| | 6.40 | Understanding an instruction book on repairing a missile guidance system. |
| | 4.20 | Understanding an apartment lease. |
| | 1.70 | Understanding signs on the highway. |
| Requires understanding short or simple written sentences that contain common words and phrases. | 1.00 | |

| A02IM00M | Written Comprehension-Importance | Means_AB | 1-5 | Importance |
|----------|----------------------------------|----------|-----|------------|

**FIGURE 18-3.** A sample entry for the data dictionary.

velopers. The delivery system should make it easy to identify and select individual data elements for personal use. It should allow users to manipulate the data directly, in a way that takes into account the complexity and hierarchical nature of the full occupational database. It should promote appropriate use by allowing users to access the metadata accompanying the database and to learn about the questions and scales used to gather the occupational data. Last, it should let users select variables and occupations and then export data to their own computers for subsequent analysis and development.

The delivery system suggested by the design committee was an "electronic codebook" for O*NET. As used within the context of this chapter, an electronic codebook is a utility developed primarily for technical users; it is designed to provide access to, and information about, data collected from large-scale surveys. The assumption is that the structure, format, and purpose of elements in a survey-related database may be unknown to consumers wishing to extract data for their own use. To help others make sense of the data, directors of large-scale survey projects often develop job aids. One of the more important job aids

to be developed by some of the federal statistical agencies is a set of reference books designed to document the questions, scales, and item values within the original survey. An ECB takes that reference information and puts it on line. In conjunction with import/export functionality, the codebooks make a convenient one-stop shop for individuals or organizations wishing to use data from the surveys for their own purposes.

As an illustration of the concept, the National Center for Educational Statistics (NCES) prepares large datasets of statistical information for use by educational researchers and policy makers. NCES ships those data on CD-ROM to technical users who request the data for analysis. On the same CD-ROM as the entire statistical database, NCES delivers an ECB. When users run the codebook application, they are presented with a utility that lets them peruse all the variables included in the dataset and acquaints them with each variable's name and format. Using the application, they are then able to select the variables they want for analysis and then download a subset of the master database for use with their own programs.

**TABLE 18-1**
**O*NET End-User Applications**

| Function of application | Assisted counseling | Self-directed counseling | Employer restructuring | Research and analysis |
|---|---|---|---|---|
| Example tasks and functions | Community college: Student plans future with counselor | Citizen comes to one-stop shop to transfer/change employment | Employer customizes job description, identifies candidates for new jobs | Browse, search, filter, sort, export, link database records |
| Gather and translate input | Academic counseling model implemented in O*NET variables | Modified assisted counseling for early or mid-career counseling | Current job descriptions and skills and abilities of incumbents | Direct input of variables, occupations, codes, and variable values |
| Match input description to occupations | $d^2$ or $r$ to identify occupations of interest | $d^2$ or $r$ to transfer to a similar job | $d^2$ or $r$ for job descriptions and job matches | Deterministic match to direct input vector |
| Create output products | Table of occupational values for selected jobs | Prose descriptions | 1) Customized job description; 2) list of matches | Exported files, test, screens, search criteria |
| User sites | Community college | One-stop shop | Employment council | Various |

### Developing Specifications for the Codebook

Our work began by developing the specifications for the ECB. In talking to prospective users, we found that it would be desirable if the codebook could

- be developed for IBM-compatible personal computers running *Windows*®; have the capability of exporting data from the master database in *dBASE III/IV*® format (*.dbf) and, perhaps, formats often used by researchers or policy analysts (e.g., *SPSS*® or *SAS*®);
- offer a user-friendly navigation scheme for working through and with the O*NET content model; and
- offer explanatory information on the origin of content model elements.

Aside from being an essential application for delivery with the O*NET relational database, the ECB would provide an example of how to acquaint end users with the structural richness of the content model. The design committee thought that this aspect of the codebook was an important part of the dissemination process. It was also thought that many of the needs of even inexperienced end users could be met by making the ECB easy to use; incorporating a number of query, search, and sort functions; and providing access to some or all of the text documenting the job descriptors and rating scales used in O*NET.

On the basis of these discussions, the design team established a set of priorities to include as specific features in the completed ECB. For illustration, these priorities and the features they generated are described below.

**Design feature: Occupational listings.** From its user analyses, the design committee determined that the ECB should be capable of displaying the list of occupations contained in the database system and

brief descriptions of those occupations and that it should be able to display this list sorted either alphabetically or by OES (later OU) numerical designation. O*NET was expected to contain information on 1,121 OUs. It was desired that the O*NET ECB be able to display the list of occupations in its entirety as well as a list of selected occupations as defined by users. It should be capable of displaying brief descriptions of each occupation that might include a list of tasks performed as part of the selected occupation.

The listing of occupations was structured according to the OES title and classification code. The project team considered it extremely valuable that users be able to access cross-walks between the OES titles and codes and alternative classification codes. These alternatives, at a minimum, included classification codes from the DOT. In addition, it was important to include cross-walks to other systems, such as the Guide for Occupational Exploration (GOE), Standard Occupational Classification (SOC), Military Occupational Specialties (MOSs), Office of Personnel Management Occupations (OPM), Classification of Instructional Programs (CIP), and Standard Industrial Classification (SIC) codes, among others. These cross-walks were obtained primarily from the National Occupational Information Coordinating Committee (1994).

Figure 18-4 illustrates the occupational listing function as it was developed in the ECB. From the primary application screen, users select one or the other of two data sets to use. At the time the codebook was completed, there were two databases available for use: one containing empirically derived data from job incumbents in 29 occupations and one containing occupational analyst data on 1,121 occupations. Users select the database they wish to use through a "dropdown" menu. The O*NET ECB can display either list of occupations in its entirety. The O*NET ECB can also display a list of selected oc-

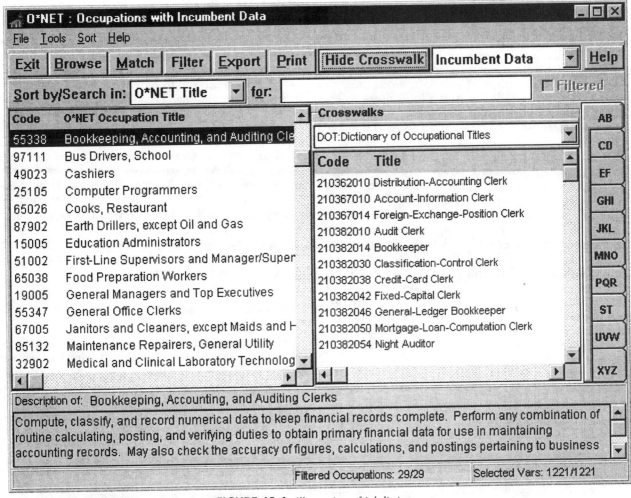

**FIGURE 18-4.** Illustration of job listings.

cupations as defined by users through the filter capability, discussed below. The O*NET ECB displays brief descriptions of each occupation as it is highlighted.

The listing of occupations includes the OES title and classification code for incumbent data and the OU titles and classification codes for converted data. Occupations are sorted either alphabetically or by OES/OU code, according to the user's preference. Users can also search the list of titles or numbers by entering an occupation label or a code. This search function can, for example, enable users to quickly locate occupations with OES Code 80000 or any other code or title.

**Design feature: Browsing through the content model.**   The list of occupational titles in the O*NET codebook should serve as an index to the true content of the database. The real contribution of the O*NET project lies in the breadth and depth of the O*NET content model and the data collected from job incumbents to describe occupations within the content model framework. The design committee determined that the second most critical feature of the codebook was that it would make the complexity

and richness of the content model available to users as they browsed through actual contents of data fields on each individual occupation.

To make the complexity of the content model available to users, the ECB was constructed to use the hierarchical nature of the O*NET content model. To do this, the codebook borrows the "look and feel" of a *Windows®*-based file manager. The primary domains of the content model (i.e., worker characteristics, worker requirements, experience requirements, occupation requirements) are depicted as folders in a "data manager" screen connected to each other at the same level of indentation with a vertical line. The user can select any one of these folders/domains and "drill down" to lower levels of the content model hierarchy. Selecting "Worker Characteristics" reveals the subdomains of "Abilities," "Interests," "Work Styles," and so on. Brief descriptions of each variable in the content model hierarchy are given as screen prompts along the way to guide users through the model. Top-level domains are also available as tabbed sections in the browser screen.

At the lowest level of the hierarchy, users are presented with actual data values. A scrollable window in the upper right corner of the screen indicates which data scales (e.g., level, importance) are available for the content model element, and it allows users to select variables for display and subsequent export. Data values are depicted numerically and graphically, with the graphical depiction showing numeric averages as points of selection along survey-based scales. A "details" button allows users to retrieve a fully documented version of the original data scale, complete with behavioral anchors and other formats.

Most but not all of the content model variables are depicted through the drill-down "data manager." Occupation-specific task information, which draws its contents from a separate dataset in the O*NET database, is available as a tabbed section in the browser window only. Selecting occupation-specific tasks presents the user with a data schematic in the data manager screen that is different for each occupation (unlike the hierarchical schematic for the rest of the content model, which is constant across occupations). For incumbent occupations, there are ratings of frequency of task performance and the importance of each task to job performance. The browsing capabilities of the ECB are illustrated in Figure 18-5.

**Design feature: Selecting occupations for review and export.** The ECB was designed to look through and select occupations and variables for export.

Users select variables for exporting in the data browsing screens just described. To select occupations, the ECB lets users establish "filtering criteria" based on content model values. Users can define parameters for each variable in O*NET that the O*NET ECB can use to narrow down (i.e., filter) the listing of occupations. The filtering function uses the standard comparison operators (e.g., <, ≤, =, ≥, >) to perform exact value searches and conditional searches. Conditional filters are often referred to as Boolean searches. Users can use the *and* and *or* statements with the comparison operators to perform simple or complex filters. The conditional statements can be used in the same field or in different domains. For example, if a job seeker is interested in finding all occupations that require a high level of oral comprehension and minimal physical strength, that job seeker can use the filter selection screen to specify the following search parameters:

oral comprehension ≧ 5 *AND* static strength ≦ 2.

The filtering feature works interactively with the listing of occupations. Results of filtering requests can be displayed in the listing of occupations with an indication of the number of occupations matching the defined parameters. In the previous example, the listing of occupations would list only those occupa-

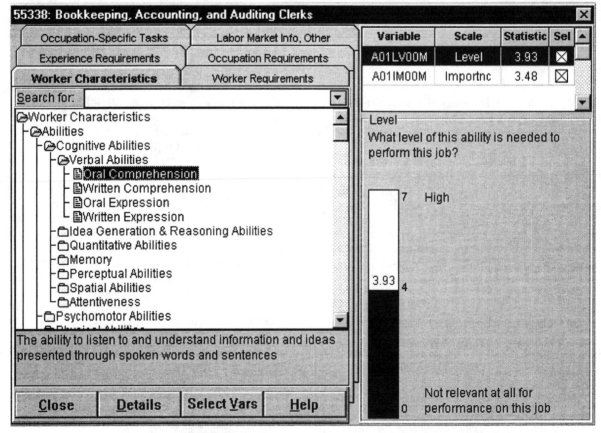

**FIGURE 18-5.** Illustration of browsing capabilities.

tions that require minimal static strength and a high level of oral comprehension.

**Design feature: Exporting.** For those users who would like to perform their own analyses on the O*NET data, a critical capability of the ECB is to offer exporting functions. Users can select the entire list of occupations for exporting or, after using the filtering or matching features, export a more refined set of occupations. Users can also select the entire list of variables or select a specific set of variables for export.

**Design feature: An illustrative matching function.** One of DOL's most important goals in funding projects like O*NET is to help build the economy by matching qualified people to available job opportunities. To help seed ideas for using O*NET as a basis for job matching, the design committee elected to include a matching function as an illustration. The matching feature uses an algorithm to estimate the relative fit of an occupation to one or all of the occupations in the O*NET database. As previously described, the database contains occupational descriptors for abilities, basic skills, cross-functional skills, GWAs, and knowledges, among others. Each of these descriptors has been rated on a 7-point Level scale (e.g., "What level of ability is needed to perform this job?"). We used these descriptors to reflect the fit between two occupations by creating a scale reflecting a "good," "fair," or "poor" fit. We assigned values on this scale according to the simple matrix depicted in Table 18-2.

The deviation between the occupation's level score on a descriptor is used as the basis of assigning a fit scale of good, fair, or poor. In this example, assume that the user is considering the fit between the current occupation—Occupation 1—and a target Occupation 2. If, for a particular variable, both occupations are rated identically, a "3" is assigned. If the occupations deviate by more than two rating levels, a "1" is assigned. For ratings that differ by 1 or 2 points, this matrix differentiates between "overqualified" and "underqualified" comparisons. If the current occupation (Occupation 1 in the matrix) is rated 1 point higher than Occupation 2 (i.e., Occupation 1 requires a higher level of the ability, or knowledge,

skill, etc. than Occupation 2), we still assign a "3." On the other hand, if Occupation 1 is rated 1 point lower than Occupation 2, a "2" is assigned. One implication of this rule is that "match" fit indices are not symmetrical: in the above example, Occupation 2 would be "underqualified" when compared with Occupation 1 for this variable.

This matching function, as noted above, is intended to be illustrative only. More fully articulated and validated matching functions could be developed for moving employees within companies to different positions, for assisting in career development, or for preparing others for career changes outside the company.

**Design feature: Printing.** The O*NET ECB offers printed outputs of various kinds. The printouts use preformatted, flexible layouts that can include different types of information. The print button on the screen that shows the listing of occupations produces a printout of all occupations currently listed. Thus, for example, if a user has used the filter function to generate a list of occupations, that list would be printed. Figure 18-5 shows the printout of the results of the filtering example described above. Similarly, if the user has matched an occupation to all other occupations (see below for a description of this function), the print button would produce a list of all occupations and the degree of fit between each and the target occupation.

**Design feature: On-line documentation.** Users of the O*NET ECB have immediate access to information on the content model. They can learn about variables with hypertext links to descriptive text. For example, users can view the scales used for each occupation characteristic. Note the "details" button in the "browse" screen in Figure 18-5; if the user would like more information about a variable, activating this button shows the user a display similar to a page from the data dictionary. The variable's definition, its value for the particular occupation, and the benchmarked scales are shown. Users can also browse through more technical information by using the extensive on-line help system.

The ECB also provides practical, on-line instructions to help users become familiar with the application. A status bar at the bottom of the interface (see Figure 18-4) displays information on the number of occupations and variables the user has selected. The help menu can display "how to" procedures, descriptions of the application and its features, and a glossary of terms. It appears on a separate screen and follows the standard *Windows*® help format.

## PLANS AND VISION

As we suggested at the beginning of this chapter, the challenge of O*NET is to reinvent the way that DOL collects and disseminates occupational information,

**TABLE 18-2**
**Weighting Matrix for Determining Relative Fit Within the Matching Function**

| Occupation 2 level rating | Occupation 1 level rating | | | | | | |
|---|---|---|---|---|---|---|---|
| | 1 | 2 | 3 | 4 | 5 | 6 | 7 |
| 1 | 3 | 3 | 2 | 1 | 1 | 1 | 1 |
| 2 | 2 | 3 | 3 | 2 | 1 | 1 | 1 |
| 3 | 2 | 2 | 3 | 3 | 2 | 1 | 1 |
| 4 | 1 | 2 | 2 | 3 | 3 | 2 | 1 |
| 5 | 1 | 1 | 2 | 2 | 3 | 3 | 2 |
| 6 | 1 | 1 | 1 | 2 | 2 | 3 | 3 |
| 7 | 1 | 1 | 1 | 1 | 2 | 2 | 3 |

*Note.* 1 = poor, 2 = fair, 3 = good.

and to do so in a manner that will enable a markedly new capability for matching people to jobs. When fully operational, this new system should have the capability of maintaining a complex web of data on multiple facets of occupations; it should serve as a bridge to link the nation's talent banks and job banks; and it should stimulate the creation of more effective career exploration programs. A key to the reinvention is to take full advantage of the country's emerging computer infrastructure.

In this chapter we have described the first phase in linking the O*NET data effort to the nation's electronic infrastructure. We have documented the decisions that led to the development of the O*NET relational databases and have explained the rationale behind developing the ECB. In this section we describe our vision for moving the O*NET concept into practice as a fully functioning and highly useful source of occupational information. Critical to our discussion is the notion that O*NET will enable a new era of research and development, one that is based on an electronic database of empirically derived occupational descriptors. This shift in paradigm should enable a new set of applications that are collectively more comprehensive, accurate, dynamic, and adaptive than was possible before O*NET. We conclude with a caution that whatever course O*NET takes, it should focus on building applications that make the complexity of O*NET easy to comprehend and simple to use.

## Enabling Research and Development

As the O*NET project proceeds into its next phase, it is apparent that there will need to be a centralized effort to ensure that the database is accurate, reliable, and up to date. Whatever organizational entity is responsible for monitoring the effort should follow a process similar to that used in the prototype phase and comparable to similar efforts from other federal statistical agencies. Data should be collected in standardized ways, checked for quality and integrity, and appropriately aggregated for dissemination. (Chap. 19 presents a broader discussion of this topic.)

## Expanded Use of the Internet

Another way of supporting research and development is through expanded use of the Internet. There has been much discussion over the past decade regarding the use of large-scale computer networks to support the work of research in the United States. Some have referred to these efforts as establishing "national collaboratories" for research (Lederberg & Uncapher, 1989). The play on words is intentional; the notion is that such structures would support a shared, virtual laboratory of resources and data to which researchers across the country would have equal access (i.e., a co·laboratory). It would also support distributed work among researchers, making it easier for colleagues who are not co-located to work with each other and share information (i.e., a col·laboratory). Such a "collaboratory" would be a valuable component of O*NET.

## New and Innovative Applications

In disseminating information, ways should be found to encourage the development of end-user applications. The ECB can be seen as one utility developed by DOL to facilitate access to the database and to promote application development. Still, what O*NET offers at this stage of production is primarily *potential* and *capability*. For O*NET to have its broadest effect on schools, employers, and job seekers, it must stimulate the development of new and more effective tools.

In our vision, we picture a future in which students explore the world of work using CIDS that are smarter and more precise than ever before. Using O*NET data, they enable students to quickly find occupations that fit their interests, to explore those and other occupations on the basis of their own aptitudes and abilities, and then to plan a curriculum based on the system's expectations for required knowledges. Displaced workers should be able to use similar tools for exploring opportunities that are similar to the jobs they have had in the past or to build plans for acquiring new skills and knowledge through training. And so on. Together, these applications have the capability of being more comprehensive, accurate, dynamic, and adaptive than ever before. How these applications might acquire these characteristics is described below.

## Building Applications That Are Comprehensive

As a dictionary of occupational descriptors, O*NET expands on the previous DOT by offering information on more than 450 content elements across the full breadth of an occupation's descriptions. By tapping into the wealth of that new knowledge base, applications developers should be able to create CIDS that are much more comprehensive than before. Furthermore, because O*NET is designed to fit comfortably with the OES and the NOICC cross-walks, applications developers should be able to create applications that tie occupational information seamlessly to labor market information, occupational thesauri, and other related information. Developers with access to digitizing capabilities can even create applications that tie occupational descriptors to pictures of people at work.

## Building Applications That Are Dynamic

Economists have posited that in a fast-paced, global economy, the demands of job seekers and employers for occupational information will be constantly changing. To support that kind of dynamism in the economy, we envision that application developers will be able to take advantage of the infrastructure we have laid for O*NET in two ways. First, by using a database of occupational information, we have created a structure that is by definition flexible. Application developers will be able to draw on as much or as little of the database as they desire. Filtering routines and advanced search routines will let users restrict the number of occupations they are reviewing at any given time to as few or as many as they wish. Second, embedding O*NET within the infrastructure of the Internet would provide the capability of distributing the most recent versions of the database as quickly and efficiently as possible, if so desired. In the on-line world, movement of information will not be limited by the time it takes to produce and distribute hardbound books, but only by the time it takes to access and download the database.

### Building Applications That Are Adaptive

With respect to computer applications, intelligence refers to the ability of a software application to bring information to users in ways that are more adaptive, interactive, and duplicative of the value offered by real knowledge-area experts. We believe that one of the more fruitful areas of development for O*NET will be to make career applications more adaptive by applying techniques borrowed from research in AI. Techniques borrowed from what used to be the arcane field of AI research are much more often found in current computer applications. Spelling and grammar-checking tools, on-line "wizards" for answering user inquiries, and "smart" database engines are all examples of AI applications that have enriched mainstream applications. Also, techniques from the field of natural-language processing can be used to tie the content of incoming resumes to the skill sets of emerging job opportunities through permutations of O*NET's matching capabilities. Expert systems can be used to query job seekers (as a human resources counselor might) to help guide them through the process of identifying matches between their own skills and aptitudes and promising occupational opportunities. Because O*NET is a database of occupational knowledge—and can support complex, numerical analyses—we believe that these advanced techniques can be used to create career applications that are adaptive and effective.

## DEALING WITH COMPLEXITY: A CAUTIONARY NOTE

As we envision a "brave new world" enabled by technology and enhanced by O*NET, we feel compelled to conclude with a cautionary note. One of the first by-products of the information age has been "information glut"; there is often too much information being produced for any one individual to process and use. The Internet, with its unanticipated burst in popular usage, threatens to bog down under its own weight as users find themselves mired in "many-to-many" communications. Finding the information that is needed in an often-undisciplined, hypertext environment such as the World Wide Web can be an expensive drain on users.

For O*NET to be effective, then, we believe that it will be important for application developers to find ways of creating simplicity out of complexity. One way of doing this is by integrating efforts across federal initiatives. A considerable amount of effort is going into the production of on-line resources to help workers become more effective in the new economy. These efforts should be communicating with each other closely, as we know they are attempting to do. The end result for citizens should not be a patchwork of disconnected, and often duplicative, information resources, but rather an integrated and seamless view of the world of work. For this reason, we applaud the "one stop shop" efforts and encourage the use of the O*NET database as part of the glue that holds those efforts together.

Another tenet to keep in mind is to tailor the interface of applications using O*NET to the purposes and capabilities of intended users. Application developers should find ways of using the wealth of information in the O*NET database to drive their own set of easy-to-use applications. It will be important to keep the specific user of each application firmly in mind and to get feedback from that user as early and often as possible. Creating applications that truly meet the needs of students, workers, and employers will be the ultimate measure of the system's viability.

# Summary of Results, Implications for O*NET Applications, and Future Directions

NORMAN G. PETERSON, WALTER C. BORMAN, MARY ANN HANSON, AND U. CHRISTEAN KUBISIAK

As described in Peterson et al. (1995), the O*NET should provide important job and occupational information for such users as employers, job seekers, career explorers, vocational counselors, and researchers interested in jobs and work. General applications of this information include employers selecting workers, individuals evaluating jobs in relation to what they are qualified for and where training might be needed, students and others exploring career options, dislocated workers trying to identify new job opportunities, educators and trainers developing programs to deliver the most relevant training, and researchers learning about similarities and differences between occupations in terms of their requirements for skills, abilities, and so on. Now that data have been gathered on the O*NET descriptors for some occupations and initial analyses of these data have been accomplished, we are able to discuss issues regarding applications with more knowledge about the kinds of information likely to be available in the O*NET database. In the next section, we review the analyses of O*NET data and comment on their implications for applications of the data.

## REVIEW OF ANALYSIS RESULTS

### Reliability

The primary statistic computed here was the interrater agreement coefficient. Table 19-1 summarizes the results for the nine domain questionnaires. It shows the observed coefficients, which are based on approximately 10 raters per occupation for most domains, and estimates for the case for 30 raters, which was our original view of the desired number of raters within each occupation. The observed coefficients are all at least .70, except for organizational context, occupational values, the dichotomous job-entry rating in skills, and the Importance scale for work styles. Possible and somewhat differing reasons for these lower-than-desired results are discussed in the respective chapters, but the major conclusion to be drawn

from these results is that the domain questionnaires produce reliable results when completed by incumbents. The estimated coefficients for 30 raters are all .79 or greater, with most in the .90s, illustrating that 30 is a sufficient number. For many of the domains, fewer raters should be sufficient, on the basis of these results. Although 30 should be the goal, 15 seems to be a reasonable number as a minimum for each questionnaire per occupation. Those questionnaires that showed lower levels of interrater agreement should be held to higher minimums, and possible reasons for the lower levels of agreement should be pursued and, if possible, corrected.

Table 19-2 shows similar results for aggregated descriptor scores. Aggregate scores were formed by computing mean values for the descriptors that were categorized into the second level of the domains' hierarchies. As shown, this was not appropriate for some domains. These results mirror those in Table 19-1, except that the coefficients are generally a bit higher, with a few exceptions. These results certainly support the use of aggregate or higher level scores for describing occupations.

Both figures show that the Level and Importance scales used in five domains are approximately equal in terms of reliability. However, this finding must be tempered by the fact that the two scales were administered in sequence, with Importance following Level. The use of both scales in this way appears to lead to reliable results for both; dropping one or the other might reduce the level of reliability for the retained scale. McCormick (1964b) found, years ago, that use of multiple scales tends to increase the reliability of all the scales.

The reliability results have implications for many if not all applications. The fact that interrater agreement was generally high for the descriptors means that descriptor score profiles for occupations have meaning in the sense that they are stable representations of these occupations' requirements. For example, when a search is initiated for the highest level skill requirements for a particular occupation, the answer is likely to be reliable and replicable.

**TABLE 19-1**
**Interrater Agreement Coefficients for Each Scale Type**

| Questionnaire | Scale | $r_k$ | $r_{30}$ |
|---|---|---|---|
| Skills | Level | .79 | .93 |
| | Importance | .79 | .93 |
| | Job Entry Requirement | .60 | .83 |
| Knowledges | Level | .86 | .95 |
| | Importance | .85 | .94 |
| Training, Education, | Instructional Program | .78 | .92 |
| Licensure, and | Educational Subject Area | .74 | .90 |
| Experience | Licensure | .85 | .95 |
| | Experience | .79 | .93 |
| Generalized Work | Level | .80 | .92 |
| Activities | Importance | .78 | .92 |
| | Frequency | .74 | .90 |
| Work Context | | .87 | .95 |
| Organizational Context | Across Occupations | .64 | .84 |
| | Across Organizations | .45 | .79 |
| Abilities | Level | .82 | .93 |
| | Importance | .82 | .93 |
| Occupational Values | | .60 | .82 |
| Work Styles | Level | .70 | .88 |
| | Importance | .67 | .86 |

*Note.* $r_k$ is the observed interrater agreement coefficient; $r_{30}$ is the estimated interrater agreement coefficient for 30 raters.

## Scale Relationships

Table 19-3 shows the correlations between scale types, computed in two ways, for those domains where multiple scale ratings were obtained. Level and Importance scales were used in five domains, and the correlations ranged from .82 to .96 for the across-occupation correlations and from .90 to .95 for the across-descriptor correlations. These are very high correlations and raise the possibility that redundant information is being obtained. However, the standard deviations of the mean correlations show that there is a considerable amount of variance across occupations in the correlations, when compared with the correlations across descriptors. The standard deviations for the across-occupation correlations are .04, .21, .11, .30, and .11 for skills, knowledges, generalized work activities, abilities, and work styles, respectively. Comparable across-descriptor correlations are .04, .04, .05, .07, and .05. This means that the relationship between the Level and Importance scales varies considerably across occupations for four of the five domains, which argues for the retention of both scales. On a practical note, completion of the Importance scale takes very little time once the descriptor definition has been read and the level rating has been completed. We would strongly argue that the Level scale should be retained because of the additional information provided by the Level scale anchors. Given these findings, and our belief that the Level scale certainly should be retained, there may be relatively little time savings (on the respondent's part) should the Importance scale be dropped from further use.

The other scales, Job Entry Requirement in skills and Frequency in generalized work activities, show somewhat lower correlations with level and importance than those two scales do with themselves. The job entry correlations range from −.66 to −.74 (lower score = not required at entry), evidently providing some unique information. The Frequency scale scores also appear to provide somewhat less redundant information, but their correlations with Importance and Level scale scores still range from .82 to .91.

## Descriptor Relationships

Some of the intended applications of the O*NET information require the hierarchical feature of the content model. Consider, for example, a student exploring the skill requirements of several occupations with which he or she is unfamiliar. As a first sweep, the student may want to enter O*NET at the higher level of the skills taxonomy and then later explore more in depth at the lower level after eliminating some occupations from consideration. To assess the adequacy of the internal structure of the descriptor variables as depicted in the content model, correlations were computed for and principal-components analysis was

**TABLE 19-2**
**Interrater Agreement Coefficients for Aggregate Descriptors for Each Scale Type**

| Questionnaire | Scale | $r_k$ | $r_{30}$ |
|---|---|---|---|
| Skills | Level | .86 | .95 |
| | Importance | .86 | .95 |
| | Job Entry Requirement | .69 | .88 |
| Knowledges | Level | .85 | .94 |
| | Importance | .85 | .94 |
| Training, Education, | Instructional Program | n/a | n/a |
| Licensure, and | Educational Subject Area | n/a | n/a |
| Experience | Licensure | n/a | n/a |
| | Experience | n/a | n/a |
| Generalized Work | Level | .86 | .95 |
| Activities | Importance | .84 | .94 |
| | Frequency | .78 | .92 |
| Work Context | | n/a | n/a |
| Organizational Context | Across Occupations | .60 | .82 |
| | Across Organizations | .41 | .77 |
| Abilities | Level | .86 | .95 |
| | Importance | .82 | .93 |
| Occupational Values | | .57 | .81 |
| Work Styles | Level | .76 | .91 |
| | Importance | .73 | .89 |

*Note.* $r_k$ is the observed interrater agreement coefficient; $r_{30}$ is the estimated interrater agreement coefficient for 30 raters.

**TABLE 19-3**
**Mean Correlations Between Scales Across Occupations and Descriptors**

| Questionnaire | Scales | Across occupations | Across descriptors |
|---|---|---|---|
| Skills | Level/Importance | .96 | .95 |
| | Level/Job Entry Requirement | −.71 | −.66 |
| | Importance/Job Entry Requirement | −.74 | −.69 |
| Knowledges | Level/Importance | .90 | .95 |
| Training, Education, Licensure, and Experience | | n/a | n/a |
| Generalized Work Activities | Level/Importance | .93 | .92 |
| | Level/Frequency | .88 | .82 |
| | Importance/Frequency | .91 | .89 |
| Work Context | | n/a | n/a |
| Organizational Context | | n/a | n/a |
| Abilities | Level/Importance | .82 | .92 |
| Occupational Values | | n/a | n/a |
| Work Styles | Level/Importance | .93 | .90 |

*Note.* Across-occupation correlations are the mean ratings on a given occupation for all descriptors for one scale correlated with the mean ratings on the same occupations for all descriptors on the other scale, averaged across occupations. Across-descriptor correlations are the mean ratings for a given descriptor for all occupations for one scale correlated with the mean ratings for that descriptor for all occupations for the other scale, averaged across descriptors.

conducted on primarily the mean occupation scores on the Level scales. These analyses are perhaps more limited by the number of occupations available to enter the analysis than are many of the other analyses. The analyses are too numerous and complex to be efficiently summarized here, but they generally provided intuitively sensible results within each domain. These analyses were not intended to exactly duplicate the a priori hierarchical structure of the domains, but they were expected to be consistent with them, which they were, for the most part. That is, descriptors from the same content model category generally load most highly on the same factor. With regard to the comparison of the empirical factor analyses and the content model taxonomies, we point out that the higher order taxonomies for some domains are not intended solely to capture past empirical findings but also to incorporate conceptual and developmental notions, notably in the skills domain.

The a priori hierarchical structure was also examined more directly. For each content domain, we intercorrelated all of the descriptors across occupations and identified those correlations that involved descriptors from the same second-order category in the content model hierarchy. These within-category correlations were then converted using Fisher's *r* to *z* transformation and averaged, and the resulting average *z* scores were converted back to standard correlation coefficients. This mean correlation *within* second-order categories was then compared with the mean correlation *across* second-order categories. The latter correlation was simply the average (again using an *r* to *z* transformation) of all of the remaining cor-

relations, that is, those that involved descriptors from different second-order categories. Table 19-4 presents the results of these analyses. Note that the mean within-category correlations are higher than the mean across-category correlations for descriptor scores in each of the six domains for which such statistics could be computed, although just barely so for occupational values. These findings support the use of the category schemes for forming aggregate scores for the O*NET, but with a word of caution for the values domain.

## Occupation Differences

Another positive finding is that almost all of the descriptors have variance across occupations. Only for

**TABLE 19-4**
**Comparison of Correlations Within and Between Second Order Categories by Content Domain (N = 29)**

| Content domain | Means for descriptors from the same category | Means for descriptors from different categories |
|---|---|---|
| Generalized work activities | .61 | .43 |
| Knowledges | .58 | .40 |
| Skills | .85 | .64 |
| Abilities | .79 | .26 |
| Work styles | .69 | .42 |
| Occupational values | .27 | .24 |

the work style and occupational value domains were the obtained data somewhat restricted. For example, Dependability (Work Styles, D12) scores were uniformly high for the 35 occupations in the sample. However, for most of the other descriptors across the domains, variance in the scores across occupations provides differentiation that is a prerequisite for many applications.

Comparisons of the same six occupations across descriptor profiles in the various domains showed intuitively sensible results and revealed that many descriptors contributed to differentiation between occupations. The fact that descriptor scores vary substantially across occupations is very important, especially for exploring career options relative to several occupations and learning about similarities and differences between jobs/occupations.

## Convergence With Analysts' Ratings

We completed these analyses for five of the nine content domains, and some of those results are summarized in Table 19-5. Generally, the pattern of ratings was similar across the two rater types; the correlations of the mean ratings provided by the two rating sources range from .53 to .74. The $d^2$ values range from .47 for the 5-point Importance scale in knowledges to 1.51 for the 8-point Level scale in skills. When the square roots of these values are taken, the average differences are all reasonably close to 1 scale point for the 8-point Level scales and between a one-half point and 1 scale point for the 5-point Impor-

**TABLE 19-5**
**Mean Correlations and Squared Differences Between Incumbents' and Analysts' Ratings**

| Questionnaire | Scale | $r_{ia}$ | $d^2$ |
|---|---|---|---|
| Skills | Level | .74 | 1.51 |
|  | Importance | .67 | .72 |
| Knowledges | Level | .65 | .86 |
|  | Importance | .65 | .47 |
| Training, Education, Licensure, and Experience |  | n/a | n/a |
| Generalized Work Activities | Level | .71 | 1.09 |
|  | Importance | .61 | .82 |
|  | Frequency | .53 | n/a |
| Work Context |  | .64 | n/a |
| Organizational Context |  | n/a | n/a |
| Abilities | Level | .70 | .99 |
|  | Importance | .65 | .39 |
| Occupational Values |  | n/a | n/a |
| Work Styles |  | n/a | n/a |

*Note.* $r_{ia}$ is the mean correlation between incumbent and analyst mean occupation ratings. $d^2$ is the mean squared difference between incumbent and analyst mean occupations ratings.

tance scale. These do not seem like practically large differences, but it must be kept in mind that these are average values. For some occupations there could be more substantial differences. We conclude, however, from these findings that there is considerable agreement between the two types of ratings, sufficient to warrant the interim use of analyst ratings in anticipation of the future availability of incumbent ratings.

These findings also raise the possibility of combining the two kinds of ratings for purposes of describing occupations. These data do not seem to preclude such a procedure, nor do they argue for complete substitutability. The occupational analysts provided some of the ratings (i.e., those pertaining to "frequency" in work context and generalized work activities) on different scales than those used by incumbents. Furthermore, some of the domains were not rated by analysts because it was judged that the stimulus material provided to analysts would be insufficient for rating those domains. On balance, these points support the notion that data from the two sources should not be combined to describe occupations.

## Other Analyses

Most of the domain chapters present additional analyses intended to evaluate the construct validity of the measures. In addition, chapters 14–17 present analyses that further evaluate the meaningfulness and usefulness of the O*NET system. The authors of each of these chapters have drawn their own conclusions, and they will not be repeated here. However, some comments are in order.

Chapter 14 presents analyses of occupation-specific data, particularly frequency and importance ratings of tasks. These analyses show that such ratings had high interrater agreement coefficients in general, with 30-rater estimates of .90 or greater for all but 4 of the 29 occupations.

Chapter 15 discusses the possible sources of variance, both desired and undesired, in occupational analysis ratings and summarizes the evidence available on this topic. Many issues are yet to be addressed in this area, and it probably is not feasible to address some of them within the foreseeable future. Nevertheless, this chapter provides a coherent organization of the issues and provides a framework for future efforts.

Chapter 16 discusses the relationships between measures across the O*NET domains. Several approaches for analyzing these relationships were used; together they provide strong evidence for the construct validity of the O*NET descriptor system. Expected relationships occurred where they should and did not occur where they were unexpected. Future analyses in this area could focus on, among other things, making estimates of scores in one domain from scores in another. Such analyses are of obvious practical use but are at present limited by the number of occupations for which incumbent data are available. This is not a hindrance for the occupational analyst database, however, because data are available for all 1,122 O*NET occupational units on five of the major content domains. A replication of the analyses that have been completed on the incumbent data, but using the analyst data, would provide a gauge for the advisability of using the analyst data to provide such estimates.

The analyses presented in chapter 17 show that the skill and generalized work activity domains are effective in forming occupational clusters. The analyses explored the impact on cluster solutions of type of variable, clustering procedure, and sample (incumbent data or analyst data), as evidenced by various evaluative statistics and the similarity of cluster solutions. Briefly put, different types of variables did produce somewhat different solutions, as one would hope, but changes in clustering procedure did not seem to have an appreciable effect within the confines of these investigations. There were some differences between the solutions based on analyst versus incumbent responses, but these were not large, and they became smaller when larger numbers of and more varied descriptors were used to derive the clusters.

## HIGHLIGHTS OF IMPLICATIONS FOR SPECIFIC APPLICATIONS

Another way to discuss the implications of the results for applications associated with O*NET is to review several general areas of policy initiatives and the occupational data needs for each of these initiatives. For each of these initiatives, the relevant aspects of the O*NET are described and the implications of results available to date are discussed.

### Educational Policy and Skill Standards

A need for this area is an occupational framework for developing skill standards. The content model clearly is responsive to this need. A comprehensive set of skill descriptors is included for describing occupational skill requirements, as well as descriptors depicting a wide variety of work activities. Data collected using these descriptors have been shown to be highly reliable, especially if data are collected from 30 incumbents per occupation. These descriptors have also been shown to differentiate between occupations in sensible ways. Thus, it is likely that this information can be used to generate occupational clusters highly appropriate for the development of occupational skill standards.

### School-to-Work Transition

Efforts in this area focus on building a school-to-work transition system for the 75% of our young people who do not go on to complete a 4-year postsecondary education. These state-led efforts will build on existing programs to prepare students to meet high academic and occupational standards and create linkages to the labor market system. These efforts require information concerning the skill requirements for occupations to help build curricula for schools. Again, the O*NET will be responsive to this need, with the skill taxonomy descriptors providing the relevant data. In addition to demonstrating appropriate psychometric properties, data collected using the skill descriptors demonstrate meaningful patterns of correlations with generalized work activities, abilities, and other descriptors, providing support for the construct validity of these measures. Accurate data concerning the skill requirements of a broad sampling of occupations will provide a good foundation for efforts to prepare students for the workplace and to facilitate a smooth transition from school to work.

### Dislocated Workers and One-Stops

Work in this area seeks to consolidate and improve an array of existing programs targeting laid-off workers. Resources and incentives have been provided for states and local communities to create One-Stop Career Centers in which employers and workers will have easy access to job and training information, postsecondary professional and technical education, adult basic education, job matching, and counseling services. The centers will be overseen by a workforce investment board. The One-Stop Career Centers, proposed as part of the Workforce Security Act, will provide laid-off workers with job-search assistance, labor-market information, and training to enable them to take control of their careers, allowing them to move into new occupations. In this case, the need is for job and occupational information to help dislocated workers find new jobs. The O*NET can help with part of this requirement by providing them with detailed information about skills, abilities, and so on, needed for different occupations. Through either formal or informal means, these workers can match their qualifications to the occupational requirements.

### High-Performance Workplaces

The O*NET can make several contributions to efforts to build high-performance workplaces. First, the content model provides for a comprehensive description of high-performance business practices, which has a strong foundation in research and theory, as well as demonstrated links to other attempts to define high-performance or high-involvement workplaces. Data concerning these aspects of the organizational context were collected from both organizational representatives (e.g., personnel managers) and incumbents in the targeted occupations. Organizational representative data were collected from more than 600 organizations; these data provide an excellent source of information concerning the relationships among these high-performance practices, their relationships with other frequently studied aspects of organizations, and the extent to which these practices are used in the workplaces sampled. These analyses revealed that business practices identified as high-performance do tend to covary across organizations. This comprehensive and empirically based description of the high-performance practices used in workplaces can provide a foundation for future research and applications.

In addition, high-performance workplaces have been described as using data to make organizational decisions and using state-of-the-art business practices. O*NET's dynamic and flexible occupational information database is ideally suited to support these activities.

Although certainly not exhaustive of important workplace initiatives, either now or in the future, we believe the O*NET is clearly responsive to the needs of these kinds of programs. Although more data are needed before this potential can be fully realized, results to date suggest that O*NET will substantially benefit all of these initiatives.

## COMMENTS ON FUTURE DIRECTIONS

The authors of the various chapters have discussed possible avenues for future research and investigation. Some broader comments are made here.

### Data Collection

With regard to methods of collecting data, the paramount lesson that has been learned is that multiple methods should be used. That data collection should be an ongoing O*NET activity is obvious; less obvious is how that activity should be organized and carried out. This is at least as much an organizational issue as it is a technical issue, but some guidance can be offered from our experiences over the first 2 years of O*NET development. First, if a variety of approaches is to be used to collect data, then a common set of demographic or identifying information must be collected. Although the exact make-up of this set of variables is not fully known, it includes the obvious personal identifiers (race, sex, ethnicity, age), but it should also include other information about the organization or establishment in which the respondent is situated. These variables are essential to allow the data to be combined across the methods to yield an accurate description of occupations. Second, some sort of incentives must be used to facilitate collection of data. The most mundane would be direct payment of respondents, but this often is neither feasible nor even the most effective method of securing cooperation. To collect data, cooperation must often be secured at many levels, such as the organization housing the occupational incumbents, including home and branch office management; supervisors of incumbent respondents; employer and employee associations; and unions, supervisors, and others. Each of these entities calls for a slightly different approach to securing cooperation and, thus, different kinds of incentives. As was demonstrated in the prototype data collection, support must be secured at all these levels to ensure successful data collection. We believe that the most powerful incentive of all will be a highly useful O*NET system with multiple, tailored applications making use of the O*NET database. These applications provide tangible evidence to users of the "fruits of labor" stemming from their cooperation in data collection. Although the prototype project has moved O*NET a long way toward this goal, much work remains to be done in this arena.

### Occupational Unit

A comment is in order about occupational unit. A major effort on the part of the Occupational Analysis Field Centers has been the identification of approximately 1,122 occupational units, which are an expansion of the Occupational Employment Statistics (OES) set of occupations. These units were identified through a thorough and careful analysis of Dictionary of Occupational Titles (DOT; U.S. Department of Labor, 1991a) information. The O*NET system presently uses these units as its basic occupational set, and they also are being considered as part of a larger federal effort to revise the Standard Occupational Classification system. The future may bring additional changes to the make-up of the basic set of occupations. One of the advantages of the O*NET system, with its multiple domains and measures, is its capability of forming alternative groupings of occupations, as demonstrated in chapter 17, thus providing the alternative groupings for special uses. However, a common set of occupational units with some degree of stability is essential for combining data across different data collection efforts, such as those conducted by the Bureau of Labor Statistics. Therefore, attention to the technical and practical utility of the occupational unit scheme used by O*NET, and its coordination with other federal, state, and private-sector data collection efforts, are vitally important.

### Continued Inclusion of O*NET Content Domains

Each content domain and its measures have been separately analyzed and reported on in earlier chapters. Although some domains clearly have stronger results supporting their continued use, collectively all the domains seem technically sufficient for continued inclusion in the O*NET system. Some fine tuning in the make-up of a few of the domains is in order and should be undertaken, but these changes are not viewed as particularly urgent. Once again, the relatively limited number of occupations available for analysis tempers our conclusions in this regard. With more data, it might become more apparent from a technical point of view that one or more domains should be drastically revised or eliminated. However, it is more likely that such decisions will be driven by the uses to which the data are eventually put, or not put. It must be kept in mind that each of these domains has associated with it a potential set of interested consumers, as found in prior user surveys and contacts with potential users throughout this project. As applications are developed and put into use, the usefulness of the various measures in the O*NET system will become more clear. If a domain clearly is useful but has some technical problems, the first order of business is to fix the technical problems. On the other hand, a technically adequate domain that finds no user base, even after some amount of time, clearly is a candidate for deletion. Likewise, it may be that candidates for addition to the O*NET content model will become apparent in the same way.

## O*NET Organization

This last comment leads to a recommendation for a possible way to organize the O*NET effort, both research and development and ongoing data collection and product development. Following some private-sector models, O*NET representatives could become familiar with data collection methods and procedures *and* the available O*NET applications. Armed with this knowledge of the benefits of O*NET that could be applied in various settings, they would be in an excellent position to recruit organizations and employee associations—and would have the knowledge to assist in the technical details of data collection. Furthermore, these representatives might specialize in particular industries or broad occupational groupings, therefore becoming much more knowledgeable in the core activities undertaken in the industry or occupational area of their specialty. These "sales representatives" could, if more detailed knowledge were required, call on a central core of O*NET technical representatives who would be working day-to-day with the details of data collection or with monitoring, cataloguing, or developing particular O*NET applications. Collectively, these technical representatives would perform the ongoing research, data quality, and technical control functions necessary to continually update and improve the O*NET system.

Such an organizational scheme is only one possible way to proceed, of course, but it does attempt to combine the working knowledge of the "input" and "output" functions of the O*NET system in a cadre of "sales representatives" so that the benefits of participating in O*NET data collection are tightly coupled with the demand on resources to engage in that participation. As O*NET grows in use, collections or associations of particular types of users could be formed, perhaps even resulting in an annual convention for O*NET researchers, data providers, and application users.

## A FINAL NOTE

We believe a tremendous degree of technical and practical progress has been made on the prototype O*NET project. Indeed, we believe the project has resulted in the production of an occupational database that is of some immediate, practical use, perhaps somewhat beyond the initial expectations and hopes of those of us most closely involved in the project. This book, along with the more detailed O*NET technical reports (Peterson, 1997; Peterson et al., 1995; Peterson et al., 1996; Rose, Hesse, Silver, & Dumas, 1996), stand as the primary documentation for the completed work. Much good work has been done, but much remains to be done.

# O*NET's Theoretical Contributions to Job Analysis Research

MICHAEL A. CAMPION, FREDERICK P. MORGESON,
AND MELINDA S. MAYFIELD

The purpose of this chapter is to draw some conclusions about the Occupational Information Network's (O*NET) theoretical contributions. It is not a discussion of the results, which have been explained quite well in previous chapters. Instead, it is more of a commentary on the conceptual or theoretical issues. Nor is it a complete summary of all the theoretical issues. Many have already been adequately discussed. Instead, it comments on an eclectic combination of topics, including those that have not been previously described and those for which a different perspective might be helpful. Finally, it does not repeat the details of the content model or various theoretical findings. Instead, it draws conclusions about the theoretical contributions and sometimes attempts to extend the ideas.

It should be noted at the outset that the authors of this chapter were not subcontractors on the O*NET project. We may be the only such exceptions in this book. The first author was the technical advisor for the U.S. Department of Labor (DOL) on the O*NET project, whereas the other two authors were not previously involved in any capacity. As such, our opinions are independent and perhaps more impartial in some ways. This compels us to offer some critique, along with the many accolades, and to raise some issues that were not addressed.

## THE THEORETICAL IMPORTANCE OF O*NET

### Develops Job Analysis Theory

The O*NET is the most important theoretical development in job analysis in recent times. Job analysis has not traditionally been considered a strongly theoretical area of research. In fact, it has often been considered rather atheoretical, consisting largely of techniques and loosely integrated terminology. Accordingly, the content model and its associated descriptors is a significant contribution to theory in the field of job analysis.

The content model was conceived by the Advisory Panel for the Dictionary of Occupational Titles (APDOT), especially Ken Pearlman, Marilyn Gowing, and Anita Lancaster. We owe a great deal of thanks to their insights. The model was then brought to life through the efforts of the editors of this book and their many associates, as reflected in the writings by the authors of the previous chapters. They both filled out and operationalized the general concept and made it a reality. Their efforts have been outstanding.

As a model or preliminary theory, the content model does many things. It provides a comprehensive, and perhaps nearly exhaustive, listing of all the possible descriptors of occupations and workers. Furthermore, the descriptors are not merely lists but taxonomies of conceptually independent and theoretically grounded constructs that fully delineate each descriptor domain. The model also depicts the hierarchical relationships among the descriptors by showing how lower level (and more specific) constructs relate to higher level (and more general) constructs.

### Synthesizes Job Analysis Research

The O*NET reflects the cumulative knowledge of more than 50 years of research on job analysis. The project was specifically commissioned with the goal of amassing all the current knowledge on job analysis, both theoretically and methodologically, and then reflecting the sum of all of that knowledge in the design of the O*NET. As is readily apparent from the citations in this book, a huge amount of literature provided input to the descriptors and methodology chosen. If a relevant citation is not included, it is probably because space did not allow it rather than because it was not considered.

It is no surprise that the people selected to lead this project included many researchers whose life's work has been devoted to determining taxonomies of human performance or job analysis measurement. In fact, all of the contractors and the various advisors on this project have substantial records of contributions to job analysis research, the details of which are too numerous to mention here.

## Supported by Data

The empirical results provide solid support for O*NET. The contractors (i.e., the authors of the other chapters) are obviously very enthusiastic about the success of the O*NET project, and it shows in their conclusions. Looking beyond that, it is our independent conclusion that the empirical results generally do provide good support for the system. Specifically, with some exceptions, the measures turned out to be reasonably reliable for job analysis instruments, the measures were able to distinguish well among different occupations, and the factorial dimensionality of the descriptor taxonomies made reasonable sense in terms of rational appraisal and past research.

## Sets New Standard for Job Analysis

O*NET will set the standard for job analysis for years to come. This is perhaps the greatest implication of the project. It will likely become a widely used database and methodology in the field. It may even become the standard of excellence against which other approaches are compared. We draw this conclusion for several reasons. First, as noted above, it represents a sort of "best practices" when it comes to job analysis, both in terms of reflecting the collective knowledge of the field and in terms of its sheer comprehensiveness. That is, you cannot disagree with it, because it includes everything. Second, like the *Dictionary of Occupational Titles* (DOT) before it, the O*NET will be used by every government agency as the primary source of occupational information and classification (as explained elsewhere in this book). Partly because of its widespread governmental use, it will have a great impact on private sector research and practice as well. Third, unlike the DOT, the O*NET provides a highly usable and inexpensive methodology for analyzing jobs. The structured self-report questionnaire format of the rating scales in the O*NET are much easier to use than the analyst-based and largely narrative format of the DOT. Because of its government funding and sponsorship, the O*NET instruments and data are both available and encouraged for use by the general public.

## SOME CAVEATS

Before we become too confident of O*NET's wonderful achievements, we must note some important caveats. We describe these caveats more as "sobering realities" than criticisms because they typically are not the fault of the contractors but are instead limitations due to the current state-of-the-art in job analysis research or due to factors beyond the contractors' control.

## Theoretical Status

The content model is not yet a theory. At this point, the content model is little more than a framework of relevant variables. Although it is fairly comprehensive, it still lacks all of the other attributes of a theory. For example, it does not specify relationships among the domains of descriptors, it does not describe any antecedents or consequences of the descriptors, and it does not make any testable hypotheses. It is an excellent start, but only that. It must be much more fully developed before it can be considered a theory of job analysis.

## Low Response Rates

The low response rates are problematic. The plural term "rates" is used because there are many ways to calculate the response rate in this project and there were several different data collections. Nevertheless, one must conclude that low response rates (such as 16% for the total mailout of employees) are problematic. The chapter on the research methods documents the response rates and does an excellent job of trying to explain them. Many ideas emerged as to how the response rates might be increased. We favor those that involve reducing the prohibitive length of the questionnaires, somehow avoiding the "gatekeeper problem," providing meaningful incentives, and developing a mixed strategy in which a variety of different data collection approaches might be used, based on the occupation, the setting, and the opportunities available. Regardless of the approach, the response rate problem is a major impediment to realizing O*NET's full potential.

## Sample Inclusiveness

The current incumbent-based sample contains only a small number of occupations. This is due, in part, to the low response rate, but it creates two additional sobering realities. First, many of the key analyses are based on $n = 29$ occupations. This violates the rules of thumb for required sample-to-item ratios. We realize that these 29 occupation-level data points are based on the aggregation of a sample of more than 2,000 respondents, and thus are much more stable than individual-level data. Nevertheless, the results must be viewed with caution until much more data are collected.

Second, with data collected on only 29 out of more than 1,000 occupations, we still have a long way to go before the O*NET database is adequate for operational use. This is a major data collection effort that is far from complete. Although the analyst-based data can be used to fill in for some short-term purposes, they do not provide a long-term solution to the need for incumbent-based data.

## OTHER THEORETICAL ISSUES

This section is devoted to a collection of issues that have three things in common. First, they are somewhat theoretical in nature. Second, they have not been fully discussed elsewhere in this book. Third, they are neither strengths nor weaknesses of O*NET per se. They apply to O*NET, but they also apply to the entire enterprise of job analysis research.

### Common Language in Job Analysis?

It may be time for a common language in job analysis (Campion, 1995a). Common language is important to the development of science because it promotes unambiguous communication of concepts and ideas. The key philosopher of science who first discussed this issue was Thomas S. Kuhn (1970). Simply put, he said that individuals in different paradigms (e.g., disciplines) find it difficult (if not impossible) to communicate because they do not speak the same language. Research programs develop and proceed with little awareness of others' efforts, in part because a common language does not exist.

There are good examples of the beneficial effects of common language in other fields. For example, in chemistry they have the periodic table, as well as common symbols for expressing equations. In psychology, the *Diagnostic and Statistical Manual of Mental Disorders* (American Psychiatric Association, 1994) is used for diagnosing mental health problems in clinical settings. The field of statistics also uses a fair amount of common language and symbolism.

There are examples of common language in every science. A key purpose of the scientific process is the development of concepts and terminology. They not only reflect key ideas in that science, but they promote efficient communication through common usage. The key question is not whether a particular field of scientific investigation should have a common language, but when is it ready to have a truly common language?

The question of readiness depends on several factors. First, it depends on whether there has been sufficient research to define enough terms to enable a common language. This is an issue of not only the number of terms but also the degree of research proof for the value of the constructs to which the terms refer.

Second, it depends on whether different researchers are ready to accept the common language. This is a function of many factors, including the usefulness of the common language, the agreement among re-

searchers within the field on the common language, the degree to which institutions (e.g., publication outlets) require the use of the common language, and other factors.

Third, it depends on whether the enhanced clarity of communication made possible by common language outweighs the stifling effects common language may have on creativity. Common language is a form of standardization, thus limiting the pursuit of new ways of conceptualizing a field. If a science standardizes its language prematurely, it may retard rather than promote the advancement of the science.

The DOT itself was a sort of common language, and that is probably one reason it had such an impact on the field of occupational analysis. It gave each job an "official" title, it described the tasks in a standardized manner, and it measured the job requirements on a common set of scales. The O*NET is an important opportunity to promote common language again in the field of occupational analysis.

### Benefits of a Common Language

There are many obvious benefits of common language in this context:

- All the many different users of the O*NET will be able to communicate with one another (e.g., employers, job candidates, vocational counselors, rehabilitation counselors, occupational analysts, labor market analysts, trainers, policy planners, and others). In fact, due to this diversity of users, a common language is especially important. Without it, an integrated system of occupational information to match people with jobs may have little realized value.
- Common language will allow computerization of the information. If the same terms are used, then the computer can easily link huge databases to make vast amounts of occupational information easily available to large numbers of people for multiple purposes.
- Common language would provide integration across government projects and between the public and private sectors. This would promote efficiencies by encouraging synergistic partnerships and avoiding duplication of effort.
- Common language in the form of the O*NET might also spread to research and practice outside the government, just as the DOT did in the past.

### Reasons for Adopting O*NET as the Common Language

There are many factors working for the adoption of the O*NET as a common language for describing occupations.

- There is some precedent established for a common occupational language by the DOT. Many people are used to a standardized terminology in this context.

- Use of the O*NET language will be required if people want to take advantage of this system. This applies more to those who have no other choice but to use the O*NET (e.g., employment service counselors, candidates using government services, etc.) than to others who may have alternatives (e.g., employers, labor market analysts, etc.).
- Most of the descriptors in the O*NET are supported by substantial research on job analysis. Thus, they already enjoy some familiarity and acceptance by the job analysis community of users.
- Some key linkages have already been established between the O*NET and other related governmental initiatives.

### Reasons for Not Adopting O*NET as the Common Language

There are also a number of factors working against the adoption of the O*NET as a common language for describing occupations.

- There are more choices today than when the DOT was developed. At that time, the field of job analysis was not very well developed. Today, there are many more alternatives in terms of job analysis instruments and taxonomies. These alternatives are widely accessible from either the extensive published literature or the large number of consulting firms that sell such systems.
- There is not a consensus in the field of job analysis today on common language. Although the O*NET adopted some of the most popular terminology in the field today, there are still large numbers of scientists and practitioners who could offer some evidence and substantial opinion in support of language other than that used in the O*NET. That is, some choices had to be made in the development of the O*NET, and others in the field of job analysis might not agree with those choices.
- Potential users of the O*NET are numerous and highly diverse. Encouraging any large and diverse group to use the same system is difficult.
- The users do not all share a common discipline that might have laid the groundwork for a common language. The users include many people who have some training in occupational analysis, but they also include counselors with training in other areas of psychology, labor market analysts with training in economics, planners and other users with training in completely different areas, and many lay-persons without any professional training.

The bottom line, however, is that O*NET provides a wonderful opportunity to adopt a common language for occupational analysis. The promotion of O*NET as a common language should be encouraged.

### O*NET and High Performance Organizations

Although O*NET is a job analysis database and not an organization analysis database, it may help us understand high performance practices (HPPs) in organizations. One of the goals in the development of the organizational context descriptors of O*NET was to collect information on HPPs. According to a DOL report (1993a), high performance organizations combine innovative human resource practices with organizational structures that facilitate employee involvement and flexibility, in order to adapt effectively to highly competitive business environments. The relationship between human resource practices and organizational performance is of great interest to practitioners and academics alike. A former Secretary of Labor went so far as to argue that people-related practices may be the only source of sustainable competitive advantage (Reich, 1990).

In this section, we first briefly review both theoretical and empirical work linking human resource practices to competitive advantages. Then, the potential contribution of O*NET to this field of inquiry is considered.

Many theoretical writings support the assertion that organizations can gain and maintain competitive advantages through effective human resource practices (Barney, 1991; Jackson & Schuler, 1995; Lengnick-Hall & Lengnick-Hall, 1988; Snell, Youndt, & Wright, 1996; Wright & McMahan, 1992). For example, the typology articulated by Barney (1991) describes three categories of firm capital: physical, organizational, and human. Any of these types of resources can be a source of sustained competitive advantage as long as it is valuable, rare, imperfectly imitable, and no strategically equivalent substitutes exist. Human resource practices can be selected that add firm-specific value. For example, when employees are molded within the company instead of being purchased ready-made in the labor market, they are both less likely to leave the organization and more difficult for other firms to duplicate. Another overriding feature of these typologies is that they emphasize the critical and often neglected link between human resource practices and organizational goals.

The relationship between human resource practices and organizational performance has been demonstrated in several studies. For example, Terpstra and Rozell (1993) studied the use of five staffing practices: the use of follow-up studies of recruiting sources to determine the best sources of high-performing employees; the use of validation studies of selection systems; the use of structured interviews for selection; the use of cognitive aptitude tests for selection; and the use of biographical information for selection. The results indicated that the staffing practices were associated with higher annual profit, profit growth, and overall performance.

Another study by Huselid (1995) used survey data and publicly available financial figures to ascertain the relationship between high-performance work practices (as defined by DOL) and organizational performance and effectiveness. Results showed that a one standard deviation increase in HPPs was associated with a 7% relative decrease in turnover, and per-employee increases of $27,000 in sales, $19,000 in market value, and $4,000 in profits.

It must be kept in mind that any research using cross-sectional data should be interpreted with caution, as association does not prove causality. It is entirely possible (and perhaps likely) that some HPPs are associated with successful organizations simply because those organizations can afford such practices. However, as Terpstra and Rozell (1993) argued, in light of the extensive literature documenting the effect of high-performance work practices on individual performance, it seems plausible that the causal chain begins with the adoption of such HPPs and then leads to increased organizational performance.

In summary, the organizational context descriptors in O*NET will provide important preliminary information on the extent to which firms use innovative human resource practices. O*NET may also help identify the knowledges, skills, abilities, and other attributes prevalent in high performance organizations. Perhaps employees in these organizations differ from those in more traditional organizations, or perhaps certain employee attributes may be emphasized in successful companies. Such attribute differences may also mediate the relationship between human resource practices and high performance.

## Potential Sources of Inaccuracy

There are many potential sources of inaccuracy in job analysis data. O*NET is an impressive job analysis system in terms of both scope and rigor. There are, however, a number of unknowns with respect to the accuracy of job analysis data in general. The purpose of this section is to briefly describe a critique of the potential sources of inaccuracy in job analysis recently conducted by Morgeson and Campion (1997) and then to illustrate some of these sources on the O*NET system. These issues were partly addressed in chapter 15.

The core of Morgeson and Campion's (1997) framework is the identification of the psychological processes that underlie inaccuracy. Shown in the first column of Table 20-1, the framework consists of two primary sources of inaccuracy: social and cognitive. Social sources of inaccuracy are created by normative pressures from the social environment and reflect the fact that individuals reside in a social context. Cognitive sources, on the other hand, reflect problems that primarily result from the person as an information processor with distinct limitations. The social sources are further subdivided into inaccuracy due to

**TABLE 20-1**
**Social and Cognitive Sources of Inaccuracy and Their Likely Effect on Job Analysis Data**

| Source of inaccuracy | Likely effect on job analysis data | | | | | |
|---|---|---|---|---|---|---|
| | Interrater reliability | Interrater agreement | Discriminability between jobs | Dimensionality of factor structures | Mean ratings | Completeness of job information |
| *Social sources* | | | | | | |
| Social influence processes | | | | | | |
| 1. Conformity pressures | X | X | | | | |
| 2. Extremity shifts | | X | | X | X | X |
| 3. Motivation loss | | | X | X | | X |
| Self-presentation processes | | | | | | |
| 4. Impression management | | | | | X | |
| 5. Social desirability | | | | | X | X |
| 6. Demand effects | | | X | | X | |
| *Cognitive sources* | | | | | | |
| Limitations in information processing | | | | | | |
| 7. Information overload | X | | X | X | | X |
| 8. Heuristics | | | X | X | X | X |
| 9. Categorization | | | X | X | | X |
| Biases in information processing | | | | | | |
| 10. Carelessness | X | | X | X | | |
| 11. Extraneous information | | | | | X | |
| 12. Inadequate information | X | | | | | X |
| 13. Order and contrast effects | | | | | | X |
| 14. Halo | | | | X | X | |
| 15. Leniency and severity | | | | X | X | |
| 16. Method effects | X[a] | | | X | | |

[a]Refers to internal consistency reliability in this case.

social influence versus self-presentation processes, whereas the cognitive sources are further subdivided into inaccuracy due to limitations versus biases in information processing. Nested within these are 16 psychological processes that constitute the specific sources of inaccuracy.

As noted in the chapter by Childs et al., the research design of the O*NET data collection does not allow a test of the presence or absence of these sources of inaccuracy. Thus, the discussion below is speculative. It asks, What data or methodologies in the O*NET project are consistent with (or might allow the operation of) these sources of inaccuracy? This analysis is only illustrative and not exhaustive. Several sources of inaccuracy that *could* operate in the O*NET data collection are discussed. Recognize that this discussion is not a critique of the O*NET system. We believe that O*NET is the state-of-the-art in job analysis. Our purpose is only to raise awareness of potential problems inherent in the entire job analysis measurement paradigm that exists today.

### Impression Management

One source of inaccuracy that is likely to occur in job analysis is impression management, which refers to people attempting to present themselves in a favorable light (Schlenker, 1980). Impression management is more likely to occur during a job analysis data collection when people are encouraged to self-monitor (as incumbents are when describing their jobs), when the audience is high status (as when a management-sponsored study, such as a job analysis, is conducted), when the situation is evaluative in nature (as when a person's own job is being analyzed), and when there is some degree of ambiguity concerning the true state of affairs (as is true by definition in job analysis). A common finding across O*NET descriptor categories is that incumbents rated their jobs more highly than did analysts. These differences were quite large, averaging about 1 scale point. Findings such as these are consistent with an impression-management effect because incumbents are more likely than analysts to inflate their responses.

### Socially Desirable Responses

These findings are also consistent with socially desirable responding (Marlowe & Crowne, 1961). In attempting to gain the approval of others (e.g., researchers, supervisors, senior managers), incumbents may distort responses in such a way as to portray their job as having relatively more socially desirable features. Again, the comparatively higher incumbent ratings are suggestive of this phenomenon because analysts are less likely to evidence socially desirable responding (Smith & Hakel, 1979). This source of inaccuracy is particularly likely when rating such desirable-sounding attributes as knowledges, skills, and abilities. Thus, it is noteworthy that the O*NET

data for incumbents showed higher mean levels compared with analysts' data for all these descriptor domains.

### Information Overload

Another source of inaccuracy likely to occur in job analysis is information overload, which occurs when individuals are confronted with large amounts of information or complex judgment tasks. There is evidence to suggest that when faced with such situations in job analysis contexts, respondents fail to make fine distinctions, in order to simplify the rating process (Friedman, 1990; Sanchez & Fraser, 1992). One common finding in the O*NET data that is consistent with this simplification process is that the various response scales are very highly correlated. It is common to find the Level and Importance scales correlated in the low .90s. Theoretically, these scales should be more independent. It is possible that incumbents sometimes simplify the rating process by giving the same response to each scale.

### Categorization

Categorization is another source of inaccuracy that refers to reliance on summary judgments about a job. It is likely to result when information-processing demands are high, when there is a small amount of information available, when information provided is category-consistent, or when respondents automatically process information. Analysts would be more likely to succumb to this problem than incumbents because they are less familiar with the jobs, and they are basing their judgments on the DOT narrative descriptions. They may rely more on simplifying heuristics by basing their ratings on general impressions of the job (e.g., overall complexity or status). One common effect of categorization is reduced dimensionality of factor structures. As the O*NET data demonstrate, analysts consistently produced less dimensionally complex factor structures than did incumbents (e.g., skills, knowledges, etc.).

### Method Effects

One final illustrative source of inaccuracy is *method effects*, which refer to the spurious covariation among responses that occurs when data are collected with the same instrument. This results in observed correlations reflecting both shared method variance and shared trait variance (Spector, 1992). Method effects are more likely when a common response format is used, the questionnaire is long, or items make very fine distinctions—all common methodologies in job analysis. Given the previous chapters' predominant findings of very large correlations among descriptors and relatively less complex factor structures than theoretically expected, it is likely that method effects occurred in the O*NET data to some degree.

This presentation of potential sources of inaccuracy is meant to challenge the thinking of future job analysis researchers. There is substantial evidence documenting the deleterious effects of each of these sources of inaccuracy in social and cognitive psychology. Thus, their operation in industrial psychology applications is likely. Historically, job analyses results have simply been assumed to be accurate. It may be time to question this assumption and devote more research to validating job analysis methodologies.

## Levels of Job Analysis Research

The O*NET project has expanded the levels of analysis in job analysis research. What is the appropriate level of analysis for job analysis? Obviously, it is the job, and also the occupation. However, O*NET has expanded the relevant levels of analysis to include not only the traditional individual level (e.g., skills and abilities) and the occupational level (e.g., education and licensure) but also the organizational level (e.g., formalization and centralization), the industry level (e.g., type of industry), and the economic level (e.g., labor market information). Unfortunately, there is a price for this expansion of the levels of analysis in terms of ambiguity in the meaningfulness of some of the data as occupational descriptors.

Traditionally, data are gathered at the individual incumbent or job level and then aggregated to the occupational level. Other times, the data are simply collected with reference to the occupational level. Differences are typically treated as random error and reduced through the aggregation process (Harvey, 1991b).

There must be both a conceptual and an empirical justification for aggregation (e.g., Glick, 1985; James, 1982). That is, it must make sense to aggregate, and the data must converge within an occupation. This is the case for most of the individual- or job-level domains in the content model (e.g., skills, knowledges, generalized work activities, abilities, etc.). Other domains explicitly involve the occupational level (e.g., education, training, experience, and licensure variables) or use the job as the frame of reference (e.g., work context variables).

On the other hand, some content model domains contain constructs that may be better theoretically articulated and empirically validated at levels of analysis other than the occupational level. For example, occupational interests and values, as well as work styles, have been typically conceptualized at only the individual level, with corresponding measurement instruments designed to measure individuals rather than occupations. Thus, it is not surprising that these descriptors demonstrated relatively lower levels of interrater reliability and differentiation among occupations when compared with the other descriptors.

Descriptors in the organizational context domain also contain constructs that are difficult to interpret at the occupational level. For example, culture is commonly recognized as an organizational-level variable (Schein, 1992). Such variables cannot logically differentiate among occupations within an organization, or show correspondence within an occupation across organizations. As another example, leadership is difficult to conceptualize at the occupational level. That is, although some researchers have suggested leadership is dyadic in nature (e.g., Dansereau, Graen, & Haga, 1975), others highlight the group-level effects (e.g., Fleishman, 1973), and still others have discussed more macro-organizational-level influences (e.g., Bass, 1985; Burns, 1978). None have suggested that it is meaningful at the occupational level. As a result, it is not surprising that organizational context variables were relatively less able to differentiate among occupations than the other descriptors.

This may be an area where the content model needs additional conceptual development. This further conceptualization ultimately may expand the levels of analysis relevant to occupational description.

## Job Analysis and the True Score Model

It may be time to revisit the applicability of the true-score model to job analysis research. The dominant paradigm in job analysis is that a "true score" exists for any particular occupation on any given descriptor. Because of this, it is assumed that measurement variation is error that can be reduced or eliminated through aggregation. Thus, reliable measurement is predicated on obtaining a reasonably large sample of respondents. O*NET also appears to be implicitly based on such assumptions. For example, it recognizes multiple sources of error, it uses averaged responses to calculate point estimates, it uses large numbers of raters to get accurate measures, and it estimates the reliability of its measures. These are all techniques characteristic of classical test theory and the true score model (Nunnally, 1978).

Although these assumptions are very applicable in many measurement contexts, perhaps the true score model should be questioned in occupational analysis. For example, some have suggested that conceptualizing jobs as static entities is no longer tenable given the dynamic nature of work settings and environments (Carson & Stewart, 1996). New innovations, such as organizing work around teams with only loosely defined tasks and responsibilities, seem to preclude the notion of single true scores for each descriptor. Others have found that as individuals work in a particular job, they perform different tasks (Borman, Dorsey, & Ackerman, 1992). This highlights the fact that jobs may change over time and leads to the question of how much variability can exist within an occupation before it is no longer considered a homogeneous entity. Relatedly, the notion of equifinality suggests that there are multiple ways to reach the same end. This is relevant to occupational analysis because there are different constellations of activities and tasks that make up the same occupation, and many may be equally effective. Finally, still others have suggested that the nature of work is changing (Howard, 1995a), which calls into question the very idea of an occupation.

As this brief review illustrates, there are many facts and recent developments that would seem at odds with the true score model. Future theorizing in job analysis might entertain alternatives that more accurately portray the nature of jobs. Generalizability theory (Cronbach, Gleser, Nanda, & Rajaratnam, 1972) is a viable alternative with its ability to segment sources of variance into effects due to descriptors, respondents, occupations, organizations, and other factors relevant to the job analysis context. The O*NET database, with its comprehensive descriptors, multiple respondents, and wide sampling of occupations and organizations, may be ideally positioned to inform the discussion.

## CONCLUSIONS

Government-sponsored projects are often criticized for not producing things of value or doing so very inefficiently. This project stands out as a shining counterexample. The O*NET serves many needs of many people, and it was developed fairly quickly and inexpensively. It is certain to provide many years of good service to the public, just as the DOT did. We would like to commend Donna Dye and the other DOL members for their vision, leadership, and support of this project.

# References

Abod, E. T., Gilbert, J. A., & Fleishman, E. A. (1996). *A job analysis method to assess the interpersonal requirements of work* [research report]. Bethesda, MD: Management Research Institute.

Ackerman, P. C. (1994). Typical intellectual engagement and personality: Reply to Rocklin. *Journal of Educational Psychology, 86,* 150–153.

Ackerman, P. L. (1987). Individual differences in skill learning: An integration of psychometric and information processing perspectives. *Psychological Bulletin, 102,* 3–27.

Ackerman, P. L. (1988). Determinants of individual differences during skill acquisition: Cognitive abilities and information processing. *Journal of Experimental Psychology: General, 117,* 288–318.

Advisory Panel for the Dictionary of Occupational Titles (APDOT). (1992). *Interim report.* Washington, DC: U.S. Department of Labor.

Advisory Panel for the Dictionary of Occupational Titles (APDOT). (1993). *The new DOT: A database of occupational titles for the twenty-first century* (Final report). Washington, DC: U.S. Employment Service, U.S. Department of Labor Employment and Training Administration.

American College Testing. (1993, August). Performing a national job analysis study: Overview of methodology and procedures. *Work Activities Survey, Form A and Form B.* Iowa City, IA: Author.

American College Testing. (1994). *The national job analysis study: Work activities survey.* Iowa City, IA: Author.

American Psychological Association. (1992). *Implications of cognitive psychology and cognitive task analysis for the revision of the Dictionary of Occupational Titles.* Washington, DC: Author.

Americans With Disabilities Act of 1990 (104 Stat. 328, 42 U.S.C. 12101).

Anderson, J. R. (1993). Problem solving and learning. *American Psychologist, 48,* 35–44.

Anderson, L. E. (1995). Education. In N. G. Peterson, M. D. Mumford, W. C. Borman, P. R. Jeanneret, & E. A. Fleishman (Eds.), *Development of prototype Occupational Information Network (O\*NET) content model* (pp. 5-1–5-12). Salt Lake City: Utah Department of Employment Security.

Arabie, P., & Hubert, L. J. (1992). Combinatorial data analysis. *Annual Review of Psychology, 43,* 169–203.

Arad, S., Hanson, M. A., & Schneider, R. J. (1996). Organizational context: Evidence for the reliability and validity of the organizational context measures. In N. G. Peterson, M. D. Mumford, W. C. Borman, P. R. Jeanneret, & E. A. Fleishman (Eds.), *O\*NET final technical report.* Salt Lake City: Utah Department of Employment Security.

Arad, S., Schneider, R. J., & Hanson, M. A. (1995). Organizational context. In N. G. Peterson, M. D. Mumford, W. C. Borman, P. R. Jeanneret, & E. A. Fleishman (Eds.), *Development of prototype Occupational Information Network (O\*NET) content model.* Salt Lake City: Utah Department of Employment Security.

Arlin, P. K. (1990). Wisdom: The art of problem finding. In R. J. Sternberg (Ed.), *Wisdom: Its nature, origins, and development* (pp. 230–243). New York: Cambridge University Press.

Arthur, J. B. (1994). Effects of human resource systems on manufacturing performance and turnover. *Academy of Management Journal, 37*(3), 670–687.

Arvey, R. D., Maxwell, S. E., Gutenberg, R. L., & Camp, C. (1981). Detecting job differences: A Monte Carlo study. *Personnel Psychology, 34,* 709–730.

Ash, R. A. (1988). Job analysis in the world of work. In S. Gael (Ed.), *The job analysis handbook for business, government, and industry* (pp. 3–13). New York: Wiley.

Ash, R. A., Johnson, J. C., Levine, E. L., & McDaniel, M. A. (1989). Job applicant and work experience evaluation in personnel selection. In K. M. Roland & G. Ferris (Eds.), *Research in personnel and human resources management: Vol. 7.* Greenwich, CT: JAI Press.

Baer, J. M. (1988). Long-term effects of creativity training with middle school students. *Journal of Early Adolescence, 8,* 183–193.

Ballentine, R. D., Cunningham, J. W., & Wimpee, W. E. (1992). Air Force enlisted job clusters: An exploration in numerical job classification. *Military Psychology, 4,* 87–102.

Balma, M. J. (1959). The concept of synthetic validity. *Personnel Psychology, 12,* 395–396.

Bandura, A., & Cervone, D. (1983). Self-evaluative and self-efficacy mechanisms governing the motivational effects of goal systems. *Journal of Personality and Social Psychology, 45,* 1017–1028.

Barney, J. (1991). Firm resources and sustained competitive advantage. *Journal of Management, 17,* 99–120.

Barnhart P. (1994). *Guide to National Professional Certification Programs.* Amherst, MA: Human Resource Development Press.

Barrick, M. R., & Mount, M. K. (1991). The big five personality dimensions and job performance: A meta-analysis. *Personnel Psychology, 44,* 1–26.

Barsalou, L. W. (1989). *Diagnosis and repair of engine malfunctions.* Unpublished report, Georgia Institute of Technology.

Bass, B. M. (1985). *Leadership and performance beyond expectations.* New York: Free Press.

Bass, B. M. (1994). Transformational leadership and team and organizational decision making. In B. M. Bass & B. J. Avolio (Eds.), *Improving organizational effectiveness through transformational leadership.* Thousand Oaks, CA: Sage.

Baughman, W. A., Costanza, D. P., Haucke, M. H. P., Mumford, M. D., Stone, L. A., Threlfall, K. V., & Fleishman, E. A. (1995). *Developing job families on the basis of ability and knowledge requirement profiles: Development of career specialty clusters* (Report to a Department of Defense Agency). Bethesda, MD: Management Research Institute.

Baughman, W. A., & Mumford, M. D. (1995). Process-analytic models of creative capacities. *Creativity Research Journal, 8,* 37–62.

Bayer, A. H. (1992). *Factors affecting human judgments regarding the ability requirements of jobs.* Unpublished doctoral dissertation, Fairfax, VA, George Mason University.

Beehr, T. A., Walsh, J. T., & Taber, T. D. (1976). Relationship of stress to individually and organizationally valued states: Higher order needs as a moderator. *Journal of Applied Psychology, 61,* 41–47.

Bentz, V. J. (1985). *A view from the top: A 30-year perspective of research devoted to the discovery, description, and prediction of executive behavior.* Paper presented at the annual meeting of the American Psychological Association, Los Angeles.

Berliner, C. D., Angell, D., & Shearer, J. W. (1964, August). *Behaviors, measures, and instruments for performance evaluation in simulated environments.* Symposium and workshop on the Quantification of Human Performance, Albuquerque, NM.

Berryman, S. E., & Bailey, T. R. (1992). *The double helix of education and the economy.* New York: The Institute on Education and the Economy, Teachers College, Columbia University.

Blau, P. M. (1974). *On the nature of organizations.* New York: Wiley.

Blau, P. M., & Schoenherr, R. A. (1971). *The structure of organizations.* New York: Basic Books.

Bloom, B. S. (1956). *Taxonomy of educational objectives: Cognitive domain, psychomotor domain, affective domain.* New York: David McKay.

Boese, R. R., & Cunningham, J. W. (1975). *Systematically derived dimensions of human work* (Ergometric Research and Development Series Rep. No. 14). Raleigh, NC: Center for Occupational Education, North Carolina State University.

Borgen, F. H. (1988). Occupational reinforcer patters. In S. Gael, *The job analysis handbook for business, industry, and government: Vol. 2* (pp. 902–916). New York: Wiley.

Borgen, F. H., Weiss, D. J., Tinsley, H. E. A., Dawis, R. V., & Lofquist, L. H. (1968). The measurement of occupational reinforcer patterns. *Minnesota Studies in Vocational Rehabilitation, XXV.* Minneapolis: University of Minnesota.

Borman, W. C., Ackerman, L. D., Kubisiak, V. C., & Quigley, A. M. (1994). *Development of a performance rating program in support of Department of Labor test validation research* (Department of Labor Tech. Rep.). Tampa: University of South Florida.

Borman, W. C., & Brush, D. H. (1993). More progress toward a taxonomy of managerial performance requirements. *Human Performance, 6,* 1–21.

Borman, W. C., Dorsey, D., & Ackerman, L. (1992). Time-spent responses as time allocation strategies: Relations with sales performance in a stockbroker sample. *Personnel Psychology, 45,* 763–777.

Borman, W. C., Hanson, M. A., & Hedge, J. W. (1997). Personnel selection. *Annual Review of Psychology, 48,* 299–337.

Borman, W. C., & Motowidlo, S. J. (1993). Expanding the criterion domain to include elements of contextual performance. In N. Schmitt & W. C. Borman (Eds.), *Personnel selection in organizations* (pp. 71–98). San Francisco: Jossey-Bass.

Botterbusch, K. F. (1992). *Suggestions for revision of the Dictionary of Occupational Titles* (Tech. Rep. Contract 92-465), Salt Lake City: Utah Department of Employment Security.

Boyatzis, R. E. (1982). *The competent manager: A model for effective performance.* New York: Wiley-Interscience.

Brown, C. (1990). Firms' choice of method of pay. *Industrial and Labor Relations Review, 40,* 165S–182S.

Bull, K. S., Montgomery, D., & Baloche, L. (1995). Teaching creativity at the college level: A synthesis of curricular components perceived as important by instructors. *Creativity Research Journal, 8,* 83–90.

Burns, J. M. (1978). *Leadership.* New York: Harper Torchbooks.

Cain, P. S., & Treiman, D. J. (1981). The Dictionary of Occupational Titles as a source of occupational data. *American Sociological Review, 46,* 253–278.

Camara, W. J. (1992). *Implications of cognitive psychology and cognitive task analysis for the revision of the Dictionary of Occupational Titles.* Washington, DC: American Psychological Association.

Camara, W. J., & Schneider, D. L. (1994). Integrity tests: Facts and unresolved issues. *American Psychologist, 49,* 112–119.

Campbell, D. P. (1971). *Handbook for the Strong Vocational Interest Blank.* Stanford, CA: Stanford University.

Campbell, J., Ford, P., Rumsey, M., Pulakos, E., Borman, W., Felker, D., De Vera, M., & Riegelhaupt, B. (1990). Development of multiple job performance measures in a representative sample of jobs. *Personnel Psychology, 43,* 277–300.

Campbell, J. P. (1977). On the nature of organizational effectiveness. In P. S. Goodman, J. M. Pennings, & Associates (Eds.), *New perspectives on organizational effectiveness* (pp. 13–55). San Francisco: Jossey-Bass.

Campbell, J. P. (1988). Training design for performance improvement. In J. P. Campbell, R. J. Campbell, & Associates (Eds.), *Productivity in organizations: New perspectives from industrial and organizational psychology* (pp. 177–215). San Francisco: Jossey-Bass.

Campbell, J. P. (1990a). An overview of the Army selection and classification project (Project A). *Personnel Psychology, 43,* 231–239.

Campbell, J. P. (1990b). Modeling the performance prediction problem in industrial and organizational psychology. In M. D. Dunnette & L. M. Hough (Eds.), *Handbook of industrial and organizational psychology: Vol. 2* (2nd ed., pp. 687–732). Palo Alto, CA: Consulting Psychologists Press.

Campbell, J. P. (1993). *Classifying jobs.* Paper prepared for the U.S. Department of Labor, Washington, DC.

Campbell, J. P., McCloy, R. A., Oppler, S. H., & Sager, C. E. (1993). A theory of performance. In R. Schmitt & W. C. Borman (Eds.), *Personnel selection in organizations* (pp. 35–70). San Francisco: Jossey-Bass.

Campbell, J. P., McHenry, J. J., & Wise, L. L. (1990). Modeling job performance in a population of jobs. *Personnel Psychology, 43,* 313–333.

Campion, M. A. (1992). *Job analysis for the proposed revision of the Dictionary of Occupational Titles.* East Lafayette, IN: Author.

Campion, M. A. (1995a). *Promoting the use of common language for occupational information.* Concept paper written for the U.S. Department of Labor, Washington, DC.

Campion, M. A. (1995b). *Some thoughts of developing a common language framework for describing jobs.* Washington, DC: U.S. Department of Labor.

Campion, M., Gowing, M., Lancaster, A., & Pearlman, K. (1994). *United States Department of Labor Database of Occupational Titles reinvention project: DOT transition team final report.* Washington, DC: United States Office of Personnel Management.

Cantor, R., & Kihlstrom, J. F. (1987). *Personality and social intelligence.* Englewood Cliffs, NJ: Prentice-Hall.

Cappelli, P. (1995). *Conceptual issues in developing a system for classifying occupations* (prepared for U.S. Department of Labor, Washington, DC). Unpublished manuscript.

Carroll, J. B. (1976). Psychomotor tests as cognitive tasks: A new "structure of intellect." In L. Resnick (Ed.), *The nature of intelligence* (pp. 27–56). Hillsdale, NJ: Erlbaum.

Carroll, J. B. (1993). Test theory and the behavioral scaling of test performance. In N. Frederiksen, R. J. Mislevy, & I. I. Bejar (Eds.), *Test theory for a new generation of tests* (pp. 297–322). Hillsdale, NJ: Erlbaum.

Carson, K. P., & Stewart, G. L. (1996). Job analysis and the sociotechnical approach to quality: A critical examination. *Journal of Quality Management, 1,* 49–65.

Cascio, W. F. (1987). *Applied psychology in personnel management* (3rd ed.). Englewood Cliffs, NJ: Prentice-Hall.

Cascio, W. F. (1995). Whither industrial and organizational psychology in a changing world of work? *American Psychologist, 50,* 928–939.

Cascio, W. F., Sacket, P., & Schmitt, N. (1991). *Use and validation of the Career Qualification Battery* (Report to the National Security Agency).

Cascio, W. F., & Zammuto, R. F. (1987). *Societal trends and staffing policies.* Denver: University of Colorado.

Cattell, R. B. (1943). The description of personality: Basic traits resolved into clusters. *Journal of Abnormal and Social Psychology, 38,* 476–506.

Cattell, R. B. (1945). The description of personality: Principles and findings in a factor analysis. *American Journal of Psychology, 58,* 69–90.

Cattell, R. B. (1946). *The description and measurement of personality.* Yonkers, NY: World Book.

Cattell, R. B. (1947). Confirmation and clarification of primary personality factors. *Psychometrika, 12,* 197–220.

Cattell, R. B. (1971). *Abilities: Their structure, growth, and action.* Boston: Houghton Mifflin.

Cattell, R. B., & Horn, J. L. (1978). A check on the theory of fluid and crystallized intelligence with description of new subtest designs. *Journal of Educational Measurement, 15,* 139–164.

Chaffee, J. (1994). *Critical thinking at Laguardia College.* Washington, DC: National Center for Educational Statistics.

Chalupsky, A. B. (1962). Comparative factor analyses of clerical jobs. *Journal of Applied Psychology, 46,* 62–66.

Champagne, J. E., & McCormick, E. J. (1964). *An investigation of the use of worker-oriented job variables in job evaluation* (Rpt. No. 7). Lafayette, IN: Purdue University, Occupational Research Center.

Chase, W. G., & Simon, H. A. (1973). The mind's eye in chess. In W. G. Chase (Ed.), *Visual information processing* (pp. 215–281). New York: Academic Press.

Chi, M. T. H., Bassock, M., Lewis, M. W., Reimann, P., & Glaser, R. (1989). Self explanations: How students study and use examples in learning to solve problems. *Cognitive Science, 13,* 145–182.

Chi, M. T. H., & Glaser, R. (1985). *Problem solving ability* (Report No. LRDC-1985/6 for the Office of Naval Research, Washington, DC). Pittsburgh, PA: Learning Research and Development Center, University of Pittsburgh.

Chi, M. T., Glaser, R., & Rees, E. (1983). Expertise in problem solving. In R. Sternberg (Ed.), *Advances in the psychology of human intelligence.* Hillsdale, NJ: Erlbaum.

Child, J. (1972). Organizational structure, environment, and performance: The role of strategic choice. *Sociology, 6,* 1–22.

Childs, R. A., & Whetzel, D. L. (1995). Scaling studies. In *Technical memorandum: Tryout of O*NET questionnaires and anchor scaling.* Washington, DC: American Institutes for Research.

Clifton, T. C., Connelly, M. S., Reiter-Palmon, R., & Mumford, M. D. (1991). *Exploring the C Division regional sales manager position: Summary of subject matter expert meetings.* Fairfax, VA: George Mason University, Center for Behavioral and Cognitive Studies.

Clinton, W., & Gore, A. (1992). *Putting people first: How we can all change America.* New York: Times Books.

Colbert, G. A., & Taylor, L. R. (1978). Empirically derived job families as a foundation for the study of validity generalization: Study III. Generalization of selection test validity. *Personnel Psychology, 31,* 355–364.

Colihan, J., & Burger, G. K. (1995). Constructing job families: An analysis of quantitative techniques used for grouping jobs. *Personnel Psychology, 48,* 563–586.

Conger, J. A., & Kanungo, R. (1987). Toward a behavioral theory of charismatic leadership in organizational settings. *Academy of Management Review, 12,* 637–647.

Commission on Workforce Quality and Labor Market Efficiency. (1989). *Investing in people: A strategy to address America's workforce crisis.* Washington, DC: U.S. Department of Labor.

Connelly, M. S., Reiter-Palmon, R., Clifton, T. C., & Mumford, M. D. (1991). *Exploring the C&I Division regional manager position: Summary of subject matter expert meetings.* Fairfax, VA: George Mason University, Center for Behavioral and Cognitive Studies.

Coombs, C. H., & Satter, G. A. (1949). A factorial approach to job families. *Psychometrika, 14,* 33–42.

Cooper, C. L. (1987). The experience and management of stress: Job and organizational determinants. In A. W. Riley & S. J. Zaccaro (Eds.), *Occupational stress and organizational effectiveness.* New York: Praeger.

Cooper, C. L., & Payne, R. (1979). *Stress at work.* New York: Wiley.

Cooper, M. A., Schemmer, F. M., Fleishman, E. A., Yarkin-Levin, K., Harding, F. D., & McNelis, J. (1987). *Task analysis of Navy and Marine Corps occupations: Taxonomic basis for evaluating CW antidote/pretreatment drugs* (Tech. Rep. 3130). Bethesda, MD: Advanced Research Resources Organization.

Cooper, M. A., Schemmer, F. M., Gebhardt, D. L., Marshall-Mies, J., & Fleishman, E. A. (1982). *Development and validation of physical ability tests for jobs in the electric power industry* (ARRO Final Rep. #3056). Bethesda, MD: Advanced Research Resources Organization.

Cooper, M. A., Schemmer, F. M., Jennings, M., & Korotkin, A. L. (1983). *Developing selection standards for Federal Bureau of Investigation special agents.* Bethesda, MD: Advanced Research Resources Organization.

Cornelius, E. T., III, Carron, T. J., & Collins, M. N. (1979). Job analysis models and job classification. *Personnel Psychology, 32,* 693–707.

Cornelius, E. T., III, Denisi, A. S., & Blencoe, A. G. (1984). Expert and naive raters using the PAQ: Does it matter? *Personnel Psychology, 37,* 453–464.

Cornelius, E. T., III, & Hakel, M. D. (1978). *A study to develop an improved enlisted performance evaluation system for the U.S. Coast Guard.* Washington, DC: Department of Transportation, United States Coast Guard.

Cornelius, E. T., III, Hakel, M. D., & Sackett, P. R. (1979). A methodological approach to job classification for performance appraisal purposes. *Personnel Psychology, 32,* 283–297.

Corts, D. B., & Gowing, M. K. (1992). *Dimensions of effective behavior: executives, managers, and supervisors.* Washington, DC: U.S. Office of Personnel Management, Personnel Research and Development.

Costa, P. T., Jr., & McCrae, R. R. (1992a). *NEO-PI-R professional manual.* Odessa, FL: Psychological Assessment Resources.

Costa, P. T., Jr., & McCrae, R. R. (1992b). *Revised NEO Personality Inventory (NEO-PI-R) and NEO Five-Factor Inventory (NEO-FFI) professional manual.* Odessa, FL: Psychological Assessment Resources.

Costa, P. T., Jr., & McCrae, R. R. (in press). Domains and facets: Hierarchical personality assessment using the revised NEO Personality Inventory. *Journal of Personality Assessment.*

Costa, P. T., Jr., McCrae, R. R., & Dye, D. A. (1991). Facet scales for Agreeableness and Conscientiousness: A revision of the NEO Personality Inventory. *Personality and Individual Differences, 12,* 887–898.

Costanza, D. P., Baughman, W., Mumford, M. D., Hauke, M., Stone, L., Threlfall, V., & Fleishman, E. A. (1995). *Developing job families on the basis of ability and knowledge requirements profiles.* Bethesda, MD: Management Research Institute.

Costanza, D. P., & Fleishman, E. A. (1992a). *Development of a taxonomy of job knowledge requirements: Preliminary definitions and rating scales* (CBCS Research Rep.). Fairfax, VA: George Mason University, Center for Behavioral and Cognitive Studies.

Costanza, D. P., & Fleishman, E. A. (1992b). *Fleishman Job Analysis Survey* (Part III–Knowledge Requirements). Bethesda, MD: Management Research Institute.

Covington, M. V. (1987). Instruction in problem solving and planning. In S. L. Friedman, E. K. Scholnick, & R. R. Cocking (Eds.), *Blueprints for thinking: The role of planning in cognitive development* (pp. 469–511). Cambridge, England: Cambridge University Press.

Cramér, H. (1946). *Mathematical methods of statistics.* Princeton, NJ: Princeton University Press.

Crocker, L., & Algina, J. (1986). *Introduction to classical and modern test theory.* Fort Worth, TX: Harcourt Brace Jovanovich.

Cronbach, L. J. (1971). Test validation. In R. L. Thorndike (Ed.), *Educational measurement* (pp. 443–507). Washington, DC: American Council on Education.

Cronbach, L. J., & Gleser, G. C. (1953). Assessing similarity between profiles. *Psychological Bulletin, 50,* 456–473.

Cronbach, L. J., Gleser, G. C., Nanda, H., & Rajaratnam, N. (1972). *The dependability of behavioral measurements: Theory of generalizability for scores and profiles.* New York: Wiley.

Crowne, D. P., & Marlowe, D. (1964). *The approval motive: Studies in evaluative dependence.* New York: Wiley.

Cunningham, J. W. (1964). *Worker-oriented job variables: Their factor structure and use in determining job requirements.* Unpublished doctoral thesis, Purdue University, Lafayette, IN.

Cunningham, J. W. (1971). "Ergonometrics": A systematic approach to some educational problems. Raleigh, NC: Center for Occupational Education, North Carolina State University. In *JSAS Catalog of Selected Documents in Psychology, 1974, 4,* 144–145.

Cunningham, J. W. (1988). Occupation analysis inventory. In S. Gael, *The job analysis handbook for business, industry, and government, Vol. 2* (pp. 975–990). New York: Wiley.

Cunningham, J. W. (1996). Generic job descriptors: A likely direction in occupational analysis. *Military Psychology, 8(3),* 247–262.

Cunningham, J. W., & Ballentine, R. D. (1982). *The General Work Inventory.* Raleigh, NC: Authors.

Cunningham, J. W., Boese, R. R., Neeb, R. W., & Pass, J. J. (1983). Systematically derived work dimensions: Factor analyses of the Occupational Analysis Inventory. *Journal of Applied Psychology, 68,* 232–252.

Cunningham, J. W., Drewes, D. W., & Powell, T. E. (1995, April). *Framework for a revised Standard Occupational Classification (SOC).* Paper presented at the SOC Conference, Washington, DC.

Cunningham, J. W., & McCormick, E. J. (1964a). *Factor analyses of "worker-oriented" job variables* (Prepared for Office of Naval Research under contract Nonr-1100 (19), Rep. No. 4). Lafayette, IN: Purdue University, Occupational Research Center.

Cunningham, J. W., & McCormick, E. J. (1964b). *The experimental use of worker-oriented job variables in determining job requirements* (Prepared for Office of Naval Research under contract Nonr-1100 (19), Rep. No. 5). Lafayette, IN: Purdue University, Occupational Research Center.

Cunningham, J. W., Powell, T. E., Wimpee, W. E., Wilson, M. A., & Ballentine, R. D. (1996). Ability-requirement factors for general job elements. *Military Psychology, 8(3),* 219–234.

Cunningham, J. W., & Scott, B. M. (1988, August). The dimensionality of USES and OAI worker-oriented job variables. In P. D. Geyer & J. Hawk (Chairs.), *Occupational analysis and the Dictionary of Occupational Titles.* Symposium conducted at the 96th annual meeting of the American Psychological Association, Atlanta, GA.

Cunningham, J. W., & Wilson, M. A. (1993). *The functions of generalized work behaviors and nomothetic job descriptors in a national computerized occupational information and classification system.* Washington, DC: DOT Review.

Cunningham, J. W., Wimpee, W. E., & Ballentine, R. D. (1990). Some general dimensions of work among U.S. Air Force enlisted occupations. *Military Psychology, 2,* 33–45.

Cureton, E. E. (1951). Validity. In E. F. Lundquist (Ed.), *Educational measurement* (pp. 621–694). Washington, DC: American Council on Education.

Cyert, R., & March, J. (1963). *A behavioral theory of the firm.* Englewood Cliffs, NJ: Prentice-Hall.

Dalton, D. R., Todor, W., Spendolini, M. J., Fielding, G. J., & Porter, L. W. (1980). Organization structure and performance: A critical review. *Academy of Management Review, 5(1),* 49–64.

Dansereau, F., Graen, G., & Haga, W. J. (1975). A vertical dyad linkage approach to leadership within formal organizations: A longitudinal investigation of the role making process. *Organizational Behavior and Human Performance, 13,* 46–78.

Date, C. J. (1995). *An introduction to database systems* (6th ed.). Reading, MA: Addison Wesley.

Davidson, J. E. (1995). In R. J. Sternberg (Ed.), *The nature of insight.* Cambridge, MA: MIT Press.

Davis, S. M. (1987). *Future perfect.* Reading, MA: Addison Wesley.

Dawis, R. V. (1991). Vocational interests, values, and preferences. In M. D. Dunnette & L. M. Hough (Eds.), *Handbook of in-*

*dustrial and organizational psychology, Vol. 2* (2nd ed., pp. 833–872). Palo Alto, CA: Consulting Psychologists Press.

Dawis, R. V., & Lofquist, L. H. (1984). *A psychological theory of work adjustment: An individual-differences model and its applications.* Minneapolis: University of Minnesota Press.

Deal, T., & Kennedy, A. (1982). *Corporate cultures.* Reading, MA: Addison-Wesley.

DeNisi, A. S., & McCormick, E. J. (1974). *The cluster analysis of jobs based on data from the Position Analysis Questionnaire (PAQ)* (Tech. Rep. No. TR-7). Lafayette, IN: Purdue University, Department of Psychological Sciences.

Department of Labor, Employment and Training Administration. (1990). Dictionary of occupational titles, issue paper and initiative. *Federal Register, 55,* 32868–32871.

Dertouzos, M. L., Lester, R. K., & Solow, R. M. (1989). *Made in America: Regaining the reproductive edge.* Cambridge, MA: MIT Press.

Dickinson, A. M. (1977). *Development of a systematic procedure for the evaluation of employee job performance based on a structured job analysis questionnaire.* Unpublished master's thesis, Fairleigh Dickinson University, Madison, NJ.

Digman, J. M., & Takemoto-Chock, N. K. (1981). Factors in the natural language of personality: Re-analysis, comparison, and interpretation of six major studies. *Multivariate Behavioral Research, 16,* 149–170.

Dowell, B. E., & Wexley, K. N. (1978). Development of a work behavior taxonomy for first-line supervisors. *Journal of Applied Psychology, 63,* 563–572.

Drauden, G. (1988). Task inventory analysis in industry and the public sector. In S. Gael, *The job analysis handbook for business, industry, and government, Vol. 2* (pp. 1051–1071). New York: Wiley.

Drewes, D. W. (1993). *The role of general work activities in the DOT review.* Washington, DC: DOT Review.

Driskell, W. E., & Dittmar, M. J. (1993). *Methodology for identifying abilities for job classification.* Brooks Air Force Base, TX: Armstrong Laboratory, Air Force Systems Command.

Droege, R. C. (1988). Department of Labor job analysis methodology. In S. Gael, *The job analysis handbook for business, industry, and government, Vol. 2* (pp. 993–1018). New York: Wiley.

Drucker, P. (1994). Jobs and employment in a global economy. *Atlantic Monthly, 1,* 132–136.

Duncan, R. (1979). What is the right organization structure? *Organizational Dynamics, Winter,* 59–79.

Dunnette, M. D. (1976). Aptitudes, abilities, and skills. In M. D. Dunnette (Ed.), *Handbook of industrial and organizational psychology.* Chicago: Rand McNally College Publishing Co.

Dunnette, M. D., & Borman, W. C. (1979). Personnel selection and classification systems. *Annual Review of Psychology, 30,* 477–525.

Dweck, C. S. (1986). Motivational processes affecting learning. *American Psychologist, 41,* 1040–1048.

Dye, D. A., & Reck, M. (1988). *A literature review and meta-analysis of education as a predictor of job performance* (OPRD-88-9). Washington, DC: U.S. Office of Personnel Management.

Ekstrom, R. B., French, J. W., & Harman, H. H. (with Dirmen, D.). (1976). *Manual for kit of factor-referenced cognitive tests.* Princeton, NJ: Educational Testing Service.

Ekstrom, R. B., French, J. W., & Harman, H. H. (1979). Cognitive factors: Their identification and replication. *Multivariate Behavioral Research Monographs,* No. 79-2.

Ellig, B. R. (1985). *Compensation and benefits: Design and analysis.* Washington, DC: American Compensation Association.

Employment and Training Administration. (1997). *Strategic Plan FY 1997–FY 2002.* Washington, DC: U.S. Department of Labor.

Erez, M. (1977). Feedback: A necessary condition for the goal setting-performance relationship. *Journal of Applied Psychology, 62,* 624–627.

Ericsson, K. A., & Charness, N. (1994). Expert performance: Its structure and acquisition. *American Psychologist, 49(8),* 725–747.

Ericsson, K. A., & Faivre, I. A. (1988). What's exceptional about exceptional abilities? In I. K. Obler & D. Fein (Eds.), *The ex-*

*ceptional brain: Neuropsychology of talent and exceptional abilities* (pp. 436–473). New York: Guilford Press.

Ericsson, K. A., Krampe, R. Th., & Tesch-Romer, C. (1993). The role of deliberate practice in the acquisition of expert performance. *Psychological Review, 100,* 363–406.

Ericsson, K. A., & Simon, H. A. (1993). *Protocol analysis: Verbal reports as data* (rev. ed.). Cambridge, MA: MIT Press.

Ericsson, K. A., & Smith, J. (Eds.). (1991). *Toward a general theory of expertise: Prospects and limits.* Cambridge, England: Cambridge University Press.

Etzioni, A. (1964). *Modern organizations.* Englewood Cliffs, NJ: Prentice-Hall.

Evans, G. W., Johansson, G., & Carrere, S. (1994). Psychosocial factors and the physical environment: Inter-relations in the workplace. In C. L. Cooper & I. T. Robertson (Eds.), *International review of industrial and organizational psychology.* New York: Wiley.

Everitt, B. (1993). Cluster analysis (3rd ed.). New York: Halsted.

Feltovich, P. T., Spiro, R. T., & Coulson, R. L. (1993). Learning, teaching, and testing for complex conceptual understanding. In N. Friedrickson, R. J. Mislevy, & I. I. Bejar (Eds.), *Test theory for a new kind of test* (pp. 181–218). Hillsdale, NJ: Erlbaum.

Fine, S. A. (1988). *Functional job analysis scales: A desk aid.* Milwaukee, WI: Sidney A. Fine.

Finke, R. A., Wand, T. B., & Smith, S. M. (1992). *Creative cognition: Theory, research, and applications.* Cambridge, MA: MIT Press.

Flanagan, J. C. (1951). Defining the requirements of the executive's job. *Personnel, 28,* 28–35.

Fleishman, E. A. (1953a). The description of supervisory behavior. *Personnel Psychology, 37,* 1–6.

Fleishman, E. A. (1953b). Testing for psychomotor abilities by means of apparatus tests. *Psychological Bulletin, 50,* 241–262.

Fleishman, E. A. (1954). Dimensional analysis of psychomotor abilities. *Journal of Educational Psychology, 48,* 437–454.

Fleishman, E. A. (1957). A comparative study of aptitude patterns in unskilled and skilled psychomotor performance. *Journal of Applied Psychology, 41,* 263–272.

Fleishman, E. A. (1958). Dimensional analysis of movement reactions. *Journal of Experimental Psychology, 55,* 438–453.

Fleishman, E. A. (1964). *The structure and measurement of physical fitness.* Englewood Cliffs, NJ: Prentice Hall.

Fleishman, E. A. (1966). Human abilities and the acquisition of skill. In E. A. Bilodeau (Ed.), *Acquisition of skill.* New York: Academic Press.

Fleishman, E. A. (1967a). Development of a behavior taxonomy for describing human tasks: A correlational-experimental approach. *Journal of Applied Psychology, 51,* 1–10.

Fleishman, E. A. (1967b). Individual differences and motor learning. In R. M. Gagne (Ed.), *Learning and individual differences* (pp. 165–191). Columbus, OH: Charles Merrill.

Fleishman, E. A. (1972a). On the relation between abilities, learning, and human performance. *American Psychologist, 27,* 1017–1032.

Fleishman, E. A. (1972b). Structure and measurement of psychomotor abilities. In R. N. Singer (Ed.), *The psychomotor domain.* Philadelphia: Lea & Febinger.

Fleishman, E. A. (1973). Twenty years of consideration and structure. In E. A. Fleishman & J. G. Hunt (Eds.), *Current developments in the study of leadership.* Carbondale, IL: Southern Illinois University Press.

Fleishman, E. A. (1975a). *Manual for Ability Requirement Scales (MARS).* Bethesda, MD: Management Research Institute.

Fleishman, E. A. (1975b). *Physical abilities analysis manual.* Bethesda, MD: Management Research Institute.

Fleishman, E. A. (1975c). Toward a taxonomy of human performance. *American Psychologist, 30,* 1127–1149.

Fleishman, E. A. (1982). Systems for describing human tasks. *American Psychologist, 37,* 821–834.

Fleishman, E. A. (1988). Some new frontiers in personnel selection research. *Personnel Psychology, 41,* 679–701.

Fleishman, E. A. (1991a). *Manual for Ability Requirement Scales.* Form A (rev. March 1991). Bethesda, MD: Management Research Institute.

Fleishman, E. A. (1991b). *The role of testing in Department of Labor/ETA training and employment programs* (Final Rep., U.S. Department of Labor). Bethesda, MD: Management Research Institute.

Fleishman, E. A. (1992a). *Fleishman-Job Analysis Survey (F-JAS).* Bethesda, MD: Management Research Institute.

Fleishman, E. A. (1992b). *Psychomotor, physical, and interpersonal requirements of work: Implications for revision of the Dictionary of Occupational Titles (DOT).* Washington, DC: U.S. Department of Labor.

Fleishman, E. A., & Buffardi, L. C. (1998). Predicting human error probabilities from the ability requirements of jobs in nuclear power plants. In J. Misumi, B. Wilpert, & R. Miller (Eds.), *Nuclear safety: A human factors perspective.* London: Taylor & Francis.

Fleishman, E. A., Buffardi, L. C., Morath, R., McCarthy, P., & Friedman, L. (1994). *Development of a model to predict human error rates from the ability requirements of job tasks.* Fairfax, VA: George Mason University, Center for Behavioral and Cognitive Studies.

Fleishman, E. A., Costanza, D. P., Wetrogan, L. I., Uhlman, C. E., & Marshall-Mies, J. C. (1995). Knowledges. In N. Peterson, M. Mumford, W. Borman, P. Jeanneret, & E. Fleishman, (Eds.), *Development of prototype occupational information network: O\*NET content model* (Vol. 1: Report). Salt Lake City: Utah Department of Employment Security.

Fleishman, E. A., & Ellison, G. D. (1962). A factor analysis of fine manipulative tests. *Journal of Applied Psychology, 46,* 96–105.

Fleishman, E. A., & Friedman, L. (1990). *Cognitive competencies related to management performance requirements in R&D organizations* (Tech. Rep.). Fairfax, VA: George Mason University, Center for Behavioral and Cognitive Studies.

Fleishman, E. A., Gebhardt, D. C., & Hogan, J. C. (1986). The perception of physical effort in job tasks. In G. Borg & D. Ottoson (Eds.), *The perception of exertion in physical work.* London: MacMillan Press.

Fleishman, E. A., & Gilbert, J. A. (1994). *A taxonomy of social/interpersonal characteristics for describing worker requirements for the new occupational classification system.* Unpublished working paper, Management Research Institute, Inc., Bethesda, MD.

Fleishman, E. A., & Hempel, W. E. (1955). The relation between abilities and improvement with practice in a usual discrimination reaction time task. *Journal of Experimental Psychology, 44,* 301–312.

Fleishman, E. A., & Hempel, W. E., Jr. (1956). Factorial analysis of complex psychomotor performance and related skills. *Journal of Applied Psychology, 40,* 96–104.

Fleishman, E. A., & Mumford, M. D. (1988). The ability requirements scales. In S. Gael (Ed.), *The job analysis handbook for business, industry, and government* (pp. 917–935). New York: Wiley.

Fleishman, E. A., & Mumford, M. D. (1989). Individual attributes and training performance: Applications of abilities taxonomies in instructional systems design. In I. L. Goldstein (Ed.), *Frontiers of industrial and organizational psychology: Vol. 3. Training and career development* (pp. 183–255). San Francisco: Jossey-Bass.

Fleishman, E. A., & Mumford, M. D. (1991). Evaluating classifications of job behavior: A constant validation of the ability requirements scales. *Personnel Psychology, 43,* 523–576.

Fleishman, E. A., Mumford, M. D., Zaccaro, S. J., Levin, K. Y., Hein, M., & Korotkin, A. L. (1991). Taxonomic efforts in the description of leadership behavior: A synthesis and cognitive interpretation. *Leadership Quarterly, 2,* 245–287.

Fleishman, E. A., & Quaintance, M. K. (1984). *Taxonomies of human performance: The description of human tasks.* New York: Academic Press.

Fleishman, E. A., & Reilly, M. E. (1992a). *Administrator's guide for the Fleishman-Job Analysis Survey (F-JAS).* Bethesda, MD: Management Research Institute.

Fleishman, E. A., & Reilly, M. E. (1992b). *Handbook of human abilities: Definitions, measurements, and job task requirements.* Bethesda, MD: Management Research Institute.

Fogli, L. (1988). Supermarket cashier. In S. Gael (Ed.), The job analysis handbook for business, government, and industry (pp. 1215–1228). New York: Wiley.

Ford, M. E., & Tisak, M. S. (1983). A further search for social intelligence. *Journal of Educational Psychology, 75,* 196–206.

French, J. W. (1951). The description of aptitude and achievement tests in terms of rotated factors. *Psychometric Monographs, No. 5.*

French, J. W., Ekstrom, R. B., & Price, L. A. (1963). *Kit of reference tests for cognitive factors.* Princeton, NJ: Educational Testing Service.

Friedman, L. (1990). Degree of redundancy between time, importance, and frequency task ratings. *Journal of Applied Psychology, 75,* 748–752.

Friedman, L., Fleishman, E. A., & Fletcher, J. (1992). Cognitive and interpersonal abilities related to the primary activities of R&D managers. *Journal of Engineering and Technology Management, 9,* 211–242.

Friedman, L., & Harvey, R. J. (1986). Can raters with reduced job descriptive information provide accurate Position Analysis Questionnaire (PAQ) ratings? *Personnel Psychology, 39,* 779–790.

Fullerton, H. N., Jr (1985). The 1995 labor force: BLS' latest projections. *Monthly Labor Review, 117,* 17–25.

Fuqua, D. R., & Kurpius, D. J. (1993). Conceptual models in organizational consultation. *Journal of Counseling & Development, 71,* 607–618.

Furnham, A., & Gunter, B. (1993). *Corporate assessment.* London: Routledge.

Gael, S. A. (1979). *Job analysis.* New York: Wiley.

Gael, S. A. (1988). *The job analysis handbook for business, industry, and government, Vols. 1 & 2.* New York: Wiley.

Gagne, R. (1985). *Conditions of learning.* New York: Holt, Rinehart, and Winston.

Galbraith, J. R., Lawler, E. E., III, and Associates (Eds.). (1993). *Organizing for the future: The new logic for managing complex organizations.* San Francisco: Jossey-Bass.

Gardner, H. (1983). *Frames of mind: The theory of multiple intelligences.* New York: Basic Books.

Gardner, H. (1993a). *Creating minds.* New York: Basic Books.

Gardner, H. (1993b). *Multiple intelligences: The theory in practice.* New York: Basic Books.

Garwood, M. K., Anderson, L. E., & Greengart, B. J. (1991). Determining the job groups: Application of hierarchical agglomerative cluster analysis in different job analysis situations. *Personnel Psychology, 44,* 743–762.

Gay, E. G., Weiss, D. J., Hendel, D. D., Dawis, R. V., & Lofquist, L. H. (1971). Manual for the Minnesota Importance Questionnaire. *Minnesota Studies in Vocational Rehabilitation, XXVIII.* Minneapolis: University of Minnesota.

Gebhardt, D. L., Cooper, M. A., Jennings, M. C., Crump, C., & Sample, R. A. (1983). *Development and validation of selection tests for a natural gas company* (Final Report 30789). Bethesda, MD: Advanced Research Resources Organization.

Gebhardt, D. L., & Schemmer, F. M. (1985). *Development and validation of selection tests for longshoremen and marine clerks* (ARRO Project #3113). Bethesda, MD: Advanced Research Resources Organization.

Gebhardt, D. L., & Weldon L. J. (1982). *Development and validation of physical performance tests for correctional officers* (Final Report 3080). Bethesda, MD: Advanced Research Resources Organization.

Gerhart, B., & Milkovich, G. T. (1992). Employee compensation: Research and practice. In M. D. Dunnette & L. M. Hough (Eds.), *Handbook of industrial and organizational psychology: Vol. 3* (2nd ed., pp. 481–569). Palo Alto, CA: Consulting Psychologists Press.

Gerrity, W. W. (1988, June). Revolutionizing the work. *Computerworld,* p. 20.

Getzels, J. W., & Csikszentmihalyi, M. (1976). *The creative vision: A longitudinal study of problem finding in art.* New York: Wiley.

Geyer, P. D. (1992). *Issues of reliability in ratings of occupational characteristics in the Dictionary of Occupational Titles.* Washington, DC: DOT Review.

Geyer, P. D., Hice, J., Hawk, J., Boese, R., & Brannon, Y. (1989). Reliabilities of ratings available from the Dictionary of Occupational Titles. *Personnel Psychology, 42,* 547–560.

Ghiselli, E. E. (1973). The validity of aptitude tests in personnel selection. *Personnel Psychology, 26,* 461–477.

Ghorpade, J. V. (1988). *Job analysis.* Englewood Cliffs, NJ: Prentice Hall.

Gilbert, J., Connelly, M. S., Clifton, T. C., Reiter-Palmon, R., & Mumford, M. D. (1992). *Describing requirements for the position of regional manager for ED&C Division: Summary of subject matter expert meetings.* Fairfax, VA: George Mason University, Center for Behavioral and Cognitive Studies.

Gilbert, J. R., & Fleishman, E. A. (1992). *Fleishman's job analysis survey: Social and interpersonal abilities.* Fairfax, VA: George Mason University, Center for Behavioral and Cognitive Studies.

Gitomer, D. H. (1992). *Cognitive science implications for revising DOT.* Washington, DC: DOT Review.

Glick, W. H. (1985). Conceptualizing and measuring organizational and psychological climate: Pitfalls in multilevel research. *Academy of Management Review, 10,* 601–616.

Goldberg, L. R. (1981). Language and individual differences: The search for universals in personality lexicons. In L. Wheeler (Ed.), *Review of personality and social psychology: Vol. 2* (pp. 141–165). Beverly Hills, CA: Sage.

Goldberg, L. R. (1990). An alternative "description of personality:" The big five factor structure. *Journal of Personality and Social Psychology, 59,* 1216–1229.

Goldberg, L. R. (1993). The structure of phenotypic personality traits. *American Psychologist, 48,* 26–34.

Goldstein, I. L. (1990). Training in work organizations. In M. D. Dunnette & L. M. Hough (Eds.), *Handbook of industrial and organizational psychology: Vol. 2* (2nd ed., pp. 507–620). Palo Alto, CA: Consulting Psychologists Press.

Goldstein, I. L. (1991). Training in work organization. In M. D. Dunnette & L. M. Hough (Eds.), *Handbook of industrial and organizational psychology: Vol. 2* (2nd ed., pp. 507–619). Palo Alto, CA: Consulting Pyschologists Press.

Goldstein, I. L. (1993). *Training in organizations* (3rd ed.). Monterey, CA: Brooks/Cole.

Goldstein, I. L., & Gilliam, P. (1990). Training system issues in the year 2000. *American Psychologist, 45,* 134–143.

Gordon, G. G. (1963). *An investigation of the dimensionality of worker-oriented job variables.* Unpublished doctoral dissertation, Purdue University, Lafayette, IN.

Gordon, G. G., & McCormick, E. J. (1963). *The identification, measurement, and factor analyses of "worker-oriented" job variables.* Lafayette, IN: Purdue University, Occupational Research Center. (Prepared for Office of Naval Research under contract Nonr-1100 (19), Report No. 3).

Gore, A. (1996, February 13). Vice President Al Gore's Address to the Armed Forces Communications and Electronics Association Conference [On-line]. Available from Internet: http://www.npr.gov/hompage/2702.html.

Gottefredson, G. D., & Holland, J. L. (1989). *Dictionary of Holland occupational codes* (2nd ed.). Odessa, FL: Psychological Assessment Resources.

Gottefredson, G. D., & Holland, J. L. (1996). *Dictionary of Holland occupational codes* (3rd ed.). Odessa, FL: Psychological Assessment Resources.

Gottefredson, G. D., Holland, J. L., & Ogawa, D. K. (1982). *Dictionary of Holland occupational code.* Palo Alto, CA: Consulting Psychologists Press.

Gottfredson, L. S. (1986). Occupational aptitude patterns map: Development and implications for a theory of job aptitude requirements. *Journal of Vocational Behavior, 29,* 254–291.

Gough, H. G. (1987). *Manual: The California Psychological Inventory.* Palo Alto, CA: Consulting Psychologists Press.

Graen, G. (1976). Role-making processes in organizations. In M. D. Dunnette (Ed.), *Handbook of industrial and organizational psychology* (pp. 1201–1245). Chicago: Rand McNally.

Graen, G., & Scandura, T. A. (1987). Toward a psychology of dyadic organizing. In L. L. Cummings & B. A. Staw (Eds.), *Research in organizational behavior* (pp. 175–208). Greenwich, CT: JAI Press.

Graves, D. (1986). *Corporate culture: Diagnosis and change.* New York: St. Martins Press.

Greeno, J. G., & Simon, H. A. (1988). *Problem solving and reasoning.* New York: Wiley.

Guilford, J. P. (1947). *Printed classification tests.* U.S. Army Air Force Psychology Research Program (Rep. #5). Washington, DC: Goverment Printing Office.

Guilford, J. P. (1967). *The nature of human intelligence.* New York: McGraw-Hill.

Guilford, J. P. (1985). The structure-of-intellect model. In B. B. Wolman (Ed.), *Handbook of intelligence: Theories, measurements, and applications* (pp. 225–266). New York: Wiley.

Guilford, J. P., Christensen, P. R., Bond, N. A. Jr., & Sutton, M. A. (1954). A factor analysis study of human interest. *Psychological Monographs: General and Applied, 68.*

Guilford, J. P., & Hoepfner, R. (1967). *Structure of intellect factors and their tests.* Los Angeles: Psychological Laboratory, University of Southern California.

Guilford, J. P., & Hoepfner, R. (1971). *The analysis of intelligence.* New York: McGraw Hill.

Guilford, J. S., Zimmerman, W., & Guilford, J. P. (1976). *The Guilford-Zimmerman Temperament Survey handbook.* Palo Alto, CA: Consulting Psychologists Press.

Guion, N. M. (1966). *Personnel selection.* New York: McGraw-Hill.

Guion, R. M. (1991). Personnel assessment, selection, and placement. In M. D. Dunnette & L. M. Hough (Eds.), *Handbook of industrial and organizational psychology: Vol. 2* (2nd ed., pp. 327–397). Palo Alto, CA: Consulting Psychologists Press.

Guion, R. M. (1992, April). Matching position requirements and personality. In L. M. Hough (Chair), *Industrial and Organizational Psychology.* Symposium conducted at the 7th annual meeting of the Society for Industrial and Organizational Psychology, Montreal, Canada.

Guion, R. M., & Gottier, R. F. (1965). Validity of personality measures in personnel selection. *Personnel Psychology, 18,* 135–164.

Gustafsson, J. E. (1988). Hierarchical models of individual differences in cognitive abilities. In R. J. Sternberg (Ed.), *Advances in the psychology of human intelligence* (Vol. 4, pp. 35–71). Hillsdale, NJ: Erlbaum.

Guzzo, R. A., & Salas, E. (1995). *Team effectiveness and decision making.* San Francisco: Jossey-Bass.

Hackman, J. R. (1968). Tasks and task performance in research on stress. In J. E. McGrath (Ed.), *Social and psychological factors in stress.* New York: Holt, Rinehart, & Winston.

Hackman, J. R. (1986). The psychology of self-management in organizations. In M. S. Pallak & R. Perloff (Eds.), *Psychology and work: Productivity, change, and employment.* Washington, DC: American Psychological Association.

Hackman, J. R., & Morris, C. G. (1975). Group tasks, group interaction process, and group performance effectiveness: A review of a proposed integration. In L. Berkowitz (Ed.), *Advances in experimental social psychology* (Vol. 8). New York: Academic Press.

Hackman, J. R., & Oldham, G. R. (1976). Motivation through the design of work: Test of a theory. *Organizational Behavior and Human Performance, 16,* 250–279.

Hackman, J. R., & Oldham, G. R. (1980). *Work redesign.* Reading, MA: Addison-Wesley.

Hakel, D. T. (1986). Personnel selection and placement. *Annual Review of Psychology, 37,* 351–380.

Halff, H. M., Hollan, J. D., & Hutchins, E. L. (1986). Cognitive science and military training. *American Psychologist, 41,* 1131–1140.

Hall, R. H. (1982). *Organizations: Structure and process* (3rd ed.). Englewood Cliffs, NJ: Prentice-Hall.

Halpern, D. (1994). *A national assessment of critical thinking skills in adults: Taking steps toward the goal.* Washington, DC: National Center for Educational Statistics.

Hammer, T. (1988). New developments in profit sharing, gain sharing and employee ownership. In J. P. Campbell, R. J. Campbell, & Associates (Eds.), *Productivity in organizations* (pp. 328–366). San Francisco: Jossey-Bass.

Handy, C. (1989). *The age of unreason.* Cambridge, MA: Harvard Business School Press.

Hansen, G. S., & Wernerfelt, B. (1989). Determinants of firm performance: The relative importance of economic and organizational factors. *Strategic Management Journal, 10,* 399–411.

Hansen, J. C., & Campbell, D. P. (1985). *Manual for the Strong Interest Inventory: Form T325 of the Strong Vocational Interest blanks.* Stanford, CA: Stanford University Press.

Harman, H. H. (1975). *Final report of research on assessing human abilities* (PR-75-20). Princeton, NJ: Educational Testing Service.

Harmon, L. W., Hansen, J. C., Borgen, F. H., & Hammer, A. L. (1994). *Strong Interest Inventory applications and technical guide: Form T317 of the Strong Vocational Interest blanks.* Stanford, CA: Stanford University Press.

Hartmann, E. A., Mumford, M. D., & Mueller, S. (1992). Validity of job classifications: An examination of alternative indicators. *Human Performance, 5,* 191–211.

Harvey, R. J. (1986). Quantitative approaches to job classification: A review and critique. *Personnel Psychology, 39,* 267–289.

Harvey, R. J. (1987, April). *Alternative factor structures for the Position Analysis Questionnaire (PAQ).* In M. D. Hakel (Chair), *The dimensionality of work: Future directions, applications, and instrumentation.* Symposium presented at the annual conference of the Society for Industrial and Organizational Psychology, Atlanta.

Harvey, R. J. (1990). *The common-metric questionnaire for the analysis and evaluation of jobs.* San Antonio, TX: Psychological Corporation.

Harvey, R. J. (1991a). Job analysis. In M. D. Dunnette & L. M. Hough (Eds.), *Handbook of industrial and organizational psychology: Vol. 2* (2nd ed., pp. 71–163). Palo Alto, CA: Consulting Psychologists Press.

Harvey, R. J. (1991b). *The Common Metric Questionnaire (CMQ): A job analysis system.* San Antonio, TX: Psychological Corporation.

Harvey, R. J. (1992). *Potential Applications of Generalized Work Behaviors (GWBs) for the Dictionary of Occupational Titles (DOT)* (Draft Interim Rep.). Washington, DC: DOT Review.

Harvey, R. J. (1993). *The guide to using the CMQ for human resource applications.* San Antonio, TX: Psychological Corporation.

Harvey, R. J., Friedman, L., Hakel, M. D., & Cornelius, III, E. T. (1982). Dimensionality of the job element inventory, a simplified worker-oriented job analysis questionnaire. *Journal of Applied Psychology, 73,* 639–646.

Harvey, R. J., Friedman, L., Hakel, M. D., & Cornelius, III, E. T. (1988). Dimensionality of the Job Element Inventory (JEI), a simplified worker-oriented job analysis questionnaire. *Journal of Applied Psychology, 73,* 639–646.

Harvey, R. J., & Lozada-Larsen, S. R. (1988). Influence of amount of job descriptive information on job analysis rating accuracy. *Journal of Applied Psychology, 73,* 457–461.

Hauke, M., Costanza, D. P., Baughman, W., Mumford, M. D., Stone, L., Threlfall, V., & Fleishman, E. A. (1995). *Developing job families on the basis of ability and knowledge requirements profiles.* Bethesda, MD: Management Research Institute.

Hayes, J. R., & Flower, L. S. (1986). Writing research and the writer. *American Psychologist, 41,* 1106–1113.

Hayes-Roth, B., & Hayes-Roth, K. (1979). A cognitive model of planning. *Cognitive Science, 3,* 275–310.

Hays, W. L. (1988). *Statistics* (4th ed.). Fort Worth, TX: Holt, Rinehart and Winston, Inc.

Hempel, W. E., Jr., & Fleishman, E. A. (1955). A factor analysis of physical proficiency and manipulative skills. *Journal of Applied Psychology, 39,* 12–16.

Hemphill, J. K. (1960). *Dimensions of executive positions.* Columbus: Ohio State University, Bureau of Business Research.

Henderson, R. I. (1988). Job evaluation, classification, and pay. In S. Gael (Ed.), *The job analysis handbook for business, industry, and government* (pp. 90–118). New York: Wiley.

Hoffman, C. C. (1989). *Impact of job analysis method on job family structure.* Presented at the annual conference of the Society for Industrial and Organizational Psychology, Boston.

Hoffman, C. C., & Lamartine, S. C. (1995, May). *Transporting physical ability test validity via the Position Analysis Questionnaire.* Current innovations in PAQ-based research and practice.

Symposium presented at the 10th Annual Conference of the Society for Industrial and Organizational Psychology, Orlando.

Hoffmann, E. (1991). *Mapping the world of work, an international review of the use and gathering of occupational information.* Washington, DC: DOT Review.

Hofstee, W. K. B., de Raad, B., & Goldberg, L. R. (1992). Integration of the Big Five and circumplex approaches to trait structure. *Journal of Personality and Social Psychology, 63,* 146–163.

Hogan, J. C. (1991). Structure of physical performance in occupational tasks. *Journal of Applied Psychology, 76,* 495–507.

Hogan, J. C. (1992). *Describing interpersonal, physical, and psychomotor skills for the Dictionary of Occupational Titles.* Washington, DC: DOT Review.

Hogan, J. C., & Fleishman, E. A. (1979). An index of the physical effort required in human task performance. *Journal of Applied Psychology, 64,* 197–204.

Hogan, J. C., Ogden, G. D., & Fleishman, E. A. (1978a). *Assessing the physical requirements in selected benchmark jobs* (Final Rep. 3012). Bethesda, MD: Advanced Research Resources Organization.

Hogan, J. C., Ogden, G. D., & Fleishman, E. A. (1978b). *Assessing physical requirements for establishing medical standards in selected benchmark jobs* (Tech. Rep. R78-8). Bethesda, MD: Advanced Research Resources Organization.

Hogan, J. C., Ogden, G. D., & Fleishman, E. A. (1979). *The development and validation of tests for the order selector job at Certified Grocers of California, Ltd.* Bethesda, MD: Advanced Research Resources Organization.

Hogan, J. C., Ogden, G. D., Gebhardt, D. L., & Fleishman, E. A. (1979). An index of physical effort required in human task performance. *Journal of Applied Psychology, 65,* 672–679.

Hogan, J. C., Ogden, G. D., Gebhardt, D. L., & Fleishman, E. A. (1980). Reliability and validity of methods for evaluating perceived physical effort. *Journal of Applied Psychology, 65,* 672–679.

Hogan, R. (1982). Socioanalytic theory of personality. In M. M. Page (Ed.), *1982 Nebraska Symposium on Motivation: Personality-current theory and research* (pp. 55–89). Lincoln: University of Nebraska Press.

Hogan, R. (1986). *Manual for the Hogan Personality Inventory.* Minneapolis, MN: National Computer Systems.

Hogan, R. (1991). Personality and personality measurement. In M. D. Dunnette & L. M. Hough (Eds.), *Handbook of industrial and organizational psychology: Vol. 2* (2nd ed., pp. 873–919). Palo Alto, CA: Consulting Psychologists Press.

Hogan, R., & Hogan, J. (1992). *Manual for the Hogan Personality Inventory.* Tulsa, OK: Hogan Assessment Systems.

Holland, J. L. (1973). *Making vocational choices: A theory of careers.* Englewood Cliffs, NJ: Prentice-Hall.

Holland, J. L. (1976). Vocational preferences. In M. D. Dunnette (Ed.), *Handbook of industrial and organizational psychology* (pp. 521–570). Chicago: Rand McNally.

Holland, J. L. (1994). *Self-directed search assessment booklet: A guide to educational and career planning.* Odessa, FL: Psychological Assessment Resources.

Holzinger, K. J., & Swineford, F. (1939). A study in factor analysis: The stability of a bi-factor solution. *Supplementary Education Monographs,* No. 48. Chicago: Department of Education, University of Chicago.

Horn, J. L. (1976). Human abilities: A review of research and theories in the early 1970's. In M. R. Rosenzweig & L. W. Porter (Eds.), *Annual review of psychology: Vol. 27.* Palo Alto, CA: Stanford University Press.

Horn, J. L. (1988). Thinking about human abilities. In J. R. Nesselroade & R. B. Cattell (Eds.), *Handbook of multivariate experimental psychology* (2nd ed., pp. 645–685). New York: Plenum.

Hough, L. M. (1984). Development and evaluation of the "accomplishment record" method of selecting and promoting professionals. *Journal of Applied Psychology, 69,* 135–146.

Hough, L. M. (1992). The "big five" personality variables—construct confusion: Description versus prediction. *Human Performance, 5,* 139–155.

Hough, L. M. (1997). Personality at work: Issues and evidence. In M. Hakel (Ed.), *Beyond multiple choice: Evaluating alternatives to traditional testing for selection* (pp. 131–166). Hillsdale, NJ: Erlbaum.

House, R. J. (1977). A 1976 theory of charismatic leadership. In J. G. Hunt & L. L. Larson (Eds.), *Leadership: The cutting edge.* Carbondale: Southern Illinois University Press.

House, R. J., & Howell, J. M. (1992) Personality and charismatic leadership. *Leadership Quarterly, 3,* 81–108.

Howard, A. (1995a). *The changing nature of work.* San Francisco: Jossey-Bass.

Howard, A. (1995b). A framework for work change. In A. Howard (Ed.), *The changing nature of work* (pp. 3–44). San Francisco: Jossey-Bass.

Huff, C., Sproull, L., & Kiesler, S. (1989). Computer communication and organizational commitment: Tracing the relationship in a city government. *Journal of Applied Psychology, 19,* 1371–1391.

Hull, C. L. (1943). *Principles of behavior: An introduction to behavior theory.* New York: Appleton-Century.

Hunter, J. E. (1980). *Validity generalization for 12,000 jobs: An application of synthetic validity and validity generalization to the General Aptitude Test Battery (GATB).* Washington, DC: U.S. Employment Service, Department of Labor.

Hunter, J. E. (1983). *The dimensionality of the General Aptitude Test Battery (GATB) and the dominance of general factors over specific factors in the prediction of job performance for the U.S. Employment Service* (USES Test Res. Rep. No. 44). Washington, DC: U.S. Department of Labor.

Hunter, J. E. (1986). Cognitive ability, cognitive aptitudes, job knowledge, and job performance. *Journal of Vocational Behavior, 29,* 340–362.

Hunter, J. E., & Hunter, R. F. (1984). The validity and utility of alternative predictors of job performance. *Psychological Bulletin, 96,* 72–98.

Hunter, J. E. & Schmidt, F. L. (1982). Fitting people to jobs: The impact of personnel selection on national productivity. In Edwin A. Fleishman (Ed.), *Human performance and productivity: Human capability assessment* (Vol. 1). Hillsdale, NJ: Erlbaum.

Huselid, M. A. (1995). The impact of human resource management practices on turnover, productivity, and corporate financial performance. *Academy of Management Journal, 38,* 635–672.

Ilgen, D. R., & Hollenbeck, J. R. (1991). The structure of work: Job design and roles. In M. D. Dunnette & L. M. Hough (Eds.), *Handbook of industrial and organizational psychology* (2nd ed., pp. 165–207). Palo Alto, CA: Consulting Psychologists Press.

Inn, A., Schulman, D. R., Ogden, G. D., & Sample, R. A. (1982). Physical ability requirements of Bell System jobs (Final Report 3057/R82-1). Bethesda, MD: Advanced Research Resources Organization.

Ivancevich, J. M., & Matteson, M. T. (1980). *Stress and work: A managerial perspective.* Glenview, IL: Scott Foresman.

Jackson, S. E., & Schuler, R. S. (1995). Understanding human resource management in the context of organizations and their environments. *Annual Review of Psychology, 46,* 237–264.

James, L. R. (1982). Aggregation bias in estimates of perceptual agreement. *Journal of Applied Psychology, 67,* 219–229.

Jeanneret, P. R. (1969). A study of the job dimensions of "worker-oriented" job variables and of their attribute profiles. *Dissertation Abstracts International, 30,* 5273–5274.

Jeanneret, P. R. (1972, September). *Investigation of a worker-oriented approach to position analysis. Directions in work analysis.* Paper presented at the annual meeting of the American Psychological Association, Hawaii.

Jeanneret, P. R. (1985, August). *Job component validity: Job requirements, estimates, and validity generalization comparisons.* Symposium conducted at the annual meeting of the American Psychological Association, Los Angeles.

Jeanneret, P. R. (1987). Future directions in the application of job analysis data. In *The dimensionality of work: Future directions, applications, and instrumentation.* Symposium conducted at the second annual conference of the Society for Industrial and Organization Psychology, Atlanta.

Jeanneret, P. R. (1988). Computer logic chip production operators. In S. Gael (Ed.), *The job analysis handbook for business, industry, and government* (pp. 1329–1345). New York: Wiley.

Jeanneret, P. R. (1990, August). The Position Analysis Questionnaire: Recent applications based on quantified job profiles. In *Quantitative Job Description and Classification: Nomothetic approaches and applications*. Symposium conducted at the 38th annual meeting of the American Psychological Association, Boston.

Jeanneret, P. R. (1992a). Applications of job component/synthetic validity to construct validity. *Human Performance, 5,* 81–96.

Jeanneret, P. R. (1992b). *Potential application of generalized work behaviors in the development of a revised dictionary of occupational titles*. Washington, DC: DOT Review.

Jeanneret, P. R., & Borman, W. C. (1995). Generalized work activities. In N. G. Peterson, M. D. Mumford, W. C. Borman, P. R. Jeanneret, & E. A. Fleishman (Eds.), *Development of a prototype Occupational Information Network (O\*NET) content model* (pp. 6-1–6-99). Salt Lake City: Utah Department of Employment Security.

Jeanneret, P. R., & McCormick, E. J. (1969). *The job dimensions of "worker-oriented" job variables and of their attribute profiles as based on data from the Position Analysis Questionnaire* (Technical Rep. No. 2). Lafayette, IN: Purdue University, Occupational Research Center.

Jöreskog, K. G., & Sörbom, D. (1993). *LISREL VIII user's guide*. Chicago: National Educational Resources.

Kahn, R. L., & Byosiere, P. (1992). Stress in organizations. In M. D. Dunnette & L. M. Hough (Eds.), *Handbook of industrial and organizational psychology: Vol. 3* (2nd ed., pp. 571–650). Palo Alto, CA: Consulting Psychologists Press.

Kahn, R. L., Wolfe, D. M., Quinn, R. P., Snoek, J. D., & Rosenthal, R. A. (1964). *Occupational stress: Studies in role conflict and ambiguity*. New York: Wiley.

Kaiser, H. F. (1958). The varimax criterion for analytic rotation in factor analysis. *Psychometrika, 23,* 187–200.

Kaiser, H. F. (1960). The application of electronic computers to factor analysis. *Educational and Psychological Measurement, 20,* 141–151.

Kamp, J. D., & Hough, L. M. (1986). Utility of personality assessment: A review and integration of the literature. In L. M. Hough (Ed.), *Utility of temperament, biodata, and interest assessment for predicting job performance: A review and integration of the literature* (ARI Research Note No. 88-02, pp. 1–90). Alexandria, VA: U.S. Army Research Institute for the Behavioral and Social Sciences.

Kane, R. J., & Meltzer, W. C. (1990). *Upgrading training for employed workers*. Washington, DC: U.S. Department of Labor Employment and Training Administration.

Kanfer, R. (1990). Motivation theory and industrial and organizational psychology. In M. D. Dunnette & L. M. Hough (Eds.), *Handbook of industrial and organizational psychology: Vol. 1* (2nd ed., pp. 75–170). Palo Alto, CA: Consulting Psychologists Press.

Kanfer, R., & Ackerman, P. L. (1989). Motivation and cognitive abilities: An integrative aptitude-treatment interaction approach to skill acquisition. *Journal of Applied Psychology, 74,* 657–690.

Kantor, R. M. (1989). *When giants learn to dance: Mastering the challenge of strategy, management and careers in the 1990's*. New York: Simon and Schuster.

Katz, D., & Kahn, R. L. (1978). *The social psychology of organizations* (2nd ed.). New York: Wiley.

Kaufmann, L., & Rousseeuw, P. J. (1990). *Finding groups in data: An introduction to cluster analysis*. New York: Wiley.

Kazier, C., & Shore, B. M. (1995). Strategy flexibility in more and less competent students on mathematical word problems. *Creative Research Journal, 8,* 77–82.

Kiesler, D. J. (1983). The 1982 interpersonal circle: A taxonomy for complementarity in human transactions. *Psychological Review, 90,* 185–214.

King, L. A., & King, D. W. (1990). Role conflict and role ambiguity: A critical assessment of construct validity. *Psychological Bulletin, 107,* 48–64.

Kochhar, D. S., & Armstrong, T. J. (1988). Designing jobs for handicapped employees. In S. Gael (Ed.), *The job analysis handbook for business, industry, and government*. New York: Wiley.

Komaki, J. L., Collins, R. L., & Penn, P. (1982). The role of performance antecedents and consequences in work motivation. *Journal of Applied Psychology, 67,* 334–340.

Kuder, G. F. (1977). *Activity interests and occupational choice*. Chicago: Science Research Associates.

Kuhn, T. S. (1970). *The structure of scientific revolutions* (2nd ed.). Chicago: University of Chicago Press.

Kutscher, R. (1989). Issues and implications. *Occupational Outlook Quarterly, 33,* 38–40.

Landy, F. J. (1986). Stamp collecting versus science: Validation as hypothesis testing. *American Psychologist, 41,* 1183–1192.

Landy, F. J. (1988). Selection procedure development and usage. In S. Gael (Ed.), *The job analysis handbook for business, government, and industry* (pp. 271–287). New York: Wiley.

Landy, F. J. (1989). *Psychology of work behavior*. Monterey, CA: Brooks/Cole.

Landy, F. J. (1992). *Alternatives to chronological age in determining standards of suitability for public safety jobs* (Vols. 1 & 2, Tech. Rep.). State College, PA: Pennsylvania State University, Center for Applied Behavioral Sciences.

Landy, F. J., Shankster, L. J., & Kohler, S. S. (1994). Personnel selection and placement. *Annual Review of Psychology, 45,* 261–296.

Landy, F. J., & Vasey, J. (1991). Job analysis: The composition of SME samples. *Personnel Psychology, 44,* 27–50.

Lawler, E. E., III. (1983). *Pay and organization development*. Reading, MA: Addison-Wesley.

Lawler, E. E., III. (1987). Pay for performance. In H. R. Halbantian (Ed.), *Incentives, cooperation and risk sharing*. New York: Rowman & Littlefield.

Lawler, E. E., III. (1991). *High involvement management: Participative strategies for improving organizational performance*. San Francisco: Jossey-Bass.

Lawler, E. E., III. (1992). *The ultimate advantage: Creating the high-involvement organization*. San Francisco: Jossey-Bass.

Lawler, E. E., III. (1993). Creating the high-involvement organization. In J. R. Galbraith, E. E. Lawler, III, & Associates (Eds.), *Organizing for the future: The new logic for managing complex organizations* (pp. 172–193). San Francisco: Jossey-Bass.

Lawler, E. E., III, & Jenkins, J. D., Jr. (1992). Strategic reward systems. In M. D. Dunnette & L. M. Hough (Eds.), *Handbook of industrial and organizational psychology: Vol. 3* (2nd ed., pp. 1009–1055). Palo Alto, CA: Consulting Psychologists Press.

Lawler, E. E., Mohrman, S. A., & Ledford, G. E. (1992). *Employee involvement and total quality management*. San Francisco: Jossey-Bass.

Lawshe, C. H. (1952). Employee selection. *Personnel Psychology, 5,* 31–34.

Lawshe, C. H., & Steinberg, V. (1955). Studies in synthetic validity: An exploratory investigation of clerical jobs. *Personnel Psychology, 8,* 281–301.

Leary, T. (1957). *Interpersonal diagnosis of personality*. New York: Ronald Press.

Lederberg, J., & Uncapher, K. (1989). *Toward a national collaboratory: Report of an invited workshop*. New York: Rockefeller University.

Lengnick-Hall, C. A., & Lengnick-Hall, M. L. (1988). Strategic human resources management: A review of the literature and a proposed typology. *Academy of Management Review, 13,* 454–470.

Lesgold, A. M. (1984). Acquiring expertise. In J. R. Anderson & S. M. Kosslyn (Eds.), *Tutorials in learning and memory: Essays in honor of Gordon Bower*. New York: Freeman.

Levine, E. L. (1983). *Everything you always wanted to know about job analysis*. Tampa, FL: Author.

Likert, R. (1961). *New patterns of management*. New York: McGraw-Hill.

Limerick, D., & Cunnington, B. (1993). *Managing the new organization: A blueprint for networks and strategic alliances*. San Francisco: Jossey-Bass.

Locke, E. A. (1968). Toward a theory of task motivation and incentives. *Organizational Behavior and Human Performance, 3,* 157–189.

Locke, E. A., Shaw, K. N., Saari, L. M., & Latham, G. P. (1981). Goal-setting and task performance: 1969–1980. *Psychological Bulletin, 90,* 125–152.

Lopez, F. M. (1988). Threshold trait analysis system. In S. Gael (Ed.), *The job analysis handbook for business, government, and industry* (pp. 880–901). New York: Wiley.

Lorr, M., & Suziedelis, A. (1973). A dimensional approach to the interests measured by the SVIB. *Journal of Counseling Psychology, 20,* 113–119.

Luthans, F., & Fox, M. L. (1989, March). Update on skill-based pay. *Personnel,* 26–31.

MacQueen, J. (1967). Some methods for classification and analysis of multivariate observations. In L. Le Cam & J. Neyman (Eds.), *Fifth Berkeley symposium of mathematics, statistics, and probability* (Vol. 1, pp. 281–297). Berkeley, CA: University of California Press.

Marlowe, D., & Crowne, D. P. (1961). Social desirability and response to perceived situational demands. *Journal of Consulting Psychology, 25,* 109–115.

Marquardt, L. D., & McCormick, E. J. (1972). *Attribute ratings and profiles of the job elements of the Position Analysis Questionnaire (PAQ)* (Tech. Rep. No. 1). Lafayette, IN: Purdue University, Department of Psychological Sciences, Occupational Research Center.

Marquardt, L. D., & McCormick, E. J. (1974). *The job dimensions underlying the job elements of the Position Analysis Questionnaire (PAQ Form B)* (Tech. Rep. No. 4). Lafayette, IN: Purdue University.

McCage, R. D. (1993). *Observations regarding the development of occupational skills clusters.* Paper prepared for the U.S. Department of Labor, Washington, DC.

McCage, R. D. (1995). *Observations regarding a revised standard occupational classification system using a skills based concept.* Arlington, VA: DTI.

McClelland, D. C. (1973). Testing for competence rather than intelligence. *American Psychologist, 28,* 1–14.

McCormick, E. J. (1959). The development of processes for indirect or synthetic validity: III. Application of job analysis to indirect validity (A symposium). *Personnel Psychology, 12,* 402–413.

McCormick, E. J. (1964a). *The development, analysis, and experimental application of worker-oriented job variables.* Lafayette, IN: Purdue University, Occupational Research Center. (Prepared for Office of Naval Research under Contract Nonr-1100, Final Report).

McCormick, E. J. (1964b). *Development of a worker activity checklist for use in occupational analysis* (Rep. No. 62-77). Lackland AFB, TX: Air Force Human Resources Laboratory.

McCormick, E. J. (1976). Job and task analysis. In M. D. Dunnette (Ed.), *Handbook of industrial and organizational psychology* (pp. 651–696). Chicago: Rand-McNally.

McCormick, E. J. (1979). *Job analysis: Methods and applications.* New York: Amacom.

McCormick, E. J., Cunningham, J. W., & Gordon, G. G. (1967). Job dimensions based on factorial analyses of worker-oriented job variables. *Personnel Psychology, 20,* 417–430.

McCormick, E. J., DeNisi, A. S., & Marquardt, L. D. (1974). *The derivation of job compensation index values from the Position Analysis Questionnaire (PAQ)* (Tech. Rep. No. TR-6). Lafayette, IN: Purdue University, Department of Psychological Sciences, Occupational Research Center.

McCormick, E. J., DeNisi, A. S., & Shaw, J. B. (1977). *Job-derived selection: Follow-up report* (Tech. Rep. No. TR-4). Lafayette, IN: Purdue University, Department of Psychological Sciences.

McCormick, E. J., DeNisi, A. S., & Shaw, J. B. (1979). Use of the Position Analysis Questionnaire for establishing the job component validity of tests. *Journal of Applied Psychology, 64,* 51–56.

McCormick, E. J., & Jeanneret, P. R. (1988). Position Analysis Questionnaire (PAQ). In S. Gael (Ed.), *The job analysis handbook for business, industry, and government* (Vol. II, pp. 825–842). New York: Wiley.

McCormick, E. J., Jeanneret, P. R., & Mecham, R. C. (1967). *Position Analysis Questionnaire (Form A).* Lafayette, IN: Purdue University, Department of Psychology, Occupational Research Center.

McCormick, E. J., Jeanneret, P. R., & Mecham, R. C. (1969a). *The development and background of the Position Analysis Questionnaire (PAQ)* (Tech. Rep. No. 5). Lafayette, IN: Purdue University, Occupational Research Center.

McCormick E. J., Jeanneret, P. R., & Mecham, R. C. (1969b). *A study of job characteristics and job dimensions based on the Position Analysis Questionnaire* (Tech. Rep. No. 6). Lafayette, IN: Purdue University, Occupational Research Center.

McCormick, E. J., Jeanneret, P. R., & Mecham, R. C. (1972). A study of job characteristics and job dimensions as based on the Position Analysis Questionnaire (PAQ). *Journal of Applied Psychology Monograph, 56,* 347–368.

McCormick, E. J., Mecham, R. C., & Jeanneret, P. R. (1977). *Technical manual for the Position Analysis Questionnaire (PAQ).* West Lafayette, IN: University Book Store.

McCormick, E. J., Mecham, R. C., & Jeanneret, P. R. (1989). *Technical manual for the Position Analysis Questionnaire* (2nd ed.). Palo Alto, CA: Consulting Psychologists Press.

McCrae, R. R., & Costa, P. T., Jr. (1987). Validation of the five-factor model across instruments and observers. *Journal of Personality and Social Psychology, 52,* 81–90.

McCrae, R. R., Costa, P. T., Jr., & Piedmont, R. L. (1993). Folk concepts, natural language, and psychological constructs: The California Psychological Inventory and the five-factor model. *Journal of Personality, 61,* 1–26.

McDaniel, M. A., Schmidt, F. L., & Hunter, J. E. (1988). Job experience correlates of job performance. *Journal of Applied Psychology, 73,* 327–330.

McGrath, J. E. (1976). Stress and behavior in organizations. In M. D. Dunnette (Ed.), *The handbook of industrial and organizational psychology* (pp. 1351–1396). Chicago: Rand McNally.

McGrath, J. E. (1994). *Groups: Interaction and performance.* Englewood Cliffs, NJ: Prentice Hall.

McHenry, J. J., Hough, L. M., Toquam, J. L., Hanson, M. A., & Ashworth, S. (1990). Project A validity results: The relationship between predictor and criterion domains. *Personnel Psychology, 43,* 335–354.

McKinney, W. R., & Greer, D. L. (1985). The construction and validation of the IDPRE: Personnel selection examination for Illinois Directors of Parks and Recreation. *Public Personnel Management, 14,* 181–189.

McPhail, S. M., Blakley, B. R., Strong, M. H., Collins, T. J., Jeanneret, P. R., & Galarza, L. (1995). Work context. In N. G. Peterson, M. D. Mumford, W. C. Borman, P. R. Jeanneret, & E. A. Fleishman (Eds.), *Development of prototype Occupational Information Network (O*NET) content model* (Vols. 1–2). Salt Lake City: Utah Department of Employment Security.

McPhail, S. M., Jeanneret, P. R., McCormick, E. J., & Mecham, R. C. (1991). *Position Analysis Questionnaire job analysis manual.* Palo Alto, CA: Consulting Psychologists Press.

Mecham, R. C. (1985, August). Comparative effectiveness of situational, generalized, and job component validation methods. In P. R. Jeanneret (Chair), *Job component validity: Job requirements, estimates, and validity generalization comparisons.* Symposium conducted at the Annual Convention of the American Psychological Association, Los Angeles.

Mecham, R. C., & McCormick, E. J. (1969a). *The use of data based on the Position Analysis Questionnaire in developing synthetically derived attribute requirements of jobs* (Tech. Rep. No. TR-4). Lafayette, IN: Purdue University, Occupational Research Center.

Mecham, R. C., & McCormick, E. J. (1969b). *The use in job evaluation of job elements and job dimensions based on the Position Analysis Questionnaire* (Tech. Rep. No. 3). Lafayette, IN: Purdue University, Occupation Research Center.

Medin, D. L. (1984). Concepts and conceptual structure. *American Psychologist, 12,* 1469–1481.

Menon, G. (1994). Judgments of behavioral frequencies: Memory search and retrieval strategies. In N. Schwarz & S. Sudman (Eds.), *Autobiographical memory and the validity of retrospective reports* (pp. 161–172). New York: Springer-Verlag.

Meridian Corporation. (1991). *The changing world of work: Implications for the DOT Review initiative.* Washington, DC: DOT Review.

Merrifield, P. R., Guilford, J. P., Christensen, P. R., & Frick, J. W. (1962). The role of intellectual factors in problem solving. *Psychological Monographs, 76,* 1–21.

Messick, S. (1989). Validity. In R. L. Linn (Ed.), *Educational measurement* (3rd. ed., pp. 13–105). New York: MacMillan.

Messick, S. (1994). *Validation designs for a new generation of tests.* Paper presented at the Bowling Green Conference on Alternatives to Traditional Tests, Toledo, OH.

Messick, S. (1995). Validity of psychological assessment: Validation of inferences from personal responses and performances as scientific inquiry into score meaning. *American Psychologist, 50,* 741–749.

Miller, R. B. (1953). A method for non-machine task analysis. USAF, WADC, TR 53-137. Wright Patterson AFB, Ohio.

Miller, R. B. (1967). Task taxonomy: Science or technology? In W. T. Singleton, R. S. Easterly, & D. C. Whitfield (Eds.), *The human operator in complex systems.* London: Taylor & Francis.

Milligan, G. W. (1981). A review of Monte Carlo tests of cluster analysis. *Multivariate Behavioral Research, 16,* 379–407.

Mintzberg, H. (1979). *The structuring of organizations.* Englewood Cliffs, NJ: Prentice-Hall.

Mitchell, J. L. (1978). *Structured job analysis of professional and managerial positions.* Unpublished doctoral dissertation, Purdue University, Lafayette, IN.

Mitchell, J. L., Ruck, H. W., & Driskell, W. E. (1988). Task-based training program development. In S. Gael (Ed.), *The job analysis handbook for business, government, and industry* (pp. 205–214). New York: Wiley.

Mogan, R. L., Hunt, E. S., & Carpenter, J. M. (1990). *Classification of instructional programs.* Washington, DC: Department of Education, Institutional Studies Branch, Postsecondary Education Statistics Division, NCES.

Mohrman, S. A., & Cohen, S. G. (1995). When people get out of the box: New relationships, new systems. In A. Howard (Ed.), *The changing nature of work* (pp. 365–410). San Francisco: Jossey-Bass.

Monahan, C. J., & Muchinsky, P. M. (1983). Three decades of personnel selection research: A state-of-the-art analysis and evaluation. *Journal of Occupational Psychology, 56,* 215–225.

Morgenthau, E. D. (1992). *Identification of how commercial products publish and disseminate DOT data.* Washington, DC: DOT Review.

Morgenthau, E. D., & Lenz, J. (1992). *International Practices: Occupational Classification and Description.* Washington, DC: DOT Review.

Morgeson, F. P., & Campion, M. A. (1997). Social and cognitive sources potential of inaccuracy in job analysis. *Journal of Applied Psychology, 82,* 627–655

Morrison, R. A. (1994). Biodata applications in career development research and practice. In G. S. Stokes, M. D. Mumford, & W. A. Owens (Eds.), *Biodata handbook: Theory, research, and use of biographical information in selection and performance prediction* (pp. 451–484). Palo Alto, CA: Consulting Psychologists Press.

Moss, F. A., Hunt, J., Omwake, K. T., & Woodward, C. G. (1955). *Manual for the George Washington University Series Social Intelligence Test.* Washington, DC: Center for Psychological Service.

Mossholder, K. W., & Arvey, R. D. (1984). Synthetic validity: A conceptual and comparative view. *Journal of Applied Psychology, 69,* 322–333.

Mumford, M. D. (1994). *Draft taxonomies of skills* [Working paper]. Washington, DC: American Institutes for Research.

Mumford, M. D., Baughman, W. A., Supinski, E. P., Costanza, D. P., & Threlfall, K. V. (1996). Process-based measures of creative problem solving skills: Overall prediction. *Creativity Research Journal.*

Mumford, M. D., & Connelly, M. S. (1991). Leaders as creators: Leader performance and problem solving in ill-defined domains. *Leadership Quarterly, 2*(4), 289–315.

Mumford, M. D., & Connelly, M. S. (1993). Cases of invention: A review of Weber and Perkins' "Inventive minds: Creativity in technology." *Contemporary Psychology, 38,* 1210–1212.

Mumford, M. D., & Gustafson, S. B. (in press). Creative thought: Cognition and problem solving in dynamic system. In M. A. Runco (Ed.), *Creativity research handbook.* Cresskill, NY: Hampton.

Mumford, M. D., Mobley, M. I., Uhlman, C. E., Reiter-Palmon, R., & Doares, L. M. (1991). Process analytic models of creative capacities. *Creativity Research Journal, 4,* 91–122.

Mumford, M. D., & Owens, W. A. (1984). Individuality in a developmental context: Some empirical and theoretical considerations. *Human Development, 27,* 84–108.

Mumford, M. D., & Peterson, N. G. (1995). Skills. In N. G. Peterson, M. D. Mumford, W. C. Borman, P. R. Jeanneret, & E. A. Fleishman (Eds.), *Development of prototype Occupational Information Network (O\*NET) content model* (Vols. 1–2). Salt Lake City: Utah Department of Employment Security.

Mumford, M. D., & Sager, C. E. (1995). Tryout report. In *Technical memorandum: Tryout of O\*NET questionnaires and anchor scaling.* Washington, DC: American Institutes for Research.

Mumford, M. D., Stokes, G. S., & Owens, W. A. (1990). *Patterns of life adaptation: The ecology of human individuality.* Hillsdale, NJ: Erlbaum.

Mumford, M. D., & Supinski, E. (1995a). *A field test of procedures for identifying occupation-specific skills.* Washington, DC: American Institutes for Research.

Mumford, M. D., Threlfall, K. V., Costanza, D. P., Baughman, W. A., & Smart, B. D. (1992). *Analysis of Kidder, Peabody account executives.* Fairfax, VA: Authors.

Mumford, M. D., Weeks, J. L., Harding, F. D., & Fleishman, E. A. (1987). Measuring occupational difficulty: A construct validation against training criteria. *Journal of Applied Psychology, 72,* 578–587.

Mumford, M. D., Yarkin-Levin, K., Korotkin, A. C., Wallis, M. R., & Marshall-Mies, J. (1985). *Characteristics relevant to performance as an Army leader: Knowledges, skills, abilities, other characteristics, and generic skills* (Tech. Rep.). Alexandria, VA: U.S. Army Research Institute for the Behavioral and Social Sciences.

Mumford, M. D., Zaccaro, S. J., Harding, F. D., & Fleishman, E. A. (1994). *The thinking leader: Developing creative leaders for a changing world* [Draft final report]. Bethesda, MD: Management Research Institute.

Murray, H. A. (1938). *Explorations in personality.* New York: Oxford.

Myers, D. C., Gebhardt, D. L., Crump, C. E., & Fleishman, E. A. (1993). The dimensions of human physical performance: Factor analysis of strength, stamina, flexibility, and body composition measures. *Human Performance, 6,* 309–344.

Myers, D. C., Gebhardt, D. L., Price, S. J., & Fleishman, E. A. (1981). *Development of physical performance standards for Army jobs: Validation of the Physical Abilities Analysis methodology* (ARRO Final Report 3045/R81-2). Bethesda, MD: Advanced Research Resources Organization.

Myers, D. C., Jennings, M. C., & Fleishman, E. A. (1981). *Development of job-related medical standards and physical tests for court security officer jobs* (Final Report 3062). Bethesda, MD: Advanced Research Resources Organization.

National Center on Education and the Economy (NCEE). (1990). *The report of the Commission on the Skills of the American Workforce, America's Choice: High Skills or Low Wages.* Rochester, NY: National Center on Education and the Economy.

National Center for Education Statistics (1993). *1990–91 schools and staffing survey.* Washington, DC: U.S. Department of Education, Office of Educational Research and Improvement.

*National Occupational Information Coordinating Committee (NOICC) Master Crosswalk* (Version 4.1) [Electronic data base]. (1995). Des Moines, IA: National Crosswalk Service Center.

*National Occupational Information Coordinating Committee (NOICC) Master Crosswalk* (Version 4.0) [Electronic data base]. (1994). Des Moines, IA: National Crosswalk Service Center.

Neff, W. S. (1987). *Work and human behavior* (3rd ed.). New York: Aldine.

Nelson, B. (1996). *Transitions in work and learning: Implications for assessment.* Washington, DC: National Research Council.

Newell, A., & Simon, H. A. (1972). *Human problem solving.* Englewood Cliffs, NJ: Prentice-Hall.

Nicks, D. C., & Fleishman, E. A. (1962). What do physical tests measure? A review of factor analytic studies. *Educational and Psychological Measurement, 22,* 77–96.

Noe, R. A. (1986). Trainee attributes and attitudes: Neglected influences on training effectiveness. *Academy of Management Review, 11,* 736–749.

Norman, W. T. (1963). Toward an adequate taxonomy of personality attributes: Replicated factor structure in peer nomination personality ratings. *Journal of Abnormal and Social Psychology, 66,* 574–583.

Norusis/SPSS, Inc. (1993). *SPSS for Windows: Professional Statistics* (Release 6.0). Chicago: SPSS.

Nunnally, J. C. (1978). *Psychometric theory* (2nd ed.). New York: McGraw-Hill.

Offerman, L., & Gowing, M. (1990). Organizations of the future: Changes and challenges. *American Psychologist, 45,* 95–108.

O'Leary, B. S., Rheinstein, J., & McCauley, D. E. (1989). *Developing a taxonomy of generalized work behaviors.* Unpublished paper presented at the 31st annual conference of the Military Testing Association, San Antonio, TX.

Ones, D. S., Schmidt, F. L., & Viswesvaran, C. (1994, April). Do broader personality variables predict job performance with higher validity? Paper presented in R. Page (Chair), *Personality and job performance: Big Five versus specific traits.* Symposium conducted at the ninth annual conference of the Society for Industrial and Organizational Psychology, Nashville, TN.

O'Reilly, C. A., Chatman, J., & Caldwell, D. (1991). People and organizational culture: A profile comparison approach to assessing person-organization fit. *Academy of Management Journal, 34*(3), 487–516.

Osborne, J. L. (1994). A survey of organizational development strategies. Arlington, VA: U.S. Army Research Institute for the Behavioral and Social Sciences.

Outerbridge, A. N. (1981). *The development of generalizable work behavior categories for a synthetic validity model.* Washington, DC: U.S. Office of Personnel Management, Personnel Research and Development Center.

Overall, J. E., Gibson, J. M., & Novy, D. M. (1993). Population recovery capabilities of 35 cluster analysis methods. *Journal of Clinical Psychology, 49,* 459–470.

Owens, W. A., & Schoenfeldt, S. (1979). Toward a classification of persons. *Journal of Applied Psychology, 64,* 569–607.

Packer, A. (1992.) *Speaking in one tongue: Integrating the NAEP and DOT via the SCANS know-how.* Washington, DC: DOT Review.

Palmer, G. J., Jr., & McCormick, E. J. (1961). A factor analysis of job activities. *Journal of Applied Psychology, 45,* 289–294.

Parker, J. F., Jr., & West, V. R. (1973). *Bioastronautics data book.* Washington, DC: U.S. Government Printing Office.

Parker, J. R., & Fleishman, E. A. (1960). Ability factors and component performance measures as predictors of complex tracking behavior. *Psychological Monographs, 74* (Whole No. 503).

Pass, J. J., & Cunningham, J. W. (1975a). *Occupational clusters based on systematically derived work dimensions: Final report.* Raleigh, NC: North Carolina State University, Center for Occupational Education.

Pass, J. J., & Cunningham, J. W. (1975b). *A systematic procedure for estimating the human attribute requirements of occupations* (Ergometric R&D Rep. No. 4 under Grant No. OEG-2-7-070348-2698 from the U.S. Office of Education). Raleigh: North Carolina State University, Center for Occupational Education.

Paul, R. (1990). *Critical thinking: What every person needs to survive in a rapidly changing world.* Rohrert Park, CA: Center for Critical Thinking and Moral Critique, Somona State University.

Pearlman, K. (1980). Job families: A review and discussion of their implications for personnel selection. *Psychological Bulletin, 87,* 80–107.

Pearlman, K. (1993). *The skills standards project and the redesign of the nation's occupational classification system.* Washington, DC: U.S. Department of Labor.

Pearlman, K. (1996). 21st century measures for 21st century work. In *Transitions in work and learning: Implications for assessment.* Washington, DC: National Research Council.

Perkins, D. N. (1992). The topography of invention. In R. J. Weber & D. N. Perkins (Eds.), *Inventive minds: Creativity in technology* (pp. 238–250). New York: Oxford University Press.

Perkins, D. P., Jay, E., & Tishman, S. (1994). *Assessing thinking: A framework for measuring critical thinking and problem solving skills at the college level.* Washington, DC: National Center for Educational Statistics.

Perrow, C. (1961). The analysis of goals in complex organizations. *American Sociological Review, 26,* 688–699.

Perrow, C. (1970). *Organizational analysis: A sociological view.* Belmont, CA: Wadsworth.

Peters, D. L., & McCormick, E. J. (1962, November). *The experimental use of various types of scales in rating job activities.* (Prepared for Office of Naval Research under Contract Nonr-1100, Rep. No. 2). Lafayette, IN: Purdue University, Occupational Research Center.

Peters, T., & Waterman, R. (1982). *In search of excellence.* New York: Addison-Wesley.

Peterson, N. G. (1992). *Methodology for identifying SCANS competencies and foundation skills.* Washington, DC: American Institutes for Research.

Peterson, N. G. (1996). General introduction. In N. G. Peterson, M. D. Mumford, W. C. Borman, P. R. Jeanneret, & E. A. Fleishman, *O\*NET final technical report, Vol. 1* (pp. 1–5). Salt Lake City: Utah Department of Employment Security.

Peterson, N. G. (1997). *Occupational information network (O\*NET) research and development.* Salt Lake City: Utah Department of Employment Security.

Peterson, N. G., & Bownas, D. A. (1982). Skill, task structure, and performance acquisition. In M. D. Dunnette & E. A. Fleishman (Eds.), *Human performance and productivity: Human capability assessment.* Hillsdale, NJ: Erlbaum.

Peterson, N. G., Mumford, M. D., Borman, W. C., Jeanneret, P. R., & Fleishman, E. A. (Eds.). (1995). *Development of prototype Occupational Information Network (O\*NET) content model (Vols. 1 & 2).* Salt Lake City: Utah Department of Employment Security.

Peterson, N. G., Mumford, M. D., Borman, W. C., Jeanneret, P. R., Fleishman, E. A., & Levin, K. Y. (Eds.). (1996). *O\*NET final technical report.* Salt Lake City: Utah Department of Employment Security.

Peterson, N. G., Owens-Kurtz, C., Hoffman, R. G., Arabian, J. M., & Whetzel, D. C. (1990). *Army synthetic validation project.* Alexandria, VA: U.S. Army Research Institute for the Behavioral Sciences.

Peterson, N. G., Rosse, R. R., & Owens-Kurtz, C. K. (1989). The use of expert judges to form synthetic predictor composites for Army jobs. In L. L. Wise, J. M. Arabian, W. J. Chia, and P. L. Szenas (Eds.), *Army synthetic validity project (report of phase I results* (pp. 67–86). Washington, DC: American Institutes for Research.

Pfeffer, J., & Salanick, G. R. (1978). *The external control of organizations: A resource dependence perspective.* New York: Harper & Row.

Porras, J. I., & Robertson, P. J. (1992). Organizational development: Theory, practice, and research. In M. D. Dunnette & L. M. Hough (Eds.), *Handbook of industrial and organizational psychology: Vol. 3.* (2nd ed., pp. 720–822). Palo Alto, CA: Consulting Psychologists Press.

Poulton, E. C. (1970). *Environment and human efficiency.* Springfield, IL: Thomas.

Prediger, D. J. (1989). Ability differences across occupations: More than g. *Journal of Vocational Behavior, 34,* 1–27.

Prediger, D. J., & Vansickle, T. R. (1992). Locating occupations on Holland's hexagon: Beyond RIASEC. *Journal of Vocational Behavior, 40,* 111–128.

Premack, S. & Wanous, J. (1985). A meta-analysis of realistic job preview experiments. *Journal of Applied Psychology, 70,* 706–719.

Prien, E. (1994). *Job activities taxonomy.* Unpublished manuscript.

Primoff, E. S. (1955a, May). *Basic formulae for the J-coefficient to select tests by job analysis requirements.* Washington, DC: U.S. Civil Service Commission.

Primoff, E. S. (1955b). *Test selection by job analysis: The J-coefficient, what it is, how it works (Test Technical Series No. 20).* Washington, DC: U.S. Civil Service Commission.

Primoff, E. S., & Eyde, S. D. (1988). Job element analysis. In S. Gael (Ed.), *The job analysis handbook for business, government, and industry* (pp. 807–824). New York: Wiley.

Pugh, D. S., Hickson, D. J., Hinings, C. R., & Turner, C. (1968). Dimensions of organization structure. *Administrative Science Quarterly, 13*(1), 66–105.

Quinn, R. E. (1988). *Beyond rational management: Mastering the paradoxes and competing demands of high performance.* San Francisco: Jossey-Bass.

Raymark, P. H., Schmit, M. J., & Guion, R. M. (1997). Identifying potentially useful personality constructs for employee selection. *Personnel Psychology, 2,* 723–736.

Redmond, M. R., Mumford, M. D., & Teach, R. (1993). Putting creativity to work: Effects of leader behavior on subordinate creativity. *Organizational Behavior and Human Decision Processes, 55,* 120–151.

Reich, R. B. (1990). Who is us? *Harvard Business Review, 68,* 53–64.

Reich, R. (1992). *The work of nations: Preparing ourselves for 21st century capitalism.* New York: Vintage Books.

Reich, R. B. (1994, November 22). *The revolt of the anxious class.* Presentation given to the Democratic Leadership Council, Washington, DC.

Reilly, R. R., & Zink, D. L. (1980). *Analysis of three outside craft jobs* (AT&T Res. Rep.). New York: American Telephone and Telegraph Co.

Reiter-Palmon, R., Uhlman, C. E., Clifton, T. C., Connelly, M. S., Deflippo, B., & Mumford, M. D. (1990). *Describing sales position requirements: GE lighting division, SME meeting report.* Fairfax, VA: George Mason University, Center for Behavioral and Cognitive Studies.

Reynolds, D. H., Laabs, G. J., & Harris, D. A. (1996). Occupational genealogies: Using job family characteristics in personnel research. *Military Psychology, 8,* 195–217.

Rist, R. S. (1989). Schema creation in programming. *Cognitive Science, 13,* 314–389.

Rizzo, J. R., House, R. J., & Lirtzman, S. I. (1970). Role conflict and ambiguity in complex organizations. *Administrative Science Quarterly, 15,* 150–163.

Rohmert, W. (1988). AET. In S. Gael (Ed.), *The job analysis handbook for business, industry, and government.* New York: Wiley.

Romashko, T., Brumbach, G. B., Fleishman, E. A., & Hahn, C. P. (1974). *Development of a procedure to validate physical tests* (Tech. Rep.). Washington, DC: American Institutes for Research.

Romashko, T., Hahn, C. P., & Brumback, G. B. (1976). *The prototype development of job-related physical testing for Philadelphia policeman selection* (Tech. Rep.). Washington, DC: American Institutes for Research.

Rose, A. M., Hesse, B. W., Silver, P. A., & Dumas, J. S. (1996). *O*NET: An informational system for the workplace. Designing an electronic infrastructure.* Salt Lake City: Utah Department of Employment Security.

Rounds, J. B., Jr., & Dawis, R. V. (1979). Factor analysis of Strong Vocational Interest blank items. *Journal of Applied Psychology, 64,* 132–143.

Runco, M. A. (1991). The evaluative, valuative, and divergent thinking of children. *Journal of Creative Behavior, 25,* 311–319.

Runco, M. A. (1994). Conclusions concerning problem finding, problem solving, and creativity. In R. A. Runco (Ed.), *Problem finding, problem solving, and creativity* (pp. 71–240). Norwood, NJ: Abler.

Rynes, S. L. (1991). Recruitment, job choice, and post-hire consequences: A call for new research directions. In M. D. Dun-

nette & L. M. Hough (Eds.), *Handbook of industrial and organizational psychology: Vol. 2* (2nd. ed., pp. 399–444). Palo Alto, CA: Consulting Psychologists Press.

Sackett, P. R., Cornelius, E. T., & Carron, T. J. (1981). A comparison of global judgment vs. task oriented approaches to job classification. *Personnel Psychology, 34,* 791–804.

Sackett, P. R., Zedeck, S., & Folgi, L. (1988). Relations between measures of typical and maximal performance. *Journal of Applied Psychology, 73,* 482–486.

Sampson, J. (1994). *A differential feature-cost analysis of seventeen computer-assisted career guidance systems* (Tech. Rep. No. 10). Available from the Center for the Study of Technology in Counseling and Career Guidance, Florida State University.

Sanchez, J. I., & Fraser, S. L. (1992). On the choice of scales for task analysis. *Journal of Applied Psychology, 77,* 545–553.

Saville, P., & Holdsworth, R. (1990). *Occupational Personality Questionnaire manual.* Surrey, England: Saville & Holdsworth.

SAS [Computer Software]. (1989–1996). Cary, NC: SAS Institute, Inc.

Schein, E. H. (1992). *Organizational culture and leadership* (2nd ed.). San Francisco: Jossey-Bass.

Schemmer, F. M., & Cooper, M. A (1986). *Test transportability study for technician jobs in the telephone industry.* Bethesda, MD: Advanced Research Resources Organization.

Schlenker, B. R. (1980). *Impression management: The self-concept, social identity, and interpersonal relations.* Monterey, CA: Brooks/Cole.

Schmeck, R. R. (1988). Individual differences and learning strategies. In C. E. Weinstein, E. T. Goetz, & P. A. Alexander (Eds.), *Learning and study strategies: Issues in assessment, instruction, and evaluation* (pp. 171–191). New York: Academic Press.

Schmidt, F. L., & Hunter, J. E. (1996). Measurement error in psychological research: Lessons from 26 research scenarios. *Psychological Methods, 1,* 199–223.

Schmidt, F. L., Hunter, J. E., Croll, P. R., & McKenzie, R. C. (1983). Estimation of employment test validities by expert judgment. *Journal of Applied Psychology, 68,* 590–601.

Schmidt, F. L., Hunter, J. E., & Pearlman, K. (1981). Task differences as moderators of aptitude test validity in selection: A red herring. *Journal of Applied Psychology, 66,* 166–185.

Schmidt, W. H., Porter, A. C., Schwille, J. R., Floden, R. E., & Freeman, D. J. (1983). Validity as a variable: Can the same certification test be valid for all students? In C. F. Madau (Ed.), *The courts, validity, and minimum competency testing* (pp. 116–183). Hingham, MA: Kluner-Nijhoff.

Schmitt, N., Gooding, R. Z., Noe, R. A., & Kirsch, M. (1984). Meta-analyses of validity studies published between 1964 and 1982 and the investigation of study characteristics. *Personnel Psychology, 37,* 407–422.

Schmeck, R. R. (1988). *Learning strategies and learning styles.* New York: Plenum.

Schmeck, R. R., & Grove, E. (1979). Academic achievement and individual differences in the learning processes. *Applied Psychological Measurement, 3,* 43–49.

Schneider, B. S. (1990). The climate for service. In B. Schneider (Ed.), *Organizational climate and culture* (pp. 383–412). San Francisco: Jossey-Bass.

Schneider, B. S., Goldstein, H. W., & Smith, D. B. (1996). The ASA framework: An update. *Personnel Psychology, 48,* 747–773.

Schuler, R. S., Aldag, R. J., & Brief, A. P. (1977). Role conflict and ambiguity. *Organizational Behavior and Human Performance, 20,* 111–128.

Scott, B. M., Cunningham, J. W., & Pass, J. J. (1989). *A comparison of two job grouping systems: Research in numerical job taxonomy.* Presented at the first annual convention of the American Psychological Society, Alexandria, VA.

Secretary's Commission on Achieving Necessary Skills. (1991). *What work requires of schools.* Washington, DC: U.S. Department of Labor.

Secretary's Commission on Achieving Necessary Skills. (1992). *Learning a living: A blueprint for high performance.* Washington, DC: U.S. Department of Labor.

Selye, H. (1980). *Selye's guide to stress research: Vol. 1.* New York: Van Nostrand Reinhold.

Shaw, J. B., & Riskind, J. H. (1983). Predicting job stress using data from the Position Analysis Questionnaire. *Journal of Applied Psychology, 68,* 253–261.

Shimberg, B., Esser, B. F., & Kruger, D. H. (1973). *Occupational licensing: Practices and policies.* Washington, DC: Public Affairs Press.

Shrout, P. E., & Fleiss, J. L. (1979). Intraclass correlations: Uses in assessing rater reliability. *Psychological Bulletin, 86*(2), 420–428.

Silver, M. B. (1990). *Summary of public response to DOT concept paper published in the Federal Register.* Washington, DC: DOT Review.

Silver, M. B. (1991). *APDOT management report: The changing world of work: Implications for the DOT review initiative,* Washington, DC: DOT Review.

Simonton, D. K. (1995). In R. J. Sternberg (Ed.), *The nature of insight.* Cambridge, MA: MIT Press.

Skinner, B. F. (1938). *The behavior of organisms: An experimental analysis.* New York: Appleton-Century.

Skinner, H. A. (1978). Differentiating the contribution of elevation, scatter, and shape in profile similarity. *Educational and Psychological Measurement, 38,* 297–308.

Smith, I. (1989). *Incentive schemes: People and profits.* London: Croner.

Smith, J. E., & Hakel, M. D. (1979). Convergence among data sources, response bias, and reliability and validity of a structured job analysis questionnaire. *Personnel Psychology, 32,* 677–692.

Smith, K. G., Locke, E. A., & Barry, D. (1990). Goal setting, planning, and organizational performance: An experimental simulation. *Organizational Behavior and Human Decision Processes, 46,* 118–134.

Smith, L. (1992). *Skills of human resource managers at the National Security Agency,* unpublished manuscript.

Snell, S. A., Youndt, M. A., & Wright, P. M. (1996). Establishing a framework for research in strategic human resource management. *Research in Personnel and Human Resources Management, 14,* 61–90.

Snow, R. E. (1986). Individual differences and the design of educational programs. *American Psychologist, 41,* 1029–1034.

Snow, R. E., & Lohman, D. R. (1984). Toward a theory of cognitive aptitude for learning from instruction. *Journal of Educational Psychology, 76,* 337–346.

Snow, R. E., & Swanson, J. (1992). Instructional psychology, aptitude, adaptation, and assessment. *Annual Review of Psychology, 43,* 583–626.

Sokal, R. R. (1974). Classification: Purposes, principles, progress, prospects. *Science, 185,* 1115–1123.

Sparrow, J. (1989). The utility of PAQ in relating job behaviors to traits. *Journal of Occupational Psychology, 62,* 151–162.

Sparrow, J., Patrick, J., Spurgeon, P. C., & Barwell, F. (1982). The use of job component analysis and related aptitudes in personnel selection. *Journal of Occupational Psychology, 55,* 157–164.

Spearman, C. (1923). *The abilities of man: Their nature and measurement.* New York: McMillan.

Spearman, C. (1931). *The abilities of man.* New York: McMillan.

Spector, P. E. (1992). A consideration of the validity and meaning of self-report measures of job conditions. In C. L. Cooper & I. T. Robertson (Eds.), *International review of industrial and organizational psychology* (Vol. 7, pp. 123–151). New York: Wiley.

Spector, P. E., & Jex, S. M. (1991). Relations of job characteristics from multiple data sources with employee affect, absence, turnover intentions, and health. *Journal of Applied Psychology, 76,* 46–53.

Spencer, L. M., McClelland, D. C., & Spencer, S. (1994). *Competency assessment methods: History and state of the art.* Boston: Hay McBer Research Press.

Spreitzer, G. M. (1992). *When organizations dare: The dynamics of individual empowerment in the workplace.* Unpublished dissertation, University of Michigan, Ann Arbor.

Sproull, L., & Kiesler, S. (1991). *Connections: New ways of working in the networked organization.* Cambridge, MA: MIT Press.

Statistical Package for the Social Sciences [Computer Software]. (1989–1997). Chicago, IL: SPSS, Inc.

Steiner, I. (1972). *Group process and productivity.* New York: Academic Press.

Sternberg, R. J. (1986). Toward a unified theory of human reasoning. *Intelligence, 10,* 281–314.

Stevens, D. (1993). The case for revising U.S. occupational classification systems. In *Proceedings of the International Occupational Classification Conference.* Washington, DC: Bureau of Labor Statistics.

Strong, E. K. (1943). *The vocational interest of men and women.* Palo Alto, CA: Stanford University Press.

Sudman, S., Bradburn, N. M., & Schwarz, N. (1996). *Thinking about answers: The application of cognitive processes to survey methodology.* San Francisco: Jossey-Bass.

Sundstrom, E., & Sundstrom, M. G. (1986). *Work places: The psychology of the physical environment in offices and factories.* Cambridge, England: Cambridge University Press.

Talbert, T. L., Carroll, K. I., & Ronan, W. W. (1976). Measuring clerical job performance. *Personnel Journal, 55,* 573–575.

Taylor, L. R. (1978). Empirically derived job families as a foundation for the study of validity generalization: Study I. The construction of job families based on the component and overall dimensions of the PAQ. *Personnel Psychology, 31,* 325–340.

Taylor, L. R., & Colbert, G. A. (1978). Empirically derived job families as a foundation for the study of validity generalization: Study II. The construction of job families as a foundation for the study of validity generalization. *Personnel Psychology, 31,* 341–353.

Tellegen, A. (1982). *Brief manual for the Multidimensional Personality Questionnaire.* Unpublished manuscript, University of Minnesota, Department of Psychology, Minneapolis.

Tellegen, A., & Waller, N. G. (in press). Exploring personality through test construction: Development of the Multidimensional Personality Questionnaire. In S. R. Briggs & J. M. Cheek (Eds.), *Personality measures: Development and evaluation* (Vol. 1). Greenwich, CT: JAI Press.

Terpstra, D. E., & Rozell, E. J. (1993). The relationship of staffing practices to organizational level measures of performance. *Personnel Psychology, 46,* 27–48.

Theologus, G. C., & Fleishman, E. A. (1973). Development of a taxonomy of human performance: Validation study for ability scales for classifying human tasks. *JSAS Catalog of Selected Documents in Psychology, 3,* 29 (Ms. No. 326).

Theologus, G. C., Romashko, T., & Fleishman, E. A. (1973). Development of a taxonomy of human performance: Validation study of ability scales for classifying human tasks. *JSAS Catalog of Selected Documents in Psychology, 3,* 25–26 (Ms. No. 321).

Thompson, J. D. (1967). *Organizations in action.* New York: McGraw Hill.

Thorndike, R. L., & Hagen, E. (1959). *10,000 careers.* New York: Wiley.

Thurstone, L. L. (1938). Primary mental abilities. *Psychometric Monographs* (Whole No. 1).

Thurstone, L. L. (1947). *Multiple factor analysis: A development and expansion of the vectors of mind.* Chicago: University Chicago Press.

Tokar, D. M., & Swanson, J. L. (1995). Evaluation of the correspondence between Holland's vocational personality typology and the five-factor model of personality. *Journal of Vocational Behavior, 46,* 89–108.

Tornow, W. W., & Pinto, P. R. (1976). The development of a managerial job taxonomy: A system for describing, classifying, and evaluating executive positions. *Journal of Applied Psychology, 61,* 410–418.

Tracey, T. J., & Rounds, J. (1992). Evaluating the RIASEC circumplex using high-point codes. *Journal of Vocational Behavior, 41,* 295–311.

Tupes, E. C., & Christal, R. E. (1992). Recurrent personality factors based on trait ratings. *Journal of Personality, 60,* 225–251. (Original technical report released 1961)

Turner, C. F., & Martin, E. (Eds.). (1985). *Surveying subjective phenomena* (2 vols.). New York: Russell Sage.

Tyler, L. E. (1965). *The psychology of human differences.* Englewood Cliffs, NJ: Prentice-Hall.

U.S. Congress, Office of Technology Assessment. (1990). *Worker training: Competing in the new international economy* (OTA-ITE-457). Washington, DC: U.S. Government Printing Office.

U.S. Department of Commerce. (1980). *Standard Occupational Classification Manual.* Washington, DC: Author.

U.S. Department of Education. (1990). *Classification of instructional programs.* Washington, DC: Author.

U.S. Department of Labor. (1979). *Guide for occupational exploration.* Washington, DC: U.S. Government Printing Office.

U.S. Department of Labor. (1991a). *Dictionary of occupational titles* (4th ed., rev.). Washington, DC: U.S. Government Printing Office.

U.S. Department of Labor. (1991b). *The revised handbook for analyzing jobs.* Washington, DC: U.S. Government Printing Office.

U.S. Department of Labor. (1993a). *High performance work practices and firm performance.* Washington, DC: U.S. Government Printing Office.

U.S. Department of Labor. (1993b). *The new DOT: A database of occupational titles for the twenty-first century.* Washington, DC: U.S. Government Printing Office.

U.S. Department of Labor. (1994). *Road to high-performance workplaces: A guide to better jobs and better business results.* Washington, DC: U.S. Government Printing Office.

U.S. Office of Management and Budget. (1987). *Standard industrial classification manual.* Washington, DC: U.S. Government Printing Office.

U.S. Office of Personnel Management. (1991). *Leadership effectiveness survey for federal supervisors, managers, and executives.* Washington, DC: U.S. Government Printing Office.

Van Fleet, D. D., & Yukl, G. A. (1986). *Military leadership: An organizational behavior perspective.* Greenwich, CT: JAI Press.

Van Maanen, J. (1978). People processing: Strategies of organizational socialization. *Organizational Dynamics, 7,* 18–36.

Van Maanen, J., & Schein, E. H. (1979). Toward a theory of organizational socialization. In B. M. Staw & L. L. Cummings (Eds.), *Research in organizational behavior* (Vol. 1, pp. 204–264). Greenwich, CT: JAI Press.

Van Meter, P., Yoki, L., & Pressley, M. (1994a). College students, theory of notetaking derived from their perceptions of notetaking. *Journal of Educational Psychology, 86,* 323–338.

Van Meter, P., Yoki, L., & Pressley, M. (1994b). Encoding of surveys when 10-to-14-years-old process isolated survey sentences: More evidence of improved encoding during childhood resulting from elaborative instructions. *Journal of Educational Psychology, 86,* 402–413.

Varca, P. E., & Shaffer, G. S. (1982). Holland's theory: Stability of avocational interests. *Journal of Vocational Behavior, 21,* 288–298.

Vernon, P. E. (1950). The validation of civil service selection and procedures. *Occupational Psychology, 24,* 75–95.

Vernon, P. E., (1961). *The structure of human abilities* (2nd ed.). London: Methuen. [2nd edition, 1961].

Voss, J. D., Wolfe, C. R., Lawrence, J. A., & Engle, R. A. (1991). From representation to decision: An analysis for problem solving in international relations. In R. J. Sternberg & P. A. French (Eds.), *Complex problem solving: Principles and mechanisms* (pp. 316–421). Hillsdale, NJ: Erlbaum.

Wallace, M. J., & Fay, C. H. (1983). *Compensation theory and practice.* Reading, MA: Wadsworth/Kent.

Ward, J. H. (1963). Hierarchical grouping to optimize an objective function. *Journal of the American Statistical Association, 58,* 236–244.

Ward, J. H., & Hook, M. E. (1963). Application of a hierarchical grouping procedure to the problem of grouping profiles. *Educational and Psychological Measurement, 23,* 69–81.

Ward, S. L., Byrnes, J. P., & Overton, W. F. (1990). Organization of knowledges and conditional reasoning. *Journal of Educational Psychology, 82,* 832–837.

Watson, J. B. (1913). Psychology as the behaviorist views it. *Psychological Review, 20,* 158–177.

Watson, J. B. (1919). *Psychology from the standpoint of a behaviorist.* Philadelphia: Lippincott.

Watson, J. B. (1925). *Behaviorism.* New York: Norton.

Weiss, D. J., Dawis, R. V., England, G. W., & Lofquist, L. H. (1964). The measurement of vocational needs. *Minnesota Studies in Vocational Rehabilitation, XVI.* Minneapolis: University of Minnesota.

West, M. A., & Farr, J. L. (1989). Innovation at work: psychological perspectives. *Social Behavior, 3,* 31–57.

Westat, Inc. (1993). *DOT user survey: A report and analysis.* (Tech. Rep.). Rockville, MD: Author.

Westat, Inc. (1994). *Sampling plan: Part 1.* Rockville, MD: Author.

Wetrogan, L. I., Uhlman, C. E., & Fleishman, E. A. (1995) *Development and validation of the Patrol Trooper Examination for the Pennsylvania State Police.* Bethesda, MD: Management Research Institute.

Wheaton, G. R. (1973). Development of a taxonomy of human performance. A review of classificatory systems related to tasks and performance. *JSAS Catalog of Selected Documents in Psychology, 3,* 22–23 (Ms. No. 317).

Wheaton, G. R., Eisner, E., Mirabella, G., & Fleishman, E. A. (1976). Ability requirements as a function of changes in the characteristics of an auditory signal identification task. *Journal of Applied Psychology, 61,* 663–676.

Windows [Computer Software]. (1981–1996). Redmond, WA: Microsoft, Corp.

Whyte, W. H. (1956). *The organization man.* New York: Simon & Schuster.

Wiggins, J. S. (1979). A psychological taxonomy of trait-descriptive terms: The interpersonal domain. *Journal of Personality and Social Psychology, 37,* 395–412.

Wiggins, J. S. (1991). Agency and communion as conceptual coordinates for the understanding and measurement of interpersonal behavior. In W. M. Grove & D. Cicchetti (Eds.), *Thinking clearly about psychology: Essays in honor of Paul Everett Meehl: Vol. 2* (pp. 89–113). Minneapolis: University of Minnesota Press.

Wiggins, J. S., Trapnell, P., & Phillips, N. (1988). Psychometric and geometric characteristics of the Revised Interpersonal Adjective Scales (IAS-R). *Multivariate Behavioral Research, 23,* 517–530.

Williams, R. E. (1956). *A description of some executive abilities by means of the critical incident technique.* Unpublished doctoral dissertation, Columbia University, New York.

Winer, B. G. (1971). *Statistical principles in experimental design.* New York: Wiley.

Wing, H., Peterson, N. G., Hoffman, R. G. (1984). Expert judgments of predictor-criterion validity relationships. *Improving the selection, classification, and utilization of Army enlisted personnel: Annual report, 1984 fiscal year.*

Wright, P. M., & McMahan, G. C. (1992). Theoretical perspectives for strategic human resource management. *Journal of Management, 18,* 295–320.

Yukl, G. A. (1987, October). *A new taxonomy for integrating diverse perspectives on managerial behavior.* Paper presented at the annual meeting of the American Psychological Association, New York.

Yukl, G. A. (1989). *Leadership in organizations* (2nd ed.). Englewood Cliffs, NJ: Prentice Hall.

Zaccaro, S. J., Gilbert, J. A., Thor, K. K., & Mumford, M. D. (1991). Leadership and social intelligence: Linking social perceptiveness and behavior flexibility to leader effectiveness. *Leadership Quarterly, 2,* 317–342.

Zedeck, S. (1975). *Validation of physical abilities tests for AT&T craft positions: Program report with special emphasis on detailed job analyses* (Tech. Rep. 5). New York: American Telephone and Telegraph Co.

Zimmerman, R., Jacobs, R., & Farr, J. (1982). A comparison of the accuracy of four methods for clustering jobs. *Applied Psychological Measurement, 6,* 353–366.

Zytowski, D. G. (1976). Factor analysis of the Kuder Occupational Interest Survey. *Measurement and Education in Guidance, 9,* 120–123.

# Author Index

# Subject Index

# About the Editors

**Norman G. Peterson** is a Senior Research Fellow at the American Institutes for Research. He received his BA (1969) and PhD (1980) degrees from the University of Minnesota in psychology. A Fellow of the American Psychological Association, American Psychological Society, and Society for Industrial and Organizational Psychology, he has conducted research in job analysis, test development and validation, classification systems, and other applied topics for a variety of government and private sector sponsors. Dr. Peterson was project director for the O*NET prototype development effort.

**Michael D. Mumford** is a Senior Research Fellow at the American Institutes for Research in Washington, DC. Prior to joining the American Institutes for Research in 1994, he was an associate professor and associate director of the Center for Behavioral and Cognitive Studies at George Mason University. He was an assistant professor in the psychology department at the Georgia Institute of Technology until 1984. He received his PhD from the University of Georgia in 1983. Dr. Mumford currently serves on the editorial boards of *Leadership Quarterly*, the *Journal of Creative Behavior*, and the *Creativity Research Journal*. He is a fellow of the American Psychological Association, the American Psychological Society, and the Society for Industrial and Organizational Psychology. His primary research interests focus on the assessment and development of high-level talent.

**Walter C. Borman** received his PhD in industrial/organizational psychology from the University of California, Berkeley in 1972. He joined Personnel Decisions, Inc. as a research psychologist and co-founded Personnel Decisions Research Institutes (PDRI) in 1975. He is currently professor of psychology and director of the industrial/organizational psychology graduate program at the University of South Florida and is Chief Executive Officer of PDRI. He is a fellow of the American Psychological Association (Division 14) and served as the Divisions

President 1994 through 1995. He has more than 200 publications, papers, and technical reports, and presently serves as consulting editor on three major industrial/organizational journals. His research interests are in the areas of job performance measurement, personnel selection, job analysis, assessment centers, personality assessment, and person perception.

**P. Richard Jeanneret** is the founder and Managing Principal of Jeanneret & Associates, Inc., a management consulting firm located in Houston, Texas. He is the co-author of the *Position Analysis Questionnaire (PAQ)*, a behaviorally-oriented, structured job analysis instrument, and he is President of PAQ Services, Inc., a data processing and research services organization. He received a BA from the University of Virginia, an MA from the University of Florida, and a PhD in industrial and organizational psychology from Purdue University. He is the author of many research articles and book chapters on the subject of job analysis, and has presented numerous symposia, workshops, and invited addresses on the topic. He was one of the Senior Investigators on the research team that developed the O*NET. Dr. Jeanneret has served on the editorial boards of the *Journal of Applied Psychology* and *Personnel Psychology*. He is a Fellow of the American Psychological Association and the Society for Industrial and Organizational Psychology, and in 1990 the Society awarded him the Distinguished Professional Contributions Award.

**Edwin A. Fleishman** has been Distinguished University Professor of Psychology at George Mason University and President of Management Research Institute. He is the former editor of the *Journal of Applied Psychology* and was the recipient of the Distinguished Scientist Award for the Application of Psychology from the American Psychological Association. He has served as President of APA's Division of Evaluation and Measurement, Division of Engineering Psychology, and the Society of Industrial and Organizational Psychology, and for 8 years was President of the International Association of Applied Psychology. His books include *Taxonomies of Human Performance: Human Performance and Productivity, Handbook of Human Abilities, Psychology and Human Performance,* and *Studies in Personnel and Industrial Psychology.* For his contributions he has also received the Distinguished Professional Practice and M. Scott Myers Awards from the Society for Industrial and Organizational Psychology, the Franklin Taylor Award from APA Division 21, the James McKeen Cattel Award form the American Psychological Society, and an honorary Doctor of Science Degree conferred by the University of Edinburgh. Most recently, APA presented him with its Award for Distinguished Contributions to the International Advancement of Psychology.